# And God Created BURTON

The Myrtle Press
London

also by Tom Rubython

*Life of O'Reilly*
- the biography of Tony O'Reilly

*The Rich 500*
- the 500 Richest people in Britain

*The Life of Senna*
- the biography of Ayrton Senna

*Dog Story - An Anthology*
- the life and death of our best friends

*Shunt - The story of James Hunt*
- the biography of James Hunt

# And God Created
# BURTON

## TOM RUBYTHON

### FOREWORD BY ROGER MOORE
### PROLOGUE BY ROBERT HARDY

First published in Great Britain in 2011
by The Myrtle Press

1 3 5 7 9 10 8 6 4 2

A CIP catalogue record for this book is available
from the British Library.

ISBN: 978-0-9565656-2-4

Typset in ITC Garamond by CBA Harlestone
Reproduction by Fresh Vision, London

Printed and bound in the UK by CPI Clowes,
Ellough, Beccles, Suffolk,
NR34 7TL, United Kingdom

The Myrtle Press
Kemp House
152-160 City Road
London
EC1V 2NX
Tel: 0207 566 1196

# Contents

# Contents

# Contents

# Contents

*Why me, why me?*
*...first account for me.*

Richard Burton in character as the psychiatrist
Martin Dysart in the film *Equus* - 1977

# Acknowledgements

I learned the hard way about how difficult it is to write about the childhood and early life of a person who had ten siblings. It doesn't matter how good a writer you may think you are, it just gets complicated. You'll be the judge of how I made out. I have to say it wasn't easy.

My chief helper in that respect was Rhianon Trowell, Richard Burton's niece but to all intents and purposes his younger sister. Rhianon was able to tell me all the intimate family details which were missing from previous biographies. Somehow, she unravelled it all. Going to her house was fascinating because of her marvellous, bulging scrapbook of her uncle's life. Sitting on chairs from Burton's childhood home in Caradoc Street, I perused the scrapbook as it rested on Burton's old dining table from his house in Hampstead.

I want to thank Rhianon for politely taking all my phone calls and responding to my requests for what were more often than not trivial pieces of information. And to apologise in advance for some of the harsh verdicts I may have delivered on one or two of her relatives.

In any book like this, there is always an anchor source; a person at the right hand who provides not only material but also advice and encouragement. In my case, that person was Robert Hardy. When I first told him about the book, he admitted that his first reaction was: "Oh no, not another one." But luckily, I managed to persuade him that mine was not simply an "oh no, not another" rendering of the saga.

Robert, of course, had a unique view of Burton's life right from when they first met at Oxford in 1944. With his unique perspective, he was of the greatest importance to me. As I tentatively sent him a few chapters for comment, he quickly saw that I was attempting something different and responded magnificently.

Robert cares deeply about his friend's legacy, and he felt strongly that previous biographers had not devoted enough energy in extracting from him everything he had to offer. I hope I didn't make that mistake.

Richard Burton was Robert's greatest friend, and a man he admired greatly. But he did not don dark glasses; he was totally honest about the good and the bad, and totally pragmatic at every stage of the process.

Sally Burton was also a rock. Despite her reputation amongst some people for being difficult, she certainly wasn't with me – in fact, the total opposite. But our first interaction was certainly very difficult for her. I sent her the first chapter to review. None of it was complimentary to her, but I was impressed when she didn't try to change it and, rather, tried to explain it.

# AND GOD CREATED BURTON

At first, her explanations seemed unconvincing, but as I got deeper into the subject, I began to understand how she had felt when her husband died.

But I had, many times, to curse Sally during the writing process because of her decision to leave her husband's papers to the archive department of Swansea University. The people in the archive department were far less helpful than one might have expected. Their excuses for not delivering me the information I requested were never-ending. It is amusing to recall now, but at the time it was deeply frustrating.

But if I have one skill, it is the ability to locate the back door when I find the front door closed. Every time I was blocked, I found another way through to the material. But it just made my life very difficult. Professor Christopher Williams, who is in charge of the archive, says he wishes to publish an edited version of Richard Burton's diaries himself. I say good luck to him, as, knowing those diaries as well as I now do, I would say it is an impossible task and not a particularly desirable one from the point of view of the Burton legacy.

The one document I particularly wanted to see was the private adoption agreement between Dick Jenkins and Philip Burton, signed on 17th December 1943. Swansea University's archive staff denied me access to this on the basis that it was the copyright of the elderly solicitor who had drafted it 58 years ago, and they informed me I would need that gentleman's written permission before it could be released. There was really no answer to that.

I was also miffed by the poor job that had been done indexing and cataloguing the archive. It was evident from Melvyn Bragg's description of the documents he had examined twenty five years ago, that many of them had not been listed. I had absolutely no way of knowing the scale of that problem.

Contrast the attitude at Swansea to that of Professor Alan Miller at Cardiff – chalk and cheese. Professor Miller is a wonderfully open man, who told me he had faced the same difficulties with Swansea's archive department as I had. Professor Miller is to be congratulated for what he is doing for Richard Burton's memory in Cardiff; the whole of Wales has reason to be very grateful for that.

Lord Rowe-Beddoe was a lifelong friend of Richard Burton's and played the organ at his funeral. I was surprised at how little he had been asked to contribute to the 11 previous biographies. I hope I have rectified that.

Another great friend during the process was Peter Egan, the actor. I continually needed the actor's view and Peter was useful because he was unconnected with the subject. I only became worried once, when he told me

# ACKNOWLEDGEMENTS

on the phone that he believed I was writing a textbook of Richard Burton's life. That silenced me and threw up all sorts of danger signs. I knew the book was very detailed, but I worried it was becoming unreadable.

A biography of this type is read almost always for pleasure. 'Textbook' was not a word I particularly wanted to hear, and it remained in the back of my mind for the rest of the writing process.

When I questioned him closely on what precisely he had meant, Peter didn't backtrack but explained that his comment had been meant as a compliment. Nonetheless, it was cause for concern.

Diane Horwood, Kate Burton's nanny, was also very helpful to me in understanding a period of Richard and Sybil's lives together.

Great thanks to Tony Palmer, not only for his help, but also his magnificent filmed biography of Richard Burton called *In From The Cold*. It's no exaggeration to say that I watched it at least eight times to take in every nuance of that great, great film.

Neither Sybil Christopher, Suzy Miller or Kate Burton were interested in helping with this book, which was a shame but not a surprise. So I had to go round them and get to the closest sources I could.

The late David Benson, the *Daily Express* motoring editor of the sixties and seventies, is actually the only journalist who ever spoke to Suzy on the record. Likewise, the late Elaine Dundy, Kenneth Tynan's wife, is the only journalist Sybil really opened up to. So my thanks to both of these fine journalists for their posthumous help. I relied on their accounts heavily. James Hunt also spoke extensively about his former wife when he was alive.

Andrew Frankl, the legendary magazine publisher, was as ever my close collaborator and, being based in California, was able to help me out more often than not. Mike Merrick helped me with 'Camelot' and April Tod was very useful as always with Sally Burton's early history.

Most of the major photographic agencies have helped my picture editor, Sophia Doe, as she sought to unearth photos that she knew existed but which had not seen the light of day before. I always take photographs very seriously, and those in this book are not the work of a moment. My thanks to Martina Oliver at Getty Images, David Scripps at Mirrorpix, Nye Jones at Corbis, Stephen Atkinson at Rex Features and Lucie Gregory at the Press Association for their contribution to the process. And also to the photographers Pete Turner and Gianni Bozzacchi. Pete Turner took the amazing photograph on the front dust cover. I must also mention Jez Douglas, who handles all the reproduction work. The effort that goes into a dust jacket and retouching old photographs to make them acceptable to print can be exhausting, but he rarely lets us down.

Also to our printers, David Browne, Jo Buck, Ian Foyster and Peter Milton, who very generously extended the deadline by a week and worked like fury to ensure the book still got to the shops on time.

I can't finish here without thanking my own staff. As one gets closer to the deadline, a different pace of life is required. My thanks go to Annie Strausa and Erin Hynes, my researchers. Every biographer needs his researchers, and these two stuck at it until every scrap of information under nearly 400 different headings was catalogued and archived so I could get at it easily during the writing process. I know I was the only biographer to undertake this task properly, and I hope it shows through in the finished narrative. Thousands of hours were devoted to this task before I even wrote a word, and that process continued to the end.

My gratitude extends also to David Peett, Mary Hynes and Kate Moravesky, who helped sell and publicise this book, and to Ania Grzesik, who designed it. Thanks also to Kiran Toor, our chief sub editor, and special thanks to manuscript readers Sarah Thomas-James, Joanne Mathers, Margaret Rubython and Merryn Tyrrell.

Also thanks to Sharon Addy for her research into the Jenkins family history and accessing birth, death and census records. And to Roger Martin for his clever execution of a highly innovative online marketing strategy.

Finally, my thanks to all of Richard Burton's previous biographers: Ruth Waterbury, Fergus Cashin, Hollis Alpert, Penny Junor, Melvyn Bragg, Graham Jenkins, David Jenkins, Tyrone Steverson, Philip Burton, Peter Stead and Michael Munn. I enjoyed all your books.

And a final thanks to the villagers of Castle Ashby, who rallied around on the night before printing and took a chapter each to check for the final time.

I am truly grateful for the efforts of all the people involved in this book and I thank you all, although the words that follow – and any errors or omissions – are naturally my responsibility alone.

*Tom Rubython*
*Castle Ashby*
*Northamptonshire*
*14th April 2011*

# Prologue

# A Welsh Prince of His Time

Rishiart of Pontrhydyfen – a legend? a myth? a Welsh prince of the time before Owain Glyndwr? Not to begin with – "To begin at the beginning", he was little Richie Jenkins, the tenth surviving child of a miner's family, of No. 2 Dan-y-Bont. There were Twm, Cecilia – but always 'Cis' – Ifor, William, David, Verdun (born 1916, you see), Hilda, Catherine, Edith, Rich and Graham. Soon after that, their mother, Edith, died. A great part of their life gone, the family circled protectively around the youngest; a family of much nobility – not the nobility of ermine, but of dignity and loyalty and pride.

Not yet a prince, but a bright schoolboy who attracted attention wherever he fixed his blue gaze; mad for Rugby football, for music, for words, for cricket 'and the run-stealers flitting to and fro'. More than one teacher saw in him promise; Philip Burton, the senior English master at Port Talbot Secondary School, himself a miner's son, saw in Richard a glow of genius, which he slowly fanned into a flame. Later, he would adopt him, with the family's blessing and to the relief of Cis, who had stepped into their mother's place and was hard put to it to look after a husband, her own children and her young brother.

From now, he would be Richard Burton 'absolutely to renounce his surname and bear the surname of the adopter and be held out to the world as if he were the child of Philip Burton.' Philip brought him forward, tutored him in literature and drama, teaching him the language of England and of Shakespeare.

So came the War, and in a crowd of half soldiers, sailors and airmen, half undergraduates, Richard, and I, went up to Oxford, met, and loathed each other – until one day poring over a map in navigation class, we spotted at the same moment the River Trent: "See how this river comes me cranking in..." said one; the other followed with "and cuts me from the best of all my land, a huge half-moon, a monstrous cantle out..." Hotspur, Shakespeare and his 'Henry IV' had formed a bond that lasted all one life (far, far too short), and still, the other.

The year of the Festival of Britain, when she strove to regain her spirits after the horrors and the gloom of war, saw Richard as a medieval prince at last: Hal, of the Shakespeare Histories, Henry of Agincourt at Stratford-on-Avon.

# AND GOD CREATED BURTON

From then, there was no stopping in the eagle-flight, bar the occasional hard landing and a stoup or two (not the falcon's stoop), and Rich became a great Shakespearean – I mean truly great, not as the word is misused now.

There had been a day near a Norfolk airfield, in the War, Easter Sunday and he and I swam in an icy sea and came back to the sands with one handkerchief to dry us both. We ran to warm ourselves, shouting bits of Hal, Hamlet, Coriolanus, Lear too probably, arguing how to play them...I was posted the next day and, in saying goodbye, told him: "Whatever you do, as actor, politician or anything else, you will do greatly." It came true, size of spirit, breadth of mind – even his life mistakes were great, his finest achievements unique, his voice unmatched.

My thoughts go back to Hampstead and to Rich with Sybil, all spirited gaiety and all forgiving love, and to Kate, the best of each of them, until one day Rich became Antony – with Cleopatra – and a huge and famous, ferocious passion ensued. Richard and Elizabeth – Dame Elizabeth – twice married, twice divorced, always in love and longing for each other, even until death.

Richard's life is famous, though only a fortunate few know of his wide generosity, his gentleness in the still centre of the fire and sometimes fury. A genius, 'perhaps a flawed genius, but there has to be a precious stone to have a flaw'. At the last, peace perhaps, writing words, reading them in his library. Now, in a sense, he is going back to Wales, which, however far he travelled, he never really left, to a theatre that will bear his name and which, I fancy, he will haunt. The Royal Welsh College of Music and Drama which houses the Richard Burton Theatre must do 'Doctor Faustus' for him one day: "The only play", he said, "I don't have to work on, I am Faustus!"

*Robert Hardy*
*Oxfordshire*
*England*
*7th April 2011*

# Foreword

# The Greatest Voice of his Time

Time magazine once called Richard's voice "one of the great wind instruments of the English speaking stage." I couldn't agree more and would even go one step further and say it was the greatest voice ever heard on the English stage.

Can anyone forget his final season at the Old Vic in 1956 in 'Othello', when he swapped the principal roles of Iago and Othello night after night with John Neville? The audience brought the house down after every performance and carried on the party in The Cut afterwards. I can't, and I suspect more than a few of you will remember.

I first met Richard Burton at the Lyric Theatre in Hammersmith, London. That was when I first came under the spell of that voice. The play was 'The Boy With a Cart' by Christopher Fry, the story of St. Crispin, who single handed constructed a church in the south west of England. We were both were young actors making our way after the war. Richard and I were more or less than same the same age but success came to him much earlier. We were both studio contracted artists in Hollywood in the fifties, he with 20th Century-Fox and me with MGM, but it took me longer to find my way through the labyrinth that is Hollywood. Richard seemed to conquer it effortlessly. He had something extra special and immediately and instinctively knew how to woo the great Hollywood moguls of the time. His relationship, when he was only in his mid-20s, with people like Darryl Zanuck and Sam Goldwyn was extraordinary and could only be looked at in envy by the rest of us young Brit actors trying to make it in Hollywood.

Richard had that way with powerful people and they just couldn't say 'no' to him, including Binkie Beaumont, the legendary impresario to whom we all owed our livings in those days. Rich and I were both contracted actors at HM Tennent in the late forties and he paid all his young actors £10 a week.

Rich got his salary increased to £30 a week and succeeded where I didn't. When I approached Binkie with the same request, he asked me if I was married and, when I said 'yes', he replied: "Well dear boy, you are very lucky to be working at all."

We were great friends at HM Tennent and I vividly remember going to see Rich's first big Hollywood film *The Robe* with my then wife Dorothy Squires, who also knew Rich very well.

In those days, I used to share a white tie dress suit with him. White tie was *de rigeur* in those days for first nights and film premieres, and we couldn't afford one each so we split the cost three ways with the theatrical costumier Monty Berman. Richard was a little shorter so the leg had to be taken up  when he wore it but we were the same chest size. If all three of us were ever invited to a premiere, only one of us could have gone, but luckily that never happened.

Of course, there are many stories of Richard's years with Elizabeth Taylor and their frequent and often quite voluble disagreements. I vividly remember in 1972, I flew to Budapest with my film producing partner George Barrie to meet with Elizabeth to finalise the arrangements for her to star in a film we were making called *Night Watch.* We booked into the InterContinental and went up to the top floor suite to meet with Elizabeth to discuss the film. Richard was there and looking very solemn; there was already tension in the air between them. When I told Elizabeth that Billie Whitelaw was playing the supporting female lead in *Night Watch*, Richard's ears suddenly pricked up. "I have a much better idea" he said. Elizabeth looked at him with her big violet eyes and said: "Who else were you thinking of, dear?" "Raquel Welch" he shouted, "a very fine actress." I'll say no more, suffice to say I was very glad to leave that hotel room at that moment.

Amazingly, by 1977, Richard had starred in 46 feature films and I had done 32, but up to that moment, as two of the best known British actors of the time, we had never appeared together in a film. That changed when Euan Lloyd brought us together for *The Wild Geese.*

It was a magical time with a wonderful, mainly British, cast. I found myself working with two of the film's industry's most famous drinkers – the two Richards; Harris and Burton. Both were contracted not to drink during filming and they told me I had to do the drinking for all three of them. Only once, during my 50th birthday party celebrations, did they break the pact. We had the most marvellous time in the South African spa resort of Tschepese and the three bungalows we lived in during filming were next door to each other.

But working with two great actors could be rather daunting. I remember vividly there was a scene where myself and the two Richards all had ten lines each. After the first run through, I asked for a cut in my own lines. Everyone looked at me askew as it was usually the other way round, as actors sought to acquire more lines. But they agreed. After another run through, I asked for another cut in my lines. By the end, I had no lines and was virtually silent in the scene.

Andrew McLaglen, the director, asked me why and said it was an unheard-of request from an actor. I said to him: "Do you think I want to act against these guys? I'll just sit here and watch them do the work." I was genuinely overawed by what I was seeing and hearing.

I'll always remember the last scene in the film with Richard and Stewart Granger and all the long-standing Hollywood rivalry that was built into that relationship. All I had to do was wait outside the house in the car for Burton's character to come out after having shot Matherson (Granger's character). Richard got back in the car and said to me in his wonderful Welsh lilt: "By heck, that Jimmy Granger, he hasn't made a film for fifteen years and he's still a bugger. When I told him not to take off his dinner suit when we finished the first take as we would be going for another take, he said, 'sod 'em!'"

Years later, in 1984, I had provisionally accepted an offer to reprise the role of Shawn Fynn in *Wild Geese II* when I heard Richard had signed up to play Colonel Faulkner again. But when Richard died, a few weeks before filming was due to start, I found my heart wasn't in it.

A very strong light went out that day.

*Roger Moore*
*Crans-Montana*
*Switzerland*
*12th April 2011*

# AND GOD CREATED BURTON

# CHAPTER 1

# Death - the inevitable outcome

## Suddenly that summer

### 3rd August to 7th August 1984

"I don't like the sound of this. Who would be phoning me on holiday?" So said David Jenkins to his daughter Susan just before three o'clock on the afternoon of Sunday 5th August. The 70-year-old was holidaying on the west coast of Wales as he did every year. The widower had been sitting in his deck chair on the hotel's front lawn, reading the Sunday newspapers in the sun, when he was disturbed by the hotel receptionist with news of an urgent telephone call. As he got up to take the call, Susan instinctively followed him to the phone.

A sixth sense told him that it was the call he had been anticipating for many years but had hoped would never come. He leaned across the reception desk and took the receiver, shaking with apprehension. On the other end of the faint line was his brother, 68-year-old Verdun Jenkins, calling from his home in Cwmafan, Wales. Verdun, not wasting any time with pleasantries, said simply: "Prepare yourself for a shock, Davy, I have some bad news for you – our Rich has passed away. He's died from a brain haemorrhage."

'Rich' was his brother, 58-year-old Richard Burton, the most famous Welshman ever born and, arguably, then the world's best known actor.

Jenkins, shaken to his core, shouted out "never" at the top of his voice and dropped the receiver onto the ground. He fell to his knees, reeling from what he had just heard. Susan also dropped to the floor and embraced her father as floods of tears ran down both their faces. She didn't need to be told what he had just heard.

The Jenkins family, some 80 strong in all, were very close, and Richard Burton (née Jenkins) was leader of the tight Welsh clan. There had been absolutely no warning of Burton's impending death, and no one had had any time to prepare for the devastating effects of there no longer being a Richard Burton in the world. This scene of family torment was to be repeated many times across England and Wales that day.

Burton's final few days had begun when he and his wife of only 13 months, 37-year-old Sally Hay, had returned to their home in Celigny, Switzerland,

1

for a fortnight's holiday before they were due to travel to Berlin for four weeks of filming on location. Burton was due to star in *The Wild Geese II*, a sequel to the original *Wild Geese* film.

A few days earlier, Burton had flown into Switzerland from London, where he had been filming a cameo role for the American miniseries *Ellis Island*. The miniseries starred Burton's 26-year-old daughter, Kate. Kate was one of Burton's two natural children by his first wife Sybil, and fast becoming an accomplished actress in her own right. His other daughter, 24-year-old Jessica, was autistic and had been sectioned in a mental asylum in America many years earlier.

Celigny in August is a beautiful place, and the Burtons were enjoying their midsummer sojourn. Especially as their friend, the English character actor John Hurt, was filming in nearby Geneva. Burton had befriended Hurt during the making of the film *1984*, which had recently wrapped. Hurt and Burton were both heavy drinkers and naturally got on very well.

Burton had been on and off alcohol his entire life. In deference to his new wife, he was now mostly off it but she agreed he could indulge himself from time to time, preferably when she was not around. The arrival of John Hurt in Celigny signalled one of those times.

In a television documentary earlier that year, Burton had admitted he was an alcoholic and that he couldn't be cured. But, having accepted that a cure was impossible, he said he had learned to control it. Burton's posthumous biographer, Melvyn Bragg, explained how the actor had learned to accommodate his demons: "He had decided to deal with it in his own way. Mostly he was sober – totally abstinent for weeks, months on end. Then he would have a binge and accept the consequences. He still smoked heavily. He was not a man to give up any of his guaranteed pleasures."

On the Friday evening of 3rd August, John Hurt arrived by taxi from Geneva. He, Sally and Burton strolled down the hill from the house to the Café de la Gare, and they enjoyed an early supper. Afterwards, Burton went out on an extended bar crawl in Celigny with Hurt. Sally stayed for another hour at the cafe before walking back home.

Both actors were simply blowing off steam that Friday evening, and by all accounts it was no different to any other boozy night out he had enjoyed with friends in Celigny many times over the years.

It was two o'clock the following morning before the pair returned to the house, both paralytically drunk. Sally, having anticipated as much, was ready and waiting. As there was no question of Hurt returning to Geneva that night, Sally put him in the guest bedroom suite. As for her husband, she knew it wouldn't be worth communicating with him in his state and was grateful she didn't have to bother. He was asleep before his head hit the pillow. Burton rarely suffered any ill effects from his drinking, and she knew he would be awake the next morning at six o'clock, as fresh as a daisy.

He was an early riser, and had been all his life. Whatever his state might have been the evening prior, he was rarely late for filming or rehearsals. But that Saturday morning was to prove different. As the early morning sun came up over Lake Geneva, he was uncharacteristically sluggish and complained of a headache. Sally fetched him two aspirin and a glass of water and enjoyed the sheepish grin on her husband's weathered face as he took the remedy. She had an 'I told you so' look on her face and he an 'I know you told me so' look on his. Afterwards, Sally would fret about not having paid more attention to the headache, but as she said: "There was never any way of telling. He scarcely ever complained, and even if it was serious, you couldn't tell."

At nine o'clock she made both men breakfast, which they enjoyed on the terrace outside, sitting in the sun. Hurt then asked Sally for the telephone number of a local taxi firm so he could return to Geneva. Burton tried to persuade him to stay the weekend but Hurt realised that, for Sally, it would mean a weekend of drinking and he wasn't about to impose that on a lady he had come to really like. Sally wouldn't hear of his calling a taxi and she volunteered to drive Hurt back to Geneva.

It was a lovely morning in Celigny and she welcomed the distraction. She also loved the roads around Lake Geneva during the summer, as the sun glinted off the lake. On the return journey, she stopped to buy groceries for the weekend meals. She was in a very good mood as she returned to the house, known famously as 'Le Pays De Galles', translating as 'The Country of Wales'.

In every other respect, it was an uneventful day. Aside from her husband, the house was empty as Burton's personal assistant, Brook Williams, was absent in Berlin. Burton spent much of it trying to shake off his headache, reading in the loft roof space which served as both his office and a library for his books. The open plan loft space had been created seven years earlier by his former wife, Suzy, who had renovated the house after they married. It featured a row of extraordinary pine wood swing-out bookcases that profiled the roofline leading out to a balcony. Burton spent many happy hours there in his rocking chair, reading his books and writing in his diaries. His meticulously-kept diaries were being readied for the day he would write his own autobiography.

His last day alive was a very happy one, and the sun shone through the windows until seven o'clock, at which time he came downstairs to Sally, who was cooking them both supper. It was still warm enough to enjoy it outside on the terrace.

Burton went to bed at ten o'clock as usual. By all accounts, he read for an hour, making notes as he always did in a little red leather-covered notebook he kept by his bed. Sally followed a couple of hours later at around midnight. By then, her husband was sound asleep and she turned off the bedside light he had left on.

On Sunday morning, Sally awoke at around seven o'clock and, unusually, found her husband still in bed next to her. Outside, the rain was coming down hard. Burton was breathing heavily and, when she shook him, he did not wake up. That was not too extraordinary as he was always notoriously difficult to wake up. So she went back to sleep believing he was enjoying a rare Sunday morning lie-in. She remembered: "Richard was still in bed, which was unusual for him. He liked getting up early. I went back to sleep."

An hour later, she woke again and he was still there in the same place. Sensing that something was wrong, since he was always up at dawn wherever they were in the world and however late he had gone to bed, she studied his inert form and realised he was also making some peculiar noises. She later described the sounds as "funny gurgling noises." She leaned over her husband and grabbed the telephone, as she remembers: "When I woke up again, I couldn't wake him." She dialled the number for Burton's Swiss doctor, who lived in Celigny. Sally woke up the doctor. As soon as he answered, he could sense trouble from her voice and promised to come immediately. He arrived at the house within 15 minutes of putting down the receiver.

Meanwhile, Sally went out and asked Harley Decorvet, the Celigny caretaker, to help her sit her husband up for the doctor's arrival. She said: "I was so frightened."

When the doctor arrived, Burton was unconscious. He ordered an ambulance to take Burton to the nearby village hospital at Nyon, a few minutes' drive away.

# DEATH – THE INEVITABLE OUTCOME

While they were waiting for the ambulance, Sally telephoned Valerie Douglas, Burton's longstanding personal manager of 31 years. She was in a state of blind panic as she dialled Los Angeles, 7,000 miles away. It was two o'clock in the morning when Douglas answered the phone. After listening, she gave Sally the only advice she could: to telephone Brook and keep them all informed. She dialled Brook Williams, who was Burton's assistant and currently in Berlin preparing for his arrival there the following Thursday. She outlined what had happened and asked him: "Could you warn them that we might be a few days late on set?" She explained: "Such was my hope over reality."

The ambulance was at the house within ten minutes, and the doctor accompanied Burton to Nyon's small hospital just a short while away. Harley Decorvet drove Sally to Nyon behind the ambulance. But vital hours had been lost.

The duty doctor at Nyon immediately recognised the seriousness of the situation and told the ambulance drivers to get Burton to the Cantonal Hospital in Geneva as quickly as possible. Sally was soaked to the skin by the heavy rain, but she hardly noticed. The doctor and Sally jumped into the ambulance to accompany Burton. Sally told Decorvet to follow in the car. The doctor wanted Sally to be with her husband should the worst happen and he should die during the journey, which he believed was a distinct possibility in his condition. But he didn't tell her that.

From the ambulance, he radioed ahead to Geneva with his prognosis. As it was Sunday, no operations were scheduled, so nurses were ordered to ready an operating theatre and to alert surgeons and an anesthetist. They also telephoned the scanner operators and asked them to come in.

As soon as Burton reached Geneva, he was wheeled into the x-ray department for a CT brain scan. The results were back in ten minutes. It was the worst possible diagnosis. The dark area surrounding part of his brain on the x-ray was unmistakable – Richard Burton had suffered an intracerebral haemorrhage. The seriousness of the haemorrhage was that it had occurred within the brain tissue rather than outside of it.

As the blood leaked, intracranial pressure continued to increase, and an immediate operation became necessary. By this time, Burton was already in a deep coma and death was close. Because doctors had been so late in getting to him, his chances of coming out of it were less than 20 per cent. Even today, with early diagnosis and new and better treatments, there is still only a 60 per cent chance of survival. The CT scan had shown the surgeons precisely what they had to do. But they had to do it quickly in order to save his life.

The haemorrhage had undoubtedly been caused by Burton's lifetime of heavy alcohol intake and chain-smoking. It seemed Burton's bad habits had finally caught up with him and, in all probability, had been the final trigger for the haemorrhage.

Decorvet drove his car straight to Geneva's Cantonal Hospital on the Rue Micheli-du-Crest and waited. Burton had already been pushed into the theatre and was being anaesthetised. Fortunately, he had not consumed any food or drink in the previous 12 hours and there was consequently no delay in getting him into the theatre. It was the only good luck he had that day.

The surgeons needed to perform very delicate brain surgery and it was scheduled to last between six and eight hours. Sally was asked for her consent to operate, and she readily signed the forms. The doctors didn't spare her the prognosis. Should the operation be successful, they informed her, her husband would be hospitalised for at least two months, thereafter requiring at least six months of convalescence at home. At this stage, the surgeons were as optimistic as they could be and believed they could save Burton's life, but they were unsure if there would be any impairment in his facilities. Sally was given the impression that it was likely there would be. Sally Burton, a highly intelligent woman, knew precisely what they meant and understood that the doctors were sparing her feelings until they had her husband in the operating theatre. She knew he was likely to die.

They told Sally to return home to Celigny and to telephone close relatives to warn them of what was happening. They told her to return later with a suitcase and to be prepared for a long wait for news.

Sally always enjoyed the journey back from Geneva to Celigny along the Route du Lac, but this time she did not. The 35-minute drive seemed to endure for hours as she went over the events of the previous two days. She thought back over the headaches, the funny noises; they all swirled through her mind as she asked herself whether she could have done anything differently. She was certainly aware that if she had taken her husband to the Cantonal Hospital earlier, he would have had a much better chance of survival. But she could not have known the seriousness of his condition at the time. She also readied herself, as much as was possible, for the worst case scenario – that he might die. But, like most people faced with such circumstances, she also prayed for a miracle.

As they drove away, surgeons went to work and performed a craniotomy to reduce the internal pressure and remove the blood clot from the brain. They very quickly realised that the condition was fatal and that they could not save him. But they continued with the effort for some 30 minutes.

As Burton was wheeled out of the operating theatre, his condition by now was hopeless. He was officially brain dead and being kept alive artificially. Doctors fought to keep him alive so Sally could say 'goodbye'. But very quickly, despite the artificial life support, his vital signs went out and he was pronounced dead at 11:45pm.

It was midday by the time Sally stepped inside the front door of the house. As she turned the key, she heard the telephone ringing in the hallway. The call was from the surgeon at the Cantonal Hospital. He could do no more than tell her that her husband had died a few minutes earlier. He merely said: "Things took a turn for the worse. We could not save him." Sally thanked the surgeon for all he had done and put the phone down in a daze.

She pulled over the chair nearest to herself and gave herself a few minutes' thought. Then, she picked up the telephone and dialled the number of Pierre and Francois Koessler, who lived nearby. The Koesslers were two of their closest friends, and Pierre was also Burton's private banker. She told them what had happened and asked if they could drive her back to the hospital. They were at the house within 15 minutes and Sally climbed into the back of the car, telling them the little she knew. As they drove, her thoughts turned to the next few days and the funeral. She couldn't help thinking that, of everyone who would come to Celigny for the funeral, she would be the one who had known Burton the least. She felt such a fraud. She couldn't help reflecting on her three years with Burton since 1982 when, at the age of 34, she had first met him. They had been thrown together on the film set of a TV miniseries about the life of the German composer Richard Wagner. Burton was playing the lead role while she was working for the film's director, Tony Palmer as continuity manager.

At that stage in her life, she was beginning to think she would never marry nor have children. But almost straightaway, she and Burton formed a sort of instant bond. She found him very attractive, despite the 21 year age gap. She recalled her joy when he had first shown an interest in her and when the sly glances across the set gradually turned into a full-blown romance. It was perfect timing for both of them – she was unmarried and unattached and Burton was in the process of separating from his third wife, Suzy.

In Burton, Sally had found everything she wanted. He was a famous man whom she genuinely adored and respected. He provided a life of luxury approximating fantasy, with two homes, in Switzerland and South America, the ultimate in financial security, and a very exciting lifestyle. Since then, she had felt truly blessed – that is, until that Sunday morning.

Upon her arrival, she was taken into a room and told what had happened by the Swiss surgeon who had led the operation. She was immediately taken in to see his body and was left alone with him. She lingered for a long time in the windowless room, now with only her memories for company. It had taken less than seven hours between her leaning over her husband to call for a doctor and her sitting in a hospital room staring at his lifeless body.

Two years later, she told Melvyn Bragg about the silent communication she had with her husband as he lay motionless on the hospital trolley and as she sat by him in that room: "I remember quite clearly thinking: 'Well done, you've thrown off that old body. You're on your next adventure. Well done.' I had a strong feeling that it was a tragedy for us, but not for Richard – that helped me through the next weeks." She added: "My feeling was that Richard had many lives in him, but not that of an old man."

She left the room and asked if she could use a telephone. She called Valerie Douglas in Los Angeles, where it was now eight o'clock in the morning. Douglas was waiting by the telephone, fearing the worse. As Sally spluttered out the news, Sally realised how difficult each individual call was going to be, and she knew it was going to be more than she could cope with. It was one thing suddenly to lose a husband, whom she loved very much, but quite another to tell people who knew him far better than she did that he was dead. So Sally asked Douglas if she would start making the calls to tell people the news. Sally told Douglas to call as many people as she thought necessary, but insisted that she would ring Kate Burton and Elizabeth Taylor herself.

Douglas, who was typically a very controlled character, found the call from Sally intensely difficult. She had known Richard Burton for nearly 32 years and been with him through thick and thin. But she knew she was beginning her last job for her boss and that she had to stay in control of the situation. Douglas, by all accounts, switched off her emotions and got on with the job, as she had so often in the past when faced with adversity. The nine-hour time difference in Los Angeles gave Douglas time to get the news out to friends and family before they heard it in the media. She herself was shattered by the news, but adrenalin kicked in and she tried to put aside her own grief.

After the formalities were completed at the hospital, the Koesslers drove

Sally back alone to Celigny and she called Douglas again with an update There were easily over 60 individual calls to make, and Douglas was left to break the news to Burton's seven surviving brothers and sisters: Cecilia, William, David, Verdun, Hilda, Catherine and Graham.

Taking the easy way out, Douglas decided to call Verdun Jenkins, whom she found the most agreeable of all the brothers, and ask him to inform the rest. He was at his home in Cwmafan when he received the news. Douglas delivered him the same monologue as she was to do many times that day and simply told him that his brother had become ill at home, been rushed to a hospital in Geneva and had died of a cerebral haemorrhage before the doctors could help him. With so many calls to make, she had time only to give everyone the basic details of what had happened. When they wanted to know more, she quickly put down the phone, insisting that was all the information she had.

Upon receiving the news, Verdun realised he also needed help. His sisters, 66-year-old Hilda and 63-year-old Catherine, were at chapel. Grabbing his car keys, he drove off to tell them in person. There was a minor commotion in the chapel as he grabbed them and pulled them outside. Upon learning of their brother's death, both women sat down on a stone wall. Verdun sat down next to them in silence as his two sisters came to terms with what they had heard. When they had recovered their composure, he told them he needed their help delivering the news to the hundreds of relatives who would need to know what had happened before they heard it on the radio or television.

The three siblings shared the calls out; they had so many to make.

So it was almost an hour after she first learned the news herself that Hilda dialled the home number of her youngest brother, Graham, in Hampshire. "Have you heard?" she asked tentatively. "Heard what?" he replied, equally tentatively. "Richard is dead", she told him matter of factly. They both struggled to talk, and there was a long silence as they cried to each other over the phone. When 57-year-old Graham put down the phone, he informed his wife, Hilary, and together they sat down on the sofa and began the process of grieving. It was then that they started ringing their own family, starting with their two sons, Richard and Alun.

One by one, all the countless nephews and nieces, cousins and uncles, aunts and great aunts all across the world received the shocking news, by telephone, that 'Rich', as they all knew him, was dead.

# AND GOD CREATED BURTON

After speaking to Kate Burton, Sally called Brook Williams in Berlin to confirm that the worst had happened. Williams was in his hotel making arrangements for his boss' arrival on Thursday. Sally knew she would need Brook in the days that lay ahead. Brook was the son of Emlyn Williams, the great playwright who had discovered Richard Burton and had given him his first major acting role. Without Emlyn, there would never have been a Richard Burton.

Brook couldn't have been more different from his father. He was a romantic drifter, whose only occupation was being the son of a famous man. For something to do, Brook had latched on to Richard Burton early in his career and was described by Graham Jenkins as a "chief gofer in the Burton household." But his loyalty to his boss remained beyond question. Now, his loyalty would pass automatically to Sally.

In truth, Brook Williams wasn't too surprised by the news of Burton's death. He, of all people, knew the state of his master's health. But he wasn't thinking of himself as he took in what Sally was saying. He knew he had to make a difficult phone call to England; to his 79-year-old father who was at home at his apartment in Chelsea, London. He knew his father, Emlyn Williams, would be devastated by the news, and indeed he was.

Meanwhile, Sally was agonising about how to tell Elizabeth Taylor. Given the eight-hour time difference between California and Europe, she had been granted a bit of breathing space to get her thoughts together.

It was 9 o'clock on Sunday morning and Taylor was in her bathroom when the call came through. The telephone was answered by Norma Heyman, the 44-year-old British film producer who was a houseguest that weekend. Sally told Heyman what had happened and she agreed to tell Taylor when she came out of the bathroom. Half an hour later, Taylor called Sally back, and what they said to each other in that most difficult of circumstances has always remained private.

Valerie Douglas phoned Taylor's personal assistant, Chen Sam, at home. Chen Sam was not only Taylor's personal assistant, but a very close companion. Douglas had never particularly liked Chen and they had been professional rivals since the days when their respective bosses were married. Rather coldly, Douglas informed Chen Sam of Burton's death and told her Sally had already called Taylor. It was all very matter of fact.

After having spoken to Chen Sam, Valerie Douglas rang Sally and asked her if she wanted her to call Philip Burton in Florida. 79-year-old Burton was the closest thing Richard Burton had to a proper father. He had effectively adopted Richard back in 1943. He had taken a rough Welsh boy who could barely speak English and turned him into a world class actor with the superb diction that became his hallmark.

Sally had never met Philip Burton although she had often spoken to him over the telephone. So Douglas volunteered to make the call to the Philip Burton, and it was then that it dawned on Sally just how close her husband had been to so many people. She was glad to have Valerie Douglas by her side, albeit 7,000 miles away. It was 9:20am when Philip picked up the telephone and heard Douglas' voice on the other end. She told him matter of factly, as she was telling everyone else, that his adoptive son was dead. It was the worst moment of his 79 years; the end of his dreams. As he remembered: "It was the greatest shock I had ever experienced because it was so completely without warning; on the contrary, he himself had led me to be believe that his physical ailments were definitely disappearing."

Philip asked Douglas if Sybil had been told. Sybil Christopher, Burton's first wife, lived in New York with her second husband, the singer Jordan Christopher. She had not spoken to her ex-husband since he had divorced her to marry Elizabeth Taylor in 1963. Douglas said she didn't know and didn't have Sybil's number, which she subsequently got from Philip. But Sybil had already heard the news, having been telephoned from London by her daughter, Kate. Sybil, in turn, had asked Kate to go to Hampstead to break the news to Burton's sister-in-law, Gwen Jenkins. Gwen was the widow of Richard's brother Ivor, who had died in 1972. Ivor and Gwen had looked after Burton from the mid-fifties to 1968, and he had bought them a house next door to his in London. Gwen was old and frail, and Sybil knew she would not take the news well.

Meanwhile, Douglas rang back to tell Sally how badly Philip Burton had taken the news. She also informed Sally that she had spoken to Sybil. This prompted Sally to ask if anyone had told Suzy, Burton's third wife, whom he had married in 1976 and divorced in 1982. No one had, and Valerie Douglas volunteered to make that call as well. Since the divorce, 35-year-old Suzy had virtually disappeared, and there was a great deal of trouble locating her.

Douglas finally found her in England at a motor racing circuit called Brands Hatch, 20 miles outside of London, on a day out with Bette Hill, the widow of racing driver Graham Hill, and Bette's daughter, Brigitte. The three of them were at Brands Hatch watching Bette's son, Damon, drive in his first car race, a Formula Ford event. It was an important day, as her son had recently switched from racing motorbikes to cars.

Suzy went cold when a public address announcement asked her to go to the circuit manager's office for an urgent phone call. She was very surprised to find Valerie Douglas on the other end of the line, as they had not spoken for over two years. Douglas asked her if she was sitting down. Although Suzy had no inkling of what was coming, she knew someone close to her must have died. Her first thought was of her parents or her first husband, the racing driver James Hunt. No one expected him to live long. But when Douglas told her that Richard Burton was dead, she became totally distraught, immediately overcome with uncontrollable grief. She simply couldn't be consoled. It was only two years since they had divorced.

Bette Hill immediately took Suzy out of the circuit manager's office and into her car. She left the circuit, entrusting Brigitte to convey the news to her son. She headed straight back into London with Suzy sobbing uncontrollably in the passenger seat. Bette simply didn't know what to do. She stopped at a telephone box to seek advice from people who had been friends to both Suzy and Burton. In the end, a friend suggested she take Suzy to the house of Alan Jay Lerner, the composer, who lived in Chelsea. The friend rang ahead and warned Lerner.

Lerner and his young wife, Liz Robertson, had been great friends of Burton and Suzy when the two were together. In fact, Liz Robertson, the actress, was one of Suzy's best friends. Bette was relieved to get Suzy to Liz's house, and the two of them gave Suzy a sleeping pill and put her to bed. It was not until the afternoon of the next day that Suzy had recovered enough to telephone Sally Burton in Celigny to ask her what had happened. Despite their obvious differences and the fact that they did not know each other at all, they spent an hour on the phone.

Meanwhile, Sally was fretting how to tell Cecilia James, the woman who had been both sister and mother to Richard Burton since 1925. 79-year-old Cecilia lived in Hadley Wood, in a bungalow in the grounds of a large house shared by her two daughters. She had taken Richard in at two years old, a few days after their 43-year-old mother, Edith, had died in 1927. She had brought him up as her own alongside her own younger daughters, Rhianon and Marian. To all intents and purposes, she was Burton's mother. After a few phone calls, it was decided that 55-year-old Marian, Burton's niece but also effectively his sister, would walk down the garden to Cecilia's bungalow to break the news. 52-year-old Rhianon was in Florence on holiday with her family and would only hear the news much later from her own daughter.

Marian, herself devastated by the news, approached Cecilia's bungalow with extreme trepidation. But she need not have worried. Cecilia was the rock of the family, and she was stoic. She had been expecting the news for years and was well prepared for it. Welsh journalists, who were gradually hearing the news by then, began contacting Cecilia and she told a news agency she had "lost the boy whom she had always loved because she couldn't help herself."

Nevertheless, despite her courage, the entire family was worried about Cecilia, who had always been affectionately known as 'Cis' by Burton and the family. After she had been informed, Hilda Jenkins comforted her on the telephone from Wales, and Cecilia whispered back to her sister: "Why couldn't it have been me?"

At the same time, Graham Jenkins was sitting at home reminiscing with his wife about his departed brother. It suddenly dawned on him that countless other members of the family would only now be hearing the same news he had heard an hour earlier. He had been so lost in his own grief and that of his wife's, that he hadn't given anyone else a second thought. He also knew Cecilia would need support, so he got in his car and drove straight to her house in Hadley Wood.

He remembered: "I sat quietly with my wife, Hilary, talking at random about the past and then, as the shock subsided, a little about the future."

It was the future that concerned him that Sunday afternoon, as he later recalled: "Richard had made known his wish to be buried at Pontrhydyfen, his birthplace, and, for him, the heart of his beloved Wales. But I guessed there might be difficulties. There were too many vested interests at stake."

Reading his mind, his wife said: "Shouldn't you ring Sally?" to which he replied: "No, I don't think so. At least, not yet."

Graham had a lot of respect for Sally, his brother's fourth wife and the role she had taken in his fight to regain his self respect after his third marriage had collapsed and he had sunk into alcoholism.

But he also personally believed Sally to be neurotic about her place in Richard Burton's life, as he explained: "Sally was also a woman made jealous by her late arrival on the Burton marital scene. After just two years of living with Rich, she resented any assumptions of intimacy from family or friends which excluded her. Most particularly, she resented the enduring love of the woman who gave Rich his happiest years – Elizabeth Taylor. A battle of wills seemed inevitable." Graham thought to himself: "To step into that contest uninvited was to ask for trouble."

When most of the phone calls had been made, Valerie Douglas typed out a short press statement, which she telexed to Reuters in London. She included with it a short embargo, which she asked the news agency to respect in order to ensure that the entire family was told the news before it hit the media. After the embargo expired, Reuters flashed the story around the world and soon teletypes clattered in thousands of newspaper offices with the shocking news. In Britain, the night editors cleared their front pages, editors returned to their offices to remake their papers, and television news bulletins were hastily extended to report the loss of the great actor.

With that done, Douglas stepped out of her house, into a taxi bound for Los Angeles airport and on to the first flight to London, where she would transfer to Geneva and then drive on to Celigny.

Meanwhile, Sally was all alone in the house at Celigny, waiting for her mother to arrive from London as well as for Brook Williams to come in from Berlin. She was totally distraught and had an attack of paranoia. All she could think about was her husband's funeral and her own role in it. But she knew that, as his last and current wife, she should and would be centre stage. But what to do about his three other wives, two of whom would most likely want to be there?

At this stage, everyone thought Burton's body would be flown to Pontrhydyfen for burial. He had arranged a plot in the cemetery there many years earlier. But five years earlier, he had changed his will and bought a new plot in the cemetery in Celigny's Protestant church. It was done purely on the advice of his lawyers, who told him that if he was buried in England, it could adversely affect his tax status and cost his heirs millions of dollars in British estate taxes. He also purchased the two lots on either side, supposedly to prevent Elizabeth Taylor from carrying out her oft-made threat to be buried with him when her time came. But he informed no one of his decision aside from Sally and his third wife, Suzy. In the confusion following his death, Sally failed to make clear to the family that it was his wish, and not hers, not to be interred in Wales. When an early biographer, Fergus Cashin, asked him in 1981 where he would like to be at the end of his life, Burton said: "Up on The Side (the name for the grassy hillside surrounding Pontrhydyfen) with the old miners and the tinplate workers, squatting one-kneed around a fire and telling yarns and peeling the sooty skins off finger-burning baked potatoes. Up there with the children of my childhood. The men of my childhood." But Tony Palmer, the film director, was equally adamant that Celigny is where he wanted to be buried. Palmer believed what he called "the romantic stuff about Pontrhydyfen" was all made up for the benefit of journalists because it sounded so good.

Having resolved to make the funeral a private affair, Sally homed in first on Graham Jenkins, the youngest of the brothers. He worked for the BBC and was best connected to the media. Assuming that media attention would focus around him and that, *de facto*, he would become the family's spokesman and go-to-guy for the press, Sally picked up the telephone and impulsively dialled Graham's house. Sally had never really liked Graham and the feeling was mutual. Hilary answered and told Sally he had gone to Cecilia's and that she could find him there. After the two women chatted briefly about what had happened, Sally immediately dialled Cecilia's bungalow, where the phone was answered by Marian.

Simultaneously, Graham was pulling up in his car at Hadley Wood. As he recounted years later: "No sooner had I walked in the door and into her arms than the phone rang. It was Sally and she wanted to talk to me."

The precise details of that call have never been recounted out of respect to Sally, but, effectively, the distraught widow told Graham, as he understood it, that the funeral would be held in Celigny and that she wanted none of his family present at all, including him and Cecilia and, certainly, all of Burton's ex-wives. They were all to be excluded. Sally denies that this was what happened, although she admits she was asked by Douglas to make some calls: "It was a crazy time and after all these years it is difficult to remember the exact sequence of events – probably because it is very painful."

But even if only half true, it was an extraordinary statement to hear for a family in grief. That night, Graham passed on fragments of the conversation to Cecilia and his sisters. He revealed his version of the full narrative the following day. Years later, he described how it was his opinion that Sally had fixated on Cecilia, recalling: "I took a deep breath, not quite knowing what to expect. Her voice was steady and clinically precise. She skipped over the clichés. Then: 'I want to make it clear. I don't want Cis to be at the funeral. She'll only trigger me off.' 'Look,' I said, 'I know you're upset. It's a terrible time for all of us. Can't we leave ourselves a few hours to think? I need to talk with the family.' She replied: 'I've done my thinking. You know what I want.'" She also told him not to say anything to the media and to leave that to Valerie Douglas.

The rest of the conversation focused on the exact circumstances of his brother's death, and Graham was angry at how little Sally was prepared to impart to him. He remembered: "We talked for another five minutes but I was feeling numb. How was I to tell Cis?" He decided the moment was not right.

Later, Sally was to regret any possible inference that the ex-wives and family were not welcome at the funeral. She insisted it was Valerie Douglas who had made the decision and that she had been misunderstood. Graham Jenkins never believed her, and there was not a rapprochement between the two of them until years later. Sally said: "It was not I who banned the family from the funeral. It was Valerie Douglas who asked Brook [Williams] to deliver the message, as she didn't think any of us could bear to look at the grief on Cis' face."

Sally maintained that she was cross when she heard what had happened, and that Douglas, as the sole executor of Burton's will, was adamant that they should not be invited. Sally recalled: "I found myself tip-toeing around Valerie, not wishing to upset her further." She added: "Remember, it was turmoil at the house with everyone in a state of shock and grief."

But family squabbles were soon forgotten as everyone became glued to their television sets.

By six o'clock that evening, the news was out and a crowd had gathered around the Pontrhydyfen terraced cottage of Hilda Jenkins, the only sibling still to remain living in the town of her birth. The house was full and there were people filling the streets, many of whom had known her brother. For Hilda, it was just like the 31st October 1927. The exact same scene as when her mother had died 57 years earlier was being played out again outside her window.

As darkness fell in Celigny, Sally no longer found herself alone. She was comforted by John Hurt, who had heard the news in Geneva on the radio and jumped into a taxi. Then her mother, Mary Hay arrived, as did Brook Williams. Williams had left behind the film set of *The Wild Geese II* in absolute chaos. In many ways, the news of Richard Burton's death was felt most keenly in Berlin, where filming had already begun and the cast and crew were awaiting the arrival of the film's star the following Thursday. A few million dollars had already been invested in the film, not counting the near US$1 million fee Richard Burton was to be paid for reprising his role as Colonel Faulkner in the sequel. He was to star opposite Laurence Olivier and the script called for him to lead a new team of mercenaries, hired to rescue the Nazi war criminal Rudolph Hess, played by Olivier, from Spandau Prison.

Williams had no idea how he would break the news to the film's producer, Euan Lloyd. Lloyd had been unable to obtain insurance on Burton and had gone ahead with the film uninsured. Now he faced disaster.

As soon as Williams put down the phone from Sally, he cancelled all the hotel rooms that had been booked for Burton and his entourage, informing the somewhat irate hotel manager that he would soon understand why. The manager had good reason to be angry. Burton and his entourage had been booked in for five weeks and had taken all the best rooms in the hotel. The cancellation amounted to a loss of over US$150,000 to the hotel.

Williams waited until he arrived at the airport and was just about to board his flight before phoning Lloyd from a phone booth in the concourse. But Lloyd had already heard the news and was trying to contact Williams himself. He gabbled out what had happened, said he had to rush for his flight and put down the phone, leaving a stunned producer at the other end, holding a silent receiver. Lloyd was coming to terms not only with the loss of US$2 million that had already been spent on the film, but also the loss of a great friend.

Lloyd telephoned Peter Hunt, the director and when they met an hour later, they went into an emergency meeting with the film's financiers. The situation could not have been worse; *The Wild Geese II* had already started filming and it had just lost its star actor. Lloyd and Hunt had no idea what they were going to do, especially without insurance. Normally, such insurance would have been standard, but in his last years, Burton had become uninsurable due to his drinking and poor health.

As Lloyd and Hunt pondered their uncertain futures, Valerie Douglas checked in at Los Angeles airport ready to take the late evening flight direct to London and then on to Geneva. The time difference meant that Douglas landed early in the morning at Heathrow and caught the first British Airways flight to Geneva. The flight gave her plenty of time to collect her thoughts on her 31 years of service to the Welsh actor who had conquered Hollywood. They had met in extraordinary circumstances in 1953; after Burton had confronted Darryl Zanuck, the most powerful man in Hollywood, and Douglas had offered to help him with the fall-out. They had been together harmoniously, with only one wobble in 1957, ever since. As soon as she arrived in Celigny, she set up a command centre in Richard Burton's main library in the grounds of the house and began making the arrangements for his funeral.

At Heathrow airport, during the changeover for Geneva, Douglas purchased three copies of each of the British newspapers to take to Celigny for Sally. That morning, Burton's death occupied the lead story on every front page of every national newspaper in Great Britain. The newspapers referred to him as "a legend" and "the great." Ironically, it was the down-market tabloid the *Daily Star* that summed him up best, quoting from a recent interview he had given to the newspaper: "I smoked too much, drank too much and made love too much."

No one would argue with that – least of all Emlyn Williams. He was sitting in Chelsea with all the newspapers spread out in front of him when he was moved to call Sally in Celigny. He said to her: "I never thought when I gave that boy his first part in a film that, when he died, he would be front page and headlines."

Meanwhile, the Jenkins family was gathering at Cecilia's bungalow in Hadley Wood. Graham Jenkins decided to stay overnight at Hadley Wood with his sisters as they toasted their brother's memory late into the night. He slept in late the next morning, but they all awoke with the same thought: that the previous day's events had been a dream.

Deciding to tell his sister Cecilia that Valerie Douglas and Sally did not want her at the funeral of her brother, Graham recalled: "I slept on it and the following morning I passed on the gist of the conversation." Cecilia thought long and hard before she replied: "So the funeral is to be in Celigny, not in Pontrhydyfen?" Graham was surprised, as he admitted later: "Curiously, the assumption built into Sally's opening words had not occurred to me. Of course, [Sally] had already made up her mind. There was to be no discussion."

But the decision that Burton was to be buried in Celigny had not been made by Sally. That had been decided collectively by his lawyer, Aaron Frosch, his third wife, Suzy, and Valerie Douglas many years earlier, although Sally got all the blame. Sally said years later: "The family were shocked that Richard chose to be buried in Celigny. And I came in for a lot of resentment and criticism. In fact, the burial plot had been purchased during Richard's marriage to Suzy. Years later, I heard that the Welsh are buried within four miles of their home. It is a cultural thing and so, many in Wales viewed it as an insult that he was not buried there." She added: "It was a resentment that burned deep for many years and, at one point, Graham said to me: 'You've only been married to him for a year, why are you making all these decisions?' That hurt. I knew that I had only been married to him for a year, but I wasn't making decisions; I felt it was important to fulfil Richard's wishes."

Meanwhile, there was a succession of phone calls for Sally to deal with as people gradually heard the news. Tony Palmer, the film director who had introduced her to her husband, was in East Germany and he simply told her: "I am on my way.

David Rowe-Beddoe, one of her husband's oldest friends, called from Portugal, where he was on holiday in Carvoeiro. She begged him to come to Celigny so he could play the organ at the funeral. He agreed to leave for Switzerland immediately.

In London, Claire Bloom heard the news on television and was more saddened by his death than she could ever have believed possible. She had thought that she had got over him 20 years before, and realised she hadn't fully.

In Celigny, Sally prepared to make what, for her, was the most difficult call of all – to Philip Burton, her husband's adoptive father and the man who had made it all happen for him 41 years earlier. He had already heard the news from Valerie Douglas, but Sally knew that what was going on in his head would be similar to what was going on in her own. Sally had never met Philip but had spoken to him many times over the phone. She told Philip, who was on his own in Key West, Florida, that she would be there for his 80th birthday in four months' time. It made him feel better immediately.

Philip said: "As I gradually accepted the fact that he was gone, I realised that it had been a merciful death for him." From that, he just counted down the days to when Sally would come visit in four months' time. Somehow, he felt incredibly close to her that night even though they barely knew each other. Their sense of shared grief united them 4,000 miles apart.

Back at Hadley Wood, Cecilia knew none of this and, pondering her banishment from Celigny, she said to Graham: "Well, you tell her I will be in Celigny for the funeral. I will be at the service and I will be at the graveside to say 'goodbye' to Richard. It is what Richard would have wanted and it is what I am going to do." Graham replied spontaneously: "...and that makes two of us."

# CHAPTER 2

# Perfect mother, imperfect father

## Fate's destiny unwinds

### 1898 to 1924

It might not have been love at first sight when a new barmaid called Edith Thomas arrived behind the bar of The Miner's Arms in Pontrhydyfen in 1899, but she did immediately attract the rapt attention of the pub's best customer, a 23-year-old coalface miner called Dick Jenkins. The tall and slender Edith towered over Dick, but he didn't seem to mind that at all. He was, by then, used to all the barbs about his height and was known locally as Dic Bach, which, when translated, meant Little Dick. The nickname was justified as he measured only a few inches over five feet.

His full name was Richard Walter Jenkins, named after his maternal grandfather, who was the manager of Pontrhydyfen mill. Born on 5th March 1876 in Efail-Fach, South Wales, he was conceived, rather shockingly, a month before his parents – Thomas and Margaret Jenkins – were married. A sister, called Jane, eventually completed the Jenkins family. Dick grew up to be a selfish young man, concerned primarily with himself – likely a relic of being an only son; a rarity in the mining villages of South Wales. Remarkably, however, he was highly intelligent, literate and spoke both English and Welsh fluently.

As soon as he turned 14, he went down the mines, where his first weekly wage packet contained 7s 6d (37.5p). Not that he had a choice; Pontrhydyfen men could either work at the two local collieries or at the copper foundry. But most went down the mines because the money was better. The coal under Pontrhydyfen was part of a huge coal seam known as the Great Atlantic Fault.

Outside of work, as soon as he had money in his pocket, he became an irresponsible, drunken gambler; undoubtedly due to genes he had inherited from his father, Thomas, who was also all of those things. He spent his free time in The Miner's Arms pub, where all of his wages were spent on beer. What was left went on the dogs. He had no other interests and, until Edith walked into the pub, he had shown little regard for the opposite sex. But all that changed when the 16-year-old blonde arrived to pull the pints.

Quickly, Dick gained a reputation as a man not to be trusted, borrowing money from everyone fool enough to lend it to him. And he never paid it back. When he got into trouble, which was frequently, his only defence was to smile broadly and to act as though butter would not melt in his mouth. It usually worked.

Aside from his character defects, he was a naturally gifted coal miner and was renowned throughout South Wales for his skill with a pickaxe. By the time he was 21, he was arguably the best coalface miner in South Wales, certainly the best in Pontrhydyfen. By then, he was earning £3 a week and, as such, was a hero of the working classes.

But all miners were heroes in those days. They worked in complete, pitch black darkness, apart from the light of their helmet lanterns, and often in two feet of water.

Verdun Jenkins recalled the difficulties faced by his father: "You must realise that, underground, it's total darkness. There's not a beam of light anywhere. The only thing you would hear was a rat scuttling underneath your feet." But Dick Jenkins thrived in this environment, where one swing of his pickaxe was known to produce a fall of 20 tonnes of coal. Jenkins was able to produce well over 1,000 tonnes of coal a year; some six times the average of his fellow miners – such was his skill.

People who remember say he knew exactly where to place his pickaxe to loosen huge quantities of coal, making his axe more potent than any stick of dynamite. His prodigious output meant that, by the standards of the day, he was very well paid. Richard Burton, many years later, recalled his father talking about coal the way other men might talk about the beauty of women. He said: "My father would look at the seam of coal, would almost surgically make a mark on it, and then he would ask his boy helper to give him a number-two mandrel – that's a half-headed pick. Then, having stared at this gorgeous black-shining ribbon of coal, he would hit it with an enormous blow. If he hit it just right, something like twenty tonnes of coal would fall out of the coal face. It was thrilling and exciting."

Like all miners, Dick emerged from the darkness at the end of a working day almost completely black from coal dust. He went straight to The Miner's Arms, as there were no pithead baths or showers in those days. The miners washed in cold water in the basements of their homes.

With a piecework element to their pay packets, crack miners like Jenkins could earn good money whenever they felt like it. The problem was that he didn't feel like it anywhere near enough, and so was always broke from drink and gambling on greyhound racing.

# PERFECT MOTHER, IMPERFECT FATHER

Throughout his life, aside from work, Dick was a relatively worthless individual, and was saved only by his intelligence and charm. What Edith Thomas saw in him isn't at all that clear, but he obviously had some redeeming qualities. He had a cheeky look and sported a moustache and a fringe of black hair that fell unevenly over his brow. Some people recalled him as a relatively good-looking man, primarily because his eyes were distinctive and set wide apart, which, combined with a finely sculpted face and high cheekbones, set him apart from other men. His son, David Jenkins, simply described him as "a strongly-built man, with intelligent brown eyes." But against that, he was short and stocky with a pock-marked face, a legacy of teenage acne. Richard Burton described his father as having "rough, masculine beauty and charm."

Dick's lack of success with women before Edith is therefore relatively surprising, and can only be attributed to his small stature.

Edith Maud Thomas was born on 28th January 1883 at Llangyfelach, near Swansea, ten miles from Pontrhydyfen.

Her parents were Harry and Jane Thomas. Unlike the rough-hewn Richard and Margaret Jenkins, they were a very respectable middle-class couple. Harry, unusually, enjoyed a dual career, first as a miner and then as a copper smelter. He eventually became part of the management.

Their eldest daughter was a very pretty teenage girl, and it is true to say that all the bachelor customers of a certain age at The Miner's Arms were interested in her. But Edith was no pushover. A strict Methodist, she went to chapel every Sunday with her mother and four siblings. The Miner's Arms, now famous, was situated in a row of three-storey residential houses, indistinguishable apart from an inlaid sign indicating it was a public house. It was less than two minutes' walk from the Jenkins family home on the Neath Road. Fergus Cashin, an early Burton biographer, described the pub as "the sentimental centre of Richard Burton's Welshness and the heaven that lay about him in his infancy." Whatever the truth of such a romantic description, it was in The Miner's Arms that the Richard Burton story began.

Almost from the start, Edith and Dick talked animatedly every day. But it was no overnight romance, Edith Thomas needed a lot of persuading to pay Dick any romantic attention. It took an entire year of wooing and nightly storytelling before she began to fall for him. But fall she did, and barely 12 months after they first met, he proposed and she said "yes". Edith later told people she had been smitten by his "eloquence and deep rooted passion." She had overlooked all his other faults, and it wasn't an obvious match: she was middle class and

23

he, most definitely, was working class.

The announcement of their engagement was not welcomed by Edith's parents, and they wholly disapproved of their daughter's choice of husband. In fact, Harry and Jane Thomas forbade their daughter to go ahead with the wedding and refused to have anything to do with the arrangements – or with Dick Jenkins. They simply did not want their daughter marrying a man they saw as a selfish drunk. They could see through Dick Jenkins even if their love-smitten daughter could not.

Edith's solution was to persuade her parents to spend more time in her fiancée's company. She began inviting him to family occasions and Sunday lunch. But the plan didn't work and, instead, made the situation worse. The more time Edith's parents spent in Dick's company, the more strongly they disapproved of him. In the end, Edith stopped trying – but never did she consider ending the relationship.

There was no question of her parents paying for a traditional wedding, so, without parental approval, a chapel ceremony was out of the question. In the end, Dick and Edith were forced to outwit her parents and planned the wedding for the 24th of December, Christmas Eve of 1900, at Neath Registry Office. Edith was then only 17 and one month short of her 18th birthday. Dick was 24.

As parental consent was necessary for a girl under the age of 18 to marry, Edith lied about her age on the marriage certificate. It seems the Swansea registry officials were noticeably lax on checking such details. To pull it off, she presented her brother's birth certificate, with the name crudely altered, to the registrar. Although the registrar did indeed notice it stated that Edith had been born a boy, he overlooked it and allowed the marriage to proceed. Birth certificates in South Wales were notoriously inaccurate in that period due to most of the registry staff being notorious alcoholics.

The deception was not without consequences as, on her wedding night, Edith was distraught by the fact that she had been forced to marry outside of a chapel without her parents' presence and after lying to the registrar. It offended every value she had. Her husband, rather predictably, spent his wedding night at The Miner's Arms celebrating and getting even more drunk than usual, and finally ending up unable to consummate their marriage. As an agnostic, he cared not at all about Edith's feelings or the deception. But Dick's fecklessness and lack of any religious conviction didn't seem to faze Edith at all, so smitten was she by then.

Both Dick and Edith signed the marriage certificate with their own names; they were the first in their respective families not to mark their names with an 'X'. Both were highly literate for their age, and the Jenkins house would later contain many books. It became one of the only homes in Pontrhydyfen with a custom-built bookcase.

When they found out what their daughter had done, Harry and Jane Thomas were furious, and they informed Edith she was no longer welcome at the family home. She moved in with her husband and his parents until Dick arranged to rent a house in Station Road, Pontrhydyfen, near the viaduct. Their first house, where they would live for 23 years, was a two up – two down modest home in a stone terrace of 12 similar houses at the end of Bont Fawr. All 12 houses were occupied by miners' families and cost five shillings a week.

Pontrhydyfen proved the perfect place for a Welsh miner to start a family. The village was built on a mountainous hillside just off the main road from Cymmer. It was four miles up the valley from the industrial seaside town of Port Talbot on the eastern side of Swansea Bay. 'Pontrhydyfen' is the Welsh name for the bridge across the vale, but there were actually three bridges which spanned the mountains on both sides: one, the old viaduct, originally carried water; another was the railway bridge; and the third carried road traffic. The River Afan ran though the town, dividing it in half.

The natural valley, green hillsides and magnificent architecture of the bridges made the mining town a Welsh paradise in which to live. Unsurprisingly, Edith fell pregnant almost straightaway and was a mother soon after her 18th birthday in 1901. The firstborn was a son named Thomas Henry, after both his grandfathers. But the pregnancy affected Edith badly, and she suddenly realised the reality of the life she had chosen. She also quickly began to recognise that her parents had been right about her choice of husband. Dick's wild celebrations after the birth triggered a drinking binge that was to continue almost unimpeded until his death.

After the birth of Thomas, Edith became put off by intercourse and, unsure if there was to be any future with her husband, she restricted sex to the six safe days before her monthly period. It was a calculated decision as, at this stage, there was some chance that Edith, strongly supported by her parents, would decide to defy convention, leave her husband and seek a divorce, taking her son with her. If she was to be a single mother, she wanted as few complications as possible.

Her parents strongly encouraged her to make a break from the errant husband who made her so unhappy. But, as divorce was virtually unheard of back then, she could never bring herself to do it. So she stuck it out. Once again, her parent's attitude intensified her resolve to prove them wrong and to make her marriage to Dick Jenkins work.

Eventually, Edith stopped sleeping with Dick altogether and moved into the spare bedroom with her son. Her resolve won a breakthrough and her husband promised to reform. He cut his drinking right down and sought to become a model father to young Thomas and a better husband to his young bride. When he was sober, the atmosphere in the house was entirely different and the change in him remarkable. He became a humorous man again and a master storyteller, enchanting his wife and child with his tales. The period of virtual abstinence was to last for a remarkable four years – the happiest Edith ever knew.

Eventually, she opened up the marital bed to him and they resumed an active sex life. She also decided to fulfil her dream of a large family. A few months after she allowed her husband back into her bed, she was pregnant again for the second time and, in 1903, Edith gave birth to a daughter named Margaret Hannah. Tragically, however, within a few months, Margaret was dead. Edith was grief stricken and, unfortunately, the death was a cue for her husband to resume his binge drinking. It was right back to the bad old days for Edith, as she struggled with her grief over a lost daughter whilst raising young Tom virtually on her own.

Once more, she stopped having sex with her husband. Repeating the same pattern as before, Dick reformed again two years later and Cecilia arrived in 1905 and Ivor in 1906. A third daughter, whom they also called Margaret Hannah, was born in 1910 but she, too, was dead within a year. It was yet another excuse for Dick to resume drinking and banishment from the bedroom, subsequent reform and an invitation back to the bedroom followed three years later.

From then on, Edith seems to have made up for lost time with non-stop pregnancy. There followed a tumultuous 12 years when the family grew from three children to nine children between 1911 and 1922, when Edith was 28 to when she was 39. In those 12 years, there came three boys and three girls. William was born in 1911, then David in 1914, Verdun in 1916, Hilda in 1918, Catherine in 1921 and Edith in 1922. By the time the last child was born, the first few of her children were almost entirely grown up: Tom was 21, Cecilia 17, and Ivor 16.

But the strains of all this and raising six more young children soon became too great for Edith, particularly as Dick spent all his time – whilst he was wasn't working or eating – at The Miner's Arms. The couple hardly saw each other and Dick had little affinity with his children. In short, he was a terrible father.

By the time Edith was 37, she had lost her looks and was overweight. Her husband had also aged beyond his 43 years and walked with a stoop like a man of 70 years old. Unsurprisingly, any physical attraction between the couple had vanished. But that did not stop her husband forcing himself upon Edith nightly. Despite her intention to have no more children, she was so weak from childbirth and hard work that she could not resist her husband's nightly advances. Dick abandoned any concept of his wife's consent and regularly arrived home drunk, taking her whether she liked it or not. In the end, she just lay back and let him have what he wanted, praying for it to be over quickly.

Edith came to detest Dick, but his actions, which would be decreed as rape and spousal abuse 50 years later, meant she was powerless to stop herself from becoming pregnant again; which meant the arrival of two more children. Both Richard Burton and David Jenkins admitted in later interviews that their father was "devious" and capable of acts of "great violence."

Edith often wished her husband dead but, in Wales, in the early 1900s, marriage was a permanent contract. With no question of divorce, they solved the problem of incompatibility by ignoring each other.

Every so often, he would start extraordinary drinking sessions that could last as long as 48 hours, and she would watch as he consumed as much as five gallons of beer in one session. She hated her life as a wife and sought solace in her role as mother to her many children.

Dick's problem was entirely alcohol. It was humiliating, but he didn't care. He earned around £3 a week and, giving half to Edith, he would spend the other half on beer – large quantities of it. 12 pints a night was not unusual for him and, when combined with spirits, as it sometimes was, the effects were lethal.

A pathetic individual, Dick would sometimes disappear for up to three weeks at a time, usually drinking in Neath or Swansea. He'd leave on payday and spend all his pay packet on beer until he was too frightened to return home. He would sleep rough, spending the nights in pubs and working by day. Then, when his money was completely exhausted, he would be forced to sober up and return home, suddenly appearing in the family kitchen. He was often filthy from nights of sleeping rough. By then, his children were understandably distraught, fearing they might never see him again.

But he always returned and was always welcomed back. His excuse for his long absence was always the same: "I met a friend." As Richard Burton later colourfully described it: "The old man didn't turn up for a week, and then two weeks and then three weeks, and everybody was fairly in despair. After all, there were, in those days, eleven children. And suddenly the kitchen door – we all lived in the kitchen – burst open, and standing there was my father with the most effulgent smile on his face." Upon his return, his older children, Tom and Ivor, would put him to bed, and Cecilia, the eldest daughter, would nurse him back to health. As he lay in bed, recovering, he would whisper to them: "I've got children in a thousand and good as gold they all are."

Whatever Edith's feelings, she put those of her children and their need for a father, however irresponsible, first. One day, he arrived back from a long absence with a greyhound in tow and announced to Edith and the children that he had the answer to the family's money troubles. "Boys and girls," he declared, "our troubles are over." He explained his plan to race the greyhound at the local track for prize money. Edith and Cecilia were furious that he had brought such a large dog into a house that was already bursting at the seams. Consequently, the greyhound was banned from the home and kennelled at the end of the garden. To everyone's relief, however, the dog dropped dead just a few weeks later.

The worst moment came after a long disappearance, during which the family almost starved. It was Christmas, and Dick undertook to work an extra long shift at the colliery to earn extra money and make some amends. But there was a gas explosion in the shaft he was working. When he was brought to the surface, he had suffered first degree burns over much of his body. He came home from the pit hospital covered in bandages, with only his eyes, nose and mouth visible. Luckily, Edith knew exactly what to do and instructed Cecilia and Hilda to rub olive oil over their father's body continually. The girls took the duty in turns, both day and night, and Dick quickly recovered and was soon back at work.

With 11 occupants, the house in Station Road was at bursting point. It was relieved only when Tom got married and set up his own home in neighbouring Cwmafan. Cecilia also moved out of the house to work as a live-in housemaid for the Handford family, a wealthy family of drapers living in Taibach, near Port Talbot. Cecilia's move to Taibach proved beneficial in more ways than one. She met a miner, a distant relation, called Elfed and they soon began courting.

Tom and Cecilia's departure left four boys sharing one bedroom and three girls sharing their parents' room. It was far from ideal, especially when Dick Jenkins arrived home drunk and demanded his conjugal rights. David Jenkins remembers: "There we were, like the proverbial sardines in a tin."

But with two wage earners in the house, since both Dick and Ivor were down the mines, the family income was healthy and plans were made to move to a bigger house. In 1924, the whole family moved to a three up – three down modern house at number 2 Dan-y-bont. The rent was ten shillings a week. Their new home was a semi detached three-storey house right by the giant viaduct that dominated the town and by then carried all the road traffic.

Edith organised the move like a military operation and was immensely proud of her new home. As her son David remembered it: "It was like a mansion by comparison. My parents and, later, baby Richard, had one large room to themselves, we rarely entered, and two beds in the other housed the three girls and the three boys respectively. Ivor had the luxury of the small room to himself."

As in most working class families, one room was set aside virtually unused. It was called the parlour and was maintained in pristine condition, with a polished table, a chest of drawers, a chair and a settee. Family photographs stood on the mantelpiece. The parlour was only used for the most special family occasions and sometimes by the adults on Sunday. The other room was a family room with soft chairs, where everyone gathered when they were not in the kitchen. The house was always warm, as miners and their dependents qualified for a tonne of free coal which was delivered every week.

Her last years, between 1924 to 1927, saw Edith always cheerful and good natured. It was a good period for her family and, determined not to become pregnant again, she excelled at being the perfect mother, keeping the new house immaculately clean and making sure the food on the table was always plentiful.

Although by all appearances they were a very ordinary family, the Jenkinses of Pontrhydyfen were known as a large, colourful clan, inclined to independence, even arrogance. As the children grew and needed less attention, Edith took the opportunity to earn extra money, taking in washing and doing some decorating for neighbours. She was particularly deft at wallpaper hanging, and her services were always in demand. She was also a superb cook and started a small catering business for special events, selling cakes, puddings and pies to friends and neighbours.

# AND GOD CREATED BURTON

David Jenkins remembers those times well: "Mother ensured that there was food in the pantry. We all had enormous appetites but never went hungry. I remember well the delicious, traditional Welsh stews she used to make; and the tarts, pastry rolled out on a flat plate – she made three of those every day."

The mid-twenties were a hard but happy time, as the younger children explored the countryside as a pack. They played in the surrounding hills and by all accounts had an idyllic childhood, especially in the summer months when they roamed free. Aside from Dick, they were a close, loving family, aware of – but not menaced by – poverty.

As David said: "Occasionally in summer, mother made up picnics which we ate on the mountain sides. Our joy sprang less from the picnic basket than from the supreme pleasure of having her to ourselves in the open, away from the pressures of home, which weighed so heavily on her."

Welsh people are a breed unto themselves and know how to enjoy life, and, with only a quarter of the population of South Wales speaking English, Welsh was spoken constantly in the Jenkins household. Like most Welsh children, Edith and Dick's children grew up in the knowledge that when their schooldays came to an end, they would follow in their parents' footsteps: daughters would find good husbands and bear them babies; sons would follow their father down the pits.

Later in his life, Richard Burton himself would describe the Welsh as "an alien race and nobody knows where they came from or what they are." His posthumous biographer Melvyn Bragg speculated that they might be "the lost tribe of Israel or Carthaginians blown north by the Gulf Stream." Penny Junor, one of the earliest Burton biographers, described Wales as a collection of "valleys filled with song and poetry and beer, where men worked hard, drank hard and played hard, and boys grew up in the expectation of a lifetime in the dark, dusty pits."

Religion dominated family life; it was the drumbeat and everything from Monday to Saturday led to Sunday. Saturday night was usually bath night, so everyone was clean to attend chapel the following day. All the children bathed once a week in the zinc bath kept for that purpose in the kitchen. It was no different from any other working class family in Britain.

The puritan influence of the Chapel ran far and deep but, despite the strict teachings, the Baptist faith also brought with it music and poetry. The Chapel was not a solemn place. It was a meeting place, a social get-together, and the minister had to call for silence a few times before he could begin a service.

Each member of the Welsh congregation had one thing in common: they all liked the sound of their own voices; and the louder and lustier, the better.

Edith attended the Bethel Welsh Baptist Chapel, and the whole family would go first in the morning and then again for the evening service. And attendance was obligatory. The children would also attend Sunday School in the afternoon. After Sunday School, the children would go to the chapel vestry for a high tea, an event in itself.

As David Jenkins recalled: "We never questioned it – it was an accepted part of our lives."

Chapel attendance across South Wales was very high because there were typically no wireless sets in households. Essentially, Sunday Chapel was the only form of entertainment for the family. According to David Jenkins, the sermons were delivered with a sense of the dramatic worthy of any actor. The minister's voice would at first be perfectly modulated and controlled. Then, slowly, deliberately, the full repertoire of his oratory would be revealed. Jenkins said: "The effect was devastating. I could not have stood or spoken if my life had depended on it! Then suddenly, to my great relief, he would lower his powerful voice almost to a whisper." He added: "In summer, we would all swelter in our 'Sunday best.'"

Although it was before his time, Graham Jenkins remembers being told that "the chapel was our other world. Within that simple building, we let our emotions rip. We sang lustily, prayed fervently and listened in awe to the thunderous declarations of moral judgment. A good preacher was a poet in action. He could spin words into a story of such power as to stop the mind." Afterwards, virtually the entire congregation marched through the village with great pomp and pride.

But there was a cloud over the Jenkins family because of the continuing absence of Dick at Chapel. He was an anomaly in those days, as non-believers were few and far between, and, even so, many a non-believer still attended Chapel for the entertainment value. Nothing Edith did could persuade him to attend and to relieve the family of the shame.

But there was one thing about which Edith was certain: as she approached her 40th birthday, she was determined that there would be no more children. But she was reckoning without considering her rampaging drunken husband, who forced himself upon her with ever increasing regularity.

# CHAPTER 3

# One birth, one death

## One legend is born, one departs

### 1925 to 1927

In March 1925, at the age of 42, Edith Jenkins realised she was pregnant once more. Richard Jenkins (later to be Richard Burton) was born peacefully on 10th November 1925 in his parents' bedroom in the presence only of a midwife. Young Richard weighed in at 12 pounds and, as one neighbour who popped in to view the new addition described him, he was a "real whopper." He was born on the eve of Armistice Day, then an important day in the calendar, which marked Germany's surrender and the end of World War I only seven years earlier. Armistice Day was commemorated by ceremonies of remembrance across Britain.

Even on the day of his birth, there was something about Richard that differentiated him from the other six sons. Edith marked him down for greatness long before that greatness became apparent to the rest of the world. Proof came when she chose to give her 12th-born the prized family name of Richard Walter, which belonged to Dick's father and his grandfather and great grandfather before him. Why Edith waited for the sixth boy to bestow the ultimate family honour is unknown. It does seem that Richard Walter Jenkins IV was, in his mother's eyes, the chosen one; the son with the best chance to elbow his way out of South Wales and shed the family's working class roots.

When Cecilia heard news of the birth, she too was struck by it and, for an entire hour, both mother and elder sister just gazed at the baby in silence, each with giant smiles on their faces. 62 years later, Cecilia told the film director Tony Palmer: "I went to see this beautiful baby called Richard."

But the feeling was not universally shared. Cecilia remembered an hour later carrying Richard downstairs for a general inspection by the rest of the family. Older brother Ivor was preparing to leave for work down in the mines. "Oh, isn't he lovely...what do you think of him?" asked Cecilia, cradling the newborn in her arms. Ivor gave his new brother a long look and said: "He's all right, I suppose, but he's another mouth to feed", adding: "I don't want to talk about babies now. I'm having my breakfast."

Knowing that her mother would be worried about Ivor's opinion on the matter, Cecilia went back and told her that he was "delighted" with the child.

Whatever his destiny, 1925 was not a great year for Richard Walter Jenkins IV to come into the world. It was an unusually bleak and cold winter in Pontrhydyfen. Pontrhydyfen was bleak anyway due to the mountains that surrounded it and blocked out the rays of low winter sun. The unusual effect created what Melvyn Bragg referred to as "rugged melancholy."

The weather wasn't the only problem in the area known as the Swansea Valley. The region also had the highest infant mortality rate in the whole of Britain. But, despite that, Richard thrived and the closest of bonds developed between the new baby and his mother. Every day, she placed him in a large shawl, which she then wrapped carefully around herself with the baby's head resting against his mother's breast; that was until he was old enough to leave his cot. Then, he would crawl around and follow his mother underfoot, never letting her out of his sight. When she did, he would cry immediately.

Already, the young Richard Burton held the women of the household in thrall. His three sisters, who were still at home, Edith, Catherine and Hilda, doted on him day and night. It was an extraordinary thing to behold, and everybody noticed it. As David Jenkins confirmed: "We all found him irresistible and were no doubt inclined to spoil him, but still there were nine other mouths in the house to feed."

But it wasn't all plain sailing. Richard was breastfed, just as all his siblings had been, and as David recalled: "Richard used to bite the breast wickedly from time to time and was smacked. On other occasions, my mother would show her displeasure by putting him down, but there was invariably someone ready to pick him up again." Despite the arrival of another baby, Edith Jenkins simply carried on as before. Melvyn Bragg would later describe her as "noble and infinitely capable, providing full meals and basic decency for her many children."

In truth, she needed to be all that and more in order to bring up her remarkable family with so little help from her husband. Edith did everything to save money and stretch the family's budget, and would spend hours devotedly over the sewing machine, making clothes for her children. Money was terribly short, and Dick was often penniless a few hours after getting his wage packet. Now that Ivor was also working and handing Edith his wage packet, Dick became even more irresponsible. Bragg called him: "A greater child, perhaps, than any of her own."

After Richard's arrival, there were ten people living in the three-bedroom house, and life was unusual and far from ideal to say the least. Richard slept in his parents' bedroom, in a cot beside their double bed. In the big bedroom next door, there were two double beds, side by side. In one bed slept the three sisters, Hilda, Catherine and Edith. While the three brothers, David, William and Verdun, slept in the other. Ivor, as the eldest son, had his own room – the third bedroom – which was really a tiny box room at the top of the house with a single bed.

All meals were taken in the large kitchen, where there were two tables to accommodate the 11 people who now turned up to be fed at meal times. One table was round, which was occupied by the children aged under 14. At the square table sat the parents and the elder children.

The financial problems, due almost exclusively to Dick's drinking, became more and more profound and eventually dogged the family. But even worse was yet to come. There were deep-rooted problems in the mining industry, and the good years that had prevailed since the middle of the previous century were coming to an end. There were then 66 collieries in South Wales, but since the end of the First World War, 21 had already been closed because of the import of cheap Polish coal, and 14,000 miners had been made redundant as a result.

Now, in the mid-1920s, there were more pressures. The industry was being hit as the domestic coal seams, heavily worked, began, one after the other, to run out. It made the coal that was left more expensive to mine. Capacity dropped sharply and Britain was suddenly exporting far less coal than previously – although global demand was going up. The British coal industry was caught in a classic squeeze as, gradually, its previously lucrative overseas markets were being taken over by the United States, Poland and Germany. All three countries had strong, efficient coal industries, and the mines were much younger.

As the coal seams in England and Wales ran out, annual output fell from 310 tonnes per man in 1880 to 247 tonnes per man in 1910. By 1920, it was down to 199 tonnes per man. In 1925, a bad situation was made catastrophic when Germany was allowed to export coal to France and Italy as part of its agreed reparations for the First World War. Coal replaced cash and, since the coal was free, France and Italy suddenly stopped buying from Welsh pits overnight.

If that was not enough, a final blow came when the then chancellor of the exchequer, Winston Churchill, introduced a new economic system called 'The Gold Standard'. The British pound appreciated rapidly, making Welsh coal much more expensive abroad. Rising production costs, rising prices and a consequent fall in demand plus cheap exports combined to create a recipe for disaster. Something had to give, and it did.

As most of the cost of a tonne of coal was labour, the solution seemed obvious. The only solution was to reduce miners' wages and make them work longer for less in an attempt to bring down the cost of a tonne of coal. The alternative was closing down all Britain's collieries and buying coal from Poland.

Historically, South Wales miners were amongst Britain's best-paid workers. They were the elite of the work force, producing the energy needed to power Britain, and they were paid handsomely as a result. They wanted the good times to continue forever.

All mines were privately owned by individual owners but they negotiated pay and conditions together as a co-operative. When the proposal of lower wages and longer hours was made, the miners' union naturally resisted it although it seemed inevitable. To fight it, the powerful union coined a new slogan: "Not a penny off the pay, not a minute on the day."

But such an approach was wholly unrealistic. The union leaders did not understand the situation that prevailed; the industry's golden days were over and an urgent restructuring was required. The union leaders turned to the government to intervene in the dispute. Prime Minister Stanley Baldwin was scared of the mine union's power in industrial Britain, and, to prevent an ugly showdown between the miners and the mine owners, he intervened before a strike could be called. But Baldwin's solution was actually a fudge.

He announced a special Commission to report on the future of coal and agreed to subsidise the entire industry until the Commission published its findings and recommendations. He also proposed temporarily to subsidise miners' wages until a solution to the problem could be found.

On 10th March 1926, the Commission's report was published and it recommended that miners' wages should be reduced by 13.5 per cent. Baldwin hoped the mine owners would accept the proposals and announced that the government subsidy would end immediately. But the mine owners were furious with Baldwin's naïveté.

Unsurprisingly, they rejected the report's findings as wholly insufficient and announced they were unilaterally imposing longer working hours along with a 25 per cent reduction in wages. The situation was serious, but the mine owners believed they had nothing to lose from a strike. Any decision to strike would be pure folly and the mine owners pre-empted it by declaring that if the miners did not accept the new terms by 1st May, they would be locked out of the pits.

By 1st May, an agreement had almost been reached but it was too late: the ultimatum expired, the deadline passed and the mine owners were in no mood to settle. Subsequently, one million miners were locked out of the pits. The industry was closed down overnight. The mine owners had effectively called the strike on its side and taken away all the miners' leverage.

The Trades Union Congress (TUC) was called in to help, and it did the only thing it could by calling for a national strike in support of the locked-out miners. Two days later began what eventually became known as the 1926 general strike. The strike's objective was to force Baldwin's government to protect the coal industry permanently with subsidies. It was an impossible request but there were no cool heads prevailing. Unionised workers all over Britain withdrew their labour, and vast armies of pickets encircled Britain's ports and power stations to stop the movement of coal in an attempt to bring the whole country to a halt. Baldwin called in the army to help keep the country going, as food ran short almost immediately. The ordeal lasted ten days, from 3rd May 1926 to 13th May 1926. Dick Jenkins went on strike along with everyone else.

It couldn't last, of course, but whilst it did, it was the most tumultuous 12 days in British history and it ended with a half-baked settlement.

The miners remained on strike but, by then, it didn't matter, and the end result was that 400,000 out of the 1.2 million miners in Britain lost their jobs almost overnight, including Dick Jenkins. Of the two mines around Pontrhydyfen, his was virtually exhausted of coal and was never again to open its doors. Those miners who kept their jobs in the adjoining colliery were forced to accept lower wages and longer hours; worse than had originally been proposed on 1st May. It had all been for nothing. The change was disastrous for the Pontrhydyfen area and right across South Wales. The Jenkins family was turned upside down.

No one can deny that the measures worked. 14 years later, in 1940, the 800,000 miners still employed were each producing 300 tonnes of coal a year, and the industry was prosperous once more. By then, Dick and four of his six sons were working down in the mines again.

The restructuring, however painful, had been necessary, and the years in between were difficult for Edith and her family. Without a place to work, there was nothing else for Dick to do but to spend his time in The Miner's Arms. After he was sacked, he was eligible for £1 10s (£1.50), a week's dole money, which he collected from the Labour Exchange at Cwmafan. Every Thursday, he would walk to Cwmafan to collect the money in cash. Although it was only half the wages he had earned whilst working, the money was still enough to pay for the family's food and rent, just as long as he didn't spend it on drink.

But every Thursday became a nightmare for Edith, as she became very frustrated and anxious waiting for his return. As her son David recalled: "I was only a child, but I was well aware of my mother's alarm and tenseness, constantly looking out through the kitchen window to see if there was any sign of him coming up the road. 11, 12 and then one o'clock would strike, and there was still no sign. Eventually, after an eternity of waiting, he would turn up after closing time, having spent a good deal of the precious dole money on drink."

The shortfall meant Edith was forced into debt, borrowing money from family and friends and taking on what credit she could. She was often left with barely ten shillings to feed and clothe the family for the week. The rent on the house at Dan-y-bont was ten shillings (50p) a week, which she eventually stopped paying altogether. She got very distressed when she could not afford the family's grocery bills. As David said: "She could not bear to go to the stores or landlord herself to explain that funds were short, and would ask one of us to go instead."

It was at this time that the true worthlessness of Dick Jenkins became apparent. Instead of caring for his family and making sacrifices, his true character surfaced as he abdicated his responsibilities and forced his wife to rely on her eldest children for money. By then, Ivor, Verdun and William were all working in the mines. As the children grew up, Edith eventually had three wage packets from which she could draw, but they added up to less than £1 10s (£1.50) between them.

But in between the misery, there was also happy family news when Cecilia announced her engagement to Elfed James, the miner who lived in Taibach. They were married in July 1927 and Edith was very relieved to see the second of her eldest children married and settled, and even happier when Ivor also announced his engagement to his childhood sweetheart, Gwen.

But the dark shadow of her husband spoilt Edith's enjoyment of her family. Out of loyalty, his sons and daughters have always protected the memory of Dick Jenkins, and historic accounts have never told the truth about a man who, in reality, was a truly evil family patriarch.

Later, his grandchildren and great grandchildren, who didn't have the same loyalty, described what he was really like. Even Dick's biggest cheerleader, David Jenkins, in the light of overwhelming evidence of his father's nasty character, reluctantly admitted before he died: "I have memories which hurt me." In his own book, published in 1992, David wrote: "Something akin to contempt for father grew in us. I certainly remember the shame and disgust his drunkenness made me feel." In his book, Jenkins called his father "self absorbed" and admitted he "humiliated" his wife in front of her children frequently.

But, despite that, Hilda Jenkins continued to remember her father rather benevolently: Many years after his death, with her memory blurred, she told the documentary film director Tony Palmer: "My father Daddy Ni always had us in fits. He loved his drink. Loved it. We idolised him because there was nothing nasty, ever." But that simply wasn't true, nor was it even close to the truth – Dick Jenkins was not a pleasant man, as later events would prove.

Determined that none of her own children should end up like their father, Edith lectured them throughout her life on the evils of alcohol.

Despite her abhorrent spouse, by the time Edith was 43 years of age, she began to experience a sense of some stability. Even though she was being continually forced upon nightly by her drunken husband, she had long since ceased complaining and simply endured it until it was over, despising him more each time.

But by then, there was some relief, as she firmly believed her childbearing days were definitely behind her.

But once again, in January 1927, she found herself pregnant. Unable to fathom having another baby at her age, she said to a neighbour: "God almighty, another mouth to feed." But the 13th and final pregnancy was to prove one too many. This time, her husband's lust had effectively served her with a death sentence.

The 13th pregnancy was highly dangerous at her age. The baby should have been terminated but her religious convictions would not allow it. Children of working class Welsh people, before the advent of the National Health Service, were all born at home in less than ideal conditions. The chances of survival for a mother and child were never that good, and Edith had been lucky up until then. The wear and tear on Edith's body after several previous pregnancies, however, had left her particularly vulnerable to infection. While many of her previous births had been followed by infections from which she had recovered, the 13th was about to prove terribly unlucky.

The risks of multiple births to a mother's long-term health were also well known in South Wales. Very few women who gave birth to more than six children lived beyond the age of 50. And, in an era before contraception, many women married to violent drunken spouses faced the same problems as Edith.

At first, however, it all went well. On the morning of the 25th October 1927, Edith had risen early to complete the family's washing. Then she packed the children off to school and started on the ironing. But, at midday, her water broke and the local midwife was called. The baby, whom she named Graham, was born three hours later.

Once again, the family was ecstatic that another baby had been delivered. It brought the family up to eleven: seven boys and four girls. But it was one too many for Edith. Septicemia quickly set in, and this time she was too weak to resist it. There were no antibiotics and her worthless husband would not, or could not, pay for hospital treatment. The local doctor called every morning and evening, but without drugs there was little he could do. Neighbours, sensing the dangers, came in to look after the children. A nurse volunteered to be with her constantly.

The problems were compounded by the fact that Edith was both physically and emotionally weak and seriously run down, as David Jenkins remembered: "We sensed that all was not well, but mother had had so many babies before and had always returned to her place, centre stage in the household, so we were not seriously alarmed at first. The doctor, midwife, my father and Cecilia were rushing about the house in a state of confused preoccupation."

It was the final indignity to his wife when Dick finally denied her proper hospital treatment with the declaration that he had no money. With the family deeply in debt, there was no alternative than for Edith to take her chances at home. Five days later, she was at death's door.

David was the only other person in the house that day, as he remembered: "On the morning of 31st October, there was suddenly a frightening atmosphere in the house. I can remember the confused, fearful feelings. I was unable to understand exactly what was going on; certain only of the magnitude of the ill-defined disaster."

That October morning of 1927, at precisely nine o'clock, Dick Jenkins came down the stairs from his bedroom and announced to his 13-year-old son that his mother was dead. He said simply: "Davey, Mae dy fam wedi marw." Translated, it meant: "Your mother has died." As David recalls: "I realised with mounting horror what he was saying to me."

Leaving the rest of his children to find out about their mother's death on their own, Dick went straight to the pub to drown his sorrows as he always did. Hilda Jenkins was on her way home from school when she overheard two women talking. One was enquiring after Mrs Jenkins. The other shook her head and slowly waved a hand in front of her face. Hilda ran the short distance to the house and on the way met Verdun, who had Richard on his back. She told them her fears. When they stepped in the hallway, the sounds of crying from upstairs told them all they needed to know. Hilda remembers: "It was all heartbreak. One minute we were all so happy for Richard to have a little brother and then, my God, Mam was dead! I was the eldest girl at home and only nine. It was like a bad dream."

The news spread quickly to rest of the family, and over a hundred people gathered inside and outside the house when they learned of Edith's passing. Meanwhile, Dick Jenkins slurped beer a few streets away, spending the money he should have invested in his wife's medical care.

The grief was unrestrained. Edith Jenkins had been known as a magnificent mother to her children. She had been universally popular and, each evening, the house filled with people. Mourners brought food and endlessly discussed Edith and her legacy. Little did they know precisely what that legacy would entail.

# AND GOD CREATED BURTON

# CHAPTER 4

# My sister, my mother

## Cometh the hour, cometh the man

### 1927 to 1931

Apart from the shock, grieving and sense of loss, the sudden death of Edith Jenkins created absolute logistical panic in the Jenkins household. Suddenly, there were seven children in the house under the age of fourteen with no mother and a useless father. Two-year-old Richard and five-day-old Graham were the immediate problem and they could not be left in the charge of their alcoholic father.

So as soon as Edith was buried, the family held an urgent meeting in the front parlour at Dan-y-bont. Dick Jenkins, then 51, sat silently on a stool in the corner. The three elder children and their partners led the discussions: Tom, 26, and his young wife Cassie; Cecilia, 22, and her husband Elfed; along with Ivor, 21, and his fiancée, Gwen. They were joined by 16-year-old William, 13-year-old David, 11-year old Verdun and nine-year-old Hilda. The two younger sisters, six-year-old Catherine and five-year-old Edith simply observed. It was a full-scale Welsh family council of war, as the siblings jointly decided what to do.

Hilda Jenkins remembered the sense of desolation that embraced everyone at the gathering. But life had to go on. Interestingly, it was Ivor who took charge and made the ultimate sacrifice. He announced that he was calling off his marriage to his childhood sweetheart and abandoning his plans to leave home. Although he was deeply in love with Gwen and wanted desperately to marry her, Ivor knew he had to set an example. When the hour came, so cameth the man; and Ivor emerged as the strong character, perfect for the task of head of the family.

His announcement had the desired effect, and the rest of the family was shocked. Any illusions the others may have had about the nature of the family crisis, and the sacrifices necessary, were immediately swept away. From that moment on, Ivor was head of the family.

It was quickly decided that Richard and Graham would be farmed out to Cecilia and Tom, and would go to live in their houses permanently. That left Ivor and Hilda to run the main family home with the rest of the siblings.

That was the easy bit. The hard bit was deciding who was to have whom. Richard was the prize, and no one really wanted the responsibility of a few-days-old baby. Logically, it made sense for Cecilia to take the baby, but she was having none of it and forced Tom and his wife to take Graham. Cecilia had formed a real bond with Richard and, years later, the girl without a selfish bone in her body admitted she was determined to get him come what may. And she got her way when Tom finally agreed to take Graham.

So, on the fateful night of the 4th November 1927, Tom and Cassie took Graham home to Cwmafan, three miles away, and Cecilia and Elfed took Richard the five miles to the home they shared at Taibach. It turned out to be a very good arrangement, and Tom Jenkins proved the perfect surrogate father for the young baby Graham. Tom was the brother closest in looks to his father, although entirely different in character. He was later described by Cecilia as "strong, kindly, fatherly, with a wry sense of humour." His wife Cassie simply fell in with her lot and she provided Graham with all the love he needed.

But Richard really lucked out as, overnight, Cecilia became his mother. The 22-year-old had grown up to be a striking young woman, capable and down-to-earth like her own mother, displaying great patience with great warmth. David Jenkins said there was never a more perfect woman than Cecilia: "She had my mother's selflessness, but with greater spirit and a keen sense of justice."

Cecilia was absolutely delighted that she had won Richard as her prize. It filled a real gap in her life and helped her immensely with the grief she felt over the loss of her mother. She told everyone that she was "half in love" with Richard, adding that she sensed the feeling was "mutual".

At that time, Cecilia was living with her new husband, 25-year-old Elfed James. They lived in a rented house in a road known as The Constant Bungalows. Cecilia had chosen a husband who was a straightforward, good man of no great distinction. Elfed didn't drink and was very parsimonious, the perfect partner for Cecilia and very unlike her father. Elfed had first attracted her attention at an eisteddfod in Port Talbot, where she was singing. She and Elfed were second cousins, as their maternal grandmothers were sisters. It wasn't love at first sight, and probably wasn't even love in the traditional sense, but they were very attracted to each other and settled into a fine, stable marriage with plenty of mutual affection and respect.

Richard immediately felt at home in Taibach, a suburb of Port Talbot.

# MY SISTER, MY MOTHER

Within weeks he had forgotten the memory of his mother, despite how close they had been. He quickly made friends with Dillwyn Dummer, Edwin and Margaret Dummer's son. Margaret Dummer was Elfed's sister and the family lived nearby at 2 Inkerman Road East. The two boys, both aged two, bonded straight away. For the next 14 years, the boys were never separated and they shared everything.

There was also the strong presence of Morgan and Mary James, Elfed's parents who lived next door to the Dummers at 3 Inkerman Road East. Morgan and Mary acted as *de facto* grandparents to Richard. Mary James was an omnipresent figure in the daily life of the family, and a strict disciplinarian. She detested liars and found young Richard wanting in that regard. Certainly, both boys were regularly beaten as they continually misbehaved. The two children were certainly in awe of their silver-haired granny, and sometimes the punishment she meted out was even more harsh than a beating. If either boy misbehaved, it was not unknown for Mary James to hold their hands on the hot iron grate of the fire for a few seconds as punishment.

But it was Richard's relationship with Cecilia that dominated his early years. As he had been so young when his mother passed, he couldn't remember much about her and Cecilia essentially became his mother. As he would say years later: "From the time I moved in with Cis, I never cried again for my mother. She was more mother to me than any mother could ever have been. She was innocent and guileless and naïve to the point of saintliness."

To keep the family together, the plan was for both Richard and Graham to return every weekend to the family home. And when they could not, their brothers and sisters resolved to visit them. The determination to maintain the family bond was pursued intensely, and David Jenkins describes the resulting family unit as "a tough, sturdy, outgoing bunch. The introverted, more reflective side inherited or absorbed from our mother was present and, to all appearances, we were extrovert and self-reliant."

But Hilda Jenkins was very worried. She would have preferred Richard to have stayed at Dan-y-bont and she had initially volunteered to bring him up despite the obvious impracticalities. She was worried that Richard understood no English, as she explained: "He had no English and spoke all Welsh to my sister while her husband, Elfed, always spoke English. So you can imagine how strange it was for Richie. It was like going to a foreign country." It was true that Elfed James had no Welsh at all, but Hilda was wrong that no Welsh was spoken in the house. In fact, the move was to have dramatic benefits for Richard's education. As no English had been spoken in the Jenkins house, the young Richard, suddenly thrust into a predominantly English speaking household, was forced quickly to learn the new language. It was to be the making of the young boy, ensuring the multi-lingual upbringing so vital to his future choice of career.

There were also hidden benefits. Richard and Cecilia were able to use Welsh to communicate in private, much to the fury of Elfed, who often had no idea what they were saying to each other. Speaking Welsh also became their daily link with the past and with their mother.

Cecilia may have been delighted with the new family set-up, but Elfed was less than enamoured. He was already burdened with the insecurity of a miner's life and did not particularly welcome a child who was not his own coming into the house. Elfed effectively became Richard's new father but, in actuality, he was the three-year-old's brother-in-law. Richard also had trouble adapting to Elfed, who was the precise opposite of his real father.

Elfed's mother and father, who lived five minutes away, were also unhappy with their son's added responsibilities, and there were tensions between the Jenkins and James families that would occasionally and suddenly surface.

But Cecilia ignored the tensions. She was living a sort of paradise existence. Marriage was still a novelty, and after four months, she had not fully adjusted to married life with a man in her bed every night. Now, an instant child made her family complete. But she was also determined to do her duty as wife and mother, and found she had exactly the same work ethic as her mother. She put her heart and soul into making a decent home for her immediate family as well as a decent home for her siblings five miles away.

After her mother's funeral, Cecilia would make the eight-mile bus ride three times a week with young Richard under her arm to perform the Jenkins household family duties. Elfed hated the fact that his wife ran two homes, and it was a terrible burden as Cecilia admitted later: "I thought: I've got to come out of this. I've got to work it off, you know. And there was plenty of work there, I can tell you."

It was only possible because of the excellent twice-daily bus service, privately run by a company called Thomas Brothers. The bus stop was barely 30-seconds' walk from Dan-y-bont, right outside The Miner's Arms. 30 minutes after boarding the bus in Taibach, Cecilia could be in Pontrhydyfen. There was one stop and a change of bus at Aberavon. The return fare was 4d (1.5p). On the return journey, if she missed the afternoon bus, she was forced to walk home – so she didn't miss it often.

Her work at Dan-y-bont consisted of cooking, cleaning, washing and ironing – all four of which she did. There were eight people living in the house and when she arrived, she was in despair not knowing how or where to begin. There were mounds of dirty clothes that needed washing, dirty floors that needed cleaning and a cupboard full of food that needed cooking. Cecilia's daughter Rhianon remembered: 'My Uncle Ivor and Uncle Davy were handsome men and were always well dressed, they even had tennis whites, and my uncle Davy had a plus-four suit. Even with all the work to be done in the house by my mother, they still wanted their white shirts and starched detached collars to be done to perfection.'

Cecilia used to start with the cleaning and would then begin cooking. And no one ever went hungry. Graham Jenkins, who was there at weekends, remembered: "We all ate plentifully and with great gusto. The main diet was fresh fish, but there was a joint once a week and, on Saturday, we had cockles and lava bread – a huge treat."

Lava bread was a staple of Richard Burton's childhood. It was said that if a woman put lava bread in front of a Welshman, of whatever age, he would forget all his troubles. Unknown in the rest of the world, lava bread is cream of boiled seaweed. When cooked, it resembles a cow pat, but to the Welsh, it is known as "Welshman's caviar."

But Cecilia found Dan-y-bont to be a very happy house, and that was all down to Ivor Jenkins and the way he ran the household. He was physically the biggest and strongest of the Jenkins clan and a natural leader. Ivor had left school and gone down the mines in 1919 when he was only 13. In 1925, when the pit closed, he went into the building trade, and his skills meant he found plenty of work.

Ivor was nicknamed 'King Farouk' by Hilda, and his secret was that he ruled the household with a very firm hand.

Graham Jenkins recalled: "Ivor knew his own mind and was capable of bringing a sense of order to the family." He was also a very moral man and became the family's conscience, wholly opposite to Dick who was relegated to a minor role in the family hierarchy. So lowly was Dick's status that even nine-year-old Hilda ranked above him in importance. In contrast to Dick, Ivor set a fine example, abhorred alcohol and never once visited The Miner's Arms. Although the hard man of the family, Ivor could also read poetry with great beauty. And despite his miserly ways, he was also capable of great kindness.

Life was certainly different for Dick with Ivor in charge. Dick was now a sideshow and, without Edith, he showed his true colours and totally neglected his children. Whilst some of his children indulged him and accepted his faults with forgiveness, Ivor wasn't inclined to do so. It didn't seem to bother Dick at all that his 21-year-old son had usurped him and reversed the role of father and son. He continued his life as a curiosity and spent most of his time at The Miner's Arms, eking out the small beer allowance granted to him by Ivor. When that was exhausted, he visited Cecilia and Tom at their nearby homes, spending as little time as he could at Dan-y-bont.

With Dick's spending on beer curtailed, the household finances were gradually restored back to solvency. Ivor allowed his father no indulgences at all and Dick's dole money was confiscated as soon as he received it. Richard Burton recalled the scene at home in those years: "It was a strong family of strong people. My father was the weak one."

Strong leadership was needed as a huge cloud lay over the entire family. It wasn't widely known, but the Jenkins family was nearly £300 in debt when Edith died; all as a result of Dick's drinking. The family owed money to almost everyone, including neighbours and local tradesmen, and was almost a year behind with the rent. But for the young children and Edith's natural charm, the family would long since have been evicted. Ivor was parsimonious in the extreme and detested debt, and he resolved to repay it as quickly as possible.

As well as cancelling his wedding, Ivor made other huge sacrifices for the family. He had developed into a rugby union player of some repute and was easily the best player in the village. So much so that he was tipped to play for Wales. But his new family responsibilities precluded that, and any possible sporting career died its own death. Richard Burton later recalled his brother as an "absolute hero", saying: "Heroes were vital to our way of life. To play rugby as well as carving out the mines was a sign of great heroism, and my older brother was my greatest hero. I worshipped him."

But not everything went as Ivor wished. In the midst of it all, he found he had an unlikely rival as head of household – his ambitious young sister, Hilda. As she grew, Hilda saw no reason to take orders from her 21-year-old brother. But as Ivor controlled the purse strings, Hilda had no independent income and her ambitions were hobbled. So she resorted to guile.

# MY SISTER, MY MOTHER

Hilda was in charge of doing the basic grocery shopping from the Pontrhydyfen Co-Operative Society store. Twice a week, Ivor made out a list of items he required, which he then gave to Hilda along with the money to pay for it. She would walk to the shop and read out the list to the shopkeeper, and the shopkeeper would pick the tins and packets from the shelves, and she would pay him; it was a foolproof system.

Allowed no luxuries by Ivor, Hilda schemed a way of adding bars of chocolate to the order. But as Ivor gave her the precise amount of money for the order, the only way she could get chocolate was by exact substitution. So instead of ordering jam, she asked for Cadbury's chocolate to the same value.

She managed to hide it from Ivor for many months. Each time Ivor spotted a discrepancy, Hilda's excuses became more imaginative. One day she even told him she had dropped one of her two shopping bags over the viaduct, the truth being that she had bought loads of chocolate instead.

But Hilda was undone when she hatched a plan to buy a new watch using the same scheme. The watch was being paid for in installments, but when Hilda was suddenly hospitalised with appendicitis, she couldn't keep up the scam. As soon as Ivor found out, the watch was returned to the Co-Op. Investigating further, he discovered her chocolate scam as well, and Hilda was relieved of her shopping duties. Despite that and other hiccups, the family continued to live happily in Dan-y-bont for many years until, one by one, they all gradually left home.

In 1929, Cecilia and Elfed moved house and put down a small deposit Elfed had borrowed from his mother and father to buy a house of their own. The mortgage repayments were £2 a month for the new three-bedroom semi-detached house at 73 Caradoc Street. There was no electricity and the house was lit by mains gas. But the house had a modern bathroom upstairs. For the first time, Richard had his own bedroom in a box room at the top of the house.

Cecilia couldn't have been happier with the novel experience of owning her own home. Coincidentally, the new house was a short walk from a baker's shop, in Commercial Road, run by a family called Hopkins. In 1937, the actor Anthony Hopkins was born there. It was an extraordinary coincidence that the same street in Wales would produce two of its most famous actors.

Cecilia kept the new house immaculately clean and prepared it for the start of her own family, which wasn't long off. She gave birth to a daughter, called Marian, followed by another daughter, called Rhianon, in 1931. From then on, Hilda took over more of the household duties at Dan-y-bont. But with the coming of their own children, Elfed and Cecilia's funds were even more stretched than before. To help pay the bills, Cecilia took in a lodger called Elliot, and Richard lost his own bedroom.

Despite that, everyone rallied round, and Cecilia's own family lived every bit as well as did the more prosperous Jenkins family at Dan-y-bont. She fed them an English diet consisting of sausages, faggots, pies, boiled ham and real cuts of meat; all invariably eaten with boiled potatoes and bread along with leeks and vegetables.

A small coal fire in the front room was the only source of heat, and a kettle was constantly boiling on the hob. She would bake bread in the oven below and sell what bread the family couldn't eat to make her housekeeping go further.

Members of the family used to stand with their back to the boiler to keep warm in winter. It was very cold and the bedrooms always had ice caked on the windows from December to March. Winters were certainly miserable. The miners' concession of free coal had long since ended.

Despite the distance between them, Richard and Graham became closer as they grew older. They also became more inquisitive. Graham believed that Cassie, his sister-in-law, was his mother and Tom his father, a state of affairs that persisted right up until 1932. As Hilda said: "A lot of children in Cwmafan thought that Tom was Graham's father." But Richard never had any doubt that Cecilia was his older sister and always said he had clear memories of his real mother throughout his life.

What he did doubt was his relationship to his other siblings, as Graham recalled many years later: "I thought of Rich as my best friend. But it took me some time to recognise a closer relationship. Just after my fourth birthday, Rich put me right. We were playing by the river one Sunday afternoon, when suddenly he clutched my arm. 'You know we're brothers, don't you?' he declared solemnly. I did not, but I was suitably overawed so I said nothing. He gripped my arm harder. 'We must never let the distance from Cwmafan to Taibach come between us.'"

After that revelation, Graham was not exactly sure who his mother or father were. Certainly, no one in the family chose to enlighten them until one day an old lady approached Graham in the park and said: "You're Dick Jenkins' son, aren't you?" to which Graham replied: "I think he's my grandfather." She told him: "Oh no, boy, you're his son all right." The old lady took Graham to his mother's grave. Eventually, as the boys grew older, Ivor realised he had to tell them the truth. Taking each boy aside, he ended the confusion.

As the years rolled by and everyone grew older, every aspect of the Jenkins family life improved. Eventually, the family's £300 debt was paid off and the whole family began to prosper; clearing the debt took five years.

Soon, Ivor, David, and Verdun were bringing home a weekly wage and, eventually, Dick went back to work in the mines as well, thereby making five wage packets coming into the house. William enrolled in the army as soon as he was old enough at 16. Whatever Dick's faults, he was never work-shy, and as soon as he could get a job, he did. But it didn't give him much more to spend, as Ivor relieved him of most of his wage packet every week without fail.

By 1937, the halcyon days before the outbreak of World War II, there was intense happiness in all the households, and the Dummer family remained very close to the James and Jenkins families, especially as they all became more prosperous.

And it was not only the wage earners who were becoming prosperous. Richard grabbed every spare-time job he could to earn extra money. He started working for Edith Evans, Elfed's sister, in the evenings and at weekends. Edith ran the fish and chip shop in Margam with her husband, and the demand for peeled potatoes was constant. So Richard and his cousin Dillwyn would work in their grandmother's backyard, surrounded by mounds of potatoes and buckets of water. They were paid very little but it was regular work. It wasn't Richard's only source of income. His money-making activities became wide and varied, as he remembered years later: "I used to get up when the miners got up about half past four. I used to go up to the top of the mountains and collect sheep dung and horse dung and cow dung in a sack. We used to work like dogs. I then used to take it home and put it in the coal shed. And, on the Saturday, I would sell the dung. Sixpence a bucket I remember I used to get. Also, most people would keep their old newspapers for me, then I would deliver the newspapers to Auntie Edith's fish and chip shop because in those days they wrapped fish and chips in newspaper. They would pay me for that." As he aged, he took on other jobs and was continually being slipped pocket money by his older brothers and sisters and an ever-increasing number of aunts and uncles. As he remembered: "I would wander about from family to family and be slipped sixpence by one and threepence by another. I would hint at the fact that one family gave me more than another." In later life, he always overemphasised the poverty in which he was brought up, although as a boy he was relatively well off.

With plenty of money in his pocket, his childhood summers in South Wales were truly idyllic. All of the Jenkins, the Dummers and the Evans families enjoyed the rugged freedom of the Afan Valley, and the younger children were continually running across the grassy hills that surrounded Port Talbot. Richard used to play with the many other children who lived in Caradoc Street in the wide open fields on the steep green hillside. As he got older, they would also go to Port Talbot docks, often stopping the local train to hitch a lift. The tracks ran past the houses in Caradoc Street and the local boys would mount the fence and get a free trip from drivers, who would slow down so they could clamber on board.

Both Richard and Graham travelled to Dan-y-bont most summer weekends and both loved sleeping over at Pontrhydyfen. As Hilda remembered: "When he stayed overnight, he would sleep in our bed. Two of us girls at the top and Richard with [Graham] at the bottom." Much later, Hilda remembered those truly wonderful years, saying: "The summers always seemed so long."

Things just got better and, by the mid-1930s, the depression was over. Even when the war began in 1939, it brought a huge new demand for coal at any price, causing South Wales to boom again. It produced a knock-on effect for the entire region. With mining back where it had been before the general strike, the Jenkins family was as prosperous as it had ever been. The miners were once more the aristocrats of the working class, superior to all other kinds of manual labourers. As Burton said years later: "In my valley, everyone's dream was to become a miner."

As the family thrived, one man became sadder and sadder. It appeared that Dick Jenkins was just serving out his time until he died. Although he would live another 20 years, and time would fade the memories of his terrible behaviour, he was for the most part a man ignored by his family and respected by no one for the way he had treated his wife. As David Jenkins described: "He pottered about the house when he was there, not greatly missed when he was not. He seemed to accept that Ivor was in charge, and never quibbled about it." And, as Richard Burton said of him rather dismissively: "He didn't believe in anything, least of all himself."

Only Hilda had any time for Dick, and she sang his praises to the end of her life: "We idolised him because there was nothing nasty, ever. I can see my mother laughing at his stories now, and Richard in his arms." But it was not a view shared by anyone else.

As Dick's star waned, Richard's rose. Ivor and the rest of the family decided that Richard was the member of the family most likely to excel. They jointly decided that the family's resources should be put behind his education. Even before he was ten, there was an ambition for him to go to Oxford, but as Burton himself said later: "The idea of a Welsh miner's son going to Oxford was ridiculous beyond the realm of possibility."

David Jenkins believes that Richard's unconventional family life at that time was actually the making of him, saying: "As the youngest-but-one, Richard never knew what it was to lack a horde of loving older brothers and sisters. It was a life crowded with affection."

And as Richard grew up, it was clear he was developing into an exceptionally good-looking boy. He had tousled hair, blue eyes and a dimple in his chin which, according to Penny Junor, made him look "disarmingly angelic."

As his obvious good looks developed, so too did the skills he would go on to use so effectively later in life. It was clear he had an outstanding memory and an excellent sense of timing together with a very strong voice. His acting skills became apparent very early on, when he would hold the whole James, Jenkins and Evans families spellbound in impromptu performances in the front room at Caradoc Street. Graham Jenkins remembered clearly: "It was home entertainment of a high order, and Rich first showed his ability as a performer not so much in presentation but in his sensitivity to the audience. He knew what they wanted and what they could take. He could adapt his routine to suit the mood of the moment – collecting laughs where none had come before, he stretched the joke; if the response was half-hearted, he immediately changed tack. But, best of all, he never outstayed his welcome."

In all those years, Richard and his siblings never once left the Afan Valley or Wales. It took 12 hours to reach London by car and the alternative was a very expensive train ride. Vacations were outings organised by the Chapel to other Welsh resorts along the coast. Everyone boarded a coach in early morning and returned home again late in the evening.

But as the years rolled by, the house at Dan-y-bont gradually emptied as his siblings married and left home. When Hilda got married and moved into a little cottage, Dick Jenkins went to live with his favourite daughter. But, for Richard, schooldays beckoned and he entered a new chapter of his life.

# AND GOD CREATED BURTON

CHAPTER 5

# Less than perfect schooldays

*Family pressures almost derail talent*

1931 to 1939

The school system in South Wales in the mid-20th century was fairly simple: first came infant school; then it was on to elementary school until the age of 12 or 13; and then a simple choice of continuing on to secondary school or entering the workforce at 14.

The first bit was easy and, in 1930, when he was five years old, Richard Burton was packed off to what is known in Wales as infant school, or nursery school in the rest of the world. Eastern Infants School was a melting pot, attended by every youngster in the neighbourhood. Fortunately, it was situated on the Port Talbot main road and only a short two-minute walk from Elfed and Cecilia's front door.

The school was effectively an annexe of the Eastern Boys School and, in reality, wasn't much of a school at all. The playing field had been concreted over and the facilities were poor. The toilets in particular were disgustingly filthy and ill-maintained. Each class numbered well over 50 boys and girls in total, but, as in most Welsh schools of the time, student discipline was excellent; if only on the basis that any punishment a pupil received at school was meted out again by their parents when they got home.

Although Richard was fluent in Welsh, his English was still very weak. Upon returning home after his first day at infant school, he told Cecilia: "I don't know what they're talking about in that school." It was a wake-up call for him and a sign that he had some catching up to do with the other pupils.

Because of his basic language problems, Richard didn't distinguish himself in any way in infant school. It took him the entire three years just to become as fluent in English as the other children.

In September 1933, two months before his eighth birthday, he transferred across to the Eastern Boys School, half a mile away, as did most of his classmates. The girls were placed in the Girl's school. Again, the class sizes were well over 50 pupils.

But it was a much rougher and tougher environment than infant school and, very quickly, Burton was introduced to smoking and drinking by some of the other boys, many of whom had come from rougher homes than his. The penalty for being caught with alcohol or cigarettes was a severe beating, the seriousness of which meant that basic discipline was very good.

Outside of school, it was rather different; the boys took the opportunity to let off steam, and drank and smoked as much as they could afford. As Burton was relatively rich from his jobs and his family's largesse, he drank and smoked the most. His early smoking was done with Dillwyn Dummer. Whilst other children spent their money on comics and sweets, the two boys bought cigarettes; namely five-packs of Woodbine, the most popular brand at the time. A pack of five cost 3d and they would smoke the entire packet together during a weekly visit to the cinema, sitting at the back of the stalls. As the dangers of smoking were relatively unknown back then, the cigarettes were unfiltered and allowed users to breathe in high levels of tar.

Burton was unremarkable in his first three years at school, which was due primarily to the quality of his teacher, Tom Howell. Howell was a mediocre instructor who simply did his job and went home to his wife. Wanting an easy life, he did as little as he had to and formed little rapport with any of his pupils. It was Burton's bad luck to be landed with such a mediocre mentor.

However, in 1937, in his fourth year at Eastern, Richard's luck changed. He was spotted by Meredith Jones, who taught the elite scholarship class which consisted of boys who would be entered for the scholarship exam. Jones was well-regarded and a brilliant teacher. He was witty and highly intellectual. He was known as a skilful promoter of the brightest boys.

The scholarship exam was the be-all and end-all of academic life at Eastern. Being entered in it was itself an achievement; and passing it was exceptional. Passing the exam enabled pupils to attend the Welsh equivalent of an English grammar school – in Burton's case, this was Port Talbot Secondary School.

Securing a place was the modern-day equivalent of graduating on to university but, back then, it meant an even more certain future. These boys were guaranteed a position amongst Wales' elite, with the promise of a well-paid and reputable job when they finally left school. It was also a ticket out of the valleys. Graham Jenkins explained just how important his brother's achievement was: "More than prestige was at stake. Those who did well in the exams and who defied the limitations of their environment, were talked about in hushed tones of respect long after they had departed to make their fortune."

But, before Jones, no one had noticed how academically gifted Richard was. Given the importance of the exam, Tom Howell's neglect of his pupils was even more poignant. As Burton admitted to his biographer Paul Ferris many years later: "If you didn't go to the grammar school, you stayed till you were fourteen and went out into the workaday world."

Jones, however, was very particular about whom he took on, and he spotted potential candidates for the scholarship exam by bombarding them with questions and arguments in order to elicit a response and engage a lively mind. In Burton, Jones found much more than he expected and, despite their age gap, the two often became entangled in long intellectual conversations. Jones had an opinion on every subject under the sun, but, mostly, he loved talking about his home and country. And Burton couldn't get enough. In fact, all the boys Jones taught were extremely lucky, gaining guidance and insight simply not available to the other pupils in the entire South Wales region.

So Meredith Jones became the first of the two great teaching influences on Burton's life, and one that undoubtedly shaped the course of his entire life.

Jones was an extraordinary man with a very powerful personality, and he bristled with self-confidence in a mostly pleasant way. A stockily built fellow with ginger hair and an extravagant ginger moustache, he had a voluble and bombastic style that was not easily forgotten. Burton later described him as "a recognisable spiritual descendant of Giraldus Cambrensis and Shakespeare's Fluellen – passionate, fluent, something of a scholar, mock-belligerent, roughly gentle, of remarkable vitality and afraid of nobody." Graham Jenkins also remembered him: "Meredith Jones was a man of great power, and a signal of approval from him was the Taibach equivalent of the Order of Merit." It was such a signal that he bestowed upon Burton.

Not only did Jones spot Burton, he also gave him special attention, and the ten-year-old quickly became what other pupils would refer to as the 'teacher's pet'. Teacher's pets tended to be the talented boys and were given special encouragement. Burton stood out anyway as, by the age of ten, he had developed into a very good-looking boy. Paul Ferris, an early biographer of Burton, described him as having "wide-awake blue eyes on a freckled face." It was before his teenage acne set in.

Jones meshed with Burton particularly well because he was very similar in background to his protégé. A scholarship boy and the son of a miner himself, he was passionate in his desire to awaken talent in young people. His intent never abated and even grew stronger as the years went on. His two main passions were rugby union and the English language, and he immersed the young Burton in both. In fact, Burton owed his interest in the game of rugby entirely to Jones. It was all part of Jones' technique to use the game to build more character into his pupils.

In the 1930s, rugby union was not the soft game it is today. It was very rough, with extremely hard tackling and no quarter given or asked for. The sport has always been recognised as the highest expression of Welsh culture and one that demands intense mental skills, including that Welsh specialty: ruthless cunning – with the emphasis on 'ruthless'. Jones embraced and encouraged the sport, but very few of his pupils were physically strong or tough enough for the required regimen. But Burton excelled at it.

Being good at rugby union became very important to Burton, and his temperament was well-suited to the game. What he lacked in terms of artistry, he made up for in raw energy. Tom Mainwaring, a contemporary of Burton at school, agreed that it created a real sense of elite, telling Paul Ferris: "Meredith got the best out of us. I don't know what happened to the weeds. They watched us, I suppose."

But Jones also had another side. He could occasionally be a fierce disciplinarian and also very cruel. He would not flinch from caning an entire class of 50 boys if he felt it necessary, and sometimes he did. Indeed, Jones was seen by some of his detractors – namely, other less successful teachers – as a tyrant. Tom Howell called him "a harsh and insensitive man." But, conversely, Howell admitted that Jones could also be very kind.

What isn't in doubt was that Burton was transformed both mentally and physically under Jones' influence. It was the making of him. Before Jones, he had put in just enough effort to get by. But, under Jones, the ten-year-old Richard began to work really hard.

It was during this period that one of Burton's most unremarked talents came to the fore and was seized upon by Jones. He was an extraordinarily fast reader and absorbed information at great speed. Jones had never before seen anything like it. Burton quickly read everything that was put in front of him, leading Jones continually to have to source more books for him to read. Later in life, Burton's main recreation became reading, eventually reading as many as three books in a 24-hour period. On some days, he was reportedly reading as many as five in a day, some 12 times the capacity of the average reader. His sister Hilda remembers him informing her, at a very young age, that "reading was the source of all wisdom." But he was not a discriminating reader, devouring books by quantity rather than quality. Burton had a voracious appetite for all sorts of literature, including comics and magazines. Most of his reading material came from the local Carnegie Library, where he went every day after school. It soon became his favourite place to be.

As a result of all the reading, Burton's vocabulary developed rapidly. Graham Jenkins recounted a typical verbal exchange during the period: "I was the first to hear of the latest acquisition in his vocabulary: 'sycophant'. He said to me one day: 'Do you know what a sycophant is?' I did not, so he told me. But it was not so much the meaning of the word as its sound which fascinated him. With Welsh intonation, each syllable given its own emphasis, 'sycophant' was a cruel and terrible word. We tried it out on our friends with devastating results. They may not have understood it, but they knew an insult when they heard one."

His sister Cecilia recalled him reading through the night at 73 Caradoc Street and falling asleep in front of the fire with a book in his hands. She said he often read in bed by candlelight before going to sleep.

Would Burton have succeeded and become an actor without Jones' early influence and tutelage? It's very unlikely. In Richard's formative years, Jones steered him on to the path that would take him towards his future successes. And later, Jones' influence on him was to become even more tangible. Jones founded the Taibach Youth Club, where Burton would eventually make his acting debut. As Burton himself said of Jones: "He was the man who changed my life."

In March 1937, when Burton was 11, he was finally faced with the scholarship exam in Wales. The scholarship exam was the equivalent of the English 11-Plus exam – but a lot tougher. Passing the exam, which consisted of two papers, in English and Maths, was vital. Only the top ten per cent of pupils at Eastern Boys School were able to pass it, and only 20 per cent were even considered good enough to enter for it. Failing to pass would mean leaving elementary school two years later and starting work at 14. Passing it would mean being in full-time education until 18. With Meredith Jones driving him forward, there was little doubt that Burton would pass. Jones was a hard taskmaster, and believed in the work ethic more than anything else. The weeks before he sat the exam were frantic ones for Burton.

The results of the scholarship exam were not announced until June. For the boys who were expected to pass, it was a nerve-wracking time. Burton duly passed, and his achievement was all the greater as he became the first-ever member of the Jenkins family to go on to higher education. Tom Howell said of his achievement: "Richie would have left and become a butcher's boy, and where would he have gone eventually? Into the steelworks or somewhere like that." Howell had summed it up perfectly, and those who left school early were effectively doomed. Burton's first biographer, American writer Hollis Alpert, put it more pointedly: "If Richard had not passed his scholarship, the world at large might never have heard of him."

In 1937, just ten boys from the entire school passed the exam. Dillwyn Dummer, who had been at Burton's side until now, was one of the casualties. Hereafter, their paths diverged to the point where they hardly saw each other again. Dillwyn was never heard of again in the Burton story.

As Burton observed his cousin's future, he realised how lucky he had been and how much Meredith Jones had been entirely responsible for his success. As he would go on to say much later: "Without him, I would probably not have become an actor."

Cecilia, his sister, was overcome with joy when she learned of Richard's accomplishment. To celebrate his passing the exam, the normally parsimonious Ivor Jenkins presented his young brother with a brand new bicycle. Possessing a bicycle was almost unheard of for a child in those days, and it was Richard's treasured possession. Owning that bicycle was a very strong symbol of his success. As Burton remembered: "It was a thing of beauty, and I went everywhere on it. It opened up the world for me. I went to Swansea and Newport and Aberdare and Mountain Ash – just me and my bicycle. I was so proud of that bike, and I was so proud of my brother who gave it to me."

Passing the exam became Burton's rite of passage. From then on, he was a member of the elite and every door was opened to him. More and more of his talents were uncovered and recognised.

So, in the autumn of 1937, the 11-year-old entered Port Talbot Secondary School, a squat red-brick building with a concrete schoolyard, overlooked by Port Talbot's giant steel mills. When he arrived, he wondered what all the fuss had been about; it all seemed rather unremarkable.

But looks flattered to deceive. Burton got the shock of his life when he attended his first classes; the teachers were exceptionally talented and capable. In fact, almost every teacher was as inspired and inspiring as

Meredith Jones. And an even bigger shock was the calibre of his fellow pupils. He was now in a much smaller class of academically-talented boys; all of whom had, like him, passed the scholarship exam. He was no longer the exceptional pupil at the top of the class. In fact, he was rather near the bottom.

He also had his first encounter with Philip Burton, the school's senior English master. Burton was a creative legend within Port Talbot and was known nationally for his work on drama radio and live theatre company. Initially, Burton was not impressed with Richard, dismissing him publicly as a "lightweight."

Without Meredith Jones to push him, he showed no sign of being a distinguished pupil and gained a reputation for being difficult. The target was to leave school at 18 with something called the 'School Certificate', and his teachers looked for over 90 per cent success rate in passing – in fact, they demanded it. The situation turned tricky when he realised he was nowhere near as clever as he thought, and Richard's only response was to ignore the problem.

So Richard reverted to sport, where he was still top dog, and his academic studies were pushed into the background. In fact, his entire focus became the outdoors and sport. During his four years at Port Talbot, he put most of his energy into rugby in the winter and cricket in the summer. But even that wasn't straightforward.

Whereas he was easily the top rugby player at Eastern, he found he was just ordinary at Port Talbot, and the play was much more competitive. Every member of the Port Talbot rugby team stood at least six feet tall. At only five feet nine and a half inches, he was the shortest in the team. So he quickly learnt to run very fast, as he remembered: "I could run fast. I had to, because if I wasn't fast enough, heavier and bigger men would bring me down and crush me." But he couldn't always run fast enough, and a legacy of those days was the back trouble he suffered because of continually being crushed underneath piles of heavy players. The pain was to plague him for the rest of his life.

As an antidote, Burton focused on physical aggression and developed it as part of his identity. He became overly aggressive to compensate for his physical inferiority. As Brook Williams later remembered: "It was on the rugby field that Rich developed his ability to land a good punch. He saw a friend being picked on by a much bigger opponent, and when the referee wasn't looking, Rich, despite being towered over by the bully, punched him hard and laid him out. He was now a hero to others; not only could he play rugby, but he could fight too. But he was never a bully. He only picked on the bullies."

Outside of his academic failure, he was now a handsome boy with sharp features and widely-spaced eyes, which had developed into a striking blue-green colour. Paul Ferris described them as "burning with excitement" and said he had the face of a "boxing poet" – whatever that meant. But most of all, it was during this period that he acquired the famous Burton physical presence that set him apart from the other boys.

His singing voice was also exceptional, and he won first prize at an eisteddfod as a boy soprano. He also became highly proficient at tennis.

Burton's all-round sports skills attracted the attention of the headmaster, who was called Pop Reynolds by everyone. Becoming a favourite of the headmaster, Richard was one of the half dozen boys in the school who were allowed to answer Reynolds back without rebuke. There was one famous exchange at morning assembly in which the headmaster, in front of all the other boys, asked Burton where his gas mask was. In those days, everyone had to carry a gas mask at all times. Burton, having previously noticed that the headmaster himself had arrived at school that day without his mask in its container, shot back: "Where is yours, sir?" The headmaster immediately shouted "dismiss", and never again mentioned the subject of missing gas masks.

He also made his acting debut at Port Talbot but found the going anything but easy. He auditioned for all the school plays mainly because acting was regarded as an elite activity. As Melvin Bragg reported, Burton discovered for the first time that he loved being the centre of everyone's attention and, on the stage, he was. Ironically, it was in acting where he first experienced any sort of failure. The first time he auditioned for a part in a play, he failed to be chosen, and a few times after that as well.

It took him until January of 1941, at the age of 15, finally to be chosen for a part in the school production of 'The Apple Cart' by George Bernard Shaw. He debuted by playing the character of Mr Vanhatten, an American. He was totally miscast and played the part with his regular heavy Welsh accent, consequently making no impact whatsoever.

But whatever the diversions from sport and acting, his lack of academic success dogged him. He could not shake off the stigma, as Graham Jenkins remembered: "Questions were asked about his seriousness of purpose. Was he not seen drinking in a pub and smoking in the street? And what about these stories of his fondness for girls? There was nothing wrong with polite conversation between the sexes. But in the woods?"

And therein lay the problem. Out of school, as he approached his 16th birthday, his behaviour was deteriorating fast. He was now fully into wine, women and song. And the older he grew, the more difficult he became to discipline. It was time for Cecilia's husband, Elfed James, finally to assert his authority.

It all started over a minor incident; Elfed was frustrated with Burton for playing football after school with other boys in the park, still in his school uniform without first changing his clothes. Elfed tried to impress upon him how expensive the uniform was, but without success. Burton continued regularly to wreck his school uniform and had to have more than one replacement purchased for him. By this time, Burton displayed little respect for Elfed and was supported in his approach by Cecilia.

There was also an ongoing problem with girls. Despite teenage acne and boils that occasionally blew up on his face, he was immensely attractive to women of all ages, and he immediately and frequently abused his good fortune. He would take girls to a dance, but he was not, as his image as a womaniser might suggest, a young man keen to sow his oats. Rather than ravishing the local girls, he treated them with great respect and they swooned as he recited poetry to them. That's what attracted the girls to him; he had natural charm and a certain elegance. Outside of school, however, he was a different character – as rough and tough as anyone.

He seems to have held back from indulging in sexual intercourse, which was against the law for anyone under 16, and didn't lose his virginity before he was of age. But he openly admitted that his hedonism was unusual in Wales at the time: "The allowance I got each week would mainly go on cigarettes and beer. When I needed extra cash to take a girl out, I borrowed from Cis." The money Cecilia loaned him came from her housekeeping, and he was never able to repay her.

Stanley Baker also recalled his waywardness: "I heard how he would come home from playing football and find Cecilia dealing with a girl crying because Rich had promised to meet her. He liked the girls but he loved rugby. That was his great passion."

For Elfed, the uniform affair was the straw that broke the camel's back, and when Burton demanded the right to smoke cigarettes and drink alcohol within the family home, the teetotal Elfed snapped and resolved to take strong and unilateral action. His resolve was hardened after a particularly disgusting incident on a train. Along with a friend, Richard dropped his trousers and urinated from the window of a moving train. This was an old Welsh schoolboy prank and was usually harmless. But that day, he had been playing rugby and was on his way home to Port Talbot. He and his friends had been drinking beer illegally on the train and decided to urinate out of the window as the train was passing through a station. Locals were horrified and the story was repeated across the valleys. Inevitably, the story got back to Elfed and Cecilia. While Cecilia was disinclined to believe it, Elfed was apoplectic.

Elfed told Cecilia that she was wholly irresponsible and had to bear some blame for Burton's behaviour. By that time, Morgan and Mary James were getting older and were unable to exert as much influence as they had in the past.

As lucky as he had been in other areas of his life, Burton's luck was about to fail him.

This time, his antics were to have consequences. Elfed had reached the end of his tether and decided that Burton was out of control with too much time on his hands and too much money in his pocket.

And the mood of the country had changed; it was 1940 and the Second World War had started in earnest. Burton's behaviour was increasingly unacceptable.

Having crossed Elfed one time too many, Burton was told to leave school and get a responsible job – to, in effect, join the real world. Being at school at 16 was an alien concept to Elfed, and Burton's behaviour got so bad that this time even Cecilia couldn't disagree.

Elfed was particularly furious as he was doing all he could to keep his family in food and clothing. He saw Burton living a playboy existence whilst still at school, squandering vast amounts of cash on cigarettes, drink and women.

Burton made little effort to earn money of his own, relying on his allowance from Cecilia and ever-increasing handouts from ever-increasing numbers of relatives. He admitted later: "My dear sister thought I could do no wrong, even though she knew I did enough wrong." Burton hadn't expected to lose the battle with Elfed and was surprised when he did, especially as Elfed had the backing of Burton's family. It was another profound shock. He felt his family had let him down when he needed them most. But what he didn't realise was that it was he who had let them down.

After much family debate between both houses, Elfed won the battle and Burton was told his schooldays were over. Elfed made the decision permanent by using every bit of local influence he had to secure his young brother-in-law a job as a draper's assistant at the Co-Operative outfitters in Port Talbot.

It was a massive reversal of fortune. From having been a member of the elite, Burton's status was reduced to that of everyone else. Passing the scholarship exam had all been for nothing. Without Meredith Jones, he had gone off the rails. His gilded life was over.

He stayed at school until the end of the spring term. In his fifth year at the school, with his school certificate looming, he left abruptly and, in April 1941, he hung up his school cap and went to the Co-Op.

He had no qualifications and, as Melvin Bragg recalled, he "seemed set for life as an unremarkable nine-to-five employee in Port Talbot." Bragg had put it exactly right: "It was a terrible fall: humiliating and very painful. It was, in one sense, his first serious test of character. Everything until then had come easy. Now, he was down and he hated it."

At this stage, the Richard Burton story seemed to be over.

# AND GOD CREATED BURTON

# CHAPTER 6

# The yobbo years

## Flouncing the Co-Op and return to school

### 1941 to 1943

Being forced to leave school by Elfed James caused Richard Burton's festering dislike for his brother-in-law to blossom into fully-fledged hatred. For the sake of his sister Cecilia, however, he concealed his feelings as best he could. In later years, the family discord with Elfed was completely airbrushed away.

Burton always referred to the incident that nearly ruined his life as "a small family crisis that demanded I should leave school and go to work." Cecilia remembered: "I broke my heart over him when he went to the shop. He hated it. Oh – he hated it." Hilda, his younger sister, concurred: "Richard detested it more than anything else in the world."

In truth, Elfed was fed up with Richard's attitude and saw no reason for financing his continued studies at school. The final straw came when Elfed read his diary and discovered that Richard had spent an entire school day playing cricket. When Elfed confronted him about it, Richard simply laughed.

Graham Jenkins, like the rest of the family, always denied any rift with Elfed and perpetuated the myth that his brother had to leave school purely because of financial problems. Graham insisted it was a joint family decision to send Richard to work.

In many ways, Richard had only himself, and his sometimes casual attitude to life, to blame for Elfed's decision. He treated his time at school lightly and often talked of wanting to leave. One day, Elfed simply said to Cecilia: "We should put him out of his misery."

When pushed, Graham did confess there was some friction between Elfed and Richard: "Elfed always harboured a resentment against his demanding and, in his view, disruptive brother-in-law. It was asking a lot of him to continue supporting Rich into the years when the vast majority of young people were fending for themselves. Rich had a mischievous streak which put him at odds with all authority. Cis let him get away with it; Elfed was not so tolerant."

In contrast, Rhianon and Marian, Elfed's daughters, were polite and well-behaved. But Elfed was also upset that his own daughters had not been able to take their exams, for various reasons, to go on to secondary school.

Philip Burton never blamed Elfed for what happened, and believes that Rhianon and Marian's lack of opportunity was a factor, saying: "To Elfed, Richard was a potential wage-earner, and there he was in school, costing money, not earning it. And the situation was made more bitter for Elfed by the fact that neither of his daughters, Marian or Rhianon, had won a place in the secondary school. I feel sure that his wife's deep and protective love for the boy also irked Elfed."

But Elfed was not the only one who was pleased to see Richard removed from school. Pop Reynolds, the headmaster, breathed a sigh of relief when Richard left. There was always sadness in seeing a talented boy depart, but the Port Talbot Secondary School was also glad to see the back of his disruptive behaviour.

In Richard's mind, however, Elfed had done him double damage by not only forcing him to give up his education but also giving him no choice but to take a job as an outfitter's assistant in the men's clothing department of the Taibach Co-operative Wholesale Society.

The Taibach Co-Op, like many others around Britain, was owned by all its customers, who became members and effectively shareholders. At the end of the year, the profits were handed back to the customers in a payment called a 'divi.' The divi ensured customer loyalty. It was a prestigious place to work. Most people were proud to work there – but not Richard.

The Co-Op was the biggest store in Taibach and had many departments, including food, fruit and vegetables, as well as a pharmacy and shoes. Elfed's father was on the committee of the Co-Op, and intelligent boys were in demand. Elfed thought menswear would be Richard's best choice. He only got the job because every other suitable person was away fighting in the war, and he would have been sacked pretty quickly had there not been a severe manpower shortage.

So when the Easter term ended on 4th April 1941, Richard went straight to work at the Co-Op. He was officially an apprentice but was still paid £1.8s (£1.40) a week, a very good salary at the time, reflecting the manpower shortage.

It was destined to be the only job he ever had and, unsurprisingly, he detested it. As Melvyn Bragg succinctly put it: "For a miner's son in a tough mining community, a rugby player, a boxer, it was the ultimate indignity." Richard agreed, saying: "I was humiliated. It was not the kind of work a miner's son should have been doing. I hated it."

So it was an ill match straight from the start and, predictably, he was completely useless at the job, having absolutely no aptitude as a retailer. Consequently, he put no effort into the job and acted as if he wanted to be fired – which he probably did.

A big part of his responsibilities included deliveries to customers' homes, which he managed with a bicycle and a wicker basket on the handlebars. He readily admitted: "I took every opportunity to break all the rules. When I had a delivery to make, I spent hours out of the shop, stopping off to chat with friends and family, or to pop into the pub."

In fact, his Co-Op bicycle was often observed by his co-workers propped up against the wall of the pub, and they envied his ability to get away with it. And get-away-with-it he did.

It was not all bad; one benefit of a regular wage was that Richard could go the cinema regularly. He took his brother Graham to the Taibach Picture Drome up to three times a week. Ironically, one of the first films they saw together was Cecil B. De Mille's version of *Cleopatra*. At the time, it was the most expensive film ever made, but Richard could have no idea what the relevance to him would be 21 years later.

Despite his continual insolence to his managers, Richard did get some enjoyment from his job. It was his duty to fold one pound and ten shilling notes and place them into a canister, which was then transported to the accounts department through a compressed air system via a tube. To his great amusement, a press of a button would shoot off the canister upstairs, and he soon began using the system to send love notes to the girls in the accounts department.

The Co-Op manager called Richard "bloody hopeless" and, as Graham Jenkins summed it up: "Rich and the retail trade were ill-suited." Philip Burton added: "Richard was getting a bad reputation at the Co-op." But there was little sympathy for him, and when Cecilia mentioned to Elfed that Richard was unhappy, he replied: "He's not paid to be happy."

His worst infraction was defying the war time rationing regulations which were then in force on clothing. He often neglected to collect the ration coupons from customers who purchased clothes. If done fraudulently and deliberately, it was a breach of the law and the penalties were high. It caused immense problems in the Co-Op's back office. But Richard claimed he was just forgetful.

Later, he admitted deliberately subverting the ration cards system: "Everything was rationed – the war was on then – and everyone had clothing coupons which they had to offer up along with their cash. I pretended to forget to take coupons from many of my customers, allowing them to come back another time and buy more than their rations allowed."

Richard spent nearly ten months as a shopkeeper and the only benefit was that he learned how properly to fold clothes; a talent he never lost and would demonstrate to others for the rest of his life. He recalled many years later: "I still fold all my suits properly and professionally. I can't bear to see someone do it badly, and I have to show them how it's done."

Elfed's plan to make Richard settle down responsibly backfired as his behaviour deteriorated further. Outside of the workplace, he was out of control, and his general behaviour, already bad, came close to landing him in jail more than once. Richard was already high-spirited and given to high jinks, and now he became an out-and-out yobbo. He mixed with some of the roughest juveniles in Port Talbot and had scant regard for the feelings of his fellow citizens. He openly smoked and drank in local pubs despite being underage. He looked much older than his real age, and behaved like it as well.

If truth be told, he was extremely lucky to stay out of prison. His gang nickname was 'Wild Jenk', and he was continually brawling with rival gang members. Many times, he seemed to defy the local hard-stretched police to do anything about it, and they chose not to call his bluff.

Were it not for the war years, and with less priority being given to teenage behaviour, he would undoubtedly have forged a criminal record that would have precluded any wider ambitions he had. But, by luck or by judgment, he managed to stay out of trouble with the courts.

The only successful part of Richard's life during this period was his membership with the Taibach Youth Club, which he joined with his nieces, Rhianon and Marian. The youth club had been set up by Meredith Jones in the mid-1940s with the financial support of the local authority in an attempt to solve the local hooligan problem – of which Richard, ironically, was a big part.

Jones broke new ground when he persuaded the local Glamorgan county council to back his youth club financially; it was the first time such a club had been established in Wales. The club was accommodated in a near derelict building in the grounds of the Eastern Boys School. There was no electricity and it was lit by gas. The first thing Jones did was to set the boys on repairing the leaky roof.

Jones received immense credit for his role in setting up the club, which became one of the best-regarded youth establishments in Wales. It became the standard for other clubs, and hundreds of similar establishments were later set up copying his methods.

During this period, Jones proved just what an extraordinarily gifted teacher he was. At the start of every club meeting, held three times a week, he would open each session with a ten-minute monologue which dealt with a different aspect of a young person's life. Marian James remembers these monologues as being inspiring and entirely original. She described them as "extraordinary."

Jones used all his powers of persuasion to improve the lot of Port Talbot's youths. But his methods also won him enemies. Some criticised him as a bully, and he readily admitted he would use any method necessary to achieve his objectives.

Richard and both his nieces, Rhianon and Marian James, were active and frequent participants at the club. As for Richard, it kept him off the streets three nights a week. He found he loved the youth club atmosphere and was a different person once inside. He played table-tennis fiercely, boxed and sang; he was a natural leader of the club's activities.

At the club, he was also to meet his third mentor; far less well-known than the other two, but still important in his life. In fact, Leo Lloyd was his first introduction to theatre. Lloyd, a teacher of English at Eastern, ran the youth club's drama group and actively encouraged Richard to participate in his dramatic productions.

Like Philip Burton, Lloyd was obsessed with the theatre and he was committed to the boys and girls who shared his obsession. He was reputed to be something of an eccentric and used to walk the pavements of Taibach in a velour, mauve-coloured trilby hat, often reading a script and reciting the lines as he went, oblivious of events and the people around him. Like Jones and Burton, he too was a highly gifted teacher.

Now that Lloyd rather than Philip Burton was running the club's drama department, Richard got a fair chance to shine. Unlike Burton, Lloyd was impressed with Richard from the very start. He quickly cast him in good parts and encouraged his stage performances. In fact, Lloyd's intervention came at a critical time when he had been all but rejected by Philip Burton. Richard said of him: "He taught me the fundamentals of the job: to stand and move and talk on the stage with confidence. He channelled my discontent and made me want to be an actor."

In truth, Richard's participation in the activities of the youth club saved him from himself, and he found it highly stimulating. Meredith Jones and Leo Lloyd treated him like an adult, and he responded in a manner which impressed them with his maturity. Later, he would recall that joining the youth club was "the turning point in my life."

An opportunity for Richard to demonstrate his skills to a wider audience came when Lloyd entered the drama group for the youth eisteddfod. The members put on a play called 'The Bishop's Candlesticks', based on Victor Hugo's novel *Les Miserables*. Richard played an escaped convict who was converted into a model citizen by one of his victims.

The whole play was performed in mime and they won first prize thanks to Richard's magnificent performance. Philip Burton was in the audience, and he was the only one not impressed. Burton continued to ignore Richard's performances on the basis that acne disfigured his face. Philip just did not believe that an actor with such an affliction could make it. But he did not seem to understand that teenage acne was a passing phase that would disappear within a few years. Only Meredith Jones and Leo Lloyd could see beyond it.

Amazingly, during this period, Meredith Jones was ignorant of the fact that Richard had left school. In all this time, Richard had been too ashamed to tell his mentor, knowing his reaction would not be good. Despite seeing him three times a week at the club, Jones had no knowledge of what had befallen his protégé. That is, until he visited the Co-Op store one day and was astonished to find Richard behind the counter. At first, Richard tried to bluff that it was a part-time job outside school hours. But Jones was no fool. When Richard lied to him, he slapped him round the face in full view of the customers and other staff, and asked for the truth. When he heard what had happened, Jones was apoplectic and horrified that his promising pupil had given up his education and taken a job without a future.

Jones immediately stormed out of the shop, found a phone box and started dialling numbers until he found Ivor Jenkins. Ivor explained the whole sorry story as Jones listened in disbelief.

From that day on, Jones and Ivor Jenkins formed an unlikely alliance in a bid to get Richard back to school. The following weekend, the two men visited Cecilia and told her: "The boy is wasted in that shop. He should be back at school finishing his education."

Ashamed, Cecilia asked Jones for his help. He agreed and returned a few weeks later, reporting: "I'm doing my damnedest, but don't get your hopes up because it's not done yet."

Jones realised he would need help and turned to Philip Burton. The apparently uninterested Burton couldn't see what all the fuss was about, but Jones browbeat him until he agreed to assist. But the wily Burton was playing a bit of a game. It turned out that he had noticed Richard's powerful performances in the youth club plays but was reluctant to admit he had been mistaken. As Jones had predicted, the acne was clearing up and Philip later admitted that he had been too hasty in his negative assessment of the boy.

The combination of both Jones and Burton proved difficult for the school governor to resist and, together, they began to lobby Pop Reynolds, the Port Talbot headmaster, to get Richard readmitted. Readmission was virtually unheard of in those days and was possible only with the unanimous approval of more or less everyone involved.

To achieve what was known technically as 'reinstatement', the highest political influence at local level was needed. Burton suggested to Jones that he enlist Councilor Llewellyn Heycock's help. It turned out that Heycock was the honorary president of Jones' youth club. More importantly, he was a member of the all-powerful Glamorgan Education Committee, which provided funding for the club.

After Philip Burton called him, Heycock promised to lobby the school governors, who would make the final decision concerning reinstatement. But Heycock ran up against stern opposition in the shape of the chairman of the education committee, who was against reinstating Richard under any circumstances. In fact, the chairman and the headmaster actively teamed up to prevent it. When Heycock reported the difficulties back to Jones, Jones insisted it was vital that he try again. He told him: "Richard is a boy of exceptional scholastic potential."

It took some tough persuasion from Heycock to get the chairman even to listen. Then, out of the blue, Heycock decided to inform him that Richard's ambition was to be a school teacher. Suddenly, the chairman's attitude changed. Teachers were in short supply, and Heycock had uttered the magic words. The inference was very much that Richard would go on to teacher training college upon leaving school. But still, it wasn't a done deal until the governors' meeting to decide the issue. The chairman had great difficulty backtracking, and Reynolds was yet to be persuaded.

Meredith Jones attended the meeting, held on a clear bright Monday night. Delivering one of his most persuasive speeches, Jones recalled the governors being visibly moved at his eloquence: "Despite the objection from the headmaster, they let Richard back into the school."

What Jones had accomplished was unprecedented, and Richard was euphoric when he heard the news. Eulogising many years later, he said of Jones: "He had breathtaking effrontery and, with his eloquent and dazzling generalisations, hurled and swept me into the ambition to be something other than a thirty-bob-a-week outfitter's apprentice." He admitted later that the intention to become a teacher had been a complete fabrication by Heycock and Jones: "I had no intention of really being a teacher but it was a good move to say I was. They went a little easier on me."

Cecilia remembers Richard coming home that day: "I was upstairs and he shouted: 'Cis, Cis, nobody's done this before. Cis, something wonderful has happened. There's a chance they're going to take me back.'"

But there was one last hurdle to overcome. Once everything was confirmed, the news had to be broken to Elfed, and Ivor agreed to go see him. The subsequent meeting did not go so well, and all the bitter family differences between the Jameses and the Jenkinses were reignited. The conversation gradually became very heated.

Eventually, Cecilia had to beg each man to lower their voices so the neighbours would not hear. Ivor told Elfed: "The boy deserves his chance." Elfed shot back: "It's all very well for you, Ivor. You're a face worker on piece rates. You earn good money. Twice as much as me, I shouldn't wonder." Ivor roared back: "And what about the sacrifices I've made and Tom has made? Don't you think we've done our bit?"

Incensed by this, Elfed said: "He's your brother. He's not my son." And there lay the rub. Elfed had no affiliation or affection for Richard; he had merely tolerated his presence. It was the final insult and it uncovered two decades of undercurrent between the two families.

The two men rose from their seats and seemed to raise their fists in slow motion. A distraught Cecilia thrust herself between them and asked them to stop. With that, they sat down again and Ivor told Elfed that the Jenkinses would finance Richard's move back to school. He said simply: "We'll all put our hands in our pockets."

But Elfed refused to accept any money from the Jenkins family. A proud man, he settled his own bills and, as Richard was his wife's responsibility, he informed Ivor he would pay. At that moment, Elfed told Ivor to get out of his house and never to return. Cecilia confirmed: "The strange thing is that, when it came to the point, Elfed would not accept a penny. He had his pride, you see." But it was all soon forgotten and the following weekend Elfed welcomed Ivor back into the house.

Elfed's quick forgiveness was typical of the happy atmosphere that generally pervaded between all the families. In reality the problems and troubles were exaggerated in the family history and Richard enjoyed a very loving childhood.

With the family issues resolved, Reynolds, the headmaster, was told to send a formal letter to Cecilia and Elfed, inviting Richard to resume his studies. It was another pivotal moment in Richard's life. The decision to readmit him was the difference between eventual success and outright failure. And, once again, the cards had fallen in his favour. So, on 5th October 1942, a date always etched in his memory, Richard returned to school.

The return to school proved to be the cementing of his relationship with Philip Burton, thanks to Meredith Jones. Jones had realised that returning Richard to school was fraught with danger because of the wild reputation he had acquired. Burton remembered: "I knew that he was potentially wild, and Meredith asked me to keep an eye on him because he might be a bad influence in the school." Philip acceded to the request willingly as, by now, he had detected a considerable sense of culture and intellect in Richard where others saw only the "rough boy who drank, smoked and played rugby like a champion."

At last, Richard was on his way. But while his return to school at the age of 16 may have been triumphant for his family and friends, it was personally rather humiliating. He had spent nearly 18 months with the grown-ups drawing a wage packet and now he had, literally, to don his school cap again and return to being a boy.

Readapting to the school routine was difficult. Later in life, he said the pure humiliation of his first day back was something he never forgot. Psychologically, it was one of the hardest things he ever had to do. Melvyn Bragg observed: "He was a man among children." Finding himself in a class of children a year younger than him, he quickly learned he was much more socially advanced than his classmates.

He also met a hostile reception from the headmaster, Pop Reynolds, who had not concurred with the governors' view that Richard should be readmitted.

Philip Burton was now paying him special attention and he had to intervene on the first day, when Richard threw a shoe across his classroom in frustration and unfortunately broke a school window. It was a serious disciplinary incident but it was hushed up as an accident. On another occasion, he attended an afternoon English class led by Philip Burton in which Richard was so clearly affected by a lunchtime drinking session in the bar of the Grand Hotel next door, that Burton had no hesitation in removing him from the class. There were other serious incidents as well, in which Richard would turn up in the morning smelling of beer. But, somehow, he got away with them all.

Philip Burton made sure the problems disappeared before they reached the ear of the headmaster. He understood the return to school was not easy for Richard, saying: "Richard returned to school a month before his seventeenth birthday. As a result of his lost schooling, he couldn't rejoin his previous class and so was at least a year older than the other boys and girls in the class to which he was assigned. With his experience of the world, he was now a young man among kids."

Richard also went out with his first proper girlfriend on his return to school. Her name was Cathy Dolan, a slim red-haired girl whom everybody called Phyllis. They hit it off because they were both interested in acting and the theatre. And, like him, she later took up acting as a career. Recalling Richard's return to school, Dolan said: "So Richard was back and you can imagine the effect on us girls. He was such an attractive young man, extraordinarily so."

Dolan and Richard had their first date at a cinema. But nothing sexual happened, as he was a late developer in that respect, and it would be another two years before he lost his virginity. She described that first date: "I don't remember a thing about the film. I was trembling so much. And he didn't even touch me. But then, Richard was never a toucher; not one of your gropers. He had more class than that. In a strange way, I became his bird. But it was all very innocent." Graham Jenkins remembered her well: "I thought Cathy Dolan was the most beautiful girl in the world with all that red hair and that shape and style. I was terribly jealous."

The two of them went on quite a few dates and read poetry to each other. It was all very wholesome, as she explained: "Richard was never a lecher. He was attracted by thoughts, feelings and ideas. I was sixteen and innocent, and he just liked me for what I was."

It seems that Richard had many other girlfriends during that time, but they all tell a similar story.

Aside from any obvious problems, Richard took a different approach to his second chance at academia and dedicated himself to his schoolwork. In fact, according to his brothers, he was a model student in that respect, working hard to make up for lost time.

This approach meant that, a year later, at the age of 17, he had passed all seven subjects in the School Certificate Exam. His superior grade in five of the subjects meant he passed to what was called 'matriculation standard', thus qualifying him to go to university and, ultimately, to take up the RAF's offer to fund him for a short six-month course at Exeter College, Oxford.

Rhianon James, his niece, remembered him telling her the news: "He said: 'I'm going to Oxford', and I said: 'Going to Oxfoooord?' He then said: 'Ox-fud', and I said: 'But I said Ox-foord', to which he said: 'You don't say "-Ford", you say "-Fud."'"

His acceptance at Oxford was the fulfilment of a Jenkins family dream that had started years earlier when their mother died in 1927. It had been Edith's dream that one of her children would attend Oxford. There and then, the Jenkins siblings decided that Richard would be the one amongst them to fulfill their late mother's dream. Just how this was to be accomplished was still unclear. As Richard recalled: "The idea of a Welsh miner's son going to Oxford was ridiculous beyond the realm of possibility."

Nonetheless, it happened just as Edith Jenkins had dreamed it would.

# CHAPTER 7

# The fateful meeting

## *The making of the man*

### 1943

Although Meredith Jones was a vital part of the Richard Burton story, there was another man, even more important, without whom Burton could never have succeeded. Philip Burton was the svengali who literally manufactured Burton: from the basic raw material he embodied when their paths first crossed in 1943 into the star he would eventually become. If ever there was proof that Hollywood superstars could be manufactured, Philip Burton's creation of Richard Burton is that proof.

But then Philip Burton was a creative genius. In a country where 95 per cent of its citizens left school at 14 and were very poorly educated, he stood out. He won a scholarship to go to university at the unusually young age of 16. In the four years he attended the University of Wales in Cardiff, he graduated in two subjects in successive years: an honours degree in pure mathematics and then history a year later.

But even armed with those qualifications, the best job the 20-year-old could get in 1925 was as an ordinary mathematics teacher at Port Talbot Secondary School. It's no surprise that he was bitterly disappointed.

However, that disappointment ensured that, 18 years later, he and Richard Jenkins would be in the same place at the same time to form the partnership that would project Jenkins to international fame – as an actor called Richard Burton.

As a young man, Philip Burton was a larger-than-life character. There was no ignoring him as he was a tall, imposing man who cut a swathe walking at high speed through the corridors of Port Talbot Secondary School, as he often did, with his long black gown billowing behind him.

His sense of style and purpose meant he was sometimes mocked by his more conventional colleagues and regarded as a curiosity by his pupils' parents. But no one doubted he was excellent at his job and that the boys and girls of Port Talbot were very lucky to have him. Melvyn Bragg described him as "a bachelor...a rather solitary man...somewhat eccentric...and, although extremely well read and very highly thought of by his colleagues, he was always regarded as something of an odd fish."

His complex personality can partially be accounted for by his upbringing. Although he was a son of Wales, both his parents were English immigrants and he spoke with a perfect English accent. He was also brought up as a devout Anglican, whereas almost all Welsh people were strong Methodists. Bragg called his Anglican religion "a serious handicap."

Despite that, his beginnings were as rough and tough as those of any of his contemporaries. Philip was born in a terraced house at 9 Arnold Street, Mountain Ash. Mountain Ash was a mining village 20 miles from Port Talbot. His father was Henry Burton, who hailed from Staffordshire. Always known as 'Harry', he had settled in the valleys after emigrating to Wales in search of a highly-paid job down the mines. Like many Englishmen, he had rushed to Wales in the boom years of the coal industry during a period that was christened by locals as "the celtic klondike of the nineteenth century."

Philip's mother, Emma Mears, originally hailed from Somerset. The Mears family moved to South Wales for the same reasons as the Burtons. Emma married John Wilson in 1881 in Newport, and her son William was born in 1887. They divorced 15 years later and Emma, whom everyone called Emily, took William and moved back in with her parents and her young brother, George. Then, at the turn of the century, she met Harry and married him in 1902; she was eight years older than her new husband.

Philip was born on 30th November 1904. His father was 36 and his mother 45. By then, the 18-year-old Will Wilson was already working down the mines.

Melvyn Bragg describes Philip as having been brought up in a "precious atmosphere" and puts it down to him having a relatively young father and older mother, citing it as a disadvantage. Bragg writes: "They forbade him the pleasures and rough and tumble of street life."

No one knows where Philip's innate intelligence came from as neither of his parents were in any way cerebral. But his artistic and cultural propensity is somewhat easier to understand as his father was a highly talented musician, playing the clarinet and violin to concert standard. His mother was also a gifted pianist.

Harry could have made a career out of music but for his hopeless weakness for alcohol. Drink made him floppy and weak, both physically and mentally. Since he was usually under the influence of alcohol, Harry's weakened personality meant his marriage was inevitably dominated by his wife.

But it wasn't to last for long. In 1919, Harry was killed in an accident down the mine when the roof supports gave way in a shaft in which he was working, and he was buried alive. Some say he was under the influence at the time and, had he been a bit more alert, he might have clawed his way out. But there was no knowing if that was true; mine accidents were common at the time and no investigation was ever carried out. Harry Burton became just another statistic.

Philip Burton was just 14 when his 59-year-old mother, Emily, took over sole responsibility for his wellbeing. Given that his mother couldn't even read or write, the death of his father was a huge loss. But although she demonstrated little intellectual ability whatsoever, Emily had strong instincts and recognised an opportunity when she saw one. She was also a very pushy woman and wanted only the best for her children. After her husband's death, she devoted herself to Philip's upbringing, and he consequently became an overprotected and rather lonely child. But he was also a very bright child, easily at the top of his class in most subjects at school, and effortlessly so. He jumped straight from second year to the fourth and completed the two-year higher certificate course in one year.

The loss of his father so early in Philip's life led him to suffer an identity crisis, which was aggravated by his creative instincts being overwhelmed by his academic talent. He had essentially lost his entire sense of self when he was saved by an unlikely event. A troupe of travelling actors visited Mountain Ash and set up a performance for a fortnight at the local church hall. Philip made sure he was in the audience for each performance, including rehearsals, and was mesmerised by what he saw. The jolting experience sparked his lifelong interest in the theatre. It subsequently dictated the course of his life and, ultimately, the life of Richard Burton as well.

In 1922, his brilliance in school saw him win a scholarship for a place at the University of Wales in Cardiff. He was only 16. He left school and travelled the 18 miles back and forth to Cardiff each day on the Taff Vale train. It took an hour each way. Philip embraced his new freedom as a student. He was startled by the cultural scene he found in Cardiff, particularly the high standard of the city's three theatres: the New Theatre, the Empire and The Playhouse.

He spent as much time as he could watching every production staged, sometimes up to half a dozen times for each one, trying to understand the creative processes they entailed. On many occasions, his older brother Will, also a theatre buff, joined him. There is little doubt Philip would liked to have become an actor himself, but he was realistic enough to recognise early on that the talent was just not there.

He thoroughly enjoyed his time in Cardiff and, by the time he left, he was as much an expert in the intricacies of theatre production as anyone in the industry. He might have achieved firsts in both of his degrees if it hadn't been for the time he spent in the three Cardiff theatres during those years.

After university, in an ideal world, he would have started his career in the arts as a production or script assistant, but it was too precarious an existence and he could not convince his mother to let him do it. All theatre personnel were freelance and hired on a production-by-production basis. Emily was worried that, between productions, even the best people experienced long periods when they were out of work.

So, at his mother's insistence, he became a schoolteacher; a career he never intended to have.

Although his first love was English, Philip was forced to begin his career as a teacher of mathematics since teachers were in short supply for that subject. But as soon as he had some influence within the school, he switched over to English. Nevertheless, the theatre remained his private passion and he started writing radio scripts for BBC Wales, based in Cardiff. But try as he might, he couldn't break out of school teaching. Although everyone recognised his outstanding talents, for some reason no one offered him a way out of Port Talbot. So he settled into the ways of school teaching and, after ten years of it, came to believe it was his lot in life despite his bigger ambitions. However, some would maintain that he did have opportunities to break away but simply lacked the courage to leave the safe and secure world of teaching.

Partially to compensate for his frustrations, he took charge of the school's drama department in his spare time and produced plays in the school and the town – sometimes acting in them, sometimes writing them. He was also continually sending spec plays he had written to West End producers in London and constantly receiving rejection slips.

Despairing of making a career for himself in the arts, he turned his attention to the most talented of his pupils and began living vicariously through them. He sought out talent that he could nurture, but found it surprisingly thin on the ground. Over the course of the next 18 years, he discovered half a dozen boys with the talent to make it all the way. Sadly, however, for one reason or another, none of them did.

But that didn't stop him dreaming of finding a pupil whom he could take to greatness, and he devoted his life to the task. Melvyn Bragg says that having no children of his own meant that Philip lived much of his life through his pupils. By his own admission, it developed into an obsession. As he once said of his own motivation: "There must be a thing called the Pygmalion complex; if there is, I have it. It's a deep urge to fulfil myself as an actor or a writer through another person. Perhaps I should be unkinder to myself and call it a Svengali complex. It is not satisfied just by teaching a class; there must be a close personal identification with the pupil."

His first success was with a very promising young boy called Tom Owen-Jones. Tom was another miner's son who had passed the scholarship exam. Philip Burton spotted him and gave him the special attention he would later bestow upon Richard Burton. The handsome Owen-Jones was very promising material indeed, and was described by Philip as a "gentle, cultured boy." He had none of Richard Burton's rough edges and developed into a very promising actor. No one was surprised when he won the Leverhulme scholarship to attend the Royal Academy of Dramatic Art (RADA) in London.

After his formal training at RADA, he appeared at the Old Vic theatre in London and, by the outbreak of war, he was one of London's better-known stage actors. He spent two seasons with the Old Vic and played opposite Laurence Olivier in 'Hamlet'. He also starred in his first feature film called *The Four Feathers*.

But when war broke out, Owen-Jones joined the Royal Air Force (RAF) as a flying officer. He was pitched first into the Battle of Britain and then the fight for air superiority over France. On a sortie over the channel, his plane was hit by enemy fire from the ground and severely damaged. He and the crew were able to parachute out of the plane before it crashed. But his parachute failed to open fully and he hit the ground too fast, badly injuring his hip. While it was a survivable accident, infection set in at the hospital and he eventually succumbed to a sarcoma.

Philip Burton was devastated and believed he would never again find anyone of Owen-Jones' ability.

But the young actor's life had not been completely wasted; the success Tom Owen-Jones achieved before war broke out in 1939 had effectively made Philip Burton's reputation.

Before Owen-Jones, although Burton had discovered other promising boys, the boys' parents had become suspicious of the teacher's true intentions towards their children and had intervened each time. In particular, there were four promising pupils, namely, Hubert Clements of Aberavon, Vivien Allen, Evan Morgan and Hubert Davies from Port Talbot being trained for stardom by Philip. But all four sets of parents interfered and halted the process, becoming suspicious of Philip's motives. And some got nasty – Morgan's parents banned Philip outright from ever seeing their son again. Philip dismissed the parents as "non-believers" and watched as his pupils suffered as a result of their parents' scepticism; none of the four were ever heard from again. It made him desperately sad.

The problems were exacerbated by the increasingly mixed opinions people held of Philip Burton. He also wasn't helped by his sometimes overconfident and glib mannerisms. People said he could be too fond of his own talents and seemed to like the sound of his own voice too much; it was a quality that irritated those who already saw more bad in him than good. But the good in Philip eventually overcame the bad.

Of course, Philip Burton's whole career was dogged by unsaid accusations that he preyed on his young pupils in an unhealthy way. In those days, this sort of activity could be carried on seemingly without consequence. But there is absolutely no evidence that this was the case, and Burton could be accused of no more than being a man who derived pleasure from developing promising careers in the theatre.

It didn't help that Philip lived such a solitary life and liked it that way. When he finally left his mother, he lived in lodgings, first in Broad Street and then at 6 Connaught Street, in Port Talbot. The lodgings were run by a widow called Elizabeth Smith, whom everyone called 'Ma.' She lived there with her two daughters, Liz and Audrey. Philip's fellow lodgers were a bank clerk and an engineer. When the Smiths moved, their lodgers moved as well.

Connaught Street was the third house the Smiths had owned, and Philip had moved with them every time. The house was relatively large with a kitchen downstairs, four bedrooms, a bathroom and three living rooms. The three Smiths shared the large front bedroom and Philip's bedroom was next door. The two other lodgers had the two smaller bedrooms beyond the bathroom. Downstairs, Philip had the large living room, and the Smiths and the engineer enjoyed the two smaller living rooms. The bank clerk did not have a separate living room.

Mrs Smith had been forced to take lodgers after the sudden death of her husband, as Philip remembered: "She was the widow of a chief maritime engineer. In 1917, he had come home on leave and had fallen victim to the widespread and lethal flu epidemic of that year. Because he had died ashore and off-duty, his widow was paid little compensation and suddenly found herself faced with having to make a living for herself and two children."

Although it became her livelihood, she detested the term 'lodger' and referred to her co-habitants as "paying guests" or "gentlemen lodgers." Over time, Elizabeth Smith effectively became Philip's mother, and her daughters became his sisters.

Philip received special attention, as Elizabeth cooked his meals, cleaned his bedroom, ironed his shirts and generally looked out for him. It was indistinguishable from a mother's role. Philip particularly enjoyed her mini rabbit pies, which she used to make from locally-shot rabbits. As he told her one night after a particularly satisfying meal: "Ma, I could write a poem about that pie."

There was no doubt he was initially attracted to the lodgings because of the cheap rent. Elizabeth Smith said that she always found Philip an odd mixture of fun and austerity. All his money was spent at the theatre and, whenever he could, he took the train to London to see the latest play.

Being a sophisticated and not unattractive bachelor meant that Philip attracted the interest of single women from time to time. But any attempts to interest him in women failed. One female teacher in particular, who also lived in Port Talbot and shared similar interests, was very keen on Philip and actively pursued him for a period. But he showed no interest in her, saying: "I'm quite happy on my own and, you know, a cultured person is never lonely." Contrary to popular opinion, he was not a virgin and the truth behind his apparent aversion to women was somewhat more poignant. In turned out that, in his university days, he had fallen in love with a waitress in a café near the university. It was a difficult but very passionate love affair, which continued for two years. But, tragically, it was cut short when the girl he loved contracted tuberculosis and, after a short illness, died in hospital. Philip, who had intended to marry her when his finances allowed it, was devastated and simply couldn't cope. He had tasted real love and had it cruelly snatched away from him. He never again spoke of the girl and he never got over it, but she remained deeply etched in his mind for the remainder of his life. After that, no other girl was to be a match, and he simply held on to his memories of her. They were to sustain him for the next

70 years of his life. As far as can be ascertained, he only ever discussed his first love with Elizabeth Smith, to whom he admitted he had been "madly in love" with the girl.

Although she lived into her late 90s, Elizabeth Smith had been long dead by the time Melvyn Bragg and other biographers conducted their research, and Hollis Alpert and Fergus Cashin were the only journalists ever to seek her out and interview her. Consequently, many of Philip's other biographers shared the view that it was Philip's lonely childhood that turned him into the very private person he eventually became. Later, Michael Munn, who claimed to know Richard Burton and people like Sir John Gielgud personally, tried to infer that Philip Burton was gay. But there is no evidence for such an assertion other than semi-malicious, uninformed hearsay from people long dead. In reality, Philip Burton was neither straight nor gay, and apart from infrequent relationships with members of both sexes remained, for the most part, celibate for virtually the whole of his life.

The success of Tom Owen-Jones nailed the lie and dispelled the rumours that he preyed on young boys, although it was too late for the careers of Clements, Morgan, Allen and Davies. Indeed, after Owen-Jones' death, opinion turned and, instead of having to persuade suspicious boys' parents that his intentions were honourable, the parents began to seek him out. According to Melvyn Bragg, parents suddenly began to see him as a "potential passport out of the valleys."

Philip also began to produce plays for BBC Radio in Cardiff. His productions were very highly regarded and he gradually became a well-known celebrity in Port Talbot. When, at the end of his first play, the announcer spoke the words "produced by P. H. Burton", any mocking amongst his colleagues ceased. As he recalled: "I was doing the radio stuff and I was known locally because I had a good theatre company."

By the time Richard Jenkins came into Philip Burton's orbit, in September 1937, his reputation was known far and wide. Richard realised that Philip Burton was a man apart. When they met, he was immediately stimulated by Philip's brilliant mind and became very conscious that he might be important to his future. He said: "I admired the way he spoke English and the fact that he wasn't afraid to demonstrate his love of books, poetry and plays."

Gradually, being in Philip Burton's company became a drug for Richard, and he simply couldn't get enough of it.

It was extraordinarily prescient of Richard Burton to pick him out as a mentor.

But getting Philip Burton's attention proved to be a process that would take several years. Burton only taught the elder boys, and he initially paid little attention to Richard.

By the time he was old enough to get into Philip's class, Richard had developed acne of the worst kind and, unfortunately, Philip could not see beyond it. He did not believe any boy, however talented, could overcome such an affliction to make it as an actor on the stage, where looks were so important. In the end, Philip told Richard outright that his spotty face precluded him from becoming a serious actor.

But apart from the acne, the truth was that Philip did not initially see any talent in the young Richard. He also foresaw a problem with what he called his "uncouth Welsh accent." Philip told him: "Well, goodness, you can't be an actor and speak like that."

Absolutely undeterred, Richard seemed to get more determined with every rejection. He went out of his way to make certain that Philip Burton took notice of him. He would often stay behind after classes, seek out and engage Philip in conversation about Welsh poets such as Dylan Thomas, Gwyn Thomas and R. S. Thomas. He would also discuss with him the plays of William Shakespeare, luring him into conversations he had rehearsed in his mind the night before. As Richard remembered: "Philip taught the last lesson and, after everybody had been dismissed, I lagged behind and finally plucked up the courage to go and talk to him." Philip Burton remembered his pupil being a "relentless questioner."

But in 1939, the relationship nearly ended. Much to Richard's chagrin, Philip decided to take a sabbatical with the aid of a travelling scholarship from the Guild of Graduates of the University of Wales. He applied for the scholarship together with 200 others and had very little hope of winning either of the two places available.

But win it he did, and with the money Philip decided to visit New York. On 8th April 1939, he left Southampton on a passenger liner called the Aquitania bound for New York. Travelling third class, he tried to make his money go as far as possible. The voyage was notable as the ship was carrying very large quantities of English and French gold, which was being used to pay the US government for war materials. For Philip, the trip wasn't pleasant; the fortune in gold in the ship's hold made him feel uneasy and he was seasick for most of the voyage.

When he disembarked, he went straight to Sloane House, the YMCA hostel where he was to stay for the first two months of his visit. Then, he discovered Broadway and resolved to see every play that was on. He attended up to three performances a day if he could fit them in. He called his obsession "an endless fascination" and, during his time in New York, he eventually saw more than 60 different shows.

As part of the scholarship, he was supposed to visit American schools and observe their teaching techniques. Although that took second place to visiting theatres, one school he did see was the Horace Mann School for Boys. Having heard of a gifted husband and wife teaching combination, he actively sought them out. Alfred and Charlotte Baruth were everything he had expected, and the three bonded almost straightaway, becoming lifelong friends. Alfred Baruth was head of English at the school, and Philip spent much of the spring and early summer of 1939 at the Baruth house.

Baruth and his wife were well known in Europe because of the tours they ran every summer on the continent for their pupils. But the advent of war made a 1939 tour impossible so, instead, they planned a tour of America.

Disappointingly, only nine schoolchildren signed up for the 1939 tour and, instead of a coach, the Baruths hired two large cars for the nine children, themselves and Philip – six to a car. They proceeded to drive 14,000 miles in seven weeks around North America. The highlight of the trip was visiting Hollywood and meeting film stars Dorothy Lamour and Eddie Cantor. It was an amazing adventure for a simple Welsh schoolteacher.

But his idyllic summer ended abruptly on 1st September, when the news came through that Germany had invaded Poland. Any sane man would have stayed put in America for the duration, but Philip wanted to get back to England as quickly as possible. He felt a huge sense of duty to be there for his country at its time of need, although, by then aged 35, he was too old to fight. After a great deal of effort, he managed to get passage back on an American passenger liner called the President Roosevelt. No one was sure if the ship would be attacked by German U-Boats despite flying a neutral flag. The crew painted huge stars and stripes on both sides of the hull and, at night, the ship was floodlit. It was a difficult trip back across the Atlantic, full of uncertainty. And it was nearly 11 days before the liner docked in Southampton.

Upon his return, Philip looked for war work and found it as a commanding officer of an RAF training squadron, a part-time role. With that secured, he was minded to leave his teaching job and work for the BBC in Cardiff full-time. But the war had changed everything, as Philip recalled: "I had virtually made up my mind to leave school teaching and devote my life to writing and acting for the theatre and the BBC, but the Ministry of Labour decided that I had to resume my position at Port Talbot Secondary School."

He had little choice in the matter, as wartime regulations dictated it, and no one was more pleased by Philip Burton's return than Richard Jenkins. In fact, the outbreak of war presented Richard an opportunity to ingratiate himself further with Philip. All British schools were guarded at night by a combination of pairs of boys and masters. Called fire-watching duty, it was scheduled by rota, but Richard schemed to ensure that he and Philip were paired together. Little by little, the crafty young boy wormed his way into his English teacher's affections.

But Philip remained far from impressed by the still spotty youth.

Interestingly, years after Richard Burton died, Philip Burton attempted to rewrite history by telling interviewers he had recognised Richard's talent from the very beginning of his time at Port Talbot Secondary School. He told Melvyn Bragg many years later: "I was fascinated by him. I thought he had incredible potential and great need."

But the truth was that it was only as a result of the constant attention he received from the young boy that he paid him any mind at all.

Indeed, Philip rejected Richard time after time for parts in his school plays. It took until January 1941 for Philip to cast him in his first role, an American diplomat called Mr Vanhattan in a political comedy called "The Apple Cart" by George Bernard Shaw. But Richard blew the opportunity by playing the American in his thick Welsh accent, leaving Philip Burton unimpressed again.

But Richard never stopped trying. When Philip Burton founded the Port Talbot squadron of the RAF Air Training Corps (ATC) in April 1941, Richard had the prescience to enlist straightaway, which gave him even more time in Philip's company. The Air Training Corps was a national cadet force that was set up for wartime training. Philip Burton was given command of the 499 Squadron with the army rank of Flight Lieutenant and he supervised the weekly drill evenings where Richard learned the basics of airforce training. As Philip explained: "The aim of the ATC was to give as much prior training as possible to future members of the RAF – membership was, of course, voluntary."

Meredith Jones also returned to Richard's life at this point. Jones was a big supporter of the ATC and coached the squadron's newly-formed rugby team. The links were made even stronger when, around the same time, Jones founded a local youth club. Philip Burton agreed to oversee the drama section, run by Leo Lloyd, so Richard joined that as well. Another brother, David Jenkins, remembered: "Richard knew he had to make the most of his chances, which meant making a real impression on Philip Burton."

Gradually, as Philip became increasingly more entrenched in Richard's life, the teacher could not fail to notice the pupil. And by October 1942, Richard's teenage acne had completely disappeared and Philip Burton finally took serious notice of him for the first time. By then, Richard was 17-years-old, had left school, got a job and returned to school again.

Philip's change of attitude did not happen overnight, but he gradually became more and more intrigued by Richard. He was undeniably impressed with the boy's determination to be noticed. Although the teenage acne had left some permanent scars on Richard's face in the shape of pockmarks, in many ways it just added to his character.

The breakthrough in the relationship came when Philip invited his young pupil back to his lodgings for tea with his landlady Elizabeth Smith. Strangely, he wanted Mrs Smith's opinion of the boy before committing to him. Luckily, she approved. Richard couldn't believe that after five years of trying, Philip was at last taking him seriously. After meeting Elizabeth Smith, he ran home to Caradoc Street and breathlessly told Cecilia what had happened.

Philip immediately got to work and began to frame Richard's future as a classical stage actor. But he soon discovered that Richard needed rather more than just the skills of acting imbued upon him. Philip found his diction barely intelligible, and he told Richard the kindest thing he could when he said that his voice was "raspy." He said of his new protégé: "He is, at best, a rough gem greatly in need of polishing" and the process is one of "preparing him for a worthwhile future."

Philip told him: "If you're going to be an actor, you've got to change your voice and your speech." The voice was rough and the accent was strong Port Talbot. And so began a difficult period of change which was to last for two years. Richard simply said 'yes' to everything Philip proposed and placed himself entirely in his hands.

Philip Burton decided to go back to basics and start at the beginning. As Melvyn Bragg explained: "The voice was strong, but the accent could have been cut with a knife; and it was no easy task to change it." According to

Bragg, Burton had to teach his protégé everything, including "breathing, delivery and movement."

Philip Burton proved a hard taskmaster. At the same time, he was giving him extra tuition to help him pass his School Certificate exam. Evening after evening, they worked tirelessly in Elizabeth Smith's front room, which Richard nicknamed "the room of terror." He later recalled: "It was from four o'clock after school until ten, 11, 12 o'clock at night." Philip used poetry to keep his pupil interested, and spent hour after hour drilling the vowels over and over again. He told Richard: "Sense must come first, and the voice, if you have it, will follow."

Gradually, a new Richard Jenkins emerged and there followed a slow metamorphosis into Richard Burton.

Burton rehearsed young Richard privately every night until his diction was pitch perfect. Philip's technique was to apply rigorous elocution training in order to hone down his Welsh accent and emphasise the pronunciation of English vowels. Philip said: "It was adolescent rough to begin with, but with constant practice, it became memorably beautiful...I aimed at giving him what I call mid-Atlantic speech, which is equally acceptable in London and New York. The vowel sounds must be clearly distinguished and the consonantal sounds distinct."

As part of the process, Richard used to climb to the summit of a mountain called Mynydd Margam and recite passages from Shakespeare at the top of his voice. As he recalled: "It was very difficult to shout in a house, with other people around and people next door thinking you've gone mad. And it sounds terribly romantic and idiotic, but in actual fact I would go to the top of the mountain and scream as loudly as I could until my voice hurt. Then when it hurt, I waited for a bit and then screamed again to fix it in some way so that it didn't hurt. And it was a very primitive way of doing it, but it worked."

The time Philip Burton devoted to his protégé was remarkable considering the many other commitments and demands on his time. Burton was deeply devoted to public service, particularly with his voluntary work at the Air Training Corps.

As Richard's diction improved, in November 1942, Philip cast him in a major role in one of the plays he was producing at the school. The play, called 'Gallows Glorious', was about John Brown, the American abolitionist, and Richard was given the part of John Brown's brother, Owen. Owen Brown himself had been played by Brin Jenkins, also a very talented and more established young actor. Richard knew he had to do something to eclipse Brin's performance.

The story centred round the American Civil War, and the closing minutes of the play called for Richard to sing 'His Soul Goes Marching On.' It was a great opportunity to be noticed and to stand out. Richard made the most of it and, although Philip criticised him afterwards for overacting, he was totally triumphant and the play would prove to be his breakthrough. From that moment on, any doubts disappeared and Richard got Philip's full attention.

He quickly cast him in a radio documentary on the BBC about the work of the Air Training Corps, called 'Youth at the Helm'. It was his first appointment as a professional actor, and Richard travelled to the BBC studios in Cardiff for the recording. He was overwhelmed, as was his younger brother, Graham Jenkins, who went along with him. Graham recalled: "I was bowled over by the melodious, seductive tones."

After his radio debut, Philip became certain he had a star on his hands and resolved to focus everything he had on Richard's career. Philip began to see him in an entirely new light.

Richard, duly encouraged, began to tell everyone his ambition was to be a professional actor. It was exactly what Philip wanted to hear, and it was the trigger for a sea change in their relationship. The sudden emergence of Richard's talent was everything he had desired, and he began to see that Richard had even more talent than Tom Owen-Jones. Graham Jenkins summed it up: "My brother had come a long way since the day Phil Burton had reported unfavourably upon his complexion. At seventeen, Rich had the rough good looks of a warrior, a stubborn jaw and compelling blue eyes. He was strong and intelligent, and he could act."

As the relationship developed, through Christmas 1942 into 1943, Philip became more and more enamoured with Richard. And it was reciprocal. Richard became restless to leave home and what he saw as the negative influence of Elfed and Cecilia. He enjoyed being at Connaught Street with Elizabeth and Philip and was increasingly unhappy living in the same house as Elfed James.

But it was not as easy as just walking out. Although he was itching to leave home, he had no income and, until he turned 21, the law dictated that he needed parental permission to leave. He confided in Philip, who, as it turned out, shared his concerns about the negative atmosphere at Caradoc Street. Philip even called Elfed an "intellectual brute".

Suddenly, though, the situation resolved itself as one of Elizabeth Smith's lodgers, the bank clerk, was called up by the army for national service. Philip Burton suggested to a very receptive Richard that he might like to take the vacant room.

But it was far from easy. For a start, Philip was unsure whether Elizabeth Smith would rent the room out to a penniless student even if the money was guaranteed by Philip. Moreover, neither man believed that either Elfed or Cecilia would let him leave the house at Caradoc Street, where he had lived for 15 years.

Philip and Richard discussed the problem continually. As they talked, it became clear to Philip that, since Elfed and Cecilia had never formally adopted Richard, there was some doubt as to who precisely were his legal parents. It turned out that his legal guardian was still Dick Jenkins, who was by now a sorry figure – a 68-year-old sozzled excuse for a man living with his daughter, Hilda.

So Philip and Richard cooked up an elaborate scheme whereby Richard would deliberately spark an argument with Elfed, walk out, and spontaneously appear on Elizabeth Smith's doorstep. Although both men denied it vigorously in later years, it was a carefully-devised conspiracy hatched between the two.

Picking a fight proved to be easy, as Elfed James was continually grumbling about Richard to Cecilia. As far as Elfed was concerned, Richard was a dead loss.

Graham Jenkins remembered the relationship between Richard and Elfed very clearly and is in no doubt about what really happened: "When I stayed there, Elfed used to fall asleep on the sofa in the living room and Richard would look at him with contempt. In the end, I reckon Richard just walked out."

And that is exactly what transpired. On St David's Day, 1st March 1943, Richard deliberately provoked Elfed and caused a huge row. He duly walked out and told Elfed he was never coming back.

As planned, Richard went straight to Connaught Street and told Elizabeth Smith what had happened. He said: "I can't go home. I have no place to stay."

Philip, in on the plan, backed him up and explained to his landlady that the student had no place to spend the night.

Elizabeth Smith fell for it and allowed him to take the vacant room upstairs. Richard not only stayed that night, but for the next two and a half years.

Philip picked up all the costs. Years later, many stories would be told and retold about Richard's exit from 73 Caradoc Street, and everyone in the Jenkins family had their own varying account of it. But what really happened was recounted by Audrey Smith, Elizabeth's daughter, who explained: "Had Ma refused to have him, there may never have been a Richard Burton. Little did we know then what fate had in store for him."

Philip Burton wrote two autobiographies; one in 1969 called *Early Doors* and another in 1986 called *Richard and Philip*, both with differing accounts. Years later, Philip Burton sought to rewrite history again and told the film director Tony Palmer that he was never keen for Richard to come and live with him. As he told it, he had to be persuaded by the family to take Richard off their hands. He said: "Richard told me that he had tried to leave home a few times and no member of the family would take him in. I didn't realise what I was saying when I said: 'Well, there's an empty bedroom in my house, you can take that.' 'You mean it?', and I said: 'No, no.' Oh, he put on such a sad act, you know. 'Nobody wants me.'"

Whatever the truth, Richard quickly ingratiated himself with the Smith family. Elizabeth Smith herself dispelled a few myths about Cecilia, and, years later, told biographer Hollis Alpert that she was none too impressed by the manner in which Cecilia had raised Richard. She was particularly horrified with his table manners and the fact that he didn't properly know how to use a knife and fork. There were also problems with his personal hygiene – particularly his feet. As she recalled: "He was a pretty rough boy then and we had to polish him up a little. I taught him everything in manners – how to hold a knife and fork; how to eat his soup." With Mrs Smith and Philip Burton, Richard acquired another mother and father, the third such paring in his life. Whereas Cecilia had indulged Richard, much to her own husband's fury, the tougher and more disciplined regime at Connaught Street was much more beneficial. As Elizabeth Smith remembered: "When Richard came here from Caradoc Street, he had nothing at all. Mr Burton bought him his clothes. He coached him, trained him, did everything. Richard has got to thank him for everything in the world he's got."

She always remembered him as a difficult boy, "strong-willed and basically unmanageable." As she said: "He didn't care whom he offended. Ask his opinion and you would get it. He had a wonderful memory, yet he could be so forgetful about his clothes. Someone gave him a new mackintosh and immediately he lost it. I remember, he had such smelly feet." But she also said he had many good points: "You had to like him. He was always in a rush, leaving it until the last minute to go to school. And I remember he used to like Shredded Wheat for breakfast."

Certainly, Elizabeth Smith was good for him in all the ways that Cecilia wasn't. The discipline she imposed energised him.

Indeed, when Mrs Smith informed Richard that he would have to clean the shoes of everyone who lived in the house as part of his household chores, Cecilia was horrified.

But the transformation from the moment he went to live in Connaught Road was astounding, and the change in Richard's outlook on life was immediately apparent. As Graham Jenkins recalled: "Intellectually and socially, he acquired a confidence which quite overawed the younger members of the family. He dressed well, at Phil's expense, adopted manners which some miners might have thought a trifle fussy, and talked fluently on topics outside the normal run of conversation."

As Richard settled, Philip stepped up the pace and made him work even harder. The coaching began in earnest and the two would often stay up until two or three in the morning. As Elizabeth Smith told Hollis Alpert many years later: "Mr Burton would be up with him at all hours, talking and studying. They would learn a play between them in a night. And sometimes they would wake me up, as I would think they were quarrelling in the front room. Then, I'd tap from the bedroom and I could hear them tiptoeing upstairs."

The application was rigorous and unrelenting. But he had a very willing pupil, and Richard was well aware that this was his moment and his opportunity. He knew that he had a short time in which to prove himself. The final school exams were only six months away and he knew that his further education required a good pass in the final exams. Richard later said of that time: "It made up the most painful and hard-working period of my entire life."

And it wasn't all sweetness and light by any means. Philip and Richard were both strong, creative characters and had their differences, and some of their arguments got quite heated. Elizabeth Smith said: "I remember once he stayed out all night after he and Mr Burton had a little bit of a fuss. He slammed out and said: 'You'll see me when I get back.' Mr Burton waited up half the night. I happened to be down early in the morning and there was Richard at the door, looking bedraggled and very sorry for himself. 'Where in the world have you been?' I asked. And he answered: 'Sitting on my grandmother's grave all night meditating.'"

# AND GOD CREATED BURTON

Despite Elizabeth Smith's tough regime, discipline was a constant problem. Philip Burton abhorred smoking and drinking, so Richard used to go to the outside toilet to smoke, with Audrey Smith keeping watch. But drinking in the outside toilet was uncomfortable, so he used to sneak off to the pub at lunchtime during school hours. Philip continually smelled drink on his breath at school but gave up disciplining him as it was ineffectual. But the other masters were not so sanguine. According to some students at the time, he came close to expulsion three times, but thanks to Philip Burton's intervention, he was excused each time. Audrey Smith remembered those days: "He would go down to the toilet at the bottom of the garden to smoke. Mr Burton would come in and say: 'Where's Richie?' And I used to say I didn't know, and smoke would be pouring out of the door of the toilet."

In June 1943, Richard took the School Certificate examination, but he would have to wait for his results until September. But it was the end of his schooldays and, from 14th June, he was a member of the RAF and, more importantly, on its payroll. A week later, on 21st June, he collected his first pay packet of £1.5s.6d (£1.32p), although he wouldn't be officially called up for over a year.

In the meantime, Philip Burton staged a production of 'Pygmalion' by George Bernard Shaw and handed Richard the starring role of Professor Higgins. Richard's performance was highly praised by a local critic in the Port Talbot *Guardian* newspaper. Years later, there was some doubt as to whether or not the production of 'Pygmalion' ever occurred, with some suggesting that Philip Burton invented it to enhance his protégé's CV. But the newspaper records indicate it did indeed take place.

His success in 'Pygmalion' led to his first paid work as an actor for BBC Radio. 13th August 1943 was a big day at Connaught Street when Richard received his cheque from the BBC for 7/6d (35p). To mark the occasion, Richard spent the money on buying Philip a poetry book, Hilaire Belloc's *Sonnets and Verse*. When he gave it to him, his mentor was overcome with tears.

While he waited for the exam results, Richard went with Philip to ATC summer camp at the RAF St Athan airfield near Cardiff. It was a blissful time and his duties were light. The two men read books continuously in the day and discussed them in the evenings.

One morning in late August, Philip Burton was sitting in a deck chair in the sun reading that day's Cardiff *Western Mail* newspaper when he came across an advertisement that had been inserted by Emlyn Williams. The then 38-year-old Williams was a well-known playwright. He also directed and acted in his own productions. Two of his plays, 'Night Must Fall' and 'The Corn is Green' were playing in London theatres to great success.

The advert announced: 'Emlyn Williams wants Welsh actors.' It stated that Williams was seeking Welsh-speaking actors for a new play he had written, called 'The Druid's Rest'. The play was to be produced in London by HM Tennent Ltd.

Tennent was a famous theatre production company run by legendary agent Hugh Beaumont, whom everyone knew as 'Binkie.' HM Tennent had been founded in 1933 after a merger. When its founder Harry Tennent died after a heart attack in 1941, Beaumont, only 33, had assumed control and rose to become the most powerful man in British theatre. Three years later, his productions dominated London's West End and Beaumont had the power to make or break an actor's career. The combination of Williams and Beaumont combining to produce a new play was exciting.

Philip applied for an audition on behalf of Richard. Simultaneously, another Welsh would-be actor, Stanley Baker, had also seen the advertisement and applied.

It was a cue for Philip and Richard to switch their efforts from his voice to his acting technique, and Philip was astonished at what he found. Armed with his new voice, Richard quickly developed what Philip called "stage presence". As he said: "Here he had something that nobody could give him. It's the quality that distinguishes the genuine star from the merely talented actor."

The auditions were being held at the Sandringham Hotel in Cardiff and attracted a long queue of hopefuls. As Richard later recalled: "There was a shortage of young men because all the young men were called up and gone. It could only have happened in wartime." As he got in the queue, he had little hope of being chosen from so many. But unbeknownst to him, Philip had already primed Emlyn Williams about "a boy he described as an exceptional talent."

Significantly, it was the first time Richard met HM Tennent's casting director, Daphne Rye. The 27-year-old Rye was a very attractive woman who recently split from her husband, the actor Roland Culver. On Philip's advice, Richard had gone to the audition wearing his ATC uniform. It was good advice as, at 17, Burton looked slightly spivvish, especially as he wore his dark, curly hair slicked down, as was the fashion of the time.

The ploy must have worked because, as soon as she saw him, Rye's mind was made up and Richard was selected to be formally auditioned by Emlyn Williams. Daphne Rye was transfixed. She said she thought his face looked as if it had been "sculpted with its high cheek-bones, his perfect mouth and eyes that held the attention of anyone they fixed upon." Richard could see Rye was very impressed and she told Richard the audition was "just a formality." It prompted the 17-year-old Richard to make a pass at her, which she found amusing. But she was struck by his presence and told Philip she thought he was "the epitome of a Welsh boy."

Despite Daphne Rye's assurances, Richard himself was none too sure of getting the role, as he remembered: "Emlyn Williams was looking for a young man who could speak Welsh and who could act. Well, I knew I could speak Welsh, but I was not too sure if I could act."

He needn't have worried, as Williams was mightily impressed. In fact, on first sight, Williams found his appearance "startling" and, never at a loss for words, described his eyes as "bold...set wide apart in a dramatic face: a clean adolescent leaf, waiting for a life to write on it." As he recalled: "After a dismal procession of no-goods, a boy of seventeen, of startling beauty and quiet intelligence, stepped forward. He read a few lines and I knew at once he would be excellent." Famously, Williams called Richard "imperishable", whatever that meant.

Paul Ferris observed in an early biography of Burton: "Burton's head already had something of the quality that would make women – and men – gobble him up with their eyes."

40 years later, Emlyn Williams recalled his memories of that first audition vividly to Melvyn Bragg: "He was a most spectacular-looking boy. Marvellous green-blue eyes and he had repose. Nothing precocious. Nothing smart-alec. Almost shy but sure of himself, you know."

As Daphne Rye had confidently predicted, Richard was selected. But Stanley Baker also impressed and he won the role of Richard's understudy. Both Williams and Rye were amazed to find two such great talents come out of one audition.

To celebrate, Williams and Rye invited Philip and Richard to lunch. But there was a problem and, over lunch, Williams told them that Richard, at 17, was too mature for the lead part of a 14-year-old Welsh boy called Tomas. They gave that part to another promising actor called Brynmor Thomas, who was the right age at 14 and was already known as a child actor.

In its stead, he offered Richard the part of the boy's elder brother, Glen.

He explained that it was a small part with only one scene, although Richard would be on stage for most of the play. Williams was mightily impressed with how Philip Burton took the news and called him a "professional adviser who knew about the theatre." The lunch was a great success.

Despite not getting the lead role he had so coveted, Richard was given a part which would take him into the West End a few months after leaving school. Williams became his fourth mentor and would later cast him in his first feature television play, his first feature film, as well as introduce him to his first wife and, through one of his sons, Brook, provide him with a lifelong friend.

Melvyn Bragg noted: "By some terrific fluke, Richard came face to face with his future at the precise time he most needed to see it. For Emlyn Williams had walked where Richard began to realise he now wanted to tread. Williams pointed in a direction and Richard followed it."

Bragg called it: "A devil longing to get out. And Emlyn's gentle comedy, 'The Druid's Rest', gave the devil its chance. The devil grabbed it and was on the loose forever after."

More practically, Daphne Rye told Richard to report in October to the Haymarket Theatre, London, to start. She told him the play would start playing in provincial theatres in November and hopefully transfer to the West End in January 1944.

But Richard was unsure whether he would be able to take up the part, which would run over the winter and early spring of 1944. He thought it almost certain to clash with his national service and his call up to the RAF.

But, as it was, his unbelievable luck held up in the most extraordinary way.

The first good news came in September, when Richard learned he had passed all seven subjects in the School Certificate Exam and received a superior grade in five of them. He had passed to what was called 'matriculation standard', thus qualifying him for entrance to university.

But there remained the problem of how to complete his education before he was called up for wartime service. Philip was desperate for him to go to university, as he believed it to be "an essential social equaliser."

Theoretically, matriculation gave an assured entry but it was expensive to attend and even more difficult to finance. Unless Richard got a scholarship, the fees would have to be paid by Philip out of his own pocket and he simply couldn't afford it. And that was assuming Richard's call up to the RAF could be delayed.

Then, Philip heard about a scheme the RAF was running for young airmen, offering a university course at Oxford or Cambridge as an incentive to attract the right sort of person. Volunteers for officer rank in the RAF could, at the British government's expense, spend a preliminary six months at university. Then, after serving their time in the forces, they could return to complete a degree.

It was one of the peculiarities of war that they would also get paid for the time they spent there. Going to university, and being paid to do so, was an opportunity not to be missed.

Philip prepared the ground for his protégé and realised it was important that he be presented to the RAF selection board in the best possible light. It was a unique situation. But Philip's influence only extended to getting Richard in front of an RAF selection board. Once there, he knew his background would count against him. The sons of miners did not get to go to Oxford or Cambridge – in fact, it was unheard of.

Paul Ferris, one of Burton's early biographers summed it up well: "If youths were to spend time at an ancient university, the authorities saw no point in wasting the privilege on bumpkins."

Philip turned his formidable intellect to solving the problem, and help came from an unlikely source. Earlier in the year, Philip had been awarded an MBE by the King for his outstanding work with 499 squadron. Philip was honoured but not surprised, as he recalled: "My squadron of the ATC became very successful."

The award of the MBE brought Philip to the attention of the Commanding Officer of the RAF in the Port Talbot region, Air Marshal Sir Cyril Cooke. According to Philip, Cooke told him: "There's a difficulty you know, this boy's name is Richard Jenkins and your name is Philip Burton and his father is living. It might be a bit suspicious about your relationship. Why don't you adopt him and give him your name honestly?" Cooke's suggestion seemed preposterous, but slowly the idea took root in Philip's mind: he could formally adopt Richard, and change his name and his parentage so that he was no longer the son of a drunken miner but of an important and distinguished schoolteacher. Cooke told Philip that the adoption would make it almost certain that Richard would be selected.

But it was with some trepidation in early October 1943 that Philip suggested to Richard that he would like formally to adopt him as his own son and to take over full responsibility for his future. Philip also explained what it would mean, including changing his surname from Jenkins to Burton.

Any trepidation was unnecessary and, when Richard was asked, he just said "great." Far from needing persuading, he was quick to see the advantages. Richard was keen to secure a place at university whatever the cost, and giving up his surname seemed irrelevant. He had no attachment to it at all. Compared to Elfed and Cecilia, he much preferred having Philip and Elizabeth as his parents and he had come to love both of them very much. It was also true that he loved Cecilia, but this was negated by the passion with which he loathed Elfed.

With Richard's acquiescence and Cooke's backing, the selection board agreed subject to the paperwork being completed. As Philip recalled: "Through [Cooke], I was able to gain admittance for Richard to Exeter College, Oxford, for six months prior to his joining to the RAF, a privilege granted to very few cadets."

In many ways, that was the easy bit; persuading the family to take such a step would be far from easy.

Although he was aware they were not Richard's parents, nor had they any legal status, Philip Burton nevertheless sought Cecilia and Elfed's formal permission to adopt Richard and went along to Caradoc Street the following weekend: "I'd never been to the house before and I went and asked them on a Sunday afternoon."

Philip explained to Cecilia why it was necessary for him to adopt Richard. He carefully told her that volunteers who qualified for officer rank in the RAF could spend a preliminary six months at Oxford at the government's expense. Then, after wartime service, they could return to university to complete their degrees at the conclusion of hostilities. He told her: "I have every confidence that, with my support and recommendation as his teacher and guardian, Richard will be chosen."

Cecilia was shocked at what he proposed and didn't say a word. But Elfed was delighted, saying: "Oh, you take him Mr Burton. You take him, you take him." After Elfed had spoken, Cecilia thought about it and whispered to Philip: "If you take him, it would be the answer to my prayers."

Philip reassured Elfed and Cecilia that money was not an obstacle and that he would provide financially for Richard from that day on. He offered himself as Richard's mentor and benefactor, an offer that was gratefully accepted. Years later, Cecilia would tell people that she had been dead set against the adoption, but that simply wasn't true. At the time, she was relieved Richard was being taken off their hands. The financial strain of raising an 18-year-old still at school was especially burdensome during the war years. They were delighted when Philip Burton said he would formally take over all those liabilities. Elfed was particularly pleased, seeing only the bad side of his brother-in-law; Philip Burton, on the other hand, saw only the good side.

Marian James, Richard's niece, admits that everyone was delighted with Philip Burton's interest in Richard. As she said: "We held him in awe. I mean, here was this man who came into our lives and was interested in one of us. He used to come and visit us quite often during all these negotiations, and he always said: 'Now, what books are you reading?' and so on. I mean, we were absolutely terrified by this man because he spoke such precise English. We had never come across anyone like this."

But his other siblings were not convinced. They were shocked at Cecilia and Elfed's acquiescence. They thought that Philip Burton was attracted by more than Richard's intellectual qualities and that there was a sexual interest in adopting him. But Philip introduced them to Elizabeth Smith and they were immediately reassured and embarrassed, and apologised to Philip for their suspicions. Even cursory enquiries revealed that Elizabeth had a reputation for being totally scrupulous, and was herself a pillar of the community. She told them that if she thought or even suspected there was any paedophile activity going on in her house, she would have thrown out the perpetrator immediately; there was no doubt about that.

But despite the assurances and success of the initial meetings, the adoption of young Richard was fraught with problems on both sides. It soon became apparent that it was up to Dick Jenkins to make the final decision. And he threw a giant spanner in the works when he demanded cash from Philip in return for handing over his son. Astonishingly, Dick Jenkins wanted to sell Richard to Philip Burton for £50.

Everyone was horrified, but it could proceed no further without Dick's permission, and he was deadly serious about wanting payment. Philip Burton himself was bemused rather than shocked. He had the £50 but, of course, any money changing hands would have been tantamount to human trafficking, for which the penalty was at least five years in jail. There was also another snag in that Philip Burton was technically not old enough to adopt Richard formally. At the time, the legal minimum age gap between adoptive parent and child was 21 years, and there were no exceptions. Philip remembered the problem: "I was 20 days short of being 21 years older than [Richard]. He was born on the tenth, and I was on the 30th of November."

Everyone became involved in the discussions to solve these twin problems. Philip's age was the easiest to resolve, as it quickly emerged that he could become Richard's legal guardian, which would give him the same rights as a formal adoption in a private agreement. Dick's demand for cash was harder to reckon with, as it was not only distasteful but also illegal.

In the end, for legal reasons, it was thought best that Philip Burton did not meet Dick Jenkins. Surprisingly, in his otherwise excellent biography, Melvyn Bragg stated that Dick was an "amiable man; who loved his son and was pleased if he was doing well." But Bragg was misled by everyone who sought to whitewash Dick Jenkins' reputation.

But at last it was settled, and the appropriate legal document was drawn up by a local Port Talbot solicitor called Ivor Rees. Meanwhile, Richard had departed for Liverpool to appear in 'The Druid's Rest' and he left it to his family to complete the legalities. For him, the deal was done and he was already calling himself 'Richard Burton.'

On 17th December 1943, David Jenkins witnessed the agreement for Philip Burton to become Richard's legal guardian. Dick Jenkins had already signed the document and been given his £50 by David Jenkins on Philip's behalf. It was accompanied by the filing of a deed poll and a confirmatory notice in the local newspaper, gave Richard Jenkins the Burton surname.

The document not only gave Philip Burton custody of Richard, but also the legal obligation to clothe, feed and educate him. The wording of the document stated that Richard would "absolutely renounce and abandon the use of the surname of the parent and shall bear and use the surname of the adopter and shall be held out to the world and in all respects treated as if he were in fact the child of the adopter and he infant shall reside in such places as the adopter think fit."

The document incorporated some stiff penalties should Dick Jenkins ever seek to try and revoke it. It actually forbade him from instituting any legal proceedings for the recovery of the custody of his son. And if Dick Jenkins were to breach that he would have to repay all the monies that Philip had spent on his son up to that date.

David Jenkins recalled: "I went along to Connaught Street, where Philip Burton was waiting for me. I had met him several times before, and had always found him exceptionally courteous and charming. I decided that we could have every confidence in Philip Burton and I was proud and happy to sign the guardianship papers."

As Philip Burton later told the film director Tony Palmer: "His father had to be found to sign it, which he did." Despite the somewhat distasteful financial shenanigans, it was a transaction made out of love and done for the very noblest of purposes. Richard Jenkins was now Richard Burton. As Philip Burton said: "Richard was my son to all intents and purposes. I was committed to him. He knew I was doing it out of love. I did feel very much his guardian and his father, and was proud of him even in those days. It was a fine relationship."

Having opened a bottle of champagne that had been kept back from before the war for a special occasion, Philip celebrated with Elizabeth Smith and her daughters that night. When he telephoned Richard, he told him to make sure he had his own glass of champagne to celebrate. Champagne wasn't an easy thing to procure in Liverpool in the war years, but he and his friend Stanley Baker ordered a glass each at the theatre bar from a dusty bottle at the theatre's wine store. As it happened, it was Richard Burton's first taste of champagne – but it was not to be his last.

# THE FATEFUL MEETING

# CHAPTER 8

# Stage debut in Liverpool

## ...and on to the West End

### October 1943 to March 1944

When Philip Burton delivered the news to Richard that the RAF didn't need him to report to Exeter College in Oxford until April 1944, he was ecstatic. He would be free to take up the offer of a part in Emlyn Williams' new play, 'The Druid's Rest'. It was a signal for more long hours in the front room at Connaught Street, as Philip and Richard dissected the script and his part line by line. Philip remembered: "It was comically ironic that he had worked hard every day for months to acquire standard English, and now he had to regain his Welsh accent for his first part on that stage."

The play was scheduled to open in Liverpool in November and the pay was £10 a week, some three times what his brothers were earning down the mines in Wales. So on 1st October 1943, he boarded the train for London in the company of his understudy, Stanley Baker, who was being paid £5 a week.

At that stage, Burton had no notion that acting would be his life's career. Believing it to be a passing phase in his life, he said: "I thought it was quite interesting that people were willing to pay me ten pounds a week for it." Baker agreed with Burton's assessment, saying: "At that stage, one's main ambition was to get out of the valleys and improve yourself. It didn't matter which way."

It was their first visit to the capital and they had two priorities. Apart from performing in the play, both boys were out to lose their virginity. They made an exuberant pair, eager to lose their innocence and surrounded by girls they thought would be only too pleased to assist.

But there was a problem; their inexperience meant that neither boy had any idea about what to do. Neither of them had ever been told the facts of life, and both were equally ignorant. As Emlyn Williams later put it: "They had heard about it and boasted about it, but what was it?"

In reality, both boys were somewhat daunted by London. They were both away from home for the first time and incredibly naïve. But, together, they forged a bond which would last for the rest of their lives.

'The Druid's Rest' was a comedy; the tale of a Welsh family – a mother, father and their two sons – living in a small Welsh village. The youngest son,

Tomas, initiates a chain of events based on mistaken identity, and his parents are persuaded that their lodger is a notorious murderer on the run. Richard was playing the part of Glen (Glan in Welsh), the older brother. It was a minor speaking role but with plenty of stage time. The major stars of the play were 36-year-old Michael Shepley and 46-year-old Gladys Henson. There were only five actors in the cast: Roddy Hughes; Neil Porter; Lyn Evans; Nuna Davies; and the lead player, 14-year-old Brynmor Thomas. Burton's part, albeit a small one, had one very important scene.

The London rehearsals were subject to a strict regime overseen by Daphne Rye. She found some digs for Burton and Baker, run by a very strict landlady, in Streatham, South London. Her ferocious regime cramped their style somewhat, especially when rehearsals went on until late. Finally, when the rehearsing was over, the company set off on tour. The first stop was Liverpool's Royal Court Theatre for more rehearsals and an extended opening run in November.

Burton may have been in unglamorous, bombed-out Liverpool during the war years, but he was living his dream. Only a few months earlier, the two actors had been in school, living in relative poverty, with an uncertain future and facing the prospect of fighting in the war. Burton, 17, appeared to be ten years older than he was. Baker, 16, was also physically mature for his age, and both had much in common – including their proclivity for beer.

Neither man could quite believe they were working for a famous theatre producer and renowned director and getting paid to act on stage. Burton was certain it was all a dream, about to end any minute. As Baker recalled: "There was a sense of unreality about the whole bloody thing; to be suddenly taken out of a Welsh valley and to be thrust into big cities totally alone."

Melvyn Bragg summed it up best when he said that Burton's outlook was "fuelled by awesome capacity and the hunger of those who cannot believe that such fortune will not vanish before their appetite is appeased."

And so it came to pass that Richard Burton's first ever public performance before a paying audience was on 22nd November 1943. He was billed for the first time as Richard Burton, a name he would not legally acquire for yet another month.

That opening night in Liverpool played to a packed house with nearly 30 people standing, and that carried through the first week. People in attendance that night had no idea they were witnessing the birth of an acting legend. But they remember Burton being remarkably confident for his age and experience. Gladys Henson recalled: "He was the most beautiful boy I'd ever seen. He was never precocious; just an ordinary boy with great talent. You would never have thought it was his first professional part. I thought perhaps he would be nervous, but not a bit of it. He was really a natural from the word go, from that first rehearsal." Offstage, she recalled he talked about nothing but one thing: "He never stopped talking about the game of rugby." Years later, Emlyn Williams also remembered Burton's debut: "He did something very rare: he drew attention by not claiming it. He played his part with perfect simplicity." The 38-year-old playwright found, to his surprise, that he was getting on famously with his 17-year-old actor: "Richard was immediately likable. He was quietly pleasant; not shy, just reserved, except for the sudden smile which – there's no other word for it – glowed."

Burton also introduced Williams to the work of the up-and-coming Welsh poet Dylan Thomas. Williams had no idea of Thomas' growing fame but Burton loved Thomas' work and, soon, so too did Williams. The actor and the playwright began what would become a lifelong friendship in Liverpool.

But it was not all sweetness and light, and Williams quickly realised he had made a mistake by bringing along Stanley Baker. By the time they arrived at the theatre in the evenings, Burton and Baker were often drunk, despite frequent warnings from the director. Williams was also worried about their obsession with chasing women. As Melvyn Bragg recalled: "They were torn between a huge urge to do everything and a huge ignorance about how to go about it."

Burton and Stanley Baker shared digs again. This time there was no Daphne Rye to keep them in check and no adult supervision. The hedonism and sudden exposure to Liverpool's seedy nightlife went to their heads and they very quickly became junior hell raisers. They spent their time during the day in bars, drinking and fraternising with what appeared to be all of Liverpool's low life, both male and female. The two liked to frequent the pubs by the Liverpool docks, which were full of people that can only be described as 'characters'. Stanley Baker later confessed that they were "like wild animals let loose to enjoy the birds and the booze." He added: "There was nobody to say 'no'. Richard could pull any bird he chose, he had the gift and the looks and the gab." Baker admitted they socialised with "completely worthless characters."

Interestingly, through all of it, the two of them virtually ran away from sex. Despite their original intentions, both ultimately seemed scared of losing their virginal status.

Their Liverpool landlady took a somewhat different view to discipline. She was in her late 30s and very attracted to Burton. But she was aware of his age and that was as far as it went. She allowed him to take her out to the cinema and, after that, for a drink and hot cocoa in her room in front of the gas fire. The following morning, Richard boasted to Stanley about his conquest: "Last night, I had her in front of the fire and, in the middle of it, I felt as though my feet were on fire and I thought I must be in hell. Then, I realised that I was too close to the fire and my socks were burning."

Initially, Stanley was very impressed, but when he questioned his friend closely, no details were forthcoming and he suspected Burton had made it up – which he had. Years later, Burton confessed to Baker that the story wasn't true, by which time his friend had already worked that out for himself.

As the play left Liverpool and rolled round the major theatres still open in the English provinces, it attracted some good local reviews and good audiences. In mid-December, it opened in Cardiff at the Prince of Wales Theatre for a run over the Christmas period. Every ticket was sold for every performance, and the Jenkins family turned out to watch Richard perform professionally for the first time. Tom, Ivor and Graham Jenkins borrowed their local doctor's large saloon car to make the trip with their partners and sister Cecilia. It was an emotional evening and would be the first of many to come over the next 40 years.

But it was in Cardiff that Burton's career almost ended. Burton and Baker's drinking reached a peak over Christmas, and one night, the two of them arrived for the evening performance completely sozzled. They climbed the stairs to their fourth-floor dressing room, which overlooked the busy Queen Street. Stanley Baker was starting to get frustrated about being Burton's understudy. Maintaining he was every bit as good an actor as Burton, he got into a disagreement with him. Burton threw Baker against the window frame, shattering the wood and five panes of glass and throwing debris onto the pavement crowds four floors below. As Baker described it: "We suddenly started fighting in the dressing room. I was thrown back against the window... the whole window frame went smash."

Fortunately, no one was hurt from the falling debris. But the police were called in and Emlyn Williams had to smooth things over. It was the cue for Williams to take action, threatening both with the sack. But it was an empty gesture, as he had no replacements and Burton knew it. Far from being chastened, the two boys started another fight the following night. This time, no one called the police, but Williams called Philip Burton and told him to get to Cardiff quickly to help restore order. Philip rang Ivor straightaway to come with him. From then on, for the rest of the tour and the hell-raising was completely curtailed.

The play moved to Swansea in mid-January and Dick Jenkins saw his son perform for the first time. He understood none of it and left at the interval for the pub down the street. It was no less than anyone expected.

The play finally arrived in the West End of London on 26th January 1944 for a run at St Martin's Theatre. At that time, the London West End's square mile of theatres and pubs was known as the most exciting place on earth and attracted audiences of mostly uniformed men and women of all nationalities, including many Americans. It was the time of the Siege of Leningrad in Russia and the battle of Monte Cassino in Italy. It was clear that the allies were at last starting to win the war and Adolf Hitler's days were numbered. Morale was high. But the West End could also be a dangerous place, with the occasional threat of a German rocket attack.

Joshua Logan, the famous American director and dramatist, was in the audience for the London opening and went backstage to tell Burton he had a great future in the business. Emlyn Williams agreed, saying: "Richard was obviously going to be a great actor. He had the looks, the ease, the deportment and the natural flair. But you couldn't foresee his future precisely because he had only the one small comedy scene, which he played with tremendous assurance – as if he had been in the theatre for years – he had tremendous reserves of natural timing."

One review by James Redfern, the theatre critic of the *New Statesman* magazine, proved very important in Burton's life. Redfern wrote: "In a wretched part, Richard Burton showed exceptional ability." Burton was entranced by Redfern's words "exceptional ability." He always claimed that the moment he read those words, he knew his life had changed and that he would be an actor. He said: "That's when the bug hit. A very powerful drug."

However, while it may have been a success for Burton, the play was exposed as a lightweight production in London and attracted only negative reviews. By the end of the first week, it was clear 'The Druid's Rest' was not destined for greatness. Its London run lasted barely eight weeks and the play would never have been heard of again had it not been Burton's West End professional stage debut. When Burton left the cast to head for Oxford, he was given a huge send-off party at the Two Brewers pub. For Burton, it had been a triumph, but 'The Druid's Rest' marked the end of Emlyn Williams' reputation as the Welsh golden boy of the theatre. And he would never be as successful again.

Ironically, that January of 1944, an 11-year-old girl called Elizabeth Taylor made her debut in British cinema at The Empire, Leicester Square, in a film called *Lassie Come Home*.

# CHAPTER 9

# Six months at Oxford University

## ...more extraordinary good luck

### 1944

Richard Burton finally left the company of the 'The Druid's Rest' and arrived at Oxford's Exeter College in April 1944. Burton's departure was a chance for Stanley Baker, his understudy, to complete the run. He arrived at Oxford in ebullient mood. In the previous six months, he had earned £250 from the performance and still had half of it left. It made him one of the wealthier students on campus. In addition, the RAF was paying him around £2 a week, so he had plenty of spending money.

On his first day in Oxford, Burton looked around him and wondered at his great opportunity. It was certainly a novel experience for the Welsh miner's son. He was immediately entranced by Oxford and its history. He said many years later: "I fell in love with Oxford and have remained in love with it. It had a curious, almost mystic, impact on me." There was much to love with the gothic triangles and medieval lanes. The contrast between Port Talbot and Oxford was bewildering at first.

He chose to study English and Italian as his subjects.

It was a strange time, as the vast majority of potential students at the universities were off fighting in the war. It was this shortage of students that gave the RAF the opportunity to train its would-be officers at Oxford or Cambridge. Burton's course was called 'short-service' and would last for six months. It was designed for students to be able to return after two years' war service, to complete their courses and then graduate.

Exeter College was situated in Turl Street and had been founded in 1314. It had long held historic connections to Welsh scholars but, in living memory, no son of a coal miner had ever crossed its gates.

Oxford was a bastion of the middle and upper classes from privileged backgrounds, the majority of whom had attended public school. Initially, Burton was totally overawed and very quiet, and he found he had little in common with his fellow students. Eventually, he fell in with the few

113

grammar school students there. The grammar school boys generally stuck together, not mixing with the others. The exception was Robert Hardy, then known as Tim Hardy, and the two actors started a friendship in 1944 that would last for life.

Burton and Hardy met at an Oxford club called the Experimental Theatre Club, which consisted of around 40 students interested in the theatre. Hardy was initially not drawn to him and thought him "vulgar." As he remembered: "We met at that meeting and he thought I was a prissy little child of privilege, and I thought he was arrogant as hell and simply not to be talked to." But Burton quickly made a huge impression on Hardy and, shortly afterwards, they met in navigation class at a table poring over a map of Southern England. As he remembered: "I had never met anyone like him before, nor have I since. He was, genuinely, a great man, a leader. Put half a dozen hell-raisers in a room with him and he would be their chief in ten minutes. Have your best conversationalists around to tea or dinner and Richard would wipe the floor with them. And there was so much danger about him, it was intoxicating. We realised we had an abiding and really quite profound love and knowledge of William Shakespeare."

Initially, Burton got frustrated by students greeting him with the line: "How are you today?" In Wales, people did not bother with such niceties and just said what they wanted to say. But he admits he soon fell in with it, saying: "I became a bit of a snob myself." He added: "Eventually, the people from the better schools treated me absolutely as an equal and I had no problem at all." It was just as well because, as his brother Graham recounted: "Rich liked to be liked."

With his personality, Burton quickly came to dominate the theatre club. As Penny Junor, his biographer, said: "Richard's handsome masculinity... was a magnet for both men and women." Hardy agreed, saying: "He had an astounding beauty, a blend of classic Greek serenity and smouldering fires emanating from that ancient troubled history of the Celts."

Burton also sought to get involved in the famous Oxford University Dramatic Society, known as OUDS. Emlyn Williams had told him all about it, as the Welsh maestro's own talents had been fashioned at OUDS when he attended Oxford's Christ Church College between 1923 and 1927. Besides Williams, OUDS had sent many promising students for their debuts on the London stage, including John Gielgud.

During the war, OUDS was officially suspended but simply carried on its activities under a different name run by its director, a very talented man called Professor Neville Coghill. It was Burton's luck that Coghill was also his English tutor at Exeter College.

Of all the classes and colleges in which he could have ended up at Oxford, it was Burton's extraordinarily good fortune to have ended up with Coghill. Eventually, the professor became the fourth significant mentor to Burton, taking over the mantle from Meredith Jones, Leo Lloyd and Philip Burton.

The 45-year-old Coghill was a fellow in English literature and an accomplished author in his own right. He was responsible for translating Chaucer's *Canterbury Tales* into modern English. The book became a best-seller. He later co-wrote a stage musical version of the *Canterbury Tales*, which was staged on Broadway and in London's West End. In New York, it won five Tony nominations. Coghill could have had a brilliant career in the London theatre but he could never cut loose from academia. Instead, he satisfied his creative urges by staging extremely high calibre productions to rival the best of anything put on elsewhere.

Coghill staged one major production every year and, in 1944, he was to put on William Shakespeare's 'Measure for Measure' in the open air theatre next to the quadrangle of Christ Church College.

As soon as he arrived in Oxford, Burton went to the OUDS office and applied for the lead part as Angelo. But he was seemingly too late and was told all the parts had been cast. Coghill's assistant told him he had already given the part to another very talented actor called Hal Fordham and it was impossible to retract the decision. But his matter of fact reply didn't perturb Burton one bit, as he said later: "I was fairly determined to play the leading part."

So, the next evening, Burton knocked on the door of Professor Coghill's study. The professor, who had no idea who Burton was, asked: "What do you want?", to which Burton replied: "I have come to recite some poetry to you." Coghill looked at him askance and said somewhat sarcastically: "Well, there's a dais over there. Stand on it and say it."

Burton, without batting an eyelid, walked to his dais and recited the "To be or not to be" soliloquy from 'Hamlet'. As the room filled with Burton's melodious tones, Coghill began to pay attention. As he recalled later: "Out came the most perfect rendering I had ever heard." He said to Burton when he had finished: "Well, you need no help from me. That was perfect. But what do you want?"

Burton told him: "I am an actor and I want to play Angelo." Coghill replied:

"I don't see how that is possible. You are here for just six months. In that time, we have only one production which is already cast and into rehearsals."

But it was clear from that moment on that Coghill dearly wanted to use Burton. After a long pause, in which the two men just stood looking at each other in silence waiting for the other to suggest something, Coghill eventually muttered, almost under his breath and expecting a negative reply: "Well, I'm afraid it's already cast, but if you care to understudy for it, you can have that." Coghill was surprised when Burton simply said: "Thank you, then, I will." As Burton turned to leave, Coghill shouted: "Hey, what's your name, by-the-by?"

38 years after it happened, Coghill recounted this exchange to Burton biographer Fergus Cashin: "I do not often recall conversations verbatim, but this one impressed itself on me."

Far from being miffed by an understudy role, Burton seized the opportunity. It meant he attended rehearsals as a fully-fledged member of the cast. It was no effort as he already knew the part off by heart. Thanks to Philip Burton's tutelage, he was well-versed in Shakespeare. The two often did impromptu performances, but Coghill wasn't to know any of this.

After their first exchange, Coghill started to focus his attention on the young Burton. He gradually came to believe he was the most outstanding drama student he had ever taught. As he told Cashin in 1982: "I have had many students of very great gifts and many of very little. But I have had only two men of genius to teach – W. H. Auden and Richard Burton. When they happen, one cannot mistake them."

And Coghill certainly did not mistake him. When he died in 1980, the file notes he wrote about Burton in 1944 were discovered. They read: "This boy is a genius and will be a great actor. He is outstandingly handsome and robust, very masculine and with a deep inward fire, and extremely reserved."

Coghill was so impressed that he made sure Burton was excused from almost all of his RAF duties with the university squadron so he could concentrate on the play. He also got permission for him to grow his hair long for the part. It was a major concession, as RAF wartime regulations specified a weekly short back and sides from the squadron barber. It seemed that Burton was not the only one determined to see him play the part.

Burton assiduously attended rehearsals and it was quickly obvious to Coghill that, as talented as Hal Fordham was, the understudy was better. Burton hoped that the incumbent Fordham would be sacked and that Coghill would reverse their roles. But it was never necessary, as Fordham was suddenly called back to his regiment and Burton stepped into the part two days before opening night.

It was the break he had been waiting for, and as soon as he got the news of Fordham's departure, Burton sent an urgent telegram to Philip Burton in Port Talbot. Philip, recognising the opportunity, took the first train to Oxford and was there within six hours of receiving the message. As soon as he arrived at Oxford Station, he went straight to Burton's rooms at Exeter College. For the next 36 hours, they rehearsed and refined his lines. By opening night, he was word perfect.

Philip remembered: "We scarcely took time to eat. We worked on it line by line, hour after hour, into the early morning. I never ceased to be astounded by how quickly and thoroughly he absorbed the notes I gave him."

On opening night, in order to steady his nerves, Richard downed four pints of beer before going out. It immediately became apparent that he was a better actor when he was under the influence of alcohol. As Robert Hardy confirmed: "Drinking produced a vein of brilliance in him."

The opening night was on a brilliant, still summer's evening in the little quad right inside Christ Church. Members of the audience that night who are still alive today remember it vividly.

The role of Angelo was a complicated one, but the part was made for Burton, who shared some of his characteristics – most notably his sex drive.

Burton made the most of the opportunity and delivered arguably his single best ever performance. It was a pure triumph, as Robert Hardy remembered: "There were moments when he totally commanded the audience by this stillness, and the voice would sing like a violin and with a bass which could shake the floor."

Coghill recalled: "Richard's stillness was overwhelming while he was being unmasked in the last act by the Duke. He stood absolutely erect, facing the audience with all the anguish in the world in his eyes, with his arms at his side, his fingers clenched and yet ever so slightly unclenching and clenching again – an almost invisible, yet overwhelming, movement; his features motionless like stone. I think I may have told him this gesture, but he did it so much more grandly (if that is the right word for something almost imperceptible) than I had expected. It was one of those manifestations that made me know his greatness as an actor. You couldn't not look at him. You couldn't not feel with him." At the after-party, Coghill was on a high and told anyone who listened that his lead actor was a "genius."

# AND GOD CREATED BURTON

And Burton could not have chosen a better place or time to impress. In the audience that evening were John Gielgud, Terence Rattigan and, most important of all, Hugh Beaumont – managing director of HM Tennent Ltd and the most powerful man in British theatre. Beaumont was also of Welsh origin and, at only 36-years-old, was already a legend in the business. As a bisexual, his style was high camp, with a high-pitched voice that could not be mistaken. His personality was ideally suited to get on well with theatrical types.

At the party, Beaumont sought out Burton and asked him what he wanted to do after the war. Burton was surprisingly non-committal about becoming an actor and a somewhat surprised Beaumont told him to come and see him when he had made his mind up. He said simply: "Look me up." Those three words, "look me up", were to rattle around in Burton's brain for the next three years. In truth, Burton was enjoying Oxford so much he wanted to return and complete his course. But Beaumont's enthusiasm upset his plans. He was stunned that the theatre's most powerful impresario was interested in him and that Neville Coghill thought of him so highly.

Once the after-party had broken up, Burton carried on partying throughout the night. Philip Burton was sharing Richard's room in Exeter College and he remembered him returning at dawn in a dishevelled state. Despite the hour, the two men indulged in some reminiscences, recalling that barely two years earlier, Richard had been behind the counter at the Co-Op. Richard reminded Philip that this was also only the second time he had been to England.

Richard's performance was such a triumph that, when word got round Oxford's campuses, he became a minor celebrity in the city overnight. He was immediately at the top of every invitation list, and he made the most of it. Naturally, Burton attended every party to which he was invited and he chased after every available woman there, often wooing them with poetry.

Besides removing any of his inhibitions around girls, the vast quantities of beer he drank at these events appeared to have no adverse effect on Burton at all. Robert Hardy accompanied him on many of these parties and said: "We all went after girls; Richard always got them. We all drank; Richard out-drank us. He had more originality than anyone I had ever encountered."

Few women have ever been prepared to speak on the record about Richard Burton. One who did was Nina Bawden, now 86 and a famous novelist. She was at Somerville College in 1943 studying philosophy, politics and economics. She met him at a university ball and was initially smitten. They had a brief affair, which ended after he asked her away for the weekend to London to stay with Emlyn Williams. Bawden, believing Burton to be a fantasist who couldn't possibly know the famous playwright, ended the relationship.

After Bawden, Richard simply moved on to the next girl. But, despite his prodigious escapades, he was still a virgin well into his 18th year. It was something he readily admitted to his friends, saying he had had a few near misses but never actually 'done it.'

He finally lost his virginity at Oxford when he met an older lady, a mature student, who fully understood his situation and predicament and guided him through the process with no embarrassment. Burton recalled the experience later: "I met a girl student there who was older than I was, and she showed me what to do."

Once he had lost his virginity, all further inhibitions disappeared and, no longer embarrassed by ignorance, he proceeded to have sex three or four times a week – rarely with the same girl. It was as if the handbrake had been released. He told early biographer Fergus Cashin: "Having discovered sex, I began looting and plundering with great delight." He told Cashin he saw the "sex urge as the sweetness of life and the origin of all affections and the root of all aspirations."

His six months at Oxford were arguably the high point of his life, when he was at his happiest. But despite the high jinks, he kept his focus on his education and was one of the 12 top RAF cadets in the passing out parade that September. Another of the top 12 that day was a student called Michael Misell. Misell didn't particularly care for Burton because of his then often-expressed anti-semitic views. But, in time, the Welshman and the Jew came to like each other and to respect each other's opinions. Misell eventually changed his name and became the great British actor Warren Mitchell. The two would meet up again at RAF Docking two years later.

The decision to depart from Oxford to take up full-time residence with the RAF was an occasion for great soul searching. Richard pledged to return to Oxford to complete his studies after the war was over. But practicalities intervened and, for the rest of his life, he regretted not sticking to his word. But he had made an indelible mark on OUDS, Exeter College and Professor Neville Coghill that would reverberate for years to come. Robert Hardy said: "He always struck me as a man of greatness. And one meets awfully few in life."

# CHAPTER 10

# Navigating the RAF

## ...Three years in limbo

### 1944 to 1947

There was never any danger of Richard Burton being killed or injured in the Second World War, as he never faced any action. Although his age spanned 14 to 20 during the war years, by chance and by luck, he never faced a German bullet.

But he didn't know that when he caught the train to Torquay in Devon to start his RAF service in early October 1944, at the age of 18. He was headed for RAF Babbacombe for two months' initiation to train as a pilot/navigator with his friend, Robert Hardy. They reported to a kindly man called Corporal Barker.

Burton may only have spent two months at Babbacombe but it was eventful. Within a week of his arrival, there was a serious incident with a woman. Burton made a pass at the deputy commander's wife, and the attention was apparently reciprocated. They were, by all accounts, caught in *flagrante delicto* by her husband, and the incident was reported to the base commander. Robert Hardy remembered: "He came back one night in great agitation because he had been arraigned and arrested by a sergeant." Although there was no obvious regulation that had been broken, it was nevertheless a tricky situation. Burton believed he would be court-marshalled and imprisoned. But he was reprimanded, warned never to talk about the incident again and asked to sign a statement confirming he wouldn't. He was sufficiently scared that he never did.

As he had at Oxford, Burton homed in on the drama department at Babbacombe, and such was his enthusiasm that they asked him to put on a production. The first-time director chose Philip Burton's production of 'Youth at the Helm' and handed Robert Hardy the lead part. He gave himself a small role, taking his directing role very seriously, although he found it all rather effortless.

Recruits underwent exams as well as physical and psychological aptitude tests, and the final decisions were taken as to whether they were of sufficient calibre to be trained as pilot/navigators. Burton suffered a serious setback

121

after a test revealed weak eyesight, which precluded him from pilot training. He was devastated and was forced to settle for the life of a navigator. It was rather an unfortunate outcome given his very poor sense of direction. In fact, according to his friends, few people could have had a poorer sense of direction than Burton.

After two months' initiation at Torquay, he was shipped to Lancashire's Heaton Park, a sprawling air force camp near Manchester, to await sea transport to Canada. At the end of January 1945, he got on the Aquitania, a passenger liner that carried him to Manitoba. It was the same ship that had carried Philip Burton on his first trip to North America in 1939.

It was at that point that he and Robert Hardy separated, as his friend went to the United States for his pilot training.

There followed ten months of intensive training, which was all wasted when first Germany and then Japan surrendered in the spring and summer of 1945. By mid-1945, the RAF found itself with tens of thousands of unwanted half-trained recruits, and the programme wound down as everyone realised it was pointless; so much so that the recruits in Canada were granted unrestricted leave if they wanted it. Burton hitchhiked to New York to visit the Baruth family, the same people who had befriended Philip Burton in 1939.

He hitchhiked over a thousand miles from Winnipeg to New York with less than two dollars in his pocket. As he recalled: "It was easy in uniform as every motorist thought they owed us something for helping to win the war." The same went for hospitality when he arrived in New York; he was invited to parties galore.

But it was all to end very abruptly. After VE Day, the Americans had been paying for the RAF training in Canada on the understanding that the newly-trained pilots and navigators would be shipped to the Pacific once it had been completed. But that funding was suddenly withdrawn after VJ Day, when fighting in Japan ended. Given that it was very expensive to have all these recruits hanging around uselessly in North America, enjoying life at the RAF's expense, it caused panic in London. Almost overnight, all the RAF personnel were flown back to England to RAF Dorking in Norfolk, and the air force desperately tried to find something for them to do in the remaining two years of their compulsory national service.

The RAF policy was last in – last out, and Richard was told he would not be demobbed until November 1947, which was over two years away.

They were all posted to what were called re-mustering stations around the country to await discharge.

It was a frustrating time, as all of them had trained for two years and it had all been wasted with no enemy left to fight. National service rules prevented them from leaving early and they simply wiled away their time at the government's expense, effectively being paid to do nothing.

Luckily, there were hundreds of old RAF airfields around Britain that were no longer in use and which absorbed all these people. Burton and his colleagues were left where they had landed, at RAF Docking. There, he was reunited with Robert Hardy again. The Norfolk airfield, built in 1940, had been a base for RAF fighter bombers. Most of the Blenheim and Mosquito aircraft that flew out of Docking had already been decommissioned and cut up for scrap. So, although the base's grass airfield was no longer operational for combat flying, the facilities remained intact.

The RAF high command issued orders for the recruits to be left to their own devices while normal air force discipline was unofficially suspended. It meant a free rein for those who were left behind, as the officers kept to themselves and the NCOs and the uncommissioned recruits were left to do what they liked. If any of the NCOs tried to impose a sense of discipline, they were turned on and beaten. Robert Hardy remembered: "The sergeants and corporals and warrant officers who should have been in charge lived in daily fear. There was a bad to-do when Richard and others practically killed a sergeant who had offended them – that was hushed up. They got away with – not murder – but not far short, I think. They were protected because they were potential rugby players for the RAF."

He continued: "What astonished me was the absolute lawlessness with which that group lived. There was a kind of protective feeling on the part of the RAF, who had sent us all out to various parts of the commonwealth and North America to train. We were all cadet volunteers, none of us was on national service, so they felt a certain responsibility for us and a lot of bad behaviour was overlooked, but it was a lawless and extraordinary time."

The evenings became one big party with the locals. Occasionally, the parties got out of hand and a local pub was damaged when a fight broke out between local lads and the air crew. Military policemen turned up and broke up the fight, but declined to arrest anyone. Each night continued in a similar vein. Occasionally, Burton was held in detention for a few days, but that was as tough as the punishment got. Drinking often got out of hand despite the wartime shortages, which did not appear to apply to the RAF. As Hardy said: "It was always there; there was always a threat with Richard even when he was young and he was only drinking as much as his age could cope."

Mick Misell, later Warren Mitchell, was also there and remembered the high jinks well: "We were just left alone by the brass. We lived an unbelievable life of absolute autonomy – reading, fucking and poaching." By all accounts, it was an accurate summary of what went on in Norfolk between 1946 and 1947.

Burton didn't always live on the camp. Soon after he arrived, he seduced the wife of the owner of Docking Hall, the local manor house in the nearby village of Docking, whose husband was a Major in the army and serving abroad. With her husband gone, Burton moved in with his wife, and because he was living in the local manor, he was nicknamed 'the Squire.'

He returned to the base in the daytime and treated it as a playground, using the RAF's cash to entertain himself and his colleagues. He started a Welsh male voice choir, although there were only two Welshmen on the base. No one cared. He also set up a drama club putting on a production of a play that Philip Burton had written. But the production was organised under the auspices of the Entertainment National Service Association (ENSA), which provided the funding and kept a strict eye on how the money was used. Creativity within that organisation did not exist, and the subsequent production was embarrassingly awful. He wiled away any time he had left translating a favourite novel into Welsh. He also turned his attention to sport and, in the winter of 1946, spent most of his time on the rugby field with an RAF team playing local teams.

The only serious activity came in 1946, when he got involved in the trial of an Italian soldier who was being held in a nearby prisoner of war camp. Because the war had ended, the prisoners were on trust with only light security in place. But one prisoner, a very good-looking young Italian, was accused of raping a local girl and found himself in very serious trouble.

There was no Italian speaker in the area to help him so Burton, who knew the young man from his hell-raising in local pubs, volunteered to defend him using the little Italian he had learned during his spell at Oxford.

Burton couldn't believe that such a good-looking, pleasant man would need to rape any girl. He also knew that the girl who had accused him was very promiscuous and he couldn't believe she wouldn't have succumbed voluntarily had he asked her. It appeared to him she had been jilted by the young Italian and resented it. Indeed, it soon emerged that the girl had been jealous of the boy's other girlfriends and had falsely accused him. Burton set out to prove this and managed to convince the military court of his case The Italian was cleared.

Aside from that trial, Burton found himself rather suited to having no responsibilities and no work to occupy him. He loved the unpressured environment and enjoyed having not a care in the world. He spent endless hours walking in the glorious Norfolk countryside discussing Shakespeare with Robert Hardy. As Hardy recalled: "When he left the RAF, Rich was word perfect in many of the great Shakespearian roles."

Eventually, Robert Hardy managed to get himself posted to London, where he lived the high life until he was demobbed. But, curiously, when Richard was given the chance to go with him, he declined. He had settled into the good life in Norfolk and didn't want to leave.

But there was one, who, many, many miles away, was very concerned. Philip Burton became worried about Richard during this period and believed he had lost his ambition. After the war ended, Philip Burton was released from his teaching duties and was hired by the BBC as its senior producer in Cardiff. Upon several occasions, he invited Richard to come to Cardiff to appear in the radio plays he was producing. But for some reason, Burton resisted. He was refusing the very opportunities which, a few years earlier, he would have killed for.

Philip grew concerned that Richard was stagnating down in Norfolk. He confided his worries to Emlyn Williams, who agreed to help. So, in January 1947, Emlyn Williams wrote to him and asked him to play the part of a character called Morgan Evans in a televised production of 'The Corn is Green' for the BBC.

The play was the story of a young Welshman of poor background who had been marked out for a brilliant career by a dedicated teacher. It was effectively an autobiographical work about the manner in which Williams, a self-professed Welsh peasant, had been groomed and educated by Sarah Grace Cooke, a Welsh schoolmistress who had taken him under her wing.

It was a rare opportunity to explore the relatively new medium of television, and the play had obvious biographical significance for Richard and Emlyn Williams. With his interest piqued, Richard wrote back and said he would do it.

# AND GOD CREATED BURTON

Cooke was also involved and was curious about a second 'Welsh peasant', as Williams described Burton. After she met him, she said straightaway: "He's going to do well. What's more, he's got the devil in him." Cooke's analysis proved devastatingly accurate.

It was a great opportunity, as the play was to be performed at the BBC's London studios. The broadcast was effectively a stage play in a studio being filmed by fixed static cameras. It went out live and was watched by approximately half of the homes in Britain with a TV set. But, in early 1947, there were only about 30,000 homes with a television, so very few people saw the production; and the technology to record it for a later repeat showing did not then exist. It was nonetheless adjudged a success by those who did see it.

Emlyn Williams was gradually becoming Burton's fifth mentor, joining Meredith Jones, Leo Lloyd, Philip Burton and Neville Coghill, all of whom were championing his career.

Burton's success in attracting such significant mentors in his early life always mystified his various biographers, including Michael Munn, who referred to it as: "The spell he seemed to cast over the older men who tended to mentor him."

Burton remained very close to Emlyn Williams and his wife Molly all his life. He became their son Brook's godfather and, during the time he was posted at RAF Docking, he spent weekends with the family in London.

His sojourn at the BBC also had other benefits. Burton started going out with his first serious girlfriend in early 1947. At the studios in London, he had met a young actress called Eleanor Summerfield, then 26 and a striking blonde. She was four years older than him and an accomplished performer. For six months, each weekend, Burton would take the train to wherever she was – usually at a provincial theatre, where she would be acting. The romance blossomed and Burton soon asked her to marry him. As she remembered: "He used to see me every weekend he could get off, and sometimes I'd be playing the provinces. I had never met anyone with quite his sort of application of word. He had all the Welsh passion of the theatre, which was fantastically invigorating."

But Eleanor Summerfield broke his heart when she revealed she had another man in her life, the actor Leonard Sachs. The competition from Burton caused Sachs to propose to her. Finding herself with two fiancées, she weighed up both her suitors and decided Sachs was the better prospect and broke it off with Burton. To ensure his victory, Sachs arranged the wedding immediately. Burton was devastated at the time and returned to Norfolk to drown his sorrows. He soon forgot her.

After 'The Corn is Green' was broadcast, Burton's interest in acting was reignited and he finally accepted Philip's invitation to return to Cardiff and take some roles in the plays he was now producing for BBC radio. From 1947 onwards, he began thinking about his career again. As his brother Graham remembered: "I have yet to come across anyone who actually saw the play. But the effect on Rich was undeniable. He was back in business and was enjoying every minute of it."

Galvanised into action, he also had to decide what to do when he was demobbed. He had turned 21 in November 1946 and was now legally free to do as he pleased. Philip Burton had finally moved to his own house in Cardiff, having left Elizabeth Smith's lodgings in Port Talbot after 20 years. That gave Richard an option to return there to make his new home. But he decided it was time to strike out on his own and opted to go to London to seek his fortune. The words "look me up" were still reverberating around in his mind, and that is what he decided to do.

That also meant that the pledge he had made to return to Oxford to complete his degree studies went by the wayside – although for the rest of his life, he was to regret that decision.

# AND GOD CREATED BURTON

# CHAPTER 11

# "Look me up"

## Metamorphosis: boy to young actor

### 1948

When he was officially demobilised in November 1947 and stepped outside of RAF Docking as a free man for the first time in three years, Richard Burton had no idea what he would do or where he was headed. Initially, he planned to return to Cardiff and take a room at Philip Burton's new house. So he got the RAF to issue him with a rail warrant that would take him back to Cardiff. To get there, he had to change trains in London and go from Liverpool Street Station across to Paddington Station.

But when he got to Liverpool Street, acting purely on instinct, he found himself on a bus heading for the offices of HM Tennent, which were situated on the top floor of the old Globe Theatre in Shaftesbury Avenue. It seems that the words "look me up" uttered by Binkie Beaumont in Oxford three years earlier were still rattling round in his head. His brother Graham recalled the unplanned detour that day: "He realised he had to change trains in London. Why not take the opportunity, he reasoned, to find out if Binkie Beaumont remembered him from his Oxford days?" Burton himself recalled: "I had four hours to wait between trains in London and it did cross my mind that that very nice man, Mr Hugh Beaumont, had told me to come and see him if I decided to become an actor. So I thought I'd have time between trains."

As he emerged from the lift that took him to the top of the Globe Theatre, the first person he chanced upon was Daphne Rye, who recognised him straightaway. She told him it was very unlikely that Hugh Beaumont would see him without an appointment, but Burton reminded her of his offer four years earlier.

Rye was right and, ordinarily, Beaumont would have refused to see a young actor without an appointment, but these were not ordinary days. As Burton remembered: "I waited for two and a half tortuous hours." As the time ticked by, he knew he would have to leave to catch his train. But just as he got up to go, Beaumont came out and took him inside his office.

Young male actors were thin on the ground in the immediate post-war period, and Beaumont was desperate to hire promising young actors for his productions. The bisexual Beaumont also had an eye for handsome young thespians. So Burton's timing was just perfect and, although Beaumont could barely remember him, on Daphne Rye's word he offered Burton a job starting in January 1948 and paying £10 a week.

Burton accepted it without hesitation, shook Beaumont's hand and was ushered out of his office by Rye before he changed his mind. He got on another bus and caught his connecting train to Cardiff as planned. The whole transaction with Beaumont had taken less than five minutes to conclude.

There was also a bonus when Rye offered him the top floor of her house in Pelham Crescent, Kensington, as a place to stay. It was only a few doors from where Emlyn and Molly Williams lived. Astonishingly, within 24 hours of leaving the RAF, Richard was all set up.

When he arrived back in Cardiff, he explained to Philip what he had decided to do. Philip, believing Richard could go all the way as an actor, was very supportive. Burton then went to Port Talbot to tell the rest of the family he wouldn't be returning to Oxford to get his degree. It's not an understatement to say that this decision was met with a great deal of disappointment. No one in the family had any inkling that Richard was going on to anything other than a career as a jobbing actor, appearing on stage from time to time in a very insecure existence. So his giving up the chance of returning to a guaranteed place at Oxford University and getting a degree seemed crazy.

Emlyn Williams thought so as well when Burton wrote to him to tell him of his decision. Williams believed time was on the young man's side in the theatre and that he should complete his studies. He wrote back and urged him to turn down Beaumont's offer and return to Oxford.

Although the family was unanimous in its condemnation, Burton's brother Ivor Jenkins saw merit in it, saying: "Ten quid a week is ten quid a week; there's no denying it and he gets it whether he's working or not." To the very practical Ivor, it sounded like a dream opportunity.

Burton arrived in London at the beginning of January but turned down Rye's offer of accommodation and decided to take up his old lodgings in Streatham, South London, with his friend Stanley Baker. Streatham was an unfashionable part of London, south of the river, but Burton and Baker hoped to recreate the good times they had enjoyed there five years earlier. And, indeed, they soon had more girlfriends than they could cope with.

He and Baker went on the rampage. The Irish nurses had all changed but the new ones were still out for a good time, and many of them were virgins. This time, the two men had none of their previous inhibitions in robbing them of that status. Baker recalled later: "We shared cheap digs in Streatham and spent our money on having a good time. We earned ourselves something of a reputation."

In fact, they went through so many women and dumped them so quickly afterwards that they did not want them to know where they lived for fear of retribution from irate parents or jealous boyfriends. As Baker explained: "It didn't seem a good idea to let the girls know where we lived. So we took them to the common and sowed our oats there."

Burton's contract with Beaumont essentially had him on beck and call to appear in whatever role and production HM Tennent was putting on – anywhere in Britain. It was akin to slavery – albeit well-paid slavery at £10 a week, which was three times the national average wage. He was guaranteed £500 even if he never got a part for the duration of the 12-month contract.

Richard Leech and Bryan Forbes were two other promising young actors on similar deals, and all the young contracted actors regarded themselves as being in some sort of competition for parts.

Leech, an Irishman who had originally trained as a doctor, eventually became a great friend of Burton's, but initially it was not so. He remembers the first time he set eyes on him in 1948 at Daphne Rye's house, where she had gathered all the young Tennent actors one evening: "When he came in, I thought, who is this? He's not an actor. He's just a squat Welsh rugby player. I won't have any trouble here. But I was wrong. Oh boy, was I wrong." Bryan Forbes, who went on to become a famous director, had similar thoughts.

Forbes remembers that they all had a crush on Daphne Rye, saying: "Daphne protected us, those of us who needed it." Burton didn't need it but she looked out for him anyway.

Within a month of starting at Tennent's, Rye had given him his first part in a play called 'Castle Anna' which opened at the Lyric Theatre in Hammersmith, London, on 24th February 1948. 'Castle Anna' was a literary play adapted from a novel by Elizabeth Bowen. It was a tale of landed gentry in Ireland.

The play was financed by a government grant; money that was available for getting theatre back on its feet after the war. The cash on offer was meant to encourage the professional staging of plays with 'artistic merit.' HM Tennent was keen to get its hands on the cash and was prepared to experiment with plays which it otherwise might not have bothered with.

'Castle Anna' was also to be Daphne Rye's directorial debut and she cast Burton for the small part of a character called Mr Hicks. He also understudied for the lead part, played by Arthur Sinclair. Pauline Letts, a well-known actress, had the lead female role.

Perhaps not surprisingly, there was more drama during the rehearsals than there was in the play. On the morning of 25th February, the cast were holding a debriefing session after the previous night's opening. Suddenly, there was a knock on the stage door and as many as 12 police officers suddenly burst in and asked for Arthur Sinclair. Naturally, Sinclair identified himself but, before he could draw breath, he was grabbed by the officers and taken away without any explanation.

It was all over in a few minutes. Daphne Rye rang the police station and demanded to know what was going on. She was told Sinclair had been hauled before a committee known as the Conscientious Objectors' Tribunal. The Tribunal had been formed to investigate people who claimed they were conscientious objectors in order to avoid national service, which had been reintroduced in 1947.

There was a real danger that Sinclair would be found to be a disingenuous objector and would be taken into custody to await trial. He would subsequently be unable to continue in the play.

The whole cast was worried and depressed about what might happen. In a panic, Daphne Rye called a full rehearsal with Burton replacing Sinclair in the lead role. No one expected much but, then, as Pauline Letts described: "Something electric happened – he was quite brilliant in the part." Suddenly, the anxiety vanished and the mood settled into one of almost hoping Sinclair wouldn't come back. Letts was amazed, saying: "Over the years, I have worked with many actors and actresses who went on to become very big stars, but he was the only one who one knew absolutely from the beginning was destined for greatness."

Sinclair eventually managed to convince the panel of the Conscientious Objectors' Tribunal that he was a genuine objector, and he returned to appear in that evening's performance. But the episode with Burton had left an impression, and word soon got around about just how good he was.

Not so, however, the play he was appearing in. 'Castle Anna' was not destined to be a hit and did not transfer to the West End as planned. The play was politely reviewed but ran for a matter of weeks before audiences dwindled. As soon as it had run long enough to qualify for the government's grant, it was pulled.

Rye immediately had another part for Burton in a touring production called 'Dark Summer'. But it was even worse than 'Castle Anna' and quickly faded away when no one came to see it. After two failed productions, Burton became restless. It was not what he had signed up for.

He also very quickly became disenchanted with his £10 a week. He believed he was a much better actor than his colleagues and thought he was worth more money – much to the chagrin of his fellow actors, who were grateful to be in paid work. All the goodwill he had earned with his co-actors disappeared and they could not believe his selfish and cynical attitude. He took his complaints to Emlyn Williams and asked for help to get out of his Tennent's contract, a contract for which he had been very grateful only six months earlier.

Indeed, Burton became very bitter very quickly and didn't want to go back to Tennent's. Brook Williams, Emlyn Williams' perceptive nine-year-old son, remembered: "What he wanted to do was earn good money. He was beginning to wonder if he had made the right decision to become an actor because the plays had not been successful, nor was he making good money. He decided that if he couldn't earn a decent salary from acting, he would quit. He was never obsessed with acting and he was not prepared to suffer for his art."

It was an extraordinary attitude to take but, even then, Burton was aware of his greater talent. Pauline Letts attempted to explain: "I can only tell you the feeling I had about him – the impact of his tremendous brain and talent. During that day, we sat around talking and became very deep about personalities and the psychological aspects of life. I remember very well him saying that he had a sort of other half, sitting on his shoulder and watching everything he did all the time, and that never under any circumstances was he non-objective. This objective self was watching everything he did. Most good actors do this, but he had developed it very early. It was there then."

His pleading with Emlyn Williams got some results. One day, while on tour with 'Dark Summer', Burton shot off to London for the day. It turned out that Williams had called him to London to audition for a part in a feature film called *The Last Days of Dolwyn*. It was Williams' first feature film, and he was to be the writer, director and the star.

The film was being made by London Films Ltd and financed by the Rank Organisation. London Films was run by well-known producers Alexander Korda and Anatole de Grunwald, both of whom attended the audition. When he turned up, Burton appeared unaware of just how important Korda and De Grunwald were.

Ordinarily, Williams would have been able to approve the casting of Burton himself but, curiously, Korda and de Grunwald told him they weren't convinced Burton was right for the part. Williams was surprised they had even heard of him.

With that in mind, Williams prepared the ground very carefully for the audition. Typically, trainees filmed auditions but Williams arranged for Burton's to be filmed by the highly talented Otto Heller, his director of photography. Burton didn't let him down, and both Korda and De Grunwald were surprised by how good Burton was. The impression was confirmed the next day when the negative was processed and viewed.

Soon after he had returned to 'Dark Summer', a telegram arrived from Williams, telling Richard he had won the part. Williams wrote simply: "You have won the scholarship." It was a line from 'The Corn Is Green'. It was a big deal and he knew Burton would understand the significance.

But when Richard Leech saw him open the telegram and asked him what it said, Burton replied nonchalantly: "I've got a sort of juvenile lead in a film that Emlyn Williams is making, called *The Last Days of Dolwyn*." Then, according to Leech, he crumpled up the telegram, drop-kicked it into a waste basket, wandered off to the pub and never mentioned it again.

Apparently, Burton never replied to the telegram and Williams was on the point of giving the part to someone else; he even had another actor on standby. It turned out that Burton was worried Tennent's wouldn't release him and he waited until the last minute to approach Beaumont about it. In reality, Beaumont was happy to take him off the books in a period when there was nothing for him to do and no productions starting.

So when Burton turned up at Isleworth for his first day's work on the set, Emlyn Williams was somewhat surprised to see him, saying: "Oh, it's you. We were just about to replace you because we thought you hadn't accepted the part."

Burton didn't say why he hadn't replied and, after all the effort he had made to get him the part, Williams found his attitude less than pleasing. He described him as "hurtfully casual" about such matters. It was something producers and directors would get used to over the coming years. But Williams soon got over it and was very pleased to see Burton again.

*The Last Days of Dolwyn* was a comedic melodrama about a scheming Welsh businessman, played by Williams, who planned to flood a fictional Welsh village called Dolwyn in order to create a reservoir to serve English towns. The story was based on fact, and Williams' co-star was Edith Evans, who played an old lady stubbornly refusing to leave the village. Burton played her foster son, Gareth.

There was also a small part for a young Welsh actress called Sybil Williams, and the significance of that would become clear a few months later.

The film had a large budget, and interior filming took place at studios near London in Isleworth in the early summer of 1948. The filming of the interiors was scheduled to last six weeks and then the whole cast would decamp to North Wales to do the outside shots during the terrible, wet, late summer. For the Isleworth shoot, Burton and Baker rented a houseboat on the nearby River Thames. And they brought two nurses from Streatham to share it with them.

During filming, Williams was continually worried about Burton's drinking and, particularly, his chain smoking. By then, Burton was smoking as many as 100 cigarettes a day, puffing continuously in the days before cigarettes had filters. Williams worried that it might have a negative effect on his voice. He was so concerned that he offered him £100 if he would give up smoking altogether for three months. Burton accepted the challenge, but managed to last only two months. When he confessed his failure to Williams, he simply admitted: "Self-indulgence overcame greed."

The filming went well, but in the course of it, Williams discovered a flaw in Burton's artistic range; he found he could not play 'innocent.' In one scene, all he had to do was appear bemused; but instead, he continually looked fierce. A frustrated Williams ordered him to concentrate on looking innocent, but it wasn't in his range and he simply couldn't do it.

The failure to be able to act innocent was put down to his inbuilt feeling of security and self-worth. Unlike most actors, Burton never experienced feelings of insecurity despite the efforts of many journalists over the years to label him as such. In truth, he was the one actor who never suffered from any form of insecurity, as Robert Hardy confirmed: "I've never known anyone as secure as Richard." In the end, Williams had to change the entire scene and do a mini re-write to get over the problem.

Despite the minor setback, filming went well and the film was ready to be released in British cinemas in early 1949. As much money was spent on marketing and publicity as on the film itself, and a small portion of that was used to promote Richard Burton to the British filmgoer. It was the first time he had been promoted in this way and he was flattered by the attention of Korda's PR people. It was also his first real taste of speaking to journalists and getting media exposure – he began to see his name in the newspapers more and more.

He told the enquiring journalists that he was from the South Wales mining community, that he was working class and proud of it. But sometimes he told them he was middle class and the son of a school teacher. Both stories were true, and which version he used depended on what he thought a journalist wanted to hear. He was very surprised to find that journalists printed verbatim what he told them without doing any checking.

The film itself was well received, and the *News of the World*'s film critic said of Burton that he had "the fire of great acting allied to good looks, a manly bearing...and an innate tenderness that renders his love scenes so movingly real."

But many years later, Burton himself said he thought his performance in the film had been "lamentable". In fact, he thought all his early acting in films to be poor. He said: "Thank God I never have to live through that again, to live through those terrible years of puerility, of idiocy."

But the film pulled in audiences and was a profitable venture for London Films, making money for Rank. In the United States of America, it was released by 20th Century-Fox studio, with whom Korda had a distribution deal. Korda understood the American market better than any other British producer, and those connections were to prove beneficial to Burton in future years.

The UK premiere of the film was held in Cardiff, and most of the Jenkins family attended. It was gradually dawning on all of them that their relative was becoming famous and had real talent. They also began to realise that perhaps the decision not to return to Oxford hadn't been so daft.

After he had completed the publicity for the film, Burton was in no hurry to return to HM Tennent, so he had his leave of absence extended to appear in Anton Chekhov's 'The Seagull' being produced by director Clifford Evans and backed by the Arts Council.

It ran for a fortnight at Swansea's Grand Theatre. Artistically, it was his best work to date and he was heavily fêted by Welsh newspapers as a result.

It was a warm up for a much bigger production he was planning in his personal life.

# CHAPTER 12

# Wedding Number 1 to Sybil

## *Suddenly a wife*

### 1949

Richard Burton and Emlyn Williams were lounging on the grass outside the London Film Studios at Worton Hall in Isleworth one lunchtime in July 1948. They were filming the interior shots for the *The Last Days of Dolwyn*. Williams casually asked Burton what he had been doing the night before, and he replied he had spent the night with a woman but admitted he was having difficulty recalling her name.

Williams, although not terribly surprised by this response, was rather concerned and said: "You know, it's really time you settled down." He then promptly turned around and fatefully pointed to a girl 30 feet away: "Now, she's a real sweet girl."

The girl in question was Sybil Williams, a pretty young actress of eighteen, who was working as an extra in the film. Williams said later: "She came from a mining village in South Wales. I knew she was right for him. I just knew. What girl could have been more perfect?"

Sybil was a very pretty, slender woman with dark hair and a very distinctive, sharp face. She was a girl it was impossible to meet without coming away with a good impression. She always appeared to be on the brink of laughter; it was built into her face, whatever her mood. Williams said she was the sort of woman any mother would want her son to marry; in short, someone everyone wanted to be with.

Burton's biographers could never praise her enough. Penny Junor described her looks as "almost Italianate, with a Roman nose and a long neck." Junor said she charmed and infected everyone who knew her with her great love of life and bustling enthusiasm for everything that was going on around her: "She had a style and an elegance of her own." According to Melvyn Bragg, she had the "surprising quality" of "consistent equilibrium." And Paul Ferris described her as "a woman radiating warmth and competence." For Graham Jenkins: "Sybil was the sort of person who would liven up a gathering just by walking in the door."

Famous actors also lavished praise upon her. Sir John Gielgud remembered her as being "very clever" and recalled an incident during the filming of *The Last Days of Dolwyn*, saying: "There were quite a number of extras playing peasant women with head scarves tied round their heads. So, at the end of the day, they all had to be lined up to be paid. Well, Sybil conceived this brilliant idea, arriving with a number of different head scarves and she'd line up and get her five pounds, or whatever it was, and then go back to the end of the queue and put on another one and receive another five pounds, which I thought was most enterprising."

Sybil could also be very amusing, as Robert Hardy recalled: "She was funny and could make you laugh hysterically when she wanted to." Stanley Baker, who knew her from childhood, said: "I used to go around with her as a kid. She was a marvellous girl, the most attractive in the village, the most mature, the most interesting, the most friendly."

So who was this extraordinary young woman for whom no one had a bad word and who, only a few months later, would lure Britain's most eligible bachelor into marriage? She originally came from a small mining village in South Wales called Tylorstown, near Ferndale in the Rhondda Valley. It was there she went to school with Stanley Baker. Her father worked at the local colliery as a clerk in the office. It meant the family was considered to belong to a higher class than those whose fathers went down the mines. As Melvyn Bragg described it: "Her background was a few rungs up from the Jenkinses."

Her upbringing was rather unremarkable and she enjoyed an idyllic childhood in the Welsh valleys. But that came to an abrupt halt when her mother died, followed by her father, when she was only 15. After that, she went to live with her older sister Elsie, who had married and moved to the midlands town of Northampton. Her sister made sure Sybil paid attention to her studies in final years at school, and she developed into a well-rounded, intelligent personality who could hold her own in a conversation with anyone.

She slowly developed a taste for the theatre and amateur dramatics and, at 18, enrolled in a drama course at the London Academy of Music and Dramatic Art.

But the one thing she wasn't was an actress. As much as she wanted it, her ambition simply didn't match her talent. It was just one of those things. Graham Jenkins recalled much later: "Sybil was not a great actress. That she landed a bit part in *The Last Days of Dolwyn* was more a tribute to Emlyn

Edith and Dick Jenkins, Richard Burton's natural parents, photographed on their wedding day on 24th December 1900. It is the only photograph in existence of Burton's mother. And this is the only coloured photo of either of his parents. Originally a black and white photo, of which 11 prints exist, the single hand-coloured version is believed to have been given to the couple by Edith's parents as a late wedding present. It was passed to Edith's daughter Cecilia on her death. But the existence of the coloured photograph, dating from 1900, was unknown until it was found by the author hanging on the wall of Cecilia's daughter, Rhianon Trowell's home in Oxford, England.

**Left:** Morgan and Mary James were the parents of Elfed James, who was married to Richard Burton's sister Cecilia. They were not Richard Burton's real grandparents but became his adopted ones and lived near his childhood home in Caradoc Street. They helped finance Burton's early upbringing, including paying the deposit of the mortgage on the family home.

*Rhianon Trowell*

*Dick and Edith Jenkins*

**Above right:** Richard Burton as a baby photographed on the grassy hillside beside his place of birth at 2 -Dan-y-bont, Pontrhydyfen. His mother, Edith, chose to give her 12th-born the prized family name of Richard Walter, which belonged to Dick Jenkins' father, grandfather and great grandfather before him.

**Above:** A copy of the original birth certificate of Richard Burton, which clearly states his given name as Jenkins. He was born on the 10th November 1925.

**Left and below:** Richard Burton as a young boy in Taibach, where he lived with his beloved sister Cecilia James and her husband, Elfed, after the tragic death of his mother when he was two years old.

*Dick and Edith Jenkins*

*Hilda Owen*

**Left:** The Jenkins' family home at 2 Dan-y-Bont, Pontrhydyfen, Wales, where Richard Burton was born in 1925. This photograph was taken around 1930, when it was still lived in by the family. It is the only original photograph of the house as it was in the 1920's.

*Rhianon Trowell*

**Above:** Cecilia James photographed in 1955 by the stills photographer of the motion picture, *Alexander the Great*. The photograph was shot in a studio in Madrid, Spain.

*Rhianon Trowell*

**Below:** Leo Lloyd was effectively Richard Burton's first drama coach at Taibach Youth Club long before Philip Burton took an interest in him. Lloyd cast him in his first play called 'The Bishop's Candlesticks' in 1941. It was Lloyd's intervention introducing him to acting that caught Philip Burton's attention.

*Kim Collis/West Glamorgan Archive Service*

**Above:** Eastern Infants School in Taibach, Port Talbot, in the mid-1930s, around the time that Richard Burton attended there. It was overlooked by the Port Talbot steel works, now demolished, and was just two minutes' walk from Burton's home in Caradoc Street.

*Rhianon Trowell*

*Tony Palmer/Isolde Films*

**Left and centre:** Meredith Jones, the first of three great teaching influences on Burton's life, and one that undoubtedly shaped the course of his entire life. Twice Jones intervened to steer the then Richard Jenkins back on course.

**Left:** Richard Burton, sitting second from the right on the second row in Port Talbot Secondary School's rugby team. His temperament was well-suited to the game, and what he lacked in artistry, he made up for in raw energy.

*Sally Burton*

*Philip Burton*

**Above:** Richard Burton and his svengali, Philip Burton, the second and perhaps greatest influence on Burton's life. Philip Burton later became his legal father in December 1943.

*Rhianon Trowell*

**Left:** The theatre programme for Burton's first school production, 'Gallow's Glorious' in November 1942.

**Below:** Richard Burton's signature as Richard Jenkins, believed to be the only one in existence.

**Below:** The theatre programme for the Swansea performance of 'The Druid's Rest' by Emlyn Williams. Burton made his first professional stage performance at Liverpool's Royal Court Theatre on 22nd November 1943.

*Rhianon Trowell*

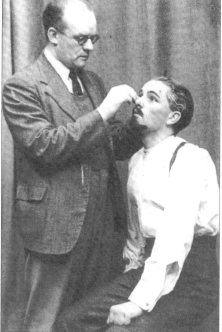

**Right:** Philip Burton applying make-up to his young protégé, Richard Burton, for his part as Professor Higgins in the Port Talbot Secondary School production of 'Pygmalion' in July 1943.

*Philip Burton*

**Left and below:** As an 18-year-old Richard Burton joined the RAF full time in early October 1944. In January 1945 he was posted to Canada where he stayed for 10 months before seeing out his national service in England at the conclusion of the war. He wrote letters and postcards to his family almost every day from Canada including this one which has been kept for 66 years by his niece Rhianon Trowell. It was posted on the 7th June 1945 and recalls how chocolate and ice cream were in plentiful supply in Canada although they were virtually unobtainable in Britain. He signed the postcard Richie.

POST CARD

CORRESPONDENCE        ADDRESS

Dear Rhian,
Wish you were here — tons of ice-cream, chocolate and wonderful little gadgets — will send you some before long.
Richie

Miss Rhianon JAMES,
Y, CARA DOG STR,
IBACH,
PORT TALBOT,
S. WALES,
GT. BRITAIN.

Made in Canada

**Above:** Andrea Lee, Richard Burton and Emlyn Williams on location in Rhydymain, north Wales during filming of *The Last Days of Dolwyn*, in September, 1948.

**Above:** Sir Alexander Korda gave Richard Burton his first big film break in 1951 with a £100 per week deal that eventually took him to Hollywood.

**Above** (left to right): Sybil Burton, Ivor and Gwen Jenkins, Richard Burton and Philip Burton on a night out in New York, where they were for the Broadway production of 'The Lady's Not for Burning' in November 1950.

**Right:** The original programme for The Lady's Not For Burning, Richard Burton's first West End play with top billing which opened in May 1949 at the Globe Theatre in London.

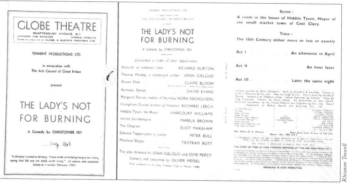

**Right:** Peter Glenville, the theatre director and Binkie Beaumont, the managing director of HM Tennent. Beaumont gave Burton his first job and Glenville sacked him from a play and nearly ended his career.

**Left:** Sybil helping her husband rehearse for his part of Prince Hal in 'Henry IV' at Stratford in the summer of 1951. She also had a part in the play as Lady Mortimer.

**Above:** Richard Burton as the title character in Shakespeare's 'Henry V' at the Memorial Theatre, Stratford-upon-Avon in 1951.

**Above:** With Olivia de Havilland on the set of Burton's first Hollywood film, *My Cousin Rachel* in August 1952. He also received his first Academy Award nomination for his part for best supporting actor.

**Right:** Richard Burton and co-star Jean Simmons in a publicity photograph for *The Robe* in 1953. Burton and Simmons were also having an affair at the same time.

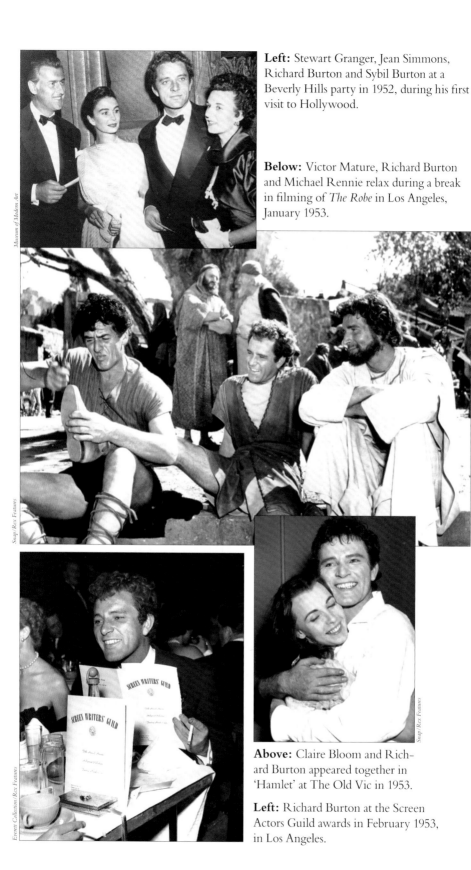

**Left:** Stewart Granger, Jean Simmons, Richard Burton and Sybil Burton at a Beverly Hills party in 1952, during his first visit to Hollywood.

**Below:** Victor Mature, Richard Burton and Michael Rennie relax during a break in filming of *The Robe* in Los Angeles, January 1953.

**Above:** Claire Bloom and Richard Burton appeared together in 'Hamlet' at The Old Vic in 1953.

**Left:** Richard Burton at the Screen Actors Guild awards in February 1953, in Los Angeles.

*Museum of Modern Art*

*Snap/Rex Features*

*Everett Collection/Rex Features*

*Snap/Rex Features*

**Left:** Richard Burton and Claire Bloom at the Wyndham Theatre, London on 28th December 1953, where she and Burton held a seminar on Shakespeare for fans.

**Left:** Richard Burton, Dick Jenkins and Ivor Jenkins at the bar of the The Miner's Arms in Pontrhydyfen in June 1953.

**Below:** Richard Burton holds court at The Miner's Arms public house in Pontrhydyfen in June 1953, soon after he returned from conquering Hollywood.

**Above:** Richard Burton walks
with his father, Dick Jenkins,
over the famous bridge in
Pontrhydyfen in June 1953 in
a visit to Wales after returning
from a year in Hollywood.

**Right:** Cecilia James, Richard
Burton and Sybil Burton, in the
garden of 73 Caradoc Street,
Taibach, Port Talbot in June
1953.

**Left:** Richard Burton takes the director's seat on the set of *Prince of Players* in Los Angeles in the summer of 1954.

20th Century Fox/Everett/Rex Features

Mirrorpix

**Above:** Richard Burton pays a surprise visit to the girls from his old youth club in Taibach, Port Talbot, on the Gala night in Margam, on 24th July 1954.

**Left:** The Burtons arrive at Paddington Railway Station in London on 26th November 1954, after the return trip from Hollywood, where he had been filming *Prince of Players*.

Central Press/Getty Images

**Above:** Director John Neville, Michael Benthall and Richard Burton during rehearsals for 'Othello' at the Old Vic in London during the 1955-1956 season.

**Left:** Richard Burton with Joan Collins on the set of the film *Sea Wife* in Jamaica, in July 1956.

**Left:** Aaron Frosch was Richard Burton's lawyer for most of his career and his closest confidante.

**Below:** Richard and Sybil Burton hold their seven week old baby daughter, Kate. She was born on 10th September 1957.

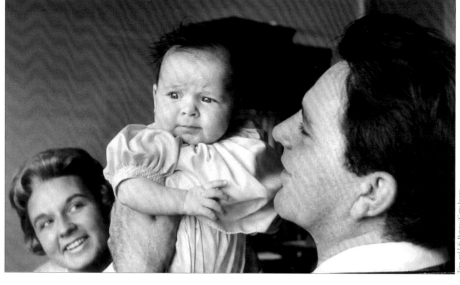

**Left:** Richard Burton and Susan Strasberg on the set of the Broadway play 'Time Remembered' in New York, in 1957. The two began an affair whilst appearing in the play.

Bertmann/Corbis

**Below:** Richard Burton with Susan Strasberg in the temporary pool at a Hawaiian-themed party in the basement of a New York hotel to mark the last week of 'Time Remembered' in April 1958.

Time and Life Pictures/Getty Images

Left: Richard Burton and Claire Bloom take time out from the filming of *Look Back in Anger* at Shepperton Studios, near London, in September 1958.

Below: Richard Burton and Mary Ure take a break from filming *Look Back in Anger* in 1958. They had a brief affair during the making of the film.

*Bob Penn/Camera Press*

*Everett Collection/Rex Features*

Below: Claire Bloom and Richard Burton share a passionate kiss during a scene of John Osborne's film of his play *Look Back in Anger*, in 1958 at Shepperton Studios, London.

*Snap/Rex Features*

Williams' generosity than to her raw talent."

Her lack of talent made it a very difficult part for her to get and she had had to use every bit of guile and cunning she possessed to convince Emlyn Williams to hire her. One of her tutors at drama school knew Emlyn Williams, and she leaned on him to give her a part in his new film. The budget only allowed for five female extras but Williams, with his arm twisted, stretched it to six. As he recalled: "Only five had been budgeted for. But then, I thought, Alexander Korda can afford six."

So six it was, and Sybil Williams' destiny was set. Emlyn Williams may have been charmed into giving her the role, but he wasn't fooled by her talent and knew her future lay in being some lucky man's wife – and he thought he knew just who that man might be.

After Williams had pointed her out, Burton went right over to her and introduced himself. He asked her out on a date that very night. All the girls on the set were interested in Burton but, up until then, he had ignored them all in favour of the imported Irish nurses from Streatham. Sybil couldn't quite believe her luck and said 'yes' straightaway. Naturally, Richard took her to a pub and, for once, constrained his drinking as he became more and more captivated by the Welsh extra. They happily chatted all night and found they had plenty of shared interests; Burton was impressed she could hold her own with him in conversation, and Sybil was in no doubt that he was her dream man. During the following week, he took her out a few times and they got along well together.

A week later, Sybil had to go to London to take her gold medal test at the drama academy. Burton was suspicious that she may have had a boyfriend in London. Burton was right to be suspicious. Sybil did have a boyfriend, but not in London; a good looking boy in Northampton called Ken Drinkwater, who was a couple of years younger than her. But she ditched him and he immediately turned his attentions to a local girl called Kay Rush as Sybil turned all her attentions to Burton.

So he got her phone number and promised to call her that night to see how she had got on. As it turned out, Sybil was successful and won her gold medal. But instead of going out with her friends to celebrate, she went back to her flat and eagerly awaited Burton's call. She was anxious to share her triumph with the man whom she now referred to as her boyfriend. She left the door open so she could hear the ring of the shared black telephone that hung on the wall in the hallway. But it was silent all night and she went to bed at a few minutes past midnight, inwardly furious and vowing never to speak to him again.

Meanwhile, Burton was carousing on the houseboat with Stanley Baker and their Irish girlfriends, who had come up from Streatham for the evening. There had been an opportunity for him to get to the phone box to call Sybil. But he didn't remember his obligation until the following morning anyway.

As she took the train back to Wales, Sybil was totally disillusioned with him and thought he was just another actor on the make, using his charms to get her into bed. She resolved that she would cut him dead if he spoke to her again. She thought that all the gossip she had heard about him must be true.

But her carefully laid plan lasted all of 30 seconds. As soon as she arrived, he bowled up to her on the set, as large as life, and said: "What the hell's the matter with your phone? I tried again and again to get through to you. But nothing – bloody nothing." He told her he had been calling all night and her phone must have been faulty. It was the first of many lies he would tell her to cover up his attentions towards other women. And then, Sybil did just as she would many times in the years to come; she instantly forgot her anger and melted under Burton's charm. She replied: "If you want to take me out to the theatre tomorrow, telephone me tonight" and turned on her heels. This time, he called.

Later, recalling the incident, she told friends she did not believe his story but admitted that she was simply seduced by his charisma.

From that moment until the duration of filming, they saw each other constantly and, soon, it was Sybil who had lost her virginity and was sharing his bed in the houseboat. The Irish nurses had been sent back to Streatham, never to return. Sybil became more and more smitten and, within days, she was deeply in love with him and desperate for him to propose. She said: "I thought him very worldly, experienced and sophisticated, which he certainly was compared to me."

As for Burton, he found her to be confident, shrewd and capable. As Sybil remembered: "I was eighteen and Richard was just reaching 23, and we were at that stage where we knew the last word about everything. We were very positive then about what was good or bad about everything." Burton nicknamed Sybil 'boot', which he told her was short for 'beautiful.'

In fact, their compatibility was immediately obvious to everyone. One night, he spoke of her with Stanley Baker, who recalled years later: "Richard had never before spoken with such genuine enthusiasm about a girl. He had named her and that meant he wasn't using her, as he never named names and never boasted on conquests. But Sybil was different; Richard was absolutely dotty about her."

Of course, Baker knew Sybil very well but it never registered with him that it was the same 'Sybil Williams' that Burton was talking about. Baker lived next door to Sybil's family in Wales and they had gone to the same school. When he did realise who she was, he was stunned: "I thought: 'the lucky bastard' – she was the best thing that ever happened to him. Talk about a perfect match. Well, it was quite incredible. They had everything in common. Not only background but in the way that circumstances had shaped them." As they got to know each other better, Baker recalled a great love affair: "She was someone you just wanted to be around. Rich was like that too, so they were a wonderful couple."

When filming of *The Last Days of Dolwyn* finally wrapped up, the two went their separate ways – he to London and she back to her sisters in Northampton. But every weekend after that, Burton took the train from London's Euston station to Northampton's Castle Station, where she would meet him, and they would walk back to her sister's house in St James Park Road. They would spend much of the weekend in her second-floor bedroom. This went on for three months until she got a job as a stage manager at the Prince of Wales Theatre in London.

He told everyone who asked: "I've met this marvellous girl."

In the middle of January 1949, Burton took her to meet the rest of the Jenkins family in Wales. Because she was Welsh, she went down very well with everyone. They stayed for two nights with Elfed and Cecilia at Caradoc Street. Burton found that, everywhere they went, people would take him aside and tell him what a wonderful wife she would make. Even his father was pleased when he took Sybil to his sister Hilda's house in Pontrhydyfen. Hilda said: "She was so homely. She was down to earth."

Philip Burton was also delighted. By then, he had followed Richard, finally left Wales and moved to London to become the BBC's chief training officer. He had already met Sybil on the set of *The Last Days of Dolwyn* and was enchanted with her, and she with him. A lifelong friendship began there and then. He considered her his daughter-in-law-in-waiting and fervently hoped Richard would propose, and told him so.

Sybil was also very keen to become Burton's wife, and the pressure on him to make an honest woman out of her became intense. When he asked Emlyn Williams' advice, he was told he would be a fool not to snap her up.

And everyone concurred. In truth, however, Burton was not the marrying kind and, at only 23-years-old, he was not receptive to the advice. In the end, he succumbed to the inevitable: while he certainly loved Sybil, it was equally certain he didn't really want to marry her.

But he very quickly found himself in too deep and, before he knew it, there was a ring on her finger. When they went home to Wales again to show off the ring, the family couldn't believe it. As Cecilia James said: "We all had a shock he was getting married."

Later, it appeared there was no one more shocked than the groom himself. He loved and adored his fiancée but couldn't believe what he had done. His antidote to what he saw as a personal disaster was to delay setting a date and to plan having a very long engagement. In truth, when he proposed, he had no intention of actually getting married but events just pushed him closer and closer to the edge until he had no choice but to jump.

Sybil, despite all her legendary equilibrium, was desperate to be Mrs Burton. It was the fulfillment of all her dreams. She would do anything to get the crown, and she was not a girl to be trifled with. Whilst Burton schemed how not to get married, she schemed the opposite with the help of Emlyn Williams and Philip Burton. It turned out that she was the better schemer.

As the pressure built up around him, Burton became desperate. Surrounded by pretty actresses, including the very special Claire Bloom whom he had met a month earlier, the temptations screamed out to him. And he was unfaithful to his fiancée more than once.

When he was unfaithful for the first time, he knew that marriage would be wrong; underneath the bravado and macho Welsh temperament, there stood a moral man who wanted to be monogamous when he finally made the decision to be married. But it was already too late for that.

The pressure to wed Sybil became unbearable. One night, he poured out his heart to Stanley Baker and asked him to voice his fears to Sybil to get him out of it. Baker told him that Sybil would understand and release him from his commitment. But Burton knew she wouldn't, and he could never find a way to inform her of his reluctance to get married. And soon, it was too late.

Baker was with him on the evening of Friday 4th February – his stag night. In those days, stag nights were always held on the evening of the wedding and, as Baker told Burton biographer Michael Munn: "The night before the wedding, he slipped into a terrible mood; really dark despair. He wasn't really ready for marriage, so I asked him why he was marrying her. He said, 'She expects it. She expects the ring on her finger.' I told him: 'Don't do it if it isn't what you want.' And he said: 'But I have to. Maybe it will save me.' And I said, 'Save you from what?' And he said: 'Myself.'"

Robert Hardy was best man and shared Burton's bedroom the night before. He barely knew Sybil at that stage and was very dubious about the whole thing. As he said: "I asked him at one point why he was marrying her because I knew what a scatterer-around he was. He said, and I remember it vividly, that it was because 'she expects it'. And that rang a sort of danger bell in my head."

Hardy believed Stanley Baker should have done more to counsel his friend and blames him and Emlyn Williams for encouraging the marriage. Hardy says of Baker: "I did not terribly like him. To me he was a sort of secondary Richard." But he blamed Emlyn Williams the most: "Emlyn was a great observer of rights and wrongs, except where he himself was concerned. Emlyn pushed him into it, there is no doubt about that."

Burton admitted his inner turmoil years later: "It was the romantic thing to do. I believed in romance. But I wasn't finding it for myself. I thought being married would give it to me."

He said at the time: "I love her dearly and she assumes that I will marry her. So I suppose I shall."

But in the midst of all his doubts, there was some certainty. He realised that she was a very special girl and he was very lucky to have ensnared her. She filled a desperate need for stability, which was something Richard always craved in his life. As Hollis Alpert said: "Sybil gave him a self-sustaining kind of love that all his bachelor conquests couldn't match." Paul Ferris added: "She conquered him, so to speak, by innocence."

Burton also saw many qualities in Sybil that were shared by sister, Cecilia. Like Cecilia, Sybil was a good housekeeper, tolerant of his unruly ways, understood his idiosyncrasies and worshipped the ground he walked on.

In the end, under intense pressure from Emlyn Williams, he thought: "Well, why not?" For Richard, Sybil was a safe and secure choice. No one would criticise him for his decision to marry her.

But the truth was that one of the most desirable men in England – one who was about to become an international film star – was getting married. His timing was terrible and the misguided marriage would cause him 12 years of uncertainty, anguish and guilt about his inevitable infidelity.

After Burton had prevaricated as much as he could, he and Sybil married on Saturday 5th February 1949, at Kensington Registry Office in London. The wedding took place at ten o'clock and, afterwards, everyone went to Daphne Rye's house at Pelham Crescent for the wedding breakfast. Rye put on a lavish catered banquet for the couple, and Binkie Beaumont paid for as many crates of champagne as they could drink that day.

The reception was a riotous affair, with the groom and best man slowly getting paralytically drunk. But even on her wedding day, the bride had somewhere else to be. Sybil's job entailed her overseeing the afternoon matinee of a comedy production called 'Harvey', which starred Sid Field, who was also a guest at the wedding. She had been unable to get the day off for her wedding, so she had to leave the reception with Field at around two o'clock for the matinee.

But it didn't really matter, as Burton and many of the male guests turned on the radio to listen to the Scotland-Wales Rugby International taking place that day at Murrayfield.

Daphne Rye was exasperated and had never been to a wedding like it, especially as all the men slowly became absolutely plastered on the champagne Beaumont had bought and started singing songs in a language she couldn't comprehend. In truth, it was perhaps better that way. After the matinee, Sybil returned to find all the guests sound asleep after lamenting Wales' loss to Scotland five points to six. She helped Daphne Rye and the maid clear up, and after making her new husband a strong coffee, Sybil and Daphne left for the theatre and the evening performance.

Later, in an extraordinary turn of events, Burton invited the maid, upstairs and, in the absence of his wife, consummated the marriage with her. It was just how it was.

When the new Mrs Burton returned to Pelham Crescent at around 11 o'clock – hoping to consummate her marriage with her new husband – she had no idea it had already happened without her. By then, the maid and the other guests had left and Burton was barely conscious. With Daphne Rye's help, Sybil got him into bed, where he did not awaken until seven o'clock the following morning. It was an extraordinary start to what would be an extraordinary marriage; the first of five for him and two for her.

None of the Jenkins family attended the wedding, and they only knew about it after the event. Only Philip Burton had witnessed it. On Monday

7th February, his brothers and sisters each received a telegram which read: "Married this morning. Pity Wales." That was it. Everyone thought 'Pity Wales' alluded to the young girls of Wales, but it actually referred to the Welsh rugby union team which had lost to Scotland – an event which, at the time, was considered a national disaster for the then totally dominant Welsh team.

After the wedding, both husband and wife would finally move into Daphne Rye's top floor flat in Pelham Crescent, signalling the end of Burton's bachelor days.

And they quickly settled in as a married couple, alternating their weekends at the friends or relatives of either Sybil or Burton. Every weekend after they were married, they sought to get out of London until they purchased their own house. Their favourite weekends away were to Northampton to visit Sybil's sister and her husband Eddie Newell. If not that, they often travelled down to Emlyn Williams' country house in the village of North Moreton, close to Wallingford on the Oxfordshire and Berkshire borders.

It was at Wallingford that Burton first met a man who was to become one of his best friends, a fellow Welshman David Rowe-Beddoe. Rowe-Beddoe was 16 at the time and attending Stowe School with Williams' son, Brook. Rowe-Beddoe was a classical music scholar and recalled: "My closest friend probably at school was Emlyn's younger son called Brook, and Richard and Sybil were staying there."

On other weekends, the couple would take the train to Northampton and spend their time at the Franklin's Gardens rugby union ground or at the county ground where first class cricket was played in the summer. Many Northampton people recall meeting Burton, who often brought his elder brother Ivor with him. One was Tony Lay and another Kay Drinkwater, who had finally married Sybil's first boyfriend, Ken. Kay recalled Burton joining them on a coach to watch the Northampton rugby team's away matches. Tony Lay had fond memories of drinking sessions with Ivor Jenkins at the County Tavern adjacent to the cricket ground.

The visits to Northampton ended very abruptly when Sybil's sister, Elsie Newell, died suddenly, soon after the Burtons were married. Sybil had lived on and of with Elsie since she was a young girl and was devastated by her sister's early death.

# CHAPTER 13

# Disaster and Triumph

## *Much pain before the glory*

### 1949

In January 1949, after he finished 'The Seagull' in Wales, Richard Burton returned to London. Strictly speaking, his contract with HM Tennent was up but Daphne Rye told him to be available and she would find him a part. Thinking he was ready for his first big part, she sent him to see Peter Glenville, who was directing a new Terence Rattigan play at St James' Theatre in London. It was called 'Adventure Story' and everyone was talking about it.

Glenville had cast Paul Scofield in the lead role as Alexander the Great, a role which would have suited Burton perfectly had he auditioned him for it. But the supporting role of Alexander's aide and companion, Hephaestion, was all that was on offer.

Glenville was initially delighted with Burton, saying: "It was a good part, a strong and important part. He auditioned for me alone on the stage and I saw at once that he was a brilliant young actor, and I gave him the part immediately."

Crucially, Burton read for the part on his own without Scofield. Hephaestion was much older than Alexander, and yet Burton was three years younger than Scofield, who looked older than his years anyway. But Glenville thought he could make it work.

The play was a great opportunity for both actors at similar stages in the development of their careers, although Scofield was better known after two hugely successful seasons of performing Shakespeare at Stratford-upon-Avon.

'Adventure Story' was one of two big new productions HM Tennent was mounting in early 1949; the other was 'The Lady's Not For Burning' at the Globe Theatre. Rye had steered Burton towards 'Adventure Story' as it seemed to have the best chance of success.

Burton biographer Paul Ferris noted: "Hephaestion was a good part. Rattigan was a famous writer, and the play was not one of the subsidised productions out at Hammersmith but a commercial venture in the West End." Burton was absolutely overjoyed to get the part. He felt it was a huge upward step. He was even more delighted when Stanley Baker also got a walk-on role in the play.

But in mid-January, on the first day of rehearsals, it was evident straightaway that there was a casting mismatch that could only be resolved by the actors swapping roles. But Schofield wasn't about to give up the lead role to Burton, even though they were great friends and liked each other very much.

As the day wore on, it became more and more obvious that it just wouldn't work and, that night, Glenville was on the phone to Binkie Beaumont complaining that Daphne Rye had forced Burton on him. It wasn't true, of course, but Glenville was desperate to cover himself for what had been a major casting mistake. Beaumont urged Glenville to give it a chance. But on the third day of rehearsals, the situation became progressively worse and Glenville visibly lost confidence in Burton and, gradually, the actor lost heart in the role. But that didn't stop Burton from wanting the role very, very badly. Another problem was that, as good as Scofield was – and he was very good – he was not as good an actor as Burton.

On the third day, Glenville held a reading of the play with the entire cast on stage and, suddenly, he turned to Richard and said: "Richard, I'm terribly sorry. You won't do." Burton just stared at him in disbelief. If an actor needed to be replaced, certainly this was not how it was done. Absolutely crushed, Richard was frozen to his spot on the stage. It was a public moment of failure that he would never forget.

Terence Rattigan was sitting in the auditorium and was shocked at the public nature of the firing; Glenville had simply snapped.

Burton took it so badly he slinked off, not bothering to say 'goodbye' to the cast. He was angry with Glenville for the manner of his dismissal but even angrier with himself because he knew he had performed badly. He had been overacting in an attempt to outshine Scofield and had subsequently mucked up the balance of the play. Burton was at his best when he underplayed roles, and he knew it. But now it was too late to do anything about it. Whatever the rights or wrongs, the sacking had done major damage to his career. One minute he was an up and coming star and, the next, a down and out has-been; it was as quick and decisive as that.

It was a double disaster as Burton was also out of contract with Tennent and, without a part, he had no income.

Glenville immediately replaced him with 37-year-old Robert Flemyng, a quiet and amenable actor who was also blessed with a wonderful deep voice. In truth, Glenville wanted a more mature, weary looking actor than one of the West End's best-looking prospects. Flemyng was a very distinguished man indeed. He was a colonel in the war and had won the Military Cross and been awarded an OBE by the King.

Not only was it catastrophic for Burton's career, but his sacking and replacement by Flemyng was a huge blow to his ego. Burton was worried about how it would play in the press. Although he was an unknown actor, theatre journalists were like bees to honey, sensing a story. He thought it would be viewed that he had failed in a straight contest with another rising young actor.

Although Burton had been in the part for only three days, press speculation forced Glenville to make an official statement about the sacking. It was by then too late to dress it up as a mutual decision for creative reasons; the excuse typically used when an actor was suddenly fired from a production. Glenville told journalists that Burton was too short. He described one of the scenes: "Suddenly, on came Paul and said: 'You're my friend, my rock, on which I lean.' He went to lean and went down about two feet. This is not entirely convincing."

But when a journalist pointed out that in fact Burton and Scofield were exactly the same height, Glenville was floored and didn't know what to say.

Burton was forced to make his own excuses to save his career, which genuinely looked to be under threat as the pressure mounted. He told a journalist, who caught up with him: "Well, I was supposed to play Paul Schofield's older friend. And who on earth can play Paul's older friend? With a face like that, he looks 108 to start with."

Glenville had pricked Burton's balloon and he didn't like it one bit. And the more Glenville tried to explain away his abrupt decision, the bigger the hole he dug for himself: "I suddenly realised when I saw him standing next to Scofield, who is well over six feet, that Richard was physically wrong. It was as simple as that. It had nothing to do with talent, regardless of what Richard said afterward. In fact, I replaced him with a less talented actor who looked absolutely right for the part." Robert Flemyng was apoplectic when he heard about this and almost walked off the set. The sacking had done Glenville as much damage as it had done Burton, and in truth, the production never recovered from the controversy. Glenville's reputation never fully recovered either.

Graham Jenkins saw it differently from his brother and put the blame for his sacking squarely on Burton's shoulders: "For Rich, the temptation to challenge and thus overact in what was essentially a submissive role was irresistible."

Noted actor Noel Willman, who was also in the cast, agreed and said that height had nothing to do with it: "Richard thought he wasn't that character. He stood there glowering in a wonderfully interesting way. The balance was wrong."

Willman, who was playing Darius, was adamant that Burton was fired because his acting overshadowed Scofield's: "Richard was sacked simply because he was far too interesting. In his part, he was meant to be a shadowy figure and Richard was never going to be a shadow no matter how hard he might try, and he was jolly well not going to try. I don't mean he was being naughty about it. He was simply a star personality who was riveting, and to play a shadowy kind of figure behind Alexander just wasn't on."

Daphne Rye was furious with Glenville over what had happened, and she sided with Burton all the way. She felt Glenville could have made it work. So too did Terence Rattigan, who was so embarrassed that he wrote Burton a letter of apology. Stanley Baker was also convinced it could have been made to work. He called Glenville's explanation "bullshit."

The truth seemed to be that Glenville could have made it work but chose not to.

But Melvyn Bragg was convinced that what really shook Burton was that he had no idea why it had happened. Bragg believes he suddenly lost confidence and, for the first time, doubted whether he would make it as an actor.

Bragg's analysis was spot on. One of Burton's enduring mysteries was that he had no idea in the first place why he was a good actor. He saw it as a gift, something as mysterious as it was simple, and if the pieces were in place with the right words and the right part, he could make it happen. To be suddenly told that he couldn't was a devastating blow and he thought his gifts had deserted him, perhaps forever. He said: "I felt suicidal. Everybody had told me this was my big chance. It made me fighting mad and I vowed it would never happen again."

He was also upset because he was denied the chance of working with Scofield, whom he genuinely admired.

Glenville never told the truth about the affair and said privately many years later: "Casting Richard was a mistake. It was a favour to Daphne

Rye." But he was lying. He had given the part to Burton for genuine acting reasons and the mistake was his, but that didn't change the fact that Burton had suffered a huge blow to his reputation

Burton retired to Pelham Crescent for a few days to lick his wounds. While there, he contemplated his future with Daphne Rye with his fiancée Sybil in attendance. He was very down and deeply depressed about what had happened, and nothing they could say made much difference.

Instead, the fiercely intelligent Burton found himself attempting to understand the fickleness of the business and analysing just how intangible and subjective it all was. He also came to a realisation about the competitiveness inherent in it, as he summed up many years later: "It has puzzled me that I have known over the years about 20 actors who are every bit as accomplished as I am and, for the most part, far better looking and the same size and weight and shape with all the accoutrements of what one would think a star should have – good voice, good presence, good eyes – and they haven't made it and I could never figure it out. I can only assume that it is some sort of diabolical, or even divine, luck. They don't know, but they worry about it because I know most of them very well. But I never worry about it, although I do sometimes wonder about it." It was a profound piece of deep thinking. But the truth was that he did worry about it in those early years; he worried very much. The conclusion he came to after the Glenville fiasco was that he had been "found out", and he genuinely believed his career was over.

But Daphne Rye was determined for this not to be so. She had invested a lot emotionally in Burton and was determined that the situation be turned around quickly. Rye was a very powerful woman in the Tennent organisation as Robert Hardy remembered: "She did really run the empire."

Glenville had taken a big risk upsetting Rye and furious with his treatment of Burton, she sought to give him a role in a play she had been championing within the Tennent organisation, a comedy entitled 'The Lady's Not For Burning' by a new playwright called Christopher Fry. It was Tennent's other big production of the year, but one that the pundits felt had much less chance of being successful, which was why Rye had initially steered Burton to 'Adventure Story'.

The play had started production at the same time as 'Adventure Story' and was already cast. But Burton's legendary luck was to strike again when a new director came on board.

# AND GOD CREATED BURTON

Rye had cajoled Binkie Beaumont to let her stage the play at the Globe Theatre. Written in verse, the play was set in the fifteenth-century and told the intertwined stories of a mercenary soldier and a beautiful witch. Set in England, it revolved around two characters, Thomas Mendip, who, returning from seven years at war, wanted to die, and Jennet Jourdemayne, a beautiful witch who had been condemned to die but who wanted to live. John Gielgud would play Mendip, and Pamela Brown the witch.

But the go-ahead to start rehearsals was delayed as Rye struggled to convince a for-once uncertain Beaumont of the play's merits and the quality of its nominated director, whom he didn't particularly care for. The turning point came when, somehow, Rye persuaded John Gielgud to direct as well as star in it. After that, Beaumont had no choice.

Burton had to go through a gruelling audition with Gielgud and Fry. The part he was up for had already been given to another boy, but when Gielgud came aboard as director, he rejected the choice and sought to cast it again. He was also unhappy with the choice of actress for the secondary female role of Alizon and wanted to recast that as well.

The part Burton was up for was that of a young, orphaned clerk named Richard who falls in love with a young girl called Alizon and runs off with her. Unlike his character in 'Adventure Story', the part was perfect for him but it was a measure of just how far his reputation had suddenly fallen that he had to face a tough audition.

Gielgud held auditions for both parts in the same late-afternoon session. The afternoon of the audition is now the stuff of legend, as Burton arrived in a terrible state and looked as though he had completely lost his way. It was also Burton's first meeting with a fledgling actress, the 17-year-old Claire Bloom, up for the part of Alizon.

Present on stage were Christopher Fry, Pamela Brown and Binkie Beaumont. In the auditorium sat John Gielgud and Daphne Rye. It was an intimidating audience, and as Burton went on stage to read the part, he had an attack of nerves. In reality, he was suffering from a severe case of stage fright caused by Glenville's brutal treatment of him just a few days earlier. Consequently, he gave a terrible audition – perhaps the worst of his career. Nobody said anything as he trooped off stage; they didn't need to. And his performance seemed even worse when Claire Bloom followed and delivered a sparkling rendition of her part.

Afterwards, Christopher Fry turned to Daphne Rye and Gielgud and said:

"Well, the girl's alright, but I don't think the boy's going to be any good."
Fry had not seen Burton before and could take a dispassionate view, but
Gielgud and Rye realised he was far from his best. The two put their heads
together and asked him to return the following day for another reading.
Being given a second chance was a very charitable act by Gielgud, who put
his arms round Burton and told him: "Have a chat with Christopher about
the part, then come back tomorrow and read it again."

Gielgud later remembered the incident: "I have never known such a gifted
actor who was so lacking in confidence. He shook, I suppose, with nerves."

Daphne Rye took Burton straight home to Pelham Crescent, where the
two had a heart-to-heart talk about the problems. She also got Philip Burton
on the telephone, and they chatted for over an hour. Sybil stood by with
cups of tea.

Overnight, Burton somehow got his head together and made sure he
drank two large whiskies in the pub before entering the theatre. It had the
desired effect of steadying his nerves and he was entirely different at the
read-through the second time around. Reading the part almost perfectly, it
was as if he had been born to it. This time, it was the same Richard Burton
that Gielgud had seen in Oxford five years earlier. Fry was astonished at
the overnight transformation and had never seen anything like it in his life.
Gielgud gave him the part on the spot. That single decision saved Burton's
career.

It didn't take long for the swagger to return. Having landed such an important
part, Burton decided that he should have a pay rise from the basic £10 a week
he had been earning from Tennent to something more suited to his new
status. It was amazing bravado for a man who the day before had been so
close to leaving acting altogether.

The negotiations for the pay rise became a legend in theatre circles and is a
story oft retold. Burton remembered it best and, for once, recounted it totally
accurately: "I went to see Binkie Beaumont and told him I thought I should
have twenty pounds a week. I made my case and, finally, Binkie compromised
at seventeen pounds, ten shillings (£17.50p). I was so flushed with success that
I took a taxi instead of the bus back to Pelham Crescent. As the taxi drew up,
Emlyn Williams emerged from his house and hailed it. He saw me inside and
asked what I was doing. I told him I had been to see Binkie about the money
I was going to get. He asked what the role was and said sharply, 'Get back in
the taxi and go back and ask for thirty.' I was caught between the two men I

was most terrified of. So I went back, and Binkie was not so pleasant. Finally, he said: 'Very well.' And as I was going out the door, he said in a sharp-edged voice, 'I suppose that old Welsh pit pony put you up to this.'"

Burton had trebled his pay and was now on some ten times what his brothers were earning back in Wales. He couldn't have been happier. It was the most extraordinary month of his life. In a few days, he had gone from disaster to triumph, from zero earnings to £30 a week; a small fortune in those days and 12 times the average national wage.

But interestingly, Burton did not see his change of luck quite so rosily at the time. He actually thought 'The Lady's Not For Burning' would turn out to be a dog. Verse drama was generally assumed to be commercially unviable and, like everyone, he believed 'Adventure Story' was destined for success and would be the big hit of 1949. Although it was to prove to be Burton's 'chance of a lifetime', he was thoroughly dismissive of the entire project.

Rehearsals started in London on 7th February. The play had a very talented supporting cast, including veterans Harcourt Williams, Eliot Makeham and Esme Percy, all in their seventies, plus Peter Bull and Richard Leech, who were contemporaries of Burton.

After the first rehearsal, Gielgud knew his decision to give Burton a second chance had been a good one. He said: "He had an immediate understanding of the part and spoke it beautifully and was perfect-looking."

When Claire Bloom arrived, she was surprised to see Burton on stage after his catastrophic audition. But she was very glad. They had formed an emotional connection and she was very unhappy when she found out that he had married the Saturday before.

As soon as rehearsals began, Bloom couldn't believe she was on stage with the same actor she had met at the audition.

But rehearsals weren't all sweetness and light and Burton continually irritated Gielgud by yawning and looking at his watch when he thought it was time for a break. His confidence returned too quickly and the other actors were irked by his apparent indifference at rehearsals. But it was born out of confidence, as the part was perfectly matched to him and he didn't need the intensive rehearsals as did the rest of the cast.

Christopher Fry was also surprised by Burton's casual arrogance during rehearsals: "Richard would loll around the stage talking passionately about everything, particularly rugby, and not seeming to show any interest in the play. I would become angry with him because he always began to yawn prodigiously."

But, offstage, it was to prove a very happy time and Burton gelled with his co-stars. He already had a great relationship with Gielgud but he revelled in Pamela Brown's infectious sense of humour. He also eventually bonded with Christopher Fry, and regular after-show impromptu parties became the norm.

John Gielgud remembered: "He was funny, gregarious and a bit of a show-off." But Gielgud also believed that Burton had been permanently harmed by his rejection from 'Adventure Story' and noticed for the first time a hint of melancholy in Burton's personality. As he explained: "He could be moody and unpredictable and had, I think, a dark Welsh streak of pessimism and carelessness." It was a characteristic that had not previously manifested itself.

There was an interesting moment when Gielgud congratulated Burton in front of the whole cast on his radio portrayal of Shakespeare's 'Henry V', which had been broadcast the night before on the BBC. He had taken the job in desperation the day after he was sacked from 'Adventure Story'. Burton was pleased with the compliment, but then, in an aside, Gielgud whispered to the cast: "So talented and so like dear Larry." Burton pretended in later life to be horrified by this back-handed comparison with Laurence Olivier, but at the time he was secretly delighted.

Rehearsals lasted barely a fortnight and the cast set off for an 11-week tour around provincial theatres in mid-March.

The play was due to tour around Britain for two months and, from the start, it played to near empty theatres. The opportunity to see the great John Gielgud on stage was lost on provincial audiences, who could not and did not want to understand the play. It was far too sophisticated for them. Graham Jenkins, his brother, summed it up best: "I have to say that the play was not well liked by many of us because, for all its cleverness, it failed to grab the emotions. The comedy of manners had an underlying tension, but it was difficult to work up any interest in the leading characters or in what happened to them."

In fact, none of Burton's Welsh relatives, who travelled to see the play, could understand it. It was aimed at a sophisticated West End audience of perceptive regular theatregoers, of which there were tens of thousands living in London. But it just didn't play well with the rest of the country.

Gielgud and Beaumont were very worried, and the play was losing hundreds of pounds a week. But Burton seemed oblivious to the problems.

As it had been during the tour of 'The Druid's Rest', he was having a fabulous time staying in a succession of cheap digs. But it was a very different type of 'good time'. As a newly married man, he had to change his style. Instead of rabble rousing with Stanley Baker, he participated in more cultural pursuits with his new friend, Claire Bloom. They spent every night in their rooms reciting poetry to each other. For now, there was nothing sexual between the two; it was entirely platonic, and Sybil often attended as well. Rod Steiger, who later married Bloom, recalled: "'That voice of his – well, that would seduce any woman. They didn't touch. And he was only just married. I don't know what he was looking for. But they fell in love during that tour."

They returned to London in the first week of May and opened at The Globe on 11th May 1949. The play's programme called it "an exciting night out for the brain." It was certainly that, and the London critics were stunned and gave it rave reviews from the start. The critics were full of praise for a play in which, as they wrote: "The author and actors revelled in the joy of imaginative language." The critics naturally focused their attention on the established stars, Gielgud and Brown, but Richard Findlater called Burton "an outstanding newcomer to the West End."

The London audiences were as good as their reputations. What provincial hicks couldn't understand, Londoners lapped up.

There was one particular scene that particularly attracted attention. It was the now famous 'floor scrubbing scene' where Gielgud and Brown were on stage in a long romantic dialogue; the centrepiece of the play. In the scene, Burton was on his knees scrubbing the floor and, in that simple act, he stole the scene from two of the greatest stage actors of the era. He had an extraordinary look, and his scrubbing action mesmerised the London audiences. The other actors were also taken in by it. Richard Leech says that when Burton was on his knees and scrubbing, "you couldn't take your eyes off him. He just did it. But because he is who he is, it was totally compelling." Alec Guinness saw the play a few times and noticed him straightaway and, as he said: "So did everyone in the profession, because of his marvellous head and shoulders."

Gielgud recalled the scrubbing scene as "memorable", explaining: "He played the boy scrubbing the floor... stopping at intervals to come into the scene with a line or two. He knew exactly what to do without my telling him. I didn't direct him at all in that play. He came into the scene and then retired from it in the most wonderful way. Absolutely, you knew instinctively, even if you had your back to him, that he was feeding the scene exactly right."

Guinness later recalled: "I couldn't take my eyes off Burton. Then I heard the same from other people. That's a rare gift, a presence. It's also dangerous because it's something neither he nor anyone else has any control over." Emlyn Williams also remembered that scene well, and said: "Somehow, he had this peculiar power, an intensity, an ability to make the audience aware of his presence."

As the play became a hit, Burton's attitude to it changed as well. He revelled in the success and, as his name became increasingly well-known, he basked in the limelight typically bestowed upon successful West End actors. He remembered: "I spent a year sharing the same stage as John Gielgud. It was the best drama education I could get." Gielgud had readily taken on the teaching role and said: "Richard Burton was, perhaps, my best star pupil."

It was the turning point in his career and barely eight months after the 'Adventure Story' fiasco, he felt entirely differently about himself. He readily admitted later that at the beginning of the year, he had been in a hurry either to "become a success or give it up altogether." Now, he felt that he had finally made it.

For Richard Burton, 'The Lady's Not For Burning' was his breakthrough part; the part that assured him leading man status for the rest of his life. Claire Bloom recalled his impact in the play succinctly: "When Richard was on the stage, he was hypnotic. It was his eyes, but also a quality that you can't define – which, I suppose, is star quality. And he was very natural. He had learned no techniques. If I made a mistake, John Gieglud would say to me: 'Watch Richard, my dear. Just be as simple and as natural as he.'"

Ironically, 'The Lady's Not For Burning' was a far bigger success than 'Adventure Story' and attracted a procession of celebrities to the Globe Theatre. All came away with a very good impression of Burton. One was Joan Collins, then a drama student. She was transfixed by the play and mesmerised by Burton, whom she believed overshadowed Pamela Brown and John Gielgud completely. As she remembered: "I barely watched Gielgud and Brown, as I was completely swept away by the mesmerising presence of a young actor called Richard Burton. He was electrifying, with an amazing voice, a faint but mellifluous Welsh accent and piercing green eyes, which gave off a luminous glow, visible even from where we were sat. I'd had crushes on a long line of movie stars…but Burton was my first flesh and blood passion, and I couldn't take my eyes off him." Collins admits she went to see the play over 12 times during its run. She used to queue for the tickets for the last row of the gallery; seats that, although no one wanted, still cost two shillings each on the night. Afterwards, she and a student friend, called Adele, hung around the stage door waiting for Burton. As she remembered: "Adele and I waited excitedly outside the stage door, autograph books at the ready, until the idol himself came out. He scribbled his name and bestowed upon us a devastating matinee-idol smile. We almost fainted, then became convulsed in giggles, watching his hunched figure in a shabby overcoat striding off down Shaftsbury Avenue. 'He's so gorgeous,' I sighed. 'Simply gorgeous.' 'But did you see his skin?' said Adele, as pragmatic as ever. 'It was covered in pock-marks.' 'Doesn't matter,' said I. 'That voice and those eyes make up for anything.'" Later, Collins wrote to Burton at the theatre and asked for an autographed photo, as she remembered: "Sure enough, back came a five-by-seven black and white glossy with the rather mundane inscription: 'To Joan. Thank you for your letter. Best Wishes. Richard Burton.' I still have it." It marked the turning point of Christopher Fry's career, who had another hit show, called 'Venus Observed', on at the same time. As for 'Adventure Story', it closed after a few months, having never recovered from the sacking of Richard Burton. 'The Lady's Not For Burning' ran to packed audiences paying high ticket prices from May to December, and made a small fortune for Binkie Beaumont and the HM Tennent organisation. And a lot of that was down to Burton, whom everyone was suddenly talking about. At Christmas, a grateful Beaumont invited Burton and Sybil to the annual Christmas party at his home, at 14 Lord North Street in Westminster. As Burton looked around the room at all the famous faces, many of whom now recognised him as well, he realised he had found his mission in life. The years of self-doubt were finally over.

# DISASTER AND TRIUMPH

# AND GOD CREATED BURTON

# CHAPTER 14

# A Leading Man At Last

## *The Boy With A Cart*

### January 1950

A t the end of 1949, 'The Lady's Not For Burning' was playing to packed houses. It would have had an extended run but for the fact that John Gielgud was committed to a season of Shakespeare at Stratford-upon-Avon the following year and couldn't stay on. Gielgud's imminent departure meant the play would have to close at the end of December.

It was a desperately sorry day when it was announced to the cast. They were a very happy bunch of people, and packed houses and high ticket prices meant the play was earning plenty of money for everyone. But Gielgud was a man of his word and was not about to let down Anthony Quayle, who ran the Memorial Theatre in Stratford, even though the decision to leave would cost him as much as £15,000 personally, a huge sum of money in those days.

When he realised Gielgud was leaving, Burton looked around for another opportunity to earn some money. And with Gielgud's help, he found it with another HM Tennent/Christopher Fry production called 'The Boy With A Cart', to be staged at the Lyric Theatre in Hammersmith.

The opportunity had come about after some scheming by Gielgud. Also looking to make some extra money, Gielgud felt he could combine his Shakespeare season with directing a play in London, which, after rehearsals, would require very little attention.

He co-opted Burton and, together, they persuaded Binkie Beaumont to finance the production of 'The Boy With A Cart', with Burton starring, Fry writing and Gielgud directing.

Beaumont was in a difficult position. After the success the four of them had enjoyed together, he couldn't refuse them; although he later wished he had. Beaumont was aghast when he read the script and saw that it was entirely uncommercial and would appeal only to a narrow few. He doubted whether even the top echelon of the London audience was ready for something this sophisticated.

'The Boy With A Cart' was a new play by Fry, albeit written by him 12 years earlier.

# AND GOD CREATED BURTON

It would never have made it to London had it not been for the success of 'The Lady's Not For Burning', which had made Fry very popular with London audiences.

But there was still some tough negotiating to be done. Gielgud wanted Beaumont to stage the play at The Globe following immediately upon the success of 'The Lady's Not For Burning.' But, realising it would be pure folly, the great impresario told Gielgud that, as much as he loved him, it was not on. Beaumont couldn't believe the performance would attract an audience in any numbers.

Eventually, Beaumont simply told Gielgud straight that it could not run in the West End and that he could barely justify a six-week run at The Lyric in Hammersmith. He told him the prospective audience was limited to the extreme intellectual side of the cultural establishment, which reduced the likely box office to only a few thousand, and a short run was the only option. Gielgud strongly disagreed and pointed to the success of 'The Lady's Not For Burning.' Gielgud couldn't see the difference but Beaumont booked the theatre for just six weeks – albeit without telling Gielgud. Burton, meanwhile, found it amusing to observe two giants of British theatre locking horns.

When the deal was done, Burton left 'The Lady's Not For Burning' and his understudy took over. Both Gielgud and Burton wanted to get rehearsals out of the way before Gielgud had to be in Stratford. Graham Jenkins remembered his brother being cock-a-hoop about it: "It was a heaven-sent opportunity for Rich, who recognised the value of playing his first stage lead under the guidance of one of the theatrical greats."

The play was in a long single act and dealt with the legend of a boy who hears a mysterious call to build a church and pushes his aged mother over most of England in a cart in search of the right site. Burton's character was called Cuthman, a simple shepherd boy who eventually ends up, with his mother, in Sussex where he has been instructed by God to build the church.

It was a formidable task for its two central characters. Virtually on their own, Richard and the 72-year-old actress Mary Jerrold had to make the entire story come alive.

Burton's extraordinary acting in this play made the story deeply moving. Much of it was mimed, as Gielgud explained: "It was a play with no set and everything was constructed out of Richard's great talent for miming."

Burton was understudied by Paul Daneman, and so daunting was the role it was the one time an understudy hoped he wouldn't be called upon. Daneman remembered: "It was strange how he tackled that part. At the first rehearsal, he read beautifully and we were all impressed. But as we rehearsed for another six weeks – which was much too long – he never did another thing. We kept asking ourselves: 'When is he going to do something?' We were all trying new things; yet he never did. And when we came to the first night, Richard's performance seemed to be exactly as it had been at the first rehearsal."

But when they were on their own, Gielgud still had to do a lot of work on Richard's performance to make the one-act play really work. Gielgud said: "He was simply splendid at it – he had to mime building a cathedral and was spell-binding." Burton said that in the scene, he felt the hairs on his neck stand on end and knew for the first time the power he could have over an audience. Christopher Fry recalled his performance as having "tremendous simplicity and youth."

Despite Burton's lack of effort in rehearsals, Daneman was blown away by his performance and was amazed to learn that it was his first leading role: "It was very unusual to see a young man walk on stage with all the maturity and quiet assurance of a middle-aged man. He had an extraordinary presence and quite fantastic repose. He seemed to know, either by experience or instinct, exactly what not to do."

But as Binkie Beaumont predicted, the play was not for everybody and the critics gave it what Christopher Fry described as "courteous reviews." But the sophisticates who turned up to see it were in raptures. They flocked to Hammersmith in huge numbers from their regular haunts in Shaftesbury Avenue. Graham Jenkins remembered it vividly: "I was there for the opening night and for the emotional scenes backstage after the final curtain. For the first time, Rich felt like a star and he loved it."

In fact, after the first week's performances, Gielgud thought that Burton could not have been bettered, saying: "It was a very simple miracle play that Fry had written for an amateur festival somewhere, and Richard's simplicity and shining sincerity were deeply moving." He added: "It was one of the most beautiful performances I had ever seen, and he and Mary Jerrold together were absolutely divine. He knew himself how good he was in it…it was his great moment and the part that made him into a star."

Once word got around, the theatrical glitterati and royalty all wanted to see the play, including one of the biggest film stars of the day – Stewart Granger. After the performance, Granger, who lived in Los Angeles with his fiancée Jean Simmons, wanted to meet Burton. Granger later told Burton biographer

# AND GOD CREATED BURTON

Michael Munn the story: "I'd seen Richard Burton in a small part in a West End play, 'The Lady's Not For Burning', so when I saw that he was appearing in a play in Hammersmith, I went to see him. He was breathtakingly good. Afterwards, I went to see him to pay my respects. I knocked on his dressing room door and he said: 'Come in', and I walked in and he stood there in just a jockstrap, clutching a glass of beer. He looked at me and said: 'Oh my God, a bloody film star.' I said: 'Do excuse me, but I just wanted to tell you that I think you're the most brilliant young actor I've ever seen, and I just wanted to tell you. That's all.' I was about to go, but he grabbed my arm and said: 'Damn it, I've only got beer, I'm afraid, but if you'd like one...' I said: 'No thanks. I've got someone waiting for me but, listen, when you get to Hollywood, come and look me up. I'll be over there in a few weeks.' He said: 'No thank you, I'm not going to Hollywood.' I said: 'Oh yes, you are. You can be sure of that. So when you do, promise to look me up.' So he promised that in the unlikely event that he ever went to Hollywood, he'd look me up. And we shook hands. That was the first time I met him."

Paul Daneman remembered Granger as just one of a queue of well-known people in the theatre coming backstage night after night, often with tears in their eyes and saying how moving Burton's performance had been.

It was a triumph for Burton and Gielgud as well as for Christopher Fry, who was at the very peak of his success with four plays being produced simultaneously: 'A Phoenix Too Frequent'; 'The Lady's Not For Burning'; 'Venus Observed'; and, now, 'The Boy With A Cart'. But 1950 was to prove the summit of his popularity, and the fashion for verse drama vanished almost as quickly as it had appeared. But for three years, between 1948 and 1950, Fry was the talk of the town.

And Binkie Beaumont's street smarts were also to be proved to be correct. 'The Boy With A Cart' played to a packed house for four weeks, but then the audience disappeared and Beaumont closed it in the fifth week. Because of the very high ticket prices, the play broke even despite John Gielgud's substantial directing fee.

But for Richard Burton, 'The Boy With A Cart' had incalculable value. He may have been 24, but he was suddenly regarded as the most talented actor on the British stage by insiders, even if only a few hardened theatregoers knew who he was.

He was a leading man at last.

# A LEADING MAN AT LAST

# AND GOD CREATED BURTON

# CHAPTER 15

# Making it as an Actor

## *The start of glory*

### 1950 to 1951

B y the time 'The Boy With A Cart' closed, Burton was a genuine British
domestic theatrical star. It quickly got him his second film part when
Associated British Pathé signed him up to *A Woman With No Name*, a
relatively low-budget wartime psychological drama set in London.

Burton had the male lead, while the established actress Phyllis Calvert
played the female lead; he played an air force lieutenant and, she, a married
woman who loses her memory after being injured in a German air raid.
The woman falls in love with Burton's character before he flies off on a
mission to Germany and is killed, at which point her memory returns and
she rediscovers her husband.

The on-screen love affair between Calvert and Burton was brief, with
Burton's character being killed before the end of the first reel of the film.
But it was not an easy production. Burton had trouble playing the love
scenes convincingly, much to the chagrin of the Hungarian director Ladislas
Vajda.

Despite some personal coaching from Calvert, who also co-produced
the film, Burton just couldn't seem to get it right. She advised him: "Film
work is to do with the eyes." But, as Vajda put it: "Burton's eyes remained
unawakened."

Burton was on set for ten days and received £100 a day for his troubles,
his biggest payday yet. But he knew his performance was only average, so
he took the money and ran.

But, despite that, and to everyone's surprise, the film made money in
Britain – thanks especially to Calvert's box office power. But it was hopeless
in America, where it was renamed *Her Panelled Door* for reasons no one
understood. In truth, it took Burton's career no further but, with the money,
he was able to buy his first house.

Afterwards, he was in demand again and moved to Brighton temporarily
to appear in yet another Christopher Fry play, called 'A Phoenix Too
Frequent' at the Dolphin Theatre, in which he co-starred with Diana Graves

and Jessie Evans. It was a typical low-budget provincial production with no aspirations, presided over by Fry, who was staging it just for fun. But 'A Phoenix Too Frequent' was, as the name implied, another verse drama and almost incomprehensible.

But Fry's verse dramas had so caught the imagination of theatregoers that the sophisticates of Brighton obligingly turned out in force and filled the theatre every night for the fortnight before it closed.

All this activity meant that Burton was noticed by one of the top theatrical agents in London, Vere Barker. He owned Connie's Agency. Barker was regarded as the top agent of his day, whose clients included Margaret Leighton, Eric Portman, Ralph Richardson and Laurence Harvey. In truth, Barker was a product of his times and had nothing like the talent or negotiating skills of a personal agent of today. He was exploited by the impresarios he dealt with, and his clients almost always came out badly. But he and few others were the only options in those days, and he was the best of a pretty bad bunch.

Up until then, Burton had done without an agent and relied on Daphne Rye's help to negotiate his contracts. Both Burton and Stanley Baker signed with Barker together, and he represented them for many years until both actors needed more specialised help.

Vere Barker became a personal friend and lent money to Burton on various occasions when he was short, including helping him with the deposit on his first house soon after he signed as well as with the purchase of his first car.

Unfortunately, Barker was a better friend than he was an agent, and he guided Burton into a terrible mistake that was to cost him nearly two million dollars over the next seven years. For reasons best known to himself, Burton was persuaded to sign a long-term five-year personal contract, and a two-year option, with London Films, run by Sir Alexander Korda and Anatole de Grunwald. They agreed to pay him a retainer of £100 a week for his exclusive services in film. Korda was contractually bound to pay it for five years, come what may. But he had the authority to place Burton in any film he liked, as well as to lend him out to other studios. Any additional money that Burton earned once the £100 had been deducted was to be split 50-50.

It was an inexplicable decision for Burton to sell himself so cheaply to a shark like Korda, particularly as he was already getting £100 a day for film work.

But Burton saw it differently. £100 a week was 35 times a typical miner's wage in South Wales and it guaranteed he would be able to pay his new mortgage. It was the first big deal that Vere Barker did for him, and the worst.

It was no surprise that Korda had snapped up Burton so early. Korda was the British film equivalent of theatre's Binkie Beaumont. He was the great impresario of the British film industry and the only Brit who understood the American market. He also ran Shepperton Studios and had a joint venture with Twentieth Century-Fox. During the second World War, the quality and effectiveness of his propaganda films for the British government won him a knighthood from a very grateful Winston Churchill.

Although very sharp and focused on the bottom line, Korda's films were lavishly budgeted and he did more than any man alive to further the interests of the British film industry while also making himself a great deal of money.

A positive side effect of the deal was the amount of publicity it generated for Burton. When the US$20,000 a year deal was announced, it was big news; few British actors earned that much. It was enhanced by the fact that, in those days, one British pound bought four American dollars.

So when Burton signed with Korda, it suddenly brought him to the attention of Britain's mainstream press. Korda's publicists went to work and were very aggressive. They did not rely on the critics for press coverage; they went out to create news. The high spot in all this press activity was Burton's press nomination as one of Britain's ten brightest acting hopes for the future. The other nine were: Jack Hawkins, Norman Wooland, Michael Gough, Jack Watling, Moira Lister, Honor Blackman, Sarah Churchill, Faith Brook and Rona Anderson.

The first tangible result of the Korda deal was the decision to cast Burton in Anatole de Grunwald's new film, called *Now Barabbas Was A Robber*, financed by Korda's London Films.

Immediately, Burton realised his mistake. His 30 days of shooting would ordinarily have commanded a fee of £3,000, but all he got was his £400 weekly wages from Korda. But it was too late for regrets; the contract was watertight. Burton, however, never forgot the lesson and would never again sell himself so cheaply to another film producer.

The film turned out to be a success and a marvellous platform for Burton's talents. *Now Barabbas Was A Robber*, directed by Gordon Parry, was based on a play by William Douglas-Home. The film featured the harsh realities of prison life and its destructive effect on inmates and wardens alike. It was a moderate success in British cinemas, and Warner Bros liked it enough to release it in the United States.

Although he was by no means the star of the film, Burton's acting attracted two important reviews. The most telling came from Caroline Lejeune, the most celebrated and respected British film critic of all time. She wrote in *The Observer*: "Mr Burton is an actor whose progress I shall watch with great curiosity. To my mind, he has all the qualities of a leading man that the British film industry badly needs at this juncture: youth, good looks, a photogenic face, obviously alert intelligence, and a trick of getting the maximum effect with the minimum of fuss."

The *New York Times* said of him: "We cannot feel we have seen the last of Mr Burton. The fact that he might almost be the double of Sir Laurence Olivier, as Sir Laurence looked fifteen-odd years ago, won't do him any harm at that."

Korda was determined to get the most out of his deal and moved Burton straight on to another film called *Waterfront*, a melodrama financed by the Rank Organisation, to be shot on location in Liverpool. As the name implied, it was about the travails of Britain's dockers in the twenties depression and was based on a novel by John Brophy. Burton played an out-of-work Liverpudlian ship's engineer called Ben Sattherwaite, and his big-name co-stars were Robert Newton and Susan Shaw. It was directed by Michael Anderson. Stupidly, the film was released in the summer and depressed audiences with its dark tone. It was not a success; it went unnoticed and soon disappeared from British cinemas. What reviews there were praised Burton. Nonetheless, it was Anderson's directorial debut and the start of a very illustrious career, in which he would go on to direct *The Dam Busters* and *Around The World In Eighty Days*.

Next, Korda contracted Burton out to appear in a film called *Green Grow The Rushes*. It was an odd film produced by ACT Films Ltd, which was a subsidy of ACT, the film technicians union. Cinema attendance was dipping alarmingly because of the advent of television, and many of the famous film studios were being sold off for development or being taken over by television. The film was an attempt by the union to give its members work and an experiment for the future to see if this type of production could work. As a favour, Korda lent Burton to the unions at scale rates.

The film was adapted from Howard Clewes' novel about a group of enterprising smugglers who make use of an ancient charter to smuggle brandy into the southern England. It was directed by Derek Twist and produced by

John Gossage. Burton co-starred with Roger Livesey and Honor Blackman and played a romantic young Romany smuggler called Bob Hammond.

Predictably, the production, presided over by the union, was a chaotic disaster and dragged on and on and, even at scale rates, Burton was eventually paid £2,000 – after deducting Korda's share.

By mid-year, Burton had made three films and, had he still been a free agent, he would have earned over £15,000, making him one of Britain's highest earners. As it was, after Korda had taken his share, Burton received less than half of that. He felt like a jobbing actor for hire, which is, of course, what he was. By signing the contract with Korda, he had lost control of his career. Years later, Burton tried to put a better spin on his contract with Korda by saying it was only for 12 weeks a year.

But by the time all these movies had been released, he was a household name in Britain and pictures of he and his wife, Sybil, out and about in London were frequently published in British newspapers. In Britain, he had made it as an actor, and that led to an opportunity for him to cross the Atlantic for the first time. John Gielgud, who could never forget the big pay packets he had earned from 'The Lady's Not For Burning', made plans to take it to the Broadway stage with himself directing and producing.

Gielgud phoned Burton from Stratford and told him to keep himself free to cross the Atlantic in late summer.

Gielgud wanted essentially the same cast that had finished the production in London, minus Claire Bloom, who had left early. Having the same cast would preclude lengthy rehearsals, expensive for a wholly British cast in New York city. Whilst British actors would accept lodging in disgusting boarding houses in England, they demanded the best hotels when abroad, and it all came out of Gielgud's share.

So Gielgud took the entire cast from London, including Esme Percy, who was 64 and in poor health. He said: "The teamwork is so honest and well-disposed that I believe any newcomer, even if more perfect in detail, might break the quality of togetherness. Gielgud planned ten days of rehearsals when they arrived in New York and went to Boston for a small pre-Broadway tour. In the event, he only got a week after the Burtons, along with Ivor and Gwen Jenkins, only arrived on the Queen Elizabeth liner on 1st November.

Leaving behind a London that was still in the grip of rationing and austerity, New York was a welcome surprise for the cast. As Gielgud recalled: "The kindness and welcome are overwhelming, but there is too much money, food and drink."

Gielgud may have found it all too much, but Burton was delighted with the job, which allowed him to escape Alexander Korda's clutches for four months as his deal did not include his earnings from live theatre. His fee was also double what he had received from the London run.

The American version of 'The Lady's Not For Burning' was unchanged and the play was aimed at precisely the same audience that had come to see it in London – the equivalent sophisticates in New York – of whom there were many more. It worked like a dream, and any New Yorker of any distinction was there.

The opening night performance in Boston's Royal Theater on 8th November 1950 was absolutely magical. Gielgud described it as "thrilling". He said: "Wednesday was a thrilling night, and I shall be able to tell my stepchildren that I played to not an empty seat."

The critics arrived a week later. Brooks Atkinson, the legendary theatre critic for the *New York Times*, was ecstatic with praise for the acting. He described Christopher Fry's script as "precocious with a touch of genius" and called his prose "sometimes soporific."

Reporters swarmed all over the play intrigued by a band of Brits that had sailed the Atlantic and were playing to packed houses, as Gielgud recalled: "All the reporters clamour for details of your life and personal behaviour till I tell them I am getting bored describing you as a dear and modest and ideal to work with."

The play received the New York Drama Critics Circle award for Best Foreign Play of 1950-51. It ran on Broadway for a triumphant five months until the end of March 1951.

For the entire month of November, Sybil and Richard had a brilliant time together in New York. They were also joined by Philip Burton, who had left the BBC and gone freelance. He had travelled over from London especially.

At the end of November, Sybil returned to London with Ivor and Gwen. For the next two months, Burton was unfaithful to her virtually every night. As Gielgud remembered: "He had various love affairs with people connected with the play, and I could see that he had enormous charm."

During the run, Olivia de Havilland came to see the play and went backstage to Burton's dressing room. She had an interesting proposal for the actor. De Havilland was trying to launch her own Broadway production of 'Romeo and Juliet.' She offered Burton US$1,000 a week to co-star opposite her. Burton didn't particularly take to her approach and turned her down flat. It was a mark of how far he had come.

The play finally closed at the end of March 1951, although Burton had left early on 7th February to return to England. He was replaced by a 23-year-old Australian actor called Ronald Faulkner.

Gielgud missed Burton desperately, saying: "We miss Burton in the play, but the boy who has taken over does pretty well – for anyone who did not see Burton."

It was an exhausted Burton that returned to London on 14th February, but he was a man with stars in his eyes.

# AND GOD CREATED BURTON

# CHAPTER 16

# Family Life With Sybil

## *A kind of domestic bliss*

### 1949 to 1955

Straight after the marriage of Richard Burton and Sybil Williams, all their friends knew it was a match made in heaven. She was the attractive, intelligent, energetic, creative, highly personable slender wife who also excelled as a homemaker. It's no exaggeration to say she was as good a choice of wife as any woman in the land. Many saw her as an extension of Burton's mother Edith, his sister Cecilia, his old landlady Elizabeth Smith and mentor Daphne Rye, all rolled into one. Burton knew how lucky he was, and their closest friends regarded their union as the ultimate match. A word that frequently came up when she was being described was "nurturing" and she just seemed to understand his *raison d'être* – his inner compulsion to prove himself time and time again – better than anyone else. Robert Hardy concluded: "There was a wonderful sort of camaraderie thing between the two of them."

And everyone thought that; no one had a bad word to say about Sybil. Her pleasant and easygoing personality combined with her sweet Welsh accent put everyone at their ease straightaway. As Hardy said: "She had a genius for engineering contentment and happiness."

Sybil nurtured his family, and the Jenkins family absolutely adored her in turn. Sybil very quickly became a fully paid-up member of the Jenkins clan. It was a clan that, once joined, made you a member for life. And no one had any doubt Sybil had signed up for a long time to come. They loved her most for her Welshness and her devotion to Burton. She encouraged him to visit Wales regularly and the two of them delighted the family by singing Welsh songs.

The universal adoration of Sybil even extended to the girls who fervently desired her husband; girls such as Claire Bloom and Mary Ure. Sybil always behaved with incredible dignity, and if other people seemed embarrassed at her husband's behaviour, she immediately put them at ease. She didn't make it difficult for them to be with her because of her husband's conduct, and that is what made her so popular – even with his mistresses.

Her popularity was built around her directness, which was so charming and so unassuming that she was impossible to dislike. She was a real personality in her own right and, combined with all her other talents, it was impossible to overstate her appeal.

But despite that, it didn't hide the fact that, at the age of 23, a consummate ladies man like Richard Burton should never have become married to any woman, however good. And so it came to pass that infidelity marked every facet of the marriage for 13 years: he was unfaithful straight after he met Sybil; he was unfaithful straight after he was engaged to her; and he was unfaithful even on their wedding night. He simply couldn't help himself.

But Sybil had an advantage over all the other women; she shared his Welsh heritage and his language. She had come from the same place as Burton, which was something none of his other women could claim. And she had known him when he was an ordinary actor just starting out.

Such an advantage meant that, despite all the infidelity, they remained together in London for the next seven years, and the marriage was an extremely happy one.

They were charmingly known as "Rich and Syb" and, to anyone looking in, it was a perfect marriage. It worked because, despite his dominant personality and ever-growing fame, when they were alone together it was a marriage of equals and Sybil was never made to feel either inadequate or inferior in his company – it was the vital ingredient to why it all worked so well. She was never at any moment in any doubt that she was his wife. She said: "He's about giving me confidence, making me feel people want to meet me equally." Although he had an instinctive urge to dominate every scene in his life, Sybil adored that side of him and was never possessive. And she never sought to change him.

Their growing circle of friends adored her as much as they did him. Robert Hardy remembered a wonderfully intimate exchange between them as they discussed their sex life: "He would talk about sex, and I remember him saying that the most wonderful thing in life is, after a good night's sleep, to wake up very, very early in the morning and think: 'I am going to have her.' She was in the room at the time and he turned to her and said: 'Isn't that right, boot?' 'Oh Rich', she said, 'Oh Rich.'" Penny Junor described them as "a delightful couple, speaking to one another in nursery talk, teasing one another and playing the fool."

In fact, Burton revelled in his status as a married man. Sybil accompanied him to every official or semi-official engagement and would often visit the theatre or film sets where he was working. When she did, he always gave her a mighty welcome, introducing her proudly to everybody – including any women he may have been sleeping with at the time.

The newly married Burtons spent the first year of their life together living on the top floor of Daphne Rye's house at Pelham Crescent in Kensington. Emlyn and Molly Williams also lived in Pelham Crescent a few doors down.

Emlyn and Molly, together with their young children, Alan and Brook, were delighted when Richard and Sybil moved in next door. Emlyn had arguably become Burton's principal mentor and was a very important part of Burton's early life. He had introduced him to Sybil and encouraged the relationship every step of the way. After they were married, he continually introduced both of them to his well-connected friends in the theatre. The value of the introductions to an up-and-coming theatrical couple like the Burtons, from one of the best connected men in the theatre, was incalculable.

The Burtons had also landed on their feet geographically. The Chelsea and Kensington areas of London in the fifties were the places to be for a rising young actor and his wife. The theatrical community clustered in either Chelsea or Kensington or, alternatively, Hampstead in North London for those who preferred a more rural environment. Famous names of the profession were well represented in the smart Georgian and Victorian terraces that littered the area. It was the era before the foreign invasion, when the pleasures of London living were a well kept secret and house prices were dirt cheap. Every weekend, the young couple rubbed shoulders with the great and the good of London theatre.

The marriage had a great first year – they were both in well-paid work and Burton's career really began to take off. But it was often a lonely existence for both of them. Sybil worked as an assistant stage manager in the evenings and Burton was away during the day at rehearsals. Many days they barely saw each other and were like the proverbial passing ships.

In February, straight after they were married, Burton went on the road with the provincial tour of 'The Lady's Not For Burning'. He was away for two whole months during March and April, and Sybil's job meant she could not join him. They were only reunited when he returned for the play's London run from May to December.

When they were together in London, in the latter half of 1949, they settled into a routine. He used to get up the moment he opened his eyes, which could be as early as four in the morning. It was a legacy from his early days in Port

# AND GOD CREATED BURTON

Talbot, where the local miners began work at 6:30am. Wide awake, he would prowl the kitchen and the living room, usually with a cup of tea in one hand and a cigarette alight in the other, deep in impenetrable thoughts.

When the urge to prowl was exhausted, he would settle in his favorite armchair and sit almost bolt upright to read for two hours before going out to work.

Never a man to waste a moment, Burton's days were packed full of activity. In his younger days, if ever he had a day without work or a planned activity, it would inevitably be an unhappy day. He was the sort of man who had to have somewhere to go. His place to go in those days was the theatre or a film set, and he was never truly happy unless he was off to either. He had one of those strange personalities that desired leisure time and freedom but, when the desire was achieved, he rejected it and sought even more work and activity instead.

On days when neither of them were working, he would inevitably go out to meet a woman; that is, unless Sybil put her foot down. When he escaped, which in truth was most days, he would invariably say he would be home for lunch, and then almost always never turn up, having found a better offer elsewhere. Often, he would not return until after midnight, having caught the last train from wherever just before the London underground railway closed for the night. Sybil hardly ever complained about his absences except when he forgot her birthday or their wedding anniversary, then there would be hell to pay.

On the few occasions that she barked, he listened. For the most part, Burton recognised that his wife was more than a match for him, and he knew better than to push his luck. If he put his coat on to go off to a liaison with a mistress – which he would tell her was a drink with Stanley or another such lie – she would tell him he was going nowhere as she had his is supper ready for him.

One of Sybil's favourite responses when Burton told her what he had planned was: "You'd better not be." And with that, he knew he had to change his plans. It didn't happen often, but it was one of the few phrases that used to stick in Burton's head and to which he would respond almost subconsciously, just as he had to Binkie Beaumont's "Look me up" all those years before. Depending on the look on his face, Sybil would often follow up her comment with: "...or there'll be trouble."

Married life in those early years was marked by Sybil's tolerance of her husband. At home, she fell into the role of the wife of a special man, subjugating her own personality to fit in almost as an adjunct to his own. It was just the way it was. But although Burton ostensibly 'wore the trousers' in the household, it wasn't cut and dried. Sybil had a very determined 'don't mess with me' streak that endured throughout the marriage and only failed her in 1962, when bigger forces overwhelmed the armoury that had held the marriage together.

In many ways, Sybil was undoubtedly much more mature than her husband and had the sense to recognise and accept her situation not grudgingly, but gracefully.

One of her secrets was that she was a very down-to-earth housewife in the best Welsh tradition. She was a superb cook and looked after her man in exemplary fashion. He had the best of everything that they could afford. The house was always immaculate and the towels and bed linen as fresh as daisies. She also excelled at managing their money.

But the real glue that kept their marriage together was their companionship, especially in the early years of the marriage in Hampstead. He loved being with her. His other relationships at the time were purely sexual. When he had dinner with Sybil, it was intellectually stimulating. She was simply a great companion, very quick witted with real intellectual depth. She also had exactly the right mix of what Burton called "front", that is, the ability to sort out day-to-day problems quickly and simply with no fuss for him. There is no question that Sybil understood Burton's foibles and undoubted inadequacies, peculiar compulsions and obsessions, and she wholly tolerated them. Their friends totally admired her for it. They believed that she was a modern day saint, as Robert Hardy said: "Sybil was born to flower with Richard."

But Hardy insisted Sybil wasn't the sort of wife who clung on: "There was nothing insipid about her. She was certainly not the little woman waiting with a boring smile when Lothario came home." Graham Jenkins summed her up best: "She never did anything that was not with his interests in mind, but in a curious sort of way she gained strength from giving so much."

Sir John Gielgud was another admirer: "She was a wonderful wife to Richard. I mean, she put up with the late nights when he'd come back with the boys and suddenly she'd have to cook scrambled eggs for five chaps. She took it all in her stride and adored it and didn't disapprove. No disapproval about it; it was part of the life she knew Richard enjoyed." Hardy remembered: "I don't know how she coped with Rich telling her he'd be back for lunch and not turning up till dinner and, then, with Stanley or some other pals. He took such chances, but Syb never seemed to bother."

# AND GOD CREATED BURTON

As for Sybil, she seemed eternally grateful to be Mrs Richard Burton. She always told people that her husband was "wonderful."

Although everyone adored them as a couple, and, as perfect a wife as Sybil was, Burton's increasing activity with other women led to increasing questions about whether he should have married at all. Graham Jenkins, his brother, was one who believed he should never have married: "Though he never said as much, at least not to me, I feel certain that for Rich marriage was a quick dash for security. He needed a fixed point, a base where he could put up the shutters and feel secure." Graham thought that the marriage could not survive long term and that it would one day blow up. It was a very prescient thought.

There is no question that Burton's treatment of his wife allayed all her suspicions about his fidelity. And if she ever did hear any whispers, she dismissed them as malicious. For his part, Burton was obsessed with Sybil not finding out about his dalliances. Not wishing to hurt her, Burton was aided in his adventures by the complicity of others in his cover ups. Everyone but everyone, including Sybil's closest friends, participated in the cover ups. Burton implicitly expected such complicity from his and Sybil's friends, and he always got it.

He got it by assuring them that the affairs were a necessary part of an enduring marriage. His friends and family realised he was not the faithful type, and he reassured them frequently and persistently that he would never leave his wife, no matter what happened. It almost became his mantra, as he stated time and again: "I'll never hurt Syb. I'll never leave Syb." Melvyn Bragg called it a "vow repeated endlessly," and, as Bragg observed, eventually the lies and deceits became so vast and so complicated that he lost track and had to rely on luck to get him through.

There was also a paradox. He never seemed to care who saw him or who knew about his infidelities. As Bragg noted: "That was life as he lived it, and that was that." Another oft-used line was: "I'll never divorce Sybil and she'll never divorce me...she thinks I'm a genius." And in many ways, and in that way in particular, it was a true partnership.

Burton got away with his womanising because he was smart about it. He had a vague heroic notion about his wife and placed Sybil on a pedestal. Whatever else he was up to on the side, she was his number one and everyone knew it, even his girls. This rule didn't change until 1962. Whilst Sybil never knew about any of his other women, all his other women knew about Sybil. This one-way transparency meant that the deception did not become too complicated - his other women knew and understood his priorities and never violated the unwritten rule.

The story of his women in this period is amazing. None of them became a problem to his marriage, but the women were far more of a problem to each other than they were to Sybil. Some of them knew Sybil and loved her, even while they were carrying on with her husband. They also became obsessed with not hurting Sybil and were thereby complicit in the cover up.

Burton had the good sense never to flaunt his extramarital affairs in front of the people he really cared about – people such as Emlyn Williams, Daphne Rye and Philip Burton. Williams, who led a somewhat peculiar life himself, being at once bisexual and happily married, did not judge, saying: "He never discussed that sort of thing with me. He knew how fond I was of Sybil."

Fergus Cashin, the journalist who was his earliest biographer, wrote of his liaisons: "It was almost invariably people he was acting with. It was not that he was a great sort of Casanova; he had to know that everybody loved him. That's a very common thing with star actors. The need to be loved is very strong. It is what they put their energy into, making audiences love them, and he carried it into his life to an astonishing extent. I think very often the affairs were not lust – only seeking reassurance that he was loved."

What bothered his friends, of course, were some of the low-life women he occasionally consorted with and also, very occasionally, the girls who were under-aged and therefore outside the law. Those girls were all highly developed and old for their age but were nonetheless risky liaisons. That predilection, albeit admittedly rare, could at any moment have destroyed his marriage and his career.

Despite Cashin being a journalist, Burton told him what he told everyone else: "It's all right, I'd never leave Sybil, you know. I'd never let her know that I've done this." According to Cashin, Burton was "absolutely convinced that he could never leave Sybil, never divorce her."

Sybil handled it by ignoring it unless her husband actually admitted it to her, which he never did. In fact, for 13 years, right up until 1962, as far as Sybil was concerned, it never happened and would never happen. But some dispute that, saying Sybil knew about each and every one of his affairs and that she simply decided it was the necessary price she had to pay to keep hold of a husband she adored and could not imagine a life without. Robert Hardy, for one, subscribes to that theory.

Sybil never caught Richard in the act because he was always very careful to shield her from his activities. He was helped by virtue of his very low fertility, which meant no girl ever became pregnant. And by luck or judgment, he generally avoided married or attached women altogether, meaning there were never any irate partners to make trouble or to give him away. As far as his other women were concerned, he led a charmed life until 1962.

Burton had something inbuilt within him which meant he never entered any situation that was dangerous to his marriage. For instance, in the first year that he knew Claire Bloom, nothing untoward happened between them despite them appearing to fall in love. Subconsciously, he seemed to recognise that if anything had happened straight after his wedding, the bond with Sybil could have been broken, and he did not want that.

Sybil simply led the double life of a well-grounded, intelligent woman as well as a fantasist as far as her husband's fidelity was concerned. She had no problems with his extramarital activities because she never knew about them and, if she did, chose not to believe them. It was as simple as that.

Sybil understood her husband was a romantic figure of deadly fascination to women, and that was that. Sometimes she questioned her husband closely when she had suspicions, but as long as he denied it, there was not a problem. On the few occasions that he might have been tempted to confess, he soon realised the folly of it by her implied reaction.

There should be no mistaking that Sybil was a very proud woman; if she had known the extent of what was going on, or had he flaunted it in front of her, she would have left him. No one should doubt the inner strength that existed within her.

That situation enabled Burton to successfully maintain his dual role as a family man and a playboy. That he was able to reconcile these two conflicting images was due wholly to the exceptional qualities of Sybil.

Robert Hardy believed that Sybil knew about many of his affairs and simply forgave him every time: "She got to know by charming friends who would report to her what he was doing with other women, but she forgave him because she loved him profoundly and passionately and that was her gift to him; to say: 'I do not like it, but if you must, you must, and I will love you forever.'"

But perhaps Sybil's biggest attribute, even more than her ability to cope with Burton's chronic unfaithfulness, was her ability to cope with her husband's drinking. His addiction to alcohol as a young man was far less of a problem than it was when he became older, when, in middle age, he would often become abusive after he drank. Only occasionally did the abusive streak manifest itself in his twenties, and Sybil tolerated and excused him as well as she could. She recognised the behaviour from her experiences with her own father.

One aspect Sybil did not have to worry about was the family finances, which went from strength to strength in the first year of their marriage. In 1949, Burton earned around £700 after tax and Sybil took home £200. It was a very large income in those days and they managed to save half of it towards buying a house, which was their focus for most of the first year of marriage. That and trying for a baby, which never seemed to come. In case a baby did arrive, Sybil decided she would like to live in the leafy London suburb of Hampstead, which was the alternative actors' community in London. They were encouraged in this by Philip Burton, who had happily settled in Hampstead, and they came to know the area well from their regular Sunday visits to his flat.

Towards the end of the year, they found a house at 6 Lyndhurst Road, only five minutes from Philip's flat. The property market was as depressed as it could be after the war, and many London houses damaged in German air raids had still not been repaired and were for sale.

The Lyndhurst Road house was a typical bomb damaged dwelling which had been unoccupied since the war and was waiting for a buyer with cash to repair it. Burton and Sybil were able to buy it for the knock down price of £2,000 against the £3 – £4,000 it would have been worth in top condition.

But the Burtons only had half the purchase price, and any sort of mortgage was out of the question. Building societies in those days would only give mortgages to people over 30 years of age with regular, long-established jobs. The Burtons qualified in neither respect. So they needed to borrow that money, and Burton's new agent, Vere Barker, came to the rescue and lent the couple £750 to complete the purchase of the house. Burton's income was then approaching £30 a week and, combined with Sybil's salary, was easily enough to pay the builders every week for the renovation. Sybil also discovered that there were government grants available to repair war damaged houses, and she managed to obtain £200 by this method.

So, as 1950 dawned, the Burtons came to own their first house together.

The builders tackled the roof first so as to make the house habitable for them to move into, which they did quickly. Another floor was quickly made good and that was let out. It took eight months to complete the repairs, which cost around £500.

# AND GOD CREATED BURTON

About the same time as the repairs were underway and the Burtons moved in, suddenly living out in the sticks of Hampstead made Burton realise that he needed a car. Up to the age of 25, he had never driven; relying on buses, the train and the occasional taxi. Now that he was becoming well known as a film actor, he decided he should learn to drive and procure a vehicle. But every penny they earned was going on house repairs and towards repaying Barker for his loan. Buying the house had left them very poor, despite Burton's high income.

He bought himself a secondhand black Austin four door saloon car that cost £175. Once he became familiar with driving, his eye fell on a secondhand four-year-old grey coloured Jaguar Mark IV saloon on sale at £600. The Mark IV saloon was beautifully styled and looked more like a sports car than a big saloon. The Jaguar suited the young aspiring actor perfectly. He talked Binkie Beaumont into lending him the money for it.

Halfway through 1950, Sybil departed for a long tour of the provinces with 'Harvey', which had finished its London run after a year. She was the assistant stage manager and had no choice but to leave her husband in their new house alone. Well, not quite alone. Stanley Baker, who was Burton's closest friend, had nowhere to live, so Sybil suggested that Baker move into the Hampstead house whilst she was away to keep her husband company and, more importantly, to keep an eye on the builders when Burton was out. With that, Sybil happily went off on tour.

For virtually the whole summer of 1950, with Sybil gone, Burton abandoned any proprietary behaviour and brought back all sorts of girls to the house and slept with them virtually every night – often in the marital bed.

Around this time, Stanley Baker met a girl called Ellen Martin, an aspiring blonde actress. Within a week of their meeting, she had moved into the house with her new boyfriend. The speed with which their relationship developed was astonishing and, within two weeks, they were engaged and Ellen had taken him to meet her parents.

And Ellen had Burton to thank for everything. They met after he took Baker along to a lunchtime omelette party in the dressing rooms at the Apollo Theatre in Shaftesbury Avenue, London. Ellen was appearing in a production called 'Treasure Hunt' and she had organised the party with her friends.

Even in 1950, five years after the end of the war, rationing was still in place and omelette parties were very popular. Entry to the party was dependent on bringing along eggs, which were then difficult to get and much prized. Burton was supposed to bring some eggs, which was what Baker believed he had in his brown paper bag. But, instead of eggs, Burton had a bag of red cherries. Ellen and her friends were about to throw him out when she spotted Baker standing sheepishly behind him.

Ellen was immediately attracted to Baker and told her friend they should not be so hasty about telling them to leave. The friend could see she was interested in the two men and initially thought it was Burton who had taken her fancy. But it was Baker. In fact, she had instantly been smitten, calling him the "tall beautiful one." But Ellen's friend warned her off and told her that Baker had a certain reputation, and his girlfriends were known collectively as 'Baker's Dozen' due to their quantity. She was warned if she pursued him, she would merely be the 13th in a group of many. Ellen told her friend that, if that was what it took, then she would gladly become number 13.

There was also another problem in that Ellen had a steady boyfriend. Burton invited Ellen and her friends to a party that same evening and Ellen attended with her boyfriend, whom she had already arranged to meet. But she dropped him that very evening and took up with Baker. They soon became inseparable. Contrary to her new boyfriend's reputation, Ellen found him to be immaculately behaved and saw no sign of the reputed 'dozen'. From that day onwards, Baker was cured of his womanising ways.

But that certainly wasn't true of Richard Burton.

Ellen hardly knew Burton but was astonished at the way he behaved, blatantly bringing women back to the house whilst his wife, whom she had never met, was away. When she challenged Stanley Baker about it, he just shrugged. So she came to believe it was Burton's normal behaviour and that Sybil must know about it and condone it. But that didn't stop her being astonished at the sheer number of affairs.

With Sybil away, Burton's activity increased five-fold and Ellen watched as he collected girls from local pubs as well as shops and even from queues at cinemas. When he was entertaining and wooing special girls, he used to ask Ellen to go out whilst he performed. She would go to local cafés and wait for Baker to come home. She could hardly complain as they were both living in the house rent-free and Baker's career took a lot longer to take off than Burton's, while Ellen worked only infrequently.

When Sybil got a rare weekend off and returned to London, Ellen suddenly realised that Sybil had no idea what her husband was up to while she was away. Ellen couldn't believe the situation she was in when Burton took her aside and swore her to secrecy. Ellen wondered what sort of naïve simple woman she was about to meet. She was astonished again when Sybil finally arrived and couldn't understand why any man would want to be unfaithful to such an amazing woman.

And she was amazed again when Burton simply picked up where he had left off after Sybil returned to the provinces. Ellen did note, however, how frightened Burton became at the prospect that Sybil might discover what he was up to. She recalled many years later to Burton biographer Penny Junor an incident with the bed sheets. It concerned a set of pink silk sheets Sybil had bought from America, where they were all the rage at the time and which couldn't be obtained in post war austerity Britain.

One night, Burton brought home a waitress he met at a local café who had deep red, dyed auburn hair done up in a bun high on her head. It was a hot night at the height of the August heat, and during the very sweaty high jinks that night, the dye she used on her hair reacted with the silk and came off all over the bedding.

The following morning, after she had left, Burton saw the stains on the silk sheets and panicked. He asked Ellen to wash the sheets and get the dye out. But, try as she might, Ellen could do nothing to shift the colour, and Burton had no idea how to explain it to Sybil.

The set of sheets had been obtained specially by Sybil and couldn't be replaced without asking her where she had purchased them. Ellen told Burton firmly that he would have to go and ask the girl what dye she had used on her hair. But she had no idea he was married, and Burton didn't wish to explain it to the girl. So Ellen had to go to the café herself and ask the girl which hair dye she had used. When she learned that, they were then able to figure out what to do to get the colour out of the sheets.

Despite her poor impression of Burton – one that never really went away despite her husband's great friendship with him – Ellen does credit him with persuading her boyfriend to propose to her.

It all happened very quickly, and Ellen Baker told Penny Junor many years later that she thought Burton was directly responsible for them getting married so quickly. As she explained, she and Burton were travelling home together on a train from Ealing studios, where they had both been working. At this point, she had known Baker for barely two weeks. Suddenly, Burton turned in his seat and said to her: "Do you want to marry Stanley?" She replied: "Yes, of course I do. But he's not going to ask me, is he?"

It was an extraordinary question and an equally extraordinary response after only two weeks of them knowing each other, but Burton said: "Just leave it to me. I think he should be married. I'm married."

That evening, when he returned home, Burton took his friend aside and asked him outright: "Are you going to marry Ellen?" Baker replied: "I've only known her two weeks" and implied he thought the question rather impertinent.

Then Burton said: "Have you met her parents?" Baker said he had.

Burton then asked him where Ellen's parents lived, to which Baker replied: "Stoke Poges", rather a pleasant village in Buckinghamshire. Burton simply told him with no explanation: "Well then, you know what they expect."

Baker was baffled but later admitted it did plant the idea in his mind where previously it had not existed. And that night, Baker duly asked Ellen if she would marry him, exactly as Burton had instructed him. Ellen replied: "Tomorrow – provided you're not like him." Baker famously replied: "Darling, nobody's like Richard."

When Sybil returned from her provincial tour in September 1950, the Burtons suddenly got itchy feet and, having completed the work at Lyndhurst Road, decided they wanted something better. As 1950 turned into 1951, Burton was earning £100 a week from his new contract with Alexander Korda and had got a one-off fee of £1,200 for appearing in his second feature film. House prices in Hampstead were still very cheap so they decided to invest in their good fortune in the shape of more bricks and mortar and buy a terraced cottage in Squires Mount and completely rebuild it. By then, they could easily afford to buy the house outright and renovate it. It became 10 Squires Mount.

They lived there for the next five years, and it was only a nine-minute walk from Hampstead railway station. They instructed builders and prepared to leave for America and Burton's debut on Broadway. But there was one special occasion to attend before they left. On 2nd October 1950, Stanley Baker and Ellen Martin were married at St George's Church in London's Hanover Square. It was a weekend of riotous behaviour. The following day, the Burtons left for New York aboard the Queen Mary en route to Broadway.

As they journeyed slowly across the Atlantic, Sybil could not have been happier. Here, she had her husband all to herself. She also resolved during the voyage to pull down the curtain on her own acting career, which, since her marriage, she had not taken too seriously. She had one commitment left to fulfil – in 1951, at Stratford. After that, she resolved, she would devote herself to being Burton's wife.

189

# CHAPTER 17

# The Summer of '51

## *The best year of their lives*

### 1951

One bright sunny day in February 1950, Sybil Burton was pottering around her house in Lyndhurst Road, Hampstead, tending to her housework when she heard the telephone ring. When she picked it up, on the other end was Anthony Quayle, the celebrated actor and director of Stratford-upon-Avon's Memorial Theatre.

The canny Sybil knew who it was immediately, and Quayle's call had been well-timed to find Sybil home alone. She was flattered that Quayle asked for her and not her husband, and after he introduced himself, he launched into what was probably a pre-rehearsed pitch. After the usual pleasantries, with her gently reminding him that they had met previously, there was some sundry conversation about the unseasonably beautiful February weather of the past few days. Finally, he came to the point and offered Sybil a part in the special Shakespeare season that he was staging at Stratford the following summer. He wanted her to play the Welsh-speaking Lady Mortimer in Shakespeare's 'Henry IV'.

Sybil had the breath sucked out of her and didn't know what to say. It was the biggest and best role she had ever been offered, and she just about managed a "yes". Her response seemed to flummox Quayle, who said: "Well, you're very much on my list." Sybil was momentarily disappointed as she thought he had been offering her the part, not a mere place on his list. Still, she thought, just being considered for it was a great honour. But then, Quayle let her in on the real reason for his call, although she didn't realise it at the time: "Now try and get your husband to play Prince Hal, and we'll see what we can do." Sybil said she would and put the phone down, shaking with excitement.

But as bright as Sybil Burton was, she had failed to spot the real motivation behind the call. When her husband returned that evening, she couldn't wait to tell him that Anthony Quayle had been on the phone and that she was on the short list to play Lady Mortimer at Stratford. At the time, a call from Quayle was a very big deal for any actor. He was probably the biggest name in classical theatre. At only 38 years of age, he had acquired a reputation as an established classical actor, a noted director and a very talented theatre administrator. His combined abilities had won him the directorship of the Memorial Theatre Group two years earlier, and 1951 would be his third season in charge at Stratford. His first two seasons had been highly successful; he had astonished Stratford's theatregoers by bringing in such top notch actors as John Gielgud and Peggy Ashcroft to Stratford for the first time.

His plans for the 1951 season were even more ambitious. He had decided to stage a programme of five of Shakespeare's plays: 'Richard II'; 'Henry IV' Parts 1 and 2; 'Henry V'; and 'The Tempest'. He would effectively merge the first four together as one continuous production with the same actors conjoining their parts and present them as a continuing story. Strangely, despite the fact that Shakespeare probably saw them as one linked play, such a continuum had never before been attempted. All previous productions had been mounted as distinct entities. To make it work, Quayle would cast the same lead actor to play Prince Hal in 'Henry IV', Parts 1 and 2, who would then go on to become King in 'Henry V'. The other running parts would also be conjoined across the three productions.

It was an unprecedented opportunity and the role of Prince Hal was a potentially reputation-making (or breaking) part.

Quayle's idea was to bring a new understanding to Shakespeare's history cycle by making Prince Hal the centre of a narrative that carries through the plays. But he needed a very strong actor with great power and presence to carry it off. Quayle knew there would be many actors who thought they could do it, but very few who actually could. Unfortunately, he couldn't think of a single actor who he believed could pull it off.

So in early 1950, realising he had a problem, Quayle began a search by going to see as many productions as he could – looking for a young actor to play the most difficult and testing role ever created for the English stage.

There was also an additional challenge. The 1951 season was very special because it was part of a larger event being held that year, known as the Festival of Britain. The Festival had been conceived to boost the morale of British citizens, which, six years after the Second World War had ended, was at an all-time low.

After the war, for reasons best known to itself, the incoming Labour government of Clement Atlee had decided to continue the system of rationing. It had also reintroduced National Service and, naturally, the effect on morale was disastrous. The Festival was Atlee's idea and was designed to try and rectify those twin mistakes now that rationing was gradually being phased out and National Service had finally ended.

There was also a need to attract foreigners, particularly Americans, to Britain again. With rationing in force, the Americans had naturally stayed away. But petrol rationing had ended in 1950, as it had on most other important items. The Festival of Britain was designed to tell the world Britain was back in business as a nation, or, at least, as Melvyn Bragg put it: "There were new teeth in the new bulldog."

Quayle's job was to serve up a season of Shakespeare in Stratford that Americans would flock to. He knew he had a big responsibility on his shoulders as he had to create a programme that would appeal to the huge numbers of culture-imbibing Americans who needed a reason to come to England. Clement Atlee hoped Anthony Quayle would be that reason. And Quayle felt the responsibility keenly.

The project was already underway and, when the 1950 season ended, a big refurbishment of the Memorial Theatre would get started with the installation of a large number of new seats to boost capacity by as much as a third.

But that was the easy bit compared with finding the right actor to play the lead role. Quayle had already decided he would play Sir Jack Falstaff and Michael Redgrave would play Richard II and Hotspur, but he had no idea how to cast the part of Prince Hal, Falstaff's young accomplice, a boy who tries to turn his back on his destiny.

Quayle decided to start from scratch and set out on a tour of the theatres of Britain looking for his Prince Hal – who, he hoped, was out there somewhere.

It was that search, or quest as he called it, which brought him to the Lyric Theatre in Hammersmith on Wednesday 18th January 1950 to see John Gielgud's production of Christopher Fry's 'The Boy With A Cart'.

When he arrived and took his seat, he was immediately spotted by members of the cast. They were all excited, as Quayle's reputation as a renowned talent spotter went before him. When Quayle cast an actor, it was effectively an advertisement of his talent. But although his power with up-and-coming young actors was absolute, it was rather different when it came to the established stars. There he had a problem, as he had to persuade them to work for half a year for a tiny stipend, probably a quarter of what they could get in the West End or on a film set. It was sometimes very tough to persuade top stars to give up so much money, even for the prestige of appearing at the Memorial Theatre.

As soon as Quayle saw Richard Burton in the title role of 'The Boy With A Cart', he knew his problem was solved. Quayle remembered: "There he was, that was Hal, straight bang-off, no question about it. He was simply magical." Astonishingly, the previous year he had seen 'The Lady's Not for Burning' in London and Quayle, for the life of him, couldn't understand why he had failed to notice Burton at all.

But although a very excited Quayle believed he had found the perfect actor to play Prince Hal, he decided not go backstage at the Lyric that night to pitch to Burton directly. He slipped out of the theatre before the end, as he anticipated all sorts of problems persuading him to do it.

Hence the phone call to Sybil Burton a few weeks later.

When Burton got home that night, Sybil excitedly told him what had happened. She expected a congratulatory hug but was very surprised when her husband just burst out laughing. For his part, Burton was genuinely surprised that Sybil, with all her street smarts, couldn't see what Quayle was up to.

Burton was not at all fooled. He guessed immediately what was going on as soon as Sybil opened her mouth. And he knew enough about his wife's acting ability to know she would never get a personal call from Quayle offering her a part.

When he gently explained the situation to Sybil, she was not in the least offended and admitted that she herself had found the approach from Quayle strange. She had already worked out she was not God's gift to the acting profession, and in her own mind, had already decided to give it up to be a full time housewife to her husband as soon as was practicable.

Quayle had been 100 per cent right about Burton's reaction. He was not desperately keen to take up the offer although the role of Prince Hal in Stratford was easily the best part he had ever been offered. Even though it would be a golden opportunity to establish himself properly as a classical actor and his first real opportunity to play Shakespeare in a lead role with the most prestigious theatre company in the world, he did not immediately grab at it.

Burton was earning a tremendous amount of money, and although he desperately wanted to do it, he calculated it would cost him around £10,000 in lost opportunities on Broadway and the West End, not to mention any film parts Alexander Korda may have thrown at him. He was also paying for two houses and was in the middle of a costly conversion of his new one at Squires Mount. All that meant it would be a difficult decision for him. Taking Quayle's offer would probably prove mighty expensive. And what if he failed?

And there was another problem which he had never revealed to anyone. Although both he and Philip Burton would often pontificate to journalists about their love of Shakespeare, the truth was that Burton wasn't that keen – he loved the idea, but not the reality. He adored Shakespeare's writings but didn't like acting it. As his brother Graham Jenkins revealed: "Rich was notoriously unsentimental in his attitude to Shakespeare. He had a hankering for the great roles but a nightly appearance in doublet and hose did not of itself appeal." Jenkins also believed that his brother was frightened of being on stage and not comparing well with Quayle, Redgrave, not to mention Harry Andrews. He was still worried about being "found out", as he put it.

Redgrave, Quayle and Andrews were acclaimed Shakespearian actors, and Burton believed there was a real risk that his own inexperience would show and bring his glittering career to a sudden halt.

He thought the likelihood that he could outshine Quayle as Falstaff, Redgrave as Hotspur and Andrews as Henry IV very unlikely. Even worse, from Burton's point of view, Quayle had hired the cream of British actors for the lesser roles. They were all younger actors who would go on to become stars in their own right, including Alan Badel, Geoffrey Balydon, William Fox, Hugh Griffith, Richard Wordsworth, Barbara Jefford, William Squire, Duncan Lamont and Robert Hardy. Playing with all these excellent actors frightened Burton to death. Against that, he really admired and liked Quayle for what he had achieved at Stratford. He was also full of admiration for the clever ploy to involve Sybil in his plan to ensnare him. In fact, far from resenting it, Quayle went up in both Sybil's and Richard's estimations. Burton said when recalling the approach years later: "That's real common Welsh slyness. If you want something, go after it – none of this English fair play or decency." Quayle agreed: "I think Richard rather enjoyed that sly approach.'

In truth, playing Prince Hal was a dream come true and Burton was tempted to say 'yes' straightaway, almost in spite of his reservations. The challenge was formidable as he genuinely had no feel for whether he could pull it off.

He probably would have said 'no' but for a concerted campaign that was begun by his family and friends. Sybil was not alone in urging him to take the plunge. John Gielgud was also strongly in favour, as was Philip Burton. In the face of that pressure, and despite his reservations, he quickly realised that Prince Hal was a part he was desperate to play.

And when Burton looked closely at the sheer quality of the cast Quayle had assembled, the prospect of not being part of it suddenly became a bigger risk than the fear of being part of it. Burton realised that, sooner or later, he would have to put himself up against this sort of talent and be compared. He figured that it might as well be sooner rather than later. After much prevarication, he finally decided to risk his career and say 'yes' to Quayle.

Burton was also delighted that he would get to spend the summer with Robert Hardy, who had been recruited to Stratford direct from Oxford in 1949. Also cast was his good friend, fellow Welshman, Hugh Griffith, who he had met on the set of *The Last Days of Dolwyn*.

But first, Burton drove a hard bargain with Quayle, who was eventually forced to pay him £36 a week, the highest fee the Memorial had ever paid an actor until then. The rest of the actors had to make do with £16 a week.

As soon as he had concluded his contract with Quayle, Burton rushed round to Philip Burton's house to give him the news. Philip was ecstatic and after his protégé left, he picked up his dairy and just wrote "wonderful" on the space for that day. Philip had dreamt that one day Richard would take his true place as a classical actor. This was that moment.

Burton knew it was going to be a great summer when Hugh Griffith called and offered to put him and Sybil up at a manor house called 'The Old House', which he had rented in the village of Oxhill. It was 14 miles from Stratford-upon-Avon, and Griffith had taken it for the whole seven month season. Robert Hardy was also invited. Griffith told Burton: "We'll set up a little Wales in Warwickshire. What do you think of that, boyo?"

The Burtons felt at home straightaway at Oxhill. True to his word, Griffith and his wife Gunda had bedecked the house in a Welsh theme and brought along his three 'Welsh' corgis, called Branwen, Olwen and Matholwch. He told Burton the insignia of the Welsh dragon would be on display in every room and that, during rehearsals, some Welsh language could be introduced into 'Henry V' where there was no dialogue available from Shakespeare's original writings. Burton loved the idea and started looking forward to going.

By the time he and Sybil arrived in Stratford, in the third week of March, they were well established as a couple. They were also rich. Burton was earning the equivalent of £12,000 a year from Alexander Korda and his stage and television work. He owned two houses in Hampstead and was a bona fide British domestic film star at the age of 26. The £1,000 he would earn for the seven-month Shakespeare season was just topping up that income.

There was barely just over a week for rehearsals and they did not go brilliantly. First, there was an unspoken division between Anthony Quayle's vision of Prince Hal and Philip Burton's vision of him. The Burtons decided it would be done their way and there was little Quayle could do about it. Quayle's vision of Prince Hal was the traditional, jolly, thigh-slapping character but Philip Burton's was a more dour but powerful character, with hidden strengths and moods and great physical presence. There was no question that the audiences preferred Philip's rendition.

Quayle later dismissed suggestions of any dispute about how Burton should interpret the character and sought to rewrite history, getting angry with suggestions to the opposite. But Burton confessed that Quayle had nearly sacked him from the part, as he said: "I remember that I was nearly fired because I tried to explain that what I was trying to do was to be solitary and removed and cold and certainly not the thigh-slapping, stamping, roaring-with-laughter Prince Hal that we'd all been accustomed to." There is no doubt that Burton risked everything in taking on Quayle and could easily have been fired.

Two years off his 40th birthday, Quayle was at the height of his powers, and his talents had already made him very rich. He was not a man to be messed about with. He was an impressive character, drove an expensive Bentley motor car and lived in some style. Aside from rehearsals, he remained aloof from his actors. As Robert Hardy recalled: "He was the artistic director but, to us, he was the boss who drove about in a Bentley and who would have you to supper once in the season if you behaved well."

Paul Ferris, Burton's biographer, who later had some long and difficult interviews with Quayle before he died, believes that the director was shocked when he came up against what he called Burton's "raw quality." And Robert Hardy remembers Quayle saying to him: "'Your chum needs a kick up the arse', or words to that effect."

As was becoming usual, Burton was laconic in rehearsals. It all came too easily to him, and he was not a pleasant actor to work with. He displayed his usually dismissive tone to the other actors. During rehearsals, he continually appeared to be distracted and "somewhere else", seemingly uninterested in the play and the part he was playing. In truth, he did not need to work at it. After a few hours, he had conquered the part totally and he thought further rehearsal was superfluous. It should have been no surprise to anyone as Burton had arrived at the first rehearsal word-perfect, and as Melvyn Bragg succinctly described it: "The part was already sewn on him like a skin." In truth, at 26, Burton was at the very top of his game and superior in talent to any other actor in Britain – including all the big names Quayle had assembled in Stratford that summer.

The full dress rehearsals often stretched into the early morning as Quayle sought perfection. By two o'clock one morning, the cast and crew had become tired and tense and unhappy with Quayle for what they saw as unnecessary attention to detail. To relieve the boredom, Burton continually drank beer during rehearsals. But, as it never affected the quality of Burton's acting, Quayle could do little about it. One evening, Richard showed up with two crates of Phipps India Pale Ale. It was a fashionable ale of the time, served in half-pint bottles.

That evening, he consumed 18 bottles, brought to him one by one by his dresser as he proceeded to empty them. He was rehearsing in a full suit of armour, which was difficult to get in and out of, making toilet breaks impractical during rehearsal. But after 18 bottles, some nine pints of beer, Burton was desperate to visit the facilities and pleaded with Quayle for a bathroom break – which was denied. So Burton simply went where he stood and filled up his armour. Eventually, it all trickled out as he moved about on the wooden stage, much to the horror of some and to the amusement of others. At that point, Quayle finally called a halt and went offstage, astonished and shaking his head at what he had just witnessed.

John Gielgud, although not involved in the 1951 production, was keeping a close eye on things and observed: "Tony discovered what a difficult task it can be to direct Richard."

Quayle admitted years later that there were two directors on stage during rehearsals – himself and Philip Burton. As he explained: "When Richard did Shakespeare, the director never directed him. Philip Burton directed him. It was Philip Burton's dream that his adopted son should play that part in Stratford above any other place, and he had virtually taught Richard how to do the play years earlier. So when I cast Burton, he sent for his guardian, and they worked on the play together."

Philip's interpretation of Prince Hal was not Quayle's. Falstaff is one of the great comic characters of Shakespeare, and Richard arrived at rehearsals playing the prince with a serious tone to it. Quayle, however, wanted no serious note to disturb the comedy of the character as written. But Burton wouldn't play it Quayle's way and tried to explain his approach: "When I play a part – any part – I don't try to become that character. I am not like Laurence Olivier who can bend himself to be whoever he is playing. Rather, I bend the character to become more like me. I had no formal training as an actor. I never learned those tricks. I am superstitious about my acting. I don't know how it happens, and if I try to discover its source, I might lose it. So playing Prince Hal was Hal becoming like me, and when I played the part, there was no way for me to change it. I can prove very unsettling for directors, I know. Tony Quayle was very unhappy with me when I was Hal to his Falstaff. But I couldn't play Hal any differently, you see."

The reviewers attended a performance on Tuesday 3rd April 1951 with an embargo which would mean that the first reviews appeared in the following Sunday's papers, on 8th April.

The evening of Tuesday 3rd April was probably the most important performance of Burton's life as it was witnessed by every top critic in England from virtually every significant newspaper and magazine that covered the arts.

The most important critic and the man Burton wanted to impress most was Kenneth Tynan. Tynan, who turned 24 on 2nd April, arrived the night before and brought his wife so they could go out to dinner in Stratford to celebrate his birthday. Elaine Dundy, then a young actress and later a novelist, was desperate to meet Burton, whom she had heard so much about.

Tynan was at the very start of his career and already attracting huge attention by writing reviews for *The Spectator*. His weekly reviews had made *The Spectator* required reading in the theatre world and the magazine was already struggling to hold on to its star writer.

Tynan and his fellow critics were bowled over by Burton that night. The reviews the following Sunday were all gushing. Tynan wrote in *The Spectator*: "His playing of Prince Hal turned interested speculation to awe almost as soon as he started to speak." He famously described the critics from the local papers in the area as "standing agape in the lobbies." He called Burton's performance that of a "shrewd Welsh boy who shone out with greatness."

Elaine Dundy remembered: "He was not only magnificent; he was beautiful to look at. I all but swooned." Dundy and Tynan made straight for Burton's dressing room after the performance to be the first to congratulate him. Dundy remembered her husband and Burton bear-hugging each other and Burton, overcome with emotion, telling her loudly: "One of these days, I'll take on Larry."

The critics all agreed that Burton's acting was "divine," which was the most common word of praise. Tynan wrote: "Burton is a still brimming pool, running disturbingly deep; at 25 he commands repose and can make silence garrulous." Harold Hobson, who had recently replaced the legendary James Agate as *The Sunday Times* chief critic, said: "The Stratford audience that night was in the presence of no ordinary player. He had an interior force, so that he is doing everything when he appears to be doing nothing." Philip Hope Wallace, *The Guardian*'s critic said: "Your eye picks him out and refuses to leave him." Even the tabloids were impressed by the play and the *Daily Mirror* stated in an editorial: "If the entire Festival of Britain can even approach this standard, the triumph over the moaners will be complete."

But not all the critics praised him. One, who has forever gone unnamed, wrote that Burton "lacked inches" in his portrayal of the prince and compared him unfavorably to Laurence Olivier's portrayal of the same character at the Old Vic a few years earlier. However, the same critic had also written, and had clearly forgotten he had written, that Olivier also "lacked inches" when playing the part a few years earlier.

Philip Burton, sitting at home reading the newspapers that Sunday morning, called the reviews "miraculous." It was the wrong word of course, but he made his point.

In the second weekend of May, Philip travelled to Stratford to see the live performances of both Parts 1 and 2. He was due to leave for the United States the following week for a holiday with his friends, the Baruth family.

It was Whitsun bank holiday weekend and the weather was beautiful. He stayed at Oxhill, and on Friday 11th May, he saw Part 1. Then, on Saturday, he saw Part 2. After seeing them both for the first time, he wrote: "Rich was magnificent and Sybil delightful. This is bliss indeed."

Philip Burton enjoyed himself so much at Oxhill, he seriously considered cancelling his plans to go to America for the summer, arrangements he had made long before he knew Burton would be in Stratford. As he recounted in his own memoir called *The Burtons,* published in 1992: "A doleful day. I had very reluctantly to leave Stratford after an idyllic weekend. I don't want a bit to go to America now."

When Philip returned to England in late September, he headed again for Stratford. He wrote in his diary that Burton's performance was: "Polished perturbation." He added: "There's no doubt about Richard's greatness. I feel proud, humble and awed by God's mysterious ways." And he genuinely was. What happened in Stratford to Richard Burton during that summer of 1951 was truly extraordinary.

Anthony Quayle was delighted by the reviews and forgot all his differences with Philip and Richard: "If he can sustain and vary this performance through to the end of 'Henry V', we can safely send him along to swell the thin company of living actors who have shown us the mystery and the power of which heroes are capable." But most people believed that he didn't sustain the performance through to the end, including Burton himself.

'Henry V' opened on 31st July, but this time the praise was more muted and the critics were anything but laudatory about his performance. There were reservations about Burton's acting now that he was playing the King, a much more mature part. They said he lacked warmth or experience and that he shouted too much.

Some reviewers were very critical, which many thought unfair including John Gielgud's mother, Kate. She rang up Burton and asked him out for afternoon tea with her in Stratford town centre. As the tea was being poured, Kate Gielgud pulled out some old newspaper cuttings of reviews of her own son's performances. As Burton himself recalled: "A wonderful thing happened. John Gielgud's mother, who'd taken a bit of a shine to me, wrote to say she was coming to see me. We had tea together and then she pulled out of her bag a whole bundle of terrible notices that John had had. I thought: 'That's it. I'll never read notices again.'"

But if Burton and Mrs Gielgud thought the reviews for 'Henry V' were poor, the reviews for the final play, 'The Tempest', were downright terrible. It was directed by Michael Benthall and Burton had no sympathy for his part at all.

He was miscast, as Graham Jenkins admitted: "His last Stratford engagement as the lover Ferdinand in 'The Tempest' was near disaster and Rich was entirely out of sympathy with the soppy youth.

Playing Ferdinand brought out all of Burton's dislike of Shakespeare, especially the Shakespearean dress; the short costume and tights, the pink and blue colours and the frills and ruffles. Even the wig he had to wear, upset him. Throughout his entire career, Burton never looked good in a wig. And wearing one had a strangely negative effect on his acting.

Quayle had included 'The Tempest' at the end of the season to "leaven the historical cycle."

Robert Hardy remembered the disaster well: "He had a terrible attitude and played Ferdinand in a curly blonde wig. He was not interested in it. We all had supper after the first night and he was so out of joint, so totally awful." Burton simply said: "I found myself incapable of playing such a role." He added: "I can be loud or soft. I have no middle range." The trouble was that the part of Ferdinand demanded a middle range. The character was a lightweight romantic with no menace or drama about him, and Burton simply could not play him. With Philip Burton in America, there was no one to help him sort it out in rehearsals. And by the time Philip returned, it was too late. The critics hammered him, and they were right to do so.

But despite the failure of 'The Tempest', overall the season had been a stunning success. Penny Junor, one of Burton's biographers, believed they were the best performances of his entire career. She said: "The roles established him as the crown prince of the British stage."

And aside from the acting, life at Oxhill that summer was truly idyllic. The Burtons stayed at the house for seven months from April to the end of October and hardly returned to London at all. They left the builders to get on with rebuilding their new home in Squires Mount unsupervised. Sybil always referred to it as "that wonderful summer".

It was indeed a glorious summer and Hugh and Gunda Griffith were superb hosts. He declared it open house and hundreds of people came through Oxhill in those few months. Philip Burton came twice and the Jenkins family all visited at one time. The house was completely full every weekend. Philip Burton declared himself "in heaven" in the company of so many fine actors.

Everyone remembered that summer. As his brother David Jenkins recalled many years later: "Stratford proved to be a place of unquestionable and delirious happiness for Rich." Robert Hardy agreed, saying: "It was one of the happiest times of his life."

The visitors included Hollywood royalty such as Charles Laughton and Humphrey Bogart and his wife, Lauren Bacall. Of all the visitors that came, the most striking were Bogart and Bacall. They were the reigning king and queen of Hollywood and had come over to experience an English summer after seeing an advertisement for the Festival of Britain in the Los Angeles Times.

Burton's youngest brother, Graham, just happened to be at Oxhill at the same time as the Bogarts. The 24-year-old was overwhelmed by the experience of sitting down to dinner at Oxhill with Bogart and Bacall, and never forgot it.

Both Bogart and Bacall took in as much as they could and were stunned by Burton's performances as Prince Hal. The Bogarts and the Burtons became instant firm friends and Lauren Bacall particularly adored Sybil, just as Humphrey Bogart adored Burton. As Bacall said years later to Melvyn Bragg: "Bogie loved him. We all did. You had no alternative." At one point, Bogart told Burton: "You're wasting your time on the stage. Come to the States and I'll look after you there." Burton's career was done no harm at all when Bogart and Bacall returned to Hollywood and told everyone who would listen that Burton was "the next Olivier".

But Lauren Bacall didn't much care for Burton personally; especially when he tried to seduce her at Oxhill while her husband was talking to Sybil in the next room. As she remembered: "Richard immediately started to flirt with me. The fact that Bogie and Sybil were there did not bother him at all."

The next day, he took her to see Shakespeare's grave and they enjoyed a picnic whilst Bogart and Sybil remained at Oxhill. Bacall described how Burton got away with it: "Bogie understood, knowing young actors, and his young wife Sybil of course understood. So he took me around and showed me the grave. He was filled with this incredible sense of adventure and was almost swashbuckling; the idea of whisking me away dramatically, kind of romantically, even though it wasn't a romance. The whole idea of it was rather fantasy like, it didn't have a lot to do with reality."

But she said of his acting: "He was just marvellous."

Kenneth Tynan and Elaine Dundy also came to Oxhill that summer. They spent hours drinking in The Dirty Duck, the famous pub that stands opposite the Memorial Theatre. There were also many parties and picnics on the banks of the River Avon, as Dundy remembered: "We did perhaps a little too much drinking, but in those days it was almost customary to drink until one got smashed or the others were under the table. We weren't aware of the potential danger in it, so we weren't alarmed by Richard's drinking. It was part of his prowess, his huge gusto."

# AND GOD CREATED BURTON

In fact, the drinking continued all summer, and it seemed that half of Wales made the pilgrimage to Oxhill. Brin Jenkins, his great Welsh acting rival, came with his wife, Mair. Osian Ellis, the great harpist, also attended and played continually, thereby contributing to the magical atmosphere while the sun shone. Frankie Howerd, the up and coming comedian, was a continuous presence at Oxhill that summer and his imitations of various Shakespearian characters had everyone in fits of laughter. It is impossible to overstate the magic of that English summer of 1951, and as Robert Hardy remembered it, the nightingales seemed to continuously sing outside: "It was the most wonderful summer in this isolated village and this beautiful house." Hardy even had a difficult experience with a ghost: "I saw a ghost and dropped a tray full of glasses. We ran into each other in a corridor and of course I did not realise that it was a ghost until it suddenly was not there at all."

There were many good times that summer, and Sybil had the time of her life. Along with Bacall, she made friends with another young actress called Rachel Roberts and they became inseparable all summer.

To his surprise, Burton found he enjoyed acting with Sybil. As his brother David recalled cheekily: "For once, he was able to legitimately sleep with his leading lady."

And they came to a big domestic decision that summer. They both decided that she would stop acting and instead take on the day-to-day management of her husband's career. During the season, Sybil had finally realised that acting was not for her and that she was much better as a stage manager behind the scenes, which really suited her talent for organising.

In late October, the season finally drew to a close and the good times came to an end. It had been the most successful season of Shakespeare at the Memorial – ever and indeed since. 332,000 people had paid a total of £132,000 to see the five plays. Burton had given Quayle good value for the thousand pounds he had paid him.

So much so that Quayle tried his damnedest to get Burton to sign up to return in 1952. He was planning to stage 'Hamlet' and 'Othello' in 1952 and told Burton: "You've a marvellous gift. You'll learn so much – become a better actor." Burton didn't exactly say 'no' but he was very non-committal. Quayle recalled his response many years later to biographer Paul Ferris: "He said a most extraordinary thing: 'I'm frightened of all that, because I've got a knack. I don't know what it is, and if I ever started to know, I might lose it.'" Quayle knew he had lost him to Broadway when Burton told Kenneth Tynan: "Quayle has asked me to come back here next year to play 'Hamlet'. I've declined. Instead, I'm going to New York to play in 'Point of Departure.'"

But the good times of 1951 were never to be repeated in his life, and Richard Burton came to regret the decision not to return to Stratford in 1952. What had happened to Burton in Stratford-upon-Avon in the summer of 1951 was an experience that most actors never get to savour. And whatever triumphs and delights the future held for Burton, life would never be that good again.

# CHAPTER 18

# Identical Lovers

## *Claire Bloom and Susan Strasberg*

### 1949 to 1958

It was around 6 o'clock on Wednesday 17th September 1958 when Claire Bloom popped into Richard Burton's dressing room at Elstree Studios to say good night. They had been working all day filming a new film called *Look Back in Anger* based on John Osborne's famous play of the same name.

A few seconds earlier, 20-year-old American actress Susan Strasberg had arrived in Burton's dressing room after flying in from New York. She was exhausted from the flight and the car journey from Heathrow Airport in rush hour traffic.

After having spent nearly four months away from Burton, the 20-year-old flung herself into the arms of her 33-year-old lover. As she pressed her lips against his, Burton had no choice but to respond in kind.

At that precise moment, Claire Bloom was skipping along the corridor. She didn't knock, she never did, and was full of the joys of life as she flipped open the door and stepped inside.

Almost imperceptibly, her mood changed and her face dropped, and in that split second, she believed she was having an out-of-body experience. She saw herself wrapped in the arms of Richard Burton, her on-off lover for the past six years. As she remembered: "For one stunned moment, I stood frozen in the doorway, thinking that it was I whom Richard was embracing and that I must be outside of myself watching this. She resembled me so much as to be almost my mirror image."

Whilst Bloom stood staring at them, Burton and Strasberg's lips remained pressed together and every other part of their bodies were similarly entwined as they turned round to face her. She said: "They were frozen, looking towards me, Richard's arms still around Strasberg."

For almost five seconds they all simply stood there – just staring at each other. Bloom was shocked, Strasberg surprised and Burton bemused; Bloom was shocked by the betrayal, Strasberg surprised by the look on Bloom's and Burton's faces, and Burton just bemused at the stunning resemblance between the two actresses. For a moment, he almost believed he was seeing double and couldn't understand why he hadn't noticed the resemblance before. He was amazed at the sudden realisation that his lovers, separated by an ocean, were virtually identical.

After what seemed an interminable length of time, Bloom, as she determined whether there might be an innocent explanation and quickly came to the realisation that there wasn't, turned away as if to leave and, suddenly thinking better of it, looked round and screamed back at them: "Fuck off, the pair of you." She slammed the door behind her and, as she left the room, emotionally she left Burton's life forever.

Bloom later remembered the incident as lasting barely five seconds, but it had seemed like a lifetime: "I finally pulled myself together and left."

Years later, in her autobiography entitled *Leaving a Doll's House*, Bloom remembered every detail, including the fact that Strasberg was wearing a white chiffon head scarf and a white mink coat, and resembled a "young nun".

It was the only time the 27-year-old English rose Claire Bloom and America's sweetheart Susan Strasberg ever came face to face. And it would be the last.

Whilst the occasion marked the end of the affair between Burton and Bloom, it was also to be the end of the liaison between Burton and Strasberg. In that single moment, Burton had lost his identical lovers. He never again shared any intimacy with Bloom and only briefly again with Strasberg, and two of the most passionate and exotic love affairs in the entertainment business were forever put to rest that night. Whilst his affair with Strasberg had only lasted a year, the affair with Bloom had been more poignant – it had lasted for seven years and had dominated both of their lives for much of that time.

The roots of that affair actually dated back nine years.

It had all started on Monday 7th February 1949, when 17-year-old starlet Claire Bloom arrived at the Globe Theatre for the first rehearsal of 'The Lady's Not For Burning', a new play in which she was to star with the up-and-coming actor Richard Burton. By day, Bloom was a highly-polished, talented actress, already making a name for herself; but by night, she was a wholly-innocent young girl who lived with her mother and had never even had a boyfriend, let alone shared a bed with a man.

It was actually her second meeting with Burton, as she had met him a couple of weeks before when they had both auditioned for a part in the film version of Christopher Fry's new play. Burton had been terrible in the audition and even worse with her. He had used a feeble chat-up line to ask her for a date – which she had ignored.

In truth, his audition had been so poor that she had not expected him to get the part, and their first meeting could not have been less memorable. As she said: "I thought little more about Richard."

But the second meeting stirred up feelings she never knew existed. The depth of her feelings for him caught her entirely by surprise.

Later, she could only imagine that the first time they met, something had been stirred in her unconscious: "Something happened that I have never been able to explain. I arrived for the first rehearsal and was just about to open the door that led to the stage when I heard Richard's unmistakable voice say: 'I was married yesterday'. I can remember the moment with absolute clarity and the dreadful leap my heart gave at the words."

Bloom was caught unawares by the news of his marriage and by her own reaction to it: "Clearly, I had felt the force of his remarkable personality, and was immensely attracted to this unknown and seductive young man with the beautiful green eyes."

She was very surprised by the depth of her feelings for a man she barely knew – and a married man at that. She was a 17-year-old virgin and feelings like that were wholly alien to her. From that moment on, she was on emotional automatic pilot, incapable of taking rational decisions where Richard Burton was concerned. She was simply transfixed by him and no longer in control of her own feelings.

Bloom was born Patricia Claire Blume in Finchley, North London on 15th February, 1931. Her grandparents were Jewish immigrants from Eastern Europe who had settled in Liverpool and, shortly afterwards, her father, Eddie, arrived. Her mother, Elizabeth, had had a more conventional middle-class upbringing in London. Her father was a gambler and his debts meant the family was forced to move house regularly. Her parents were divorced when she was 16 and she stayed close to her mother as she quickly found fame as an actress, which is how she found her way to the stage of the Globe Theatre a year later.

It was barely four weeks after his marriage to Sybil, but when 'The Lady's Not For Burning' went on its provincial tour prior to opening in London, Bloom and Burton were thrown together in the most intimate way.

During the tour, the young actors were booked into lodgings that all had one common denominator: they were the cheapest available with some of the most disgusting sleeping quarters imaginable. As Bloom put it: "Some of these boarding houses were indescribably vile, cold, dirty and with the worst of English cooking while others could be cozy, run by landladies who would make endless cups of tea and spoil the lucky actors for the week that they were there."

So Burton and Bloom began their relationship, the first phase of which was completely platonic. They fell in love but never touched. It appears that both of them were afraid of disturbing his young marriage and of the potential consequences. They didn't trust themselves enough to have physical contact; Burton feared that his marriage would fall apart and Bloom was scared she would become a home wrecker. That fear dominated the early days of their relationship, as she described: "We never touched each other, never physically shared more than the rather chaste kiss that I looked forward to every night on the stage; and yet we had unquestionably fallen deeply in love.

"Richard, who had an encyclopedic memory for poetry, would recite poems to me late into the night", she continued. "He would be seated in my room, very properly, on a chair pulled away from the bed on which I silently lay, fervently listening to the sound of his beautiful voice."

Amazingly, Sybil would often join them, as Bloom revealed: "I felt no guilt, as I didn't seem to understand my own feelings and I knew that I had nothing to be ashamed of."

After ten weeks, the play moved to London and the actors moved back to their own homes in London – Burton back to Sybil and Bloom back to her mother. The relationship reverted to two actors in a play and the intimacy instantly disappeared: "Richard and I went back to leading our own lives and, for the time being, our relationship changed into the cooler one of two young actors who were playing opposite each other, who were fond of each other and sometimes had a lemonade shandy with other members of the company when the curtain came down. At least, *I* had a lemonade shandy."

But Bloom was totally besotted with Burton. As a virgin, she had little idea what sex or intimacy with a man was, so the lack of it wasn't a problem to her. She described him as "hypnotic." She explained: "It was partly due to the mesmerising beauty of his eyes, but also a quality he had that was quite indefinable and that I have never seen in any other actor."

When she was at home, she confessed that she "longed for the hours when I could leave for the theatre."

The rest of the cast were convinced the two were having an affair, but Bloom was adamant they were not: "I had never slept with any man, and Richard was faithful to Sybil."

There was an air of delusion surrounding Bloom during this period, as she figured she could keep Burton as her lover as long as she did not have sex with him and did not thereby threaten his marriage. His behaviour was certainly totally out of character and he appeared genuinely frightened of what might happen to his marriage if he did sleep with Bloom. In truth, he was as equally mesmerised by her as she was by him.

Then it all ended suddenly. Bloom was offered another role in another play. She got a lead role in Jean Anouilh's 'Ring Round the Moon', to be directed by Peter Brook, opposite Paul Scofield and Margaret Rutherford. It was a dream part but she took it reluctantly, as she admitted: "I knew it would be ideal for me in every way, but just as strongly I wanted to stay with Richard and my family of friends in 'The Lady's Not For Burning'. Of course, I made the decision, which was the only one I could have made, to take the new role, and Richard and I parted as friends."

As time went by, though, somehow their love didn't just die; it turned to hate. As Bloom revealed: "There grew up between us competitiveness, a jealousy, and almost a dislike of each other, which was only the mirror-image of the love that we both felt but had never expressed nor even quite understood."

Bloom's early departure from 'The Lady's Not For Burning' meant she missed out when the play moved to Broadway later in the year. But Bloom was the flavour of the moment and her career advanced much faster than Burton's. She got a part at the Old Vic as Jessica in 'The Merchant of Venice' and returned the following season. She also got her first film role on location in Berlin starring opposite James Mason in Carol Reed's film *The Man Between*. Then, in 1952, she got her big break when she was discovered by Charlie Chaplin. He turned her into an international star by putting her opposite him in a film called *Limelight*, a comedy drama. Chaplin and his wife Oona became her lifelong friends

And then, four years later, in the summer of 1953, she returned to within Richard Burton's orbit. She was cast as Ophelia opposite Burton in 'Hamlet' at the Old Vic. By then, Bloom was 22 and Burton 27. She was shocked when she realised Burton was to play Hamlet. The four years in between had dulled their memories and the fact that they had never even properly kissed caused them both to forget what they had meant to each other.

Time and events had moved on, but in many ways they were still the same people. Much had changed in their lives; Burton was now a genuine Hollywood star, having been nominated for an Oscar, and seemingly still happily married to Sybil. Bloom was an established actress, but still a virgin living at home with her mother.

But one thing had changed. Burton was no longer innocent in her eyes. She was fully aware of his reputation as a lothario and had learned all about his wild escapades in New York during the Broadway run of 'The Lady's Not For Burning'. She was genuinely frightened of that reputation.

So much so that when she heard they were playing opposite each other, she said about him in front of the rest of the cast: "My God, not that uncouth man." It was a defensive remark that was unfortunately reported back to Burton, who was heard to say in response: "I'll make her pay. I'll have her; I'll have her whichever way I like." His response, when it got back to her, merely confirmed that her opinion was correct. But Burton's response had been pure bravado and the truth was that neither of them had forgotten what they meant to each other – they were just frightened of it.

Burton's reputation genuinely scared Bloom, and she tried initially to keep him at arm's length, fearing the consequences if they rekindled their relationship. She was also frightened of losing her virginity to a married man. That was not part of her dreams.

What had changed was that Burton was no longer frightened of his marriage; he had had so many affairs in the intervening years that he considered it to be indestructible. On that basis, he was now ready to sleep with Bloom. Bloom felt this keenly and it scared her to death.

Having heard so many lurid tales of Burton's womanising, Bloom asked fellow actor William Squire to take care of her and to keep Burton away. It was a ridiculous notion, of course, as the last thing she really wanted was for him to be kept away. But she probably didn't trust herself, as she told Squire: "You will keep him away from me, won't you, Billy?"

Squire, believing the request was genuine and knowing Burton's unsavoury reputation with women, agreed to be her unofficial guardian and carried out his task as dutifully as he could. He remembered: "When they were in 'The Lady's Not For Burning', Richie was on the Guinness and, I suppose, she thought that any man who drank Guinness was condemned to hell."

Squire was so attentive to Bloom that Burton suspected them of having an affair, a situation with which he was most unhappy. One day, he sidled up to him at The Olive Branch, the pub opposite the Old Vic, and said: "Getting on well with Claire, then?" Squire nodded back: "We're just good friends." He replied: "Are you fucking Claire, then?" Squire said: "Good God, Richard. Good God, no" to which Burton responded: "Well, it looks like you are."

Burton sat down next to him and sunk into a morose mood as a wave of jealousy overcame him. Sensing this, Squire said to him after a few minutes: "Look, it's no good, Rich. She won't do it with anybody. Especially not you." Burton perked up when he realised his friend was telling the truth. Quickly back to his usual cocky, self-confident self, he replied: "I bet I'll get there." Squire retorted: "You won't." Burton said: "What you bet?" "A pint," said Squire. "You're on," said Burton.

Later that week, Squire and Bloom were sitting at the back of the theatre watching Burton rehearse, when Bloom said suddenly: "You have to admit. He is rather marvellous." Squire, noticing a glazed look coming over his friend, said: "Yes, he is rather marvellous."

Squire suddenly realised that Bloom was no longer a virgin and that he owed Richard Burton a pint of beer.

It had all happened the night before. As Bloom recalled: "The spark that had only fitfully ignited those few years ago now sprang to flame with an incandescence that astonished us both. We both knew that something very serious had come into our lives."

Rediscovering each other after a drink in The Olive Branch, Bloom had shaken off Squire and taken Burton back to the Chelsea house she shared with her mother in London's Godfrey Street. She recorded the precise events of that night in her autobiography. Under pressure from her publishers, Bloom was astonishingly candid and was forced to reveal more than she might have cared to. She wrote: "We made love quietly in my room in the little house with my mother sleeping upstairs, who may or may not have known what was happening on the floor below. I was almost ignorant about sexual matters and found this first experience perplexing. Richard was tender and considerate, and later we laughed and joked in relief at getting over this first hurdle.

Richard left me in the early morning to go back home, and I went to sleep happy and childishly thrilled that I was a 'woman' at last. I felt absolutely no guilt about anything because I knew that making love with Richard was something that had to happen."

She continued: "We knew each other so well, were so intimate with each other already, that this further intimacy was just the physical consummation of an already-accepted fact."

When she saw him the next morning at the Old Vic, there was a magical reunion from the night before. As she put it: "I felt we truly belonged to each other."

The change in their relationship was obvious to the rest of the cast. After rehearsals, they would drive to Regent's Park in Burton's grey Jaguar car. There, they lay on the grass just talking. She said: "I found his Welsh working-class masculinity and vigour excitingly different from the Englishmen I had known."

After rehearsals concluded in London, 'Hamlet' opened in Edinburgh and Burton's wild ways appeared completely unchecked. He frightened everybody during the pre-London run by staying up one night drinking and then attending an early morning rehearsal, an afternoon matinee and an evening performance and, afterwards, going to a party with Bloom, still having had no sleep at all. After another all-night drinking session, he went straight to a sound studio the following morning to record a radio play for the BBC after downing two what he called "stiffeners". Only then, at around two o'clock in the afternoon, did he finally go to bed. William Squire recalled: "It was his happiest time, it was all going to happen for him, and he knew it."

Burton and Bloom, with Sybil absent, carried on their affair with gay abandon in Edinburgh. William Squire recalled to Melvyn Bragg that he was walking down Edinburgh's Princes Street with Robert Hardy when they came upon Burton and Bloom wrapped round each other under a lamp post. Squire, anxious to avoid a confrontation, ushered Hardy in the opposite direction so he wouldn't see. Hardy disapproved strongly of his friend's betrayal of Sybil and was later one of the few people to tell him so.

There were six Shakespeare productions at the Old Vic that year, and Burton and Bloom starred opposite each other in five of them. The Burton-Bloom affair became well-known to the rest of the cast, but not to Sybil. Bloom said: "We were always discreet and supportive; everyone knew that this was not just an affair, but something precious and deeply spiritual for us both."

Sybil had no idea what was going on and Bloom admitted she went to great lengths to deceive her: "We behaved on these occasions as colleagues and friends." When they weren't on stage, Bloom spent most of her time in Burton's dressing room and they were inseparable.

Bloom said she never knew how much Sybil knew, nor did she care: "I am sure she knew that she had Richard's love and affection. He was, in his own way, a loyal and devoted husband."

The Globe Theatre's doorman was briefed by Burton to call him when Sybil approached the stage door so that Bloom could return to her own dressing room.

No one, including William Squire, could understand why Burton didn't simply leave Sybil for Claire Bloom during that period. As Squire remembered: "It was the happiest I ever saw him and it was the first time Sybil was in danger." Even Melvyn Bragg wrote: "The classiness of Claire Bloom, her undoubted talent, quality, beauty, promise, made her, in that world of sexual roulette, a winner to break the home. There were no children in the way, and Burton was not a religious man. Times were far stricter then, but actors were not expected to behave themselves. Yet Sybil held him and he held on to her. The bond between them was proof against tremendous pressure."

But Lauren Bacall was not surprised at all that he stuck with Sybil. She had become great friends with Sybil in Stratford in 1951 and said: "Richard adored her and he knew how valuable she was to him. She was the class act; always a woman of tremendous integrity and values and standards, absolutely straight and clear, no question."

It appears that Bloom's total passivity, her willingness to accept the situation – any situation – meant Burton was under no pressure to alter the status quo, and so he didn't. Bloom was totally prepared to accept that he would make love to her and then go home and make love to his wife.

In that period, Burton effectively had two wives – one at work and one at home – and he was enjoying a full sex life with each. It was every man's dream. And Claire Bloom was also living her dream and was not as deluded as an outsider looking in might have assumed.

She was prepared to put up with it, as she said, rationalising it in an extraordinarily honest way: "Perhaps we both instinctively guessed that Richard would never be completely true to one woman, and that Sybil and I between us filled the roles that Richard needed most: the mother he had never had and the dream woman that he would search for, and only temporarily find, all the rest of his life."

Again, Lauren Bacall was not surprised when she heard what was going on: "Richard's values were not very good and his standards, I don't think, were either. The wicked side got wickeder and wickeder as time went along."

In that period, Bloom saw as much of Burton as did his wife. She gave him a key to her house in Godfrey Street and he would often arrive late at night, let himself in, and they would make love. He would leave before dawn to go back to Sybil, apparently telling her he had been up drinking all night with his friends. Bloom said: "How much of this Sybil guessed I can never know." She added: "The secrecy that surrounded our offstage life was necessary but miserable. I came to dread the moment before dawn, when Richard had to dress and go back to his wife."

Bloom's life was often a miserable one, and she found herself rarely leaving her house in case he called. As she admitted: "I waited at home, already fearing to miss one of his precious visits. I lived with a great deal of tension and loneliness."

Astonishingly, her mother moved out of the Godfrey Street house and rented a nearby flat in case her presence put Burton off. When he didn't come, Bloom simply looked forward to going to work at the theatre and being with him there. It was a difficult existence but it somehow made her happy. They even arranged it so that their dressing rooms had connecting doors and, as Bloom described it: "We had a private life in the theatre we were unable to have outside. Sometimes even our lovemaking took place in the darkened room, between the matinee and the evening performance."

During that summer, when Sybil was away, they enjoyed a long weekend together in Norfolk over four days, as she remembered: "We went to a hotel in Norfolk, and called ourselves Mr and Mrs Boothby. We had a log fire in our room and spent most of our time there making love – we had never had such luxury before – no strain, no getting up to go home. In less than the year that had passed since we had first become lovers, I had come a long way."

From her comments, it appeared Bloom would have been content to let the situation continue for the rest of her life, sharing Burton with Sybil. She admitted as much, saying: "It seemed to me, at the time, that this situation was really quite normal; that we would go on being together always, in spite of the seemingly insurmountable difficulties we faced."

But then calamity faced her at the end of the Old Vic season. Burton told her he would be going to Hollywood for three months to make a new film called the *Prince of Players* and Sybil would be going with him. Bloom was in despair.

Before that, at the end of the Old Vic season, the company had two overseas engagements in Denmark and Switzerland before disbanding. Sybil decided to accompany her husband and, for the first time, Bloom found the situation with Burton very difficult. Sybil on the road was a very different proposition to Sybil at home. As Bloom confessed: "I remember it as a confusing and difficult time. I had come to hate the hiding in corners, the secrecy that accompanied

Richard's visits to my hotel room." She added: "Our sexual need for each other seemed to increase; I waited only for the times when we could be alone together."

Bloom knew the time was coming when the company would disband and her idyll would end: "As the time to part grew nearer, I began to feel desperate and unsure. The only times I now felt secure and happy were when we were making love. Then everything else seemed unimportant."

From Denmark, they travelled to Switzerland. As Bloom described: "Our next stop was Zurich, and we travelled by train. Richard and Sybil travelled in one compartment and I in another, separated from theirs only by a sitting room. It seems incredible to me now that we got away with this, but Richard actually came into my compartment during the night and we made love in the moving train." It had turned into a great love affair going on right underneath Sybil's nose.

At the end of the Swiss run of the play, Bloom went to Vevey on the north shore of Lake Geneva to stay with Charlie Chaplin and his wife, Oona, and the Burtons returned to London.

There was supposed to be a brief reunion in London before Burton left for Hollywood, but it all went horribly wrong. As Bloom recalled: "Our parting was painful, as Richard had planned to come to my house on his last night in London. I was exhausted with strain and weeping and was also very young. I fell into the kind of sleep only young people can know; deep and heavy with strange dreams. Richard did come to the house, but hadn't got his key, and I didn't hear his quiet tapping at my door. I awoke the next morning to realise that I had missed him, and he telephoned in a fury to say that I hadn't heard him and that he must now leave without saying 'goodbye'. I felt I had failed him miserably."

Extraordinarily, they wrote to each other every other day he was away in Hollywood. She routed her letters through Valerie Douglas, his manager in Hollywood, and he replied to each one at Godfrey Street.

Bloom later destroyed most of his letters, on the eve of her marriage to Rod Steiger. Only a few remain and were published by Bloom in her autobiography. The letters are markedly different to those he later wrote to Elizabeth Taylor and show that Burton was deeply in love with Bloom, a much more genuine love than he was ever again to display with anyone. The letters show none of the puerility present in his later so-called love letters to Taylor. He also claimed in the letters that he was faithful to Bloom during their relationship, which could well have been true at that point.

But, amazingly, she wasn't faithful to him. When he had gone, she got an offer from Laurence Olivier to play the part of Lady Anne opposite him in a film version of *Richard III*. She accepted immediately. At the time, Olivier was married to Hollywood actress Vivien Leigh.

Bloom fell into an affair with Olivier during the period filming took place. When filming ended, so too was the affair. Bloom admitted: "I was lonely, sad and, when I started to work on *Richard III*, I was extremely vulnerable." She somehow rationalised the affair with Olivier by saying: "I was always aware that I had no lasting claim on Richard's affections beyond the fact that we loved each other. I knew that he would never leave his wife for me, that the ties of a shared Welsh background and of their very real delight in each other's company would hold them together more strongly than a more passionate relationship would ever do."

She described the affair with Olivier as: "The classic situation of the young actress bedazzled by the attentions of her mature co-star, and ending without any rancour on either side. I had absolutely no further role in Laurence Olivier's life, and the only relationship we had in later years was purely professional."

It was to be January 1955 before Burton and Bloom got together again. They were cast opposite each other in a 1955 film called *Alexander the Great*. It was filmed in Spain.

In the intervening period, Burton's career had really taken off whilst Bloom's had stalled, as she admitted herself: "Although I was featured on the cover of *Life* magazine, I had not become the international star I longed to be. The offers did not appear, and there was no question on producers' lips that it had to be 'Bloom or nobody.'"

Bloom hoped her affair with Burton could resume, but it soon became clear that the magic had faded. And it also became clear that Sybil knew what had been going on. She was with Burton for the entire six months that *Alexander the Great* was filming and she never left his side, especially when Bloom was around. Nevertheless, they made love on a continual, if random, basis.

She had one of the best suites in a very grand hotel, where Burton was also staying on the same floor with Sybil. The proximity made it tricky and their get-togethers became increasingly rare. Bloom became a hermit and would not dare leave her suite lest she missed one of his visits. She remembered: "Quite understandably, this time Sybil was more wary and Richard more careful. I would wait in my room for days on end."

During this time in Spain, Bloom began seriously to question what she called her own "passivity" in the relationship. Burton was clearly the great love of her life and yet she did not have him. It didn't seem to have mattered in 1953 at the Old Vic, but now it increasingly did. She tried to explain in her autobiography: "My first affair had come fairly late in life; I was completely inexperienced. But there is a missing component in this rationale, a truth which is as old as human relationships: to have an affair with a married man is a recipe for disaster. Even so, if I was handed the same set of circumstances and given another chance to relive those anguish-ridden years with Richard, I would unhesitatingly choose to do so. He was my first, my greatest, love; the only man to whom I have fervently and completely given all of myself. To feel so much pleasure from the body, mind, voice, mere presence of another, is a gift I am profoundly grateful to have received. Even though it lasted only a few years, I realise now how lucky I was. Many women go through life without ever knowing such happiness."

They were thrown together again at the Old Vic in the 1955/56 season, but by then she knew she had to make the final break for her own sanity. She finally made the decision to leave him and accepted an offer she had twice turned down to go to the United States touring with the Old Vic Company.

But parting for good proved much more difficult than either of them had envisioned. Her new production went on a provincial tour of England prior to leaving for America. Neither of them could believe that the relationship was coming to an end. As Bloom recalled: "I would say a final 'goodbye' to Richard only to find him waiting at the London railway station to meet the train that had returned from one of the provincial towns where we were trying out the productions for the US tour. Then he would definitely say 'goodbye' to me, and I would leave messages with his secretary, desperately asking him to telephone. We couldn't let go of something that had meant so much for the past five years."

Their final meeting was in Hyde Park on a rainy day in a muddy grass park. The image of her sodden lover waving to her is one she has carried in her mind ever since. As she recalled: "We knew that there was no other way. The rain dripped down, and the sound of it was muted and hopeless. We were not to see each other again for three years."

Bloom found she was very relieved when she finally got on the aeroplane and it took off bound for America. She explained: "I felt a weight drop, as though it was a physical sensation. I knew that however painful the parting from Richard might have been, I had done the only thing possible to protect my future. I was now 26; an age when young women of my generation had already started to think seriously about marriage and children. My mother felt strongly that I was doing the right thing in leaving England, at least for a while; there was no question in either of our minds that this was, however, only temporary and that my real future life and career still waited for me at home."

Meanwhile, Burton had a sea change in his life as he left London and moved to tax exile Switzerland and filmed a few forgettable movies in between. He continued with his same old routine of slash-and-burn sexual encounters with his leading ladies and other assorted actresses, along with the continued consumption of large amounts of alcohol. That is, until he arrived in New York in 1957 and met a very special lady who stole his heart. Remarkably, she was a younger, more streetwise and more volatile version of Claire Bloom, and she spoke with a different accent.

Susan Strasberg was already a star when Richard Burton came into her life. She had started acting at the age of 15, pushed by her parents, a famous theatrical couple, Lee and Paula Strasberg. At 15, she starred in a play about the life of Anne Frank and became a household name in America. By the time she appeared in her second stage play in 1957, she was, as she put it, "a star": "I had been working for five years; I was making a good deal of money and receiving a great deal of adulation. But, for a girl who had everything, I felt I was long overdue to meet my prince." As soon as she laid eyes on Burton, she believed her prince had arrived. It was September 1957.

Strasberg's parents were very successful acting coaches. Paula had notably mentored Marilyn Monroe and Marlon Brando, and Lee had parlayed those skills into running a very successful theatrical school called The Actors' Studio. Where acting was concerned, the Strasbergs knew what they were about.

Consequently, they had found little trouble getting their daughter into the business and establishing her career very successfully. Inside four years, they made her into one of America's top young film stars. At the age of 19, Strasberg was America's sweetheart.

After starring in three hit movies, her parents believed she was ready for her second Broadway appearance to consolidate her growing reputation as a serious actress. Her second Broadway play was to be 'Time Remembered', a romantic French comedy starring Richard Burton and Helen Hayes. When a journalist asked why she had chosen the role, she replied: "I get to wear beautiful clothes and I get a prince. What more could I want?" Not much more as it turned out.

She had first met Burton briefly in England the year before, when Helen Hayes had introduced them on a film set. But Strasberg, like Claire Bloom before her, was seemingly unimpressed with their first encounter. As she remembered: "Richard had a reputation as a charmer, a ladies' man, but at that first meeting in England, I had not been impressed. He was a little too theatrical; another older man and, besides, he was married." But nonetheless, as he had with Bloom, Burton had left an indelible impression on another young actress which could not easily be wiped away.

Their second meeting was more significant after Burton flew into New York from Geneva to begin rehearsals on 'Time Remembered' at Broadway's famous Morosco Theatre at 217 West 45th Street. The first read-through was scheduled for 10:30am on 12th September in a dingy rehearsal hall, and Burton arrived bleary-eyed from having flown in late the night before.

Rehearsals were already behind schedule, as Burton had been delayed in Europe by the birth of his daughter, Kate, on 10th September.

Before he arrived, Jimmy Gelb, the stage manager, took Strasberg to one side and warned her about Burton: "Listen, Susie, if anyone gives you any trouble, I'll be there. This Burton, I hear he's a Casanova, a heartbreaker. If he comes near you, I'm ready." All the crew were very protective of Strasberg, who was a strikingly beautiful young girl.

But, in reality, it was Burton who needed protecting from her. She described the moment he arrived as "etched in my memory." She continued: "He was dressed in a blue sweater; his skin was slightly pockmarked from a childhood illness. I thought the scars were beautiful because they made him look vulnerable. His face was classically featured: straight nose, high cheekbones, full bottom lip. A lock of his fine hair fell over his forehead."

She was particularly struck by his hands, which she called "peasant hands". She described them in her autobiography, entitled *Bitter Sweet*: "His hands, which he hated, were similar to my father's; although not physically beautiful, there was great sensitivity and feeling in them, so that when they were used, they took on the colour of what was being said." But she was most taken with his voice. Americans generally love British accents and she adored Burton's: "He used his voice as a weapon to charm and seduce people, and the enormous energy radiating from his compact frame made people gravitate toward him." She realised that she wasn't the first woman to fall for those charms and, despite the warnings from Jimmy Gelb, Strasberg was utterly smitten and had almost exactly the same sort of feelings Claire Bloom had felt nine years before: "I admired him silently, secretly; watching him covertly when he was rehearsing, but keeping my distance. He began to pay more and more attention to me. He called everyone 'love', but I detected an extra passion in his voice when he said it to me."

From that moment on, she was lost to him and desired him more and more each day. Burton recognised the attention he was getting from her and one day strode into rehearsals, swept her off her feet, swung her round in the air and said to her: "My beautiful Hebrew princess." Strasberg remembered: "I was ecstatic, though trying to hide my infatuation." From that point on, an affair was inevitable.

Burton had arrived in New York, alone. His wife, Sybil, and his newborn daughter, Kate, would not arrive until 10th November, some eight weeks hence. Philip Burton, Richard's stepfather, had by then moved permanently to New York and become a successful director. Part of the reason Burton had accepted the role was so that the three of them could have six months together in New York as a family with Philip. He wanted his new daughter to bond with the man Richard regarded as her grandfather.

Sybil's absence was a golden opportunity for Strasberg, which she grabbed with both hands: "I was afraid he was just flirting with me and that it could never lead to anything, but by the time we went on the road to Washington, Boston and New Haven, my feet were firmly planted in mid air." But she immediately realised that Sybil and Kate were a formidable barrier, as Burton made no secret of them and his feelings for them. As she admitted: "I told myself that Richard was married and that when his wife and child joined him I would be forgotten."

The relationship began slowly. Burton seemed unduly conscious of his greater age and maturity and the fact that he was married. He knew Strasberg was America's sweetheart and was wary of what any bad publicity could do to his career in America. But, like he had with Claire Bloom, when he encountered a woman he really liked he was ready to take it slowly.

Helen Hayes, Burton's 57-year-old co-star in the play, was very protective of Strasberg and concerned by Burton's burgeoning relationship with the 20-year-old. Hayes feared that Burton was squandering his talent and Strasberg was jeopardising her marriageability. Hayes said: "Richard Burton fell in love with Susan, or, more accurately, Susan fell in love with him and he was not about to turn her down."

Hayes was not a figure to be trifled with. She was one of America's biggest stars and one of only 12 people ever to have won an Oscar, Emmy, Tony and Grammy. Not for nothing was she known as the first lady of American theatre, and she would later be awarded the Presidential Medal of Freedom, America's highest civilian honour, by President Reagan.

As well as Hayes, Strasberg also had to contend with her mother, Paula, who hovered protectively. Before she could begin an affair with Burton, she had to shake off these two formidable ladies.

She remembered: "I was not free of her until I saw her lights go out at night and could slip out the door to meet Richard in his hotel suite." But, interestingly, like Claire Bloom's mother, Paula Strasberg seemingly approved of her daughter's liaison with Burton, as Strasberg admitted: "Richard lived up to Mama's standards of a prince, too."

But there was a logistical and practical problem to the affair getting started, which Strasberg recalled in her autobiography: "There was another, more immediate, intimate problem I faced which I could not discuss with my mother. I longed to consummate Richard's and my relationship but was unable to. I had not brought my diaphragm with me. In the fifties, no nice girl premeditated or anticipated sex. Too embarrassed to tell Richard, I pretended instead to have qualms about going further."

Although she was concerned that Burton would feel rejected, it proved an excellent tactical ploy to ensnare him, and the delay and anticipation caused him to fall in love with her. She said: "The more I held back, the more persistent he became."

His courtship was relentless and he bombarded her with love notes and gifts, including an expensive heart-shaped diamond and pearl brooch that she took to wearing everywhere, including to bed. They began to spend every moment together and he taught her appreciation of the works of Shakespeare, Keats and Shelley. She recalled: "I learned to say 'I love you' in Welsh, and it became harder and harder to leave him at night. I carried an alarm clock when I went to his room, as I was afraid I would fall asleep in his arms and my mother would be confronted with my empty bed in the morning."

The provincial tour went well, but it was meaningless; what counted was what happened when the play opened in New York. Although a vastly experienced actress, Strasberg hadn't been on the stage since debuting in 'Anne Frank' five years earlier. And as they got closer to New York, deep anxieties began to surface about her acting, and her mother began coaching her intensively. She had achieved good reviews throughout her career, but she now worried about flopping. She had never before worked with such big stars as Hayes and Burton and it terrified her. She was intimidated by them and it affected her acting. The burgeoning affair with Burton also distracted her and rendered her unable to focus. She explained: "I was terrified and as my terror mounted, my voice became tight and a little too shrill. My mother was frantic. I wasn't bad, but it was obvious something had gone awry. She didn't know how to deal with it, and the more she pressed me about it, the worse the condition became."

But what was really worrying Strasberg was the imminent arrival of Burton's wife and child. They were flying over from Geneva via Lisbon. All she could think of was holding on to Burton, as she wrote in her autobiography: "How could I continue to please Richard yet still hold him at arm's length?"

Opening night in New York was 10th November, which was also Burton's 32nd birthday. The evening started badly when Strasberg got stuck in the ladies toilet and had to be rescued by the stage crew – getting on stage with only seconds to spare. Against the odds, she turned in a great performance. At the curtain call finale, Burton kissed her passionately on the lips for ten seconds in front of the audience and Hayes embraced her. She knew by the looks she was getting from the rest of the cast that her performance had been good. As she recalled: "I floated back to my dressing room; I thanked God it was over." Friends from the audience began to flood backstage praising her performance. But not everyone was pleased. The performance hadn't lived up to her mother's and father's very high standards and expectations for their daughter. Her mother berated her publicly in her dressing room, embarrassing and upsetting her, although everyone who witnessed it understood it was all part of the complicated mother/daughter relationship they enjoyed.

The first night party was held at Sardi's restaurant, which had been taken over for the evening. It was also doubling as a celebration of Burton's birthday. After the row with her mother, Strasberg was the last to arrive.

When she got there, she had a shock. Just inside the door stood Burton and Sybil, who had come virtually straight from the airport to be there for her husband's birthday. Strasberg hadn't been told Sybil would be there and recalled the moment: "I froze and I could see my father knew exactly what I was feeling." And Burton was feeling it too. He got drunk and Sybil, oblivious to all the undercurrents flowing, left the party early to attend to her daughter back at the apartment Burton had rented for them. Burton eventually left with

Philip Burton to go to his West 67th Street apartment, and Strasberg left with her father to return home.

Burton needed urgent counseling from Philip, his adoptive father. They had earlier both gone to the airport to greet Sybil, Kate and Diane Cod Kate's new nanny. By now he was deeply in love with Strasberg and was badly affected by what had occurred at the party when Sybil and Strasberg had met. Although there had been no outward embarrassment, Burton's inner turmoil was tearing him apart. He also couldn't understand Strasberg's reluctance to sleep with him. Philip remembered it well: "An almost imperceptibly drunken Richard came back with me to my apartment. He was flooded with guilt. Why did he feel so guilty? Partly because he was ashamed of me seeing him the worse for drink – he always tried to avoid that – but chiefly I'm sure because of the well-publicised affair he was having with Susan Strasberg."

Seeing Sybil with her husband for the first time had a deep psychological effect on Strasberg and she threw caution to the wind. As she admitted in her book: "I threw myself into my affair with Richard with total abandonment and passion. He absorbed, demanded my complete attention. Up until then, my relationships had revolved around me. Now, I was ready to lose myself in someone else."

Strasberg became determined to win Burton from his wife – whatever the cost. She started having sex with Burton straightaway, even though she risked pregnancy: "I did not care about the consequences. Richard didn't seem to either. I was overwhelmed."

The first time they made love was a revelation to her. Unlike Bloom, she was not a virgin, but she was still terribly inexperienced: "He surpassed all my childhood fantasies when he laid his passion at my feet."

Both were so infatuated with each other that they dispensed with any sense of propriety. Sybil was totally absorbed with her new daughter and did not read the New York newspapers. So, with his wife tucked away in a New York apartment, and Philip Burton in attendance doting over his new granddaughter, Burton and Strasberg began a very public affair and started living life by their own set of rules. As she recalled: "His charisma and charm set him above the ordinary man, allowed him his own rules of life, including acceptance of our affair. You could not judge someone like Richard. He was too alive to restrict."

Burton completely threw any caution to the wind, relying on his brother and stepfather to protect him from the consequences of Sybil finding out. As Strasberg recalled: "He introduced me to his legions of friends as his 'baby girl,' his 'angel.' I was reticent at first, afraid of what people would think, but no one seemed to take it amiss." But she admitted she felt guilty about Sybil being tucked away with her baby: "I was torn between pain and ecstasy."

At every step of the way, there were reporters and photographers who couldn't quite believe what was happening themselves. Usually, celebrities hid their mistresses and illicit affairs from public view. Burton flaunted his. When reporters asked Strasberg: "Are you in love?", she would answer: "Yes, with life."

It was an extraordinary situation, and Burton seemed at one point to have abandoned Sybil altogether. Strasberg said: "His wife, Sybil, was always somewhere with the children. I had never been to their home. That whole part of his life didn't seem real to me, as he seemed so free to come and go as he pleased."

And the infatuation wasn't a one-way street. Burton seemed absolutely besotted with Strasberg and told her so: "Forever and a day, you belong to me."

Meanwhile, Sybil, taking advantage of her husbands long abscences was developing her own social life in New York. She found that she made friends easily and was always out for lunch or dinner. She seemed oblivious of her husband's activities and never once did it affect the atmosphere in the apartment. But others were concerned, Ivor Jenkins now back in London, rang his brother and warned him of the potential consequences. Burton assured them it was just a fling and that Strasberg was no threat to Sybil. Ivor had no option but to take him on his word. Philip Burton was also reluctantly drawn into the cover-up, and kept his adoptive son's secret from Sybil.

Meanwhile, Strasberg and Burton, with reporters trailing their every move, became the talk of New York. They were constantly together and partied from dusk to dawn, as she recalled: "We dined in every restaurant, visited every nightclub." Burton and Strasberg were photographed every night. She said: "I was in a daze half the time and Richard was totally verbal and extroverted about 'us'. He wore me like a flower in his buttonhole."

It was an exhilarating time on Broadway. Peter Ustinov was playing in 'Romanoff and Juliet'; Rex Harrison and Julie Andrews were appearing in 'My Fair Lady'; and Laurence Olivier was in 'The Entertainer'. They would all gather at The Baque Room around midnight to listen to music with other American stars such as Lena Horne.

Acceptance of the pair as a couple was absolute. Lee and Paula Strasberg started acting as though they were already Burton's in-laws, despite the fact that they knew Sybil was just a few blocks away, much to their daughter's surprise, as she recalled: "If I had expected my affair to be a gesture of defiant independence or a rebuff to my parents, I was totally mistaken. Instead of being angry or outraged, my mother was delighted. She adored Richard. But I began to feel there was something indecent about having my parents as co-conspirators in my love affair. I confided to Richard: 'My mother says she hoped I'd fall in love with you.'" Paula Strasberg said that she simply took the view of life that it was better to be extraordinary and miserable than ordinary and happy.

Burton attended Sunday lunch at the Strasberg's apartment regularly. One Sunday, he regaled them with the (untrue) story of his grandfather's death in a wheelchair, crashing, drunk, into a brick wall. When they heard that, they all laughed out loud for ten minutes. Susan Strasberg often thought in these moments: "I wondered if Sybil knew where he was and whether she knew about us. If she did, I thought she must be the most understanding wife in the world."

Burton and Lee Strasberg got on particularly well. Both were literary scholars and Burton found that Strasberg knew just as much as he did about Shakespeare and the great English playwrights.

Burton stayed with Strasberg in her bedroom every night until dawn, when he would go back to Sybil. Like Claire Bloom before her, Strasberg hated that moment and said years later: "After he had gone, I would cry myself to sleep; 'This is too painful, we mustn't see each other,' but I would die if I couldn't see him."

Strasberg was delighted when Meredith Evans and his wife, old friends of Burton's from Wales, came backstage after a performance and Burton introduced her as "my pocket princess." She then delivered a speech in Welsh which Burton had taught her specially. He said to her in English: "Whom do you love?" She replied in Welsh: "Ti rwyn dy garu di rimy na neb arall yn y byd." After she had rendered it, they laughed and clapped. She later admitted Burton had taught her the words but she had no idea what they meant: "The only thing I cared about was that he had wanted them to meet me. That was as good as being asked home for dinner." The words actually translated as: "I love you more than anyone else in the world."

Burton also took Strasberg to visit Philip Burton at his apartment. Philip was enchanted and reminisced with her about Burton's boyhood. On that visit,

# AND GOD CREATED BURTON

Strasberg remembered vividly Burton saying to her: "Little one, we actors, madmen, are capable of experiencing not just the moment, but the nostalgia and anticipation of it." She admitted she didn't understand what he meant. But she did note how relaxed and comfortable her boyfriend was in Philip's presence.

For some reason, that visit with Burton's adoptive father affected her more than any other moment in her short time with him. Afterwards, she wrote Burton a letter, which read: "It's horrible not to be with you all the time. I wish I had known you as a child, you know. Last night, for the first time in years, I said my prayers and wasn't embarrassed. I don't want to hurt anyone, but I can't give you up. I love you more than life itself. I belong to you, so I prayed to God to make it alright. I'm not sure. I'm either regressing or growing up. All my heart, forever and a day, Susan."

At Christmas, they exchanged expensive gifts. He gave her a white mink hat and scarf set plus diamond earrings from Tiffany's. She bought him the most expensive Omega watch in the range with 'forever and a day' engraved on the back. But she was miffed when he bought Sybil an even more expensive full-length mink coat.

The relationship developed so much that they rented an apartment to share together.

There was one moment in the play 'Time Remembered' where Helen Hayes says to Strasberg's character: "The moment is now, seize it with both hands, be greedy, for it will never come again. You are twenty years old and in love. You will never be stronger." Strasberg adopted that as her mantra and began to make a play to take Burton away from Sybil. She pressed him to ask Sybil for a divorce.

Meanwhile, Hayes was furious with what was going on and said: "My God, what a mess. I was the unwilling voyeur, or auditeur if that's the word, of their intermission couplings. Susan and I had the only ground-floor dressing rooms, and she and Richard would make love in her dressing-room between the matinee and evening performances. Moans of ecstasy reverberating through the walls kept me awake. Even my radio turned up full blast couldn't drown them out. In more than 50 years as an actor, I had never seen a theatre used that way. For me, theatres were temples, and this one was being sullied. Couldn't they have rented a room in a Broadway hotel?"

But the renting of the flat and Strasberg's ambition to be his wife marked a turning point in their relationship. It lost its innocence and they began to quarrel furiously. As Strasberg recalled: "We began to fight passionately, but we made up even more passionately. I was jealous of his wife and any woman he talked to for more than five minutes. He was possessive and furious when I went out with other people."

She said of the time: "I was thrilled. We were living every emotion to its fullest, playing our parts onstage and off. I believed it would never end." He told her: "I shall keep you in my pocket day and night. We will grow old together."

But he was telling other people a very different story. When Ivor Jenkins reported what was going on, the entire Jenkins family gathered together to see if they could intervene. Ivor told the family that Burton was playing a very dangerous public game with Strasberg that could backfire and wreck his marriage. Graham Jenkins recalled the time: "My brother parted himself from any remaining vestiges of discretion." Of Strasberg, he said: "Her affair with Rich was, for her, a matter of deadly seriousness. Rich was warned of this, by Ivor among others, but he ignored all the danger signals until it was too late to disentangle without causing great distress all round. Sybil alone retained her dignity. This she achieved by flatly refusing to believe that anything untoward was happening."

When the family's concerns were relayed to him, Burton wrote back and assured them the affair would end when the play's run was over and he returned to Europe.

But he admitted he had fallen dangerously in love with Strasberg: "I was obsessed and possessed by her. Obsessive and possessive. Does that constitute love? If so, then I was in love. But it feels now like it was more of a sexual compulsion. If anything, I love love. I am in love with being in love. And I love to make love."

Meanwhile, the publicity of the Burton/Strasberg relationship was doing ticket sales no harm at all. Audiences packed the Morosco Theatre to see what was in reality a very mediocre comedy that was far less entertaining than the drama going on outside the theatre. In one scene, where Burton delivers a long monologue to Strasberg's character, she became so moved she began crying real tears every night – overcome with genuine emotion. The New York audiences loved it.

The play's publicists sought to exploit the situation and astonishingly persuaded Burton to appear on a round of early morning breakfast TV shows with Sybil and eight-month-old Kate. Ticket sales spiked again and the prices were raised for the play's final month. Burton was being paid US$8,000 a week and he had no choice but to go along with the publicity people's requests.

The same night of the TV interviews, one of Strasberg's movies, called *Stage Struck*, opened in New York. They went together to the premiere at a midnight showing. Afterwards, Burton told her: "I wanted to make love to you on that screen."

As a result of the publicity and his rising profile, Burton received a huge US$1 million offer from the Warner Bros studio for a three-picture deal. It was a career-defining offer, but he didn't like any of the scripts and turned down the offer, much to the chagrin of his manager, Valerie Douglas. But the real reason he turned it down was more simplistic. The Warner deal would have meant him staying in America, and he knew his marriage wouldn't survive it. Although he was in love with Strasberg, he was frightened by her passion for him. By now, he wanted to leave and chose his marriage over the money. But despite that, he was determined to enjoy his last few weeks in New York with his young lover.

On 22nd May 1958, Strasberg turned 20 and, as she recalled succinctly: "I turned 20 with the world on a string, but there were strings attached, too." Burton told her he had to spend the evening with his manager and couldn't see her. She was depressed and, after the performance, was going home alone. To cheer herself up, she booked an appointment at an all-night beauty parlour to have her hair done. As she described in her autobiography: "I took off most of my makeup, put on my old pink raincoat and pink dress, and prepared to leave the theatre. I noticed that a number of the cast were all dressed up, carrying gifts off to some party or other, which made me feel more neglected. Richard came round to my dressing room and said he'd walk me to a cab. As we passed through the alleyway, we saw that the door of the empty theater across the alley was unlocked and ajar." Burton said to her: "Come, my beautiful princess, let's go in." She replied: "I'm late for my hair appointment now." He said: "Just for a minute, I really do love an empty stage."

She stepped into the darkness of what she thought was an empty stage clutching Burton's hand. Suddenly the lights went up and cheering started. Inside, Strasberg found hundreds of people, including the actors Henry Fonda, Anthony Perkins, Julie Andrews, Peter Ustinov and Laurence Olivier, chanting "Susan, Susan, Susan" at the top of their voices. Then they all started singing: "Happy Birthday to you."

Practically every actor playing on Broadway was there. *Pathe News* was covering the party for its newsreel and press photographers were snapping away for the front pages of next day's first editions. It had all been arranged by Burton. Strasberg broke down when they all started singing, crying tears of joy, despite the fact that she looked a mess. Afterwards, she said: "I wanted to strangle Richard. How could he not warn me? I became self-conscious and, to this day, I loathe surprise parties."

Strasberg's birthday party kicked off a whole fortnight of parties to signal the play's run coming to an end. The following week, Richard and Sybil together hosted a spectacular Hawaiian party in a hotel. They set up the entire themed evening, complete with a huge portable swimming pool and Hawaiian-style cabanas brought in for the occasion. It was attended by a host of famous actors but dominated by Susan Strasberg, with Sybil seemingly oblivious to her.

The following week, Laurence Olivier gave a party to say 'goodbye' to the Burtons. He rented a boat to sail around New York harbour. On the gangplank before they boarded, Strasberg and Burton posed for photos with Douglas Fairbanks, Peter Ustinov and Laurence Olivier. It made the front pages of virtually every single American newspaper that week.

But there was a sting in the tail of Olivier's party when a well-known journalist called Igor Cassini, who wrote under the pseudonym Cholly Knickerbocker, became confused. He knew one of the famous actors in the photograph was having an affair with Susan Strasberg, but couldn't remember which one. She recalled in her autobiography: "A few days afterward, I picked up the *Journal-American*, an afternoon New York newspaper, and went into shock. There, on the front page, was a picture of me in a low-cut dress, hair falling over one eye, trying to look like Rita Hayworth, the headline proclaiming: 'OLIVIER TO DIVORCE.' I was named as the femme fatale who had taken him away from Vivien Leigh. The story was totally untrue; someone had confused the rumours about Burton and me with the rumours about Olivier and Joan Plowright."

The story went around the world and there was even more confusion in England from the people who knew about Olivier's dalliance with Claire Bloom and Burton's affair with Strasberg. This was one newspaper that Philip Burton made sure Sybil did read.

The story caused mayhem, and Burton himself believed it and accused Strasberg of actually having an affair with Olivier and arranging the story to be printed to make him jealous. She told him: "I swear on the Bible it's not true." Igor Cassini admitted to Strasberg that he had made a mistake and told her:

"Yes I know. I made a mistake but what do you care. It's Laurence Olivier, not Al Capone. You should be flattered. It's the front page." Strasberg consulted lawyers but they told her as it was a genuine mistake and not written with malice; under US law there was nothing she could do about it. As the story had been reprinted in Britain, Burton offered to pay for a defamation suit to be issued in London where the libel laws were more progressive. But a journalist friend called Joe Hyams told them: "Just remember, today's newspaper is tomorrow's fish wrapping." Lee Strasberg gave them his sage advice: "If it's true, ignore it because it is true. If it's not true, ignore it because it's not true." After that, they soon forgot it and so did everyone else. But it certainly pleased Sybil and the Jenkins family.

As time neared for Burton to leave, Strasberg started agonising over the future. She wrote Burton long, impassioned letters explaining how she felt, but never sent them. She started taking sleeping pills to numb her feelings. Groggy with the pills, she would roam her apartment, unable to sleep. She said: "I was frightened by the jealousy and anger I was feeling. In the worst moments, I contemplated suicide to punish him. The contrast of the intense pain and pleasure was too much."

Towards the end of his stay in New York, Burton gave up drinking. The mood of the relationship changed and became introspective. Burton knew it was coming to an end but he was also deeply in love with Strasberg. They talked about his childhood in Wales, his life dreams and his family. Sober, she found him a different, less flamboyant man.

The last few weeks were a blur of un-shed tears, as she described: "The day before his departure, I ached to cry out: "You can't go, please don't leave me, you promised."

On the last night he was in New York, they took a horse and buggy ride through New York's Central Park. The park was lit by the moonlight and the stars were out. They were wrapped together under a blanket and when it, ended Burton told the carriage driver to "go round one more time", which he did again and again and again.

As Burton left New York, they had made no plans and their future was unsaid. After Strasberg saw him and his family off, she returned to her apartment in a daze and wrote in her autobiography years later: "I felt anaesthetised. I made it across town, home, through the lobby, up the elevator, past my mother and father, into my room, where I collapsed in despair and disappointment. He had promised 'forever and a day', but he was leaving. It had to be a mistake.

He would change his mind; he would send his family home and come to claim me."

That night, she took a sleeping pill and he phoned her from the docks as he boarded the Queen Mary to return to Europe with Sybil. He told her he loved her. She fell asleep and dreamed he had left Sybil at the docks and returned to her. She woke up after a few hours and took four more sleeping pills but couldn't sleep again. She watched a late movie on television, ironically starring Laurence Oliver. She said: "But I saw only Richard's face."

As dawn broke, she slept fitfully, awaking every half hour from what she described as "unremembered nightmares." She recalled in her autobiography: "I forced myself to lie there in limbo until 12:30, when I knew he had really gone, that the ship had sailed and the phone would not ring. It was a relief not to have to pretend any longer. I barely left my bed, and when I did, the floor seemed to undulate like the ocean. The food lay untouched on my plate. Trying to swallow would release a flood of tears. I slept with an old t-shirt of Richard's clutched in my hand like a security blanket, comforted by the familiar scent of him. I smoked to try to stop my trembling. Trying to read made me nauseous. I was undone."

Her father came into her bedroom, cradled her and rocked her as he had when she was a baby. He told her: "Some people never live their lives. They never feel or have a great passion or love. You are fortunate. It's within you, this capacity, and no one can take it away from you. There will be other loves for you, while some people have none at all. Be grateful that you can feel so much." Her mother was as distraught as she was when Burton left.

A few days later, her parents left for the west coast to go and stay with Marilyn Monroe, who was a great friend of the Strasberg family. Susan was due to go but couldn't face it. As she recalled: "I was alone in the house with my misery. Perhaps I should have known Richard would leave me. I had been warned that 'he'll never leave Sybil, ever,' but I had never accepted it. I lay in my bed day after day, waiting for his boat to land so he could call or cable or write as he had promised. There was only silence."

In the end, she drove to California with her brother across country.

The summer in California – in company with Monroe and Cary Grant, Audrey Hepburn, James Stewart, Lauren Bacall and the Fonda family – helped to restore her sanity. She bonded with Marilyn, who was enjoying the happiest time of her life with her husband, the playwright Arthur Miller.

Back in Europe, Richard Burton was spending the summer resting at his home in Celigny, Switzerland, before he would fly to London to take the starring role in *Look Back in Anger*. He had decided to ignore all of Strasberg's letters and resolved to forget her. It was more difficult than he thought.

Strasberg, meanwhile, was getting more and more frustrated, as she explained: "The weeks passed. I rested, partied, and deluged Richard with love letters." Burton had a private Geneva mailbox Sybil didn't know about. But he didn't reply until Strasberg threatened to ring him at home in Celigny. She said: "There had been a long silence from Richard. He had not answered my letters. I wrote: 'If I don't hear from you, I'll call you at home. I'm worried about you' and it resulted in an immediate telegram with protestations of love and 'Letter to follow' but no explanation of the time lapse." She had no idea that it was over and said of his reticence: "I was sure there was a good reason that I just didn't know."

Then, out of the blue, Strasberg's agent called her and told her about an offer to appear in a play in Belgium at the Brussels World's Fair Expo, which was starting in September. The play was Saroyan's 'The Time of Your Life'. They would also do a television production for showing on English television at the same time. The financial offer, effectively from the Belgian government, was huge and the currency exchange rate at the time made it very attractive. She said: "I was sure it was fate bringing us together. I would see Richard again."

She wrote to Burton: "I will actually see you in two months." She thought to herself: "It seemed too good to be true, too easy."

Burton was in a panic and tried to persuade Sybil to stay in Celigny and not accompany him to London, but to no avail. He knew he could not get away in London with what he had got away with in New York. And he knew Strasberg would not understand that.

Burton was heartened when he heard that her Brussels play had collapsed when the government decided they couldn't afford to fund the production even with the millions they were pouring into the Expo.

Some people believe to this day Burton had a hand in getting the funding withdrawn and called in some favours. But if he did, it would not have mattered. By now Strasberg was so determined to go that she financed the production costs herself, confident anyway she would see a profit. She said: "Everyone complimented us on our patriotism. But it was the love of Richard, not America that motivated me."

And then Burton got some news in Celigny that really cheered him up. Claire Bloom had accepted the lead female role of Helena in *Look Back in*

*Anger.* He had no real hope or expectation of resuming their affair but he had deep feelings for Bloom that had never been extinguished, and he was looking forward to seeing her again.

In September 1958, when they arrived at Elstree Studios in North London, he and Bloom had not seen each other for nearly four years. The first get-together of the cast was for a pre-rehearsal script read-through in the first floor room of a London pub. Bloom remembered the trepidation she felt as she waited for him to arrive, but thought: "I was not going to be caught in his spell – neither to be hurt again nor made emotionally vulnerable."

But that resolve didn't last for long and almost immediately they picked up their affair where they had left off four years before. Burton was somewhat surprised himself: "As soon as I saw Claire, I knew I still had strong feelings for her." Bloom was astonished at her own lack of control, as she said: "As our mutual caution disappeared, we began our conversation where we had left off some years before; we knew each other so well that we were still able to talk in a kind of shorthand." The affair was on again for the fourth time, as Bloom admitted: "Our old intimacy quickly came back: too quickly."

Simultaneously, Burton also began an affair with his other co-star, Mary Ure, who was married to John Osborne, the film's writer. But that didn't stop Burton pursuing her despite Osborne's close proximity. Mary Ure said: "I made sure I kept a low profile and have no idea if Claire knew that Richard was fucking me."

Bloom quickly realised some of the magic had gone out of their relationship, but she could not pin-point exactly why. The three previous incarnations had been exclusive relationships, except for Sybil, but this one seemed different. As she admitted: "I viewed the resumed affair this time with some suspicion." There was good reason for her to be suspicious although she never worked out why, as Mary Ure admitted many years later: "Poor Claire. She'd had no idea."

But Bloom wasn't completely stupid and, for the first time, she started to have reservations about her hero and her opinions of him were no longer untarnished. Eventually, she summed it up: "Richard's former, youthful charm had become somewhat spurious; it was too facile, too widely spread. I no longer saw the talented and handsome young boy from Wales; although only just over thirty, Richard already had some of the airs of a practiced rogue."

Bloom didn't like the "practiced rogue" as much as she had and this time she could see through him.

While all this was going on and he was simultaneously sleeping regularly with three women, Burton was concerned that a fourth might be too much even for him. Burton was very worried about Susan Strasberg's trip to Europe. It was the last thing he wanted, but he kept up the pretence, frightened she would call Sybil. He managed to restrict her visit to London to a day and a half and booked her into a suite at the Savoy Hotel, overlooking the river.

Strasberg had called him as soon as she landed at Brussels airport from New York, and he realised she would not be put off. She said in her autobiography: "At the end of the week, I would fly to London for a day and a half and he would meet me at the airport."

Strasberg had rented a large house in Brussels, where the ten Americans involved in the production were staying with her. But she was not interested in her play and was counting the hours until she flew to London to see Burton.

Burton decided not to meet her at the airport and sent a studio chauffeur to pick her up. As Strasberg remembered: "When I got off the plane in London, my knees were shaking and there was a knot of energy that kept shifting from my throat to my solar plexus. I couldn't see him. All the faces were unfamiliar blurs. Then I saw my name on one of those hand-printed signs drivers hold up at airports. A chauffeur stepped forward. 'Miss Strasberg? Mr. Burton sent me. He's still working, so I'm to take you to the studio.'"

Once in the security of the car, her trembling stopped. As she put it: "The knot melted perceptibly. In the back of the car, I tried not to think. I concentrated on the grey buildings, the sky, anything."

But she hadn't realised the distance between Heathrow Airport and Elstree Studios. The one and a half hour journey in rush hour traffic was stressful after her flight and she was relieved when the car pulled into the gates of the studios. "The driver opened the gate for me: 'This way, Miss.' Rich appeared at the top of the stairs and I was so excited I didn't hear what he said or notice how he looked. We embraced and moved into his dressing room. I felt shy, awkward, as if we had just met."

And then fate intervened. Claire Bloom pushed open the door and, from that moment, life would never be the same again for either of them.

Bloom was absolutely furious with herself as she got into the studio car to take her back into London: "I was left with a profound sense of loss, of panic and humiliation. I was extremely angry at myself for resuming my affair with Richard, an affair that should have died out naturally."

Strasberg, of course, was the only one of the three who did not know what was going on. She had no idea who Claire Bloom was. So when Bloom left, swearing and slamming the door, she was somewhat bemused. She knew nothing of Burton's relationship with Bloom, nor that it had mirrored her own and that there was a striking resemblance between them. To her, Bloom was just another moody actress saying goodnight after a bad day of rehearsals. At least that was the way that Burton explained, telling her that Bloom was a friend of Sybil's and had reacted badly when she saw them embracing.

Burton didn't choose to enlighten her any further, but Strasberg did start to wonder and thought to herself: "Why would she care?" She remembered years later: "My pulse quickened; I wondered if they were more than friends."

Burton said to her: "Love, I'll take you for a drink at a pub and then to your hotel, but I'll have to go home tonight. We'll arrange something tomorrow." Strasberg was upset and thought to herself: "'Something'? What was 'something'? I hadn't come three thousand miles for a guided tour of London. What had happened since I last spoke with him? I was afraid to ask. We went to a pub and then drove to the hotel while he made small talk."

Suddenly, reality hit Strasberg like a thunderbolt and she realised that they would not be resuming their affair nor having dinner that night, and that she was being dumped in a suite at The Savoy and would be on her own for the remainder of her trip. She said: "I looked at him and realised he seemed more than withdrawn. He acted frightened. I lost control and by the time we reached the Savoy Hotel, my face and eyes were distorted and swollen from my tears."

She pleaded to him: "Please, just walk me into the hotel. I can't go through that lobby alone looking like this." He replied: "I can't, someone might see us." She was stunned by that reply, as for a whole year he had flaunted her in New York and now he was suddenly afraid someone would see them together in a hotel lobby. She thought it was incomprehensible that he was behaving as if they were virtual strangers.

She got very angry as he drove off and remembered years later how she felt: "Dear God, I wanted to kill him."

As she went upstairs and stared out of the windows of her suite onto the River Thames, she had never known a lower moment in her life. Suddenly, reality hit her square in the face as she sat on the bed. She remembered: "In desperation, I walked aimlessly through the evening mist, drifting with the fog until I reached Waterloo Bridge. In one of my favorite films, Vivien Leigh had thrown herself off this bridge after the loss of her great love. I leaned over and tried to see my reflection in the murky water; a sharp, cold wind moved through my hair. Slipping over the rail would have been so easy; I could see myself lying on the ancient cobblestones of London like Ophelia, like Vivien. Yes, I thought, I'd rather die than feel this…this abandonment. I felt the railing pressing against me. My coat had fallen open, my costly mink coat that I had bought myself; if I drowned, it would be soaked, ruined. In a flash of intuition, I realised that if I could worry about a coat at a moment like this, my life wasn't over yet…I could survive."

With a new sense of purpose, she walked back along the embankment to the Savoy and booked a flight back to Brussels for first thing the following morning. She arranged for a car to take her to the airport and fell into a deep sleep, surprisingly without the aid of any sleeping pills. She knew it was over and resolved she would never speak to Burton again. It was a relief and, despite the heartache she knew was to come, she could now finally get on with her life. Almost precisely to the day the year after it had started, it was over.

That morning, coincidentally, Paula Strasberg flew into Brussels from New York and found her daughter in distress. Strasberg said: "I could see the pity in her eyes and it made my humiliation worse." When the play's run was concluded, they all flew back to New York and Strasberg gradually recovered.

In the event, she did see Burton again, but only once – when he returned to New York six months later. She had resolved not to, but she weakened in the moment. As she recalled in her book: "He called and I met him at the airport in a limousine. In his hotel, we drank champagne and he took me to bed."

But, just like Claire Bloom's reality check the previous year, she also saw Burton in a completely new light, as she explained: "I saw what I had refused to see before, that he was human. On his lovely, strong, peasant fingers I noticed the nicotine stains; on his firm, godlike body I saw the excess; in his green eyes I saw the red veins of dissipation; on his sweet breath I smelled the alcohol; and in his poetic words I heard the lies. Someone said: 'The height of indifference is forgiveness' and it was true. I had made him a god. Now, I forgave him for being mortal. I even forgave him for London."

But when they parted this time, she told him they would never meet again.

In the space of a few months, Burton had lost both of his identical lovers in almost identical circumstances. His marriage to Sybil had survived its two biggest tests. It seemed indestructible.

As for Claire Bloom, the encounter in Elstree had broken the spell and the hold that Burton had over her. She confessed in her autobiography, written years later: "This encounter marked the end of another phase of our involvement. Although, on the surface, more for the sake of our work on the film than anything else, we remained on speaking terms; the tie that had bound us for almost six years, even before we technically became lovers, was finally broken.

I made a vow that I would never, ever again have an affair with a married man."

On the rebound, she met and married actor, Rod Steiger, but eventually found he was a pale imitation of Richard Burton. But what man wasn't?

Although the final split with Strasberg was traumatic, Burton deeply regretted the end of the affair with Bloom. Melvyn Bragg summed up their relationship as "one which seems over the years to have gone from genuinely innocent adolescent friendship through sexual obsession to humiliations, bitter broken promises, exhausted recriminations and, finally, a violent rupture."

# AND GOD CREATED BURTON

# CHAPTER 19

# Sudden transition to Hollywood star

## *Big time beckons*

### 1951 to 1952

As the 1951 Stratford upon Avon season wound down, Richard Burton resisted all the blandishments of Anthony Quayle to return for another season. The refusal was more to do with money than anything else. Appearing in Stratford had cost him at least £3,000 and he had fended off film offers for the entire time he was there. All his American visitors, notably Humphrey Bogart, had told him he must go to Hollywood and earn his fortune. Although he resisted the prospect – and he did actively resist it – there was no doubt at the back of his mind that the advice was sound. Bogart knew that Burton was as big and charismatic a talent as other stars who were earning as much as half a million dollars a picture in Hollywood.

One night, when they had both consumed far more alcohol than was safe for their health, Bogart confided to Burton how much he had earned over the previous two years. In that time, he had completed five films, *Chain Lightning*, *In a Lone Place*, *The Enforcer*, *Sirocco* and *The African Queen*. Burton did literally fall off his chair when Bogart told him he had taken home US$5 million for his work on those five films. Burton quickly worked out this was more than one and a half million British pounds, some 5,000 times what he had earned in the previous two years. He knew he would not be able to resist that goldmine for long and decided there and then he wanted to earn that sort of money someday. The first step was telling Anthony Quayle where he could put his £36 a week.

But with all the wishing and hoping and thinking, the reality was that Burton had no offers from Hollywood studios. So he did what he was to do many times in the future when his career hit a dry patch, he signed up for a lucrative high-profile Broadway play to put his talents on display in New York.

He accepted an offer to take another trip to America for Christmas and signed a deal to play the male lead in a Broadway production of 'Point of Departure' by Jean Anouilh.

# AND GOD CREATED BURTON

Anouilh was a fashionable writer and regarded as France's most important and interesting postwar playwright. The play, starring Dirk Bogarde, had been a success in London's West End. Once his signature was on the contract, he also managed to get his friend Hugh Griffith a part.

Burton sailed for America with Sybil almost as soon as he left Stratford, pausing only for a few days to view progress of the refurbishment of their new house in Squires Mount, Hampstead. They found that, with the owners away, the builders were making very slow progress. Burton told Sybil it didn't look as though they had been there for months, despite putting in regular invoices. The truth was that builders were in big demand as the property market picked up and there were plenty of bomb-damaged houses still to repair. Burton just shrugged his shoulders. They were very happy living in Lyndhurst Road but were rarely there. Burton had barely slept in his own bed for the past two years. So once again they boarded a Cunard liner to take to the United States. Burton loved the six-day transatlantic luxury of a first class suite where he could devour his books and drink beer all day unmolested.

Arriving in New York in early November, they started rehearsals and three weeks later embarked on a short provincial tour of Washington and Hartford before the play's Broadway opening. During rehearsals, Burton struck up a close friendship with 33-year-old British actor Noel Willman, who was appearing with him. They had acted together before but had never gotten to know each other. Both were heavy drinkers and liked to stay up all night with a bottle of scotch whisky. Willman later recalled that Burton spent much time boasting about the future he saw for himself: "It was made quite clear that he was the one; he was the crown prince, he was the actor who would take the mantle of both Gielgud and Olivier."

When Burton arrived back in New York at the Plymouth Theatre, he was delighted to see his name up in lights over the front together with that of his co-star Dorothy McGuire. Although he had already achieved much success, never before had his name been on a theatre's hoardings as the main star. But his name was not destined to remain in lights for long.

The production was doomed from the start. On Broadway, it was renamed 'Legend of Lovers' but the provincial tour failed and exposed problems, which the producers attempted to fix. They tried to make the play clearer to American audiences, only to make it more confusing. They imposed swingeing cuts but the changes only served to warp the delicate Anouilh material. But the worst mistake was the casting of McGuire. Although a big star in America, she was hopeless in this European play.

Hugh Griffith could sense the problems immediately and had no confidence in the director or the producers. After one fiasco in rehearsals, he stormed out saying: "I will stay no longer, I am going home." Noel Willman recalled: "It was the classic example of an American management mucking up and mishandling an English production. Dorothy McGuire was simply not right for the role. She is a darling, and in many ways a good actress. But in this instance, she was badly miscast." Burton shared his disenchantment and called the production 'A Streetcar Named McGuire'. Otherwise, Burton, who was being paid a great deal of money, held his tongue but knew Griffith and Willman were right. He didn't hide the fact that he was doing it for the money – some US$1,000 a week. In truth, he knew the play was not really Broadway material and would probably fail. Christopher Fry's success had caused producers to dare to try all sorts of obscure material. But, by then, even Fry's productions were starting to fail.

Opening on 26th December, the play was panned by critics who found it "pretentious and wordy" and "cheerless and muddled", although Burton received good reviews for his performance. In particular, the *Herald Tribune* called him "an actor of tremendous promise" and the *New York Times* said he was "intelligent and persuasive."

But Burton's stellar performance could not save it and the play shut down on 12th January 1952 after just two weeks. Burton was paid out his full fee of US$12,000, some £3,500 when finally translated back to sterling.

Interestingly, the play was Burton's first and only commercial failure on stage. More or less every other stage production he appeared in was a financial success. The failure briefly shook his confidence and it was not a particularly happy journey back to Europe on the ship from New York that winter. Graham Jenkins called the saga: "Disaster on Broadway."

It was certainly not an auspicious start to the year, and by the beginning of February Burton was back in London with no work and no prospect of any as word got around about the quick closure in New York. Burton knew acting was a fickle business but he didn't reckon on it being this fickle. Failure in any form, he found, was contagious. He filled in his time with some work that Philip Burton arranged for him at the BBC. It felt like he was starting again.

Once again, Daphne Rye sensed what was happening and came to his rescue. HM Tennent was putting on a new play called 'Montserrat', adapted by Lillian Hellman, at the Lyric Theatre in Hammersmith. Rye offered Burton the title role and he seized the opportunity even though it paid only £50 a week, a fraction of his earnings in New York. Coincidentally, the play marked the directorial debut of Noel Willman, his new friend from New York.

The play had a brief run in Brighton and then opened at the Lyric on 8th April. It was set in Central America during Venezuela's fight for independence in 1812 and based on a true story. Burton played an idealistic Spanish captain who is left alone with six hostages and told that if he does not betray the revolutionary leader, Simon Bolivar, they would all be shot. The hostages beseech him to save their lives, but one by one are taken out to die.

The play was not very commercial but once again attracted London's culture-imbibing audience, who loved it, and the opening night was a huge success. After the final curtain call, the audience got to their feet and called for the cast to return for another bow. When they returned, they stood and cheered. Burton was prompted to make a short unscheduled speech and said: "We are overwhelmed." Someone shouted back: "So are we." Back in the dressing room, with the whisky bottle uncorked, Burton was on a high and told Noel Willman: "One day, I tell you, they'll have to queue up to see me."

The play ran the full six weeks and the critics called his performance "memorable." But its audiences had dwindled by the sixth week and Binkie Beaumont did not have the confidence to transfer it to the West End as had been hoped. Burton found himself out of work again.

Beaumont sat on the board of Stratford's Memorial Theatre as a governor and tipped off Anthony Quayle that Montserrat was closing and that Burton had no work.

Quayle, sensing his moment, once again visited the Lyric Theatre and this time went backstage and urged Burton to return to Stratford for the 1952 season. But he said to Quayle: "I'm not in the mood for it."

Quayle turned on his heels and left, unaccustomed to having his offers dismissed in such a perfunctory manner. He never really had any time for Burton after that. Burton later said of that career-defining moment: "It was just a hunch. I have always tried to follow my hunches, not always with much success. In this case, I was right to step back because, if I hadn't, I wouldn't have gone to Hollywood which, despite the material I had to work with there, was a major step in my career."

# SUDDEN TRANSITION TO HOLLYWOOD STAR

But Burton was being slightly disingenuous when he said that. There was already talk of him going to Hollywood and Alexander Korda had also visited him in his dressing room at the Lyric.

By 1952, Burton had made five films in England and was a fully-fledged domestic movie star. Hollywood was now the only place to go, and everything fell into place perfectly – as if it had been pre-ordained.

Unbeknownst to Burton, Hollywood director George Cukor had seen him on stage in 1951, at Stratford, but had left the Memorial Theatre quietly and hadn't gone backstage to make himself known. So Burton was unaware that he had already been scouted by Hollywood.

At the time, the casting for a new film called *My Cousin Rachel* was being done by Cukor, who was scheduled to direct it in Los Angeles a year hence. Cukor was methodical in his search for a leading man, which had led him to Stratford to look over Richard Burton. He very much liked what he had seen and wrote a memo to Darryl Zanuck, the head of 20th Century-Fox in Los Angeles, advising him to contact Burton's representative and make him an offer for the actor's services. As is the way in Hollywood, the recommendation took a long time to get through the system and, eventually, Zanuck sought opinions by writing a studio memo, which every Fox executive would see. It was dated 21st April 1952 and stated that Burton would be "wonderful for a war film Fox was planning to make."

Zanuck had become confused and had mistaken *My Cousin Rachel* for *The Desert Rats* but, nonetheless, the memo had the desired effect and, unbeknownst to Burton, Fox opened negotiations with Korda. And Burton would eventually get the war film as well.

Korda negotiated with Zanuck through Fox's production head in Europe, Freddie Fox. Zanuck and Fox wanted to hire Burton as a contract actor in America for three films for the balance of 1952. The money on offer was huge. Zanuck was potentially offering a maximum of US$600,000 and a minimum of US$350,000 for the three films, which would be just over 12 months of work. If the maximum was paid, after Korda's share, Burton would get US$350,000. But on the first film, the fee would be US$90,000 with Burton's share US$50,000. The minimum Burton was guaranteed on a typical Hollywood pay-or-play deal was US$150,000, and the larger amount would be dependent on an option being taken up. After meeting Korda at his London office in mid-June, Burton was astonished by what was on offer. The money was potentially three times for just a year's work what he had made in his entire six-year career.

Sybil remembered him walking around the house stunned at the enormity of the figures. She said: "Richard wrote those figures on a piece of paper that he kept with him all the time. US$50,000 times three – US$150,000. He kept thinking of how many times he had gone hungry as a boy and he would take out that piece of paper from his pocket and look at it again and again. He just couldn't believe there was that much money in the world and that it was coming to him." But the contract was carefully worded and the small print also stated that, if he flopped, Burton could be sent home with just US$50,000 after one film. Even that smaller amount was as much as Burton had earned in the previous three years.

Zanuck wanted Burton in America almost immediately, and as soon as the deal was signed he had to leave on virtually the next flight. It was agreed that Sybil would take a week to pack up and join him by taking the next Cunard crossing from Southampton to New York and then come to Los Angeles by train.

But Burton had no choice but to catch a plane; it was his first transatlantic trip by air. A half a dozen of his close friends, including Stanley Baker, arranged to travel with him to the airport to see him off.

That evening, Alexander Korda threw a farewell party for Burton at his house in London. Such was the hype surrounding his first Hollywood movie that many leading British stars turned out for the party anxious to meet Burton, whom they really didn't know. It was a who's who of the film and theatre world.

It was only at the party that Burton learned from another guest that *My Cousin Rachel*, adapted from the novel by Daphne Du Maurier, was to be his first film. That delighted him as it was the film of another Du Maurier novel, called *Rebecca*, that had made Laurence Olivier's name ten years earlier.

Against that, Burton was not convinced that an old-fashioned costume melodrama would work in modern day Hollywood. When he heard, Burton collared Korda and Fox at the party and demanded a copy of the script so he could read it on the long plane journey. Korda fobbed him off but eventually Fox fished out a copy of the film's treatment, which showed Burton in 189 of the 196 scenes planned. He knew then it would be his launch pad to fame. Upon his arrival, he decided he would get nowhere in Hollywood by being timid and so he prepared for the greatest performance of his life. He decided he would cast modesty aside and act like a star from the get-go. And he did.

# AND GOD CREATED BURTON

# CHAPTER 20

# Party Time in Los Angeles

## *A real Hollywood welcome*

### 1952 to 1953

In 1952, it took the grand total of 30 hours to fly from London to Los Angeles, and Richard Burton's journey to Hollywood stardom was a gruelling one – albeit in first class comfort. Ordinarily, Burton would have preferred to sail to New York aboard the Queen Mary and then taken the train to Los Angeles, but once the contract was signed Darryl Zanuck, the head of the 20th Century-Fox studio, insisted he got there immediately. With US$150,000 at stake, Burton didn't have an option – he did as he was told and hardly had time to pack a bag. So he made the best of it, read nine books during the journey and drank beer for the entire 30 hours. Glass after glass was brought to him by the stewards, every quarter of an hour.

Finally, Burton arrived at Los Angeles airport just before dawn and was met by Ted du Brey in a stretched chauffeur-driven Lincoln. Du Brey worked for Charles Feldman, the 48-year-old Hollywood agent who had been appointed by Burton's English agent, Vere Barker, to represent him in America. Feldman was a legend in the film business and managed the careers of Howard Hawks, John Wayne, George Stevens, Claudette Colbert, Irene Dunne, Charles Boyer and many other stars.

Burton was not in a pleasant mood when he walked down the steep gangway off the plane at Los Angeles. Wearing a corduroy coat over a crumpled shirt and baggy trousers, he had two days' growth and was badly hung over.

Punch drunk, he was feeling very cocky and barked orders at a startled Du Brey, whom he had met only minutes before: "I'm expecting my wife to join me in ten days – tell whoever it is one tells in Mr Feldman's office to find a house for us." They were the only words he spoke and, once inside the limousine, he curled up on the back seat and went to sleep whilst he was driven to the Beverley Hills Hotel. Du Brey checked him in while Burton looked on uninterested. When he got to his bungalow in the lush 12-acre grounds of the world's most famous hotel, he slept for another eight hours undisturbed.

Before leaving him, Du Brey told Burton he would pick him up at seven o'clock and that he should be ready. Burton stared at him and yawned.

Burton's reputation went before him. Humphrey Bogart had done a brilliant job promoting him and it seemed all of Hollywood was awaiting his arrival. In fact, the anticipation of his arrival in Hollywood was extraordinary. At one point, it seemed that every hostess worthy of the name in Hollywood was planning a party to welcome Richard Burton.

The first of the welcoming parties for him was given that same night, by the producer Nunnally Johnson at his lavish Beverly Hills home. Johnson was producing and writing the script for *My Cousin Rachel.*

When he woke up in his bungalow, Burton dived into the big iron roll top bath and slipped on one of the luscious bath robes supplied by the hotel. After he had bathed and shaved, he put on the dinner jacket he had bought three days earlier in Saville Row. It was one of those flawless dinner jackets that only London tailors know how to make. As he looked in the mirror, he knew he looked great and was ready for anything Hollywood could throw at him.

Before Ted du Brey arrived, Burton made a start on the cocktail cabinet in his room so as to be perfectly prepared. The limousine arrived on the stroke of seven. As Burton emerged from the lobby of the hotel, Du Brey couldn't believe it was the same man he had collected from the airport just 12 hours before. At that moment, the young agent knew what Burton's destiny would be. He had never seen such star quality in a newcomer.

It took just eight minutes to drive to the Johnson house. The thrice-married Nunnally Johnson was arguably Hollywood's most successful producer of the time. He lived the high life in a lavish mansion in Beverly Hills with his wife, the 37-year-old actress, Dorris Bowdon and their three young children.

Johnson put on a big show to welcome Burton, and the party was stuffed with stars, including the Bogarts and Darryl and Virginia Zanuck. Burton did not wait to be introduced. Knowing everyone was curious about him, he immediately shed his own skin and went into character. People who were there remembered his magnetic green eyes scanning the room. His eyes seemed to mesmerise the other guests just as it did his audiences when he was on stage.

Somehow, Burton knew that the performance he put on at his first Hollywood party would be just as important as his first film role. How he showed himself in Hollywood would eventually translate to the respect he was given in what was known as the city of dreams. He sought to conquer Hollywood, not to be conquered by it – as so many hopefuls had been in the past. He didn't let himself down, and those who were present remember him giving the performance of a lifetime.

But Burton was surprised by the general dullness and reserve of most of the people he met. It was his first introduction to Hollywood reserve. For a moment, he was taken aback and looked round for a fellow Brit to lock onto – in vain.

That was until the grand entrance of James Mason. The 43-year-old Mason had come to Hollywood in 1938 and conquered it. He arrived at the party late with his vivacious wife, Pamela. Straightaway Burton recognised a kindred spirit in Pamela and made a bee-line for her.

As Burton introduced himself to the Masons, he suddenly felt all his inhibitions depart. After a few minutes of conversation, he turned around and burst into song. It was so completely unexpected that the whole room immediately hushed to listen to their new star singing a simple Welsh song, unaccompanied. According to Pamela Mason, who recalled the event 13 years later, his fine voice produced a most delightful effect on the entire room: "We all had the impression of an extremely lively, joyous person. Richard was quite noisy, riotous and full of fun." When he had finished singing, he began reciting poetry. He beguiled everyone, as another guest recalled: "He makes anyone feel 20 again, just by watching him."

Then Stewart Granger and Jean Simmons arrived. At the time, the newly married couple were regarded as the prince and princess of Hollywood. Burton immediately renewed the acquaintance of Granger, whom he had met at the Lyric in Hammersmith two years before. But he couldn't keep his eyes off Jean Simmons, then just 23-years-old. And she couldn't keep her eyes of him. Granger didn't appear to notice.

Granger asked Burton where he was staying, and when he told him, ordered him to pack his bags and come and stay in his guest house until he found something permanent. Ordinarily, Burton would have refused but, just as he was about to open his mouth, Simmons' smile closed it for him and the arrangements were made. Granger said he would send a car for him the next morning.

Burton left the party at midnight as it broke up and, for once, he returned to his bungalow at the Beverly Hills Hotel alone. The next morning, just as Granger had promised, a car arrived at ten o'clock.

The Grangers had a particularly beautiful house, high on a mountain top, with fantastic views that stretched far over the city, to the east of Los Angeles, west over the Pacific and the San Fernando Valley, and north to the Sierra hills.

Burton was amazed by the Granger house and, particularly, its gadget-laden kitchen. It contained gadgets he didn't even know existed: it had a waste-disposal unit built into the sink outlet; an automatic dishwasher; a coffee percolator; an electric food mixer; and a wall-mounted built-in oven. But he was most taken with the electric can opener.

Sybil arrived a few days later. The Burtons were delighted to be guests of the Grangers, and the Grangers were delighted to have the Burtons living with them. And it would stay that way for the next seven months. Sybil joined the party whirl and was a huge hit. Everyone in Hollywood loved her as much as they did her husband.

Every night was taken up with parties at homes in Beverly Hills, and they all followed the same pattern with the same people. Burton did his party act and put on a different performance every night with Welsh songs and then poetry. Sybil invariably joined in and she proved every bit as good a singer as her husband. As Pamela Mason remembered: "After that first meeting, James and I kept meeting him in every place we went because Hollywood enwraps itself around people when they first arrive and invites them out night after night."

Stewart Granger was about to go away on location to film *Scaramouche*, and Sybil arrived just before he left. It was a cue for Burton to commandeer Granger's white Jaguar XK120, which his wife, Jean, liked to use.

Sybil's arrival and Granger's departure was also the signal for Burton to begin an affair with Jean Simmons, which he proceeded to conduct right under Sybil's nose. When Sybil thought he was out roustabouting in Los Angeles, he was actually in the main house with Simmons.

Even when Granger returned, the affair carried on. The gay party life continued all summer and into the fall but, with the approach of the Christmas holidays, the party season in Hollywood got into full swing. And Richard and Sybil Burton were at the heart of the festivities.

So much so that Darryl Zanuck was forced to intervene and asked Burton to curb the partying. Zanuck was under scrutiny from America's religious lobby and was worried that the sight of the star of his soon-to-be religion-themed epic, *The Robe*, partying too hard would attract the wrong sort of publicity.

Zanuck would probably have liked him to stay at home for the holidays but Burton refused to turn down a single party invitation. And Burton did nothing to tone down the hedonism that Christmas as he staged two party stunts – one planned and one unplanned – stunts that are still being talked about at

Hollywood dinner parties to this day.

The first came on 23rd December at Humphrey Bogart and Lauren Bacall's annual Christmas party at their home. The party was also to celebrate Bogart's 52nd birthday on Christmas Day.

At the stroke of midnight, signalling the beginning of Christmas Eve, Burton walked into the middle of the Bogart's lounge waving his hands and hushing the 150 or so people in the room. Straightaway, he launched into a festive recital of Shakespeare. And, as he had previously arranged, Jack Buchanan, a star of British musical comedies, suddenly joined in and began dancing to the rhythm of Burton's voice. Burton went from 'Hamlet' to 'Richard III' to 'Romeo and Juliet' and 'The Merchant of Venice', all from memory and without pause, as Buchanan danced to his rhythm. Then, in an unplanned move, another guest, in a white dinner jacket, whom nobody seemed to know, jumped up and began playing jazz tunes on the Bogart's cream-coloured grand piano. Buchanan began to dance to the tune while Burton strutted Shakespeare to it, in the manner that Mick Jagger would today.

It was a stunning, impromptu cabaret spectacle such as no one in Hollywood had ever before seen. Certainly, no one had ever seen Shakespeare set to jazz before. Amazingly, fuelled by whisky, the three of them kept it up until four in the morning as the audience formed a human stage and clapped along. No one who was at the Bogart's house that night did not carry away from it the awareness that they had been watching a very great star performing for them. He had literally revelled in his artistry, assisted by Buchanan. It was a performance of such scope it was close to genius.

Burton never did catch the name of the piano player and wondered afterwards whether he had been specially hired by Lauren Bacall, who had guessed what Burton had planned. If she did, she never admitted it.

On Christmas Eve, the following evening, Nunnally Johnson invited guests to his mansion's screening room for a private showing of *My Cousin Rachel*, which was being released in cinemas on 26th December in time for the Oscars season. The Masons, the Grangers, Bob Dolan and his wife were all invited. But strangely, the idea of it spooked Burton and he didn't turn up, although he allowed Sybil to attend on her own. His no-show was the talk of Hollywood's gossip columnists after Christmas. He later explained why he had declined to attend: "I never see any of my pictures. This is the sixth film I've made. I did see all of my first picture; walked out midway through the second and haven't seen one since. It's too frustrating. I see a gesture, I hear a line I'd like to improve, and there is nothing I can do about it. So now I stay away."

Burton was perhaps wise to have stayed away. After witnessing Burton's stunning performance the night before, the guests in Johnson's screening room were expecting something very special on the screen. But afterwards, they were strangely quiet as they left the room. And all of the guests felt the same way. His performance was good – very good – and highly competent but it wasn't the stunning acting they had witnessed the night before. Somehow, Burton's outrageous talent didn't translate to the screen. It was a problem that would follow him his entire life. Philip Dunne, the screenwriter and later director, summed it up best: "Something Burton had right there before you on a sound stage, something exciting, vivid and flawless, did not register at all on the finished film."

As Pamela Mason recalled many years later, as they left the screening room, everyone instinctively knew something, somehow, had gone wrong with *My Cousin Rachel*. It was not a patch on Laurence Olivier's *Rebecca* ten years earlier. But Mason said everyone was "too infatuated with him, too beguiled by him to believe the evidence of their own eyes."

Luckily, the Fox studio executives had viewed the final cut of *My Cousin Rachel* the day before and loved it. They were certain it was an Oscar-winning performance.

The second stunt that Christmas was completely unplanned and was an unintentional joint production with his wife, Sybil. Traditionally, the Hollywood in-crowd gathered at the house of Charles and Anne Lederer on New Year's Eve, and 1952 was no different. The director's 42nd birthday was on 31st December and it was a glittering party with a double celebration. The Cristal champagne flowed all night and the high point of the evening was the deep gong of Lederer's grandfather clock at midnight. There was no better place in the world to be on New Year's Eve.

As it was, Burton was dancing with Jean Simmons as the first gong sounded. It was a signal for them to move closer towards each other and embrace. Seemingly in a trance, Burton kissed Simmons full on the lips and they stayed in that position for all 12 gongs as 1953 was clapped in by over 220 people gathered in the Lederer House – as balloons fell from the ceiling. But no one noticed the balloons, they were all transfixed by Burton and Simmons.

It was custom at Hollywood parties on New Year's Eve that, as midnight struck, husbands and wives who had been separated would find each other. All the other couples had rushed across the room and kissed one another; all except Simmons, who did not rush towards Granger and Burton, who did not rush towards Sybil. Sybil was left stranded on her own staring at her husband kissing another woman.

Everyone in the room had heard the whispers about the affair between them and now the couple were seemingly confirming it for them. No one could take their eyes off them, and Stewart Granger sought to laugh it off and started clapping as their lips finally parted. The couple carried on dancing, oblivious of the commotion they had caused.

Both Burton and Simmons seemed in a trance and very visibly had eyes only for one another. Stewart Granger continued to laugh it off, but not so Sybil. She was livid. She could put up with anything but a public humiliation. She rushed to where Burton was and, summoning up all her strength, slapped him across the face with a slap that was heard by everyone in the room – even over the music of the band. Pamela Mason remembered: "It sounded like a bomb blast." Burton was momentarily stunned and the music stopped. Simmons retreated to the arms of her husband, and everyone wondered what would happen next. The moment froze in time. But Sybil simply turned on her heels, headed for the front door and asked the Grangers' driver, who was waiting outside, to take her home.

The party wound down quickly after that, and Burton followed his wife home realising he had overstepped the mark. He got a lift in the Mason's car and the astute Pamela suggested that if, the next morning, he found he needed a new place to live, then they would be pleased to have him and Sybil as their house guests.

When Burton got home at around one o'clock, he found Sybil packing. He feared she was leaving him but when he asked what she was doing, she explained to him that they could hardly stay on at the Granger house after what had happened. It hadn't even occurred to Burton that it might be a problem.

Almost immediately, the next morning the Burtons moved out of the Granger residence to the Mason's house. They ordered a taxi and Burton sheepishly handed over the keys of the Jaguar XK120 to Granger, who actually seemed sad to see them go. Granger apparently had no idea about the affair and hardly remembered what had happened the night before.

When the taxi containing the Burtons pulled into the Mason's drive, they were greeted with open arms by James and Pamela. They were both delighted to have the Burtons as their new house guests. The Mason house was nowhere near as grand as Granger's residence but it was a welcome change for the Burtons, who realised they had outstayed their welcome at the Grangers anyway.

Pamela Mason recalled the moment of 1st January 1953: "After five or six weeks of encountering them everywhere, we learned to like them immensely and equally, I should say, because Sybil, herself, is a great character...on impulse, we asked them to become our house guests."

James Mason lent Burton his red convertible Cadillac to replace the Jaguar. Burton couldn't get over how smooth and comfortable it was after the rickety Jaguar. Mason was left with just his silver-grey Rolls Royce to use. One morning, when the Rolls was in for servicing, Mason said to Burton: "May I have my Cadillac for a few days?" to which he replied: "I'll think about it." Mason made do.

After a month, and frightened of again outstaying their welcome, the Burtons moved to a rental house owned by Pamela Mason. She recalled: "I had been dabbling in real estate following the birth of our daughter, Portland, and had bought four houses for speculation and income. The house that the Burtons rented from me was a tiny one, really just an apartment with a garden. It was up in the foothills and it was exactly right for them. Sybil loved doing her own cooking and housework, and was expert at both of them. A legend has arisen since, that we gave them the house rent-free, but that is not true. They paid. They also rented a car from us. This was not because they were mean about money, as everybody now says, but because they had no intention of staying in America."

Surprisingly, the relationship with the Grangers was barely affected by the New Year's Eve incident. And indeed, Burton carried on visiting the Granger house, although he never seemed to bump into Stewart Granger there, just his wife.

Granger remained seemingly oblivious to the affair that was going on right under his nose. He simply didn't appear to believe that Burton would do such a thing to a friend. But he didn't know the man.

But there it was, for all the world to see. It reflected itself on screen in their love scenes in *The Robe*, which had started filming right after New Year.

Eventually, a friend of Granger's decided to put him fully in the picture and told him what had been going on. Granger refused to believe it and confronted his wife, who admitted everything. Sensing the danger to her marriage, the affair stopped in its tracks. But it reflected itself on Granger's hurt and unhappy face, as, from then on, he drove his young wife to and from the studio every day and visited the set of the film with increasing regularity.

But, for the sake of harmony, Burton and Granger agreed to be cordial and there was even some renewed social contact between the Burtons and the Grangers. It was, after all, Hollywood and not real life.

Even Sybil could not ignore the talk of the Jean Simmons affair, but she also didn't appear to believe that it had been anything more than a good friendship. She said: "Knowing Richard, I'm sure he didn't deliberately set out to confound anyone. But he did nothing to prevent it either, taking such an impish delight in being himself. He takes a delight in shocking stodgy people."

She believed 100 per cent in her husband, and added: "I've watched Rich being just as charming to a seven-year-old or an eighty-year-old female as he is with the reigning Queen of London. As long as he keeps it that way, it's all right with me. After all, I'm Welsh, too, and was brought up on the same motto. Our motto says: 'Whatever thy hand finds to do, do it with all thy might.' So I guess I can't complain that Rich flirts with young and old with the same intensity that he puts into everything else he tackles."

As time went by, James Mason and Richard Burton became best friends despite the fact that Mason didn't like to drink. Their link was their love of literature. Both men were avid readers and would sit for hours in silence in each other's company, their noses buried in a book. Mason said: "What we both had was a love of books. He read avidly, and so did I." In between takes on *The Desert Rats*, Burton and Mason discussed the books they had read.

The four of them became very close and discussed doing a television drama series together, in which both Pamela and Sybil would have roles and their husbands would play the leads. The series was to be named *The Sea Squall* and was actually green-lighted by studio executives who authorised the production of a pilot. But then, James Mason landed a very lucrative part in a new film called *The Berlin Story*, to be made in Germany, and had to leave Los Angeles at short notice, so the TV project never happened.

Soon, after a year that couldn't have been more eventful, the Burtons would also be leaving Los Angeles. But, before that, there were some films to finish.

# AND GOD CREATED BURTON

# CHAPTER 21

# From Rachel to Robe to Rat

## *Three movies define his future*

### 1952 to 1953

My *Cousin Rachel* did not get off to a good start. Fox had paid the novelist Daphne du Maurier US$80,000 for the film rights for the book three years previously – well before it was published.

45-year-old Du Maurier had written a simple story about the mysterious widow of a wealthy Cornish gentleman called Ambrose Ashley. Upon Ashley's death, his heir falls in love with his widow. Burton's character, the heir Philip Ashley, eventually suspects the widow, Olivia de Havilland's character, Rachel, of killing Ambrose – an issue that is left unresolved at the end, when she dies in an accident he arranges.

The huge sum paid for the book was based solely on the success of the filmed version of one of Du Maurier's previous novels, called *Rebecca* and starring Laurence Olivier ten years before. *Rebecca* had been a huge hit and had turned Olivier into a star. But that was then and this was now and, in the intervening few years, with the advent of television, old-fashioned melodramas made for the cinema had gone out of fashion.

But having paid so much, Fox was forced to make the film. Unsurprisingly, there were problems trying to adapt it to the screen and to keep it relevant to an audience that had had its horizons massively widened by the television sets that were creeping into every American home.

So, when director George Cukor wanted to start filming, he found there was no proper script. This annoyed Cukor intensely as the script was being written by the producer, Nunnally Johnson, who was supposedly very experienced and expert in his craft. Cukor had some harsh words for Johnson and quit the picture. Johnson tried desperately to persuade him to stay, but Cukor was unconvinced by Johnson's talents.

Cukor was a brilliant, methodical director who liked everything in place before he started filming and he detested what he called "half-baked scripts." He held Nunnally Johnson personally responsible. Johnson's failure to provide a workable script was surprising as, up to that point, he had done no wrong and enjoyed a glittering career. He had written and produced 45 films in his career for 20th Century-Fox and was then basking in the success of his previous year's box office hit, *The Gunfighter.*

It was apparent to Cukor that, in the past, Johnson had been lucky and his success had all come too easily. Cukor believed he had gotten slack and become overconfident about his ability. He told Johnson that his decision to quit was irrevocable.

Cukor's departure was Johnson's first serious reversal and a blow to his reputation. He was quickly replaced by Henry Koster, a German-born director who was known more for his reliability in turning out a serviceable final negative than for creative filmmaking. From that point onwards, with Cukor gone and Koster hired, *My Cousin Rachel* was destined to be only mediocre at best, and Burton had lost his chance of making a film with the brilliant Cukor.

Such were the ways of Hollywood, even 60 years ago, that Burton was forced to wait for nearly two months while the studio cleared up the problems on the script so filming could finally get started in late July.

Burton found working in Hollywood entirely different to England. In England, the director you started with was the director you finished with. The resources allocated to the film were also of a different scale to anything to which he had been accustomed.

When he arrived at the Fox sound stages, situated on the studio's vast back lot right in the middle of Los Angeles, he found that everything was big – from the budget to the buildings.

He was allocated two dressing rooms. One was a normal trailer adjacent to the set and the second, in a separate building, was a luxurious air-conditioned suite of rooms including a lavishly furnished lounge, a dedicated make-up room and en suite bathroom. He took one look at his suite and never went there again. He was overwhelmed by the luxury and feared it could affect his acting. Coming from war-ravaged England, he was embarrassed by the ostentatious display of money and found his set trailer more than adequate.

He was also surprised by the intensity of the journalists that covered the filmmaking community in Hollywood. But he soon caught on, and Hollywood's press pack took to the newcomer as he regaled them with stories of his tough upbringing in Wales and colourful relatives. Very few of the stories he told them were true. The story of his wheelchair-bound grandfather killing himself in a drunken frenzy after winning a small fortune betting on a horse called Black Samba became Hollywood folklore, despite being completely made up. But Hollywood's correspondents loved it – true or not. In return, they went back and typed up their stories, which depicted him as a typical du Maurier hero and a worthy successor to Laurence Olivier.

*The New Yorker*'s Hollywood correspondent in particular lavished heavy praise and commended Burton for his raw sex appeal, calling him "lean, handsome, troubled and upstanding." And that was even before he had seen him act.

The crew on the film also adored him. Every morning, when he arrived on the set, he brought them coffee and clowned around with them – remembering all their names in a way that big stars generally don't in Hollywood. He was continually bounding around the set, cracking jokes, singing Welsh songs and charming everyone.

But Burton also had to get used to one other small change – whilst English film sets overflowed with alcohol, American film sets were what he called "bone dry." But when pushed, he admitted that it was no bad thing at all.

But despite his relationship with the crew, the atmosphere on the set was marked by his relationship with his co-star Olivia de Havilland. She appeared not to have forgotten the perfunctory way he had dismissed her offer to play Romeo to her Juliet in her own Broadway production two years before. His decision still rankled with her and she made no secret of the fact that she had wanted Gregory Peck for Burton's role. After turning her down, Burton really upset her by revealing his decision to a reporter called Fergus Cashin. Cashin's subsequent story in a down-market paper had circulated around the world and De Havilland felt humiliated.

Although he couldn't have known how their paths would cross again, Burton had upset the wrong person in De Havilland, who was a very important star indeed. She had won two Oscars, been nominated twice and starred in numerous hit pictures, including the greatest box-office film of all time, *Gone With The Wind*. In her contract, she took revenge on Burton by specifying the size and position of his name on the adverts and posters used to promote the film. When they appeared, it was Burton who was left humiliated – as he found his name a quarter of the size of hers and right at the bottom of the adverts.

But there were problems for the 36-year-old star. She was aging fast and now playing a woman much younger than her years in *My Cousin Rachel*, and it showed. Burton sensed this and, for once, he didn't bother hitting on his leading lady.

But despite her miscasting in *My Cousin Rachel*, De Havilland was a real pro and she knew how to act and make the most of what she had. She went out of her way not to help her co-star, who was not versed in the ways of sophisticated lighting and other Hollywood techniques that made actors look good on screen. In fact, she used all her feminine wiles to outshine her co-star and sabotage his performance.

She didn't hide her dislike of Burton either. When she first arrived on set, she said with a remark pointedly aimed at Burton: "By heaven, I'm going to be the greatest actor or what's the point of acting?"

Initially, Burton played her at her own game and tried to match her; one prima donna move for another prima donna move. But he found she knew every trick and he was no match, so he eventually gave up – but not before some amusing histrionics which the crew were in on, while the bemused director, Henry Koster, was not. One day, Koster just stared at Burton in disbelief after one such chimpanzee-inspired incident. He was completely bewildered at the strange man from England. But De Havilland knew precisely what he was up to and was unaffected by the stunt, as Burton soon realised.

With her, he was out of his class and he knew it. As Pamela Mason recalled: "None of us knew why Olivia hated him. My impression is that he thought she was a bit of a snob. She had a drama coach on the set all the time, telling her what to do and how to do it. Richard despised that, which may have been part of the trouble. It may have been, too, that Richard made a few sporty remarks to her which she thought were in bad taste."

A few weeks after filming began, the enmity between the two was the talk of Hollywood and filled the gossip columns of the Los Angeles newspapers. De Havilland told some reporters that had gathered around her on set one day: "Burton goes berserk when he is frustrated. He had these violent departures from control." And then, famously, she uttered: "He's a coarse-grained man with a coarse-grained charm, and a talent not completely developed, and a coarse-grained behaviour which makes him not like anyone else."

The film's publicists went into overdrive after De Havilland made those remarks and, soon, she was singing a different tune. She was furious when Fox's publicists put out a press release with a quote from her saying Burton was "the greatest leading man in a decade." She may have been forced to say it, but she certainly didn't think it.

Pamela Mason publicly defended Burton against De Havilland's attacks and said she didn't agree at all: "Of course, I do not agree with that; not back then, nor now. It's true that Richard is not precious. He's a canny, down-to-earth

Welshman of great appeal."

Despite not agreeing with the change of director, Burton got on well with Henry Koster, who was patient and considerate with him. Playing young Philip Ashley, the central character, called for a softening of his rough edges, so he sought to de-emphasise his toughness. It was a part, as Melvyn Bragg described it: "With no verbal bite and no guts."

With all the delays, filming didn't begin until mid-July, and the first decision Koster made was to dispatch a second unit to Cornwall in Britain to get authentic exterior shots. He found the painted backdrops that Nunnally Johnson had commissioned totally inadequate.

As was the way in Hollywood, the Cornish and Italian scened narrative was played out entirely in Los Angeles on special sets built on one of Fox's giant sound stages. The actors did all their work on the sound stages. The exteriors were shot against a green screen and later superimposed on the Cornish and Italian scenes shot by the second unit. Koster would have preferred to take the actors to Europe but Zanuck would not authorise the extra cost.

Despite all the problems, Burton's acting was superb. With all the constrictions, the film was never going to be a classic, but Burton played his part well. He was also becoming a heartthrob around Los Angeles. Koster remembered the hypnotic effect Burton had on women and, in particular, on a young actress who appeared on the set regularly watching Burton "with tears in her eyes." When Koster asked her what she was doing, she replied: "I just want to see him." Her reaction was not untypical. Somehow, Burton set off a chemical reaction in women that no one could explain. There were plenty of very good-looking young actors in Hollywood, dispensing gas at petrol stations. But Burton had an extra ingredient that everyone recognised but no one could define.

John Gielgud visited Burton on the set of *My Cousin Rachel* and afterwards Burton took him to dinner at the house of Hollywood's most successful independent producer, David O. Selznick. Selznick, who had produced *Gone With The Wind* and also *Rebecca*, was married to the actress Jennifer Jones. It was a mark of how far Burton had come that he was invited to dine with the Selznicks. Charlie Chaplin was also a guest that evening. Gielgud later described the experience: "Burton is a huge success here. Last night, he and his wife drove me to Malibu Beach to dine with the Selznicks. She is Jennifer Jones. Chaplin was there."

Gielgud had a wonderful time in Hollywood with Burton. He described it as only he could: "The parties are grand, but clumsy – awful food, too much drink, rather noisy and the weirdest mixture of clothes, women in beach clothes or full evening dress, and the men in every crazy variety of sports clothes. But it is not difficult to pick out the people one wants to talk to, and the rest of the guests don't seem to trouble one or expect one to trouble about them."

Gielgud viewed some rushes of *My Cousin Rachel* during his visit and was impressed with Burton's performance. He colourfully described him as: "Stocky, Welsh, tough, yet beautiful in repose – only he is a bit phlegmatic and may lack power and aristocratic authority. But on the screen, all that could easily be emphasised with close ups and clever photography and direction. Besides this, he is the new rage, and really a good actor; intelligent, sensitive and full of potentialities." Any doubts Gielgud might have had about Burton by this stage had been completely dispelled. He recommended his talents to everyone and anyone, and had become a huge fan.

The filming of *My Cousin Rachel* wrapped in late October and was followed by a hasty editing schedule in order for the film to be released before the end of December 1952 so it could qualify for that year's Oscars.

Darryl Zanuck was delighted with what he had seen of the rushes of *My Cousin Rachel*, but still he prevaricated with Charles Feldman about taking up his option on Burton for the remaining two films. Zanuck thought he had the upper hand and could negotiate the price down, despite the impact Burton had made in Hollywood. Zanuck was playing a dangerous game as Burton, unbeknownst to him, had already been cast in *The Desert Rats* in the lead role with James Mason.

When Feldman phoned Alexander Korda in London to tell him what was happening, the canny Korda knew precisely what to do. Korda was 17 years Zanuck's senior and been around the film industry a lot longer. He understood the game better. He called Zanuck and told him that, since he wouldn't be taking up Burton's option, he was casting him in a British war movie called *The Last Enemy*. *The Last Enemy* was the true-life story of Richard Hillary, a Battle of Britain pilot who was burned when his plane caught fire and crashed, and who then went back to the RAF and was killed during a routine training flight.

But Korda knew Zanuck would be no pushover and had chosen a genuine project with which to call Zanuck's bluff. Korda even put out press releases announcing Burton would play the part of Hillary. And Zanuck swallowed the story hook, line and sinker, as Fox had been offered the book itself and knew Korda had optioned it.

# FROM RACHEL TO ROBE TO RAT

When a shocked Zanuck heard what Korda had to say, he spluttered and said he had no intention of letting Burton's option drop. In the process, he accidentally blew his lit-cigar halfway across his desk, dropping the phone receiver to recover it before it set fire to his papers. At least, that is what is supposed to have happened. What most certainly did happen was that Zanuck told Korda he was mistaken and that Feldman must have misheard him on the telephone. Zanuck told Korda he was taking up the option and to back off. It was exactly what Korda had wanted to hear, and he couldn't believe his deception had been so easy to pull off. Korda never intended *The Last Enemy* to go beyond a script outline and a press release. It was a ruse to force Zanuck to keep Burton, and Korda never made *The Last Enemy*.

A letter confirming the option was waiting on Feldman's desk the next morning and confirmed that Burton's total take from the three films would rise to US$500,000 with him getting US$300,000 and Alexander Korda US$200,000. Even after the fees of both his agents, Burton would be taking a quarter of a million dollars back to England with him.

As expected, Zanuck also confirmed that Burton would be taking a lead role in a new film by Fox called *The Desert Rats*, co-starring with James Mason. But there was no word of the third movie. *The Desert Rats* was an inconsequential war film from which no one expected much. But then Burton's legendary luck came into play as, first, Tyrone Power, then, Marlon Brando and finally, Laurence Olivier turned down the role of Marcellus in a planned new Fox epic film called *The Robe*. *The Robe* was a big budget movie, essentially the story of the early years of Christianity, and was scheduled to be Fox's big summer film of 1953 – commonly known in Hollywood parlance as a 'tentpole'.

To play Marcellus, an actor was needed who had a strong romantic image but who would not appear out of place in a religious epic. Burton could have been tailor-made for the role. That he had romantic appeal was undeniable. He also had what was described as a "rough sensuality", which made him believable as a Roman tribune caught up in a personal struggle between duty and conscience.

With three refusals, Zanuck called Burton and offered him the part of Marcellus. Zanuck told him he could do both films and Fox would juggle the shootings schedules to suit. Zanuck also told Burton he was now seen in Hollywood as an actor with the right star quality and a real seriousness of purpose. Burton was surprised, as it wasn't like Zanuck to compliment the talent, but he was unaware of what had gone on behind the scenes with Korda.

# AND GOD CREATED BURTON

Suddenly, Burton was Fox's most important star. 20th Century-Fox's publicity department put out a press release announcing that the part was Burton's and confirming the spiritual significance of the role of Marcellus. The news was broken in the *Los Angeles Examiner* the day before by its legendary 70-year-old columnist, Louella Parsons, who quoted Burton as saying: "I'm really called the poor man's Olivier." She also wrote that he was "one of the most delightful and unaffected actors ever to come to our town", adding he was the "hottest thing in Hollywood."

With those words ringing in his ears, Burton made plans to stay in Los Angeles until mid-1953 after which he decided he would return to the UK and do another season at the Old Vic.

The production of *The Robe* came first. It would be the first film to be shown in the newly invented widescreen Cinemascope system. Cinemascope was the cinema's attempt to fight back against the erosion of its audience due to television. The threat to Hollywood from television was real and, between 1946 and 1951, no less than 5,000 cinemas had closed in America and ticket sales had been halved.

It was believed that Cinemascope could reverse this trend, and it aimed to create an effect that black and white televisions could not possibly give. Instead of a square screen, Cinemascope employed a slightly curved screen, two and a half times the normal size. It also gave the impression of a three-dimensional picture. Up to that point, American cinema screens had been square format and had shown films mostly in black and white. Cinemascope was championed by Spyros Skouras, the Greek-American president of 20th Century-Fox, much against Zanuck's better judgment, who saw nothing wrong with square screens.

It emerged that there had never been any logical reason for the cinema screen to be square, so the opportunity to widen the field of vision was seized upon. It also meant cinemas could charge higher ticket prices – half of which went to the studios. *The Robe* would also be Burton's first colour film. Hollywood had somewhat belatedly realised it had fully to adopt the colour process in order to fight television, which was then only available in black and white.

Cinemascope, which was championed by Fox, competed with another widescreen system called Cinerama, which had been introduced the year before. But Cinerama was a cumbersome system that required three projectors in cinemas while Cinemascope needed only one.

# FROM RACHEL TO ROBE TO RAT

The adoption of Cinemascope was even more risky than it looked, as millions of dollars were needed to convert cinemas to be able to show *The Robe*. Fox inevitably had to subsidise the cost. When Burton asked Spyros Skouras what would happen if Cinemascope didn't take off and *The Robe* flopped, he reportedly replied: "We start by hanging you by your thumbs." Fox insiders believed he was only half-joking.

But in reality, there was little danger of *The Robe* flopping. In Hollywood parlance, it was a slam-dunk. The film was based on a best-selling novel of the same name by Lloyd C. Douglas. It was basically the story of a Roman tribune who carried out the execution of Jesus Christ. Later repenting his actions, he became so obsessed with the guilt of what he had done, that he converted to Christianity and was himself martyred.

The rights had been sold by Lloyd Douglas to Frank Ross, an independent producer, ten years earlier – before the book had become a success. It had taken Ross all that time to sell it to Zanuck, and Fox finally agreed to make it in 1952.

But Douglas, who didn't start writing until he was 50-years-old, had died in 1951 at the age of 73. At the time of his death, *The Robe* had sold two million copies in hardback.

Darryl Zanuck staked the entire future of 20th Century-Fox on the success of the film. He was so pleased with *My Cousin Rachel* that he handed directing duties to Henry Koster. It was all very neat. He also lined up a starry cast, including Victor Mature, Jean Simmons, Dawn Addams, Michael Rennie and Richard Boone.

The film was due to start shooting in the first week of November 1952, but the script had not been properly adapted for the new widescreen scenes. The screenplay was by Philip Dunne, who was out of his depth on such a big film. The delay meant Burton could get on with *The Desert Rats*, and Fox brought the filming schedule of that forward once it realised *The Robe*'s script was having problems.

*The Desert Rats* was a war film set in North Africa but acted out in the vicinity of the Palm Springs desert. Burton co-starred with his British friend James Mason, who played Field Marshal Rommel. Burton played Captain MacRoberts, a young English captain in the second siege of Tobruk, who defeats Rommel's tanks at a crucial moment in the North African campaign in World War II.

Burton was initially flustered, as it was an all-male cast with not a female in sight. He proceeded to secure a cameo role for his wife, Sybil, who was the only woman in the film. But, ultimately, he enjoyed the male company, particularly that of Robert Newton, who he found was the first man who could out-drink him.

Robert Newton, by then declining spectacularly into the final stages of alcoholism, was, with amazing irony, apparently warned by Burton that too much drinking would kill him. It was a lesson as hard for Newton to learn as it would prove for Burton later in his life. Burton said at the time: "I've told him; we've all told him: If he doesn't lay off, it'll kill him."

One weekend, Burton and Newton assumed American accents and crossed the border into Mexico without the proper visas that Britons needed to enter Mexico. He remembered: "We became absolutely paralysed with tequila, and on the way back we were so stoned that we completely forgot about our accents, and we landed in the pokey for the night."

Aside from the male bonding, Burton found he excelled at acting in an action film, which he had never before attempted. The style fitted him like a glove. Robert Wise, the director of *The Desert Rats*, concurred and found Burton agreeable, hard-working and reliable, as he said: "I was very glad we had no women in the film because I'm sure that would have distracted him. I'd expected Burton to be resistant to the kind of role he had – that of an army officer. I thought he would have preferred a script with some lovely language, but he said to me: 'You know, I am really enjoying being an action star. It's tremendous fun.' So he was having a good time, and he was perfect for that kind of role because you really can believe that he is a leader of men."

Filming began in the desert near Palm Springs in the middle of November and took less than three weeks to complete. The crew was back in Los Angeles to finish the studio work by mid-December and would do the interiors on the sound stage as soon as *The Robe* was finished.

Meanwhile, back in Los Angeles, the delays to *The Robe* seemed to add to the hype, and the film was creating tremendous excitement across America. It seemed that everyone had read the book.

Once again, Burton couldn't believe the amount of money being pumped into the film. If Burton had thought that *My Cousin Rachel* was a lavish production, then he had no idea what the word 'lavish' could be stretched to mean. *The Robe*'s budget, at US$6 million, was almost ten times that of *My Cousin Rachel*, a fact that led Burton to say in an unguarded moment to a journalist: "I am appalled by the amount of money the studio is putting into *The Robe*, and it makes me feel a terrible, awesome responsibility."

Rex Features

**Above:** Richard Burton smoked between 60 and 100 cigarettes a day from the age of 14 to the day he died, at 58. Along with his alcohol consumption, it contributed to his early death on Sunday 5th August 1984.

**Left:** Richard Burton, Julie Andrews and Robert Goulet appeared on the Ed Sullivan show on CBS on 19th March 1961. They performed a sequence from 'Camelot'. Ticket sales at the box office exploded the next day and the show never looked back.

**Above:** Richard Burton and Julie Andrews backstage at the Majestic Theatre in New York after the opening performance of 'Camelot' on 3rd December 1960.

**Above:** David Hurst, Robert Goulet, Julie Andrews, Richard Burton, Robert Coot and Roddy McDowell read through the 'Camelot' script (such as it was) in New York in July 1960.

**Right:** Richard Burton arrives at Rome Airport from New York, with his wife Sybil and daughter Kate, to begin the filming of 'Cleopatra' on 27th September 1961.

**Left:** An LP was recorded from 'Camelot'. The album reached number one in the spring of 1961 and stayed in the top 40 charts for three years.

**Left:** The Burtons visit a toyshop in Rome, Italy with their daughter Jessica during the filming of *Cleopatra* in October 1961.

**Left:** Richard Burton chats casually to Elizabeth Taylor and husband Eddie Fisher on his first visit to the set of *Cleopatra* in September 1961. No one had any idea at that stage of the dramas that were to come.

**Below left:** Richard Burton and Elizabeth Taylor in costume on the set of *Cleopatra* in January 1962.

**Above:** Jack Brodsky and Nathan Weiss were the publicists who worked for 20th Century Fox on *Cleopatra*. They later wrote a book called *The Cleopatra Papers*.

**Above left:** Eddie Fisher shows off a ring, a present from his wife, Elizabeth Taylor, to reporters and denies any rumours of a breakup of his marriage on 31st March 1962.

**Above right:** Richard Burton and Elizabeth Taylor left the road in their Lancia sports car, returning to Rome on Easter Sunday 1962. Taylor had a bruised eye and facial cuts and filming of *Cleopatra* was delayed while her injuries healed.

**Left:** Richard Burton drives Elizabeth Taylor home in his Cadillac on the night of the 22nd January 1962. Still in their theatrical make up, legend has it that they made love on the back seat for the first time that night.

**Below:** Elizabeth Taylor and Richard Burton with director Joe Mankiewicz on a break from filming *Cleopatra* in Rome on 5th April 1962.

**Above:** Walter Wanger, the producer of *Cleopatra*, was a nice man but his ineptitude cost 20th Century Fox millions.

**Below:** Richard Burton leaves The Dorchester Hotel in London with a patch over his injured eye after an unexplained incident when a man attacked him allegedly in reprisal for his treatment of his wife Sybil on a train 21st January 1963.

*Camera Press/Robin Douglas-Home*

*Daily Mail/Rex Features*

**Above:** A paparazzi sneak photo of Richard Burton and Elizabeth Taylor in a pub near Shepperton Studios before they were married. Burton was filming *Becket* with Peter O'Toole in 1963.

Sybil Burton ignores a reporter who attempts to question her about her husband's affair with Elizabeth Taylor in New York as she tries to hail a cab outside Hotel Westbury, on 4th April 1963.

*Bettmann/Corbis*

**Above:** For two extraordinary weeks in April 1963, *Cleopatra* fever took over America as cinema goers queued around the block to see the film. It was featured on the covers of both Life and Time magazines on successive weeks on the 19th April and the 26th April. The film was premiered at the Dominion theatre in London. *Cleopatra* eventually managed to make a small profit on the $37 million it cost to produce.

**Above:** Richard Burton and Elizabeth Taylor talk to journalists at a press conference in London in December 1962 to publicise *The VIPs*.

**Above:** Sybil Burton with Kate and Jessica on 24th September 1964. She divorced her husband on 20th December 1963; the grounds were stated as abandonment and cruel and inhuman treatment.

**Right:** Richard Burton on location in Northumberland shooting the exterior shots of the film *Becket* in the summer of 1963.

**Above:** Sue Lyon, Deborah Kerr, Ava Gardner, Richard Burton and Liza Todd during filming of *The Night of the Iguana* in Puerto Vallarta, Mexico in 1964.

**Left:** Hugh French was Richard Burton's agent for most of his career. French also acted for Elizabeth Taylor, Marylin Monroe (pictured) and many other Hollywood stars of the era.

**Right:** Darryl Zanuck of 20th Century Fox was a prime player in Richard Burton's life from 1952 to 1963. The two men had a love hate relationship that was finally resolved when Burton did a cameo role in Zanuck's *The Longest Day* for no fee.

**Left:** Burton and Taylor in the Hotel Oceano Bar in Puerto Vallarta, Mexico, on 22nd December 1963. The couple visited the bar everyday whilst Burton was filming *The Night of the Iguana.*

**Below:** Richard Burton, Elizabeth Taylor and Philip Burton at the Lunt Fontanne Theatre in New York on 22nd June 1964. The pair gave a successful poetry reading in benefit of Philip Burton's acting academy.

**Above:** Philip Burton, Elizabeth Taylor and Montgomery Clift at the premiere of *The Night of the Iguana* at the Philharmonic Hall in New York on 30th June 1964.

**Left:** Taking instruction from director, John Gielgud at the O'Keefe Center in Toronto during rehearsals for the production of 'Hamlet' on 6th February 1964.

Time Life Pictures/Getty Images

**Above:** Elizabeth Taylor and Richard Burton in New York with the company of 'Hamlet' on 27th February 1964. Taylor prepares to cut her 32nd birthday cake with a prop sword from the play whilst the company sings 'Happy Birthday' to her.

**Left and below:** Richard Burton and Elizabeth Taylor on their wedding day at the Ritz-Carlton in Montreal on 15th March 1964. They are with Burton's valet, Bob Wilson, who was the best man at their wedding.

Getty Images

Getty Images

**Above:** The cast of 'Hamlet' take their curtain calls following the gala opening at the Lunt Fontanne Theatre on 9th April 1964. (left to right): George Voskovec, George Rose, William Redfield, Alfred Drake, Eileen Herlie, Richard Burton and Hume Cronyn.

**Above:** The Burtons getting ready for the premiere of *Lido* in Paris in 1964. Elizabeth Taylor is wearing a set of yellow diamonds, the latest expensive gift from her new husband. Taylor's hair is attended to by her favourite hairdresser, Alexandre de Paris.

**Right:** Richard Burton with brother Graham Jenkins and Elizabeth Taylor at Cardiff Arms Park watching Wales v. England in the Five Nations Championship, on 16th January 1965. Wales won 14 – 3.

**Left:** Sybil Burton with second husband Jordan Christopher in New York at the premiere of *The Graduate* in December 1967.

**Above:** Sybil Burton with her great friend, actor Roddy McDowell in 1967. He was also a lifelong friend of Elizabeth Taylor and the two women met for the first time since *Cleopatra* at McDowell's deathbed on 3rd October 1998.

**Left:** Director Mike Nichols, George Segal, Elizabeth Taylor and Richard Burton on the set of *Who's Afraid of Virginia Woolf?* in November 1965.

**Below:** Richard Burton and Elizabeth Taylor, in character as George and Martha on the set of *Who's Afraid of Virginia Woolf?* in November 1965.

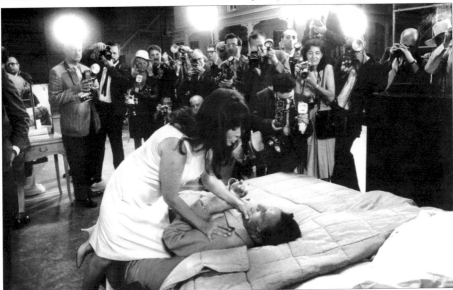

**Left:** Richard Burton and Elizabeth Taylor at Merton College, Oxford University, on 1st February 1966, when they arrived to perform 'Dr. Faustus' with students. They are accompanied by Professor Neville Coghill (far right) and Burton's understudy, Bob Scott (fourth from left).

**Left:** Elizabeth Taylor, Peter Sellers, Brit Ekland, and Richard Burton at London Airport on 19th November 1966. The four stars had flown in to appear in a television show to raise money for the Aberfan mining disaster appeal fund.

**Below:** Richard Burton and Elizabeth Taylor with Clint Eastwood on board their chartered yacht, Beatriz, on 16th February 1968. The yacht was moored off of Tower Pier in London whilst Burton and Eastwood were filming *Where Eagles Dare*.

**Right:** Richard Burton and Elizabeth Taylor with Noel Coward at the wedding of her great friend Sheran Cazalet to Simon Hornby at Fairlawne in Kent on 15th June 1968.

*Getty Images*

**Left:** Richard Burton and Elizabeth Taylor with their adopted daughter Maria Burton and Taylor's daughter Liza Todd at Chalet Ariel in Gstaad, Switzerland, on 8th December 1968.

*Popperfoto/Getty Images*

**Right:** Elizabeth Taylor shows off the 33.19 carat Krupp diamond ring on 20th May 1968. Burton had paid US$305,000 for the ring at Sotheby's a few days before.

*Mirrorpix*

**Left:** Richard Burton and Elizabeth Taylor arrive at RAF Abingdon, Oxfordshire in their private jet in October 1967. Burton paid US$960,000 for the plane.

**Below:** Richard Burton at Sotheby's auction house on 4th July 1968. He was on the lookout for old master paintings to spend some of the vast amounts of money he was accumulating.

**Above:** Richard Burton bought Monet's 'Le Val de Falaise' at the auction on 4th July 1968, for £50,000 and afterwards posed with his purchase. Today it is worth 200 times what he paid for it 43 years ago.

**Above:** Kalizma was purchased by Richard Burton in 1967 as a present for his wife. Burton paid £80,000 for the yacht and re-named it after his daughters, Kate Burton, Liza Todd and Maria Burton. The yacht was originally named Minona when it was built in 1906 and was used in both World Wars by the Royal Navy. This photo was taken on 1st June 1969 when the Burtons were staying on board during filming of *Anne of the Thousand Days* on the River Thames.

**Left:** Richard Burton leaving Professor Neville Coghill's house in Oxfordshire on 5th February 1966 after discussing a new production of 'Dr. Faustus' that they were putting on at the Oxford Playhouse. By then he owned at least a dozen cars including the Rolls Royce pictured.

**Right:** The view over the Bay of Banderas from the top floor of the Burton Taylor villa in Puerto Vallarta was called Casa Kimberley, which they purchased during the filming of *The Night of the Iguana* in 1963.

# The Burton-Taylor jewellery collection

*Elizabeth Taylor*

**Left:** The famous La Peregrina pearl set on a choker designed by Cartier. Burton bought Taylor the pearl for Valentine's Day in 1969 for US$37,000. The pearl was reportedly discovered in the early 1500s by a slave in the Gulf of Panama and has had various different owners, including Mary Tudor of England and the Bonaparte family. However there is some doubt that the Burton-Taylor Peregrina is genuine and it may be a clever replica. The genuine Peregrina is believed to be part of the Spanish crown jewels

*Elizabeth Taylor*

**Left:** The 33.19 carat Krupp diamond, bought for Taylor by Burton for US$305,000 at Sotheby's in 1968. It was the highest price ever paid at auction at the time for a diamond ring.

**Left:** The Bulgari 18.61 carat emerald and 10 carat diamond necklace which Burton bought for Taylor during the filming of 'Cleopatra'. The piece was designed so the pendant could be detached and worn as a brooch. This was the only piece of jewellery Taylor wore during her nuptials to Burton. It was pinned to her wedding dress.

*Elizabeth Taylor*

**Below:** The 69.42 carat pear-shaped Taylor-Burton diamond, bought for Taylor by Burton in 1969. Burton instructed his lawyer, Aaron Frosch, to bid as high as US$1 million, but was outbid by Cartier who bought the diamond with an additional bid of US$50,000. Burton then purchased the diamond from Cartier for another US$50,000, bringing the total price to US$1.1 million. It was the first million dollar diamond sold in a public auction.

*Elizabeth Taylor*

*Elizabeth Taylor*

**Above:** The 17th century heart-shaped Taj Mahal diamond, set on a gold and ruby chain by Cartier. Burton purchased it for a reported £350,000 as a gift for Taylor's 40th birthday. The diamond was originally given by Emperor Shah Jahaan to his third wife.

Once again, Burton was untiring with the press and gave endless interviews about his Welsh coal-mining ancestors, his passion for Shakespeare and his determination not to be seduced by the glamour of Hollywood. As well as Louella Parsons, he attracted the attention of Los Angeles' most famous journalist, 77-year-old Hedda Hopper, whose syndicated column in the Los Angeles Times was read by virtually every American. She said he was the most exciting story since Gregory Peck's film debut ten years earlier. Burton told *Look* magazine that his success was "damned gratifying to a man who came up from the lowest depths of the working class."

Burton was captivated by the idea of playing Marcellus, who starts off the film as a drunken, debauched womaniser and ends up a model citizen. He gave a long, rambling interview to Hollywood correspondents when he waxed lyrical about the responsibilities that had been placed upon his shoulders. He was stunned when, subsequently, all the Los Angeles newspapers and magazines printed his comments word for word, almost as the gospel of Hollywood. He told them: "I am not customarily nervous about roles, but I am challenged by Marcellus. In one scene, for instance, this man goes from belligerence to acute agony and terror, then to the peace that passes all understanding. On a lesser plane, playing Marcellus is like playing Hamlet. There will never be a perfect Hamlet because the part demands too much. No matter how many facets all human beings may have, Hamlet has all of them. As an actor, if you find the performer who speaks verse well, you generally find a man who has no strength. Reversely, the man who has strength and tremendous power, generally can't speak verse.

"For example, John Gielgud can wipe up the floor with Laurence Olivier when he says 'To be or not to be,' but a couple of speeches before that, Olivier could wipe up the floor with Gielgud when he speaks: 'Oh, what a rogue and peasant slave am I.' The great attraction of 'Hamlet' is in its enormous variety for the actor, and in a more limited way, Marcellus in *The Robe* has the same attraction."

In truth, Burton was totally out of his depth and just about getting by. Later, he admitted he had been talking mostly rubbish and was scared he would be found out at any moment. However, he found the more rubbish he uttered, the more he was taken seriously. He knew Marcellus was no Hamlet, and he thought the extensive preparation for the role insisted upon by the studio was unnecessary.

Fox had insisted he take lessons in fencing and tone up his muscles with weightlifting sessions in the gym. The studio even hired an Olympic weightlifting champion to train him for several hours every day. He told *Variety*, the Hollywood trade magazine: "If I don't play Marcellus, I shall go mad thinking how I shall use all these bulging muscles." James Mason told him that no other Hollywood leading man would have put up with it and he thought Burton's naïveté in agreeing to the studio's demands hilarious.

But, typically, Burton became overconfident and caused a furore when he told the *Hollywood Citizen-News* newspaper that "the only satisfaction of being an actor is getting away from your own disgusting self." He was quickly forced to deny he had said that by Fox's public relations department but it was clear to everyone that it was the sort of quote a journalist could not make up.

It prompted Darryl Zanuck himself to emerge from the executive offices and to take Burton aside on set. He told him that Americans regarded *The Robe* as a very important film for religious reasons and that he should be careful how he conducted himself. Zanuck told Burton he must be on his best behavior at all times. Astonishingly, Zanuck said nothing about the twin affairs Burton was running on set with his co-stars Jean Simmons and Dawn Addams, but merely told him to desist from smoking on the set lest it created the wrong image. As it was, Burton was embraced by America's religious lobby but did not welcome their interest in him. According to his brother Graham Jenkins, he "despised their cloying hypocrisy."

The only sensible article written in the period came from Richard Hubler in the *Saturday Evening Post*, which sounded the first warnings about Burton's sometimes irascible behavior. In the language of the time, Hubler said he detected an "inward uncertainty" and a "wry defensive humour" which may make Burton "miss by miles being a matinee icon." Hubler said Burton had neither the "patience with the public" nor the "calculated personality" of a top-drawer motion-picture star. He described Burton as being "a firm follower of the fiery Welsh left politician, Aneurin Bevan." Burton, he continued, had "invaded the social purlieus of the movies like a shaggy Welsh griffin, invariably wearing a leek-green tweed coat and green, unpressed corduroys. His procedure was to devour the *hors d'oeuvres*, lay down a basis of beer and go on from there – meanwhile reciting, singing and wooing, Welsh-style, any unwary lady within reach." If anyone understood it, it was probably the only really perceptive analysis of Burton's character attempted by any writer in America during that period.

Filming finally started in January 1953. But it was fraught with early difficulties, as the new Cinemascope system required more attention to focus the camera lenses and much higher levels of lighting. The extra lighting created almost double the heat of normal lighting levels, making filming very uncomfortable for the cast and crew.

But as soon as the script was straightened out, the professionalism of the actors, led by 40-year-old Victor Mature, came to the fore. Mature led the cast and they skipped through the scenes, requiring very few retakes.

The swift progress was aided by the excellent relationship between all the actors. Jean Simmons, who played Diana, the Roman girl who falls for Marcellus, was completely devoid of the ego normally associated with lead actresses. She adored Burton and respected Mature, and continually deferred to them without argument or drama.

Burton and Mature also got on famously. He played the slave Demetrius, and Burton said of him: "When it came to cinematic technique, he knew the business from A to Z. I learned a lot from him. I've never known an actor so happily aware of his limitations. He rejoiced in them. He liked to joke that he was no actor, and he said he had 60 films to prove it."

When Burton asked him what he was thinking while acting, Mature replied: "I'm thinking of the money they're paying me." The two actors enjoyed great camaraderie on the set, and in one scene, where Mature's character was to be filmed massaging Burton's back with olive oil, Mature substituted ice cold water instead of oil. Burton didn't mind a bit.

Burton was once again the crew's darling, and they worshipped him. He, in turn, loved them. One day, an aging stuntman, who was just about to retire, came up to him and asked a cheeky favour, as Burton explained: "He was getting on a bit and came to me one day to talk about a scene we were doing together. We had to fight our way up a flight of steps so that he could fall off the top of the battlements. 'It's simple,' he said, 'but please make it look difficult.' I asked him why. 'Because I get a hundred bucks for every retake and I could do with the money.' So, on the first take, I dropped my sword; on the second, I had a sneezing fit; and on the third, I was the one who nearly fell over the side. After that, I couldn't think what else to do except get it right. So my friend walked off with four hundred dollars. He was very grateful. It was my one good turn at Hollywood."

The other actors took their lead from the stars even though the film was hindered rather than helped by its huge budget. Despite the harmony and lack of problems, Burton realised that *The Robe* – rather than being a brilliant epic – was sinking into what he called "competent mediocrity" typical of a Henry Koster film.

By coincidence, Emlyn Williams arrived in Los Angeles for a separate engagement at another theatre, where he was reciting the works of Charles Dickens on stage. Sybil invited him to stay with them, and Burton told him that *The Robe* was an "indifferent epic" and that he was bored by its mediocrity. He also told Williams he thought his own performance was poor. He said: "I tried so hard, and the harder I tried, the worse I got." When Williams saw the rushes, he couldn't disagree, but he told him he still thought it would be a hit.

Burton treated Williams like royalty when he arrived, and he returned all the favours Williams had done for him four years earlier in London's theatrical community. One night, while Williams was reciting Dickens in a Los Angeles theatre, Burton led a pack of Hollywood stars including Humphrey Bogart, Lauren Bacall, Robert Newton and Clifton Webb to see him perform.

In the end, *The Robe* took only 58 days to shoot and, afterwards, Burton finished off the remaining scenes for *The Desert Rats*. Then, he had to wait a month kicking his heels in Los Angeles whilst waiting for both films to be edited in case any retakes were required.

The Burtons killed time by taking a short-term rental on a beach house in Santa Monica, a smart suburb of Los Angeles. They spent an idyllic month on the beach getting deep suntans in the Los Angeles sun. Burton even learned to surf with local boys until Fox's insurers found out and banned him from the activity.

As he was about to leave Los Angeles to return to London, he received a huge offer from Metro Goldwyn Mayer to play Marc Antony in MGM's new production of *Julius Caesar*. But Fox, backed up by Korda, forbade him from taking the role. And, as Fox held his contract, he had no choice but to refuse.

Marlon Brando got the role and the half million dollars it paid. The stupidity of Vere Barker's advice to sign the contract with Korda became more and more apparent as each day passed.

# FROM RACHEL TO ROBE TO RAT

# AND GOD CREATED BURTON

# CHAPTER 22

# Turning down
# one million dollars

## *No one could believe it*

### 1953

Before the Burtons left Los Angeles for London, there was one more drama to be played out, far more exciting than anything Burton had done on celluloid that past year. The drama concerned Burton's future and who owned it.

Alexander Korda's ruse to get Darryl Zanuck to take up Burton's three-picture option had worked too well. Zanuck was now obsessed with Burton and wanted to sign him up and commit to a ten picture – ten year deal with 20th Century-Fox. Zanuck had viewed the rough cut of *The Robe* and knew it would be a summer hit. In the parlance of Hollywood, it was a blockbuster. And, somehow, Zanuck was convinced it was all down to Burton.

In fact, he really believed Burton was going to be the next big thing in Hollywood and didn't want to share him with other studios. He also didn't want to pay him the going rate of US$250,000 to US$500,000 per film that the big stars earned. So, he tried to tempt him to sign a long-term deal whilst he was still young and naïve – and unschooled in the devious ways of Hollywood moguls.

Zanuck thought he had the answer to snaring Burton. Step one was buying Burton out of his contract with Korda – which he duly did very quietly. To buy Burton out from Korda cost him less than US$200,000.

The canny Korda was glad to get out of his deal with Burton. He already knew that Burton had agreed to a season at the Old Vic for 1953 and was committed to return to England to perform 'Hamlet' for £45 a week. The decision seemed so strange that Korda wondered whether Burton would ever return to films again, and he didn't want to take that chance.

Korda had another concern. He had viewed *My Cousin Rachel* and seen rough cuts of *The Robe* and *The Desert Rats* in his private screening room. He wasn't sure Burton was as good as Zanuck thought he was. He could see that his undoubted acting skills weren't exactly translating to celluloid as they should have been. Korda had seen outstanding talent crash and burn before, so he took the money and let him go. After taxes, the US$200,000 equated to only £7,000 but was enough to buy a Canaletto which Korda hung on a wall of his new house in The Bishops Avenue, North London.

Once that was done, Zanuck turned his full attention to contracting Burton to Fox. He decided to offer him a guaranteed US$1 million to make ten films for Fox over ten years. The US$1 million would be a pay-or-play contract, which, in Hollywood parlance, meant the money would be paid out to the actor come what may, even if no films were ever made. But the sting in the tail was that Burton would be entirely at the beck and call of Zanuck and Fox in everything he did. He would also have to move to Los Angeles full-time.

Burton's American agent Charles Feldman arranged a meeting in Zanuck's office to conclude the deal. With US$1 million on offer, he didn't foresee a problem getting Burton to sign.

When Burton arrived for the meeting, he kept quiet whilst the two men laid out the deal in front of him. Burton noticed that Zanuck already had an agreement drafted. Feldman was very much in favour of Burton signing the deal there and then, and he and Zanuck did all they could to persuade him to do just that.

But Burton feigned complete disinterest in what they had to say; in truth, he simply wasn't interested. But both men thought this indifference was just a negotiating ploy to get more money and better terms. They just couldn't believe that a Welsh boy like Burton could possibly turn down a million dollars. Like Feldman, Zanuck couldn't understand why Burton didn't jump at the contract.

But what neither Zanuck nor Feldman understood were the vagaries of the British tax system. In Britain at the time, one could earn UK£15,000 a year and pay moderate taxes. But anything much over that as much as 94 per cent went to the British Inland Revenue department. Burton had worked this out. It meant he could afford to work at the Old Vic for £45 a week and not be significantly poorer than he would be earning a hundred thousand dollars a year in Hollywood.

All that was magnified by the exchange rate, which was then three and a half dollars to the British pound. $100,000 watered down to £30,000, which then dwindled to less than £3,000 once the tax man had had his share. In fact, Burton had already worked out that his actual pay for the past 12 months would be only £12,000 from the US$300,000 he had already earned.

And Burton was not quite the Welsh hick that Zanuck and Feldman believed him to be; he realised they were trying to buy him up on the cheap. Burton was not unaware of the fact that he had just been nominated for an Academy Award for his performance in *My Cousin Rachel*. He was equally aware of the favourable previews of *The Robe* and what they would do for his career.

So both men were stunned when Burton walked out of Zanuck's office, having turned down the offer flat. He said to Zanuck: "When once you've felt the power of the stage, you don't want to do anything else." And he truly meant what he said – or at least he did when he said it.

Zanuck was so shocked, he couldn't believe it. He was a man used to getting his own way. No one ever said 'no' to him. There was an oft-quoted story that did the rounds in Los Angeles, in which he had shouted at an assistant who had interrupted him while he was speaking by saying: "Don't say 'yes' until I've finished talking."

Feldman was also furious. He stood to lose his US$50,000 commission on the deal, which Fox would arrange to pay him out of Burton's share immediately after the deal was signed. Feldman thought his client had taken temporary leave of his senses and was worried that Zanuck would withdraw the contract and that he would lose his commission altogether.

What happened next is lost in the sands of time. But it appears that Feldman tried to rescue the situation by telling Zanuck he would sort out his client and then signing the contract on behalf of Burton. Feldman believed that Zanuck had the whip hand anyway, as he had already bought Burton's contract from Korda – and therefore a contract of sorts already existed. He didn't believe his client had any choice but to accept Zanuck's offer.

There was some logic in what Feldman was thinking, but it didn't excuse the agent's actions that day.

As soon as he left Zanuck's office, Burton himself couldn't believe what he had done. As he drove back to his house, all he could think about was the million dollars. He admitted years later that the thought in his mind during the car journey home was: "Oh my God, what am I doing?"

And he didn't know how he was going to tell his Welsh relatives that he had turned down one million dollars: "When I tell them what I've done, what will they think of me in the village?" Melvyn Bragg recalled the moment: "He turned down flat the king's ransom, the pot of gold, the answer to his poverty-prayers he had always dreamt of. And in the process, he showed his steel of independence."

As he pulled up in front of his house in James Mason's red Cadillac, a wave of insecurity came over him. He was suddenly very frightened and very lonely. Soon, he and Sybil would be leaving this world of unreality for the total reality of London. All of this could be theirs forever, and yet he was turning it down.

In time, as Burton tried to rationalise his own decision, he finally put his refusal to sign down to his own tremendous intelligence. He argued that it kept telling him that he would not be living up to the artist within him if he signed.

Later that evening, Feldman phoned him and said he had left the contract open with Zanuck and that he should "consider it signed if he wanted it to be signed" – whatever that meant. Later, those words would cause Burton much aggravation when Zanuck tried to enforce the unsigned contract as a done deal anyway.

Despite the conflict with Zanuck and his distrust of Feldman, Burton was floating on air. He wrote to his brothers back in Wales about the offer: "It's fantastic. They are offering as much as fifty thousand sterling per picture and are absolutely convinced when I turn them down that I'm a clever boy after more money."

But Burton was mystified when, a week later, Fox's publicists issued a press release saying he had agreed to a long-term deal. Burton thought they were referring to his deal with Korda and let it go. But that was a mistake, as Zanuck mistook his lack of action over the press release, which he knew was wholly misleading, as acquiescence. It transpired later that Burton had asked Victor Mature's advice over what to do about the press release. Mature advised Burton to play along with the studio's publicity efforts as, sooner or later, the studios tended to believe their own publicity – which he told Burton he had always found was "no bad thing."

When Zanuck realised that Burton was intent on returning to London and that he would be leaving Los Angeles for a whole year, he threatened to sue him. A stiff lawyer's letter was hand-delivered to Burton with that threat.

Burton was shocked and took the letter round to James Mason and asked him to look at it for him. He told his friend: "I haven't signed a fucking contract, and as far as films are concerned, I much prefer *acting*. I did all right in London and, as for suing me, I've got £30 in the post office."

After the letter was sent, Zanuck asked Burton to come to his office for a meeting. Ominously, he told Burton: "Bring your lawyer." But Burton didn't have a lawyer. And by then, he was also very fed up with Feldman. Burton had belatedly realised that Feldman was not really acting as his representative. When Burton told Vere Barker he wanted to sack Feldman, Barker flew in for the meeting himself.

Burton later described this meeting in Zanuck's office as a court hearing, and there was a general misconception for years that Fox had actually sued Burton for breach of contract. But it was never anything like that. It now appears that there was never any signed contract, and the gist of the affair was Zanuck trying to force Burton to honour a unsigned contract that he claimed had been agreed verbally, indicated by Feldman's initials on that contract. In truth, Zanuck and Feldman had been conspiring together to get Burton to sign. Feldman had acted unethically and laws were eventually passed in America preventing agents from acting as managers and vice versa to outlaw these type of conflicts of interest, which were all too common in Hollywood at the time.

At the meeting, Burton was on his own and representing himself, while on the other side of the table was an entire assortment of Fox executives with their own in-house corporate lawyers – but it was not a courtroom.

Zanuck argued that Burton had agreed to a contract and shook his hand and that his agent, Feldman, had initialled it to signify that understanding. Feldman backed up Zanuck's version of events. One of the Fox lawyers shouted at Burton: "You shook hands with Mr Zanuck on an agreement in this very office." Burton replied: "I don't believe Mr Zanuck told you that happened, and if he did, then he's a fucking liar."

The room hushed as not many people dared to use that sort of language about Darryl F. Zanuck.

Years later, Burton told biographer Michael Munn: "It was true that Mr Zanuck had offered me a seven-year contract. I'd turned it down. He knew that and I knew that, and he kept very quiet about it while the lawyers ran around making plans to sue me, which they didn't, of course, because there was no agreement." But Burton's recollection was very hazy and he got the length of the contract wrong and, in the end, even he appeared to believe he had been in a courtroom rather than Zanuck's office. He told journalists: "On one side of the courtroom was Darryl Zanuck and half the corporation boys in America. On the other side was me, alone; I didn't have a lawyer. I played it very English, very Ronald Colman."

In the end, the issue was settled quietly with Burton agreeing to honour the terms of the original Korda contact and to make some more films for Fox. In truth, it was all forgotten about soon enough. But there was plenty of bitterness at the time.

As Burton was leaving Zanuck's office, Zanuck shouted after him: "You know, I could stop you working in Hollywood. But for me, you might never make another picture." Burton looked over his shoulder and said: "I believe you, but I can go back to the theatre. I have an offer from London. I might very well take it. You can't stop that, can you?"

But there was a positive side effect for Burton that was to have a big impact on his life. Before he left for London, a woman called him up and without any introduction said to him: "Did you call Darryl Zanuck a fucking liar?" Burton replied without knowing who she was: "Yes, I think I did." She said: "Then you need help. I'll be right round." The woman was Valerie Douglas, a lawyer, who helped Burton to sort out the contractual problems with Zanuck and to manage his business affairs for next 31 years. Douglas was a 30-year-old tough-minded woman who gradually got more and more involved in Burton's affairs until she joined his staff permanently, working out of a small office in West Hollywood.

# TURNING DOWN ONE MILLION DOLLARS

# AND GOD CREATED BURTON

# CHAPTER 23

# Oscar nomination is catapult to fame

## The high wire ride begins

### March 1953

O n Sunday 19th March 1953, the Burtons attended the 1953 Academy Awards ceremony at the Pantages Theatre in Los Angeles. That year's Oscars were a historic occasion in more ways than one.

The Oscars were organised by the Academy of Motion Pictures Arts and Sciences, which was effectively the trade body representing the film community in Hollywood. Until 1953, the ceremony and awards had been largely a domestic affair, of interest only to the film community in Hollywood. But that year the ceremony was broadcast on television for the first time.

So in 1953, to accommodate live television schedules and the five hour time difference between the east and west coasts, the ceremony was split between two venues in New York and Los Angeles simultaneously. Bob Hope hosted the awards in Los Angeles at the Pantages and Conrad Nagel in New York at the NBC Theatre. Against all expectations, the dual ceremony worked a treat and resulted in the largest audience in commercial television history.

Hollywood had been reluctant to let television into its main event. After all, television was the great enemy of the cinema and had decimated the business. But, for many members of the Academy, this attitude was madness and the wiser heads in the industry had begun to realise that the future of cinema was inextricably bound to television. The televising of the Oscars was the first tangible evidence of a change in mood. Almost overnight, the huge audience made the awards much more important and relevant.

1953 also marked the first time in Oscar's history that all of the top six prizes – best picture, director, actor, actress, supporting actor and supporting actress – were won by six different films. All of Hollywood was astonished when this happened and didn't think it actually possible. They certainly never thought it would happen again, but it did – twice; the last time as recently as 2005.

It was certainly a very bizarre night as far as Richard Burton was concerned. He had been nominated in the best supporting actor category. But anyone

283

who had seen *My Cousin Rachel* knew he was the male lead, and not in any way a supporting actor. He was in the wrong category and was insulted by it. But Darryl Zanuck didn't think he had a chance as best actor so he somehow finagled the Academy to put Burton in the best supporting actor category, where he thought he would have a better chance of picking up an Oscar.

In the category of best supporting actor, Burton was up against Jack Palance in *Sudden Fear*, Arthur Hunnicutt in *The Big Sky*, Victor McLaglen in *The Quiet Man* and Anthony Quinn in *Viva Zapata*.

Burton's nomination itself – in any category – was a mystery to his friends, who thought he had put in a merely average performance. In truth, Burton was very surprised that *My Cousin Rachel* had been nominated for anything after George Cukor had been sacked as director. As it was, the film received five nominations in all; for best supporting actor, cinematography, art direction, set decoration and costume design.

In the end, however, *My Cousin Rachel* got what it deserved and won nothing. Burton yawned his way through the entire five-hour ceremony and just wanted to get out of the theatre to have a drink. Sybil, on the other hand, was thrilled just to be there.

When the winner of the best supporting actor category was announced as Anthony Quinn for his performance in *Viva Zapata*, Burton was actually relieved. He had no speech prepared as he had not wanted to tempt fate. In any case, he felt a fraud sitting alongside the cream of the acting profession and pretending to be one of them. He did not feel he had yet earned that right. Years later, he would change his attitude and desperately want to win an Oscar – but, back then, he was not at all bothered.

Afterwards, he and Sybil went to the traditional Governors' Ball and quaffed champagne and ate a three course meal, courtesy of the Academy. Sybil made sure he got home before he got too drunk.

After the Oscars, Hollywood traditionally quieted down and the parties stopped as the film community got down to the serious business of filmmaking for the coming year – before the fun started again. Almost every actor worth their salt in Hollywood was working between March and June. But the Burtons were forced to cool their heels waiting for post-production to finish on *The Robe* before they returned to Wales in mid-June.

The action thus switched to England, where Burton's first big movie, *My Cousin Rachel*, was about to be released in his home country. The film's box office takings had disappointed in America, but great things were expected in his home country and the film's performance in Britain was an acid test for Burton's future as a big name actor.

The anticipation was felt most keenly in Wales and its citizens had been worked up into a state of frenzy as Welsh newspapers had reported how Burton had conquered Hollywood during his year away. For them, there was a world of difference between being in low-rent British domestic films and big Hollywood productions. The Jenkins family back in Wales was very excited with his three films, which were all scheduled to be released in 1953.

The Welsh premiere of *My Cousin Rachel* caused a minor outbreak of patriotic fever in Wales. Bill Hall, the manager of the Capitol Cinema in Cardiff, where the premiere was due to be held, sent a telegram to Burton in California and asked him to send over one of the suits he had worn in the film. He wrote: "It's a great day when a son of Wales conquers Hollywood, and something special is called for." Burton was surprised by the request but didn't question it and asked the wardrobe department on the Fox lot to send Hall one of the suits he had worn for the role of Philip Ashley.

The entire Jenkins family, except Dick, attended that first showing at the Capitol in the company of the Lord Mayor of the city. It was a great occasion, with some family members making the trip to Cardiff for the first time. David Jenkins remembered: "This was no tiny, second-rate suburban picture house, but the grandest, most opulent cinema around."

The family was given special seats by Bill Hall, and David Jenkins was stunned at the special treatment and the new fame of his brother: "We were agog. Richard on stage in London or Stratford was one thing; Richard projected on a giant screen twenty feet high surrounded by all the storytelling artifice Hollywood had at its disposal was altogether something else. Our family pride knew no bounds and we wanted to tell the world, or at least all South Wales, which amounted to the same thing, that it was our brother up there on the screen, taking his place with the stars – good, bad or indifferent but always magical – of our trips to the tiny, shabby cinemas of our childhood days."

The film was hugely enjoyed by the great and good of South Wales that night.

Fifteen minutes before the end of the film, Graham Jenkins went out to the back of the cinema and changed into the period suit that Burton had sent Hall. Hall thought Graham was the spitting image of his brother, and it was true that there was a close resemblance. Indeed, he would later get work as his stunt double in his brother's movies.

Graham Jenkins described what happened next: "With the help of a full-length mirror, I hunched my shoulders and jutted my chin in a way that I hoped resembled a typical Burton stance. Then, holding that position, I made my way to the wings to hear the manager announce to the audience the arrival of an honoured guest. I walked on."

As the closing credits rolled, Bill Hall kept the lights low and Graham Jenkins walked up the centre aisle. Hall actually announced that Richard Burton had arrived in person, straight from Hollywood. Graham did his bit and climbed onto the small stage area in front of the screen. Everyone in the cinema, except Bill Hall, thought it was Burton, including his own brothers and sisters in the audience. As Graham remembered: "The applause was tumultuous. My first reaction was relief and delight that the impersonation had been so successful. But as the clapping continued, I could not help wondering if this audience could take a joke. I had not wished to be hounded offstage by a fusillade of well-aimed ice cream cartons. I held up my hands to beg silence: 'Ladies and gentleman,' I began, 'I am not Richard Burton.' But the trouble was, by projecting my voice, I even sounded like Richard. 'Who are you then?' shouted someone. 'Olivia de Havilland?' That broke the ice. 'Truthfully,' I said, 'I am not Richard. He is working in Hollywood and cannot be here. But he has sent me along, his brother Graham, to thank you for this wonderful reception.' There was silence for a moment, but as I turned to walk off, the applause was renewed. I breathed a sigh of relief."

None of the family had known in advance what was to happen. As David Jenkins said: "There were gasps all round when Richard, in full make-up and authentic nineteenth-century costume, made his entrance. It took several moments for the realisation to sink in; this was Graham, who then bore an uncanny resemblance to Richard, gamely impersonating our brother."

The routine had taken just five minutes, and when he left the stage, most people still thought they had seen the real Burton and gave Jenkins a standing ovation that lasted a few minutes.

Afterwards, Bill Hall held a champagne reception for his guests. Tom Jenkins, the eldest brother, couldn't quite take it all in, especially his brother's acting in the film. It was his first trip to a big cinema like the Capitol and he had never seen anything like it. Tom, a gentle man, who, with his wife Cassie, had brought up Graham, muttered to his nephew and adopted son almost in disgust: "Kissing that actress with all those people watching."

The next day, the story of Graham's impersonation was big news in all the

# OSCAR NOMINATION IS CATAPULT TO FAME

Welsh newspapers, and the Jenkins family was featured prominently in all of them. Suddenly, they were all famous. They looked a very handsome family posing with Graham in his period suit.

Whilst all this was going on in Wales, Burton's natural father, Dick Jenkins, finally realised something special was happening but couldn't understand what it was. So his daughter, Hilda, with whom he was living with by then, took him to the Odeon cinema in Port Talbot to see *My Cousin Rachel*. Afterwards, when she asked him what he thought of it, he said: "Well, I'm not sure I liked all that kissing and cuddling. It wasn't decent. What will Sybil say?" Hilda told him: "It's a film, Dad. It's only acting." He replied: "Acting is it? Well, all I can say is, it looked real enough to me."

*The Desert Rats* followed *My Cousin Rachel* into British cinemas in April. Philip Burton first saw the film on 24th April in London. He recorded in his diary that he was "overwhelmed with tearful pride." Not only Philip but all of Great Britain was overcome. *The Desert Rats* was very well received in Britain and reinforced Burton's reputation as a coming man in films. But, inevitably, it was overshadowed by his debut film, *My Cousin Rachel*, and *The Robe*.

20th Century-Fox publicists created huge hype over the release of *The Robe* in American cinemas that summer and in Europe over the Christmas holiday season. The novelty of being the first film in Cinemascope excited audiences the world over, and the film took in millions at the box office. Any box office problems with *My Cousin Rachel* were forgotten.

The press dubbed it the most ambitious picture in the 14 years that had passed since *Gone With the Wind*. But film critics were not impressed on either side of the Atlantic. In America, *Time* magazine said it "contained more piety than wit and more spectacle than humanity, but is ably served by a competent cast, headed by Richard Burton." Hedda Hopper in the *Los Angeles Times* welcomed Burton permanently to Hollywood and described him in *The Robe* as: "One of the most exciting actors I've seen in Hollywood in the past ten years."

British critics generally dismissed the film as lightweight but praised Burton's performance. Caroline Lejeune in *The Observer* damned the film with faint praise but said of him: "If his attempt is not crowned with very great success, it is not the fault of the actor who does his best with the material."

Graham Jenkins brought everybody back to reality: "Happily for all concerned, the studio bosses were more at home reading the box office returns than the press reviews. The popularity of *The Robe* was undeniable.

This was partly thanks to Cinemascope, which, on the whole, was favourably received and which gave the film a curiosity value. But Richard Burton was the star they all came to see. In 135 minutes of running time, he was scarcely off the screen. Someone calculated that of 700 speeches, Rich had to deliver 313."

In early 1954, *The Robe* was nominated for best picture, and Burton earned his second Oscar nomination – this time in the correct category as best actor – and established himself beyond doubt as a global film star.

The second nomination was an extraordinary achievement. To be nominated for an Oscar for both of his first two Hollywood films, in successive years, was something that had never happened to any actor before, or since.

The event was held on 25th March 1954, again in dual venues, at the Panatages Theater in Los Angeles and the Century Theater in New York. This time, he was in the best actor category up against probably the strongest ever nominations for that category; Marlon Brando for his role in *Julius Caesar*, Burt Lancaster and Montgomery Clift, both nominated for *From Here to Eternity*, and the eventual winner, William Holden, for *Stalag 17*. Burton knew he wouldn't win against that line-up of talent and performances and made no effort to attend the ceremony, being on stage that night at the Old Vic in London. Burton was surprised when Holden won; he thought it was going to Montgomery Clift.

Meanwhile, *The Robe* had opened in Britain and was breaking box office records at the cinemas equipped with Cinemascope. British audiences had never seen anything like it – including the Jenkins family.

David Jenkins said: "We, in the family, thought it was marvellous; Tom, Hilda and Cassie, especially. I saw it on the widest screen I have ever encountered and was more impressed than ever by Richard's screen presence; a kind of quiet, resonant dignity in which his great on-screen professionalism shone through."

Philip Burton said when 1953 was over: "I went to see Richard's first three Hollywood films; *My Cousin Rachel, The Desert Rats* and *The Robe.* Whatever reservations I had about the films, I had none about Richard."

He may not have won any Oscars for his two nominations in his first year in Hollywood, but Burton did not end those two years without any official recognition. The Hollywood Foreign Press Association presented him with a Golden Globe for the most promising newcomer. Burton had no idea what a Golden Globe was, and in those days, it did not have the same prestige as it does today.

# OSCAR NOMINATION IS CATAPULT TO FAME

When he returned to his house in Hampstead, he didn't know what to do with his statuette, which he regarded as a bit of a joke. So he used it as a doorstop for the toilet door. His brother Graham was shocked and said: "Can't you think of a better place to put it?" Burton shook his head and replied: "You've got the wrong idea, I want people to see and admire it. Now, what chance is there of that if I put it up on the mantlepiece with the other ornaments? But, in the loo, what else have they got to look at?"

It summed up Richard Burton's attitude towards Hollywood.

# AND GOD CREATED BURTON

# CHAPTER 24

# Return to the valleys

## *And a quick escape back*

### July 1953

On 16th June 1953, the Burtons arrived back in London after an absence of nearly a year. Much had changed while they had been away. The country had finally started to emerge from its post-war economic blues and everything was on the move again. In London, they found things much as they had left them and they settled into domestic bliss in their new home at Squires Mount in Hampstead. The renovations at Squires Mount had finally finished and the builders had moved out. They decided not to sell the house at 6 Lyndhurst Road in Hampstead and kept it as their official address to ensure privacy from Burton's fans. Over the past four years, they had gradually converted the property into four separate flats, which were all rented to tenants. The Burton's own flat, called the garden flat had been rented by his 21-year-old niece, Cecilia's daughter, Rhianon James, who was sharing it with another friend.

After a few weeks at home, they were enjoying life in their new home but the pressure from both their families to visit Wales became too much and they succumbed. In truth, neither Richard nor Sybil were that keen to return at this juncture in their lives. It was a life they had escaped and they were not keen to revisit. Although Burton romantically praised his place of birth whenever he could, the truth was that he had never really liked it and, as a child, couldn't wait to escape.

He may not have cared for the place of his childhood but he did care for the people he was brought up with, and he deeply loved his family, all of whom still lived in the Port Talbot area.

So at the beginning of July, Richard and Sybil Burton headed down to South Wales in their grey Jaguar saloon and were determined to enjoy the four days they were back in Pontrhydyfen and Port Talbot to reunite with their families – most of whom they hadn't seen for a whole year.

But before he left, he went to his bank and withdrew £1,000 in cash. £1,000 was a huge amount in those days and special arrangements were needed for his local bank to accommodate his request. He would most likely have been given the money in 500 £2 notes, the highest denomination bank note at the time. He stashed the envelope containing the cash under the spare wheel in the boot of his Jaguar and tried to forget it was there.

Long gone were the days when Burton could slip back to Wales unnoticed. He was now a famous film star. Everyone in Wales knew who he was and virtually his every move was shadowed by reporters from the Welsh newspapers – certainly it was impossible for him to return to South Wales quietly.

The Welsh valleys seemed greener than Burton remembered them. It wasn't just his imagination. With the closure of most of the coal mines, the local councils were covering up the slag heaps and replanting them with grass and trees.

As soon as they arrived, Sybil headed off to see her family in the Rhonda Valley, and Burton stayed with Cecilia and Elfed at Caradoc Street in his old bedroom. 73 Caradoc Street was a far cry from the luxury he had been living in Los Angeles. As Graham Jenkins recalled: "It could so easily have been a disaster…but he was so unlike what everyone imagined a star to be. He stayed with Hilda, he visited the pubs he had known since he was a boy, and he enjoyed the company of old friends."

Burton was happy to play for the cameras as journalists followed him around his place of birth. As he toured the streets around Port Talbot, he visited his old schools and said 'hello' to his old mentors Meredith Jones and Leo Lloyd, both of whom had faded into the shadows now that his career was launched. Leo Lloyd was still a teacher but Meredith Jones was now a top executive at the Glamorgan's education authority. As Burton looked those old men in the eyes and grasped both their hands, he knew that they knew it was they who had made him. And he was happy for them to know that he knew that too. Through the tears that welled in all their eyes, they embraced and remembered the struggle of that which had brought them to this point. Meredith Jones was not an emotional man, but that day he was.

Of the few people who remain in Port Talbot and who remember Burton's first visit in 1953, most of them were young children at the time but remember him giving them a ride in his Jaguar that summer and, then, in his Rolls-Royce in subsequent summers when they had grown up into teenagers. These ritualistic visits would continue, every five years or so, until all the Jenkins had left the Port Talbot area.

After two nights, Burton headed back to Pontrhydyfen to stay for a night in his sister Hilda's house. It was when he got to Pontrhydyfen that the photographers got excited. This was the place of his birth and where his father, sisters, brothers, nephews and nieces still lived.

It was time for a reunion with his father, Dick Jenkins, whom he had not seen for at least five years – not that he cared. He was still smarting from the £50 Dick had forced Philip Burton to pay when Philip had taken over Dick's parental responsibilities ten years earlier. Burton later recalled the moment they were reunited: "I think my father believed Hollywood was a small place on the other side of the Welsh mountains. He just greeted me with: 'Well, Rich, how are you getting on?' as though I'd been down to Swansea for the weekend."

A series of iconic photographs emerged from that visit, in which he was photographed in company with his 77-year-old father walking around Pontrhydyfen. As writer Penny Junor romantically recalled in her biography of Burton: "He was happy to play the part of boy-from-the-valleys-made-good...brooding wistfully against the backdrop of the Welsh hills; gazing into the middle distance with his brothers; and walking alongside his old father." And Melvyn Bragg also joined in with colourful rhetoric to describe the homecoming: "Photographers snapped the strapping young giant crossing a bridge with his bemused and diminutive father, looking wary in the pub as his father waved a finger over a pint, glancing obligingly into the middle distance as the wind from Swansea Bay blew his hair."

Graham Jenkins, recalling the occasion, was more realistic: "Even if there was a certain amount of calculation in this playing the ordinary-boy-from-the-valley, it worked a treat. Every evening, there was a gathering in the Miners Arms or the Copper House, both just a short walk from where Hilda and Tom lived. Both pubs did good business that week. Rich had to put up with a lot of ribbing, but he took it all in good part."

His interactions with his father that weekend consisted of the most words he had ever spoken to him in his entire life. Even if Burton didn't care much for Dick Jenkins, he wasn't going to let that show. It was good for his image to show respect and affection for his father, and he obliged. In reality, he would have liked to have pushed Dick Jenkins off the bridge in Pontrhydyfen if he could have gotten away with it. As it was, he decided the only way to get through the ordeal was to go drinking with him, so they retired to the Miners Arms to do what both men did best.

Burton himself, many years later, recalled to film director Tony Palmer what happened next: "He was a very old man by this time, about 80, I think. I took him to the pub and he was sick, he had flu. I said: 'beti mon – what would you like?' and he said: 'Oh, I don't know' and he was really streaming with cold, with flu and everything, and I said: 'Well, I'm going to have an American drink. It's called a boilermaker', and he said: 'What's that?' and I said: 'Well, in my case, it's a double shot of scotch with a pint of beer to chase it'. He said 'Ahh, I'll have that, but make mine's rum', and I said: 'Well, we'll all have rum.' There were five of us in a row, six of us with my father. So we ordered six double rums and six pints of beer. Before the fella had served me, my father had finished his, so I said: 'Do you want mine?' and he said: 'Alright' and took mine and drank it. And then the other brothers said: 'Do you want mine?' and he drank those too. He drank them all in a row. Absolutely extraordinary. He went home, and the next day, the temperature had gone. 'Best cure in the world', he said. 'Best cure for flu in the world, boilermakers. Very good of the Americans, very clever race.' And he would look at us all, and we'd all look at him and he'd sing: 'Forgive and forget all the troubles we've met, we'll be friends with each other again.' In English he'd sing it. And everyone would say: 'Ohh, put him to bed.' You couldn't resist him."

Dick Jenkins called Hollywood 'Hollywell' and said to his son: "Is it true, Rich, they've paid you $50,000 for 12 weeks' work in that Hollywell?" Burton turned to his father and said: "No, it's not. They paid me $150,000." "What for?" said his father, and for once his son didn't have an answer. Burton said many years later, retelling the story: "I couldn't explain it then, and I still don't understand it."

That evening, he turned the phrase "What for?" over and over in his head, trying to find the answer to his father's question. 'What for', indeed, and his father had unwittingly asked the question that continually vexed his son for his entire life.

Burton also took his father out for a ride in his Jaguar car. It was believed to be the first time Dick Jenkins had ever been in a car. Burton turned round to him and asked: "What you think of the car, our Daddy?" He answered: "It isn't a car, mon, it's a bloody boat." To him, it might as well have been – father was not like son.

Most of the time Burton spent with his father was for the cameras but, in reality, Burton spent as little time with him as he could get away with. He keenly remembered the stories he had heard of how his father had treated his mother, and he really wanted as little as possible to do with him. But as much as he disliked him, Burton never said a word against his father in public, quite the opposite.

Not so his brothers and sisters – who couldn't hide their joy at having their brother at home again. For his siblings, he was like a returning hero with his tales of Hollywood over beers at the pub. He brought presents for all the family and friends. The most memorable was a Russian squirrel coat for Cecilia, his elder sister. She had always wanted one and was amazed her brother had remembered. And he now had the money to buy it for her.

As they spent time together, Burton was also visibly proud of them. He loved them and told them he wanted them involved in his life and urged them to leave south Wales as soon as they could for England and a better life. And with only two exceptions – his brother Tom and sister Hilda – they all did. But that was in the future and, then, only his eldest brother, Tom, was still going down the mines. The others had all escaped and had jobs above ground. David was a police sergeant, Verdun a machinist in a factory, Graham an administrative clerk for the town council, and Ivor a builder and highly-skilled bricklayer.

That weekend, he handed out the cash he had in the boot of the car. Over £1,000 was handed out to various family members in those few days with instructions from Burton to use the money as deposits to buy their own houses.

Stanley Baker recalled it: "He wasn't showing off, he was repaying his family. And he was giving them what they would otherwise be unable to afford. They were gifts of love. He wanted to earn money, not just for himself, but for his family."

On the long drive back to London, he reminisced with Sybil about the trip and the four days they had spent in Pontrhydyfen and Port Talbot. They both agreed he had outgrown it and that, whatever happened in the future, there would be no going home again, ever.

# AND GOD CREATED BURTON

# CHAPTER 25

# Burtonmania

## *The superstar at the Old Vic*

### 1953 to 1954

During 1953, a new word entered the English dictionary of slang: 'Burtonmania.' The term was coined to describe the new phenomenon that was Richard Burton, who joined Stewart Granger and James Mason as genuine home-grown British movie stars. But Granger and Mason attracted nowhere near the passion and interest from fans that Burton engendered.

Burtonmania started on 16th June 1953, when Burton flew into London Airport on his return to Britain after a year away in Hollywood. Unlike his arrival in Los Angeles a year earlier, this time he had changed into new clothes as the aircraft had begun its descent onto the runway at Heathrow, and he looked as fresh as a daisy. He had been warned by 20th Century-Fox's publicists to expect a big crowd of fans, journalists and photographers at the terminal to welcome him home.

Burton may often have been feckless but he was no fool, and he realised how important his homecoming would be. If he had rolled off the plane looking like he had in Los Angeles, the negative publicity would have been huge. He was right to be careful, as over 400 fans were waiting for him at the airport, along with around 50 photographers and journalists. Burton put on his best smile to face the press pack.

Burton had left England a relative unknown and come back to a country where most of the 40 million citizens knew who he was. *My Cousin Rachel* had opened, *The Desert Rats* was about to open and *The Robe* was getting pre-release publicity and would open soon. And they were all big budget movies where he had the lead role. It was difficult to open a newspaper or a magazine in Britain during that period without seeing Burton's face.

Although *My Cousin Rachel* had been a box office flop in America, in Britain it was playing to full cinemas. Full page adverts for *My Cousin Rachel* were everywhere, although, interestingly, Burton's name was at the bottom; a quarter of the size of the typeface of Olivia De Havilland's billing on the posters and adverts. Burton knew the reason for that and was glad no one else did.

# AND GOD CREATED BURTON

But the appropriately named Freddie Fox, the vice president of 20th Century-Fox in London, knew it was Burton selling the tickets and not De Havilland, so Fox's publicity people were pushing him for all it was worth. They had hired a room at the airport for Burton to give an impromptu press conference. He was flanked by Sybil, who also looked spectacular in a flowing patterned dress that seemed as though it had come straight from Paris.

Unsurprisingly, most of the questions from journalists were about how he had turned down a million dollar offer from 20th Century-Fox to return to Britain to perform at the Old Vic for £45 a week. Freddie Fox bit his tongue; it was not exactly a story in his employer's favour, but it guaranteed publicity the next day.

After the conference, Burton faced his fans outside the terminal and signed autograph after autograph. With the gaggle of people surrounding him, it was difficult to get a decent photograph, so the photographers took Burton around the back and put him and Sybil up against a wall and blasted away. What emerged the next morning on the front page of all the newspapers was a marvellous photograph of the beaming couple, with their arms round each other. He looked every inch the young superstar returning from conquering Hollywood, and she looked every inch the superstar's wife.

They then caught a taxi back to Hampstead, and Burton carried Sybil over the threshold into their new whitewashed cottage at Squires Mount. After a few weeks' rest and a visit to Wales, Burton began rehearsals for his 39-week, £45-a-week season at the Old Vic theatre in London's Waterloo Road, which would keep him occupied until June 1954.

Starting in 1953, the Old Vic theatre in South London had decided to present all 36 plays of what was known as Shakespeare's First Folio, over the following five years. The 1953/54 season was the first of the five, and Burton would star in five of the six plays that season, beginning with 'Hamlet'. The others were 'Twelfth Night', 'King John', 'Coriolanus' and 'The Tempest'.

Burton saw his defection from Hollywood to South London as a victory for artistry and artistic integrity. But the nearer it got, the more nervous he became. As he said: "I'm looking forward to the Old Vic with a kind of belligerent apprehension. I wake up sweating with fear in the middle of the night, and smoke and walk myself and mutter myself back into some semblance of confidence. 'Hamlet' is the mischief, of course."

But he had to admit that being back in London that early summer felt very good.

Career-wise, removing himself from Hollywood when he was at his hottest was to prove a huge mistake, and his career was to suffer as a result. Amusingly, when he heard that Burton was not going to stay in Hollywood and was returning to England, Darryl Zanuck was reported to have said: "Who is Old Vic and what's he paying? I will pay him double."

It later emerged that it had been British theatre director Michael Benthall who had snatched Burton from the grasp of Zanuck.

Benthall had first directed Burton at Stratford in 1951. As director of the Old Vic, he was responsible for its artistic direction. Benthall was highly regarded and lived with another distinguished actor and director, Robert Helpmann. Benthall had been in New York visiting his old friend, the actress Katherine Hepburn, who told him about the sensation Burton had caused in Hollywood and how he had informed her at a party that what he really wanted was to play 'Hamlet' at the Old Vic.

Benthall's ears pricked up at this. He was scheduled to direct 'Hamlet' at the Old Vic a year hence and was astonished by Burton's interest. Hepburn urged Benthall to call Burton immediately and offer him the part. She was apparently sitting by his side when he made the call to Los Angeles.

When Burton answered the phone, Benthall introduced himself and said: "I think it's time you tried 'Hamlet.'" Burton replied: "Oh, I don't know about that. I'm not sure I'm ready for it." Hepburn, listening by his ear, snatched the telephone receiver from Benthall and told Burton: "Now, look here. You are going to play 'Hamlet' and that's final." In Hollywood, it was one of the unwritten rules – folklore, even – that no one turned down a request, any request, from Kate Hepburn; and Burton was not about to be the first. And once Burton had made his commitment to Benthall, he intended to honour it.

But the financial consequences of honouring it were huge. If he had stayed in Hollywood, he would have been earning a minimum of US$100,000 a year; some £30,000. As it was, he had to settle for £2,000 at the Old Vic in London.

But it wasn't anywhere as bad as it looked because of the high British tax rates of the time. Tax levels for the rich were at an all-time high in post war Britain. For earnings over £15,000 a year, the true tax rate was about 92 per cent. Burton had earned US$550,000 during his year in America, but after Alexander Korda, Vere Barker and Charles Feldman had all had their cut, he had received US$330,000, which translated into around £95,000 in sterling. Of that, after the taxman's ravages, he actually got to keep a mere £11,000 for his year's work, although it was still enough to make him one of the highest paid people in Britain, earning some 45 times the national average wage at the time. And he was able to save most of that money as the studio had been paying him a living allowance of US$140 a week for the year he was in the United States.

So he gave up a lot to accede to Benthall's request and Hepburn's urgings.

The big production at the Old Vic that summer was 'Hamlet'. Michael Benthall had assembled a superb cast including Robert Hardy, Claire Bloom, Fay Compton, Michael Hordern, William Squire and John Neville. Rehearsals began in July and were immediately marked by that new phenomenon, Burtonmania.

The Burtonmania started at rehearsals, and the fans besieging the stage door put Burton in a good mood every day as he arrived at rehearsal eager to take up the challenge of the role of Prince Hamlet.

Philip Burton took time off from his job at the BBC to coach Burton and remembered: "My being in London enabled me to work in depth with Richard on his Hamlet. I was sent the script of the cut version that was to be used, and on 30th June we began work. We had seven sessions, some of them long ones, all in my apartment, the last taking place on 9th July."

He added: "Once again, Richard arrived at the first rehearsal word perfect and the director glided over the monologues, saying: 'They're yours.'" Benthall didn't like the interference but he had put up with Philip's unofficial presence, together with his "encyclopedic knowledge of Shakespeare's text." As Philip Burton didn't hide his motives, he said honestly: "My only chance of ever playing 'Hamlet' was through Richard." Benthall just let the Burtons get on with it.

In the end, Michael Benthall stopped trying to direct Burton, hence his use of the expression "they're yours" in rehearsals, as he delegated passages of the script to Philip Burton's direction.

Philip believed Hamlet to be the "most naked of all parts, un-actable except in terms of, as he said: 'the Hamlet that is in you.' But left to Philip, a melancholy dark Prince Hamlet emerged, and one certainly not to everyone's taste. It was 'Hamlet' to suit Philip Burton's taste but not popular taste, including that of director Benthall. Burton moulded the role around his own personality, instead of what Shakespeare had imagined and what Benthall wanted.

Many years later, Philip Burton seemed embarrassed by the problems with Michael Benthall to the extent that, in his book titled *The Burtons* published in 1992, he denied they had ever happened. He even denied he had attended any of the rehearsals at the Old Vic, which was simply untrue.

Burton's young actor friend Richard Harris best summed up Burton's relationship with the part: "He was always Hamlet. He became a middle-aged Hamlet, ever introspective, easily disillusioned."

But it cannot be denied that, right from the first performance at the Edinburgh Festival, where it had a difficult initial run, the critics were unsure of Burton's interpretation of Hamlet. The venue caused some of the difficulties. It was a theatre created within the Assembly Hall, situated just below Edinburgh Castle. There was a platform stage, with the audience on three sides and little in the way of scenery.

Burton didn't feel at home in rehearsals on that stage and Philip Burton had to take a train north to advise his protégé how to make the best of the difficult conditions. Burton needed him close as he believed that Philip had an appreciation of the "very particular difficulties that actors continually faced." Burton believed Philip could bring considerable learning and intuition to any analysis of his acting. Whatever the value of the input from Philip, Burton improved quickly and felt more at one with his personal Hamlet by the time of the Old Vic opening.

Philip himself recalled: "I saw the performance again two days later from a well-placed seat and was totally satisfied by it, so much so that I returned to London the next morning."

The first night at the Old Vic was on Monday 14th September. As a prelude to it, Richard and Sybil had lunch with Philip Burton. Richard had a few stiff drinks to calm his nerves and, for once, Sybil and Philip joined him. All three were desperately nervous about the night that lay ahead.

When they arrived at the Old Vic, Burtonmania was in full swing and the queue for tickets for future performances was around the block. Burton's Hamlet attracted an intelligent, appreciative young audience. It was a portent of things to come, and even though 'Hamlet' was performed 101 times as part of the season, every house was jam-packed full. In the gallery at the Old Vic, there were some wooden benches where tickets could be had for two shillings. Those benches overflowed with youngsters out to catch a glimpse of Burton. Even when all the tickets were sold out, fans besieged the box office all day, every day, to snap up returned tickets.

When the Burtons arrived, there was a 30-strong crowd outside the stage door, just as there was for almost every performance. When he left, there were as many as 500 people waiting for him. On some evenings, there were thousands of fans crowding out across the road, blocking traffic and attracting the attention of the police. In fact, Burtonmania became a daily ritual at the Old Vic; Waterloo Road had never seen anything like it. It was the start of an extraordinary ten months.

Burton's performance as Hamlet may not have been what everyone wanted, but it was extremely well received that night. As Graham Jenkins described: "The old magic of Phil Burton seemed as powerful as ever." Philip said: "His performance that night was thrilling."

So much so that eight distinguished British actors who had previously played the role of Hamlet on the professional stage made the pilgrimage to the Old Vic to watch Burton's rendition. They were: John Gielgud, Paul Scofield, Alec Clunes, Michael Redgrave, Alec Guinness, Ernest Milton, Esme Percy and Robert Helpmann. Helpmann sat through three consecutive performances, absorbing it all.

John Gielgud said he did not like it much but then backtracked when he saw how popular it was with audiences. One night, he came to take Burton out for dinner after a performance. On the way to Burton's dressing room, he had to fight past the well-wishers and fans in the corridor outside. When he made it to the dressing room door, Burton was not ready and Gielgud said: "Shall I go ahead or wait until you're better – I mean, ready?" What he said was heard by everybody in the corridor and was soon being quoted in newspapers, with the precise meaning of it being disseminated by critics and columnists. Gielgud later said that the line had come out of his mouth spontaneously and called it "an amusing accident", but everyone who knew him thought it couldn't have been. Years later, Gielgud said he believed that Burton was not holding his audience and that there was "no emotional backing to the façade." It may have been true, but there was no denying of the popularity of it.

Philip Burton commented on Gielgud's reaction to it in his book in 1992: "I'm not suggesting that Richard's Hamlet, which was mine, was right and Gielgud's was wrong. Far from it. Gielgud's Hamlet had been one of the most treasured experiences of my theatre-going. Every actor reveals himself in every part he plays, but this is particularly true of Hamlet. One man's Hamlet cannot be another's."

The reviews were generally good, although the critics did not give Burton's Hamlet a particularly easy time, but they liked it. The comments printed included such phrases as: "aggressive rather than thoughtful"; "moody, virile and baleful"; "a sturdy creature of blood and thunder" and "dash, attack and verve." One kinder reviewer said: "He looked and sounded like the Olivier of fifteen years earlier, his passions running away with him, his voice close to hysteria." *The Times* said: "This Hamlet has charm which, for all its melancholy, is not to be resisted."

But Harold Hobson, the *Sunday Times* critic, sounded a real note of caution: "Richard Burton appeared to have selected from Hamlet all the most unsympathetic traits he could find. His playing had power, but it was curiously without charm."

Robert Hardy said honestly about the performance: "Rich was good, but not great in that production of 'Hamlet.'" But Michael Hordern, who played Polonius, strongly disagreed with Hobson and Hardy, maintaining that Burton turned in "a staggering performance." He added: "But then, Richard only has to walk out on the stage, open his mouth and the rest of us can go home. He has such charisma. But he didn't hog the stage. He didn't mean to take it away from you – unless you tried to take it from him; then he put you down and you couldn't defeat him."

The highlight of the performance was the stage sword fight between Burton's Hamlet and Robert Hardy's Laertes. Hardy was a skilled fencer and Burton a natural street fighter, which made for an interesting situation. Although supposedly scripted and choreographed, every night the two men turned it into a fencing challenge and audiences loved it; particularly the night when Burton's blade brushed Hardy's forehead, drawing torrents of blood. That night's audience believed it was all part of the production.

Burton later told Kenneth Tynan, who had by then moved from *The Spectator* to *The Observer* newspaper: "I played it as if I would like to be John Gielgud." But Burton's way of speaking verse was far removed from what was known as Gielgud's "poetic diction." Ten years later, in America, Gielgud would direct Burton in 'Hamlet' and have all the same old problems.

One evening, Prime Minister Winston Churchill came to see the play and sat in the front row of the stalls. It was a Monday evening performance, well into the run, and Churchill entered just before the lights went down. Burton had been pre-warned by the manager of the Old Vic, who popped his head round the dressing room door and said: "Do be good tonight because the old man's in front." Burton knew immediately whom he meant and recalled: "The old man, as you know, only means one person in England, and there he was sitting in the front row of the Old Vic. He was literally at arm's length." Burton later remembered his reaction: "I'd been on a slight binge over the weekend and I wasn't my usual self and it's a very exhausting part, even at that age." So he was full of trepidation when he took the stage feeling well below his best. At first, he couldn't pick out Churchill in the dark but, soon, and much to his amazement, he heard a familiar voice and recognised it as coming from the familiar silhouette in the front row. He said: "There is no orchestra pit at the Old Vic and Churchill was sitting in the front stalls, so I was acting almost in his lap." He soon realised that Churchill was muttering the lines along with the Prince and knew the part perfectly, except when Burton was deviating from Shakespeare's original words. As Burton remembered: "I heard this dull, thunderous kind of rumbling in the stalls and it was Churchill, who spoke every line with me. Now this was fairly disconcerting so I tried to shake him off and I went fast and then slow, I went backwards, I went edgeways, but the old man caught up with me all the time."

But the version at the Old Vic had been substantially cut and this annoyed Churchill, as Burton remembered: "A four and a half hour play in the full version, it had to be cut. And whenever we came to a cut and the old man lost his place, he'd get a bit annoyed." Burton tried to keep to the original as much as he could to accommodate Churchill, saying: "That night, I acted above myself."

Churchill was a familiar presence in London's theatres and often coming in unexpected and unannounced and, as often as not, only staying until the interval. As Burton explained: "One of the things that happened in those days was to see whether you could keep Churchill after the first act. So I looked through the spy hole at the end of the first act and, my gosh, he was leaving. And I thought: 'That's it, we've lost him.'"

A very disappointed Burton returned to his dressing room to be consoled by Claire Bloom, who was waiting for him. But unbeknownst to Burton, Churchill had got up from his seat and wandered back stage to say 'hello' to Michael Hordern and had then asked him for directions to Burton's dressing room. He knocked and pushed the door open to find Burton and Bloom inside looking very surprised. As Burton remembered: "I went back to my dressing room and suddenly the door opened and standing there was Churchill, and he bowed to me very courteously." Ignoring Bloom, the prime minister said: "My Lord Hamlet, may I use your lavatory?" A shocked Burton almost fell to his knees, but recovered himself and pointed to the toilet door. Bloom disappeared to her own dressing room and, when Churchill emerged, he simply smiled at Burton, who smiled back, and left to return to his seat.

At the end, as the final curtain dropped, Churchill climbed onto the stage and shook hands with all of the cast. He then spoke to Burton and told him he was a "virile Hamlet."

It was also the first time Robert Hardy met Churchill, the man who was to shape his later career.

Burton told the story of Churchill's accompaniment and visit to his lavatory many times in his life, but few people believed him – including his own brothers, David and Graham. But it was one Burton story that was 100 per cent true.

Humphrey Bogart and Lauren Bacall, now almost Burton groupies, also came to the Old Vic one evening to see Burton's Prince Hamlet. Afterwards, they took him and Sybil, together with William Squire and Claire Bloom, back to their suite at The Dorchester for dinner. It was the first time Burton had been to the hotel and he was very impressed with the splendour of the Bogarts' suite. It was also the first time that Squire and Bloom had met Bogart. They were both impressed and were in obvious awe at his presence.

Graham Jenkins recited a story of that night in a book about his brother published in 1988. Apparently, Bogart's monogrammed 'HB' pyjamas had been folded over a chair in the dining room of the suite. Desperate to get in on the conversation and feeling awkward at his long silences, William Squire finally told Bogart that his "pyjamas were splendid" and the most "luxurious" he had ever seen. Bogart looked at him for a long time and everyone else fell silent as the host's pyjamas were not a usual conversation point at a posh dinner party. Bogart told Squire: "Take them, they're yours." Squire spluttered that he "couldn't possibly" but Bogart said it was too late for that and he risked offending by refusing his generosity. So Squire had no choice but to accept the pyjamas as a gift.

All through the rest of the meal, Squire found himself wondering what Bogart would wear in bed that night after he had made off with his pyjamas. The gesture had a huge impact on Burton and he could see how a big film star could make a relatively inexpensive gesture and create such a big effect. But what Burton didn't know was that Bogart had a box full of the pyjamas, which he had been given by the manufacturer. The pyjamas hadn't casually been placed on the chair either; they had been deliberately put there by Bogart ready for someone to comment on them. It was Bogart's party trick, but Burton knew none of that and the seemingly spontaneous gesture impressed him as much as it did the recipient.

# AND GOD CREATED BURTON

One of Burton's old school friends, Trevor George, who had replaced Dillwyn Dummer as his best friend when he moved to Port Talbot Secondary School, also came to visit during the run. Claire Bloom remembered that Burton was as pleased to see him as he was Bogart and Bacall. George was in London on his honeymoon and came backstage. He and his new wife were thrilled when Burton introduced them to Bloom and the pair took them to dinner.

Burton's pleasure at the success of his Old Vic run was rudely interrupted on 9th November, when he suffered a personal reversal. Philip Burton phoned him to say that his great friend and idol, Dylan Thomas, the Welsh poet and playwright, had died in New York of bronchial pneumonia brought on by a combination of alcohol and the notorious New York smog of the time.

Thomas was a heavy-drinking womaniser and a man after Burton's own heart. Burton believed him to be a genius and told everyone he knew about a Welshman far more talented than he.

But he believed he had contributed to Dylan Thomas' death by refusing him a loan of £200 before he had left for New York – just before he died. Burton could easily have afforded it, but for some reason he prevaricated and turned him down, believing he would spend it on drink and prostitutes. A desperate Thomas even offered to sell him the copyright to his new play called 'Under Milk Wood' for £200, but Burton still refused. Burton had given the poet money on innumerable occasions over the years – but not this time. After Thomas died, Burton was rather disingenuous about the refusal to journalists: "I told him I simply did not have the money, although I suppose I could have raised it by selling things." It was disingenuous; the truth was that he had thousands of pounds in the bank.

Whether the refusal contributed to Thomas' death is unknown. He had arrived in New York on 20th October 1953 to take part in a recital of 'Under Milk Wood' at the city's prestigious Poetry Centre. On 2nd November, he had nearly killed himself by knocking back 18 whiskies, one after the other, in a New York bar. But it was the smog that finally got him a few days later, attacking his chest and causing him to lapse into a coma.

Following his death, his body was brought back to Wales for his burial in the village churchyard at Laugharne, on 25th November. Burton remembered his friend to journalists in interviews at the time: "We all gathered around like vultures, including those who really didn't care for him at all. He was an extraordinary talker; the best talker I think I ever knew. One spent endless hours with Dylan just to hear him talk."

The death shook Burton badly and, afterwards, he never again refused a friend a request for a loan. In fact, he often used to ask old friends that he thought might be short if they needed a loan. And that caused offence on many occasions, especially to Philip Burton for whom he was always palming US$50 notes when he saw him in New York – causing Philip much personal humiliation.

Philip Burton, who was also upset at Dylan Thomas' death, was keeping a fatherly eye on his adopted son during the entire run of 'Hamlet' and kept appearing at the Old Vic when he could get tickets, by doing surprise critiques of Burton's ongoing performance. As he noted in his book in 1992: "I kept an eye on Richard's performances from time to time, sometimes without letting him know in advance that I would be there. Thus my diary for 4th December says: 'To the Old Vic to see "Hamlet". I was very worried by R's performance – absurdly sing-song and with incredible pauses – but he took my subsequent sermon very well.'"

When 'Hamlet' closed after 101 performances, the final audience clapped and cheered for ten minutes, not wanting to leave the theatre. Outside, they chanted Burton's name as he emerged to go home.

Next came 'King John', in which Burton played the role of Philip the Bastard. It was much the same cast, but without Claire Bloom and directed by George Devine. Once again, Philip Burton was assisting Devine directing Burton's performance in rehearsals. The role of Philip, a quasi-chorus, required Burton to sit unobtrusively at the side of the stage between choruses. Even though he was sitting still off centre, Burton's presence commanded such attention that Devine eventually had to remove him between the speeches. Philip Burton remembered: "Nobody could take their eyes off Richard."

Halfway through the run, Burton got bored and pulled off a stunt that no other actor would have been allowed to get away with. In a scene at the siege of Moulins, his character was to appear on the stage and deliver a short speech to each of the aristocrats involved in the siege. It was described by author Tyrone Steverson as "tedious oratory." So Burton decided to liven it up by inserting extra lines and saying something outrageous and out of context to each of them. As Steverson recalled: "One after the other, the actors fell out of character and out of control in laughter."

The third play was the production of 'Twelfth Night' by director Denis Carey. The critics didn't like Burton's portrayal of his character Sir Toby Belch. Michael Hordern recalled: "In 'Twelfth Night', he was a disappointing Toby

Belch. I couldn't wear a crown and Richard couldn't wear a wig. Disguise diminished him, and he knew it." For once, Burton was too sober and too withdrawn in the part. When Richard Leech saw it, he said to Burton: "Well, it's lovely. It's enchanting and you're so sweet, but what about the old man bit?" Leech said he replied: "You've got to think of the fans, haven't you?" Burton was right again; the fans loved it.

But Richard's best reviews came for his performance in the fourth production of the year, in 'Coriolanus'. Michael Benthall returned to direct Coriolanus and had trouble persuading Burton to do it. He had to enlist the support of Philip Burton. Burton had decided he didn't want to do 'Coriolanus', and it took heavy pressure from Philip to change his mind. According to Philip, it was because he had no sympathy with the character. Philip recalled: "Michael Benthall called me up in great distress. Although it had long been announced that Richard would play Coriolanus, he had suddenly decided not to do so, and wouldn't budge; could I get him to change his mind? I said I'd try."

Philip guessed what was wrong, as he explained: "He could find no jot of sympathy for the character, whose unmitigated contempt for ordinary folk was completely at variance with Richard's abiding identification with the working class. And there was no let-up in the character, not one soliloquy in which he questioned himself."

Burton and Philip met late one night in Hampstead to thrash out the problems.

As Philip remembered: "There followed a never-to-be-forgotten long night of discussion. I pointed out that it was Coriolanus' very lack of ambivalence that was admirable. However much we disagreed with his values, we had to admire his devotion to them. And he had no ulterior motive; he refused to benefit from his victories. He was a man of action, happy only in action. He had derived his heroic values from his mother, but she had taught him too well; in a moment that called for compromise, she could do so but her son couldn't. He was the quintessential soldier's hero." But Burton told Philip that he couldn't do it, as he was "the socialist product of a socialist family." It was only when Philip replied with: "You don't have to commit murder to play a murderer", that Burton saw the logic and instantly changed his mind. Michael Benthall was mightily relieved, and any previous differences with Philip he had had over 'Hamlet' were instantly forgotten.

The play was a total triumph for Burton, as Robert Hardy said: "His Coriolanus was without parallel; quite easily the best I've ever seen. But you couldn't rely on it happening the next night. Already, he was quickly, openly bored." In Hardy's opinion: "Once the puzzle was cracked, the conquest made, the enemy taken", Burton's interest fell away.

Philip Burton said: "There's no such thing as a definitive Hamlet because he's such a multifaceted character, but there is a definitive Coriolanus, and it was Richard's."

And there was one incident that is etched in the memory of the cast. There was more sword play in 'Coriolanus', this time in the final scene with his old stand-in, Paul Daneman, who played Tullus Aufidius. Daneman fancied himself as a swordsman and so too, after 101 jousts with Robert Hardy, did Burton. But one night, it all went wrong and Daneman almost lost a finger. As he recalled many years later: "We had short Roman swords, no gloves, and the lighting was very low. Anyway, in our enthusiasm, we fought rather too furiously and I suddenly felt a tremendous wallop around the knuckles. I was carried off in some pain and then the hand went numb and it wasn't until I was at the bottom of the steps underneath the stage that I saw my hand was streaming with blood. The nurse at the theatre bound it up and we finished the performance. Later, I went to Charing Cross Hospital and found that the blow had cut through the tendon of the index finger of the right hand. For the next six weeks, I had to go on stage wearing this bloody great plaster, and I was still wearing it when we were playing 'Twelfth Night'. I still can't completely bend that finger. After that, it became a firm rule at the Old Vic that gloves should always be worn for sword fights."

The final production was 'The Tempest', which Burton had struggled with at Stratford-upon-Avon two years earlier. Burton played Caliban and this time had an easier run at it, directed by the legendary Robert Helpmann. Helpmann had a new take on the play, which included Robert Hardy playing the part of Ariel nearly naked.

The actor came in for some abusive reviews by the critics and outraged some of them with his state of undress. The performance was called "obscene and disgusting." So much so that *The Times* newspaper refused to review the play unless it had Helpmann's assurance that Ariel would be appropriately dressed.

Robert Hardy was deeply upset by the controversy. But Burton couldn't care less. When Hardy, seeking solace and sympathy, asked him: "What's wrong? Am I really as awful as they say?" Burton got angry and shouted at him: "No, you're too good. They don't understand what you're at. Stop worrying about it; don't panic." Hardy was wholly reassured by his friend, and from that evening never looked back. His confidence was renewed.

Despite Burton's false nose falling off on the first night, Harold Hobson in the *Sunday Times* said: "A fine end to this actor's astonishing display of vigorous versatility in five major roles."

But by the end, the stress of five mighty performances took its toll. At the end of the run, Burton became ill and was ordered by the Old Vic doctor to rest and, subsequently, he missed a few performances of 'The Tempest'. But after two days, he recovered and resumed the role.

The stresses were considerable during this period; while performing at the Old Vic, Burton was also working hard for the BBC, appearing in radio and television productions, many produced by his friend Frank Hauser. His narrating skills were also much in demand.

Burton was also a regular guest on the Frankie Howerd television comedy show. Howerd was an old friend, and the shows on which Burton appeared garnered huge ratings. Burton briefly enjoyed being Howerd's sidekick and thought it was money for old rope. It was nothing compared to what he earned in Hollywood, but one hour's work for the BBC could yield what his brothers in Wales took three months to earn. Graham Jenkins remembered: "In between rehearsals and performances at the Old Vic, the likeliest place to find Rich was the Broadcasting House, where his distinctive voice was much in demand. The disembodied voice could take its listeners anywhere, do anything." The radio and television work all added to Burton's fame.

One of his greatest achievements on radio had been his performance of 'Under Milk Wood', the late Dylan Thomas' last play. 'Under Milk Wood' was produced by Douglas Cleverdon. Cleverdon was the patient radio producer who had waited three years for Thomas to write his play. Thomas had worked on the play intermittently for nearly ten years, and had died within a month of completing it. Cleverdon cast Burton in the role Thomas himself would have played had he been alive. Burton, like the other actors, acted for free and donated his fees to Dylan's widow, Caitlin, and their children.

When the Old Vic season came to a close at the end of May 1954, there was a near riot outside the theatre. No one knows how many people came down for that performance, but the crowds certainly outnumbered the seats available. When Burton emerged from the stage door, there could have been as many as 2,500 people outside. The road was completely blocked, despite the efforts of the police, who gave up and set up a diversion. Philip Burton was there and recalled: "Richard's fans nearly tore the place apart. He had to be smuggled away in a taxi." Melvyn Bragg called the mass of fans "rabidly enthusiastic."

The company then went on a brief tour of the north of England theatres before leaving for Denmark for ten performances of 'Hamlet' at Elsinore Castle. It included a glorious week of overindulgence for the actors and crew, who were treated like royalty by the Danes. And then, it was briefly on to Zurich for three special performances.

In his biography of Burton, entitled *Rich*, Melvyn Bragg said of Burton at the conclusion of that season at the Old Vic: "He was now, beyond any doubt, the heir to Olivier and Gielgud both."

And Burton's rocketing fame had been noticed by Queen Elizabeth, who invited him to one of her annual garden parties at Buckingham Palace along with seven thousand other guests. The Burtons attracted far more interest and attention than the Queen at her own party that day.

Immediately afterwards, Burton flew off to Paris for a long-scheduled meeting with Darryl F. Zanuck, the most powerful man in Hollywood, who had come to Europe specially to see Burton.

# AND GOD CREATED BURTON

# CHAPTER 26

# The Three Stinkers

## *Burton's career goes down the tube*

### 1954 to 1955

When Hollywood insiders talk about films they have seen and wished they hadn't, they talk about three types of films: commonly known as 'Dogs', 'Turkeys' and 'Stinkers', in that order of awfulness. Although no one in Hollywood has ever officially bothered to grade them, 'Dogs' are poor films which lose money but break even eventually; 'Turkeys' are very poor films that lose money, but not much; and the term 'Stinker' is reserved for movies that not only lose fortunes but are essentially unreleasable, i.e. not fit for human viewing. Over half the films made in Hollywood are placed in the first two of these three categories, and always have been. But hardly any make the latter category – to do that, a film has to be very poor indeed, and very expensive.

Between 1954 and 1955, Richard Burton managed to make three movies, all of which fell into the latter category, and although the studios 20th Century Fox and United Artists lost fortunes, Burton himself got rich out of them and earned US$650,000 for his appearances.

The first stinker was called *Prince of Players*, the product of Burton's return trip to Hollywood in the middle of 1954.

In June 1954, straight after the 1953/54 season closed at the Old Vic, Burton flew to Paris to meet with Darryl Zanuck, who was on a tour of the Fox offices in mainland Europe. After a year away from Hollywood, Burton had no offers of work and he quickly concluded a deal with Zanuck to return to Los Angeles to take the lead role in a film called *Prince of Players*. The fee was US$200,000 and was settled quickly and without argument. The old contractual disputes were seemingly forgotten. Both men had the same objective; Zanuck wanted Burton back and Burton wanted to go back. This time they kept it simple.

Burton was sent the script for *Prince of Players* before he left England for New York, so he was able to learn his lines during the Atlantic crossing. The day after he arrived, on Wednesday 4th August, he met his adoptive father, Philip Burton, for lunch and showed him the script. Philip went home and stayed up until 3am reading it.

When he had finished, he threw it down on the floor of his apartment in disgust. Horrified, he referred to the script as a "disgrace" when Burton called the next day. He couldn't understand how a studio like 20th Century-Fox could come out with such rubbish. He was even more staggered when he learned that the script had been written by Moss Hart, a distinguished theatre director and well-regarded writer.

*Prince of Players* had been deliberately green-lighted as a comeback vehicle for Burton in Hollywood. Darryl Zanuck, obsessed with getting Burton back to Hollywood and out of the claws of Old Vic – who he believed was a person – had ordered up a script to suit him.

The script was adapted from a novel about Edwin Thomas Booth, the brother of John Wilkes Booth, who had assassinated Abraham Lincoln in 1865. Both brothers were nineteenth-century Shakespearian actors, like their father, Junius Brutus Booth, who was actually English. Burton played Edwin, and the young actor John Derek, who later married Bo Derek, played John Wilkes Booth.

The novel, by Eleanor Ruggles, recounted the life of the theatrical Booth family and how Edwin took a troupe of actors to mining camps to perform Shakespeare's plays after his brother was killed following the assassination. Zanuck saw it as a way for Burton to indulge his love of Shakespeare in Hollywood instead of at the Old Vic.

As such, Zanuck took a hands-on role in the film and made all sorts of bizarre decisions to try to create what he termed 'special material' – whatever that meant.

Despite Zanuck's enthusiasm, Burton was very worried by Philip's analysis of the script and wondered what he was getting into. He also wondered aloud whether *Prince of Players* could be Zanuck's way of getting back at him for his snub the previous year. So he asked Philip to come to California to help avoid a fiasco.

Right from the start, *Prince of Players* seemed to be a disaster in waiting. There was nothing wrong with the original story, just Moss Hart's very poor script. It also had a very inexperienced director, Philip Dunne, who had written the screenplay of *The Robe*.

When Richard and Philip Burton arrived on set, they found that Dunne had no directing experience and the final screenplay from Moss Hart was little better than his draft script. Philip agreed to help where he could.

Dunne was an admirer of Burton's from the moment he had seen him in

'The Lady's Not For Burning' at the Globe Theatre in London in May 1949. But Zanuck seemed to be in charge and acting as producer. He thought of it as a great opportunity to exploit Burton's appeal as a leading Shakespearian actor while holding to a familiar Hollywood story line of an unlikely character emerging victorious from a seemingly hopeless position. In fact, up to now, Zanuck had never failed to make money from that sort of film.

From Zanuck's point of view, the key to the success of the film was Burton's performance of the Shakespearian extracts, which included the singing of some songs. But that style of acting just did not work on the big screen, and as the days went by, Burton knew it was all going wrong.

Philip Dunne, however, was pleased with the film and thought Burton's extraordinary acting would compensate for the problems of a poor script. So much so that Dunne began to have dreams of an Oscar. But it was all an illusion, and what he thought he saw through the viewfinder was not the same as what he was getting on film. As he said: "The personal magnetism Richard had on the sound stage didn't come through the camera. The fire and the intensity were there, but that was all. He hadn't yet mastered the tricks of the great movie stars such as Gary Cooper, who knew them all." Hollis Alpert, a journalist who followed Hollywood, explained: "In Hollywood, a studio could build a star through publicity and suitable vehicles, but at a certain point the would-be star had to learn the intricacies of his trade. Lighting could enhance or destroy. It was wise to have friends among the assistant directors and the soundmen, to entrust oneself to the director for guidance through the intricacies of a shooting schedule. Richard, one of the finest actors ever to come to Hollywood, had not yet learned enough about starring."

Apart from the problems, Burton enjoyed his usual good time during filming. He had abandoned the set trailer and was now using and enjoying the lavish dressing room suite allocated to stars in the main building. He found it rather convenient for his off-set activities and it became a conveyor belt of different women who had caught his eye on set, sometimes two or three a day. In fact, the female traffic in and out of his dressing room was even heavier than it had been in 1952 and many of the women were married – to men he knew. He said of himself and his own dubious behaviour with his friend's wives: "I was not the best of men back then."

In particular, he chased after his co-star, the 26-year-old starlet Maggie McNamara. He started a brief but passionate affair with the fragile McNamara after a short pursuit. In an astonishing display of arrogance, he told a journalist: "I was confident and could never understand why any girl would resist me."

Although the studio itself was dry, Burton was drinking heavily in the evenings throughout the production, literally drowning his sorrows. Halfway through filming, it finally caught up with him after he tried to shake off a flu virus with his father's solution of a row of boilermakers. Proving he did not have his father's legendary capacity, he totally overdid the cure. It induced alcohol poisoning, an experience he had not suffered before. He was in bed for a week with a combination of poisoning and the flu.

No one was unhappy when filming finally wrapped; post-production was finished and Burton went home to London.

British cinemas, that had so embraced Burton with his three films the previous year, deserted him for this one. It was a real stinker and, to this day, it is hard to find anyone who actually saw it.

Burton had laid an egg and he knew it. *Prince of Players* became the first flop in Cinemascope, giving Burton a unique place in Hollywood history as having starred in both the first hit and the first miss of the new widescreen format. Afterwards, when the disaster of *Prince of Players* unfolded at the box office, he told his brother Graham: "I'd give anything to do the whole bloody thing again."

In London, it was soon back to business and Burton and Valerie Douglas met with the American director Robert Rossen, who wanted to cast him as the lead in a new film version of *Alexander the Great*, being financed by United Artists, to be filmed in early 1955.

Interestingly, at that time, there were two *Alexander the Great* film projects to choose from and both of their producers considered Burton the only actor who could play the title part. As well as Rossen, producer Frank Ross, whom Burton had worked with on *The Robe* and was backed by 20th Century-Fox's money, had a film that would focus on the last two years of Alexander's life. But there was no script and Burton preferred Rossen's vision over that of Ross'. Or maybe he just wanted to send a message to Darryl Zanuck. Whatever it was, Burton chose the wrong Alexander, a decision that was to have terrible consequences for his career.

When Burton accepted the role, he insisted, as part of the conditions, that Rossen secured him a 'no consequences' release from Darryl Zanuck, as his contractual position with Fox was still far from clear. Zanuck released him all too quickly, which made Burton very suspicious. Burton settled for a fee of

US$250,000, and Aaron Frosch made the arrangements and handled his first film contract for his new client.

Frosch also secured parts and good pay packets for Burton's friends Stanley Baker, William Squire and Michael Hordern. Burton also insisted that Rosen cast Claire Bloom in the lead female role. Rossen simply said 'yes' to anything Burton wanted, especially when he knew Frank Ross was lurking with a deal.

Determined to absorb the part, Burton immediately bought all the history books he could find on the period and studied every aspect of *Alexander the Great*. The movie was filmed in Spain from February to July in 1955 in the rolling sierra hills outside Madrid. Rossen, who was to be director, producer and screenwriter, had been attracted to Spain because of the favourable exchange rate, good studio facilities, low taxes and the Spanish Army, which could be rented *en masse* at the right price from General Franco, the dictator who ruled the country.

Rossen was an interesting character, and Burton warmed to him. He had made a number of hard-hitting, gutsy dramas including *All the King's Men*, which had won the Oscar for best picture in 1949. He was a former member of the communist party and had been blacklisted during the Hollywood witch hunts of the late 1940s, when he was accused of being un-American. He had been luckier than many other Hollywood writers and directors of the time, who were actually imprisoned for being un-American.

Rossen told Burton he had been researching the subject for some years to ensure historical accuracy and it would be a great spectacle. He promised to be devoted to excellence in every aspect of the film and to pay meticulous attention to detail. But he was also adamant that there would be a genuinely warm human story behind what he called the "sweep of historical events." Unfortunately, that was precisely what was missing, and it brought down the film.

The budget was enormous and United Artists allocated US$4 million to the project. When he heard the budget was US$4 million, Burton quipped that it was more money than Alexander had spent conquering the whole of the Persian empire. But without a good story, all the detail and money in the world wouldn't matter. But Burton believed what Rossen told him and thought everything was set for a classic movie, and he was actively looking forward to it in the weeks before filming started. Despite his high hopes for the film, it was to turn out to be his second stinker.

At that time, neither Burton nor Sybil cared to fly and went to great lengths to avoid it if they could. So they sailed for Lisbon and hired a car, drove across Portugal into Spain, stopping at small inns along the way. They made a whole week of the journey, criss-crossing Spain and choosing the most minor roads to drive for eight or ten hours a day, absorbing everything the country had to offer. Some days, they didn't see another car at all and found themselves in remote areas of Spain, forced to accept what accommodation was at hand, however dubious, and finding only bread and cheese to eat. Along the way, they celebrated their sixth wedding anniversary. It was a perfect week and, despite the leisurely drive, they were amongst the first to arrive in Madrid on 10th February at the Castellana Hilton Hotel.

United Artists had taken over the whole of the Castellana, one of Madrid's best hotels for the duration of filming. It allocated each of the stars of the film a spacious suite, all of which were situated on the same floor. Burton made sure he had his close friends around him. Stanley and Ellen Baker were next door. Michael Hordern and his wife, Eve Mortimer, were one down. At the end of the corridor was Claire Bloom's suite, which she occupied on her own, and next to hers was William Squire's. Squire was the perfect foil for Sybil, although Ellen Baker wasn't fooled for a moment and marvelled at how Burton maintained his mistress and his wife in such close proximity.

But throughout the six long months they were there, Bloom was no threat to Sybil Burton. But their cover was nearly blown on the first day when Bloom arrived at the Castellana and Burton was in reception talking to a bunch of reporters. They hadn't seen each other for nearly four months and embraced enthusiastically. As one reporter remarked the next day: "He was enthusiastic about his leading lady and she about him."

Bloom was Burton's mistress in the film as well as in real life. She was playing the part of Barsine, one of Alexander's three wives, who, as she explained to the press, was "really his mistress". Her hotel room door was always open to him and she spent most of her time alone in her suite waiting for Burton to call on her – it was all she lived for. As she said: "It wasn't much of a part for me. Most of the film was about the men conquering Greece and Persia."

Burton confided to one or two reporters, who were in on the secret and could be relied upon to be discreet: "I find it almost impossible and unbearable to leave her. But she needed much more than I could give her, I do believe. I think she would have married me if she could. But it wasn't written, and other destinies awaited us."

Because Spain was easily accessible to Britain, many members of the Jenkins family came out to Madrid and stayed for as long as they were able that summer. Ivor and Gwen were there for most of the time. Cecilia also came with her young daughters, Marian and Rhianon.

The Spaniards were delighted to have all their famous American and British guests in Madrid, and gave parties for them almost every night. Even the puritanical Generalissimo (Franco) got in on the party act and opened the doors of his palace.

The first few weeks of filming went well until the actors realised which way the film was headed – which was nowhere. For some unfathomable reason, Rossen insisted Burton wear a poorly-made yellow-coloured wig, which took away all his natural authority and turned his character, Alexander, into a figure of fun. Wearing that wig, Burton lost the plot and didn't look as though he was there. Alexander was undoubtedly the worst performance of his entire career. He looked like a ham, and modern audiences watching it today would be forgiven for asking why there was so much fuss about Burton. The film was terrible, and he was even worse.

Not without good reason, Burton blamed the director for his troubled performance. Rossen was overburdened in his three roles: writing directing and producing.

There was actually no story to the film besides the rather lengthy 161-minute history lesson, which wasn't particularly interesting anyway. Rossen was at his best when dreaming up momentous oratory and there were one or two finely written lines of dialogue in the film. As Michael Hordern noted: "I think Robert Rossen thought he *was* Shakespeare.

After a fortnight, it was clear that Rossen should be sacked, but there was no one at United Artists strong enough to do it; because Rossen was screenwriter, producer and director, he was a law unto himself.

Rossen was a gifted director of social dramas, but directing a grand historical saga was not in his repertoire although he did his best to prove otherwise. But his brain was simply not big enough to pull it off, and he quickly lost his way – especially on the day he dropped his only copy of the latest version of the loose-leaf script, which had unnumbered pages, and the strong winds blew them all over the Spanish sierras.

The film meandered everywhere and he lost grasp of events. Burton called him a "troubled man", saying: "He would say one thing and mean another, and after the first few weeks, he seemed to lose heart in the film." He added: "I know all epics are awful, but I thought *Alexander the Great* might be the first good one. I was wrong."

The critics were merciless when they finally saw it. They called the film 'Alexander the Bore'. Campbell Dixon, the *Daily Telegraph*'s film critic actually called the film "unpleasant." Hollis Alpert, who visited the set and was close to Burton said: "The speeches came out hollow and pompous. The pace was agonisingly slow, the battle scenes stodgy. So much for fidelity to historical truth. Audiences fell asleep."

Two hours and 41 minutes of military history was too much for any audience, and those who saw it told their friends not to, ensuring the film's demise and consignment to ignominious history.

Because they were in Spain, with no access to normal studio facilities, no film was viewed before the end of shooting and no one had any idea what had been shot. Burton actually returned to London believing he had acted well. The deluded Rossen assured him that it may have appeared stodgy, but good editing would create the "spectacle to end all spectacles."

But just as one stinker wrapped, Burton was about to embark upon another. He took a few weeks off and tried not to think about it.

In August, he sailed once again to New York aboard Cunard's Queen Elizabeth liner in company with Sybil and his brother Ivor and his wife, Gwen. He and Sybil occupied the best first class suite in the ship, and it was an idyllic crossing. Burton was no longer shying away from the luxuries of life and believed he had enough money to indulge himself, encouraged by his new lawyer, Aaron Frosch, who told him that all film-related expenses, including travel, would be tax-free. It was a luxury Burton didn't refuse, especially when it was effectively being paid for by the Inland Revenue department of the British government. He really enjoyed the crossing, with his books and his beer for company.

They were headed for Los Angeles for Burton to co-star in a film with Lana Turner called *The Rains of Ranchipur*, in which he played an Indian doctor called Dr Safti. *The Rains of Ranchipur* was a remake of the 1939 Tyrone Power film *The Rains Came*. The excuse for its remake was a massive tidal wave in the middle of the film that would translate very well to the new Cinemascope widescreen.

The essence of the film was a love affair between the wife of an English lord, played by 34-year-old Lana Turner, and the Hindu doctor, played by Burton. In the hands of a gifted director, writer, make-up artist and voice coach, it could have worked, but in the absence of all four, it bombed. Burton was miscast as the doctor and Turner equally miscast as an English aristocrat – say no more.

Filming began late because Lana Turner was injured after slipping on a wet floor while exiting her bathtub. As a result, the film was shot in a rush so that it would catch the Christmas season.

When shooting did begin, it was Hollywood at its absolute worst, as Melvyn Bragg summed up: "He was very bad. The film was very bad." Graham Jenkins observed: "Not even the make-up was convincing. They imported an elocution expert to help him with his accent, but after a couple of lessons they agreed his case was hopeless. Dr Safti, as portrayed by Rich, must be the only Indian doctor on screen to sound as if he came from Cardiff."

Burton could not be bothered to play a Hindu doctor, however black the makeup was. The astonishing miscasting was amplified by the weak directing of someone called Jean Negulesco; Under his direction, Turner overplayed her role while Burton underplayed his.

The Romanian-born American Negulesco had won an Oscar and a Bafta in his career, but, clearly, they had been down to someone else. Negulesco was by all accounts "a charming man with a fine sense of humour" and believed he was making a "wonderful picture." But he should have been ashamed of himself, as the story on which the film was based – the 1937 novel *The Rains Came* by Louis Bromfield – was a good one.

Burton, who described Negulesco's directing style as "beyond human belief", couldn't wait for the picture to end. He saw none of the director's so-called "charm or sense of humour" as mentioned in his press cuttings.

Negulesco eventually wrote his autobiography and entitled it: *Things I did and Things I Think I Did*. It summed him up. But he did great damage to Burton's career, which, after this stinker, came to a dead halt.

The only other bright spot was that Burton picked up another US$200,000. And this time, with sterling gradually declining in value and Aaron Frosch practicing some expert tax avoidance, he got to keep a bit more of it.

No other film actor in history had starred in three stinkers in succession and survived. When his brother David Jenkins saw the film in Wales, he called it "risible." When Burton was asked by a journalist to explain the dreadful film, he fixed him with a stare, smiled and said: "Ah well, they do say it never rains but it Ranchipurs." It was all he could say.

He had no choice but to ignore the critics and his attitude toward them was recounted by Penny Junor in her biography of Burton: "Forget critics, he used to say. If they're good about you, they're not good enough. If they're bad about you, they'll only upset you. So don't read them on either count."

In his lifetime, Burton never watched *The Rains of Ranchipur* and he never read the reviews. It was the only way he could stay sane. With no film offers forthcoming, he signed up for another season at the Old Vic. But in truth, he was a desperately worried man and he saw the life he envisaged for himself slipping away. He now had to support a team of six people looking after him, and for the first time, he realised he wasn't as set up for life as he had thought he was.

Hollywood no longer wanted anything to do with him.

He said ruefully of that terrible period: "It was not the most interesting period of my life from the artistic point of view. I tried to rise above the material; some good film actors can. I didn't.

"I did some films which I enjoyed and a lot of films that I didn't want to do. And there was no way of my persuading anybody that I wasn't right for them or that the scripts weren't good. I had no self-criticism at all. I firmly believed that if people would pay money to see me in the theatre, or in the films, that's their responsibility and not mine."

His arrogance was not appreciated – not least by the studios who had financed those movies.

# THE THREE STINKERS

# AND GOD CREATED BURTON

# CHAPTER 27

# Meeting his rainmaker

## *Aaron Frosch changes his life*

### 1953 to 1956

When Richard Burton left Hollywood in June 1953, the last thing Humphrey Bogart said to him was: "I never knew a man who played Hamlet who didn't die broke." The thought rang in Burton's ears, as those profound throwaway thoughts always did with him.

But a year later, he proved Bogart wrong. Although the taxman had taken most of it, Burton's bank account exceeded a credit balance of £10,000 for the first time when 1954 rolled round. In a period when the average earnings of a Briton were around £350 a year, it was a momentous achievement. Of course, by Bogart's standards, Burton was effectively broke. Bogart was worth US$6 million, an unimaginable sum in England in the fifties.

But, added to his cash, Burton also owned three houses in Hampstead worth close to £12,000. The previous year, he had purchased a small cottage opposite his own house in Squires Mount for his 49-year-old brother Ivor and his wife, Gwen. By then, Ivor had given up his job and effectively become Burton's road manager, organising his life and his logistics. Ivor was a powerful character, 100 per cent honest, trustworthy and a very good administrator and organiser.

The house was not only a good investment but it meant Ivor was always on hand. Gwen, although much older at 45, was a good companion for Sybil.

Ivor Jenkins had had no hesitation accepting his new role. After tasting a different life in his travels with his brother, he had been desperate to get out of Wales and the new arrangement suited him down to the ground.

So life was good in 1953, after three successful films and with the three stinkers still on the horizon. And Burton so enjoyed having his older brother, Ivor, around permanently.

Ivor was, and always had been, a father figure in his brother's life. 19 years his senior, he spoke with a strong South Wales accent and the two brothers had the advantage that they could always switch to speaking Welsh to keep conversations private – which they often did.

Penny Junor, Burton's biographer, described Ivor and Gwen as the perfect couple: "Kind, gentle, loyal and a pillar of honesty and respectability, and his wife, Gwen, was a gentle and intelligent woman. The great sadness in their lives was that they had no children."

But most of all, Burton respected his brother's judgment and the elder brother seemed gradually to become Burton's conscience, filling the void that existed in Burton's relationship with his adoptive father Philip Burton. Junor believed that Philip was never a father figure in anything but name. She said: "He was a mentor, yes; a coach, a critic, a friend, and someone to whom Richard remained indebted, but never a man to whom he looked for pastoral guidance."

She believed that some disillusionment with Philip had set in as Richard grew older: "Now that he was established in the business, owned a house, was married and no longer the new boy in London, he found Phil a bit of an old woman and his pedantic ways a little irksome." The assessment was very astute – although Burton still loved Philip as though he was his own father.

David Jenkins thoroughly approved of his brother's new role, saying: "It seemed natural that Ivor should adopt this supportive role, just as he had taken the lead in our childhood days, organising the household after the death of our mother. Richard looked to him for fathering in the same way that he looked to Cecilia for mothering. He could laugh at him too." Burton told people that Ivor was his new "henchman."

But there was inevitably some jealously from other family members envious of the high life that Ivor and Gwen were now leading – not least youngest brother, Graham Jenkins, who considered that the role should have been his: "I was not over the moon about the appointment. My reservations were chiefly personal. While I admired Ivor as the driving force in the Jenkins family in the years after our mother's death, I was never able to get close to him." Graham also believed Ivor lacked the creative and cultural knowledge, advice that Burton often needed, as he said: "Though an intelligent man, he knew little of the theatre or films. For him, Rich was the creative genius who could do no wrong."

Graham was not alone in his view, and other members of the family were also worried that Ivor would be a too willing drinking partner for Burton. Both men were dangers to themselves when they got together on benders, which occurred rather too frequently, especially now as Gwen and Sybil were able to amuse themselves in their absence. Ivor was easily as big a boozer as Richard, and the tales of Ivor's nights of drinking abound even today. And Ivor was indiscreet when he drank with strangers, which resulted in many negative stories about his brother appearing in newspapers. Ivor would drink with anyone he liked, and he didn't always take enough care to find out exactly who they were. It annoyed Graham because when these stories appeared, he always got the blame. Nobody thought it might be the fault of good old Ivor. Surprisingly, none of the many biographies of Burton, including those penned by two of his brothers, mention Ivor's drinking problems, which were every bit as serious as Burton's and eventually directly caused Ivor's accident and subsequent death in 1972.

Ivor may not have been very creative and he may have drunk too much, but no one doubted his courage. He was always ready to act as a bodyguard or minder when his brother needed one. He was tall, powerfully built, something of a fitness freak and ideally suited to the role. David Jenkins explained how Ivor once prevented disaster on a film set: "On one occasion, Richard was sitting astride a horse waiting for his cue to start; Ivor was standing by him. The horse suddenly reared fiercely and started galloping towards a couple of hundred extras. Ivor boldly ran towards the horse, held on to the reins with all his might, managed to stop the animal from bolting further and, while Richard hung on with tenacity, brought the horse to a stop. Richard held the view that if Ivor had not taken this decisive action, the horse would have dashed into the hordes of waiting extras, causing terrible injuries, if not death."

With Ivor on his payroll taking care of things at home, Burton felt a lot more secure about his future when he and Sybil sailed for New York in late July 1954 on the French liner, Liberté. They had planned to stay over in New York for a few days with Philip before going to Los Angeles to begin work on *Prince of Players*.

After a two day stopover in New York, they caught the Express Super Chief train to Los Angeles. Escorting Burton and his wife on the train to Los Angeles was a young 20th Century-Fox executive called Aaron Frosch.

The two men found they liked each other immediately and they fell into deep conversation about the ways of Hollywood. Burton had been musing for some time on his need for management and legal assistance with his business affairs. Valerie Douglas had filled a big hole and was an excellent day-to-day organiser and a tough negotiator when required, but she was not a legal or contract person.

Frosch was 30 years old and hailed from Brooklyn. He was also a lawyer who knew his way around film contracts. As they got talking during the journey, Burton realised that Frosch was very sharp indeed and could hold his own in a wide range of subjects. Burton tested his knowledge time and again without Frosch knowing it. The young lawyer passed every time. They discussed the intricacies of film finance and Burton was really impressed when Frosch told him two ways he could minimise his British tax bill, firstly by spacing out his income over several years and secondly by taking full advantage of studio allowances to their maximum value.

Burton was impressed by these two pieces of simple advice because no one had mentioned them before, certainly not his sleepy British accountant who had been recommended by Vere Barker. His only interest seemed to be in making him pay as much tax as possible to avoid any trouble. Burton had long thought that when the British Inland Revenue said "jump", his accountant just asked "how high."

Frosch was doing a relatively low-level meet-and-greet job for Fox in New York, escorting studio visitors who arrived there to LA. His career was in the doldrums and his problem was that Fox employed literally hundreds of sharp young executives like him – many with Harvard law degrees. He had graduated from the far less prestigious Brooklyn Law School and it was difficult for him to climb the ladder. At 29, he was getting frustrated at being little more than an errand boy.

But Burton quickly realised whilst talking to him that Frosch was the answer to his prayers and that his talents had been overlooked at Fox. He was just what Burton needed at the time.

Frosch also liked Burton more and more as the 12-hour train journey unfolded. Suddenly, between the conversations, Burton could wait no longer and said: "I want you to represent me." A very surprised Frosch agreed on the spot but said there were difficulties; he would need to set up an office in Manhattan and get out of his job contract at Fox. He told Burton: "I have to set up my own office and this will cost a lot of money, and I don't have a lot of money."

Burton told him he would finance his office and that he would straighten out his departure from Fox with Daryl Zanuck. Frosch nodded but told Burton that he doubted Zanuck would know who he was. Burton, realising that as well, said: "If I solve the first of the problems, can you solve the second?" Frosch nodded at that and they just shook hands on it there and then, sealing a relationship that would endure until the day Burton died. Burton agreed to pay him 10 percent of whatever he earned as a fee.

So Frosch set up his own little office in Manhattan, and Burton was his first client. Later, he would merge his one-man-band firm with a larger New York outfit before eventually going on to found his own multi-partner practice called Weissberger and Frosch in 1973, with offices in East 56th Street. Frosch would gradually add clients such as Marilyn Monroe and Margaret Leighton and, eventually, Elizabeth Taylor. Frosch later achieved fame when he drew up Marilyn Monroe's will and was the executor after her death.

With both Frosch and Douglas on board, Burton had the perfect team. They were not only colleagues, but all three of them also became firm friends and they all eventually became wealthy as a result.

So Burton felt very good about life when he arrived in Los Angeles, that is, apart from the usual problems with the script. Straightaway, he rented a small two-bedroom house from the ballet director Roland Petit, who was going on tour with his company.

Once there, he resumed the celebrity lifestyle and it was as if he had never been away.

Philip Burton joined them a week later.

On his second visit to Hollywood, Burton found he was no longer the naïve youngster, and this time he saw Hollywood through different eyes. He started to realise how false and fickle it all was. He hated the way everything revolved around the dollar, and he did not enjoy his stay half as much as the first time around. Almost immediately, he found himself longing for Waterloo Road again.

Burton was also a little non-plussed. Although he was warmly welcomed, no one regarded or treated him like the star he thought he was. He noticed he was still well down in the pecking order, after people like Stewart Granger and James Mason. It was then he realised that it took more than three films, even a blockbuster like *The Robe* to establish genuine stardom.

Doubts were also surfacing in Hollywood about his screen presence. As Darryl Zanuck, now one of his biggest fans, said: "I put him among the three finest actors in the world, but this doesn't automatically make him a star. He has acted his parts so far, but as for his personality, he hasn't had the opportunity to show it yet." But Zanuck was a true believer and said what he thought: "Burton would creep up on audiences slowly."

Arriving in summer, he found the party scene different as well. Sundays were the great party day in late summer in Los Angeles. They were invariably set around swimming pools in lavish houses. This time, he had nothing to prove and was more circumspect in his behaviour. He entertained his fellow guests with romantic stories from his first season at the Old Vic. But the Old Vic he described was nothing like the real Old Vic, but the stories went down well nevertheless – unless, of course, any of the guests had actually been to the South London theatre.

Before leaving Los Angeles, Burton went to a Sunday afternoon party at the home of Michael Wilding and Elizabeth Taylor. A demure Taylor was five-months pregnant with her second son, Christopher, and took little part in the socialising. She and Burton hardly exchanged more than two words. But Burton was smitten by the 22-year-old, who was already one of Hollywood's highest-earning stars. But even he didn't think it proper to hit upon a pregnant woman in her husband's home. He didn't forget her, and when he left the party with Sybil that night, there was only one thought in his head: "Maybe, maybe, one day, one day." And that thought rattled around in his head for the next few days.

The filming of *Prince of Players* lasted until mid-October, and four weeks later, as soon as post-production was finished, Burton headed straight back to New York on the train with Sybil and Valerie Douglas, who was coming back to England with them for an extended visit to Europe over the Christmas holiday season.

The three lingered in New York to see Philip Burton's new apartment. Philip had now definitely decided to settle in New York permanently. He had also been appointed as creative head of the newly formed Cowan-Chrysler Productions Inc., and he took them to see his elaborate wood-panelled office in the famous Chrysler Building, where the company was based. His office walls were hung with paintings worth over US$1 million from Walter Chrysler Jr.'s private collection. Walter Chrysler was one of the world's most famous collectors of art, and his collection was then rumoured to be worth well over US$100 million, an unimaginable sum in 1954. Burton was delighted to see his adoptive father doing so well and becoming so well established in the creative community in New York. At the behest of Burton, Douglas had also started managing Philip's burgeoning career in the film world.

After six days, the three of them left for England again on the Liberté liner. After the crossing, they disembarked at Plymouth on 26th November 1954 and caught the train to Paddington Station in London, where 20th Century-Fox PR minders were waiting for them. They had arranged for photographers to meet the train, and pictures of the arrival at Paddington were printed in every newspaper the next day, along with some colourful quotes about Burton's new film.

After he had contracted to make *Alexander the Great*, and with his immediate future secured, Burton could relax and enjoy the upcoming Christmas holiday. It was his first Christmas at home for three years.

There was only one thing troubling him: his inability to get his wife Sybil pregnant in nearly six years of trying. The two of them took the opportunity to have hospital tests. The tests found no reason why the couple couldn't conceive, so they just kept on trying.

That Christmas, the Jenkins family implored them to come to Wales, and Burton felt obliged to comply. To ease the boredom, he invited Valerie Douglas to join them and she also made the trip to Wales, staying at 73 Caradoc Street with Elfed and Cecilia James.

Douglas' presence was not entirely accidental. Burton actually needed her help for a special mission. He had planned a very special Christmas present for Sybil and would present it to her on Christmas Day.

The present was a brand new, bright red MG TF sports car with a black canvas convertible hood. In those days, it was the ultimate dream car to own. Douglas' task was to collect it from the London Morris car showroom and drive it down to Port Talbot. There, she would hide it away safe in a garage until Christmas morning.

Burton rose early on Christmas day without waking his wife and went downstairs to find a huge roll of red canvas ribbon material, an inch and a half wide, which he had purchased from a local haberdasher. He collected the MG from where Douglas had left it and parked it round the corner from Caradoc Street and got his young niece Marian to stand guard. Luckily, it was a sunny Christmas morning and he dropped the canvas hood down and threaded the ribbon round the steering wheel and attached the other end to the car keys. He then unwound the ribbon right up Caradoc Street to no. 73 and up the stairs, and he gently put the keys in his wife's hands with the ribbon attached – as she slumbered blissfully all the while.

When Sybil awoke, she found the car keys in her hand and had no idea what was going on. She put her dressing gown on over her shoulders and followed the ribbon, winding it up as she went. It led her all the way up the street until she came to the red MG with its hood down, ready for her to drive. There was a note from her husband telling her to take her new car for a spin and to drive it back to the house. Marian jumped in with Sybil, and the two of them – with Sybil still in her dressing gown – drove around Taibach, although Sybil could hardly see through her tears of joy.

It was the most extraordinary Christmas present and it caused a sensation in Taibach as everyone came to take a look. On Boxing Day, Sybil drove it to Taylorstown to show her Welsh relatives and the following day drove it back to London with Valerie Douglas in the passenger seat. She was on cloud nine the whole way home.

Rhianon Trowell, who was there that day and witnessed Sybil's delight, kept hold of the ribbon and still has it today in her house in Oxford as a memory of that wonderful Christmas.

With Christmas and New Year over, Burton filled in the month before he would leave for Spain to film *Alexander the Great* with voiceovers and some radio plays and television work for the BBC. From February to June, they were in Spain shooting *Alexander the Great*, and straight after that, they left for New York to begin shooting the disastrous *Rains of Ranchipur*.

Principal photography on that ended in early October and Burton had to hang around for another four weeks for post-production. He, Sybil, Ivor and Gwen rented rooms in a hotel on the beach at Santa Monica and went surfing before departing on the Queen Elizabeth and arriving back at Southampton on 1st November 1955.

When Burton arrived back in London, he was hugely depressed over the three films he had completed. He was certain all three would fail and that he would find it difficult to get well paid work in the future.

He then proceeded to make the most catastrophic judgment of his career. Although it was five years before shooting would eventually begin, Burton was approached by director David Lean and legendary producer Sam Spiegel to take the lead role in a new epic to be called *Lawrence of Arabia*, to begin filming in 1961. Both Spiegel and Lean thought Burton perfect for the part and envisaged him as T. E. Lawrence. It was an exceptional story, based on the life of an extraordinary man. But after the strains and disappointment of *Alexander the Great*, Burton was reluctant to do another big budget epic film, believing them a waste of his talent and unlikely to be a success. By then, he had seen a rough cut of *Alexander*. He had tried to sit through it but couldn't.

But Burton couldn't see that *Lawrence of Arabia* had a storyline that *Alexander the Great* didn't.

Lean gave him a week to decide but, as his brother Graham ruefully recalled, he inexplicably turned down the role: "In the critical week or so when the part was his for the asking, Rich could not bring himself to sign away a year of his life on another historical epic. The torture of *Alexander the Great*, not to mention *The Robe*, was too fresh in his memory."

Lean quickly gave the once-in-a-lifetime part to a newcomer called Peter O'Toole and, when it was made in 1962, turned him into an instant star. *Lawrence of Arabia* was one of the most significant films ever made, a genuine classic and a huge box office success. Turning it down was a mistake of epic proportions.

By now, Burton had little faith in the artistic judgment of his Hollywood masters. In that period, he also turned down another extraordinary part; he was offered the role of Douglas Bader in a British film called *Reach For the Sky* about an RAF ace in World War II who lost both his legs in an accident and flew again in combat. When he passed, it went to another newcomer called Kenneth More, who also became a star as a result of the hugely successful film.

Burton tried to make sense of the six films that were the product of his three excursions to Hollywood between 1953 and 1955. His first three Hollywood endeavors were all, in their own way, successful; while the next three were not. But he had no idea why. In advance of production, he simply had no idea how to distinguish how they would turn out. And he had no idea why Hollywood studios would pay him so much money to make so much rubbish.

Burton was not reassured when he was told a story about Gregory Peck and James Stewart by his friend, the British journalist Fergus Cashin. Cashin told him: "Gregory Peck, when he was new to Hollywood, met James Stewart, who asked him how many movies he had made. He told him: 'Two. One good, one bad', and Stewart replied: 'Well, I've made sixty-two and you're already ahead of the game. All you need here is two good movies out of five to keep the old bicycle wheels turning.'" It was good advice, but Burton was too depressed to absorb it. Nothing could make him feel better after the three stinkers.

But he hardly had time to draw breath after arriving back in London in December 1954 as he plunged into the 1954/55 Old Vic season for his second go at Shakespeare in Waterloo Road. In the intervening period, Burtonmania had tailed off. The three stinkers had severely damaged his reputation along with his popularity, and the scenes at Waterloo Road were very subdued in comparison to those in 1953.

Although his performances weren't.

# AND GOD CREATED BURTON

# CHAPTER 28

# Back on the Waterloo Road

## *Old Vic to the rescue again*

### 1956

By the end of 1955, Richard Burton's star was on the wane. At only 30 years of age, his career was all but extinguished. The gradual appearance of the three stinkers in British cinemas finished him off. No one going into a cinema as a Richard Burton fan would emerge outside still a fan – they were all that bad. It didn't matter in America, where he had no real fan base, but in Britain it was a disaster.

Even the Old Vic company wasn't as enthusiastic, sensing he might be yesterday's man. But he gladly took their £45 a week to play his second season of Shakespeare. He knew he needed to pull a rabbit out of the hat to stay in the business and fell back on the stage, as he would many times in his career, to revive his fortunes.

And he was no longer a one-man band. He had responsibilities, with overheads of £200 a week to meet. He now effectively had five people on his payroll and had to start running hard just to stand still. But at least with Aaron Frosch and Valerie Douglas handling his affairs, all his expenses came out of pre-tax income but he knew he could carry on for only so long without topping up the money he had in the bank.

As was his want, Burton realised that if he never earned another penny, he would run out of money in ten years' time at his current rate of burn – he would be 40 years old. That thought frightened him, as he genuinely believed that he would never be offered a well-paid film role again by anyone – especially when he realised that the losses to 20th Century-Fox and United Artists on the three stinkers clocked up to close to US$6 million.

At the time, newspapers both in America and Britain were full of articles saying Burton was a "failed genius", following an anonymous quote from an unnamed Hollywood director in the *Los Angeles Times*. Frank Hauser, the BBC radio producer, described by Melvyn Bragg as "a man of cutting judgment", was angered by the remark. He didn't subscribe to that view. As Hauser told journalists, there is no such thing as a "failed genius – either you are or you aren't."

# AND GOD CREATED BURTON

Burton had come late into the Old Vic season and 'Henry V' was the fourth of six Shakespeare plays scheduled. Three had already come and gone. John Neville was appearing in all six. Neville was now the established Old Vic star and had signed up for the full five-year cycle of Shakespeare's history plays. Neville had made a real name for himself at the Old Vic, although he hadn't made any money. In theatrical circles, he was every bit as famous as Burton.

So as soon as Burton arrived, a turf battle with John Neville was expected to begin. But, instead, Burton found Neville very supportive and he didn't behave at all like they were in some sort of competition to be Britain's best young actor – although that was exactly how it was.

Neville was the same age as Burton and every bit as good looking and every bit as good an actor, without the flamboyance. He was also noted for his classical good looks and distinctive voice and, at the time, was frequently described as John Gielgud's natural successor, just as Burton was Olivier's.

At that time, Burton was known as the 'Welsh wonder' and Neville the 'Willesden wonder', alluding to their birthplaces. Upon Burton's arrival, Neville positively gushed about his rival to journalists: "It was an extraordinary thing at that time, you know, to be Welsh or a Cockney and unashamed of it. We took to each other and, with Richard, that was that. He was serious about friendship. He had a wonderful mind in another league from that of any other actor around."

Neville's intervention was timely as, one by one, the three stinkers began appearing in British cinemas. It was a very bad time for Burton and he was glad of any public support he could get, and he never forgot how kind Neville was to him at the end of 1955.

The stress and strains of that period were reflected by some of the weird interviews Burton gave to British journalists at the end of 1955. He talked to them about far ranging subjects, including his views on acting as a job and homosexuality in the theatre world. Penny Junor, in her brilliant biography of Burton published after his death, summed up the mood from those interviews: "He was beginning to question what he was doing with his life. Having struggled with such single-mindedness to leave the valleys, and having successfully freed himself from his working-class origins, he found they haunted him still. He could not shake off the knowledge in the back of his mind that the work real men did was difficult, dangerous and dirty, taking them from their beds at dawn and bringing them home exhausted at the end of a day. Here he was dressing up, making up and parading on stage. Acting was not a job for a real man, no more than a draper's apprentice had been, and this feeling was to remain with him all his life. Furthermore, he feared acting eroded his masculinity. The theatre world was, as it still is, liberally populated with homosexuals. It was commonplace for young actors, particularly good-looking ones, to be propositioned especially by men who were in a position to give them a job. Indeed, many of the men who had given Burton jobs were homosexual, as were a lot of his friends."

'Henry V' opened at the Old Vic on 13th December to full houses and ran for 71 performances. The critics were ecstatic and it was an immediate success – the first of any kind of success for Burton in almost two years. Directed by Michael Benthall, John Neville played Chorus. The part of Chorus was second billing to Burton's role as Henry V, but that didn't stop Neville turning in an extraordinary virtuoso performance. But his brilliance didn't please everybody, as Burton's friend and now Britain's leading drama critic Kenneth Tynan, observed: "The compere who steals the show is by definition a bad compere."

But that was Tynan's view and not anyone else's. Partnering the two men was a masterstroke by Benthall, and to some extent Burton basked in Neville's reflected glory. The critics went wild and over the top, seemingly desperate to praise Burton again after a very barren period. Many were the same people who had been reviewing his recent films and were glad he was back. Burton was very popular with the English press because he always had time for them and many of them were his late-night drinking buddies. *The Times* newspaper noted his recent fall from grace politely, saying: "He is able to make good all the lacks of a few short years ago…and excitingly combined all the qualities of Shakespeare's ideal king."

They all agreed that, despite what had been going on in Hollywood, Burton had "matured and developed as an actor." Typical praise included: "steely strength", "hard brilliance" and, best of all, "a romantic sense of a high kingly mission and the clear consciousness of the capacity to fulfill it."

His performance was marked by the arrival of his second major award after his Golden Globe. In January, he won the very prestigious Evening Standard Drama Award for best performance by an actor. The award was effectively a gift from Lord Beaverbrook, who owned the *Evening Standard* and who was said to have been heavily influenced by his close friend Winston Churchill's opinion of Burton.

Kenneth Tynan, now ensconced at *The Observer* newspaper, was ecstatic about his old friend's return to the theatre and renewed success. He had become the arbiter of what was good and bad in British theatre. So what Tynan said really mattered, and when he called Burton "the natural successor to Olivier" and announced that he believed Burton would come to be regarded as the "greatest living classical actor," it resonated around the world.

In February, rehearsals started for 'Othello' and Michael Benthall, also directing, had the idea to revive a concept that hadn't been seen since 1949. It was a tradition begun by Macready and Young at Covent Garden in 1816, in which two complimentary actors alternated the lead parts of a play. But Benthall took the concept one step further and suggested they alternate on successive nights – throughout the run. It was with some trepidation that he asked Burton and Neville to be both Othello and Iago on alternate successive nights.

At first, Neville hesitated to accept the challenge, saying: "In a sense it meant that we were rehearsing two plays and normally you would get four weeks to rehearse one play. We did both in six weeks; moreover, we didn't have a week between the openings. We opened one night and swapped parts the next."

The idea had obvious audience appeal but it was a bold gamble by both actors, effectively to be judged by their peers, who made sure they were there to see both performances. The critics needed little encouragement to hype up this contest, although they were not impressed and took the line that the exchange of roles was nothing but a publicity stunt.

There was also another problem; at 30 years of age, Burton and Neville were the youngest actors ever to attempt the roles of Othello and Iago on the English stage. Kenneth Tynan was entirely opposed to it on this basis and said: "The parts demand an unfeignable quality, which some call weight and others majesty, and which comes only with age." Nevertheless, with Tynan's warning words ringing in his ears, Michael Benthall went ahead with it.

A natural but friendly rivalry soon developed between Burton and Neville, and the two men attracted rival sets of theatre fans as might two football competing teams. But Neville insisted there was no acrimony between them, just very good-natured competition: "To say I was trying to compete with Richard, as some critics suggested, was absolute balls. I certainly don't look upon acting as a competition, and Richard and I were always great friends. Yet there was still this invented rivalry between us, and it seemed to us that many of the critics were preoccupied by this aspect rather than by the plays."

In the end, Neville, by common consent, proved the superior Othello. But

Burton, with a supreme effort, shaded Neville's Iago and the acting contest was declared a draw by the critics.

The swapping of roles meant the play generated huge enthusiasm from audiences, who were booking seats in consecutive performances to see both actors. The audiences went wild at every performance, cheering from the gallery and drowning out what was happening on stage.

The start of Othello also brought Burtonmania back to the Waterloo Road as word got around of Burton and Neville's stirring performances. But, this time, the fans didn't just turn out for Burton. John Neville had also become the object of his own mania, as he recalled: "It was incredible and those crowds were really enormous, stretching right across the road and blocking the way from Waterloo Station. They screamed and wore all sorts of things, such as scarves and jumpers with our names on."

The attention from the vast crowds coming in and out of the theatre every night meant the strain on the actors was tremendous. To play Othello one night and Iago the next was bad enough, but to perform in circumstances more appropriate to a rock concert pushed Burton's endurance to the limit. As Graham Jenkins noted: "On more than one occasion, I discovered Rich slumped in a chair in his dressing room, drained of all energy, unable to move. I would load him into the car and drive him to Hampstead, all without a single word spoken."

Sybil Burton was providing maximum support during this time and made sure all her husband had to do was perform at the theatre; everything else was taken care of. For the period when he was most vulnerable, she came to the Old Vic every day to look after him, sitting through performance after performance, supporting him from the stalls. Sybil's main effort went towards keeping her husband in good condition, both mentally and physically. She threw herself into supporting him, and impressed everyone with her devotion.

Sybil's example was followed by his entire family, who came up from Wales to offer moral support. David Jenkins admitted he was wholly caught up in the moment: "I was completely enthralled by his sheer nerve and guts in playing Othello one night and Iago the next. This extraordinary mellifluous voice, I thought, this subtle change in the atmosphere, this demeanor, language and emotion. I could hardly believe I was witnessing it, over and over again."

Once, before watching him play Othello, David said to his brother jokingly: "The Welsh contingent are here in strength this evening." Burton replied: "I want you to shake the very foundations of this building so that the roof vibrates and the walls cave in." And David obliged: "I could not help responding with all of myself – proud older brother, patriotic Welshman, the lot. I was spellbound. Good God, I thought, is that really Rich? Is this truly the little boy from Pontrhydyfen who has taken London by storm and won the hearts and minds of all these men and women? I simply could not hold back the tears and was thankful that the theatre was dark and that no one could see me."

Kenneth Tynan said, after seeing Othello twice, with Burton in both roles: "We may now define this actor's powers. The open expression of emotion is clearly alien to him: he is a pure anti-romantic, ingrowing rather than outgoing. Should a part call for emotional contact with another player, a contemptuous curl of the lip betrays him...Mr Burton keeps yet his heart attending on himself. Which is why his Iago is so fine and why, five years ago, we all admired his playing of that other classic hypocrite, Prince Hal. Within this actor there is always something reserved, a secret upon which trespassers will be prosecuted, a rooted solitude which his Welsh blood tinges with mystery. Inside these limits, he is a master. Beyond them, he has much to learn." Whatever all that meant, it cheered Burton up no end and Tynan seemed to be admitting he had been wrong.

The run ended on 12th May 1956, after just fewer than 50 performances over two months and each one was a sell-out.

The closing of 'Othello' proved to be the end of Burton's Shakespeare season. He was due to perform in 'Troilus and Cressida', but two weeks before the play was due to open, he was forced to pull out, ostensibly suffering from exhaustion. A press statement said that his doctors had advised him to slow down.

But this was nonsense, and the truth was somewhat more interesting. There was a clash of personalities between him and director Tyrone Guthrie which could not be resolved. Guthrie and Burton had not worked together before. Guthrie came into the production not liking Burton and considered him an overrated film star and not a proper actor. When he tried to direct him, Burton ignored him. One day, there was a fight on stage and they had to be dragged apart by the other actors. It was clear they could not work together so Burton resigned the part, which was taken over by Clifford Williams. Graham Jenkins said: "For Guthrie, there was no such thing as a star, only bigger or smaller roles. He was not at all sensitive to the delicate matter of actor's status."

Guthrie appeared not to bear a grudge and later described Burton as "one of the six gentlemen who mean anything in the box office and also can even begin to make a showing in the great parts."

Near the end of the run of 'Othello', Frank Hauser, his old BBC radio producer, came to see him in his dressing room at the Old Vic. Hauser was trying to revive the Oxford Playhouse Theatre and needed cash. Without hesitation, Burton agreed to invest £2,000, a huge sum of money in those days. It was a large amount designed to help attract matching funding from the Arts Council. But Burton's manager, Valerie Douglas, strongly disagreed with the investment and tried to stop it. Douglas was worried about money at the time, but Burton insisted. He still had on his mind his refusal to lend Dylan Thomas £200 a few years earlier and the consequences of that.

Burton strongly believed his high earning days would soon return and that he was to be proved right.

In the event, Hauser made a huge success of the Playhouse and ran it personally until 1973, making Burton a good return on his £2,000 investment.

John Neville also experienced Burton's spontaneous generosity at the same time and never forgot the day Burton lent him £680 to buy a new car. At the time, he drove a very old Austin A16 that was falling to bits. He recalled Burton looking at it and saying: "You ought to have a proper car." Neville replied: "I'm very happy with the car I've got." Burton said: "That's not a car – what car would you like if you lost this one?" Neville told him he would choose a convertible Morris Minor, which was the fashionable car of the day and had a list price of nearly £700. Cars were very expensive in those days, as Neville said: "It was a fortune. You could still buy a good small terraced house in a decent district of London for that."

Burton took Neville home to Hampstead and went upstairs, as Neville recalled: "We went into his bedroom and from under the bed he hauled a suitcase stuffed with notes. It was like being in a gangster movie. He counted out £680 and said: 'I had a good day today.'" Burton had apparently earned the money from voiceovers and it was money he didn't need. Neville eventually paid him back, and Burton said to him: "You're the only man in the world who's ever paid me back."

Neville and his wife, Caroline, and Richard and Sybil were very close in that period, before Burton moved to Switzerland and Neville to Canada. He told Melvyn Bragg in 1988: "Richard did what he wanted to do. He chose the path he wanted and he stuck to it. Acting wasn't the most important thing to him. Living was: and he hoped one day to be a writer or a scholar. But he was a star. And the Old Vic proved it beyond all question. It was unmistakable. He just had to walk on to the stage. Nobody can take that away."

Finding himself with no work in June 1956, Burton looked forward to a leisurely summer at home before serendipity struck and the famous Italian director, Roberto Rossellini, appeared from nowhere and offered him the male lead in a new film he was shooting that summer in Jamaica. The film was called *Sea Wife*. Rossellini had procured financing from 20th Century-Fox for the venture. *Sea Wife* was the story of an RAF officer who finds himself shipwrecked on a desert island with a nun and falls in love with her. It was a delicate subject and required the most skillful directing.

Aaron Frosch negotiated Burton a fee of US$200,000 for the role, only because Rossellini was somewhat desperate to start shooting and had no leading man in place. It was amazing luck, and got Burton back in the big money movie game.

And he also reasoned that, with the talented Rossellini on board, it would be a good film. The screenplay was adapted from the oddly named novel *Sea-wyf and Biscuit* by James Scott, which had been published to great acclaim a few months before. Joan Collins, a promising 23-year-old actress, was to play the lead female role. She was a sensation and in six years had already starred in 16 films. *Sea Wife* would be her 17th. But was she right to play a nun? Rossellini thought so and he had a vision.

But after the crew and cast had arrived in Jamaica, there was a creative disaster before shooting had even begun. 20th Century-Fox sacked Rossellini as director for reasons that were not fully explained. They replaced him with a non-entity called Bob McNaught. At the time, Rossellini's life was complicated by the break-up of his marriage to Ingrid Bergman and a well-publicised affair with an Indian writer. It seemed that Fox executives lost confidence in him and he walked off the set as it was being built, never to be seen again. Afterwards, it was revealed that Rossellini was sacked when he insisted that there be romantic scenes in the film between Burton's RAF officer character and Collins' nun. Fox objected because of America's religious lobby, which would not have liked to see a nun become sexually aroused.

McNaught had no finesse and was a complete disaster, and he brought out the worst in Burton. There was an absence of any real passion and the casting of Joan Collins as a nun was described as "perverse" by Burton's brother Graham.

What McNaught should have filmed was Burton's offscreen pursuit of Joan Collins' affections – that was interesting. Seven years earlier, in 1949, Collins as a 16-year-old young student had been obsessed with the then 23-year-old Burton and waited at stage doors to catch his eye, although all she got was his autograph. Now, at 30, the attraction had waned and she saw more of his faults than his virtues.

Burton stalked Collins for days before making his move. She listened to the stories of his conquests, calling them a "lengthy saga of lust and intrigue on sets and in dressing-rooms and elegant boudoirs." Finally, they kissed passionately but when she asked him about his wife, Sybil, who was sunbathing back at the hotel, he said: "My dear, what the eye does not see the heart does not grieve for." But she rejected him. His response was to tell her that women always gave in to him eventually, but she retorted: "Richard, I do believe you would screw a snake if you had the chance." He laughed and replied: "Only if it was wearing a skirt, darling, and it would have to be a female snake." Collins eventually fell for a young cameraman on the set, much to Burton's disgust. It was the first time he had tried and failed to bed his leading lady.

Afterwards, when Collins gossiped about Burton's amorous advances, he denied her claims outright, saying: "She had a much exaggerated view of her own importance, but then so did everybody else on the picture, including me. We deserved our disaster." The disaster to which he was referring was at the box office. When Philip Burton saw the film in New York, he said: "I was ashamed of his performance."

There was no one more ashamed than Burton for acting out another stinker, his fourth in a row, and for having earned plenty of money for doing so. With 1956 almost over, when Aaron Frosch did the sums, he discovered his client had earned over a million dollars in 24 months but had kept only a fraction of it after British taxes. Frosch rang Valerie Douglas and told her that Burton would have to leave Britain for tax exile as soon as possible. He could no longer afford to live in the country of his birth.

# AND GOD CREATED BURTON

# CHAPTER 29

# Switzerland and tax exile

## *No more English taxes*

### 1957

In the late Autumn of 1956, the Burtons were back at home in Hampstead, London, deeply suntanned from nearly three months in Jamaica. Burton had no work except for occasional excursions into the Broadcasting House for the BBC. The consequences of the three stinkers plus poor word of mouth about what had gone on in Jamaica in *Sea Wife* had finally rendered him truly unemployable. But he hadn't a care in the world as he was rich beyond his dreams and set for the next ten years. Although there was no sign of it, he believed the next big money film offer was just around the corner, and all he had to do was wait.

So Burton's ears pricked up and he smiled widely when Valerie Douglas called him with the good news to say he had earned a million dollars in the past two years. It was one of his personal milestones and he immediately reached for his latest bank statement, which had lain unopened in its envelope for a couple of weeks. He found his credit balance to be just under £20,000. Added to his property assets and a company bank account he maintained, he calculated that made him worth £35,000 in all. He knew that Aaron Frosch had deferred around US$300,000 of what he had earned to minimise his tax bill – but where was the rest?

That question prompted him to put in an immediate phone call to Aaron Frosch in New York, which was precisely what he was supposed to do when he put the telephone down to Douglas.

Frosch, as he admitted many years later, had used Douglas as a stalking horse to get inside Burton's brain and to find out how he felt about leaving the UK permanently. Frosch thought that if he had called Burton himself and put the proposition to him directly, it would have fallen on deaf ears. For all his fierce intelligence, Burton could be a remarkably stubborn man sometimes and, as Frosch used to say to friends, "close his ears." In fact, Burton had become practiced in "closing his ears" when accountants and lawyers started talking, and sometimes subterfuge was necessary to get him to open them. One of Frosch's weaknesses was that he easily lapsed into the foreign language that lawyers and accountants sometimes speak and assume their clients can understand. Burton, with his creative brain, could understand little of the legalistic mumbo jumbo that Frosch expounded when he was being serious.

Frosch could see only too clearly the folly of Burton earning so much money in Hollywood, exporting most of it back to the UK and losing it to a punitive income tax rate of 93 per cent, or whatever calculation a faceless Inland Revenue official decided was appropriate. And Burton was an easy target for the British Inland Revenue department. In those days, its officials had plenty of time to track down missing taxes and were right on top of its citizens' wily ways to avoid it. In the days before mass immigration and globalisation made their jobs all but impossible, they got every penny of what they were owed, and more.

As soon as he realised Burton was on the line, Frosch kept quiet and let him speak over the crackly transatlantic line. Burton's opening gambit was basically: "Where's all my money?" It was exactly the response that Aaron Frosch had wanted. It was a cue for him to deliver some home truths.

Frosch told him that in his whole career since 1946, he had in fact earned over US$2 million and was now left with only £30,000 plus the deferred income he had not yet received from 20th Century-Fox and United Artists. Frosch pointed out that the Inland Revenue would eventually take three quarters of that as well – and there was little he could do about it whilst his client remained resident in Britain.

The problem was clear: the Inland Revenue was taking virtually his entire income. And this would go on for year after year unless something was done. Burton's argument had always been that other high earners, such as Laurence Olivier and John Gielgud, lived in Britain and managed, so why couldn't he? But this time, he didn't bother to deploy it.

Frosch, however, anticipated the question and replied to it, even though it hadn't been asked. He told his client that he had earned five times what both Olivier and Gielgud had made combined in the last two years, and that they were both "relative paupers" compared to him. Frosch was firm in his assertion that the only solution, which Burton would be forced into sooner or later, was to move abroad – preferably Switzerland.

In fact, Frosch gave him two options, both of which were equally viable; move to Switzerland and pay no tax, or move permanently to Hollywood and pay around 50 per cent tax. In the lawyer's view, either was a palatable option. Burton told Frosch he would consult Sybil and call him back. Before he put the phone down, Frosch reminded him he would still be able to spend 90 days in the UK if he decided to leave. But he omitted to tell him he would not be able to return at all in the first year.

When he put down the receiver, Burton realised that the moment of truth had finally come. This was a decision from which he could not shrink away, defer or hide. It was a life changer and one of the biggest decisions of his life, as he said: "Look at Larry, all he has is a house in London and a Rolls. I'm not settling for that."

Burton immediately saw what he had to do. He went off to persuade Sybil. He told her they were rich but they didn't have any serious cash to speak of and that it was time to leave. As they sat down and he spelled it out for her, he gave her the choice of Switzerland or Los Angeles and told her he would go to wherever she decided.

The thought of living in Los Angeles permanently filled them with horror, so, by default, they chose Switzerland. They had visited Switzerland for three days in the autumn of 1954 and had liked it. It soon became clear that the area around Geneva was the most attractive to them for lifestyle and communication reasons. Later that evening, Burton put another call into Frosch, who was waiting nervously in his office, and said they had made their decision.

Frosch breathed a sigh of relief and told him he should leave for Switzerland as soon as he could pack his bags; but at the latest by 31st December, or he faced losing another £100,000 immediately.

Frosch bluntly explained to him that, potentially, if 1957 dawned and he was still a UK resident, it could cost him as much as £200,000 in further taxes. When he did finally leave, the savings were to be enormous. For every £100,000 of income, the tax in Switzerland was to be a mere £700 rather than £93,000. Burton reasoned that nothing about the British way of life could be worth £93,000.

Burton's decision was everything Frosch had hoped for. He knew he could now make his client rich beyond his dreams and transform his life and that of those around him.

As soon as the decision was made, Frosch and Douglas went into action. Douglas took the train to New York and set up a war room in Frosch's office for an entire month to plan every aspect of the move. Nothing could remain in Burton's name in Britain. The properties were transferred out of his estate, and he no longer beneficially owned them. Once he was offshore, Frosch formed a company in Bermuda into which all Burton's earnings could be paid and his UK income kept out of tax. The Inland Revenue monitored companies far less severely than they did individuals. Frosch's aim was to make Burton invisible as an individual in Britain.

But when the decision was made, there was still plenty of time for regrets. Once or twice, Burton almost picked up the phone to Frosch and told him to stop the proceedings. The stark reality of what they were doing hit him hard in the face – the pleasant, worry-free life they led in London, with complete freedom to come and go as they please and do virtually whatever they pleased, was over. In the future, they would be the prisoners of the tax man. They would no longer pay taxes, but they would pay a very high price for not doing so.

Burton put on the best face he could as he popped over the road at Squires Mount to tell Ivor and Gwen and as he phoned his brothers and sisters, one by one, in Wales. He assured them that Geneva airport was only an hour and a half from London, with Paris just 45 minutes away and Rome within two hours. He told a tearful Cecilia that with the money he saved in tax, he would be able to afford to fly them to Switzerland regularly.

Ivor Jenkins took the news the best. He was not all surprised by the decision and asked why he had waited for so long. Ivor had already told some journalists that it was inevitable he would leave Britain eventually, but he had always believed it would be to live permanently in Los Angeles.

The most difficult call was to his adoptive father, Philip Burton, in New York. Burton knew Philip would be against it, indeed they had discussed it in the past and it was Philip who had persuaded him it would be a bad move. At the time, Richard had promised Philip he would never do it.

Burton thought about making the call for a day and then copped out and rang Valerie Douglas and asked her to go round to Philip's apartment and tell him in person. However, Douglas was scared of Philip's reaction as well, so she subsequently told him that "Richard is seriously contemplating" the idea, not that it was decided. The news was broken to Philip gradually over the next four weeks in order to soften his opposition. Philip recalled: "My conversation with Valerie was largely about a major move Richard was contemplating, one of which she heartily approved. My instinctive reaction was to oppose this because it would take Richard away from the world in which he was at his best and happiest, the London theatre. For Valerie, Richard's world was

Hollywood, which existed to make big money, which should be protected by all possible means." Philip immediately wrote to Richard, setting out all the reasons for not doing it – but it was too late.

Burton saw the move in two ways. There was a recognisably bad side to it, but also benefits. On the negative side, he was cutting himself off from any work in the British theatre as his 90 days allowance would not allow it. He was also leaving behind all his theatrical friends; people he and Sybil were close to, such as Stanley and Ellen Baker, Paul and Joy Scofield, and John and Caroline Neville.

The good side was the benefit to his marriage. He would have to say 'goodbye' to all his girlfriends in London, of which there were probably a dozen with whom he was enjoying a casual relationship. One was a schoolgirl called Rosemary, whom he had reportedly been seeing for a few years. It was a dangerous liaison as she had been underage when it began and he was glad of an excuse to end it. The girl later claimed, after he died, that she had become pregnant by him and had an abortion; but that was never proved.

The biggest and most difficult farewell was to Claire Bloom. She was his official mistress and the affair had endured for nearly six years.

Burton decided right away not to hide the move but to tell journalists openly what he was doing and the reasons for it. He knew it would be controversial and that he would be criticised heavily. But he felt that the British government under the premiership of Sir Anthony Eden and the incumbent chancellor, Rab Butler, needed to know that its high tax policies were very negative for the country and were restricting the economic recovery.

Burton had a point. It had been 12 years since the war had ended and the country was still mired in recession. High personal taxes and the consequent loss of incentive were the main causes, although the politicians couldn't grasp it. Britain was still caught up in a mood that had endured since the end of the first World War in 1918. The British people, regardless of whether a socialist or conservative government was in power, had turned against wealth, privilege, enterprise and capitalism in a big way, and a reversal of that mood would take another 20 years. But before that, Britain lost its place in the world economic pecking order to America, Japan and Germany.

The net result was that the country was about to lose the man who was, at that time, probably its single largest individual tax payer. If the top tax rate had been 50 per cent or even 60 per cent, he would never have left. In the next 27 years, Burton's departure was to cost Britain's exchequer at least £20 million in lost taxes.

But whichever way he dressed it up, it did not make him popular and he was inevitably labelled a tax dodger. Nonetheless, he decided to be up front and gave journalists as many interviews as they wanted on the subject. He spelled out the numbers time and time again and they were inarguable. Burton spoke honestly about what he called "Britain's vicious, punitive tax situation." He explained: "As it is, it's not worth bothering after the first fifteen thousand. Most of it goes straight to the Inland Revenue." He told journalists that he wished "someone like Olivier would leave and really shake up Rab Butler."

Only joking, he suggested to journalists that actors should be "entitled to be exempt from tax." But some journalists reported his remarks as serious, and it was made worse when he repeated: "I'm not against high taxes for Britain. I believe everyone should pay them; except actors." He added by way of explanation: "I would earn about £100,000, and in England I'd pay £93,000 of that in tax. But as a Geneva resident, all I pay is £700. Do you wonder that I don't want to live in London again? Ours is an uncertain profession. We make a lot of money for a few years – then nothing."

But whilst all this was going on, Burton was adamant that he was only going for three years to accumulate serious money and then he would be returning to England. There was no intention or even a thought of the move away being permanent.

But before he could go, he had to find somewhere to live, and Valerie Douglas was put in charge of the house search. She went into overdrive and bombarded all the Geneva real estate agents to find what they had. Aaron Frosch demanded that she look for a modest house with plenty of land. Frosch had to negotiate his move with the Swiss authorities and settle what his client's tax rate would be. The cheaper the house, the lower the rate he would pay and, once set, it would remain at that level for his lifetime. Frosch argued that a modest house with plenty of land could easily be extended and rebuilt, and that is exactly how it turned out.

In the meantime, they rented a house in the village of Celigny, on the outskirts of Geneva, in the French speaking section of the country. It was a typical split level Swiss house, about a half mile from where they finally ended up. The house was called Le Bosquet and they lived there for the first eight months.

With Douglas' help, they eventually found a house they liked in the same village of Celigny. The Burtons inspected it, liked it and virtually bought it on the spot. It cost around £15,000, something Burton could easily afford now that he had no taxes to pay. Frosch just took it out of the deferred income he had built up, as that tax saving measure no longer mattered anymore. The house was in good condition but needed extending and renovating. Although they could have afforded something bigger and better, the important factor governing tax assessment overruled every other consideration.

And as soon as the purchase closed, Burton named his new house 'Le Pays de Galles' and ordered a sign for the gate. It was simply the French term for Wales, and as David Jenkins happily noted: "Wales was literally his home again."

Their unpretentious house was on a hill only half a mile from the shores of Lake Geneva, with a lightly used domestic railway line a hundred metres away. But it had large grounds and Ivor organised for the open boundaries to be surrounded by a high wire fence to provide his brother with immediate privacy. Ivor also installed large electric gates. Almost immediately, Ivor instigated moves to extend the house and build him and Gwen a guest chalet in the large garden. Ivor was in his element as he recruited an army of builders to get to work.

It was a beautiful setting and, apart from the odd train rumbling along to the little stop at the bottom of the hill, it was very quiet. The air was beautifully clean and fresh, and Sybil, who suffered from terrible hay fever, found it disappeared straightaway.

There was a bar and restaurant called the 'Café de la Gare' at the bottom of the hill, and both he and Sybil were soon close friends with the owners. They soon found they had some sociable and illustrious neighbours, who included the Aga Khan, Charlie Chaplin, Peter Ustinov, Jean Anouilh, Deborah Kerr and the most popular novelist of the day, Alistair MacLean.

The fact that neither Richard nor Sybil spoke French didn't matter either. Switzerland was attracting so many British tax exiles at that time that there was quite a sizable English-speaking community in the area. They soon learned a sufficient amount of French to get by.

The Jaguar stayed in Britain, and Burton imported a convertible Cadillac from America and eventually bought a Rolls-Royce to keep in Switzerland. Sybil gave her MG to Graham Jenkins to use in Wales before it was driven over to Switzerland.

From the beginning, it quickly became one of Burton's favourite rituals to drive to Geneva airport on a Sunday morning and pick up all the British Sunday newspapers which had been flown in overnight. It was the only place they could be obtained reliably on the very day they were published.

But some days they weren't in and the 20-minute car journey turned out to be a waste of time. So Burton obtained the telephone number of the kiosk and would always phone before setting out. For the next 27 years, whenever he was in Switzerland, he would perform this ritual every Sunday.

It set the pace for Sundays and he often used to pause at the airport for a coffee opposite the newspaper kiosk and scan the sports pages and take a first stab at *The Observer*'s crossword puzzle. He also paused at the bookshop and inevitably found a book he wanted to buy. Sometimes on the way home, he would go off the main road and stop at a Swiss village for another coffee and settle down to read the newspapers in the sun. Sometimes, he would even linger for lunch if the mood took him.

If not, he would have lunch at the Café de la Gare and always order the local fish dish with the local wine. In the afternoon, he would play a game of tennis or table tennis with whoever was around before sinking into his favourite chair at home to read. When he wasn't working, or had house guests, that became the pattern for every day.

Ensconced at Celigny, Burton encouraged British reporters to come and see him. In those days, Fleet Street reporters had plenty of expenses and latitude. Many of them took him up on his offer as film stars normally craved privacy, but Burton did the opposite.

He told all of them that, for the first time in his life, he had no money worries and pointed to his new Cadillac convertible parked outside, saying: "Our whole family had to exist on five shillings a week. Now I have enough money in the bank here never to have to work again."

He revealed that he already had accumulated US$100,000 tax-free. It was money he considered free money; money that he had effectively stolen away from the British tax man. He also told journalists about his new Swiss numbered account: "You don't use your name – just a number. Heaven help you if you lose it. Mine is written down in Welsh all over the place."

But not everyone was pleased or as convinced about the move, Philip Burton for one. He thought it a huge mistake for Richard to effectively remove himself from the London theatre scene. When Burton finally spoke to Philip about it, he told him he had no choice but to leave: "As a resident abroad, I can work three months a year in this country without getting into trouble with the

Inland Revenue. That gives me plenty of time for stage acting. The rest of the time I would probably want to be abroad, anyway, in Hollywood or on film location. So why don't I make the best of it?" But Philip was not moved and believed that Richard also eventually came to regard it as a mistake. If he did, he certainly never told anyone. But Philip had been right about the divorce from the British stage; when he left London for Geneva, Burton turned his back on the classical stage in Britain forever and would never again perform at the Old Vic or the Memorial Theatre.

The Burtons settled enthusiastically into what he called the "Lake Geneva lifestyle" and there was a constant stream of visitors from London to Celigny during that first summer of 1957. Melvyn Bragg said that, during this period, Burton acted as "the prince across the water".

Burton found he had no need to visit Britain in that first year. His first acting role was a war film called *Bitter Victory*, co-starring with Curt Jurgens. It was shot in five weeks in the Libyan desert and he left in late February and returned at the end of March, happy to leave Ivor and Sybil to sort out the new house.

The film was based on the novel of the same name by Rene Hardy, who co-wrote the screenplay. It was financed by Columbia and a European consortium, which had approached Burton just after he left London, in January. He looked at the building site where he was living and quoted them his regular fee of US$200,000. Expecting a "we'll think about it" response, he was amazed when they agreed to it.

The film was a confused psychological melodrama about two soldiers fighting in the desert who love the same woman. It was directed by Nicholas Ray, and Burton played a British Army captain leading a patrol in the desert to capture important secret German documents. Curt Jurgens was the major who had had an affair with the captain's wife, and amid all the fighting, there was a personal conflict between the two officers. Nicholas Ray attempted to show how the horrors of war could affect the human spirit. It was a bold attempt at a different kind of war film but, as Hollywood's trade magazine *Variety*, wrote: "The script was basically flawed by the unclearly delineated key character of the major." But *Variety* also noted the "fine thesping" by Richard Burton." The film was not a success but not a failure either; it was a non-event and probably the least remembered film of his whole career.

When he returned, the house was still unfinished so he and Sybil rented a villa on the Côte d'Azure and spent a few months sunning themselves in luxury whilst Ivor and builders continued to toil away at Celigny. Burton suspected that his brother was enjoying himself so much in the Swiss sunshine that he was deliberately dragging out the job.

So they drove down to Nice in their new Cadillac convertible and Philip Burton came over and stayed with them on the French Riviera in April. When they returned to Celigny, their home was still a building site, so Burton decided to look for more work. But after *Bitter Victory*, Burton was once again faced with a lack of film work and realised he was only getting the film roles no one else wanted and only when the producers were desperate. It was well paid, but it was rubbish. So he cast around for a good stage role to try and redeem himself. With London ruled out that meant Broadway. His new Swiss agent subtly put the feelers out hoping to catch a big fish.

It worked, and an American producer called Milton Sperling took the bait and came calling at Celigny. Sperling headed up a small studio grandly called United States Pictures.

Sperling was a highly intelligent, civilised man, and Burton bonded with him straightaway.

Sperling realised Burton was down on his luck and wanted him to sign not only for his new Broadway production of a Jean Anouilh play called 'Time Remembered' but also for two films to be made in 1959 called *The Bramble Bush* and *Ice Palace*, with funding from Warner Brothers, where Sperling had family connections.

Sperling vividly remembered the meeting in Celigny: "In 1956, his record was one of failure. That was because he did not understand film acting. But nevertheless, he survived what would have permanently killed a man of lesser talent."

Sperling admitted he had come to Switzerland hoping to find an actor down on his luck whom he could sign up for a cut price fee for all of his three projects. But Burton completely seduced him, as Sperling revealed later: "In person, I soon discovered he is one of the most attractive men I have ever known. He's compelling. It's impossible to take your eyes off him, or your ears. He's marvellous to listen to and the fund of information he has is extraordinary. He can quote Dylan Thomas in his entirety and he remembers lesser poets. He can quote whole books of the bible and he remembers, I'm sure, every role he has ever played."

A deal was done for the three projects. 'Time Remembered' would take them away for nine months and it was a big payday at US$10,000 a week.

# SWITZERLAND AND TAX EXILE

It was decided that Ivor would stay behind in Switzerland to complete the building work and that David Jenkins and his wife Betty would accompany Burton to New York instead. David managed to get some extended leave from his job as a police sergeant.

Before he left, virtually the entire Jenkins family visited Celigny that summer. They were put up in a luxury hotel on the shores of Lake Geneva at Burton's expense. He found that, now that he wasn't paying any tax, he could throw his money around with gay abandon. David Jenkins said: "Over the years, we all visited Celigny and enjoyed Richard's considerable hospitality." The family loved the Swiss environment. They swam in Lake Geneva and then played cricket, badminton, squash and bowls all day in the sun.

His sister, Catherine Jenkins, remembered Celigny being very much like Wales, as she said: "My impression of Celigny when I first came here was that it was the next place to Wales, delightful. I thought it was so similar."

One immediate side effect of the move to Switzerland and the enormous tax savings was the export of money to Wales. No longer was it a thousand pounds shared between all of them but it became £1,000 each and every year. Aaron Frosch set up a limited company called Atlantic Productions Ltd to absorb any money Burton earned actually working in Britain, which the Inland Revenue would still tax at high rates. Atlantic was designed so that he didn't pay any tax on the distributions he made to family members. It enabled the family to sort out the tax on the money they were given. They paid tax at the normal rate of 30 per cent, which was different to the 93 per cent he paid.

The shareholders of Atlantic were all the senior members of the family and they were paid £750 each August and £250 in December. Those standard payments were mostly a legacy of money in Atlantic's bank account before he went into tax exile and kept being paid out until they day he died.

He simply wanted to improve the lot of his brothers and sisters, all of them now with families of their own. So, one by one, he bought for them the houses they lived in along with their cars and holidays and anything else they asked for.

Graham Jenkins remembered it well: "That we were able to buy our own homes when none of us were particularly well-off was thanks entirely to our brother's generosity." His eldest brother, Tom, had been made redundant from his colliery around this time and Burton helped him out with extra money. He wrote to him: "Enclosed is a little cheque. I hope you will accept it. I know how a few weeks' unemployment cripples your finances, and I don't want you to scrape through Christmas. You can pay me back sixpence a week out of your old age pension! If Wales beat the All Blacks, I'll give it to you as a present." Tom bought his own bungalow for himself and his second wife, Hyral.

Cecelia and Elfed finally sold off 73 Caradoc Street and bought a detached house with a sea view on Baglan Road. He also bought Elfed a big pension for his old age.

Hilda, by now married to Dai Owen, decided to stay in Pontryhdyfen and he bought her a terraced cottage. He also gave cash to his growing band of nephews and a £25 bonus for passing their 11-plus exams, which would see them into grammar school.

The generosity was not just confined to his family and he paid for an annual coach trip to take pensioners living in Taibach to go the seaside at Porthcawl for a day. He knew that most of them couldn't afford holidays and how much this single day could mean to them every year.

The money he was saving living in Switzerland was huge, and Burton could scarcely believe just how much disposable income he had available. It was so much that he gradually lost all sense of the value of money; he could afford to spread so much of it around.

Before the end of 1957, his first year of tax exile, he had US$500,000 in his Swiss bank accounts, some £200,000 when converted to sterling.

That year, he paid tax in Switzerland of just US$2,000.

# SWITZERLAND AND TAX EXILE

# AND GOD CREATED BURTON

# CHAPTER 30

# Life and Death

## *Kate lives and Dick dies*

### 1957

1957 was to prove the most eventful year of Richard Burton's life. By the time the new year of 1958 dawned, his life would be totally different from that of 12 months earlier – his father was dead, his daughter was born and he was a millionaire. And he was effectively no longer British.

The first shock came a few weeks after they had arrived in Switzerland. Either it was the air, the water or simply the change of environment, but after eight years of trying to conceive, Sybil announced she was pregnant.

The news was immediately flashed to New York and Wales. Valerie Douglas, who was still working away in Aaron Frosch's office, ran round to Philip Burton's apartment to tell him he was to be a grandfather. Philip was overjoyed; childless himself, he could once again fulfil his life's dreams through his adopted son. He said: "I longed to see him, and was to do so sooner than I expected." And then Burton was on the telephone, insisting that Philip come to the south of France on holiday with him and Sybil in April.

But Douglas, as she sat down to discuss the baby with Philip, also had "news of her own." She told Philip she was thinking of leaving Burton's employment.

Douglas had been in New York for almost three months organising her boss' move to Switzerland and the logistics of a new tax exile. It had been a tense time, as any mistake made in the paperwork or procedures could have been an expensive one. In the event, she and Aaron Frosch performed the task seamlessly, meticulously and tirelessly.

According to Philip, she was upset about being under-appreciated and underpaid. With all the extra cash flowing in because of the tax exile, she was still on the same salary she had been when she first started in 1953. She was the one who had pushed for the move to Switzerland from the start, which had generated all the extra cash, and now she felt hard done by.

She was also nursing an old wound. A few months earlier, Douglas had secured him a deal with Warner Bros for three pictures worth a guaranteed US$450,000 whether the films were made or not. Burton, for reasons best known to him, had refused to sign it. Douglas thought he was endangering his career, which was in the doldrums, by not taking what she called "the bird in the hand," an expression she had picked up in England. Burton believed there might be a better deal around the corner and he was eventually proved right when an independent producer called Milton Sperling, with Warner Bros backing, offered him twice the money for effectively the same arrangement.

Douglas' heart-to-heart was a cue for Philip to spring into action. A few days later, he called Burton in Celigny and, after much talk of the new baby, he subtly began talking about "Aaron and Valerie and what a great job they had been doing over here" and he hoped that Richard was "showing his appreciation appropriately." That was all Burton needed to hear and as soon as he put down the phone, he realised his laxness. He had been taking them for granted, especially Valerie Douglas. He also worked out what must have happened in New York for Philip to make those comments to him. Although he strongly suspected that Douglas, who was a clever and capable woman, was manipulating Philip, he knew he couldn't afford to lose either her or Frosch. He also knew she was a proud woman and he had to handle it carefully. Suffice to say, four weeks later, Douglas had banished any thoughts of leaving Team Burton.

Sybil could not have been happier being pregnant. She was convinced it was the move to Switzerland that had triggered it. She felt healthier and healthier every day now that she had escaped the London smog.

She found a new inner peace.

Few people at the time knew how anxious the Burtons had been about wanting children. So much so that they had taken secret steps to start the process of adopting two Welsh babies, believing they could never have any of their own. Burton's sister, Cecilia James had been leading a secret search in Wales to find a suitable boy and girl. Those plans to adopt were now abandoned.

Burton was also on cloud nine about the baby. For him, it was the fulfillment of a dream come true as Stanley Baker remembered: "Richard was profoundly happy in a way I had never seen him before. He seemed to be at peace with himself." After a month not tempting fate, 20th Century-Fox's London office put out a press release announcing Sybil's pregnancy and saying both parents were "tremendously happy." Claire Bloom read the news like everyone else – in the newspapers – and had mixed feelings. She was happy for Richard but also unhappy for herself. The news finally dashed her dreams of ever being with Richard permanently.

# LIFE AND DEATH

By the end of March, Burton had returned from Libya, where he had been filming *Bitter Victory* in the desert. He was resting at Celigny looking after Sybil and looking forward to going to the south of France for the early summer and then spending the latter part of the summer with the extended Jenkins clan on the shores of Lake Geneva before going to New York in September. Ivor was still fully occupied with building his chalet in the garden, although he had virtually finished the interior changes in the main house.

Then, on the morning of 25th March, came the news, by telegram, that Dick Jenkins had died at the age of 81. Burton read it just as his brothers, who had gathered at the hospital in Neath on that morning to meet the undertaker, were removing Dick's body from the hospital to a funeral parlour, prior to burial.

Dick Jenkins had been taken to Neath General Hospital a week before, suffering with severe respiratory problems. Very quickly, his vital signs began gradually to shut down, indicating death was near. His bodily functions had finally been overwhelmed by his alcohol intake and it was amazing he had survived for so long.

For the last four days, he was unconscious for most of the time, showing only the occasional flickering of life. The hospital stopped giving him food or drink, and Tom, William, Verdun and David Jenkins organised a rota to be with him at his bedside, so that at least one of them would be with him when he died. David Jenkins was with him on the night of 24th March, when he stopped breathing at half past four the following morning. As David noted: "So it was that I was the one present at the death of both my parents. My father's death was nowhere near as traumatic as my mother's had been for her young children, but it was nonetheless a great wrench."

Dick Jenkins had been retired for one year and had finally given up work at the age of 80. He had been forced to carry on working into his old age to get enough money to buy drink, which he lived for. He had spent fifty years down the mines, and when he was retired from the colliery, he became a night watchman for a company in Port Talbot and walked the four miles from Pontrhydyfen and back every day.

When the telegram arrived in Celigny, the news didn't upset either of the brothers although it became an occasion for some memories to be aired. Neither son had cared much for their father, if they cared for him at all. They had only bad memories of him being drunk and abusing their mother. They believed he had caused her death by burdening her with so many children, by forcing her to have unprotected sex with him time and time again when he got drunk.

Equally, when he died, Dick hardly knew or cared of his son's fame or achievements. The only film he ever saw was *My Cousin Rachel.* He simply preferred going to the pub and getting drunk to any other activity.

Although they only praised their father in public, Richard and Ivor's real feelings were perfectly obvious to anyone who knew them. And it became publicly obvious what Burton thought of his father when he declined to attend his funeral.

Normally he would have done so, as it would have been an opportunity to see the family. But he was in the first year of tax exile and could not stay overnight in the UK during that first year, as there was the risk the Inland Revenue might step in and demand additional taxes. But he could fly in and out for the day. The only way to feasibly do it would have been to fly from Geneva to Cardiff by private plane. It was easily arranged, he could afford to do it, but he chose not to.

His refusal to fly to Wales was a public unsaid demonstration of the contempt he had for his father. Although he would never say it publicly, it seemed he wanted the world to know. And everyone in the family understood but never commented on it.

Ivor fully backed the decision and also declined to travel, although he had no tax considerations to worry about. Ivor was 100 per cent behind his brother and believed it would have been the height of hypocrisy for them to make any effort to attend the funeral of a man they didn't like, regardless of the fact that he was their father.

When asked by reporters that, if he loved his father as much as he had often professed, why hadn't he attended the funeral? Burton replied: "My father was a very unsentimental person and he would be shocked if he knew I had travelled more than seven hundred miles to go to his funeral." It was rubbish and Burton knew it was as he said it.

Melvyn Bragg was the first of Burton's biographers not to be fooled by Burton's public pronouncements, writing: "For such a family-story-telling man, this was a tremendous decision and his joking excuses will not do." Bragg knew the real reason for Burton's absence at the funeral and said: "He saw in him the wreckage of a woman's life; his mother's." Burton's decision not to attend was the first time the truth of Dick Jenkins' tawdry life had been revealed, as Bragg recounted: "It was a rare slap in the face of his past."

David Jenkins merely said of his brothers' non-attendance: "Richard and Ivor were, I recall, too busy to attend the funeral." But he was being very disingenuous and knew full well they were sunning themselves by Lake Geneva at the time.

Graham Jenkins joined in the whitewash, saying: "We assumed they would come back for the funeral, but they decided against it. Their absence naturally created some gossip locally and in the press, which thankfully was treated lightly by Rich. He told reporters that Dadi Ni would never have approved the extravagance of a plane ticket just to attend a burial."

There was great hypocrisy in Wales over Dick Jenkins' funeral. It was well-attended, not because of who he was, but because of who his son was, and no less than seven Welsh ministers presided over the funeral service of a man who had never attended church. David Jenkins said: "Dadi Ni would have chuckled had he known." Those seven ministers were clearly publicity seekers and did themselves, or their church, no credit at all.

Jenkins had cared little for the church or his family throughout his life. So any time he did show any emotion was eagerly remembered, especially by his daughters and granddaughters, who took a much rosier view of him than did his sons or grandsons. Cecilia told journalists that her father had taken her to eisteddfods to sing, but that was all the good she could remember of him.

Burton in Switzerland just held his tongue when asked about his father. He refused to eulogise him but, equally, never said anything remotely critical.

Not so Graham Jenkins, the youngest son, who knew him the least.

Graham Jenkins made up some absurd story about his brother's failure to attend the funeral in his own book published in 1988. He spoke about Richard Burton's need to "keep his distance from suffering and grief." It was total baloney, and he was well aware why his two brothers did not attend the funeral. Jenkins said it was because his brother was "never altogether sure what his father thought about him."

Burton himself felt the need to write his youngest brother a letter afterwards by way of explanation: "I didn't know Dadi Ni very well – he was always an enigma to me – but blood is blood and I feel very empty today. Ivor has been hit much harder of course, but is as taciturn as a rock. Feels a lot, says nothing."

Graham Jenkins felt desperately the need to totally whitewash his brother's real hatred of his father and said: "The contrast between all-embracing warmth and what seemed to him to be chilly incomprehension made it difficult for him to get close to Dadi Ni. He assumed, wrongly, that Dadi Ni took no interest in his work." It was the most incredible disingenuous tosh, but it got worse as Jenkins tried to maintain that Dick had seen all of Burton's films. It simply wasn't true and Graham's need to wash his father's reputation, a man he hardly knew, in what was supposed to be a serious book about his brother, was not his finest hour. It misled future biographers, distorted history and inevitably cast doubt on some of the other content in the book.

David Jenkins, in his book, published four years after Graham's, was more circumspect. David said that his father's death "must have affected Richard very deeply." The word 'must' in that sentence was no accident.

But David also felt some need to whitewash Dick Jenkins' reputation by saying: "Our father Dadi Ni spent the last years of his life as a gentle old man sitting by Hilda's hearth." That, at least, was true.

David excused his father's obvious indifference to his sons and daughters, which had been noticed by journalists over the years, by saying: "Some writers have pondered long and hard about his occasional confusion over his many children. I recall that the confusion was over his grandchildren, which I feel was entirely understandable since there were such a lot of them all about the same age. My daughter remembers being taken to see him and being regarded quizzically: 'Which one is this, then?' he would ask. Certainly, his muddles were not directed with any ulterior motive at Richard alone. We all encountered them."

That was nonsense as well. It is true he appeared to care more for his grandchildren than his own children; it was just a different level of indifference. Wherever he was or whatever he was doing, he was always thinking about his next alcoholic drink.

Richard and Ivor did make one concession to mark their father's funeral. Every drink they took that day on their way to alcoholic paralysis was accompanied by a toast to their father's demise. It was, in the circumstances, highly appropriate.

Today, the various whitewashes seem to have worked and his living grandchildren speak warmly of him, especially Rhianon Trowel, who remembers him as a "quiet, kindly man" but, when pressed, admits she hardly knew him. The grandchildren, for obvious reasons, were never told the stories of his treatment of their grandmother. But many people believe that Graham Jenkins' eulogy to his father was an insult to his mother, Edith, whom he never knew.

Dick Jenkins was quickly forgotten as the whole Jenkins family, and it seemed the whole of Wales, looked forward to the birth of Richard Burton's first child.

# LIFE AND DEATH

The baby arrived on 10th September 1957, and it was a desperately tight-run affair as Burton was due to leave to go to New York for the rehearsals for 'Time Remembered'. But in the end, it was timed to perfection as the baby arrived a week early.

He was present for the birth at Geneva's main hospital and stayed there overnight with Sybil before flying to London the next day to travel to New York. Sybil and their daughter would follow two months later.

The baby weighed 6lb 4oz and they named her Katherine after Katherine Hepburn and, like Hepburn, she was known from that day on as Kate.

Kate's nanny was to be a young girl called Diane Cod, the daughter of a friend of Sybil's late sister, Elsie, from Northampton in England. Cod would stay with the family and travel with Sybil for the next two years, looking after Kate before leaving to eventually marry the well-known Northampton Saints rugby union player, Roger Horwood.

The birth of Kate "reanimated" the marriage, and Sybil now felt absolutely secure in the relationship. As Melvyn Bragg described it: "She knew what she had, what she wanted and what she would put up with." The birth reignited the intensity of Burton's devotion to his wife, although that would not manifest itself in his conduct in the months after the birth.

But his confidence in the union was the highest it had ever been. Burton genuinely believed his marriage to be indestructible; and the more indestructible he believed it to be, the more determined he seemed to test it.

Stanley Baker recalled: "Kate was the child they had wanted for so long. Sybil was particularly happy because she had what she wanted: a child, a life she enjoyed with wonderful friends, and a husband she was sure would never leave her, despite his games."

It was to be two months before Philip Burton would see his grandchild, and Sybil arrived in New York in time for the whole family to spend Christmas day together. Philip spent a wonderful seven months with his baby granddaughter, aside from one unpleasant incident. The Broadway theatres were open on Christmas Day and Burton had to leave for his performance, and as Philip recalled: "An otherwise happy Christmas Day was marred when Richard returned from the theatre that evening, already the worse for drink."

When 'Time Remembered' finished, Sybil and Diane returned to Celigny and so did Burton for a few weeks rest before he started filming *Look Back in Anger* in London.

Sybil had quickly regained her figure and they immediately began to try for a second baby, hopefully a brother for Kate. After eight months, the Swiss air worked again and Sybil found she was pregnant for the second time. On 28th November 1959, Jessica Burton was born.

But Burton was in Alaska filming *Ice Palace* for Milton Sperling and the Warner Bros studio and missed the birth. It was a terrible film and Burton was devastated he could not be back at Celigny to see his second daughter.

On the night of the birth, he telephoned Philip Burton in New York to discuss the new arrival and told Philip that Sybil had been wonderful about his absence. That night, Burton celebrated in the only way he knew; by getting paralytically drunk with his co-star, Jim Backus. They had been up since five in the morning filming scenes in the freezing cold of Alaska. He told Backus that he should have been at home with his wife, but instead: "Here we are, drinking at three o'clock in the morning, sitting on top of the world and making this piece of shit."

Burton had been desperately hoping it would be a boy as he had always longed for a son, but he was enchanted by his two girls. Not only were the parents delighted, but the resident Uncle and Aunt, Ivor and Gwen, treated the two girls as though they were their own. By now, their chalet in the garden had been completed and they were living in Celigny full time.

The two summers the family spent in Celigny were to prove as happy as they were idyllic. Ivor taught Kate to swim whilst Gwen nursed Jessica. Burton was totally thrilled by the family scenes he witnessed, but was reluctant to show it. They were delighted they had two children to look after.

Anyone looking in on the delightful family set up in Switzerland would not have believed it had only two years to endure and would, in a few short years, be torn asunder.

# LIFE AND DEATH

# AND GOD CREATED BURTON

# CHAPTER 31

# At last a good movie

## ...and two more stinkers

### 1957 - 1959

R ichard Burton's life got better when Milton Sperling, the producer who headed his own small studio called United States Pictures, had come calling at Celigny in the early part of 1957. Sperling sensed that Richard needed the work, and he was right. Only the day before, Burton had been looking back on a film career that to all intents and purposes appeared to be over. He had no offers.

Sperling traveled to Switzerland hoping to take advantage of Burton's plight and to sign him cheaply, but as soon as he sat down he realised that was never going to happen. Burton was never a man who sold himself cheap. And quickly, Sperling knew that Burton sensed he had the advantage as well. He knew Sperling had made a great deal of effort to get to Celigny and that he must therefore want something. Almost as soon as he sat down, Burton told him that his wife was pregnant and that he was taking the rest of the year off to look after her. The inference was that he was unavailable. He also told Sperling how rich he was now that he was in tax exile; the inference being that he didn't need the money. Very quickly, Sperling was having to sell his proposition very hard to get his man.

But Sperling had an unusual proposition that was very attractive. He wanted to sign Burton for three projects: 'Time Remembered', a play he was financing on Broadway, which would run from October 1957 to June 1958; *The Bramble Bush*, a movie financed by Warner Bros, which he would film in early 1959; and *Ice Palace* which was to be filmed in Alaska in August 1959. Burton had never before been offered a film and stage package together and was intrigued.

The offer to do 'Time Remembered' was a godsend for him; it took Burton away from films, where he was failing time after time, and gave him an American theatre platform to display his acting talents.

Sperling had sat down hoping to pay US$250,000 for all three projects- US$500,000 at the most. But the 45-year-old Sperling would end up paying Burton a sum close to US$1 million for just over 12 months' work – spread

369

over two and a half years. In one stroke, Sperling revived Burton's career, made him substantially richer and filled out his diary for years which would otherwise have been very empty, indeed. In fact, without him, Burton's career may never have been revived. But it was not the first time in his career that Burton had sensed a producer with a dire need and exploited it. When Burton called Aaron Frosch to tell him about the deal, Frosch was astonished. He had expected two years of inactivity whilst Sybil was pregnant and his client wasn't hot. Now, as he looked forward to the million dollars, he reminded Burton they would owe his new American agent US$100,000 commission for finding Sperling. As Burton put down the phone, he thought to himself that lawyers always managed to find the negative in any situation.

Years later, Sperling would admit he had been "taken." He always believed that Burton's career survived the three stinkers purely because of his looks. As he explained: "Burton survived because he is startlingly good looking. Even his defects add to him; that peculiar pock-marked cheek he has somehow adds to his appearance."

Sperling was a powerful friend to have. He was Harry Warner's son-in-law by virtue of his marriage to Warner's daughter, Betty. Harry was Jack Warner's brother and one of the founders of the Warner Bros studio. Hence, Sperling had access to Warner Bros funds. Interestingly, he had originally been a protégé of Darryl Zanuck until he married Betty Warner, which forced a switch of loyalties.

The arrangement with Sperling and Warner Bros meant that a final split with Darryl Zanuck and 20th Century-Fox was inevitable. The only contract that existed between them was the original one signed with Alexander Korda in 1950, and it was about to run out anyway. Burton met with Zanuck in New York for old time's sake. In return for tearing up the Korda contract, Burton agreed to do a cameo role in one of Zanuck's movies in the future, gratis, to settle any outstanding arrangements. Zanuck had a movie in mind but didn't tell him which.

It was, in the end, all very amicable. And when Burton left Zanuck's New York office that day, he truly felt a free man for the first time in his life. The contract that his then agent, Vere Barker, had advised him to sign with Alexander Korda all those years ago had been an immense burden, and now it was lifted.

With the last obstacle removed, Milton Sperling promised Burton that his films would be superior productions and he wrote it into his contract. But what, precisely, was to be the definition of a 'superior' production? Burton had no choice but to accept Sperling's word at face value. And when he said it, Sperling genuinely believed it.

Burton made no promises to Sperling about his acting, but Sperling believed he had been mishandled at Fox, saying: "It is very hard to determine why an audience doesn't want an actor at one point, then does want him at another. But to me, Burton had demonstrated ability. He was always interesting, never dull. He was handsome and his voice was glorious. It is probably the best voice on the stage today."

Despite Sperling's affability and the cultured veneer, he was, like many Hollywood executives, a producer in name only; he did not have a creative bone in his body.

But he could talk the talk, and he paid well.

For 'Time Remembered', Sperling had signed up two of America's biggest female stars, the very young Susan Strasberg, at 19, and the much older Helen Hayes, 57, to star with Burton. The three stars only had one thing in common – all were being paid US$10,000 a week. The high overheads made it financially impossible for Sperling to turn a profit on the production, even though it played to full houses for virtually every night of its eight month run. And, thanks to the antics of Strasberg and Burton, the play enjoyed immense free publicity in the New York newspapers every day. Even before it opened, 'Time Remembered' had advance sales of US$600,000, a record for a straight play in New York.

But 'Time Remembered' couldn't live up to its billing. It was an overweight fable written by Jean Anouilh, a French playwright considered by many to be overrated. Anouilh was actually a neighbour of Burton's in Celigny. The romantic comedy directed by Albert Marre was indeed very average, although Sperling was deluded about it to the day of his death. As he said: "The play was a critical success. People came to it, but it lost money because the salaries were staggering and so was the cost of operating it. I closed the play because we were steadily operating in the red." 'Time Remembered' was the first Broadway flop of Helen Hayes' career, and *The New York Times* summed it up best: "Richard Burton plays the bemused suitor as if it were part of a masquerade. It is elegant and a little stuffy on the surface, but a little ridiculous too, for Mr. Burton never forgets that the author's tongue is in the cheek."

Sperling dusted himself down and moved on to his next project, called *The Bramble Bush*.

# AND GOD CREATED BURTON

So did Burton. Whilst he was appearing in 'Time Remembered', he somehow found time to star in a two hour drama version of *Wuthering Heights* for the ABC television network. It was a critical success and earned Burton a US$60,000 fee for very little work and a lot of critical kudos. By general accord, Burton was a magnificent Heathcliff and the presence he lacked in the cinema seemed somehow better suited to television. He certainly seemed more comfortable acting with a TV crew in a smaller studio than on a giant Hollywood sound stage.

The extra work coming through was no accident. Now that Burton was safely in tax exile and able to take full advantage of earning opportunities, Aaron Frosch and Valerie Douglas sharpened up the selling of him. They effectively cut him off from Vere Barker and Charles Feldman and appointed a new agent to handle him called Hugh French.

French was immediately bringing in a lot of opportunities and Frosch wanted Burton to be able to pick and choose projects for a change. Thus, they were very disappointed and very sceptical when he returned to England for the first time in nearly two years to film a British production called *Look Back in Anger.* As far as Frosch and Douglas were concerned, it had disaster written all over it.

But *Look Back in Anger* proved to be his critical salvation. Burton had met the writer, John Osborne, at a party given by Laurence Olivier in New York in May 1958.

It was a wild party with over 200 people crowding onto a boat for a midnight cruise up the Hudson river. Burton got into the spirit of it by having a red jersey printed with 'HMS Olivier' across his chest.

Olivier was at his most mischievous and entertained his guests with barrels of stout beer and a buffet of jellied eels and fish and chips served in English newspapers. The band played English classics such as 'Knees-up-Mother Brown', and it was as Burton was pounding up the deck to that tune that he literally bumped into England's foremost playwright of the time.

The collision on deck performing to 'Knees-up-Mother Brown' was not as accidental as Burton might have thought. Osborne had been watching Burton move around Olivier's boat, and he thought that he would make a perfect Jimmy Porter, the anti-hero and lead character in *Look Back in Anger.* The original play had been a brilliant success in the theatre but, despite the acclaim afforded to Kenneth Haigh – later to achieve fame as Joe Lampton in the classic TV series *Man At The Top* – it needed a bigger name to play Porter for the screen version.

So Osborne arranged to bump into him, and Burton was very glad he did.

Osborne's stage version of 'Look Back In Anger' had defined a generation. He was a highly strung but fiercely intelligent man, and Burton was immediately struck with him – as was Osborne with Burton. They immediately discovered they had something in common because Osborne, like Burton, had a Welsh father and a former barmaid as a mother.

Melvyn Bragg called Osborne "fastidious and wonderfully rude", and Burton loved him for it.

Just at the moment Osborne met Burton, he was trying to raise the finance to make the film. He offered the part of the heavily cockney-accented Jimmy Porter to Burton there and then. Osborne was straight forward enough and told Burton, if he signed up, it would enable him to secure the backing that would make the film possible. Burton apparently said 'yes' immediately.

When he told Aaron Frosch and Valerie Douglas the next day what he had agreed too, they were angry and upset and told him he was never to do that again. They pointed out that Osborne had no funding and there was effectively no film, and by committing to nothing he had lent out his name for nothing as well.

Frosch called Osborne and negotiated a fee of US$125,000 – half what Burton had been getting. But in the circumstances, Frosch thought he had done rather well as his client was determined to honour his commitment to Osborne, paid or unpaid. Burton was attracted by the originality of Osborne's ideas and wanted desperately to test his range as an actor. He found the challenge too irresistible to ignore and admitted he would have done it for nothing if pushed.

As Frosch predicted, Osborne went out and told everyone Burton was attached to the film, which would begin filming that September. It was the hook he needed to get the cash. But it also made it impossible for Douglas and Frosch to secure for Burton other more lucrative deals that might have been available to him during that period.

It also dismayed Philip Burton, who at the time was trying to set up a film version of Shakespeare's 'Coriolanus'. Philip worked on a screenplay of 'Coriolanus' while Burton ostensibly tried to raise money for the project. The money never materialised and Philip shelved it. By then, Philip was an independent producer; his Cowan-Chrysler Productions company had folded after the two partners fell out.

# AND GOD CREATED BURTON

Interestingly, Warner Bros, which Burton had turned down earlier in the year, were still hungry to sign him. It was the Hollywood disease in which rejection just made the Hollywood heart grow fonder, and Jack Warner was now in the same place that Darryl Zanuck had been five years earlier. Interestingly, the relationship was also to develop and conclude in the exactly the same manner.

So with Burton's name attached, Tony Richardson, the director, and Osborne formed a production company called Woodfall Films Productions Ltd to make the movie. Warner Bros brought an experienced producer called Harry Saltzman on board to keep an eye on things for them.

Jack Warner came up with a relatively modest budget of US$625,000 after all previous attempts to raise money in Britain had failed. Frosch had been right - Burton was the catalyst to it all.

It was a defining moment as Richardson and Osborne smashed the closed shop of the British film industry and introduced American financing to British films; things were never quite the same again.

'Look Back In Anger', which had opened on stage in London in 1956, had created more interest and controversy than any other new play since the war. Osborne's writing was pure genius and he was at the vanguard of a revolution in British theatre.

For Burton, the attraction was that at last he was working on a film full of genuinely talented people. The Oxford-educated Richardson, who would later win an Oscar for *Tom Jones*, hired Claire Bloom, Edith Evans and Mary Ure for the lead female roles.

The story itself was adapted for the screen by Osborne and Nigel Kneale. It portrayed a stark picture of youth and disillusionment set in the 1950s. Burton's Jimmy Porter, a tormented and angry young man, is an intellectual barrow-boy who cannot cope with his wife's middle-class background. The fury of his class resentment against what he sees as the unearned privileges society gives the woman he has married, compared with how it treated his former landlady, is truly enlightening. The essence of the story is the revenge Porter takes on the establishment by marrying his wife.

The acting called on Burton to extend himself on film as he never had before, and it was just what he needed at this stage of his career. Being directed by Richardson was also exactly what he needed. As Melvyn Bragg observed, in a manner that only he could: "He comes over as a man consuming the world and himself in an anger which feeds on every swallow of oxygen he takes. And he manages to portray, with ferocity, the hopelessness of idealistic love."

Bragg also believed Burton had matured as an actor enormously in ten years: "The chubbiness is gone, the boyish glamour looks are forsaken. He is a mature, virile, wonderfully and intelligently handsome man, who is generous but also dangerous."

Richardson had not directed a film before and allowed the actors to act the parts as they saw them, which included improvising the dialogue. It made for a great atmosphere on set and it was the first film Burton really enjoyed making. As Claire Bloom remembered: "Tony Richardson gave the actors every encouragement to be as natural as possible, answering our questions with a noncommittal: 'I have no idea; do what you like.'" It was also the first time Burton looked forward to seeing one of his own films. Today the movie is considered a classic, and Burton's performance one of his finest.

On the romantic front, it was business as usual for Burton, who carried on simultaneous affairs with both of his leading ladies during the filming and seemed to get away with it. The role of Jimmy Porter's wife was played by Mary Ure and she in particular pursued him vigorously, which was potentially difficult as she was married to John Osborne at the time. But the marriage was virtually over and she and Burton were very discreet. The relationship with Claire Bloom ended halfway through filming, after Susan Strasberg famously turned up in his dressing room.

Ironically, with all the sexual tension crackling and Burton sleeping with both of them, Bloom and Mary Ure gave the performances of their lives. Many people also believe it was Burton's finest film acting.

When filming ended, Burton believed the film had gone extremely well and, for once, he was right. He wrote to Philip Burton that he was "unusually pleased with the whole experience." And added: "For the first time ever, I am looking forward to seeing a film in which I play."

Osborne and Richardson believed the same culture-imbibers who had made Christopher Fry's plays such a success would come out to see *Look Back in Anger*. But they had not reckoned on the intervention of Harry Saltzman.

After filming finished, Harry Saltzman was to prove – as Burton put it – a "pain in the arse." The rough and ready, shoot-first-aim-later Canadian producer, who later found fame producing the James Bond films, had no feel for it. The 42-year-old producer didn't understand the film, the director, the writer or the acting.

He had no confidence in the film at all, and to protect himself and his reputation in the United States, he bad-mouthed the film to journalists before it even opened. He told them he had fought hard against the choice of Burton for the lead, and he later blamed him when the film failed at the box office. He told journalists that Burton had not been his "first or even his second choice." Saltzman concluded that it had been "a monumental miscalculation" to give the part to Burton, who was "too old". Apparently, when Saltzman showed the film to Jack Warner in the studio screening room in Hollywood, Warner asked: "What language were they speaking?" Saltzman replied "English", to which Warner said: "This is America" and walked out of the screening room.

Proof that Saltzman sabotaged the film in America came when all the critics repeated the criticism that Burton, at 33, was too old to play Jimmy Porter.

*Look Back in Anger* was a film that desperately needed the critics' support and, of course, the English critics, to an extent, followed the American ones and put people off seeing it.

Burton did his best to help offset the damage Saltzman was doing, and he sought to encourage people to see the film by announcing at a press conference: "The film has a sex message. Sex is the overwhelming urge and driving force in all human beings."

His words were printed everywhere but the damage had been done, and a fine film attracted a poor box office.

Saltzman's behaviour was selfish and crass; protecting his own back by predicting failure, he distanced himself from the film and, in the process, ensured its failure.

Saltzman, who eventually made some good films in his career, also made a lot of enemies and was eventually booted off the James Bond films by his partner, Cubby Broccoli, for similar behaviour when things did not go well. In his lonely retirement, he was forced to build a big wall around his country house in Denham and to hire bodyguards to protect him from people who, frankly, wanted to harm him. He died a miserable and unhappy man in 1994 at the age of 78, but there was no truth in the rumour that his wife danced on his grave.

Saltzman's worst barb had been to say publicly that Burton was "monumentally miscast." Melvyn Bragg, who was a huge fan of the film, reflected everyone's views when he said: "Mr Saltzman is monumentally mistaken."

Graham Jenkins, an astute observer of his brother's performances throughout his career, said: "It was the first time I had seen Rich expose weakness and emotional inadequacy. *Look Back in Anger* was, for my money, the best thing he had done on stage or screen. The pity was that because the film was not a financial hit, he failed to recognise the importance of what he had achieved."

David Jenkins said of it: "The finished film had undeniable power, assaulting the senses with violence of language and extremes of feeling. Rage, cynicism, unkindness and rank brutal selfishness were transferred, without diminution, from the play. Impressive it certainly was; escapist it was not. There are audiences for unflinching film dramas from time to time, but they are fickle. It is a gamble which Richard later won on *Who's Afraid Of Virginia Woolf?* – but this time, he lost."

Halfway through filming, Burton and Sybil drove down to Wales for their first visit for 18 months, and his first as a non-resident. His newfound wealth was obvious. He had bought a new Rolls-Royce Silver Cloud, which had cost £6,000. He intended to drive it back to Celigny.

But before that, he drove down to Wales in the Rolls-Royce, where it caused a sensation in Port Talbot. The boot of the Rolls was full of expensive presents for his old neighbours, and he was described as being "like Father Christmas come to the valleys." He also gave the local people in Caradoc Road rides in his Rolls. They had never before seen one – let alone been in one. Many locals, who were children then, still vividly remember that weekend and the rides in the Rolls-Royce, just as they remember the rides he had given them in his Jaguar when he first returned to Wales as a film star in 1951.

Graham Jenkins recalled: "When Rich arrived in his old village of Pontrhydyfen in his Rolls-Royce, he went straight to The Miner's Arms and bought drinks for everyone. He was greeted as a hero and he enjoyed the adulation." He told his old friends that he was so rich since he had moved to Switzerland that "I need never work again."

Burton himself said of the trip: "There was no point in pretending I was still one of them. I could have arrived in a cab, but I drove up in my Rolls. I wasn't showing off; I was just saying this is what a Welshman from the valleys can achieve. I think my friends and family back in Wales have always celebrated with me that fact. I wasn't better than any of them. I was just someone who had done well. But my heart was, is, always back there." Whether that last part was actually true is still a moot point today. Many people insist that after he left, he began to hate the place of his birth but kept up the pretence for his relatives' sake.

Burton saw a lot of his brother Graham during the filming of *Look Back in Anger* and sought to make amends for excluding him when he appointed Ivor as his road manager. As Graham said: "He seemed to want family and friends around him. It was as if he was making a deliberate attempt to reinforce the domestic security he had so nearly lost over the affair with Susan Strasberg."

After *Look Back in Anger* wrapped, Burton got on a non-stop treadmill in 1959 to fulfill his commitments to Milton Sperling and Warner Bros. He travelled to America in March 1959 but, this time, he found his home at the Warner Bros lot in Burbank, where the facilities were surprisingly similar to those at Fox in Los Angeles. But he found the Warner Bros publicists to be far less effective than those at 20th Century-Fox. The Warner people quickly stopped trying, and they told Burton that, as far as journalists were concerned, he was no longer interesting. They told him his novelty value had worn off and he was not considered to be a major star. "Not considered a major star" became more words that rang around in Burton's head. It was a situation he swore he would change even if, at that particular moment, he didn't know how. However, there was a consolation at not being considered a major star – it still "paid just as well."

The first film for Warner Bros and Sperling was called *The Bramble Bush*, which was described by columnist Louella Parsons as a "poor man's *Peyton Place*." It was an apt description.

As Burton arrived, there was a minor drama going on behind the scenes. Because of what he had heard from Harry Saltzman, Jack Warner was already cooling on Burton. Milton Sperling was forced to defend his star and assured Warner that Burton had "unexplored possibilities as a romantic leading man." Sperling won the day.

*The Bramble Bush* was directed by Daniel Petrie and written by Philip Yordan from Charles Mergendahl's 1958 novel of the same name. Burton was the only recognisable star and played a doctor standing trial in Massachusetts accused of blackmail, adultery and a mercy killing.

*The Bramble Bush* also marked the debut of Bob Wilson in Burton's life. Burton had recently decided he needed a valet to assist him domestically day-to-day and to that end had hired Wilson, a tall, slim black man from New Jersey. Wilson was effectively an old-fashioned man servant, which most Hollywood stars had on their payrolls.

Daniel Petrie grew to like Burton during the filming and, particularly, the style with which his first alcoholic drink arrived on set at precisely five o'clock in the evening. As Petrie remembered: "He had a trailer, both on the set and on location, and on the wall a big round clock with a sweep second hand. When that second hand coincided with the minute hand precisely at five o'clock, Bob Wilson would slip a drink – vodka and tonic – gently into his extended hand. I was there one time when Bob was a few seconds late getting the drink to him. Richard exploded: 'Dammit, Bob, it's five o'clock.'"

Burton found that the rules regarding alcohol at Burbank were much less stringent than they had been at Fox. Drinking was permitted after five o'clock and Burton took full advantage, not wanting to waste a second.

But the film, despite it also having the young starlets Angie Dickinson and Barbara Rush in it, was not a great one. Petrie was yet another director who quickly became aware of the difference between Burton on stage and Burton on film: "I used to say about him that, pound for pound, he's the best actor in the English-speaking world in terms of equipment – his voice, his body, his looks. But something happens to him on film. A coldness seems to assert itself. He doesn't have the compassion or warmth that some of the great film actors have had. Off the screen, he is one of the best of raconteurs. He is articulate, vivacious – delightful company. Some of that warmth and wit translated to the screen would be rewarding. But he doesn't use himself in his roles, and perhaps that's the reason that in any of his films I haven't seen the kind of thing you'd see in his dressing room."

Burton said simply: "It was one of those films that looked good on paper, but a lot less so on film. I'm not sure I've ever learned that lesson. I don't believe any actor does." In later life, Burton declared it was the worst film he ever appeared in.

Despite its mediocrity, the film made a small profit at the box office – but only because it was made very cheaply.

The same could not be said about the second film, *Ice Palace*, a filmed version of Edna Ferber's novel about feuding families in Alaska. The film rights to the novel were bought by Jack Warner for US$350,000 and handed to Sperling to produce. Warner had bought it against the advice of his script department and the department's head penned him a famous memo that stated: "*Ice Palace* is a rambling, plotless social tract with cutout characters that never come alive." It was that assessment which prompted Warner to give the film to Sperling to make, thus providing him with an excuse if it turned out badly.

Burton's co-stars were Robert Ryan, Carolyn Jones, Martha Hyer and James Backus. Burton went straight to Alaska from Burbank to film *Ice Palace*. The exteriors were set entirely in Alaska and the interiors were filmed on very expensive sets at Burbank.

The director, Vincent Sherman, was furious with screenwriter Harry Kleiner, and he told Jack Warner the script was so poor that he doubted he would be able to find any actors to do it. But he didn't know Burton had already signed without seeing the script.

The novel on which *Ice Palace* was based was a sweeping saga chronicling the development of Alaska from 1918 to 1958, when it became a state. But the story line was seemingly forgotten about and not properly defined in the film script.

No one participating in *Ice Palace* emerged from what one critic called a "monstrous misconception of a movie" with their reputations intact. It was absurdly long and, in an unguarded moment, Burton let his attitude to it slip to British journalist, Fergus Cashin: "If you're going to make rubbish, be the best rubbish in it."

Sherman's experience of Burton was not unlike Petrie's. Filming started in August at Petersburg, in bad weather. Petersburg was a back-of-beyond Alaskan town with less than 1,500 people. August was the height of its winter. Sherman said that, despite the difficult conditions, Burton was completely co-operative on the set; nothing was too much trouble for him. There were a few weeks of filming on location in Alaska in temperatures below freezing.

But Sherman quickly discovered Burton's limitations: "He was such a facile actor but I'm sure sometimes he doesn't dig deeply enough and, god knows, *Ice Palace* didn't require any great depth of digging."

Sherman liked him personally: "Richard was most pleasant to work with. The women were crazy about him. The crew loved him, too. He was a very democratic type of guy. He had what is always I think attractive in a man, you felt he had a working-class background, he wasn't afraid of having dirt under his fingernails, which gave him a certain reality. There wasn't anything affected. In some ways, he reminded me of Clark Gable, with whom I once did a Western – the genuine professional, always on the set on time, never gave you a moment's trouble as long as you explained to him what you wanted."

Burton also struck up a good relationship with his co-star Jim Backus, and they both enjoyed long evening drinking sessions together. They both called the film "a piece of shit", and Backus recalled Burton telling him: "Here we are, sitting on top of the world, having a drink at three o'clock in the morning with the sun out and the dogs barking, making this piece of shit. If they want to pay us, let them. But they must be out of their minds."

Burton and Backus' assessment of the film was correct, and it died a death at the box office as well as with the critics. *Time* magazine summed it up best: "*Ice Palace* is the sort of film that will be described by misogynists as a good women's picture. The tearful vapidity of Edna Ferber's novel about Alaska is faithfully reflected."

In between filming *The Bramble Bush*, with some time on his hands, Burton appeared in *The Valiant Years*, a 26-part television documentary collaboration between the BBC and ABC on the life of Winston Churchill. He spoke the voice of Churchill reading from his war-time memoirs and it was amongst the best work he ever did. His secret was not to try impersonating Churchill, but to take him over and make the great man his own – which he did. Jack le Vien, the producer, told him he wanted a 'Churchillian type of voice.' So he used his own deeply mellow delivery of narrative to suggest the Churchill style while, at the same time, sticking to the well-known Churchillian rhythm of well-timed pauses and variable inflections.

Apparently, when *The Valiant Years* was at the planning stage at the BBC, Churchill was approached and asked which actor he would like to play him, and he said: "Get that boy from the Old Vic." Burton was delighted when he heard that story and said: "It was a challenge to convey the old man's greatness without melodrama, to try to give the essence of him without mimicry."

As the narrator, Burton did not appear on screen at all, but it was a superb display of non-present acting which viewers found convincing on both sides of the Atlantic. Burton said: "The actor and the politician have a lot in common. It takes one to know one. I was successful with Churchill because I knew his secret. He was the greatest actor of them all."

*The Valiant Years* was a big ratings hit on ABC in America when it was broadcast, just as it was on the BBC in Britain.

Burton also starred in a BBC television play called *A Subject Of Scandal And Concern*, in 1960. The BBC paid him £11,000, then its largest ever fee to an actor. It was also written by John Osborne and directed by Tony Richardson, which had prompted Burton to travels thousands of miles to London to do it. Burton played a character called George Jacob Holyoake, a 19th-century schoolteacher. But it wasn't a ratings success and was dumped in the BBC archives, where it lies today, a black and white gem unseen for fifty years.

But, by then, Richard Burton was off to Camelot; the castle of his dreams.

# AND GOD CREATED BURTON

# CHAPTER 32

# The three geniuses

## *Recreating Camelot for Broadway*

### 1960 - 1961

In early January 1960, Richard Burton was languishing at home in Switzerland, wondering what on earth he was going to do next. He had just endured another three box office flops in a row and, this time, the word really was out about him. There were no more Milton Sperlings to come to his rescue. As much as he may have wished for it when he was working, he was loathing the freedom of having nothing to do and, worse, nothing to look forward to. He was bored stiff.

Not so his wife Sybil, who was blissfully occupied looking after her two babies, two-year-old Kate and five-month-old Jessica. He was being a good husband, but that bored him as well. He hadn't had sex with a woman who wasn't his wife for at least two months.

At that moment, a horrible thought came into his head; if the phone had rung and someone had offered him the part, he would have gone into a Punch and Judy show. There was only one job on the horizon and that was a 90-minute drama for CBS called *The Fifth Column*, an adaptation of an Ernest Hemingway play for television, to be directed by John Frankenheimer. It was well beneath him and meant him flying to New York for a few days' work and US$10,000.

But salvation was at hand, although he didn't know it. There was a message on the hallway table that had been routed to him via the concierge desk at the Beverly Hills Hotel saying that a Mr Moss Hart had asked him to return his call. But Burton couldn't be bothered. His last experience with Hart had been on *Prince of Players* five years earlier, and he didn't wish to revisit that. Hart had written the screenplay of *Prince of Players* and it had been a disaster, initiating the downward career spiral he had experienced since.

Suddenly, the phone rang and on the line from New York, as clear as if he had been next door, was Moss Hart, full of the joys of life. The gaiety in his voice cheered up Burton immediately, and old differences were immediately forgotten. Everything changed with that telephone call – his opinion of Hart as well as the course of his own future.

What Hart had to say intrigued him. He told Burton he had been hired by

Alan Jay Lerner and Frederick Loewe to direct a new musical, which was bizarrely called 'Jenny Kissed Me.' The subject of the new musical was King Arthur and the Knights of the Round Table.

Whilst Burton may not have had a great opinion of Hart, he did of 42-year-old Lerner and 59-year-old Loewe – their reputations went before them as the creators of the most successful musical ever, 'My Fair Lady'. But it meant they had a problem selecting an equally good subject for their next venture.

In their desperate search for another hit, Lerner and Loewe had bought the partial theatrical rights to a series of fantasy novels called *The Once and Future King*, written by British author Terence Hanbury White. The four novels were: *The Sword in the Stone*, published in 1938; *The Queen of Air and Darkness*, in 1939; *The Ill-Made Knight*, in 1940; and *The Candle in the Wind*, in 1958.

They bought the latter three but Walt Disney already owned *The Sword in the Stone*, which dealt with King Arthur's childhood.

Lerner, the writer-half of the duo, needed the novel's storyline of King Arthur and his knights, an old fable. He wanted an ownership hook for his story and there were some nice twists in White's books and luckily, he didn't plan to include Arthur's childhood in his play.

Both Lerner and Loewe knew how important ownership of a story could be; in the mid-fifties, they had fought the MGM studio for the rights to George Bernard Shaw's *Pygmalion*, which 'My Fair Lady' was based on. The rights were controlled by Chase Manhattan Bank, which was in charge of the estate of the owner, film producer Gabriel Pascal. Ultimately, they acquired the rights and it went on to set the record for the longest run of any major musical; followed by a hit London production, a popular film version, and numerous revivals. Its success made Lerner and Loewe multi-millionaires.

Raising the cash to stage what quickly became Camelot was no problem. When Lerner and Loewe went to see CBS boss Bill Paley, he gave them the US$400,000 funding they needed for 'Camelot' on the spot.

With the material and finance secured, all they needed was a director and a script. They found the director they wanted, or thought they wanted, in 45-year-old Moss Hart. They had worked with Hart before and it had been a success. Hart was a complicated man, a homosexual who had nonetheless married and had two children by his wife, the actress Kitty Carlisle.

Lerner and Loewe signed Hart in January 1960 to direct the new project and to hire a team to produce it. But Hart was not the man Lerner and Loewe thought he was. His success had been very patchy.

One associate, who worked with them at the time, nicknamed the trio 'The Three Geniuses', mainly because of the early brainstorming sessions he witnessed and the obvious self-regard they had for themselves and for their collective talents. In fact he said that Lerner, Loewe and Hart were "awash with self-regard" and foresaw problems ahead. He wasn't wrong.

At the time of their coming together, all three had personal problems. Fritz Loewe had had a coronary and been seriously ill in hospital. He really wanted to retire and not write another show, but felt he had been forced into it by Lerner, whom he had started to resent. Alan Jay Lerner, a peculiar man at the best of times, was in the middle of a mighty fall-out with his fourth wife and had recently had a nervous breakdown. Moss Hart was depressed about his sexuality and his relationship with his wife. At any other time, the three of them might have been able to carry it off, but in the circumstances in which they found themselves, it was a recipe for disaster.

Initially, it appeared to go well. Immediately, they decided upon Julie Andrews for the lead female role of Guinevere. Andrews had acted and sung beautifully in 'My Fair Lady' and was delighted to be invited to repeat the success. Lerner described her as "lissom, lovely and pure-voiced." She was all of that.

But the male lead role was extremely difficult to cast. Rex Harrison, the obvious choice and Andrews' other half in 'My Fair Lady' was ruled out immediately. Lerner and Loewe knew, to their cost, that Harrison couldn't sing, although he mimed beautifully. They had only just got away with it before and didn't want that risk again.

They needed an actor of great presence to play King Arthur; an actor of regal bearing and one who, as Lerner described it, had "manly fire" – whatever that meant. The chosen one also had to be able to sing beautifully and dance credibly. The only actor in frame was Howard Keel, a very famous singer of the time, who could also act. But Keel had a charisma shortfall which had prevented him from becoming a great actor, and no one was too keen.

Then Moss Hart suddenly suggested Burton and, as Ruth Waterbury wrote in her book about Burton in 1965, the following verbal exchange took place: "'Richard Burton? He can sing?' asked Loewe. 'Richard Burton,' said Alan Lerner, thinking out loud, 'He'd look at it. He could act it. But...' 'But nothing,' said Hart, 'I have never forgotten him since I wrote the script of *Prince of Players*. He is an absolutely stupendous actor.' 'All his films have been turkeys,' said Lerner. Hart replied: 'Yes, I know that, but I don't know why. It has to be some preposterous type of mishandling.'"

But then Hart poured cold water on his own idea and questioned whether Burton could sing and dance. Lerner answered that straightaway. He told Hart he had been at a party at George and Ira Gershwin's house in Los Angeles and had heard Burton and his wife, Sybil, sing what he called "some charming Welsh songs" together. But Lerner was also worried about how much Burton would cost: "What's his situation regarding contracts? Is he free?" Hart replied: "I'll check his agent, Hugh French. You know, of course, he's high priced." "Give it a try," said Lerner and Loewe almost in unison.

And that was why Moss Hart came to be calling Richard Burton that snowy morning in New York and sunny afternoon in Celigny.

Hart found Burton very affable and keen to promote his talents. Burton told him: "I've been trying for years to get into a musical. Way back when I was in 'The Lady's Not for Burning' on Broadway, I tried to get the lead in 'Guys and Dolls'. They wouldn't give me a chance, but I went to a matinee of it every single week that I was in New York." Burton told him: "Would you like me to warble 'Take Back Your Mink' right now?" Hart laughed and said: "Not at long distance prices." After some more small-talk, Hart cut Burton short and said: "We'll work out the details with French, have him send you the contract, okay?" Burton replied: "Okay." Before Hart put down the phone, they agreed to meet the following week when, conveniently, Burton would be in New York filming his television drama for CBS.

When he put the phone down, Burton allegedly danced a jig of delight in front of his wife and children. He was back from the dead and, as Melvyn Bragg described it so poetically: "Plump at his feet like wind-dropped fruit, came the offer from Moss Hart to play King Arthur."

When Hart put the phone down, he also felt like dancing a jig. He certainly breathed a sigh of relief. Burton had not asked to see a script, which was just as well since the script had not yet been written. He did not even ask who else would be in the show. It all had been too easy, he thought uneasily.

Hart was right to be uneasy. By the following morning, when he had the chance to think about it, Burton was full of remorse. For once in his life, Burton prevaricated and was unsure of his own abilities. He picked up the telephone and placed a transatlantic call to Valerie Douglas in Los Angeles. When he got through, he asked her to call Hart and backtrack.

The following week, Burton flew into New York's Idlewild Airport to make *The Fifth Column* for CBS. The jet age had arrived suddenly and Burton flew on a Boeing 707 jet with Pan-Am for the first time. The transatlantic crossing could now be made in less than nine hours, with only one stop for refuelling.

With a week to think about it, Burton was far more cautious when he finally met with Moss Hart in New York. He told him straight that he didn't think he was a good enough singer to carry off a Broadway musical. Without the songs, he said, he wouldn't be hesitating. The meeting didn't go well, as Hart had expected to get a firm decision.

Burton may not have said 'yes', but he didn't say 'no' either and wasn't about to let it go. But for the first time in his life, he doubted his own abilities on a stage. As he walked back to the CBS studio, he decided to ask Laurence Olivier and John Gielgud for some advice. Back at the studio, he put in two transatlantic calls to both men. Olivier's advice was simple: "The money's good, so I should say nothing and carry on." Gielgud hummed and hawed, as he always did, and could offer nothing in the way of constructive advice.

Burton then spoke to Alan Lerner on the telephone and voiced his fears to him. Lerner listened and then told him: "We had the same problem with Rex Harrison in 'My Fair Lady'. Rex said he couldn't sing. But he learned to talk in tune, and everyone thought he had a wonderful voice." Burton was appalled at what Lerner said: "But I can't do that. What would they say at home to a Welshman who was in a musical and wasn't allowed to sing? I'd be classed as a traitor." Lerner asked him: "But do you have a singing voice?" With that challenge, Burton cleared his throat and sang to Lerner over the phone the tune of 'A Cry in the Wilderness' in Welsh. Lerner was convinced, and so finally was Burton.

Burton rang Hart that same afternoon and agreed to do it subject to a satisfactory financial deal being worked out with Aaron Frosch. Then he rang Frosch and told him how much they wanted to hire him and to ensure that he got the maximum money he could – which Frosch proceeded to do.

The deal was by far the richest Broadway had ever seen; Frosch got his client a basic pay of US$4,000 a week. But he also negotiated a share of first dollar gross, then almost unheard of on Broadway. Frosch asked for 15 per cent and Hart finally negotiated him down to 11 per cent. It was a great deal and would eventually earn Burton around US$750,000 for 18 months' work. With ticket prices for the production sky high, the top price was US$50, Burton ended up getting around US$3 for every seat sold.

Burton signed up for six months of rehearsals and try-out performances in Toronto and Boston and a whole year playing on Broadway until the end of 1961; at least that was the plan.

# AND GOD CREATED BURTON

As soon as Hart put the phone down on Frosch, he convened a meeting with Lerner and Loewe. He told them Burton had agreed a deal and it was a lot more money than they wanted to pay, and three times what Julie Andrews had asked for, but it was a definite deal.

Fritz Loewe whistled at what Burton was asking, thought about it, and Hart braced himself for a row for having agreed to such a lucrative deal for the actor.

But Loewe seemed unconcerned about the money and just wanted to know whether or not Burton's reputation for womanising was true. As he blurted out: "Wait a minute. I'm thinking about this fellow's reputation with women. If he plays Arthur, how are we going to persuade audiences that Guinevere would choose Lancelot?"

Moss Hart just smiled with relief. He told Loewe that he knew all about Burton's reputation with women first hand, and said: "Alan will write it that way." Lerner said: "Nothing easier for you two. But let's remember this, fellows: we won't have to worry about any backstage romance this time. Julie's like that old Pond's cream slogan, remember? 'She's lovely. She's a new bride. She adores her husband.' There will be no heartbreak atmosphere around our theatre."

Moss Hart kept his thoughts to himself when he heard that. Personally, he didn't think that Julie Andrews – newly married or not – had a hope of staying out of Burton's bed. Loewe and Lerner had no idea what they were dealing with.

The sudden realisation that both Burton and Julie Andrews were on board and would be arriving for rehearsals in just four months' time shocked Alan Lerner and Fritz Loewe into action. Although they had been hugely successful with 'My Fair Lady', they had also had their fair share of less successful musicals. Lerner, in particular, laboured hard at his craft. And before he could write the lyrics for Loewe's tunes, he had to craft the basic story. And therein lay the problem. White's three novels were very long, meaning Lerner's story and his script were equally long. That affected Loewe, whose songs were also too long. Both men kept pondering how to make them shorter, but it was a riddle they didn't solve.

Meanwhile, after completing the CBS drama, Burton flew back home for four months before returning to New York for rehearsals in May.

When he got home, he told Sybil all about his first flight in a jet airliner. Soon afterwards, Sybil bought Philip Burton a Pan-Am air ticket so he could come and visit them at their new house and see his new granddaughter. A few weeks later, Philip flew into London and quickly hopped on a flight to Geneva to spend two weeks with the Burtons in Celigny. Paul and Joy Scofield were also staying at the same time.

After a joyous two weeks with his grandchildren, Philip flew back to London to spend a month in Britain before returning to New York to await the arrival of his adoptive son for 'Camelot' rehearsals.

Burton arrived a week early so he could spend the time with Philip learning the script and rehearsing his singing, which he was still worried about. Philip remembered: "As soon as Richard got hold of the script and score of 'Camelot', we set to work on his three big solos and duet. I had some pleasant sessions with Richard in which we went over his lines, and I felt the show had potential."

Luckily, Philip had a piano in his apartment. It brought back memories of Elizabeth Smith's front room in Connaught Street, where he had first met Richard: "My mind flashed back to the time when, at Richard's insistent request, I had taught him finger-by-finger to play the first movement of Beethoven's 'Moonlight Sonata' and he had become sufficiently adept at it to surprise people when the show-off mood was on him." Philip played as Richard sang, and eventually 'Camelot's' rehearsal pianist took over as it got more polished.

A week later, Sybil, Kate and Jessica Burton, together with their nanny, Diane, made the same trip into Idlewild, experiencing their first taste of jet travel. Sybil and Diane loved it, but the children were sick. They arrived at the same time as rehearsals started.

Philip was pleased that the family would be staying at an apartment nearby, which he had found them in a building called 'The Beresford'. It was within walking distance of both his apartment and that of Aaron Frosch's in Central Park West. They lived there until the spring of 1961, when Lauren Bacall lent them the lavish apartment she had shared with Humphrey Bogart.

Rehearsals were scheduled to last six months or more. Robert Goulet, a handsome newcomer, had been signed to play Sir Lancelot, and both Burton and Julie Andrews thoroughly approved of the choice of their talented co-star. The star lineup was completed when Roddy McDowall signed to play the supporting role of Mordred.

Richard Burton reported for his first rehearsal in the last days of spring. That day, the Burton magnetism was ablaze and Julie Andrews was distinctly shaken as to just how attracted she was to her co-star. As it was, her new husband, Tony Walton, looked on in horror as he saw what the rest of the cast saw. Walton watched his wife with the same frightened and disturbed look that Stewart Granger had worn when watching Jean Simmons during filming of *The Robe*, seven years earlier. Julie Andrews struggled to stop looking at him. Burton was so confident he would bed her, he decided to play it very cool, which gave Andrews time to get over the initial shock and to pull herself together.

On that first day, rehearsals went well as the cast gelled together. Moss Hart had cast it well. Burton knew his lines perfectly right from the start and surprised Lerner and Loewe as to just how good he was.

But that was as good as it got; the problem was that their script was nowhere near as good as the casting. This was no ordinary musical, it was the live creation of a new work in rehearsal. The script was in a terrible state and the 61-strong cast laboured day on day, hour on hour, and seemed to be going nowhere. As Burton said: "Everything is wrong in 'Camelot.'" He wasn't joking; the book was too long, the songs were too long, the script was too long, and the play was subsequently too long. Two words summed it up: "too long."

There was also a fundamental problem in that it was a play of two very different halves, which was confusing. The first half was light comedy, humorous and romantic, but the second half was the opposite, a leaden-footed tragedy, and the story seemed to fall apart when Guinevere two-timed King Arthur with Sir Lancelot. But the ending was good, with a touching moment when King Arthur finds out that his wife, Queen Guinevere, and Sir Lancelot are in love with each other, but decides that, because he loves them both, he will do nothing about it. He decides that, with God's help, they will live through it.

But overall, it was a disaster that became more and more obvious as each day dawned. The three geniuses just weren't used to this kind of failure and they wondered where their genius had gone – although they didn't wonder too much. Alan Jay Lerner got the blame, and there was more acrimony between him and Loewe. It proved to be the beginning of the end of his relationship with Fritz Loewe.

Both Lerner and Loewe found Moss Hart to be of very little help in resolving the difficulties. Lerner just sweated out the book, writing and re-writing continually, but he simply couldn't see wood from the trees and had no one to help him.

Spring merged into the heat of the New York summer. Everything was being continually re-written and re-harmonised but, in truth, they were going round in ever increasing circles and 'Camelot' was nowhere near ready. As summer cooled into autumn, Burton began to realise there was a serious problem. Every day they seemed to be changing everything, with the actors learning the changes, trying them out, discovering they were wrong, forgetting them and learning new changes. It was so bad that the first full run through of Act One was not ready to perform until 12th September, some three months after rehearsals had first begun.

The creative side may have been flagging but, commercially, the musical was already a success long before it opened. The combination of Richard Burton and Julie Andrews on the billing was selling huge numbers of tickets months before it was due to open on Broadway. The advances were breaking all records for any type of Broadway production. Officially, US$3 million of advance ticket sales were made before rehearsals finished. Although the figures were undoubtedly hyped for press consumption, Alan Lerner called ticket sales "astounding."

Not so the production itself. By the night of the first tryout in Toronto, in the middle of October, the show was far from ready and still hopelessly long, to the point of being ridiculous.

The venue in Toronto was also causing problems. Lerner and Loewe, whose own money was tied up in the production, had received a lucrative offer to open it in a new theatre called the O'Keefe Center, which was been financed by the O'Keefe Brewery Company. It was a very large hall that had cost US$12 million to build but like all brand new theatres had terrible acoustics. It was also unfinished and Julie Andrews remembered: "They were hammering carpets and installing seats, and we were trying to get the show ready."

The opening night show on Saturday 1st October 1960 ran for a full four and a three quarter hours and, with the intermission, did not finish until over five hours after it started. The first curtain did not come down until 40 minutes after midnight. It was an hour and a half too long. The following day, one witty critic in a local newspaper praised the show for "helping considerably to shorten the winter."

By then, the three geniuses had completely lost the plot – especially Lerner – and they needed saving from themselves. Entirely certain of their genius, it was difficult for them to accept that they were on the verge of failing.

Lerner had the heaviest workload and had been rewriting scenes almost every night for six months until he finally cracked. The strain on him was immense, and it was not helped by the breakdown at the same time of his fourth marriage to the French lawyer Micheline Musseli Pozzo di Borgo. She had been a wealthy woman when she married Lerner, but Lerner had managed to squander all her wealth, and much of his own, through poor investments. This had naturally upset her, and she was suing him.

Lerner, who, despite his charm and wealth, was a disaster with money and women, had been warned not to marry a lawyer, but chose to ignore the warnings. Now he was paying the price. He eventually went through eight wives in his 67 years. He said of himself: "All I can say is that if I had no flair for marriage, I also had no flair for bachelorhood." One of his ex-wives reportedly summed it up by saying: "Marriage is Alan's way of saying 'goodbye.'"

Somehow the show struggled through the Toronto run and in late October the show and its huge amount of scenery was trucked to Boston's Shubert Theatre for another month of try-outs.

Two days after the opening in Boston, Lerner's ulcer burst. Everyone had known his ulcer was a problem before production started and he was being prescribed strong drugs throughout the rehearsal and tryout period. When the drugs were withdrawn, he had to adhere to a strict diet, which he constantly broke. Unsurprisingly, in the third week of October, he finally collapsed at a dinner party where some rich food was being served. There were immediate fears for his life but, amazingly, he was back at work two weeks later. Two days after that, Moss Hart had a heart attack and was hospitalised. Lerner remembered: "I was carted off to the hospital with an internal hemorrhage. I was there for ten days, and as I was going out, I saw someone on a table being wheeled into the room I had vacated. It was Moss Hart with another heart attack."

With no director, an audience to play to nightly, a cast of sixty one people, and an entire musical going wrong, the show was set to close down. And instead of cutting it as they planned to do, before they were struck by illness, Lerner and Hart had actually managed to lengthen it to just under five hours.

But Moss Hart's heart attack actually saved the show. It was a cue for Richard Burton to insist that Philip Burton be brought in to take over directorial duties. Philip was already very familiar with the play from his work with Burton. Finally, faced with no choice, Lerner approached Philip on 10th November, Burton's 35th birthday, with an offer to take over the show.

So over lunch the following day, Lerner asked Philip formally to take over as director and replace Moss Hart. Lerner agreed to pay Philip a good salary but told him he would not have any credit as director; that would remain solely with Moss Hart. It was Philip's dream job and he immediately agreed, as he remembered: "I readily agreed to the terms of my engagement. I was to be adequately paid, but Moss Hart, quite rightly, was to retain billing as director. I was to receive no billing."

The following day, Philip began three weeks of intense work. He had no preconceptions and could slay all the sacred cows that Moss Hart could not deal with, as he said: "It was the most strenuous time I can remember. I saw all the performances and gave notes after every one, rehearsed the allowed five hours a day and had sessions with Alan Jay Lerner that lasted until the early hours of the morning. Rarely did I get more than four hours' sleep."

Philip took an hour and half out of the running time and still managed to add three songs that Lerner had left out. There was also a whole new set. The script overhaul was total, and the changes were gradually incorporated into each performance in Boston. But the strains of creating virtually a new production alongside the old one being performed simultaneously were huge.

Richard Burton rose to the occasion. He gave up drinking and womanising completely and focused on the production. Alan Jay Lerner and Frederic Loewe could only watch in wonder as the two Burtons singlehandedly saved their skins and reputations. When the other actors grew panicky over the changes, Burton calmed them down and told them all would work out well – and it did.

Philip Burton recalled: "It was a great strain on the company to play one version by night and rehearse another by day until, gradually, scene-by-scene, the new material was incorporated into the show the public saw."

It became a team effort between father and son, as Melvyn Bragg recounted: "It was Burton who held 'Camelot' together and it was his leadership alone which got it to Broadway." But the Burtons proved they had what it takes as they rose to the challenge. As Burton said: "It sounds perverse, but when you're given a perfectly written part, like Hamlet, there's not much you can do with it after the first few performances. The Burton Hamlet is the Burton Hamlet and that's that. But in a show like 'Camelot', when the changes are coming thick and fast, all things are possible. You can make something of the part that is yours and yours alone." It helped that Burton thoroughly enjoyed working with Philip.

The Boston tryout was coming to an end and Philip realised he was still a week short of getting it right. It was much better but he was still struggling to get the musical into shape and balanced. The cuts he made had reduced the running length, but they had also distorted the balance. Lerner and Philip worked on it day and night to try and sort it out, but in the process of restoring the balance, the show's length went back up to four hours. It was a nightmare, and now Philip found he had become too absorbed and could no longer see the wood from the trees.

But Richard Burton was adamant that Philip had prevented the show from closing: "Phil saved 'Camelot'. He cut the running time to a more manageable three and a half hours and yet managed to add three new songs." Roddy McDowall added: "Philip's contribution cannot be underestimated, and he was very generous in agreeing to allow Moss Hart full credit as director."

Alan Jay Lerner always kept quiet about Philip's contribution but later paid substantial tribute to Richard Burton's efforts, saying: "I can't remember any actor as loved by a company as he was. He radiated a faith and geniality which infected the company. God knows what would have happened if it were not for Richard Burton. If ever a star behaved like a star, it was he." He added: "Camelot might never have reached New York had it not been for him."

When the show finally reached Broadway, it opened on 3rd December 1960 as planned. But for the one and only time in Richard Burton's career, the opening night was not a rip-roaring success; this time, there were no standing ovations or cheers from the first night audience – in fact, quite the reverse. Although Alan Jay Lerner, in his autobiography, insisted it had been a success, it wasn't. At three hours, people started to leave and, by the end, 300 people had left early. It was particularly embarrassing because it happened in front of a host of celebrities, including Noel Coward.

The walkouts continued night after night. The advance bookings carried the show forward and theoretically guaranteed full houses for the first three months but, as they began to tail off as word got around, it looked like the show might have to close – 'Camelot' seemed doomed to die.

Considering the scale of the disaster, the critics were relatively kind to 'Camelot'. There was a sort of sympathy and conspiracy developing gradually, whereby the real truth, which would have immediately killed the production, was never told. Perhaps the critics feared for the future of big Broadway productions if that happened, or perhaps the fear of the Majestic Theatre being dark for a long period frightened them as well. Rather than be hypocritical in their praise for 'Camelot', they praised Burton instead and were justified. *Time* magazine said: "Richard Burton gives Arthur the skillful and vastly appealing performance that might be expected from one of England's finest young actors." Walter Kerr, the doyen of New York theatre critics, who then wrote for the *New York Herald Tribune* went further: "It is clear that everyone admires Arthur, including the actor who plays him. Richard Burton slips down from his hiding place in a pretzel-shaped tree to put two uncompromising feet upon the earth. He speaks of his kingship as though he were right out of Mallory. Mr Burton, superb actor that he is, might easily have condescended to the musical form, might have reserved some of his power and some of his majestically satisfying, vocal precision for the next time he tangles with Shakespeare.

"There is no such half-hearted nonsense. The syllables sing, the account of his wresting the sword from the stone becomes a bravura passage of house-hushing brilliance, and when it is time for Mr Burton to join Julie Andrews in 'What Do the Simple Folk Do?', there is at once a sly and fretful and mocking accent to take care of the humour without destroying the man."

With notices like that, whatever happened to the production, Burton emerged with much credit, with one critic even calling him: "The new king of Broadway."

Lerner heaped praise on Burton's performance and even had to rewrite some scenes to bring him articulately into them. As Lerner explained, Burton was dominating the scenes even when he had no lines to speak, thereby detracting from the other players: "I've never known anyone else with that kind of presence on the stage. There was a moment when he was merely standing by the fire, supposedly deep in thought, while others in the scene were speaking. But I saw that no one was interested in what was being said. His peculiar power of concentration was so great that he just sucked all the energy of the stage into him. I spoke to him about it and he told me he had done a play once that had failed for that reason. I rewrote the scene to eliminate many of the lines of the others, and made sure to include him in it." Roddy McDowall agreed: "Richard had a not-so-secret weapon that gave his King Arthur the power and brilliance which turned 'Camelot' into a massive hit. It was his voice. He could have stood on stage and read the obituaries in the newspaper and he would have made it sound like an epic poem."

The positive reviews for Burton's performances gave them breathing space, but half an hour still remained to be cut to stop audiences leaving early. Whilst that problem remained, it was debilitating for the audiences and the cast.

And then, suddenly, a reinvigorated Moss Hart arrived back to rescue the production. Newly refreshed and away from the day-to-day problems, he could immediately see what was wrong. His recovery and return spurred Philip Burton and Alan Lerner to make the changes that finally made the show right. When failure became a real option and the egos of Lerner, Loewe and Hart finally subsided, the three geniuses, now much humbled, seemed to find their original passion and talent again. After a supreme effort, the play was reduced to three and half hours, and this time it was superbly balanced.

Almost overnight, as though a switch had been flicked, 'Camelot' had been turned into a magical evening, and as one critic who saw the new version put it: "Camelot is the timeless dream of Broadway." But it was too late; word of mouth from early patrons had already done great damage, and once the advance sales ran out, the theatre was only half full.

To save it, drastic action was needed. So, Lerner and Loewe hired a new public relations team in a do-or-die effort. Somehow, they managed to persuade Ed Sullivan to feature a 20-minute sequence on his show on CBS. *The Ed Sullivan Show* was the most popular television show in America at the time and the PR firm persuaded Sullivan to do a special to mark the fifth anniversary of 'My Fair Lady'. Sullivan allowed Lerner and Loewe to virtually produce the segment themselves and do what they liked. So they brought on half the cast of 'Camelot' and devoted the entire 20 minutes to its best songs. Sullivan was expecting a tribute to 'My Fair Lady' but actually got a 20-minute preview of the new version of 'Camelot'. As it was a live show, there was nothing the show's director could do short of pulling the plug. But viewers were ecstatic with what they saw: Burton and Julie Andrews singing 'If Ever I Would Leave You', 'Where are the Simple Joys of Maidenhood' and 'What Do the Simple Folk Do?', with the backing of the full chorus.

The following morning, there was a queue for the Majestic's box office that ran halfway down the block. 'Camelot' was suddenly a smash hit and set for a very long run, indeed.

Once the problems were sorted, the good times started to roll and there began a six-month period of fun for the cast and crew, who felt like celebrating. They were joined almost every night by a slew of stars, including Alec Guinness, Mike Nichols, Phil Silvers, Tammy Grimes, Lauren Bacall, Jason Robards, Robert Preston and Elaine May.

Once the run was assured, Burton spent US$750 refurbishing and decorating his dressing room. Sybil helped him and they furnished it with lumpy couches and armchairs. They also installed a bar with a refrigerator, which Bob Wilson restocked every night and acted as barman. He hung a sign outside which read 'Burton's Bar.' Backstage at 'Camelot' became a very merry place and every night Burton's Bar was heaving before the show, in the intermission and after the show. Young secretaries and copywriters who worked for advertising agencies on Madison Avenue block-booked the front stalls every night and were often invited by Burton backstage. The conversation in Burton's Bar was both brilliant and racy, as Burton said when the theatre manager challenged him about the number of people being invited backstage: "Why shouldn't this place be crowded? It's the cheapest bar in town."

The most riotous nights were when there was an afternoon matinée; then, the evening started early and never really stopped.

1961 turned out to be Burton's most remarkable year ever, and one in which he never missed a single performance of 'Camelot'. In April, he won a Tony Award for best actor in a musical. After it was announced, hordes of fans besieged the stage door before and after every performance, chanting Burton's name. That continued for the rest of his run.

The good news now just kept coming. A record album recorded from the show was selling like hot cakes and making Burton and Julie Andrews a small fortune in additional royalties. Whatever cock-ups the three geniuses had made, and there had been many, the songs were brilliant, and the musical arrangements superb. The album reached number one in the spring of 1961, and stayed in the top 40 album charts for almost three years. Warner Brothers also bid US$1 million for the film rights to the musical.

Burton also became an unlikely hero. In June, a fire broke out backstage and Burton, his bravery enhanced by the amount of vodka he had drunk, put the fire out singlehandedly with a fire hose, before it could take hold. For that, he was made an honorary fire chief by the New York Fire Service.

Even President Kennedy was caught up in 'Camelot' and thought King Arthur's court and the story reflected the spirit of his own administration. So much so that the Kennedy White House was nicknamed 'Camelot' by First Lady Jacqueline Kennedy, and the name stuck. President Kennedy invited the Burtons to the White House and declared 'Camelot' to be his favourite musical of all time.

Almost as interesting was the competition between Burton and Robert Goulet to get Julie Andrews into bed. The 25-year-old's husband was absent in London. Burton decided to bide his time and circled her whilst his younger rival, Goulet, made the early running. Goulet made his pitch again and again, and failed. Andrews could easily see off a young stud like Goulet and she found his good looks and charm much too obvious, calling them a "commodity."

Burton was different altogether, and she was intrigued. But by the time

Burton moved in, her husband had returned to New York and he missed his chance. It was one of the few times he had failed to bed his leading lady. As Burton admitted to Robert Goulet when the two of them compared notes: "I tried everything on her myself. I couldn't get anywhere either." And for the first time, he appeared to be in genuine awe of a woman. He told Goulet that Andrews was pure wholesomeness and that he didn't want to defile her, as he confessed: "Every man I know who knows her is a little bit in love with her."

But probably the truth was that Burton didn't really have the time to pursue Andrews. He had a lot of girls during the run of 'Camelot'. There were 20 or so chorus girls in the cast and each one of them was a very good looking woman. No one knew whether or not Sybil knew what was going on, but it seemed hard to believe that she didn't because it was so open and there was so much talk about it amongst the New York newspaper columnists.

Eventually, a new favourite appeared called Pat Tunder, whom Burton met soon after he got to New York. She was tall, blonde and brassy, in direct contrast to Andrews. She was a dancer at the famous Copacabana Club and Burton squired her around town as openly as he had Susan Strasberg three years before. Tunder's arrival marked the end of his attempts to woo Andrews, but not his movement through the chorus girls. He eventually went to bed with virtually every single one. A running joke emerged in the form of a song, performed by the girls, in which the lyrics: 'I wonder what the King is doing tonight' were manipulated to sound surprisingly like: 'I wonder who the King is screwing tonight.' Burton enjoyed the joke immensely.

On many evenings, after a performance, many of the cast and crew would adjourn to Downey's, a popular actors' bar on Broadway. Noel Behn, a friend of Philip Burton's remembered: "The place was filled with young actresses and chorus girls, and Burton seemed to have the pick of the lot."

Burton entertained many of his women at actor Robert Webber's New York flat. Webber was away in Los Angeles during the entire run of 'Camelot' and had left Burton the keys. People still talk of the "enormous energy that flowed from the bedroom" where he entertained.

Once the success of 'Camelot' was assured, Burton began drinking again and took his consumption of vodka to new heights. There were stories of legendary drinking sessions lasting well into the morning hours. Alan Jay Lerner, newly separated from his wife and a single man again, joined in the fun. He remembered: "I decided to see for myself. So I went out with him one night, determined to stay by his side. We visited a couple of bars and, while I nursed one drink, he would down double vodkas with beer chasers at an absolutely incredible rate. I've never in my life seen anyone drink like that. Finally, I gave up. It must have been three or four in the morning, and I left him in the bar of our hotel. I came down again at noon, and there he was, still at the bar, still drinking, with an entourage he had collected." Lerner believed that there was no one in the world who could outdrink Burton: "I would have matched him drink for drink against anyone in the world. If anyone had watched and clocked him, he would have made the Guinness Book of Records."

Lerner was so shocked at Burton's capacity for alcohol, and so worried, that he began to wonder if he would survive Camelot's run; he feared Burton might actually die of alcohol poisoning before the end. So he consulted his doctor in Boston, who told him that Burton was not unusual and that he knew of other severe cases, as he explained: "Welsh livers and kidneys seem to be made of some metallic alloy quite unlike the rest of the human race. One day, like airplanes, they eventually show metal fatigue."

Burton never ate before going on stage, and this caused more concern about his drinking. His brother Graham Jenkins said: "This was in the days when my brother's drinking was treated as a joke. Because however much booze he got through, it never seemed to affect his performance. Colleagues who might otherwise have delivered a friendly warning indulged his choice of relaxation. I remember someone telling me: 'To Richard, the bottle is like a second wife; and who wants to break up a happy marriage?'"

One day, Robert Preston, another actor, proposed a bet: that Burton could not drink a bottle of hundred-proof vodka during a matinee and another bottle during the evening performance without noticeable effect. As Graham recalled: "Richard promptly took the bet, and others clamoured to get in on the action." In Burton's own account of it: "I popped off the stage every so often, and there was a glass waiting for me." The unknowing judge was Julie Andrews as, after the performance, Burton asked her: "Julie, how was I today?" She replied: "Rather better than usual." Andrews said: "Whatever Richard did on stage was magical. Even on the nights when he had imbibed too much, he managed to pull something out of his bag of theatrical wonders."

But she was not as impressed when the cast adjourned to her apartment one night after a heavy drinking session. As she remembered: "One night, Richard and his pals got so drunk that they went into our kitchen and, unbeknownst to me, competed with each other as to who could urinate the farthest distance. I didn't notice it until the following morning, when I discovered the kitchen floor and ceiling saturated with beer and urine. I remember saying to Richard later: 'You are disgusting; sophomoric.'"

Andrews, who had more than her fair share of problems with Burton throughout the production, eventually forgave him.

After a wonderful nine months as King Arthur, Burton's run came to an end when he was replaced by William Squire on his own recommendation. His final night, at the end of September 1961, was by all accounts an extraordinary experience. Graham Jenkins, who was present, recalled: "It had me in tears when, after a dozen curtain calls, the company disappeared into the wings to leave the king alone on stage to abdicate his throne."

Moss Hart hosted a last night party to mark the departure the following day of the Burton family. He made a speech as he toasted Burton's future: "Great actors, like you, are born once in a lifetime. You are as big a personality off the stage as on the stage, and you are, in every sense, larger than life. I beg you not to waste your wonderful gifts. You must know you have it in you to be one of the greatest stage actors of this century."

Although Burton was the undoubted toast of New York and had been christened the king of Broadway by the press, Sybil Burton had become the belle of Broadway. She had made a very successful social debut in Manhattan. On this trip she had been freed from her responsibilities to her children as Philip Burton, the doting grandfather, continually babysat whilst she lunched and dined with the many friends she had made in New York over the year. She became one of the leading ladies-who-lunch in New York and was as big a success in her own circle as her husband. It prompted her close friend Roddy McDowell to say: "Sybil was, and is, such an extraordinary woman. Her sense of family, Richard's extended family of all his friends in the theatre, provided the glue in his life. We were all glued together by Sybil's concern for people, her vitality and love – this was a very important part of any friendship with Richard."

The trip ended with a huge profile of Burton in the *New York Times*. Barbara Gelb, one of the top writers there became obsessed with Burton – the life he led, his relationship with his wife and the many women he squired around New York.

She timed the publication of the profile for the eve of his departure, before he left New York. It was virtually a psychological analysis. With considerable perceptiveness, she wrote: "A tug-of-war began in him at the age of two [referring to the loss of his mother], and the two sides of his nature have never been reconciled. He appears to be at once self-possessed and uneasy with himself, unsure where the caustic Welsh clay stops and the silken veneer begins. He is simultaneously the dark and self-destructive Celt and the glossy idealisation of a classical actor, circumspect and disciplined. In his bemusement over which of these selves to champion, he often takes refuge in a third and safer self – the little boy lost."

Nobody disagreed with the sentiment as Burton embarked on the next and most colourful chapter of his life in Rome, leaving behind his adoptive father with all his memories of a fantastic one and a half years. Philip Burton had saved the show from oblivion, but all he got was a small paragraph thanking him for his contribution in the Majestic Theatre's programme. The three geniuses preferred to airbrush him from their success, which had really been Philip's success.

17 years later, there was a regrettable postscript when Alan Jay Lerner wrote his autobiography, called *The Street Where I Live*. It was a self-serving tissue of lies and pure fabrication from pages 171 to 223, as he described the gestation of 'Camelot' with barely a sliver of truth in his descriptions of any of the events.

Not only that, he also whitewashed his own failings and excused his conduct during 'Camelot' by describing how he had had a breakdown when his French wife removed his son, Michael, to Europe. And then he described his seemingly equal distress when she brought him back – all told with not a trace of irony.

He failed to mention hardly any of the problems with 'Camelot', bar a mention that it might originally have been too long. He failed to mention Philip Burton's name at all. In fact, Philip's contribution to Camelot's success was completely erased in Lerner's version of events. Lerner gave the strong impression, without actually saying so, that he had taken over as director after Moss Hart's heart attack and saved the show.

Burton was apoplectic when he read it, although not completely surprised. The following year, in 1979, Lerner approached Burton about appearing in a 20-year anniversary tour of the show across America. Burton took the opportunity to tell Lerner what he thought of him, saying: "I gave Alan Jay Lerner five minutes of ice cold hell for not mentioning in his autobiography that it was [Philip] who saved the show."

Anyone reading Alan Jay Lerner's autobiography will immediately understand why he had eight wives and feel intense sympathy for each and every one of those ladies.

# AND GOD CREATED BURTON

# CHAPTER 33

# Blazing Magnetism

## *The thousands of women*

### 1944 - 1962

Of all the men that have ever walked the planet, it is probably true to say that Richard Burton, between the years of 1948 and 1962, was the most attractive. During those fabulous 14 years, there was virtually no woman with whom he came into contact that could resist him. And those women ranged from young, naïve schoolgirls to the world's most desirable film stars.

He was a magnet to women, and if two words can be used to sum up his appeal, then they are 'blazing magnetism.' It was as if he used to rehearse and practice the extraordinary effect he could have on people who met him for the first time – especially on the first day at a film set or a rehearsal stage.

The secret of that magnetism was the extraordinary glint in his blue-green eyes, which were often described as "wicked." On those days when his magnetism blazed and those eyes glinted, there was no telling what could happen.

That blazing magnetism was never more apparent to Julie Andrews than in the summer of 1960. Andrews was one of the more chaste women ever to work in Hollywood. In her whole life, she was only ever intimate with two men: her childhood sweetheart and first husband, Tony Walton; and the love of her life, her second husband, director Blake Edwards.

Yet this most chaste of women was sexually challenged by Richard Burton and only managed to get out by the skin of her teeth, as she readily admitted: "I was introduced to Richard Burton and was immediately enthralled, as was everyone present, by his charm. He was simply one of the charismatic people who attracted attention from every man, woman, child or animal the moment he walked into the room. His voice was a magnificent instrument, mellifluous enough to make any woman swoon; that, and his piercing grey-green eyes and full, beautiful mouth. The first time I heard him sing 'How to handle a woman', I simply melted."

Andrews was totally smitten, as she confessed: "I'm grateful that Richard remained professional with me and didn't press his luck until much later in the run. In all honesty, had he turned his considerable charms on me early in rehearsals, I do not know what my reaction would have been. He was that attractive." She was relieved when it went no further, but watched Burton bed a succession of women during rehearsals; including virtually the entire cast of chorus girls.

Andrews should not have been surprised; Burton's success rate with women in his younger years was around 95 per cent. And for 32 years, he used the magic he had to play havoc with the opposite sex.

Burton was happy having sex anywhere and couldn't have cared less about the venue. If he couldn't take them home to the marital bed – something for which he had no respect at all – a dressing room couch, a vacant room in a pub, anyone's bedroom or a garden bench would do. He also had no hesitation about calling on his friends and family to cover for him.

He found there was no better venue for attracting women than a film set or theatre stage, and many of his conquests were in his set trailers or dressing rooms. In his heyday, between 1947 and 1975, on average he slept with at least one new woman every other day and sometimes more than that. His promiscuity cannot be underestimated; from the day he lost his virginity, he slept with a different woman, other than his wife, sometimes on almost a daily basis.

So much so that he became one of the greatest lotharios who ever lived, certainly on a par with the great free-loving playboys of the seventies, Warren Beatty and James Hunt, two men he knew well. But they were for the most part single, unattached men. Burton slept with all his women whilst being happily married and strongly attached to his wife, Sybil, making his sexual achievements all the more extraordinary. Where sex was concerned, he had few morals, so it's hard to estimate the number of women he slept with, but the best guess is 2,500.

He was undoubtedly assisted by his alcohol consumption. Like most men, he discovered that his inhibitions completely disappeared when he was under the influence. Allied with his great charm, his extraordinary voice and good looks, he found the more women he asked, the more succumbed – it was as simple as that. The actress Mary Ure said of his seduction technique: "Other men can spend days or weeks getting to the point, but not Rich. He has a system which always gets results."

Being in the acting profession meant there was always a good supply of women available. Many of these women were of good character but fell in with the easy sexual atmosphere that existed around most stage and film sets.

He had no shame about the women he seduced either. The wives of friends were fair game –and, often, with their husbands not far away. And he never made excuses for being married himself, as Penny Junor famously recounted: "He didn't even pretend to other women that his wife didn't understand him; he didn't discuss her – his problem was that his wife *did* understand him."

Ruth Waterbury, his very first biographer, who witnessed his assault on the women of Los Angeles in the mid-50s, said: "But from a man's point of view, he seems to make no noticeable passes. He is just there, and then the ladies are there. He had a kind of availability about him, and the girls come running. He does not implore. He just quietly demands full surrender as a passport to his attention, but during the short period of the romance, he is very attractive. He is solicitous. He directs most of his conversation to the lady and involves her in everything he is doing. He seems to be caught up by her exclusively, and he forgets everything else."

Frank Ross, who produced two of Burton's earliest films in Hollywood, *The Robe* and *The Rains of Ranchipur*, was astounded by the respect women had for him, even when he signalled that a relationship was over: "I have watched some of his girls and you can see they are bewildered, first by their good luck – and then by their loss of him. Yet when he rejects them, they all go away. He apparently instills in them such respect for him that they do not annoy him further. They act as though they had been momentarily blessed – and that's enough for them."

If he had been alive today, Burton would have been classified as a sex addict and probably sought treatment. As he said of himself: "Whenever I see a pretty girl, I begin telling her the nicest things."

For him, love and sexual fidelity did not go hand in hand at all.

Robert Hardy said of his friend: "He was Don Juan, and it was a necessity in his nature to have any female who was not under age or terribly ugly. He simply had to conquer." Burton admitted as much himself: "I was a terrible Don Juan. I would make a remark or two to my leading lady of the moment, and if she replied with good humour, I knew we were going to work well together. And if she showed real interest, then I was going to make my move sooner or later. Usually sooner. I have no explanation of my insatiable sexual appetite. I assume it is the same for all men. Some are able to control it. I didn't want to control mine. I wanted to pursue it and satisfy it." Brook Williams, probably his closest friend in his lifetime, believed it was a lot more straightforward than that: "Rich was simply a man who loved chasing women.

# AND GOD CREATED BURTON

It was as simple as that."

No one could ever deny that.

There were nine principal women in his life; his four wives: Sybil Williams, Elizabeth Taylor, Suzy Miller and Sally Hay; and six mistresses: Claire Bloom, Jean Simmons, Susan Strasberg, Pat Tunder, Jeanne Bell and, later, during his marriage to Taylor, Geneviève Bujold. But in between those wives and mistresses, there were thousands of women with whom he enjoyed more casual affairs.

Part of his sexual chemistry was undoubtedly formed by his transformation from rough-edged, angry boy from the valleys, who could hold his own with rough and tough mine workers three times his age, to a sophisticated urbane individual who, just eight years after leaving Wales for the first time, was effortlessly rubbing shoulders with the likes of the Kennedy brothers, Frank Sinatra and Humphrey Bogart.

Burton was helped in his sexual escapades by his extraordinarily quick wit. He always seemed to have an answer for everything. And just as his eyes were always described as "wicked", so too was his intelligence defined as "fierce."

And he used that innate intelligence as a seduction tool, whenever he required it. His seduction specialty was poetry recital. He used his grasp of the extravagance of the English language to recite verse to suit the moment at hand. If that failed, he tried Shakespeare and, in the rare event that failed, he would sing. When a woman needed wooing, there was no man better at it.

As sophisticated as he could be one minute in wooing a woman, he could switch and use the ruthlessness of any a red-blooded male with absolutely no discrimination and zero emotion.

At his most rampant, in London and Hollywood in the early and mid-50s, he could leave an assignation with no remorse and he slept with many women without knowing, or caring to know, their names.

He could also be highly manipulative to get what he wanted. When he finally decided to go after Julie Andrews in 1961, she described what happened in her autobiography: "About nine months into the run, Richard began to behave in a very odd way. Up until this point, ours had been a good relationship – easy, friendly, both of us sharing the stage with joy, giving strength to each other. Our families were often social and I never once sensed anything between us that was the least bit unpleasant.

"One evening, his demeanour onstage completely changed. He flinched when I touched him; he withdrew from me as if I were acutely distasteful to him. I was utterly thrown by this manner. I slammed on my brakes, so to speak, and continued the performance observing this strange attitude, puzzling as to what his problem might be. Had he had a row at home? Was he tipsy? Was he trying some new characterisation to keep himself fresh? Was he just in a foul mood? But his behaviour was almost calculatingly deliberate, and I became very angry and deeply hurt. I felt demeaned in front of the audience and embarrassed, for there was no mistaking his displeasure with me. I had no idea how to handle the situation. I admit that at that moment I had not the courage to confront him, especially since I didn't know what was going on. As the final curtain came down, I made for my dressing room, and neither of us spoke about it.

"When actors work together, there is a tacit understanding that the show and its messages are what matter above all else. Personal issues are set aside once the curtain goes up. I didn't say anything to Tony that first evening. Perhaps Richard was just having a rotten night. But when he behaved the same way at the next performance, my anger became icy. I then spoke to Tony and he came to the theatre to observe the odd phenomenon. He asked me if I would like him to speak to Richard. I replied: 'Don't you dare. This is between us. I have to figure it out for myself.'

"Tony said that for roughly a week, our performances in 'Camelot' were quite electric. I realise now I was an idiot not to stop the foolishness. I should have asked Richard what the hell he was up to. But I began to sense something, which was confirmed the following matinee when he knocked at my dressing room door. He was all smiles and tenderness, looking for a hug, asking if I was alright. I suddenly guessed that he had been trying to manipulate me into a state of despair concerning his behaviour. I think I was the only woman in the company who hadn't succumbed to his allure – and maybe this was supposed to be my moment. 'Piss off, Richard!' I said to him, surprising myself with my venom. A smile played around his mouth and he dallied a little longer. But I meant what I said, and he eventually got the message. It didn't help matters, for we then suffered through two more miserable performances. But at the end of the third show, he took my hand as we made our bows and said cheekily: 'Who do you love?' I was staggered by his audacity and was caught off guard. I replied something dumb like: 'You, I think.' As the curtain finally settled, he threw up his hands and said: 'Okay I'm sorry.' He pinched my bum, I pinched his and we never had another bad moment after that."

More or less every Burton biographer and interviewer has attempted to analyse Burton's sexuality without any success. Penny Junor tried when she said of his attitude to women: "He did not enjoy caressing them, he did not enjoy their company. He used women to boost his own confidence, to hide his insecurity, to feed his ego, and to make him feel wanted. He also used them to prove his heterosexuality which, like his intellect, he felt was threatened by his chosen profession." But Junor described the opposite of what Burton was. He got absolutely no thrill in the sense of conquest. The essence of his sexual drive was that he enjoyed the act and had an insatiable desire for it that didn't abate until his late 40s. He didn't need to love them, or to be loved by them; nor had he any desire to possess them.

It would also be easy to say that Burton had no respect for women, but that wasn't true either. He put certain women, such as Claire Bloom, Julie Andrews and Sophia Loren, on a pedestal and worshipped them. So any attempt at sexual pigeonholing by Junor and many others with such analyses were fruitless and almost always wrong.

Stanley Baker summed him up when he told of how his wife, Ellen, accepted his proposal of marriage with one proviso: "That you're not like him" And Baker summed up his friend perfectly when he replied: "Nobody's like Richard." Three words that were wholly true; there was no one like him.

Burton's sexual adventures all started in 1943, when he left Wales in company with his friend, fellow Welsh actor Stanley Baker. Both men were travelling outside of Wales for the first time in their lives. They went first to London and then to Liverpool to make their professional stage debuts, although in reality they were far more concerned and anxious about losing their virginities. Both were aged 17 and desperate to get off their mark, but neither of them actually had any idea how. They had both grown up in god-fearing, closed communities, where sex was never discussed openly and where the last thing a parent or teacher would contemplate was taking a young boy to one side and telling them the facts of life. It may sound strange, bearing in mind their later reputations, but that is how it was then.

The closest either man came to sex was touching a girl's top half, over their clothes, of course – any wandering to the lower half was totally unthinkable.

Despite all these self-imposed restrictions, Burton was known as a rampant ladies man from the age of 15. The unimaginable frustrations that were built up over the next three years can only be guessed at. His first proper girlfriend, Cathy Dolan, said Burton was the perfect gentleman and never groped her improperly; a story that all his early female acquaintances confirm.

It was not until October 1943 that Burton began the serious task of finding a woman who would have sex with him. He had the swagger and would never admit for a moment he didn't know what sex actually entailed. Burton and Baker even kept the secret from each other, and neither man would admit to the other that they didn't know. They also gave the impression to others that they did know, which also made the voyage of discovery so much longer.

As it was, whenever they got close, they stopped simply because they didn't know what came next. The ridicule they would face stopped them in their tracks.

After a false start with his Liverpool landlady when he got to Oxford University in 1944, at the age of 18, he was still a virgin. He went out for a while with a girl from Somerville College called Nina Bawden, but nothing happened between them sexually, as the old problems emerged.

He finally lost his virginity at Oxford to an older mature student he met in a pub. She guided him through the process with the minimum embarrassment.

And Burton proved a very quick learner. Once initiated, he never looked back and simply started to make up for lost time. Afterwards, he could barely believe what all the fuss had been about as he rampaged through the female population of Oxford before he was posted to active service in the RAF.

In the RAF, there were two extraordinary situations with the wives of two officers – both instances sailed very close to the wind, and both of which he got away with.

After the war he fell in again with Stanley Baker and the two of them lived near a nurses' home and proceeded to run through most of them.

In 1949, he only got married under pressure from Emlyn Williams who was concerned about his addiction to women, alcohol and cigarettes. The final straw for him was when Burton couldn't remember the name of the nurse with whom he had spent the night and left just a few hours earlier.

Almost immediately after his marriage, he began an affair with Claire Bloom, which took well over a year to consummate. With her, he took an opposite approach; putting her on a pedestal and waiting until it was right to bed her, which occurred over a year later. Bloom was his second serious relationship with a woman, and he seemed to put it in another category along with that of his wife.

His rampaging ways moved up a gear when he and Sybil moved to their first home at Lyndhurst Road in Hampstead. His wife was frequently away touring with her theatre company and her husband's behaviour was witnessed by Stanley Baker's new wife, Ellen, who could not believe what she was seeing as the women came in and out of the marital bed at their home in Hampstead as he collected girls from pubs, cinema queues and buses. His personal magnetism, armed with an alcohol-fuelled lack of inhibition, meant there was a regular supply of women. The disposal of the women after he had finished with them was almost as skillful as the collection of them. Stanley Baker, now happily married, was in awe of his skills, which were without any parallel in his recollection.

Ellen Baker remembered him entering a party and walking into a room containing a couple of dozen people. Soon, no less than three of the women present were in tears when they saw Burton, and it was clear he had loved and left all three in less than pleasant circumstances. Ellen Baker continually marvelled at the sheer quantity of women he got through.

London's women had a rest when Richard Burton arrived in Los Angeles for the first time in 1952. That period is the stuff of absolute legend. In a town that thought it had seen everything, it found it had never seen the likes of him.

At 27 years old, he was absolutely at his sexual prime. He was known as 'beau-about-town' and it seemed that virtually every woman gazed on him with hungry and inviting eyes.

His devastating magnetism was at its peak in 1952. In particular, the frustrated married women of Hollywood flocked to him.

One particular married starlet in her mid-20s, who was never named because of her powerful husband, walked into his trailer on the set of *My Cousin Rachel*, locked the door, took off her white mink coat to reveal only her underwear, and said to him: "Nobody would introduce us because they are all afraid of my husband." But Burton was unafraid.

Pamela Mason, James Mason's wife, recalled Burton saying to her: "Imagine me, Richard Jenkins, being such a hit with these Hollywood dames." Burton told her Hollywood ladies were "sitting ducks" and said: "It is not really a triumph to be a success with these ladies because they have so little opportunity with men."

His main relationship during that first visit to Hollywood in 1952 to 1953 was with actress Jean Simmons, who was married to Stewart Granger. The relationship between Simmons and Burton started when the Burtons were house guests at the Grangers' home in Beverly Hills and had continued when they co-starred in *The Robe*.

Granger and his wife slept in separate bedrooms and, after her husband had gone to bed at night, Burton would get into the house through the flap the servants used to access the wood shed outside. Each night, he would completely empty the shed of its logs to make a passageway through to the flap, which Simmons would have left unlocked.

She occupied a huge bedroom which was dominated by a modern open fire with a flume. Burton made love to Simmons in front of the fire on a big cream sheepskin rug and, afterwards, exited through the woodshed, piling up the logs behind him. Recalling the events many years later, Burton said: "If you dismantle the entire contents of a wood shed, log by log, you've got to be pretty determined to do anything at the end of it."

Eventually, Burton was shopped to Granger reputedly by a friend, and there was a confrontation at Granger's house in his study. This famous confrontation has two versions – one recounted by Granger and one recounted by Burton – and both vary considerably. Burton's version went: "He [Granger] invited me over for a drink. When we were alone, he told me he had something important to say. Then he went behind a desk, opened a drawer and took out a gun. He put it down in front of him, all the time talking about me and his wife, accusing me of forcing her into an affair. He wanted me to swear on the bible that I would never see her again." Burton admitted he duly swore on a bible Granger had on his desk. But as he confessed, he broke his vow almost immediately: "You know what they say about a promise made under duress, don't you? It's not really a promise at all. Still, I was more careful. I didn't want my head blown off."

Granger's version was that as soon as he learned of the affair, he telephoned Burton, who was eating lunch at 20th Century-Fox's commissary. He said to Burton: "Get over here to my den tonight – I know all about you and Jean. You be here." Burton knew that Granger's den was lined with hunting trophies and guns. Granger remembered: "I was going to kill the bastard but I knew he was a tough guy, this Welshman, so I looked for something to protect myself with. I opened the drawer of my desk and took out several rolls of dimes and put them in my fist just in case he came at me, so I'd be ready. He came across to the house and he said: 'Forgive me, forgive me,' and he knelt down and dragged my knees and said: 'Please, please, I promise, I promise I'll leave your wife alone, don't hit me' and I kicked him away and said: 'Get out of my house.'"

Years later, Burton also told a very different story to Elizabeth Taylor. This one went: "He [Granger] phoned me in the commissary and said: 'Get over to my den tonight.' And I said: 'Of course.' I knew his den. There were guns and daggers and trophies, and I thought: 'Christ, he's going to kill me. I don't possess a weapon.' Then, I saw the commissary's cashier opening those nickel coins and I said: 'Here, I'll have two of those.' I went to meet him with those in my pocket. As I went into his den, Jimmy fell on his knees and came towards me, and said: 'Give her up, give her up. I'll give you anything.' I said to him: 'You can have her, you weak bastard', and I kicked him in the goolies and walked out."

Whatever the truth of it, Burton ignored Granger and carried on unconcerned. As well as Simmons, Burton was also having an affair with 24-year-old Dawn Addams on the set of *The Robe*. She admitted it years later: "I was in my early 20s and still new in films, and Rich swept me off my feet and into bed." But that was also fraught with problems.

At the time, Addams was engaged to be married to Prince Vittorio Massimo, head of one of the oldest noble families in Italy. A year later, in 1954, Stanley and Ellen Baker had an embarrassing moment when they were invited to their nuptials in Rome. It was the society wedding of the year, and Sybil Burton, who wasn't invited, asked Ellen to give her and Richard's love to the bride. The unknowing Ellen promised to do just that. When she and Stanley got to the end of the receiving line at the reception, as she was moving off, she turned round and blurted out to Addams: "Oh and by the way, darling, Richard and Sybil send their love." Prince Vittorio turned round and shouted to her: "Well, fuck him for a start." Ellen stared in horror at Addams and mouthed: "Oh no, not you too." As they moved away, her husband said to her: "Didn't you know? It was the talk of Hollywood."

Many Hollywood executives suspected that Burton had slept with their wives. In the end, he was so prolific that they could only joke about it and wait until he returned to England to reclaim their marriages. One even cracked an oft-repeated line about Burton's prowess, saying: "For this guy, the women bring their own mattress." It was a clever gag, but there was also a lot of truth in it.

When Burton finally left Los Angeles to return to London in mid-1953, Hollywood husbands breathed a sigh of relief. It is said he caused more than a dozen husbands to file for divorce, their marriages blighted by Burton.

In early 1954, he began his most dangerous relationship, although, at the time, he had no idea just how dangerous. He met a girl, called Rosemary, in a café. She was just 14 years old and still at school. He was 28.

It happened after Rosemary's father had taken her to a dance at Morley College, on London's south bank. She was bored as her father chatted up local women and wandered off to the café called The Cave, situated right opposite the Old Vic.

Killing time, she was staring at a poster on the wall when a voice suddenly said: "It's Amalfi." She turned around and was face to face with Richard Burton, who had popped in for a coffee before that night's performance of 'The Tempest', in which he was appearing as Caliban.

She knew exactly who he was, having seen all his films.

To Burton, she was another girl, one with big brown eyes, flawless skin, 5ft 4in tall, with thick, dark, shoulder-length hair, wearing a green taffeta party-dress.

The girl was the author Rosemary Kingsland, now 70 years old. She later recalled her first impressions of Burton: "Magnetism, instant magnetism. He just had presence, quite apart from the fact that he was exceptionally good looking." She also noticed his bone structure and the shape of his lips, which she called "striking."

Burton did most of the talking and they started chatting about the poster and about life. Burton was curious about how old she was, but she deflected the question by telling him she was at finishing school. She was too terrified to tell him the truth, fearing he would lose interest in her and walk off. Like many girls before, Rosemary was instantly smitten with Burton. As she readily admitted many years later: "Girls of 14 are very sexual creatures. I was like a little puppy on heat."

They parted after an hour and Rosemary returned to the dance, but not before he had told her about his life – about which she pretended to be completely ignorant so he wouldn't stop. She said: "I would have listened to him just for the sound of his voice."

From then on, she started going up to the Old Vic on term-time afternoons instead of going to her hockey practice, hoping to see him again. She had no idea he had returned to Los Angeles. She recalled: "I'd go to The Cave and drink sixpence-worth of orange juice."

In November 1955, Burton returned to the Old Vic to rehearse 'Henry V' and inevitably ran into Rosemary again on one of her Wednesday afternoon visits to the café – exactly as she had planned. By then, she was 14 but looked 18. She remembered she was wearing a pink woollen jumper.

This time they walked across the River Thames to a pub called The Griffin. As they sat down, she admitted: "I think I was flaunting myself a bit, too. I wasn't being coy." Eventually, he took her back to a flat in John Adam Street. Burton told her it belonged to a friend.

She remembered it had a thick green carpet.

Within moments, Burton had removed Rosemary's pink jumper and was making love to her. At the end of it, she was no longer a virgin.

From then on, they met at the flat every week, mostly on Wednesdays, as Rosemary recalled: "I was having a good time. It was exciting, it was sexy." Rosemary admitted that Burton was intoxicated on many of the times they met.

Years later, David Thomas, a writer on the *Daily Telegraph*, questioned Rosemary closely about the affair and whether Burton suspected she might be under age, she told him: "He certainly liked young women. A lot of his girls were young and boyish-looking, although I was never boyish. But I think it was simple sex appeal. He didn't look at the age. I kept trying to pretend that I was older than I was, so I never thought of him looking at a young girl. I thought perhaps I'd fooled him; that I'd got away with it. So he might not have thought I was as young as I was."

She also described how it felt being a schoolgirl having an affair with Britain's most famous actor: "It was somewhere else, like a different world. He talked to me as if I was an adult, instead of being dismissed as a child all the time, as I was at home." She said: "I thought that when I grew up and finished school, I would have a wonderful life and travel to Hollywood and be Mrs Richard Burton."

In 2003, Rosemary published a memoir that contained a graphic description of how she lost her virginity to Burton at the age of 14. It caused controversy at the time and most people who were asked to comment said they did not believe her story and decided that she had made it up. But David Thomas believed her, and after forensic examination, it was found to be almost certainly correct. There were things in that book that she couldn't have known unless it had happened; especially as she recounted some things Burton told her about his adoptive father, Philip. They were diabolical untruths and exactly what Burton would have said when he was drunk – the same nonsense he sometimes wrote in his diaries when he was drunk – she simply could not have made that up. She said: "When he'd had a lot to drink, he was very, very black and angry about Philip." Burton led Rosemary to believe he had had a sexual relationship with Philip, although he never did. She admitted to David Thomas: "It was mostly drunken rambles, and I didn't really understand what Richard was talking about."

In her book, years later, she realised she was just one of many mistresses and that he was carrying on a simultaneous affair with Claire Bloom.

Around Christmas 1956, she realised that he was married and also discovered she was pregnant by Burton. She said Burton's response was immediate: "You'll have to get rid of it", and he paid for her to visit a Harley Street clinic where she had an abortion.

She admits the pregnancy was her fault and said to David Thomas: "I didn't resent him, far from it. I was the one who'd said: 'Don't stop,' when he wanted to pull out. The reality is a woman is always in control of a sexual situation, unless the man gets violent."

The trauma of the abortion cooled the relationship and it was essentially over until a chance meeting during a school trip to the Old Vic, when he saw her in uniform. It was the first time he realised that she was a lot younger than he had thought. But by then, he knew she could be trusted, and seeing her in the uniform made him want to see her again. As he wrote out autographs for her classmates, he scribbled a note to her which read: "Come to the flat in half an hour; don't change."

The affair started again but this time Burton knew that she was still at school. She told him: "You must have known that I was quite young." He said: "Of course, I knew. But I thought you were seventeen or so."

Rosemary said he told her he was scared that he might be jailed; but said to her it was every man's fantasy to make love to a schoolgirl.

In the summer of 1956, Burton went to Jamaica to film *Sea Wife*. When he came back, they met once more and he told her he was moving to Switzerland into tax exile and wouldn't be back for a year. And that was that – she never saw or heard from him again.

Five years later, she met and married the journalist Gerald Kingsland and became a writer herself. She never mentioned her relationship with Burton to anyone until 2003, when she published a memoir of her life. Under pressure from her publishers, she revealed the affair with Burton. By then, he had been dead for nearly 20 years and she didn't think it mattered anymore.

She was surprised when the publishers chose to put his picture on the cover and the book became something she had never intended it to be.

In truth, most people didn't believe her story – except those people who really knew Burton, including Robert Hardy, who said: "He couldn't resist conquering a woman, and when I heard the story, circumstances made me believe it and I realised that it was Rich. That was Rich operating, including the extraordinary false attack on Philip, which reminds me of the similar attack he made on Winston Churchill."

Years later, Rosemary felt no guilt for her or him, as she admitted to David Thomas: "It wouldn't have happened if I'd had more self control. I think I was just dying for it, if the truth be known. But I was never wronged. And actually, I don't think he did do anything wrong. I never felt that I was harmed."

Burton returned to Hollywood halfway through 1954 and carried on where he had left off. The actor Raymond Massey witnessed Burton's shenanigans on the set of *Prince of Players* and was quoted in the *Los Angeles Times* when asked by a reporter, somewhat tongue in cheek: "Is there any actress in Hollywood that Richard Burton failed to bed?" He replied: "Yes, Marie Dressler." The reporter said: "But she's dead." Massey retorted: "Yes, I know."

This time, Burton left the wives alone and scythed through some of Hollywood's leading actresses, including his leading lady on *Prince of Players*, Maggie McNamara. Lee Remick, then a struggling starlet in the mid-50s in Hollywood didn't even bother to try denying an affair after spending a night with Burton: "He has the marvellous quality of making a woman feel as if she's the only one in the world worth talking to, and its bliss. It really is." Tammy Grimes also admitted: "I was madly in love with him for at least four days. He makes women feel beautiful."

On the set of *The Rains of Ranchipur* in 1955, producer Frank Ross witnessed all sorts of shenanigans with his co-star Lana Turner and a whole troupe of dusky extras that populated the film, which was set in India. Ross famously called Burton a "born male coquette."

Burton naturally wooed and won his leading lady, Lana Turner, and enjoyed sexual escapades with her in his trailer during make-readies. He reportedly said of her: "I didn't set out to catch her. She set out to get me, and I let myself get caught. Why not? Who's going to turn down Lana Turner?" But the affair began and ended with the filming.

His frequent dalliances with the extras led Turner to quip to a journalist: "For someone who didn't like playing an Indian, he did seem to enjoy playing with them."

Frank Ross said after filming had finished: "Richard is probably the most notable seducer of our time. He is absolutely incredible and his powers are incomparable. He is a man who is sexually inexhaustible and, apparently, he gives a satisfactory performance any time, any place, anywhere, under any conditions, and is always available. I have never heard of any dissatisfied woman who knew him."

# BLAZING MAGNETISM

In 1957, his affair with Susan Strasberg was the talk of New York.

On his return to London to film *Look Back in Anger*, he was sleeping with both of his leading ladies for much of filming and one of them was the screenwriter and producer's wife. Mary Ure had pursued him ruthlessly in the way he often pursued women, and it was witnessed by his brother Graham Jenkins, who said: "Her undisguised determination to get Rich into bed was all the more embarrassing because she was married to John Osborne. More than once, I heard her proposition Rich in a way few men could have resisted. For the first time, I could see that the problems were not all one way." Burton shrugged it off and told his brother: "It's an occupational hazard." Later, Mary Ure said: "Richard didn't just want to fuck. He liked to wine and dine and recite poetry. You knew you were only in it for the short haul, but he made you feel the most special thing in his life at the time."

He went back to Hollywood again in 1959 for back-to-back filming of *The Bramble Bush* and *Ice Palace* for Warner Bros. At the studios in Burbank, Burton found a rich new seam of women; he was rampant. Whilst filming *Ice Palace*, he had an affair with 19-year-old blonde starlet Diane McBain whilst also carrying on with the 30-year-old actress Roberta Haynes. It was all out in the open, with Haynes and the columnist Hedda Hopper quoting Haynes talking about Burton in her syndicated column, which was carried in newspapers across America: "You can say that Richard and I are very close friends. Aren't we?"

Daniel Petrie, the director of *The Bramble Bush*, recalls a flight he took with him from Los Angeles to Maine. They were served by a stewardess, who gave Burton a smile. Burton said: "By god, she's gorgeous, isn't she? Too bad there's a rule they can't go out with passengers." Petrie said: "Ask her for a date." It was all the invitation Burton needed, and a few weeks later, Petrie was amazed when she turned up with him on location.

In 'Camelot', he reached the heights of philandering before leaving for Rome to film *Cleopatra*, where he was finally to meet a woman who at least had a chance of holding on to him.

He was only faithful to two women in his life; his last two wives. And that was because he literally ran out of steam on 10th November 1975, his 50th birthday. A lifetime of alcohol abuse and smoking 60 cigarettes a day had aged him by 20 years, and at 50, he felt like a man of 70. He had been burned out by a life of debauchery that had begun when he was 18 and had continued more or less unabated until he was 50.

But he had had a very good run by then, indeed.

# AND GOD CREATED BURTON

# CHAPTER 34

# Fate and fables

## *The scene is set for Cleopatra*

### 1961

Time and time again, extreme fate intervened in Richard Burton's life and was about to do so again. It all started when Darryl Zanuck resigned as head of 20th Century-Fox in 1956 and moved to Paris. Zanuck's irrational decision to abandon the captaincy of his company was never fully explained, but, once again, his actions were to have a big impact on Burton's life.

Zanuck, Fox's largest shareholder, was a very rich man and had dallied with many of Fox's contract actresses. It appears that his wife, Virginia, had found out and was going to divorce him. California's community property laws meant he could lose millions, so he moved to Paris permanently and put his wealth outside Virginia's clutches. He would effectively be an independent producer for Fox in Europe and would not return to California for six years.

Spyros Skouras, the president, effectively took over the studio. But Skouras was not Zanuck, and within a few years, calamity reigned where peace and order once had. Skouras had little flair for filmmaking and sat uneasily at the controls. Groucho Marx said of him: "Mr Skouras faces the future with courage, determination and terror."

Soon after Zanuck had left, a senior Fox producer called Walter Wanger brought Skouras a project to remake *Cleopatra*. He had already bought the film rights to an Italian novel called *The Life and Times of Cleopatra*, on which to base his script. It was a time when films with an ancient world setting were fashionable in Hollywood and, with a good script, could be made with moderate budgets and therefore make money.

The story of Cleopatra was an old fable that had already spawned five remakes in Hollywood. Georges Melies, a Frenchman, made the first one in 1899. Helen Gardner played Cleopatra in a 1912 version. Theda Bara was Cleopatra in 1917, and Claudette Colbert starred in Cecil B. De Mille's 1934 version. Finally, Vivien Leigh played Cleopatra in George Bernard Shaw's 'Caesar and Cleopatra', directed by Gabriel Pascal in 1946. All the remakes were hits and made money, which is why the film kept getting revived.

Wanger thought the story was ready for a sixth remake and convinced

Skouras of the same. All the numbers made sense, so they went ahead.

The story of the Queen of the Nile was apparently irresistible to Hollywood. It was attractive because it contained all the classic Hollywood ingredients: lust, seduction, sex, love, power and the fate of an empire. Its main character, Cleopatra, was not only a queen but also a vamp.

The storyline never changed; when Julius Caesar's Roman army conquered Egypt, Cleopatra proceeded to seduce and conquer him. When Caesar was assassinated, the Roman Empire was split between the inheritors of his power, Marc Antony and Octavius. To unite the nation, Marc Antony married Octavius' sister, but he soon left her for Cleopatra, whom he eventually married. This precipitated a civil war with Octavius, which Marc Antony and Cleopatra eventually lost, and both committed suicide.

Wanger and Skouros planned a relatively modest film which would cost a few million dollars. To keep costs down, it would be made at unglamorous Pinewood Studios, outside London, and be directed by 65-year-old Rouben Mamoulian, with Joan Collins, Stephen Boyd and Peter Finch in the title roles, all of whom Fox had under contract – so far so good.

The first change of plan came when Skouros decided that the film could be a Fox tentpole movie for the 1961 Christmas season. For that to happen, it needed bigger stars as Collins, Boyd and Finch were all B-list stars. Skouros decided that Elizabeth Taylor would be perfect as Cleopatra. So Collins was dropped and Taylor hired.

But it was well known that the 28-year-old was not in the best of health and had become difficult in her demands. She had been an A-list star virtually since she was ten years old and now acted like one. Her contract terms were horrendous and Fox agreed to pay her US$750,000 for three months' filming and US$100,000 a month for overages plus two suites at The Dorchester for herself and her husband, the singer Eddie Fisher, plus innumerable rooms for her entourage and two chauffeur-driven Rolls-Royces.

Skouros was delighted. He called a press conference in Hollywood and announced Taylor's contract. In the process, he hyped up her fee to US$1 million. Hence, she became the first actress in history to earn US$1 million for a film. Skouros got his publicity, but in the process kicked off an inflationary spiral in star salaries that continued throughout the sixties, and landed himself with a whole heap of union demands as seemingly everyone on Fox's payroll in Hollywood sought parity with this new benchmark.

All 20th Century-Fox got for its generosity was trouble – big trouble.

# FATE AND FABLES

*Cleopatra* was now a big budget epic starring Elizabeth Taylor in the title role of Queen Cleopatra of Egypt. Peter Finch and Stephen Boyd kept their roles as Julius Caesar and Marc Antony. Shooting was scheduled to start on 30th September 1960 at Pinewood.

But it soon became obvious that the plan to make the film at Pinewood was impractical, if not ridiculous. Egypt was effectively recreated in the English countryside. No expense was spared; palm trees were flown in from Hollywood and lorry loads of sand were trucked up from the English coast and spread on English fields. Rouben Mamoulian, a very sensible director, was reported to have been astonished when he first saw the city of Alexandria reconstructed in an English field.

Almost immediately, the worst of the English weather closed in and the hardboard Alexandria was smothered in old-fashioned English fog. One day, Mamoulian had 600 extras in Egyptian costume in front of his English Alexandria, but he couldn't see them, let alone film them, because of the fog. After an hour, he sent them home. Belatedly, it was discovered that the English climate was ill-suited to the recreation of ancient Egypt.

Meanwhile, the fog and smog of London was causing havoc with Elizabeth Taylor's uncertain health. She was installed at The Dorchester, with Eddie Fisher in attendance. But straightaway, she was put to bed with a severe cold.

On the very first day of shooting, Mamoulian received confirmation that Taylor was ill. First laid low by the cold, it turned into flu and she missed the whole of the first two weeks' filming. On the following Monday, it was announced she was to have her wisdom teeth removed as soon as she had recovered from the flu. Two weeks later, they were removed in hospital and she took a fortnight to recover from that.

But it was mainly the smog and poor air quality that were causing Taylor's catastrophic health problems. London was a dreary place before the benefits of the clean air act started to make a real difference. Taylor was a delicate person who thrived in the Californian sunshine, and London nearly killed her.

By then, it was early November and she was diagnosed with meningitis. By Christmas, Taylor had not been on the set once, and only a few minutes of film had been shot of what was now a rain-sodden Alexandria at Pinewood.

Aside from Taylor's problems, the film was also having script, management and union troubles. Skouras' press release meant that everyone wanted more money. And all the peripheral problems were magnified by the nonsensical decision to shoot such an epic film, set in Egypt, during an English winter.

# AND GOD CREATED BURTON

Mamoulian kept receiving urgent telegrams from Skouros insisting that he keep filming, even without his star, as he remembered: "It was sheer lunacy. The insurance people were full of nervous chickens. They said: 'Shoot some film, shoot anything as long as you can keep the film going.' Well, we tried – rain, mud, slush and fog – it was stinking weather. We didn't have one inch of film with Liz in it."

Finally, Skouros had to call a halt to the lunacy. Production was suspended indefinitely until Taylor was well.

In January, Taylor got the flu again but by mid-January she was finally ready to start filming.

But now there were new problems. Time was running out and it was apparent that Peter Finch and Stephen Boyd would be needed elsewhere before filming was completed.

But even worse news was to follow. Taylor had finally recovered enough to read the script and deemed it not good enough. She wanted her friend, the director, Joseph Mankiewicz, to rewrite it.

By then, Mamoulian had had enough. He knew there was nothing wrong with the script and resigned in disgust. He swore he would never work with Fox or Taylor again.

Production was suspended again, and the 12 minutes of celluloid Mamoulian had already shot was dumped. Mankiewicz was hired first to rewrite the script and, then, at Taylor's insistence, to direct it as well. By then, Skouros and Wanger were completely in thrall to Taylor and would agree to anything she wanted.

But Mankiewicz was already working on a film project of his own, adapting a novel called *Justine* by Lawrence Durrell. Mankiewicz's agents demanded and got a US$600,000 salary for their client and then another US$100,000 or so in abandonment costs on his own picture. Mankiewicz set about writing a new script, to be ready as soon as Taylor got better again.

Up to that point, Fox had spent US$4 million on the picture plus US$750,000 on Taylor and US$250,000 on Mamoulian, a total of US$5 million and had got nothing.

Mankiewicz laboured throughout February on the new script, consulting with Taylor every day for her approval. In between she and Fisher went to Zurich for a holiday, cut short when Fisher fell ill. They quickly returned to London and Fisher went into the London Clinic to have his appendix removed.

After her holiday it looked as though Taylor had fully recovered, but then the London weather closed in again and Taylor's health spiralled downwards. She went back to bed and celebrated her 29th birthday with another bout of the flu.

By now, she was also suffering from depression and becoming irascible. It emerged that there were deep psychological scars from the death of her previous husband, Mike Todd, in an air crash two years earlier. As she said: "It was my subconscious which let me become so seriously ill. I just let the disease take me." She also made it clear to anyone who listened that she had only married Eddie Fisher to help exorcise her grief for Mike Todd and said she wished she could live in a 'dream world' with the dead Mike Todd rather than the 'real world' with the live Eddie Fisher.

Her condition gradually deteriorated during February, when there was serious concern. The situation was considered so serious that the Queen was alerted and put her own personal physician, Lord Evans, on standby should Taylor's condition get worse.

The smog outside was awful and the flu once more turned into pneumonia. On 4th March, in the early evening, there was a sudden crisis. Taylor's throat had swelled up and she couldn't breathe. She was literally choking to death. Lord Evans was summoned, but it was clear he would not arrive in time. So waiters were ordered to rush round the hotel shouting: "Is there a doctor in the house?" Luckily, there was a young doctor at a party in the ballroom who just happened to be a respiratory specialist. Being told what was wrong, he didn't waste any time going to her room and ran straight to his car, grabbed his black medical bag and then rushed to Taylor's suite to examine her.

That split-second decision saved Taylor's life. When he got there, he saw that the diagnosis was correct and he fed a thin plastic tube down her throat just as an ambulance arrived outside. That plastic tube and the anonymous quick-witted doctor saved her life.

Lord Evans was diverted straight to the London Clinic's operating theatre, where he performed an emergency tracheotomy. On four occasions in the course of the operation, she stopped breathing and Evans got her going again. All through the night of 4th March, 11 doctors, including Evans, were at her bedside struggling desperately to keep her alive. Regular 15-minute bulletins were issued on her condition to the more than 100 journalists and photographers from around the world who were camped outside the London Clinic.

Somehow, they kept her breathing and she gradually regained her strength. Her parents caught a flight from Los Angeles that night and by the following morning were by her bedside. After blood tests, it was discovered that she had a type of pneumonia called staphylococcus. Dr Carl Goldman, the clinic's spokesman, told journalists: "Out of every one hundred who have Miss Taylor's type of pneumonia, rarely do two survive."

But she did survive and the drama was over, less than a week after it had begun.

Her deteriorating condition was front page in all the American newspapers as well as the British ones. In New York, Richard Burton had been shaken by the news of the tracheotomy, especially when newspapers reported that there was little hope of her survival. The last report he read before going to bed that early morning of 5th March was that she was going in and out of a coma and was not expected to last the night.

Finally her doctors realised that it was the London smog that was causing her problems and ordered her back to California to recuperate. When she was stretchered out of the hospital a fortnight later, she was wearing a strip of plaster across her neck in place of the normal string of pearls. She said to waiting journalists as she was wheeled out on her way to the airport: "This scar is my badge of life. I wear it with pride because it reminds me of the time my life was saved."

A few weeks in the California sun and she had almost completely recovered and attended that year's Academy Awards at the Pantages Theatre in Los Angeles, where she was nominated for best actress for her role in *Butterfield 8*, a film she had made the previous year. After all the dramas, the Academy members were so pleased she was alive they all voted for her regardless of her performance. She was presented with her Oscar on stage by Yul Brynner. In her acceptance speech, she was honest enough to say that her Oscar was a reward for not having died and confirmed to a hushed audience that she had come "within a breath of dying from pneumonia."

In New York, Richard Burton read about her recovery and her Oscar, and thought to himself: "What a fantastic little creature she is."

By then, *Cleopatra* was a movie that should have been wrapped and post-production editing completed in time for a summer 1961 opening. But it wasn't. The film hadn't really got started but, even so, it had already had twice its original budget spent on it.

It had closed down for what everyone believed would be for the last time, and the producer, Walter Wanger, and new director, Joseph Mankiewicz, flew home to Los Angeles soon after Taylor.

But no one had counted on producer Wanger's determination. He had become obsessed with the project and believed it could revive the 20th Century-Fox studio, which was struggling after Zanuck's departure.

Somehow, he managed to persuade Spyros Skouras to keep the production going. He came up with a new plan that involved writing off the US$6.35 million already spent; he intended to start again with a new cast and to move production to the Cinecittà Studios in Rome, where he would spend another US$2 million getting it right with a new start and new stars.

He really didn't have any choice. His two male leads were now unavailable and unwilling, and a return to London would have been foolhardy.

Wanger's big problem was recasting his two male leads. Rex Harrison quickly agreed to play Caesar, but no obvious Marc Antony was available.

Then, Wanger went to New York and found that the talk of the town was 'Camelot' and Richard Burton. Queues for tickets were round the block at the Majestic Theatre, and the revised production was being widely fêted. But the biggest praise was for Burton. When he went to see the production himself, Wanger realised what all the fuss was about and also realised that Burton could be his Marc Antony.

Wanger seemed completely unaware of Burton's history with Fox and his patchy record as a movie actor. He also seemed to know nothing of Burton's problem in getting his extraordinary stage presence translated successfully onto celluloid.

After the curtain came down, he went backstage to pitch Burton directly. He had to push through to Burton's Bar to find him and seemed unfazed by the commotion going on in his dressing room. Wanger was intoxicated by what he had just seen on the stage and went for broke. After the introductions, and without thinking, he offered Burton US$250,000 to take the role of Marc Antony in *Cleopatra* and asked him if he could be in Rome for late September. When he had blurted it all out, Wanger said: "Are you interested?" Burton looked at him askance wondering if he was for real.

After a moment's pondering, Burton said: "We can't talk about it here. How about our going over to 21?" As Burton stood up to go, the crowd cleared out of the dressing room and he motioned to Bob Wilson to lock up. Wanger noticed that a tall blonde girl, who obviously wasn't his wife, followed them out and he wasn't really surprised when she sat down with them at a table in 21. No one in Hollywood, not even Wanger, was unaware of Burton's reputation with women.

Wanger and Burton got on well and were soon swapping stories. The 67-year-old Wanger was an interesting man. He was a former president of the Academy of Motion Picture Arts and Sciences and had worked for most of the major studios in his career.

But his main claim to fame was the four months he had spent in jail in 1951 for shooting and wounding a man he suspected of having an affair with his second wife, Joan Bennett.

Wanger's lawyer ran a temporary insanity defense and obtained a very light sentence for his client in an open prison with no gate or fence. He even managed to research a treatment for a film whilst he was inside, by gathering experiences from other inmates. It was released in 1954 and called *Riot in Cell Block 11*. Hollywood being Hollywood, Wanger got out and simply just resumed his career as if nothing had happened.

Burton really warmed to Wanger as he proceeded to outline the history of *Cleopatra* and its future. He told him that a new script was being written and that Mamoulian had been replaced as director by Joe Mankiewicz.

Wanger said he thought the role of Marc Antony should be played by an actor with classical experience and that Burton fitted the bill. Wanger was saying exactly what Burton wanted to hear. He had been looking for a way back to big-budget Hollywood and this appeared to be it. But he didn't let Wanger know that. He just let him talk, and the more he talked the more he sensed a growing desperation in his voice.

So Burton did what he always did when he sensed desperation, he turned Wanger down. In any case, he told him he couldn't start filming until January 1962, when his 'Camelot' contract ended.

In reality, that was when Burton would be needed. But Skouras, a real duffer when it came to scheduling and logistics, as he had already proved, didn't realise that Marc Antony only appeared in the second half of the film and wouldn't be needed until January. Instead, he told Burton he would have to be in Rome for the start of shooting **in October.** He also appeared to have given no consideration at all to the possible outcome of throwing Burton and Elizabeth Taylor together on a film set.

But Burton insisted he wouldn't be available. So he called for the bill and winked at Pat Tunder. His gesture worked perfectly. Wanger put his hand on Burton's wrist and said: "We'll buy you out." Burton knew exactly what he meant and replied, feigning disinterest: "I haven't the vaguest idea as to whether they would agree to that."

Underneath, Burton was getting really agitated and struggling not to show it. The idea of ending 'Camelot' early and going to Rome excited him. No one had any idea of the hard work he put into his stage acting night after night. After a year, he needed a break and longed to get back to Europe, despite the good time he was having in New York.

He had also achieved all he could in 'Camelot', and returning to the stage had just been a way of putting his talents on display for a big money film offer.

Wanger thought about what Burton had said, and replied: "Let me start negotiations and see what happens." He was delighted when Burton rose and proposed a toast to "the future", and Wanger clinked glasses with him and Pat Tunder.

Before he left, Burton told Skouras that, as well as the US$250,000, he would need US$20,000 a week for any overages on shooting. He explained it was what he was earning on 'Camelot'. Wanger just nodded. Burton had been paid overages for the first time at Warner Bros, who had routinely inserted it into his contract. It had made him an extra US$250,000 on *Bramble Bush* and *Ice Palace*, whereas Fox had previously paid him nothing for hanging round Hollywood to complete its movies. The overages on *Cleopatra* would eventually earn him an extra US$750,000.

Although he perhaps should have known better after the disastrous experience of *Alexander the Great* in Madrid only five years before, Burton was intrigued at going into a big budget historical epic. He was also attracted by the appeal of playing opposite Elizabeth Taylor, who he desperately wanted to go to bed with. A mischievous thought entered his head: If he couldn't have Julie Andrews, he most certainly would have Taylor.

After Wanger left, it all went quiet and Burton heard nothing for two weeks. Neither Alan Lerner nor Moss Hart said a word to him. He assumed that Wanger had talked to Spyros Skouras and that the people at Fox had gone cold on the idea. He wasn't unduly surprised at that. After his history with Fox, it would be very dumb of them to sign him up again.

Then, Aaron Fox called and told him he had received a call from Hugh French. Lerner and Hart had accepted US$50,000 to let Burton leave 'Camelot' on 16th September, three and a half months early.

It turned out that Wanger had contacted them the day after he had met Burton. They had decided to release Burton early purely for financial reasons. 'Camelot' was effectively sold out to 31st December, and to keep Burton would have cost US$280,000 against a cost of only US$28,000 to replace him. Added to the US$50,000 from Wanger, they would be US$330,000 ahead. Lerner was, in any case, not convinced that Burton, with his prodigious drinking, would make it to the end of the run.

Two weeks later, Hugh French came to Burton's dressing room with the 20th Century-Fox contract to sign. At US$250,000 and US$12,000 expenses, plus US$20,000 a week overages, it was his biggest film contract to date. And both men knew that there would be at least three months' overages.

Included in the deal was a country house in Rome, plus a household staff and two chauffeur-driven cars. Burton laughed as he signed the contract and thought: "Just how stupid are these Hollywood people?" French simply said: "Now the fun will start."

But as soon as Burton had signed, he felt only remorse as he was having such a good time in New York. Paul and Joy Scofield had arrived from London, and the night before, they had enjoyed a magical dinner at the Plaza Hotel's Oak Room restaurant with Philip. Afterwards, they had all jumped in a horse and carriage and circled Central Park.

The following week, Laurence Olivier and Joan Plowright were getting married and he was hosting their wedding reception in the Bogart apartment. He was also having great fun with Philip, developing a screenplay of Dylan Thomas' *Beach of Falesa*, for which he had bought the film rights from Caitlin Thomas, his widow.

Cecilia and Elfed James were also due to come to New York for the first time in August.

But the next day, Moss Hart received a hand-delivered cheque for US$50,000, signed by Spyros Skouras. Suddenly, the departure from New York was confirmed and irreversible.

So, Burton put his regrets aside and made the best of it. With the deal done, Burton's thoughts turned to Elizabeth Taylor and the excitement that lay ahead. He could barely contain himself.

The family flew home on 18th September, direct to Geneva for a week at Celigny before going on to Rome.

In the VIP lounge at Idlewood Airport, Burton gave his final interview to a pack of journalists who were all asking him about Elizabeth Taylor, perhaps sensing some of the drama that lay ahead. Bizarrely, he told them: "I've known Liz for twelve years. I realise it is a little ridiculous to say that she is a dear friend of mine. Let's say we know one another and respect one another. And we will, I'm sure, find it very interesting to play together."

The following day, journalists made nothing of the Freudian slip. But they might have if they had taken the trouble to check out his extraordinary statement. The truth was that he barely knew Elizabeth Taylor. He had met her five years earlier at her house in Beverly Hills, when she was Mrs Michael Wilding. But she had not said two words to him.

Back in Celigny, Burton turned his mind to the film itself and tried to stop thinking about Taylor. According to his biographer, Paul Ferris, Burton envisaged the film would be "an artistic success and that he would speak well-written lines in a psychological drama in which the vast settings, the battles and processions, were mere backcloth to a serious study of the character of Marc Antony as he ruins himself for the charms of Cleopatra."

But by now, he really should have known that, in Hollywood, what you see is not what you get. But despite that, he was looking forward to arriving in Rome with both anticipation and trepidation.

Soon, his life would be changed forever.

# AND GOD CREATED BURTON

# CHAPTER 35

# Cleopatra changes everything

## *A life changing year*

### 1961 - 1962

In September 1961, Elizabeth Taylor made her second stab at playing Cleopatra and started to earn the US$1 million 20th Century-Fox was paying her. This time, the conditions were more favourable. They were to recommence filming at the Cinecittà Studio in Rome, in a warm, sunny climate. The whole production had been shifted from Pinewood in London to Rome, leaving the hardboard Alexandria to rot in its English field.

Cinecittà Studio had been built by Benito Mussolini before the war and was huge, with every possible facility. Further south, at Anzio, a private beach had been rented for the exterior shots and another hardboard Alexandria had been erected there. This time, there was no mud and rain, just sea and sand.

The script was also said to be in better shape under the new director, Joe Mankiewicz. Or, at least, that is what everyone thought. As it turned out when filming started, Mankiewicz, despite having been on the film for six months, had barely written anything, so straightaway he was writing every night for the following day's filming. It was a recipe for disaster, and so it was to turn out.

Taylor set up home in Rome with her husband, Eddie Fisher, and her three children, Michael, Christopher and Liza, plus the family's five dogs. For living quarters, the family was allocated a beautiful Roman house called Villa Papa, situated in eight acres of parkland just off the Appian Way, not far from the studio. It was a ranch style house with 15 rooms, a heated swimming pool and tennis court. As she suspected they might be there for a long time, Taylor put her two elder children, eight-year-old Michael and six-year-old Christopher, into the American Day School in Rome. Liza, who was only three, attended a local English speaking nursery.

Taylor was treated like a princess by the film's producer, 67-year-old Walter Wanger, who supplied her with US$3,000 'flash money' every week to spend on anything that took her fancy. Every other expense was paid for by the studio.

At the Cinecittà Studio, she had a new dressing room built to her specifications, and her husband and personal staff were allocated a suite of offices at the studio. Eddie Fisher had his own contract with the studio – as his wife's minder – and was being paid US$50,000 to make sure she arrived at the studio on time every day.

Elizabeth Taylor's arrival enlivened Rome. For Italians, she epitomised Hollywood glamour. Italians really appreciate beautiful women, and Taylor easily fell into that category; she was an icon. It meant, as soon as she arrived, the Italian paparazzi followed her wherever she went. They camped outside her house in the evenings and weekends, and outside the studio gates during the day. Whenever she left the house or the studio, they followed her on scooters and motorbikes. She kept the policemen in a continual state of agitation, especially when she got out of her car and walked the Roman streets.

The intense interest in Taylor was not a real surprise. She was the number one film star in the world and had been since Grace Kelly had retired and gone to Monaco. She had seen off upstart challengers like Marilyn Monroe and Lauren Bacall with ease.

Taylor had a beguiling beauty, different from other women. It was a beauty that affected every man she met. To fully appreciate her appeal, it had to be seen in person. Her screen appearance or photos did her no justice at all. Melvyn Bragg described her best, as only he could: "Sex and danger beam off her as directly as the shaft from a lighthouse." And for once, reality was truer than the hyperbole, with Bragg calling her a "cynosure for neighbouring eyes."

She was undoubtedly, at that time, the most famous woman in the world; eclipsing even First Lady Jackie Kennedy in the White House.

As an actress, she was also at the peak of her career. Before *Cleopatra*, she had completed two of her best films: *Cat on a Hot Tin Roof* and *Suddenly Last Summer.*

So who was this one-woman phenomenon with whom the entire world appeared to be obsessed? She was born on 27th February 1932 in Hampstead, North London, to American parents. 34-year-old Francis and 36-year-old Sara Taylor both hailed originally from Kansas. Her parents couldn't have been more different. Francis was quiet and considered, while Sara was brash and the very opposite of considered.

Elizabeth was born with her father's big eyes and dark distinctive eyebrows offset by her mother's finer features. By accident of birth, she acquired dual British and American nationality.

Her father was a very talented art dealer who ran the London office of Howard Young Galleries in Bond Street. His job was to buy art in Europe and to ship it to the United States for sale. Her mother was a moderately successful stage actress, who had retired from the stage in 1926, when she was married.

Francis Taylor had joined the Manhattan-based gallery run by his Uncle Howard in the 1920s, and it had grown to be one of the biggest art dealers in the world. It was the perfect partnership, with Howard Young running the New York office and Francis Taylor managing the London office. As the European business grew, Francis became very wealthy when he met the British artist Augustus John. John specialised in post-impressionist works but had no exposure in the United States, the biggest market of all. Meeting John was the pivotal moment in Francis Taylor's life, and he did not waste it.

Taylor was immediately struck by his work when he first went to his Chelsea studio in London. During that visit, he found an old crate of discarded canvases of portraits and landscapes that John was about to throw out. Taylor thought they were excellent works and asked if he could buy them. What happened in the next five minutes changed Taylor's life. John said: "They're not for sale." When Taylor asked why not, he said: "They're not any good." He replied: "Then may I take them?" "With my blessings," said John, delighted to be rid of them.

Taylor sent the canvases to Howard Young in Manhattan, where they were sold immediately for huge sums. After that, Howard Young Galleries became Augustus John's exclusive agent in the United States and everyone, including the artist, became very rich from it. Taylor eventually amassed a substantial personal fortune which enabled his family to live in some style in a six-bedroomed mansion in Hampstead and to be looked after by half a dozen servants.

Relieved of any household duties, Taylor's mother, Sara, focused on her children. She became extremely pushy and her style was to treat Elizabeth and her elder brother, Howard, as adults as soon as they were old enough to understand. Elizabeth began ballet lessons at only three years old and developed great poise at an early age. It was also clear she was going to be a great beauty; her double-width eyelashes and huge, violet-coloured eyes were described by her mother as "otherworldly."

Her father was very astute and, in 1938 and 1939, whilst travelling extensively in Europe and selling art to people like Hermann Goering and other Nazi leaders, he saw the writing on the wall and quit England, selling up in early 1939. He was therefore able to leave with his fortune intact before prices plummeted a few months later, when war was declared.

The Taylor family re-settled in Los Angeles, California, and Francis established a west coast office for the gallery.

By chance, Sara Taylor became friendly with a wealthy English girl called Andrea Berens, who happened to be engaged to Cheever Cowden, the chairman of Universal Pictures. Berens thought Elizabeth was an extraordinary child and introduced her to Cowden, who was dazzled by Elizabeth's breathtaking dark looks. A film test was quickly arranged and she proved to be a natural. On 18th September 1941, Universal signed her on a six-month rolling contract at US$100 a week. Sara Taylor hired David Selzncik's brother, Myron, as her daughter's agent.

She appeared in her first film, called *There's One Born Every Minute*, at the age of nine. But it proved to be her only film at Universal. Inexplicably, the studio didn't renew her six-month contract. It was the decision of Edward Muhl, Universal's production chief, who had taken a strong dislike to Elizabeth's mother, Sara. He famously said of Elizabeth: "She can't sing, she can't dance, she can't perform and, what's more, her mother has to be one of the most unbearable women it has been my displeasure to meet."

But Sara Taylor was Elizabeth's indispensable manager, PR lady and chaperone, and Muhl's inability to get on with her and his inexplicable decision to fire her had dire consequences for Universal. But for Taylor, her sacking at the age of nine proved to be her lucky break, when, eight months later, in October 1942, Metro-Goldwyn-Mayer paid her US$1,200 for *Lassie Come Home*, turning her into a star at the age of ten. She followed it up with *National Velvet* in 1944. The film was a huge hit.

After that, she was signed to a US$3,000 a week deal at MGM and she never looked back, making 28 films between then and her 28th birthday. In between, she was nominated for four best actress Oscars, picking up the award once and earning herself an estimated US$2 million.

Her life was lived like a dream, as Melvyn Bragg described it: "Elizabeth grew up in a fantasy land. She was like a princess in a fabulous story, pampered and petted, schemed over and manipulated, made to please as exactingly as the foot of a Chinese child would be strap-bandaged to perfect tininess. It is no exaggeration to say that she belonged to the nation. They treated her as the fairy sister, daughter of the family – to be idolised and idealised."

But it was too good to be true. No human being could have that much adulation, fame and wealth and not be adversely affected. The success, at so young an age, distorted her personality and she developed some character defects which eventually manifested themselves in seven husbands and eight marriages.

The character defects were not congenital but acquired through her extraordinary life pattern. Inevitably, great fame and great wealth did not lead to happiness and she started drinking too much. She was a delicate person and could not stand the damage that alcohol inflicted. She was also susceptible to cold weather. She thrived in hot climates and declined in cold ones. She could also be very accident prone and some of her accidents were truly bizarre, such as one recounted by journalist Paul Ferris: "Dancing a rumba with Joe Mankiewicz at a party, she stepped on a match, which ignited and set fire to the ostrich-feather fringe on her dress and musicians leaped to her aid."

She also picked up husbands and marriages almost effortlessly. By the age of 18 she had married her first husband, Nicky Hilton, thinking it was for life. She famously said: "Your heart knows when you meet the right man." And added: "There is no doubt that Nicky is the one I want to spend my life with."

On paper, Hilton sounded good. He was the son of legendary hotelier Connie Hilton. But Hilton, busy building his great hotel empire, had never given his son much of his time. When he grew older, he compensated by indulging him with everything he desired. He was spoilt and became a violent gambler; he also developed mental problems.

The marriage lasted eight months and Taylor quickly moved on to husband number two, a good-looking, charming English actor called Michael Wilding, who was twice her age. They had two sons, Michael and Christopher, before that marriage collapsed, and, in 1957, she moved on to husband number three, impresario Michael Todd. He was also twice her age and divorced. But it was third time lucky for Taylor, and this time it was the real thing. Todd was the love of her life, and they had a dreamy few years together. Todd produced the film *Around The World In Eighty Days* and earned millions of dollars from it. Todd lavished gifts on his wife, including very expensive jewellery. It led to the start of a fabulous jewel collection that remains intact to this day. She found she loved to receive presents and would almost demand them from her many admirers. She gave birth to a daughter they called Liza.

Taylor developed her personality under the tutelage of Todd. Although she was not an intellectual, he imbued her with shrewdness, cunning and life lessons she never forgot. She, like him, became a vociferous reader.

But it was all shattered when, fourteen months later, he was killed in a crash in his private plane. Taylor's life collapsed and she was dealt a blow from which she never fully recovered. On the rebound, in grief, she turned to Todd's best friend, singer Eddie Fisher, for support and inadvertently broke up his marriage to actress Debbie Reynolds when Fisher became besotted with her. They married on 13th May 1959, the same day Reynolds divorced him. America deemed it unseemly and, for the first time in her life, Taylor faced a hostile press. Although she and Fisher were happy and compatible, the marriage was a huge mistake and it made her grief for Todd worse rather than better.

After Todd's death, she decided to dedicate her life to money and success. She became very self-absorbed and acutely aware of herself. One of her major preoccupations became sitting in front of a mirror trying out new looks to impress film producers. It worked, and she was offered more and more money to appear in films – until she was easily the highest paid actress in the world.

Ultimately, there was a price to pay for all the success. By the age of 29, she started to exhibit severe prima donna tendencies. By then, she had the power to make or break Hollywood studios, and when she was signed up to play Cleopatra, she almost broke 20th Century-Fox with demands that crippled the production in London and led them to Rome in September 1961.

So it is true to say that Richard Burton could have had no idea what he was getting himself into when he and his family arrived in Rome in the last week of September 1961.

Richard, Sybil and the children, Kate and Jessica, plus a nanny and Ivor and Gwen Jenkins drove down in two cars from his house in Celigny, ready for a long stay in Rome. They were allocated a handsome villa off the Appian Way and quickly settled in, attended to by servants.

Burton was surprised when he wasn't called to the studio to begin work straightaway, as usually happened. But when the script outline and schedule arrived, it soon became apparent why he hadn't been called upon. There was nothing for him to do, and there wouldn't be for several months. He had been called too early. His character, Marc Antony, didn't appear until the second half of the film, which, as far as Burton could see from the schedule, didn't start filming until January. He quickly worked out that Fox would be paying him US$250,000 to lounge around for three months in luxury. After three months, he was on US$20,000 a week overtime. He decided that in those circumstances, he would not make an issue out of it.

At first, it was a welcome rest after New York, but soon he got thoroughly bored and frustrated by the weeks of inactivity. He called it "expense-account boredom" and invited all his friends to come and stay at the villa to relieve the tedium. Rachel Roberts, Caitlin Thomas and Stanley Baker all answered the call, along with most of the Jenkins family. He also arranged for Roddy McDowall, who was playing Octavian in the film, to vacate his hotel and come live at the house.

Philip Burton also visited Rome, arriving from New York, in November. Burton prepared a big welcome for him at the house and arranged for Rex Harrison, Rachel Roberts, Hume Cronyn, Jessica Tandy and Ricardo Montalban to come to meet him. Cronyn and Tandy liked Philip so much they gave a lavish dinner party for his 57th birthday. Burton had principally invited him to Rome to read the script of *Cleopatra* and to coach him in the part. But he could only view the script that had been completed, which wasn't very much, and Philip said: "I thought it better than I had expected, and I found the sets for the film to be unbelievably impressive in size, lavishness and attention to detail."

When Philip flew off to London, Burton got bored again and started granting interviews to journalists, just to give him something to do. When one journalist, who hadn't been briefed, asked him what he was doing in Rome, Burton stared at him before answering and said finally: "I've got to don my breastplate once more to play opposite Miss Tits." The journalist had no idea what he was talking about and just reported it verbatim in his newspaper the following day, much to Burton's amusement. Luckily, Elizabeth Taylor thought it was funny.

The only relief came when Burton got permission from Joe Mankiewicz to go to New York for a week to appear in a television special on CBS about Alan Jay Lerner and Frederick Loewe. Sybil joined him for the weekend.

To wile away his days, Burton spent some time on the set of *Eve*, which was also filming at the Cinecittà Studio and being directed by Joseph Losey. It starred Stanley Baker and the 32-year-old French actress Jeanne Moreau. Losey was distraught when he saw Burton on the set and was terrified he would begin a scandalous affair with Jeanne Moreau and wreck his film. Baker warned Burton off and stood guard over the deeply sensual and ethereal Moreau.

When he saw Burton making eyes at Moreau, Losey became so frightened that he banned him from his set. Interestingly, despite the concerns of Losey, Mankiewicz, who watched Burton lust over Moreau with some amusement, showed no apparent concern about any disruptive effect Burton might have on the female star in his film.

Meanwhile, Joe Mankiewicz was busy shooting with Elizabeth Taylor and Rex Harrison, and he called Burton onto the set only sporadically. One day, while watching Taylor perform, he commented to Joe Mankiewicz: "I expect she shaves."

# AND GOD CREATED BURTON

In the 19 weeks in Rome between September and December, Burton spent only five days on the set. But it was time enough to observe that there were already flaws in Mankiewicz's direction. Burton recognised one problem very quickly as a result of his nasty experience on *Alexander the Great* seven years earlier; Mankiewicz was both director by day and screenplay writer by night. It hadn't worked in *Alexander* and it wasn't working in *Cleopatra*. Doing both jobs was too big a strain on Mankiewicz, and neither could be done properly.

But the worst problem was the lack of a finished script. Mankiewicz was directing by day and writing by night for the following day's shooting. He couldn't understand why the studio had let production begin without a completed script – it was one of the first rules of filmmaking. In truth, the script was only a page or two ahead of the camera, leaving the actors very little time to learn their lines.

Very quickly, Mankiewicz couldn't see the wood from the trees and began crafting an overlong epic without a strong enough human storyline. It was exactly what had killed *Alexander the Great.*

Burton was also unimpressed with the management style of Walter Wanger. It was clear to Burton that millions of dollars were being spent on the film without much regard as to why or how. One consequence of moving filming from London to Rome was that it had become a licence for every Italian connected to the movie industry to overcharge Fox for their services. Hundreds of extras, who never donned a costume and never appeared on film, ate three square meals every day at Fox's expense at the commissary and still queued up and collected US$50 each evening. As the writer Sheridan Morley observed: "The Italian film industry knew a gift from heaven when it saw one coming over the Atlantic."

As regards actual day-to-day producing chores, Walter Wanger proved absolutely hopeless and clueless. The budget had now ballooned to US$15.2 million and US$500,000 was being sent to Rome every week by 20th Century-Fox. Fox could only afford it because it had sold off half of its Century City back lot to developers.

As early as November 1961, Peter Levathes, a Fox vice president, told Wanger: "We are the laughing stock of the industry; this is the greatest disaster in show business." If Levathes had had the power to sack Wanger, he would have done. The main problem of cost continued as shooting carried on without a finished script, and no one felt able to control Mankiewicz. Spyros Skouras flew in and held court at a huge suite in the Grand Hotel in Rome. He appointed a new executive called Sid Rogell to take charge of spending. But Mankiewicz and Wanger ignored him and let him hang himself, which is what he quickly proceeded to do.

Rogell decided to save money by having Rex Harrison's set trailer towed away, ending the rental contract of his studio Cadillac and sacking his chauffeur. From then on, Rogell declared Harrison could use his studio dressing room and drive himself. Harrison, a big star, went on strike and said he would be leaving the film. A meeting was hastily called and Harrison, knowing he held all the cards, blasted Rogell and told him he would not work until his trailer was towed back and his Cadillac and driver returned. If Harrison had carried out his threat, the whole film would have had to start again at a cost of US$5 million. As soon as he realised that, a shocked Rogell quietly reinstated all of Harrison's perks. As it was, a day and a half of filming was lost at a cost of US$75,000. Rogell looked very foolish when it later emerged that the savings on the car and the trailer would have been less than US$15,000.

But Burton, watching all this, was being paid too much to rock the boat and didn't interfere. Instead, he adopted an air of detachment, even staying calm when he was allocated Stephen Boyd's leftover costumes and shoes, which were all the wrong size. He set out to enjoy his time on the film as best he could.

On one of his visits to the set, Burton witnessed Elizabeth Taylor shooting a nude scene and he returned to his house that day in a daze. According to Roddy McDowall, he was acting "like a man possessed, raving about her beauty." He told McDowall he couldn't wait to get started. He was already besotted with Taylor.

As the holiday season neared, both Burton and Taylor attended the *Cleopatra* Christmas party, a late-night dinner party at Bricktop's, a famous underground jazz club on Rome's Via Veneto, run by an American woman. As the evening drew to a close, Burton asked Taylor to dance. Afterwards, Burton whisked her back to her seat, kissed her on the cheek and wished her a happy holiday. To anyone who had witnessed the kiss, it seemed innocent enough. To others more astute, the eventual outcome, when Burton and Taylor finally got together on set, was not in doubt – the game was afoot.

Burton enjoyed the party so much that he hired Bricktop's for his own New Year's Eve party on 31st December 1961 and invited Taylor and Fisher as his guests of honour. Secretly, he hoped for a repeat of the New Year's Eve of 1952 in Hollywood, but this time Sybil made sure her husband got nowhere near

Taylor as midnight struck. Instead, Fisher and Taylor smooched all night and any observer that night might have assumed theirs was the happiest marriage in show business.

Despite that, Burton just knew it was going to happen; he had never been more certain of anything in his life. He started counting the days to 22nd January, his first day on set.

Finally, the long awaited day arrived; it was Burton's turn to act opposite Taylor in their first scene together. But when the day came, Burton was about as unprepared as he could be. He had been up all night drinking with his brother Ivor and Roddy McDowall and could hardly walk. And then he made the worst possible start, as Elizabeth Taylor herself memorably recalled in her own memoirs: "He said 'hello' to Joe Mankiewicz and everyone. And then he sort of sidled over to me and said: 'Has anyone ever told you that you're a very pretty girl?' I said to myself: Here's the great lover, the great wit, the great intellectual of Wales, and he comes out with a line like that. I couldn't believe it. I couldn't wait to get back to the dressing room and tell all the other girls."

But despite the unpromising start, both Taylor and Burton seemed to know in advance what was going to happen. Almost immediately, they began circling each other on the set. Taylor's unsaid rejection just made Burton more determined and he went in heavy straight from the start, not wanting to repeat his mistake with Julie Andrews.

In their first scene together, he was terribly hung over. At first, Taylor thought it unprofessional and then, seeing how helpless he was, she held a coffee cup up to his lips for him to sip from. As she described it: "He drank a lot, all Welsh men do. And I felt my heart just went: 'Oh, poor baby'. And he said: 'Could you help hold this cup up to my lips, please? My hands are shaking too much'. So I did. And I looked into those green eyes, and it was like, huh, here I am." She ultimately claimed that, with this one simple gesture, a bond was forged and said she found in him many of the traits she had previously identified in Mike Todd; power, strength, intellect and vulnerability.

Burton soon recovered himself and found acting with Taylor very different to what he had been used to. He was amazed at the lack of effort she put into it. So much so that on the first day he went to Mankiewicz and complained: "She's doing nothing, I cannot act with this, it's a plank. And also I can't hear what she's saying. I can't hear my cues, this is a farce." Mankiewicz replied: "I tell you what, come and see the rushes tomorrow, see that scene you've just done." When Burton went to the studio screening room, he couldn't believe what he saw on screen and said: "This magic personality came off the screen." He didn't complain again; he just watched and wondered.

And then, suddenly, it all happened and neither of their lives were ever the same again.

Later, on that first day, Taylor joined Burton in his dressing room. What went on then is anyone's guess. But if they didn't make love that first day, they certainly did the next day. The affair started almost immediately. She wanted him and he wanted her – that was clear.

According to Chris Mankiewicz, the director's 21-year-old son, who was running errands, Burton briskly strode onto the set the following morning and told him that he had "nailed" Elizabeth Taylor the night before in the back seat of his Cadillac. Mankiewicz explained: "I was amused by his use of the word 'nailed'. I hadn't heard it used that way since my earliest days in high school." Whatever the truth of that story and whenever it happened doesn't matter now. By the end of January, it had happened and, from then on, it happened regularly.

Most people connected with the film thought little of the affair. They believed it was just a leading man/leading lady affair that happened on many films and would end when filming did. The official set photographer, Bert Stern, was one of the first to realise that the romance was real and not just a casual affair. He said: "At first, the romance struck some people as too campy; too Hollywood to be true. I remember telling my editor at *Life* about Liz and Burton. 'There's a love story here,' I said. 'What're you talking about? They're merely having an affair,' he countered. 'No,' I said. 'It's a real relationship.' 'Don't be absurd,' he told me."

Louella Parsons, the syndicated columnist of the *Los Angeles Examiner*, and the most influential writer in Hollywood, was the first to break the news and got it precisely right, reporting that Elizabeth's marriage was in trouble and that the ever-tempestuous actress was in the midst of yet another torrid affair that could "possibly lead to the dissolution of not only her marriage but someone else's as well."

No one read Parson's story that morning with more interest than Eddie Fisher, who was back in New York on business. He immediately put through a call to his wife in her dressing room in Rome and asked her to call a press conference to deny any kind of romance with Richard Burton. "It needs to stop, all this talk," he told her. "And you're the only one who can do that." After a few seconds of thought, she told him: "I'm sorry, Eddie, but I can't. It's just not the right time." He replied: "Thanks a lot," before slamming down the telephone. A very worried Fisher caught the next plane back to Rome to find out precisely what his wife had meant. His nightmare had just begun.

When Walter Wanger challenged Burton over what Parsons had written, he replied casually: "Actually, it might just be a once-over-lightly."

When Fisher arrived back in Rome, he and Taylor had a quiet dinner at Villa Papa and there was some very uneasy conversation. Without getting to the point, they went to bed. As they lay in bed, Taylor went to sleep almost immediately, and suddenly, the phone rang. Fisher answered it quickly, so as not to wake his wife. On the line was Bob Abrams, Fisher's best friend, who had come to Rome to visit him, calling from his hotel. He said: "There's something you need to know: Elizabeth and Richard are having an affair." Coming from Abrams, Fisher knew it had to be true. At that moment, Taylor stirred and Fisher asked: "A friend just called to tell me that you and Richard Burton are having an affair. Is it true?" Taylor said quietly, in a whisper: "It's true." And turned her head away.

A week later, Joe Mankiewicz, who was beginning to realise the consequences of the affair, said to Taylor: "What is going on here?" and she replied: "Nothing, we're just good friends." The next evening, Mankiewicz heard a knock on the door at his house at three o'clock in the morning. When he opened the door, he found a dishevelled Richard Burton on his doorstep asking him to help him choose – "Was it going to be the wife or the lover?"

Years later, Elizabeth Taylor spoke about it, saying: "It was so intense. All Welsh people, I think, are extremely intense. Just by the nature of being Welsh. They are musical, they are poetic, they are visionaries, there is something very mystic about all Welsh people. And that sense of poetry and wildness was where I had always wanted to be. I had wanted to be free, running in the rain on the grass, and nothing to tether me, I just wanted to go. And Richard and I went that route together. And neither one of us pulled the other back. We just went forward. We were soul mates."

Ron Berkeley, who was Elizabeth Taylor's personal makeup artist and part of her entourage, consequently observed everything at close hand and recalled: "Elizabeth was not used to assertive men. Oh, they might put on an act for a while, but they nearly all ended up showing love by deference, paying tribute to her beauty. Only one other man had taken her by sheer force of personality. When she encountered Richard Burton, it must have seemed to her that she had rediscovered Mike Todd."

# CLEOPATRA CHANGES EVERYTHING

Graham Jenkins also believed his brother was a Mike Todd substitute: "He was right; there were many similarities between Burton and Todd. Neither was overawed by Taylor. Both had aggressive personalities and both were capable of extreme extravagance, which Taylor had always found very attractive."

By the beginning of February, within a week of their first scene together, Taylor told Mankiewicz: "I love him and I want to marry him." Mankiewicz was shocked and told no one; he tried to forget that the conversation had ever happened. But he, too, soon realised it was more than just a romance that would end when the movie was finished. The powerful combination of Burton and Taylor together in Hollywood made him shudder. Graham Jenkins said: "From then on, my brother was a prisoner of his own emotions. He loved Sybil and was spellbound by Elizabeth. To act decisively was beyond him. He lived from day to day hoping decisions would be made for him, willing the fates to direct him. He was confused."

But once it had begun, however hard he worked to turn back the clock, he found there was no going back.

And therein lay the problem; this time it was different. Whilst he could easily carry on with other women openly in New York and Los Angeles where no one cared, it was just not possible in Rome. He had never been discreet about his other affairs, and he saw no reason why this one should be any different. But it was the first time Burton had been to Rome, and he had not encountered the famous paparazzi before. Paparazzi is the collective name given to freelance Italian press photographers. They are the best in the world and specialise in taking photos of celebrities. They operate with telescopic lenses and are able to get photographs at great distances, which other photographers would view as impossible. Burton simply didn't realise that the rules of a celebrity affair in Rome were different to anywhere else. He didn't understand that no one kept secrets in Rome, period.

Burton also seemed very naïve about Taylor's special status and her place in the peoples' hearts. He had never encountered anyone with iconic status before. He didn't seem to know what he was dealing with nor just how big a star Elizabeth Taylor was. He genuinely saw no difference in having an affair with Taylor than with Claire Bloom or Susan Strasberg. He had no perspective whatsoever, and that misjudgment undid his marriage more than anything else.

Equally, he saw no obstacles to his desire to gain the ultimate prize of the hand of the most beautiful and famous woman in the world, and he didn't even think about the consequences of actually achieving that ambition. So far, his life since the age of 18 had been a magic carpet ride, with everything going his way. Suddenly, the carpet was about to be pulled from underneath him and he was totally unprepared. Time and time again, he ignored the warnings of his closest friends, Stanley Baker and Roddy McDowall, who told him he was playing out of his league.

Despite Fisher's press conference, the relationship with Taylor remained more or less an unconfirmed rumour for at least three weeks. Most editors thought it so obvious, and Fisher and Taylor's stunt at the press conference so ridiculous, that the rumours couldn't possibly be true. During that period, Burton went to dinner at Villa Papa almost every night, and he continued to do so even when Fisher returned from New York. He continually taunted him in front of his wife.

Taylor loved listening to Burton tell his stories about Wales. And she loved the fact that, unlike her husband, Burton was never worried about staying up late and having a good time.

One night, Fisher returned to the house and found Burton and his wife drinking. About to go to bed and leave them to it, he heard Burton shout to Taylor so that Fisher could hear: "Who do you love?" She replied: "You," and he said: "That's the right answer…but it wasn't quick enough." Taylor suddenly became hysterically upset by his rebuke and left the house to walk in the gardens, leaving Burton and Fisher alone to discuss their situation and get drunk together on Fisher's brandy. Fisher was confused by Burton's continual presence in their house, and whilst he accepted that they might be having a clandestine sexual relationship, he confessed later: "It never occurred to me they were falling in love."

Sybil Burton was also suspicious and was worried early on in a way she had never been before. She found everything was so different to New York. To her, Rome was like a goldfish bowl and everything was so public. At a studio party in late January, she noticed her husband staring at Taylor, and Eddie Fisher noticed it too. She said: "I suddenly looked at Richard, saw him looking at Elizabeth. It was the way he kept his eyes on her and I thought: 'hello.'"

Two days later, Burton, suffering from a bout of depression, pounded his fists on the front door of Villa Papa, demanding entry. The butler opened the door to see Burton standing there, reciting Shakespeare. He entered the house and demanded to see Taylor.

Taylor was hosting a dinner party for 12 guests. Eddie Fisher had already gone to bed and got up to investigate the commotion. According to a person who was at the dinner party, Fisher stood at the top of the stairs, dressed in a blue terry-cloth dressing gown with matching slippers, both of which had Fisher's initials embroidered on them. He shouted down the stairs to Burton: "What are you doing here?" Burton responded: "I'm in love with that girl over there", as he pointed to Elizabeth Taylor. Fisher replied: "But you have your own girl; you have Sybil. Why are you trying to ruin my marriage? Go away; go home." Burton shouted: "Sybil and Elizabeth are both my girls." He turned to Taylor and said: "You are my girl, aren't you?" A terrified Taylor looked at Fisher and then at Burton, and said quietly: "Yes."

Satisfied, Burton retreated as the butler held the door open and then turned his head back to Fisher and said: "Keep her warm for me, won't you?" The butler closed the door. But Burton wasn't finished. Keeping the door ajar with his foot, he came back into the hallway to say to Taylor: "If you're my girl, come over here and stick your tongue down my throat." Taylor apparently went to Burton and gave him a long passionate kiss in full view of her dinner guests and Fisher. A disgusted Fisher turned around and walked slowly back to the bedroom and Burton finally left.

The full story did the rounds of the set of *Cleopatra* the next day.

As newspaper and magazine editors gradually learned what was going on, there seemed to be no other story of interest for them. Nothing in the history of entertainment journalism had ever attracted as many column inches and for so long a period. Cinecittà Studio became the centre of the world as far as the world press was concerned. Burton and Taylor both acquired bodyguards, while the studio gates were kept shut and the perimeter fence regularly patrolled to keep journalists out.

Editors continued to be in denial. They could not believe what was happening. They simply couldn't believe that such a big story could be handed to them on a plate; that two of the world's biggest film stars, both married, had started an affair with both their wives and families present. It seemed so improbable it was hardly possible.

Because of that, 20th Century-Fox publicists' attempts to deny the story had, at first, met with success. Editors believed they were being double-bluffed in order to goad them into giving the *Cleopatra* film publicity.

The improbability of an affair also made Jack Brodsky's initial denials very easy to believe. Brodsky was a Fox public relations executive on the set for much of the film. He faced the brunt of the media questions and had to tell lies daily.

Brodsky's boss in the New York office was called Nathan Weiss. They were two of the best film publicity men in the business. Brodsky and Weiss exchanged letters every day during the production of *Cleopatra*, detailing events in Rome and later publishing them in a book called *The Cleopatra Papers*. Their correspondence became the best contemporary account of what happened 50 years ago. The letters also show what a difficult job the two men had trying to keep a lid on the affair.

Not only were Brodsky and Weiss lying to reporters, they were also lying to their own staff. As early as 15th February, Brodsky was forced to tell the head of Fox's Italian office that there was no truth in the story. When she told Brodsky that Burton was visiting Villa Papa every night to see Taylor, Brodsky looked her in the eye and said it wasn't true.

But Brodsky knew it was and wrote to Weiss in early February, saying: "Burton's affair with Taylor is plain fact and not rumour."

Privately, Brodsky blamed Eddie Fisher for the crisis that had arisen and believed that the affair would have stayed private if it hadn't been for Fisher as by mid-February 1962, Fisher had had enough of Burton and, in Brodsky's words: "Fisher started squawking."

Then, as Rex Harrison described it: "The balloon went up."

Desperately frightened of the consequences, Joe Mankiewicz kept denying the affair to himself – even though he knew first hand that it was true. He famously said: "When you are in a cage with two tigers, you don't let them know that you are terrified."

Mankiewicz and Walter Wanger discussed the Burton-Taylor affair at length and its likely impact on the film in terms of publicity. Both men, by then, knew how important *Cleopatra* was to the future of 20th Century-Fox. Wanger asked Mankiewicz to delay filming any scenes which might be judged controversial, so as not to fuel the fire.

Richard Burton became apoplectic when he heard that Fisher was talking to journalists. Once Fisher talked, Brodsky's denials became very hollow – but editors still didn't believe it. The paparazzi stepped up their efforts to get a photograph that would put the matter beyond doubt.

Fisher himself had felt he had no choice but to go public after his wife had admitted to him that she loved Burton. Somehow, he could tolerate the infidelity – inwardly, deep down, he knew he could never expect to keep the most beautiful woman in the world exclusively to himself – but he expected her to stay faithful to him in her mind at least. That was what he couldn't accept.

Ironically, if Fisher had tolerated the situation, it may well have gone away naturally. But he was complicit in the entire affair. Fanning the flames in desperation, he made the result he didn't want even more likely. His initial reaction had been to leave the house and to move to a hotel to try and shock Taylor to come to her senses. He went to Mankiewicz to ask his advice about what to do next. Mankiewicz told him to return home immediately before the press found out, which he did. Taylor didn't even notice he had been gone.

Fisher would probably have liked to have left Rome altogether, but he couldn't. He was tied by his own contract with 20th Century-Fox, which retained him on a substantial salary with his own office and staff. His job was to organise his wife's schedule and to make sure she turned up to work every day – healthy and ready for filming. It was an obligation which Joe Mankiewicz constantly reminded him of.

Whilst all this was going on, Mankiewicz was desperate to keep the cameras rolling and was having his own problems keeping to schedule. He knew the film had to be finished by the end of June and be in cinemas for Christmas or the 20th Century-Fox studio might actually run out of money and have to file for bankruptcy – the stakes were that high.

Mankiewicz and Wanger huddled with Brodsky to plan strategy. Knowing what they knew, and aware that the story must eventually break; they were concerned about Taylor's reputation and the possibility that the inevitable subsequent moral outrage might endanger the film's prospects. Together, both men paid several visits to the Villa Papa in an attempt to calm the troubled waters. On one such visit, they found a very disturbed Eddie Fisher wandering around talking to himself. He told them he had bought a gun and that he wanted to shoot Burton. Mankiewicz tried to persuade Fisher to leave Rome before he did something rash.

Fisher was eventually convinced to go to a house that he and Taylor had purchased in Gstaad. But when she found out he was leaving, Taylor asked him not to. They had only recently arranged to adopt a German baby called Maria, and Taylor was worried that the German adoption agencies would not go through with the adoption if they found out her husband had left her. Taylor had fallen in love with a three-year-old crippled girl in Germany, abandoned by her parents, and was desperate to adopt her. To that end, Taylor took Fisher away to Paris for the weekend in early February to soothe his damaged ego, and for a short while all seemed well again. But it wasn't.

Eventually, the crescendo of publicity meant it was no longer possible to contain the story and, very quickly, the media began referring to the affair by its own name: "*le scandale.*" Brenda Maddox, Taylor's biographer labelled it "the most public adultery in the world."

The Associated Press (AP) bureau in Rome became the nerve centre of the story and began to fuel it. AP's sale of stories from the bureau suddenly went up over 500-fold. One AP staffer said it was a "bigger story than the death of the Pope." The respectable news agency decided to throw caution to the wind and suddenly became an outlet for scandal and gossip. Once that happened, the story could not be contained and Reuters and the Press Association were forced to follow AP. As Walter Wanger put it, "the snowball became an avalanche."

This time, there was no keeping the newspapers away from Sybil; the affair was on every television show, every magazine and every newspaper continually. As she became increasingly desperate, everyone in the Burton household, without exception, took Sybil's side. If Burton expected loyalty from his friends and family, he received none. They were behind Sybil 100 per cent. His only defence was continually to deny the affair, but even Sybil was not that naïve.

Ivor Jenkins harangued Burton, and Stanley Baker backed him up. They urged him to end it immediately, telling him he risked losing everything he had. Emlyn Williams phoned the house to reinforce the message. The entire time, Burton told himself that it was no different to all his other affairs and shrugged off the warnings, just as he had when all his friends had ganged up against him over Susan Strasberg five years earlier.

But then, on 13th February 1962, Eddie Fisher upped the stakes. He had gone away to Florence on his own to think things over. Almost on impulse, he picked up the phone and dialled Burton's house. He knew Taylor and Burton were filming at the studio and that Sybil would be alone. Sybil answered the phone and Fisher informed her straight out that her husband was sleeping with his wife. Fisher's motives were clear. He thought Sybil would put pressure on her husband to end the affair. But Sybil allegedly told Fisher that she already knew about the affair and said: "Ever since Richard and I have been married, he's had these affairs. But he always comes back to me. The thing with Elizabeth is over."

Walter Wanger was apoplectic when he heard that Fisher had telephoned Sybil Burton. Wanger said: "Eddie broke the cardinal rule as the cuckold in any affair – he called the wife."

Despite what she had said to Fisher, Sybil may have suspected the affair, but she certainly did not know of it. Afterwards, she went down to the studio and confronted Burton. When he did not give her the reassurance that she wanted – that it would not happen again – she returned to the house and told Roddy McDowall that she was moving out and going to New York. McDowall said she could borrow his apartment and tossed her the keys. She left Kate and Jessica with Ivor and Gwen. Her departure was designed to frighten Burton to his senses. The family certainly believed it would have the desired effect as Sybil had never done anything like that before.

Roddy McDowall panicked and rushed down to the studio to tell Burton. Sybil was packing to leave. But there was nothing Burton could do as he was in the middle of filming. He rang the house but she had already gone. Her sudden departure affected him more than he cared to admit and he was momentarily stunned.

As soon as he pulled himself together, he marched off to Taylor's dressing room and told her that the affair was over. He said that Sybil had to come first and that it had been "great fun while it lasted", but it was just "one of those things." When he left, Burton genuinely believed that was the end of it and that he had sorted out the problem just in time.

But Sybil did not go to London as she had said to her husband; she went to New York on her own to seek advice from friends she had made in the city and to see Philip Burton.

Sybil's departure shocked him to the core, especially when he returned to the house that afternoon to find that she had carried out her threat. The rest of the household virtually refused to speak to him.

As it happened, Burton was leaving Rome on a late evening flight on Friday 16th February to go to Paris to film a cameo role in *The Longest Day*. It was to fulfil a long-standing promise he had made to Darryl Zanuck years earlier. Before he flew off he called Ivor, Gwen and the family together and told them he had ended it with Taylor and asked them if they would please convey the news to Sybil and ask her to return.

The situation was made worse when he phoned his house in London from Paris and received no answer. In their 14 years together, Sybil had never once been out of contact. It was also clear that Ivor and Roddy McDowall knew where she was but wouldn't tell him. Suddenly, he felt very lonely and insecure. He was also profoundly shocked as he realised for the first time that he had been monumentally stupid and was about to lose everything he held most dear.

And that might have been that, but, once again, Burton had no idea who he was dealing with when it came to Elizabeth Taylor. She was the world's biggest movie star and was not about to be dumped by the man she loved for a simple Welsh girl, which is how she regarded Sybil.

When Sybil got to New York, she went secretly to the empty apartment that belonged to Roddy McDowall in Central Park West. At seven o'clock on the evening of Friday 16th February, Philip Burton got a surprise when his phone rang and on the end of the line was Sybil, calling to tell him she was in McDowall's apartment in New York.

Philip Burton was totally shocked and unprepared to find the very distraught Sybil on the phone. As Philip recalled, she didn't make any excuses and told him straightaway that she had left her husband because of his involvement with Elizabeth Taylor. Philip rushed out of his front door and walked straight round to McDowall's apartment. He talked to her for an hour as she explained the events in Rome over the last three weeks, events of which Philip had absolutely no knowledge. He then arranged to return and to take her to dinner later that evening.

When he got back to his apartment, he was so cross with his adoptive son that he dictated a telegram over the phone to be delivered to the set of *The Longest Day* in Paris the following morning. It was an angry message, ordering his son to his senses. That night, he and Sybil went to dinner and, afterwards, he put a phone call through to Ivor Jenkins in Rome, who assured him that Burton had told Taylor it was over.

But on Saturday morning, Philip's phone rang early and on the line was an angry Richard Burton. Burton started haranguing Philip over the contents of the telegram, which he said had already been leaked by telegraph operators in Paris to local journalists. Publicists on the film in Paris were already getting calls about it. Burton told Philip he had been "very indiscreet." Philip exploded when he heard that, as he remembered: "Richard's anger was met by mine. As soon as we hung up, I wrote him a very strong letter. I didn't speak to him again for two years."

When Burton put down the phone in Paris, he was shocked by how angry Philip had been. But he was also relieved as he now knew Sybil was in New York, and he set about trying to find out precisely where.

Philip Burton cancelled all his engagements that weekend to devote himself exclusively to Sybil. On Saturday night, he took her to see an old Marx Brothers movie that had been re-released and then to dinner. It cheered her up, especially when he told her the latest news from Rome.

Meanwhile, Elizabeth Taylor had taken Richard Burton's rejection very badly indeed. She was distraught after he left. That night, by accident or design, she took too many sleeping pills. She was so upset and desperate to sleep, that she swallowed what appeared to be an accidental overdose. Her delicate constitution was unable to cope and she slumped into a deep sleep.

She did not report for work the following day, and, when a worried Mankiewicz and Wanger went to Villa Papa, they found Fisher absent and Taylor confused and apologetic. The following Saturday afternoon, 17th February, Walter Wanger returned to Villa Papa to check on Taylor's condition. They chatted but at around 5pm she told Wanger she was very tired and that she was going to bed. Desperate to sleep, she took another big dose of sleeping pills, said to be Semecols.

Wanger, with nothing better to do, decided to stay at the house and he chatted to the staff. When he finally decided to depart, Wanger went upstairs to check that Taylor was alright. She was propped up in bed reading, but said she had taken some tablets and was sleepy. Wanger suggested she have something to eat and so she ordered some milk and sandwiches before she slipped off to sleep.

Vivian Zavits, who was one of Taylor's hairdressers, volunteered to take the tray upstairs. But when Zavits opened the door, Taylor was slumped on her pillows with her head lolling over, fast asleep with the pill bottle by her side.

Zavits, never the most stable of characters, panicked, dropped the tray and screamed at the top of her voice: "Oh my God, she's taken pills." Her screams caused panic in the household and an ambulance was called as events got out of control. Wanger just stood there being useless, and by his own account, just let events unfold.

Someone at the hospital also rang the newspapers to tell them an ambulance had been dispatched to Taylor's house for a suspected overdose.

The paramedics found a surprised Taylor who, by then, had woken up and was befuddled in a sleepy stupour. She hardly knew what was going on. She was rushed in the ambulance to Salvator Mundi International Hospital.

But as doctors discovered when she got there, it was a simple accidental overdose with the previous night's pills still in her system. It was no more than the combined effects of two nights of too many pills by a confused and desperate person wanting to sleep and being unable to. It was not, as portrayed by many later biographers of both Burton and Taylor, a suicide attempt. As Graham Jenkins said: "Elizabeth had indeed been taking sleeping tablets, but with the innocent intention of getting some sleep."

Once the hospital doctors realised that there was nothing seriously wrong, they did not even order a stomach pump. But they decided to retain her in hospital for the next few days for observation.

Taylor could hardly argue with that and surmised that the news would have Burton running to her bedside, and she was right.

The following day, on Sunday 18th February, Burton finally tracked down Sybil. He had guessed she must be at McDowall's apartment and called her in a foul mood after a night of drinking in Paris with John Wayne, who was also appearing in *The Longest Day*. They argued over the children, whom Sybil had left behind. She told him she would be returning shortly and taking them to London with Ivor and Gwen. He ordered her to take them to Celigny, but she refused. In the end, he put down the phone and left her in tears. However, before that, he told her he had definitely split with Taylor and she told him she didn't know if she could ever forgive him.

On Monday, Philip took Sybil, who was unaware of events in Rome, to Idlewild Airport and she left to return to Rome.

Meanwhile, back in Rome, 20th Century-Fox was in damage control mode. Walter Wanger called Taylor's hospitalisation "a minor incident" and Brodsky's subsequent press release called it "food poisoning", which, in a way, it was. Brodsky also suspected it might be a manipulative attempt by Taylor to draw Burton back to her. And if it was that, then it worked like a dream.

It was not until the morning of 18th February that newspapers carried the story of Taylor's attempted suicide and, as soon as he heard what had happened, Burton rushed back from Paris, where he had finished filming. All thoughts of a separation vanished from his mind. Graham Jenkins said Burton had originally planned to go and see Sybil before he heard of Taylor's hospitalisation. As he revealed : "He hoped to persuade Sybil that their marriage could yet be saved. But the pulling power of Elizabeth Taylor proved too strong."

Chris Hoffa, Burton's personal press officer, met him at Rome's airport when he flew in on 18th February. As soon as he got in the car, Burton said: "What the hell else is going on?" Hoffa said he had no real idea other than what had been reported. Burton, in a high state of dudgeon, decided he had to do something about a situation that he had entirely lost control of.

During the half hour journey, he decided to issue his own statement, put together with Hoffa's help in the car.

It was entitled "Elizabeth and myself" and read:

# CLEOPATRA CHANGES EVERYTHING

*For the past several days, uncontrolled rumours have been growing about Elizabeth and myself. Statements attributed to me have been distorted out of proportion, and a series of coincidences has lent plausibility to a situation which has become damaging to Elizabeth.*

*Mr Fisher, who has business interests of his own, merely went out of town to attend to them for a few days. My foster father, Philip Burton, has been quite ill in New York and my wife, Sybil, flew there to be with him for a time since my schedule does not permit me to be there. He is very dear to both of us.*

*Elizabeth and I have been close friends for over 12 years. I have known her since she was a child star. And I would never do anything to hurt her personally or professionally.*

*In answer to these rumours, my normal inclination would be to simply say 'no comment' but I feel that in this case things should be explained to protect Elizabeth.*

The statement then went on to deny there was any kind of romantic relationship between the two of them and ended with the hope that the statement would end the rumours. Hoffa should have known better. First, he didn't clear the release with Jack Brodsky and suddenly, because of it, for the first time, journalists could report the story unheeded, by effectively printing the stories that Burton was denying.

It was a PR disaster, and suddenly Walter Wanger's phone lit up with journalists wanting comment. Wanger was entirely at a loss as to how to respond and finally told callers that he did not believe that Burton had issued the statement.

A furious Wanger called Burton when he finally got back to his own house and demanded that he retract the statement and say that it was the unauthorised work of Hoffa. In effect, Wanger told Burton to "deny his denial." It was pure farce but that is exactly what Burton did, and Hoffa became the fall guy. Of course, the denial of the denial started another press frenzy.

An unintended consequence of the publicity of Taylor's hospitalisation was that Fisher also rushed back from Gstaad, and so Taylor ended up with both men glowering at each other at her bedside. The separation with Burton had lasted all of three days, and people in the know say it was exactly how Taylor had planned it.

By the time Sybil returned, the news of Taylor's illness was all over the newspapers, which were also reporting that Burton was at Taylor's bedside as she recuperated. Almost immediately, Sybil and the entire family left for London, leaving Burton alone with McDowall. And they weren't speaking to one another either.

At Villa Papa, the situation became impossible as Fisher and Burton competed to keep Taylor company in her bedroom while she recovered.

Fisher blinked first and left for Gstaad until Taylor was better. This time, Taylor didn't try to stop him. Fisher, like Taylor, couldn't escape what was happening to him. The *Cleopatra* set, and everything revolving around it in Rome, for a period, had become the biggest thing going on in the world in 1962.

Although there was no sign of Taylor, Burton returned to the set of *Cleopatra* on Tuesday 20th February as though he hadn't got a care in the world. He walked around the set with a glass of beer in his hand, spreading *bonhomie*. As Walter Wanger watched him, he thought: "I realised that a strange thing had happened to this canny Welshman. When he came to this picture some months ago, he was a well-known star but not famous. His salary was good but not huge. Suddenly, his name has become household word…his salary for his next movie has skyrocketed. The romance has become the biggest thing in his professional life. But I don't think he realises that this is not going to be one of those casual passing things."

Wanger was right; he didn't.

The next day, Burton astonished Wanger by turning up on set with Pat Tunder, the dancer at the Copacabana Club he had squired the previous year during 'Camelot'. He showed her off around the film set and in the restaurants and nightclubs of Rome, thoroughly confusing everyone.

The news of Tunder's arrival was relayed to Taylor, still convalescing at home at Villa Papa. It caused her suddenly to rise from her sick bed and report for work that Wednesday afternoon.

Taylor's response to the arrival of Tunder was to remove Mike Todd's wedding band, which she had worn since his death two years earlier. Todd had been wearing the ring when he was killed and it had been damaged by the crash. The removal of the symbolic ring from her finger made headlines around the world. Burton was exasperated and, when the photographs appeared with big question mark headlines, he said to Jack Brodsky: "Jack, I've had affairs before. How did I know the woman was so fucking famous she knocks Khrushchev off the front page?"

Tunder's arrival and the subsequent publicity caused Fisher to return to Rome once more, and he was severely depressed when he found his wife brooding about Burton. He wandered around Villa Papa all day in his pyjamas, drinking vodka and wondering what had happened to his life.

# CLEOPATRA CHANGES EVERYTHING

Taylor was also distraught and told Walter Wanger: "My heart feels as though it is haemorrhaging." Brodsky observed: "Taylor is nuts about Burton and he's on the spot trying to pacify everyone."

On 27th February 1962, Taylor's 30th birthday loomed. She loved parties and getting expensive presents. Burton decided that, in the circumstances in which he found himself, it was prudent to stay away from the birthday celebrations. Fisher saw Taylor's birthday as a chance to rescue the marriage. But for once, Taylor was not much cheered by the lavish party he threw for her at the Hostaria dell'Orso, a downtown Rome hotel. Nor was she impressed by the surprise birthday present of a large Bulgari diamond ring, brooch and earrings from a husband who was trying to buy his way back into his wife's affections. What she wanted most was some sign from Burton, but he did not even send a card and totally ignored the occasion, leaving her distraught. With the Dom Perignon champagne flowing, everybody did their best to have a good time but no one's heart was in it. Walter Wanger left early and thought: "What trials and tribulations she has had – the girl so many envy."

When Tunder went to visit friends in Milan, Burton went back to Celigny to avoid getting involved with Taylor's birthday celebrations. When he got there, he found the Jenkins family had convened a meeting to discuss the problems. Ivor and Gwen Jenkins were already there, but Burton was surprised to find that his eldest brother, Tom, and his second wife, Hyrel, had been sent over to represent the rest of the family. Tom explained to his brother that there was a great deal of turmoil and agitation within the family. Ivor was not as calm and threatened to punch his brother's "lights out" if he didn't come to his senses.

After much discussion, he agreed to end it with Taylor once and for all, and Sybil once more agreed to return to Rome with the children.

Burton returned to Rome and, on the night before St David's Day, went on an extraordinary drinking binge with Pat Tunder, which was excessive even by his standards. He went to the studio the next morning without any sleep and unfit for work. Taylor, seeing photographs in that morning's newspapers of him out with Tunder, phoned in sick and another week's filming was lost.

On Monday 6th March, Taylor returned to work but was in great distress as Burton was still flaunting Tunder on the set. It finally caused Walter Wanger to lose his temper and he asked her to leave. Tunder finally realised she had outstayed her welcome, and returned to New York the next day.

Taylor's response to Tunder's continuing presence had been to cozy up to her husband again, and they had a brief reconciliation. Taylor's reconciliation with Fisher worked as well on Burton as his flaunting of Tunder had worked on her, and the great love affair resumed almost as soon as Fisher's plane took off for his return to New York.

In New York, Fisher was persuaded to give a press conference in which he denied the rumours that his marriage was in trouble and that his wife had left him for Burton. Then, Fisher did something really stupid. During the press conference, he called for a telephone and placed an international phone call to Taylor direct to her dressing room on the set in Rome. He placed the receiver on a hands free unit so that journalists could hear her answer as well. When she answered, he explained what he was doing and asked her to deny that the rumours were true. She thought about it and said: "Well, Eddie, I can't actually do that because there is, you see, some truth in the rumours." Fisher was stunned, and when Sybil read what had happened, so too was she.

Fisher collapsed from nervous exhaustion and was hospitalised in New York, where a succession of journalists went to his bedside and found him disoriented and rambling inconsistently, under the influence of medication. They reported his inane ramblings almost word for word.

As soon as he was better, he left for Rome to confront his wife once more.

In between all this drama, Spyros Skouras flew in to try and make sense of what was going on at Cinecittà Studios in Rome and left again, none the wiser. Skouras was justifiably upset. After five and a half months of filming at US$500,000 a week in overheads, less than half of the film had been shot. But he found the film and events in Rome were now wholly beyond his control. He just hoped for the best and he wasn't the first Hollywood boss to do that.

With Sybil still in London, in a desperate way herself and being comforted by her friends, Emlyn Williams was deputised to fly to Rome to meet with Burton on behalf of Sybil to try and bring him to his senses.

Burton drove to the airport to collect his old friend and mentor. He owed his old friend plenty for what he had done for his career, but this was a favour too big to grant. And Williams had no high moral ground to stand on. Although happily married to his wife Molly, with two children, he enjoyed regular affairs with young homosexual lovers. In the car on the journey back into Rome, Burton turned to him and said very calmly in Welsh, so that the chauffeur did not understand: "Dwi am briodi'r eneth 'ma [I am going to marry this girl]."

Burton took Williams straight to the set, where he met Elizabeth Taylor, who said she knew him by reputation. Williams allegedly said to Taylor: "Why not have a lovely affair?" He said afterwards: "She didn't warm to my suggestion and walked out." Williams turned to Burton whilst Taylor was still in earshot and said: "She walks like a chorus girl." Burton roared with laughter as he watched Taylor indignantly walk away.

With that, Williams realised that it was no casual affair. But on the way back to the airport two days later, Williams still urged his friend to do the sensible thing and return to Sybil. Burton listened and agreed that it made good sense, and told him he would think about it. Williams took that message back to London.

With Sybil gone and his own house empty, Burton continually turned up at Taylor's house in the evenings, often sitting down for dinner with her and Eddie Fisher. On one particular occasion, in the middle of March, after a long day of filming, Burton joined the Fishers for dinner and, once the children were in bed and the wine was flowing freely, he said to Taylor: "Who do you love?" Taylor made no reply. "Who do you love?" he repeated more loudly. She looked first at Eddie, then at Burton and said: "You."

With that, Fisher snapped and quietly got up from the table and went to his car to retrieve the gun from the glove box. But he found it empty. Walter Wanger had asked Fox's studio security chief to remove it a few days earlier. It had proved a wise precaution.

Fisher left again for Gstaad, frightened he might do something he would regret. He had no doubt that if he had found the gun that night, he would have shot and killed Burton, as he admitted many times.

Meanwhile, the press attention was relentless, and Burton and Taylor, with both their spouses absent, decided to confront the press by appearing in public for the first time socially, leading to the famous Fettuccine incident. Burton invited Taylor out to dinner at a restaurant called Alfredo's on the Via Veneto, where they stayed drinking until three o'clock in the morning. Burton famously told Jack Brodsky, in an endlessly repeated quote: "I just got fed up with everyone telling us to be discreet. I said to Liz: 'Fuck it, let's go out to fucking Alfredo's and have some fucking fettucine.'"

But the photographs of them together, with Taylor in a fetching leopard skin, set another newspaper frenzy going and dragged the Pope and the Vatican into the story. The Vatican had been forced to respond to the moral outrage caused by two married people with children openly cavorting with each other just a few streets from the holy city.

The warning from the Vatican condemned the "caprices of adult children... which offended the nobility of the heart, which millions of married couples judge to be a beautiful and holy thing." The statement was read out on the Vatican radio station and did not mention Burton and Taylor by name, but no one was in any doubt who it referred to.

Burton was astonished by the controversy but also found he was secretly enjoying it, as Jack Brodsky recalled: "It seemed to me that Burton was half in love with her and half in love with the idea of what the relationship might do for him. In the beginning, it was simply that she was one more leading lady he was having an affair with. It seemed it was something he expected. He was always involved with his leading ladies, with a couple of exceptions. But this affair was different. He was suddenly famous, as he had never been before. With an avalanche of publicity, whether wanted or not, he was, for the first time, a genuine international movie star. He felt a new sense of power."

When his brother Graham spoke to him on the phone about the statement from the Vatican, Burton told him: "The Pope's never been on my party list." Graham laughed but warned his brother never to make any such remark to a journalist, as it would not be taken well.

After the Vatican had done its worst, Burton and Taylor decided that discretion was no longer called for and they began openly consorting by day and night. The occasional late-night suppers at Alfredo's for the famous fettuccine became regular nights out.

One night, they were leaving the restaurant and some Italian women spotted them and started shouting down the street. As Taylor got into the car, she asked Burton, who knew Italian, what they were saying. He wouldn't tell her, so she asked the chauffeur. Burton snapped: "Don't tell her." Taylor swatted him and said: "Quiet." She leaned closer to the chauffeur and asked: "*Favore*, tell me what they're saying." The chauffeur looked in his rear view mirror to the backseat and said: "Home wrecker, whore, unfit mother." Taylor brushed it off and later told journalists: "I had to be with Richard. I knew it was wrong. I knew it would hurt people. I knew. I knew. But I also knew what I had to do. God help me, I had to be with Richard." Burton said: "We were hurting a lot of people and we knew it. Christ, you don't eat the forbidden fruit and gob the pips in the public eye."

Publicity surrounding the making of the film was now greater than for any other film in the entire history of cinema, and Burton and Taylor's open association made the story even hotter. For weeks now, the affair had been on the front pages almost every day, in every major English language newspaper. Every day, there were pictures of Burton and Taylor together.

Art Buchwald, America's best-known columnist, noted that the affair had driven the talks concerning nuclear disarmament and what was known as the Berlin settlement off the front pages. He said: "There was a kind of international hysteria over the relationship that had never before been seen." Buchwald was right. At the time in the United Sates, President Kennedy was having affairs with all sorts of women, including mafia molls and Marilyn Monroe, but they were never reported.

Amazingly, internally, Eddie Fisher was getting the blame for the affair. On 2nd April, Jack Brodsky witnessed an astonishing four-way conversation between Burton and Taylor and Joe and Tom Mankiewicz, the director's son who was assisting his father with the script. What Brodsky heard convinced him that they had all lost the plot, as he relayed to his boss Nat Weiss in New York: "Can you imagine a conversation where everybody starts putting Fisher down? After a while, I began to feel 'maybe I'm wrong; maybe it is his fault.'" Brodsky admitted he even began to feel sorry for Taylor and her treatment by Fisher.

Italian newspapers now declared open season on Burton and Taylor and the film. On 6th April, the most remarkable story in the whole saga appeared on the front pages of that morning's newspapers. The stories quoted an anonymous but authoritative source claiming for the first time that Burton and Taylor were not having an affair. The story insisted that it was Taylor and the director Joe Mankiewicz who were having an affair, and that they had successfully used Burton as a cover. The source for the story was quoted referring to Burton as a "shuffle-footed idiot." The story, although ridiculous, was reported seriously. Burton could have taken it the wrong way, but he delighted the whole cast and crew that morning by walking into the studio and doing his best "shuffle-footed" impression. He then went up to Mankiewicz, cocked his head to one side, doing the best "idiot" impression he could manage, and said in a moronic voice: "Do I have to go out with her again tonight Mr Mankiewicz?"

But Jack Brodsky took it very seriously and asked Mankiewicz if he wanted to respond. Mankiewicz told Brodsky: "Yes, actually, the truth is that Mr Burton and I are in love – and Miss Taylor is being used as a cover up." Brodsky repeated what Mankiewicz had said to any journalists who asked. Astonishingly, Mankiewicz's words were reported in that night's evening newspapers and many Italians believed it.

But the levity was short lived. The Vatican's statement meant a series of attacks were launched by various publications against Elizabeth Taylor, who appeared to be an easier target than Burton. In France, *Paris Match*; in America, *Life*; and in Britain, the *News of the World* all savagely attacked Taylor, leaving Walter Wanger distraught.

Meanwhile, Burton had started avoiding Villa Papa as Fisher returned and took to the vodka bottle. Burton thought he might be dangerous after Walter Wanger finally told him about the gun incident. So he and Taylor started meeting in her secretary Dick Hanley's flat near Villa Papa. What had begun as a sexual conquest for Burton had deepened into an infatuation and inexplicable thirst to be with Taylor all the time. That had never happened to him before with any woman, and he was in new territory.

Mankiewicz and Wanger finally realised that Fisher's continued presence was now counter-productive and released him from his contractual obligations. With that, he departed to seek solace with an old girlfriend, who flew over from New York to console him. With Fisher gone, Burton returned to the Villa Papa for dinner every night and sometimes didn't bother going home, even though the paparazzi were outside, tracking and reporting his every movement. One night, Fisher called Villa Papa to speak to his wife. Instead, it was Burton who answered the telephone. Surprised, Fisher said: "What are you doing there? What are you doing in my house?" Burton replied: "What do you think I'm doing? I'm fucking your wife." Fisher slammed down the phone.

Meanwhile, Walter Wanger urged Taylor to issue a statement ending her marriage but she refused. The truth was that Taylor was unsure what the future held. It was clear to Wanger that she was still enjoying sex with Fisher whilst she carried on with Burton, and some aspects of their marriage were still very happy. In fact, Wanger believed them to be a well-matched couple in many ways. He recounted visiting the house at the height of the scandal in the early evening, going up to their bedroom and finding them both happily tucked up in bed reading the newspapers together.

Meanwhile, Burton went to Paris to complete filming his part in *The Longest Day*. When he alighted from the plane at the airport, 40 photographers were at the bottom of the steps to record his arrival. Sybil also flew in from London separately and they spent the weekend together.

But they flew back with nothing resolved, as Burton discussed the possibility of a divorce for the first time with his wife. When Roddy McDowall heard that, he had had enough and he packed his bags and moved out of Burton's house to an apartment. He remained cordial with Burton on the set, but was disgusted with his treatment of Sybil, whom he adored.

Meanwhile, on set, Mankiewicz was filming love scenes between Marc Antony and Cleopatra and having difficulty separating the actors after he had shouted "cut." He told the pair: "I feel as if I'm intruding."

On 12th April, there was another bombshell when the Vatican City official weekly newspaper published an open letter to Elizabeth Taylor in its letter pages. It was a vicious attack on her and just stopped short of accusing her of abusing her children and being a bad mother as well as of being a woman of dubious morals. The accusations were picked up and reported all over the world.

At the time, the incident threatened to wreck Taylor's career. In New York, 20th Century-Fox's executives huddled and conferred with board members. There was serious consideration given to sacking Taylor and making what they could of the footage that had been already shot.

Both Taylor and Burton were on very tricky ground legally. In every Hollywood talent contract, there exists what is called a "morality clause." It is a clause that is rarely referred to once a contract is signed, but it is nonetheless very damaging if a studio ever called it in. Fox came very close to that with Burton and Taylor, and if the studio had cancelled their contracts, they would both have been uninsurable and would have never worked again. Fox could have also sued them and probably won millions in compensation.

Somehow, they both avoided censure, with Fox unwilling to take what would have been at that stage a US$22 million write-off. The loss would have been covered by insurance but Taylor was saved only because there was some doubt as to whether she was insured at all after what had happened in London the previous year. Fox already had a big claim of US$12 million outstanding with its insurers from Taylor's illnesses from the closing down of production at Pinewood. But the insurers were refusing to pay the claim, inferring that Taylor had not disclosed all of her previous health problems. Fox was disputing it.

The insurers had refused to confirm or deny they were covering her. If there had been no doubts about the validity of the insurance, Fox would probably have invoked both actors' morality clauses and closed the production after the Vatican article. In the event, all the Fox directors ordered Skouras to do was to write a stiff letter to Wanger. All six pages of it arrived by courier on set the next day.

That night, with the controversy raging, there was, of all things, an industry testimonial dinner in honour of Spyros Skouras in New York. It had been scheduled more than a year earlier. The dinners are the greatest possible honour bestowed on a Hollywood executive. Now it was entirely inappropriate and embarrassing, with Fox's losses and the cock-ups being reported back daily from Rome in *Variety*, the Hollywood trade paper. Skouras realised it and said to Nat Weiss: "I would rather go to my own funeral than to the dinner for me tonight. Why don't one of you boys come up here and put a knife through my heart? It would be kinder than to force me to go to that dinner." Groucho Marx was scheduled to make the keynote speech that was supposed to praise Skouras' contribution to the industry. But he realised it would have been too hypocritical and instead delivered a humorous address, mildly lampooning Skouras: "Mr Skouras is president of a company dedicated to good picture making and some very peculiar bookkeeping." And in a direct reference to *Cleopatra*, he said: "Mr Skouras never made a horror film intentionally."

It was a brilliant speech in the circumstances and some wags in the audience muttered to themselves that maybe Groucho Marx would make a better president of Fox than Skouras; at least he was funny.

Meanwhile, in Rome, Walter Wanger claimed he was at the time unconcerned about the Vatican attack and its aftermath. But he was almost certainly being disingenuous. For a few days, the whole production was in shock. But Wanger was insistent and believed that the American public only "claimed" to be puritanical. And he said the morality clauses in actors' contracts were the height of hypocrisy and that "motion pictures glamourised the same immorality their contracts forbid."

Astonishingly, Wanger also defended Taylor's morality and doubted whether most women had "as strong a code of personal ethics" as Taylor. He also said, laughingly, that not many women would have been able to "resist Burton's charm." He added: "She goes where her heart leads her. Most people don't dare to follow their heart and, in envy, attack those who do."

Wanger's views went to the heart of what had gone wrong with *Cleopatra* and reflected the fact that he had lost control of the production and his employers' money.

Finally, though, Wanger did stand up to both Burton and Taylor and told them they would not be paid on days they were unfit for work. He also told Burton that his valet, Bob Wilson, was no longer to serve him drinks on the set and that he was to remove all alcohol from his dressing room. Burton didn't like it, but he did it. And he admitted to Roddy McDowall that he had a grudging respect for Wanger now that he had finally made a stand.

But it was too little too late as the profligate spending went on. Burton himself was observing the machinations of the filming of *Cleopatra* with growing disbelief. He was now being paid US$20,000 a week on top of his initial US$250,000 fee. As filming ran into April, then May and finally June, he realised that everyone on the set must now be on overages and calculated the extra bill must be over US$200,000 a week. Money was literally being thrown around everywhere as Spyros Skouras gambled his and Fox's future on this one last throw of the dice.

It was no more apparent than in the middle of April, when Mankiewicz shot the big scene in the film where Cleopatra enters Rome uncertain whether she will be fêted or executed. It could have all been modelled with special effects, but Mankiewicz chose to do it live with literally thousands of extras all expensively costumed.

Burton later described how a member of the public eating an ice cream caused it to be aborted: "Elizabeth had to make an entrance into Rome. They built the forum, half as big again as the original forum, I shall never know why. And there were black panthers and there were elephants and 80 nubian slaves who weren't black enough so they were painted blacker than they were. There were 40 dwarves, painted as zebras, sitting on 40 donkeys, also painted as zebras. So they had to start at two o'clock in the morning, making up these people. And the dancers had been rehearsing for months.

"Joe Mankiewicz, the director, said: 'Okay, roll 'em' and we had something like, I think, five cameras going and the whole thing starts and the music starts and the tambourine goes and on come the dancers and the panthers and the elephants, and Elizabeth is on top of this thing and these thousands of extras and, suddenly, Joe says: 'Cut, cut, cut godammit' and then: 'Get that guy out of here.' There was a chap sitting, eating an ice cream in the crowd."

Everything had to go back to the beginning to be re-choreographed and start again, adding five hours to the day. That one ice cream cost Fox US$155,000 extra in costs and overtime for thousands of people. The knock on delays to the schedule as a result wasted another US$200,000.

One journalist witnessing all this was Walter Lippmann, who wrote the syndicated newspaper column, 'Today and Tomorrow'. Lippmann was America's most respected journalist and had won two Pulitzer prizes. He had come to Rome to see what all the fuss was about and to interview Mankiewicz. Lippmann's view of the situation was refreshingly simple and reflected why his column was America's best read, as he said: "All that to-do about Liz and Burton is a good thing. It gets the newspaper readers' minds off the daily world crises."

AND GOD CREATED BURTON

But in the midst of all the chaos, Burton continued to marvel at the excellent performances Taylor continued to give. Her acting in rehearsals looked to be nothing, but when the cameras rolled, she would then characteristically come to life and steal the scene. As Sheridan Morley recounted: "He [Burton] had never come across an alliance of stardom and sexuality in quite such high definition as was then apparent in Taylor. Nor had he ever met anyone who was so totally and utterly the creation and creature of film."

But trouble followed the film around; most of it self-inflicted, with Burton and Taylor contributing their fair share. For the Easter holidays, in the third week of April, the whole set shut down. Burton and Taylor went on their own to Porto Santo Stefano together without telling anybody what they were doing. They were followed by the paparazzi, who predictably swarmed everywhere.

The paparazzi ruined the holiday for them, but that was not the main consequence. On Easter Sunday, Sybil flew in from London to Rome unexpectedly with a copy of the London *Sunday Times* newspaper under her arm. It was the only newspaper Sybil read. In it, there was a huge photograph of her husband kissing Taylor and sitting on rocks in Santo Stefano eating oranges and staring out into the Tyrrhenian Sea.

Sybil read the newspaper on the plane and was in tears for the duration of the flight. She had missed most of the newspaper coverage of the affair simply because she never read them. But she knew that the story must be important if the *Sunday Times*, her newspaper, was covering it in such a big way.

Immediately upon her arrival, she got to the house, which was empty apart from the servants, and called Walter Wanger at his suite in the Grand Hotel in Rome. Wanger realised that he had a difficult situation with a distraught woman on her own in Rome and didn't want any adverse publicity. So he sent his car to bring her to the Grand Hotel for dinner to soothe the situation. He also contacted Brodsky and told him to drive out to see Burton and to tell him Sybil was in town.

During dinner, Wanger was very impressed with the way Sybil carried herself and called her a "worldly-poised woman." She left the hotel, reassured by Wanger, to await the return of her husband.

Meanwhile, the message had been delivered to Burton and he and Taylor cut short their break and drove home in the little Lancia soft-top sports car they had borrowed. However, as a result of the dreadful weekend and the return of Sybil, it appears they had an argument in the car and Taylor made a lunge at Burton, causing him to swerve off the road. The little sports car ended up in a ditch and only narrowly avoided turning over. Taylor's head hit the dashboard and bruised her eye and nose. It was a scary moment for both of them.

They left the car and managed to get a lift back to Rome.

Taylor returned home at 11 o'clock. Her secretary, Dick Hanley, took one look at her and her drove to the hospital, where her wounds were treated. From the hospital payphone, Hanley rang Wanger at midnight and told him that Taylor was in hospital after a minor car accident and would not be able to work the following day.

Meanwhile, a shaken Burton arrived back at his house for a tricky reunion with Sybil.

The following morning, on 24th April, there was a crisis meeting at the studio between Wanger and Mankiewicz as they realised Taylor would probably be away for a week until the bruises disappeared.

When Taylor called Mankiewicz, she told him that she was returning to Rome from Santo Stefano alone when her chauffeur braked suddenly and she "fell forward and hit her nose." Mankiewicz's anger at the blatant untruth was tempered by relief that she had not been more seriously hurt. Burton said nothing. Taylor was distraught by the accident and was worried about permanent scarring to her face. She called her parents in Los Angeles and asked them to come over, and they arrived the next day to support their daughter.

A press release was issued to say that it was a small accident. But this didn't stop speculation raging in the Italian newspapers that it was a second suicide attempt. The real story of the accident did not emerge for many years later when a photo appeared of the crashed car, believed to have been taken by a passer-by, who didn't realise who were the two people he had photographed until years later.

A whole week's shooting, at a cost of US$250,000, was lost as a result of the crash.

Three days later, Burton had another car accident, writing off his Cadillac on the Appian Way.

The situation went from bad to worse when Bianca, Taylor's Italian housekeeper, sold her story to an Italian tabloid. She was immediately fired.

By this time Eddie Fisher had disappeared from Rome and gone back to New York. He was not to return again. He had given up and went home to lick his wounds.

Meanwhile, it seemed everyone was talking to the newspapers. Stanley Baker had also given a bizarre interview to Roderick Mann, the show business correspondent for the *Sunday Express* in London. The story appeared on Sunday 6th May. Baker attempted to excuse Burton's behaviour by saying it was necessary for a leading man on a film to sleep with his leading lady for artistic reasons. He said it was "absolutely essential for an actor to establish some sort of emotional rapport with an actress if any sort of performance is to be given on screen." He added: "I always take my leading ladies out and my wife Ellen knows it." And then said: "How else could one establish any kind of relationship?…It shows in real life and it shows on the screen." The astonishing interview was reported and repeated around the world. He ended it with: "It's hard, of course, for one's wife."

What Ellen Baker thought of the interview was never recorded.

In the middle of May, Burton and Sybil decided to follow it up with a joint interview of their own with the *Daily Express'* David Lewin. Lewin was really only interested in what Sybil had to say. She told him she "understood" the affair her husband had with Taylor but that "there was no question of a divorce between Rich and me." She added: "There never has been and there is not now." She went on to praise Taylor and said she was an old friend of ten years standing and needed her husband's attention because she was "alone here in Rome." She explained: "I was away in London and Elizabeth's husband had left her and she was alone with very few friends in Rome. Should Rich ignore her? Certainly not. He took her out as I would expect him to do if, for instance, Rex Harrison or anyone else were to be alone in Rome."

It proved to be the most incredible interview of all, and when the newspaper arrived on set two days later, Wanger and Mankiewicz read it together, finishing at the same time and both looked up at each other in wonderment. Mankiewicz said to Wanger: "Walter, it just goes to show that if you live long enough, you get to see everything." A speechless Wanger could only agree as they both read the article again to make sure they hadn't been dreaming.

Meanwhile, Taylor had read the article and so had her parents. She had insisted to her parents that Burton would leave his wife and would marry her. Francis and Sara Taylor believed a man like Burton would never do that and that it was the time for some straight-talking with their daughter. There was a row as Taylor told her parents they didn't know what they were talking about, and she cried all night. Her eyes were so swollen she missed two days of filming.

A whole three weeks of filming had now been lost as a direct result of the Burton-Taylor affair, and there was renewed pressure from 20th Century-Fox to cut the film short and to close down.

Both Wanger and Mankiewicz resisted it. 20th Century-Fox president, Spyros Skouras, was in a very difficult position as he strongly suspected that a very good film would emerge from the chaos and make Fox a lot of money. But he couldn't be sure.

Eventually, he flew into Rome to see for himself. He was very concerned about the scandal and the daily bank transfers of ever-increasing amounts of cash from Los Angeles to Rome. *Cleopatra* was supposed to save Fox; instead, it was starting to kill it. So much so that Skouras was in negotiations with real estate developers to sell off more of the Century City site that housed Fox's studios to raise cash, principally to pay *Cleopatra's* bills.

The meetings between Skouras and Wanger were very tense. At one point, Skouras told Walter Wanger he would never work in Hollywood again after what he had done.

Before he returned to New York, Skouras held a press conference and famously made a statement to a noisy room that included the phrase: "It's all rubbish." But no one had heard the question, so they didn't know why he had said it and whether he was referring to the film, the Burton-Taylor affair or the Taylor overdose; and he never had the chance to make his intention clear.

Although Skouras had put on a virtuoso performance for the world's press, with the sale of the real estate underway, it was clear 20th Century-Fox would never be the same again. Fox's financial problems were magnified because it was also simultaneously funding the very expensive production of Darryl Zanuck's *The Longest Day* in Paris – but that was on budget and on schedule.

And as the studio's bank account went more into the red, the ultimate performance of the film became more and more important. Taylor was the key to everything and it became vital that she continued to turn up on set, and the studio did everything it could to keep her happy. If that meant indulging her and Burton and their affair – so be it. As one of the assistant producers on the film observed: "If Taylor coughs, Fox catches pneumonia."

Her discipline and time-keeping got worse and worse, although Joe Mankiewicz dared not complain, as he said: "A late Taylor was still better than no Taylor at all." He found it meant a lot if she could be kept happy.

Mankiewicz was also worried about her health and also her weight. With all the strains, she had put on weight and her costumes had to be adjusted to hide it. Mankiewicz tolerated it but it was detracting from his movie and he knew it.

By now, *Cleopatra* had become a kind of black farce in which the actual filming itself seemed secondary. Both Mankiewicz and Wanger could no longer see things clearly and, in the end, it took Rex Harrison to call for what he termed "cinematic discipline."

Morale had sunk to an all-time low with the realisation that there were still several more months of filming left and that the only public interest now was on what Antony and Cleopatra were getting up to in their dressing rooms – not on the celluloid. It was also patently clear that they had already fallen deeply for each other and that the photographer Bert Stern had been right from the start.

Mankiewicz and Wanger wondered whether they were in fact making a film of the wrong story. Others thought that too, and, in London, producer Anatole de Grunwald was working on a script of the Burton-Taylor saga with writer Terence Rattigan for a new film called *The VIPs*, where the Rome protagonists would essentially play themselves in an airport rather than on a film set.

Meanwhile, in London, the hardboard Alexandria that was still standing in the field at Pinewood had finally found a purpose. The set was bought from 20th Century-Fox by the producers of the *Carry On* films. They did not tell Fox what they wanted it for until the deal to buy it was signed. Spyros Skouras was apoplectic when he heard that the title of the film would be *Carry on Cleo*, a comedy spoof of the serious film he was making in Rome. For Skouras, it was almost the last straw.

There seemed no end to the problems when a crucial day's filming was lost when the unprocessed film was 'fogged' on the plane journey to Los Angeles. It had been a physically demanding scene between Cleopatra and Marc Antony, and no one looked forward to filming it again.

At the end of May, Wanger and Mankiewicz took a calculated gamble. Fearing that Skouras might order the production shut down at the end of May, they decided to shoot the last scene of the film, in which Cleopatra and Marc Antony die. With that in the can, they felt they would have a workable film if the worst happened. But the filming was kept secret, as once Skouras heard it had been shot, he would close it down anyway.

Closure was considered likely as there had been more bad publicity in the United States when a US congresswoman suggested that Taylor not be allowed to return to the United States when filming had finished.

Meanwhile, in Wales, the Jenkins family greeted the news about what was going on in Rome with disbelief and then anger. They were frightened of the future, as David Jenkins said: "We began to long for privacy, for anonymity.

We kept wishing that all this was happening to someone else – someone not related to us. It was very hard to accept, but by the nature of things, somehow, we had to deal with it all."

The Jenkins family's reaction to these rumours, when reports first reached it, had been one of total disbelief. Having had a renowned film star in the family for fifteen years, they had become hardened against the questions of dubious journalists and their capacity for unfounded exaggeration. It was also not the first time that their brother's name had been romantically linked with a co-star, but nothing serious had ever come of the entanglements, as David Jenkins said: "Sybil and the children came first, always. Whatever was happening now was no threat to the stability of Richard's marriage and family. Or so we convinced ourselves at first. The self-delusion, however, was impossible to keep up for long. Unlike Ivor and Gwen, the rest of us had never spent much time with Sybil, but we felt very close to her now. She was Welsh, she was one of us, she was part of our family, and we felt she must be suffering terribly."

Finally, Sybil got fed up as her husband continued to see Taylor and she realised that staying in Rome was untenable. She had behaved with dignity throughout and had refused to panic, staying loyal to her husband. But enough became enough and she realised that what was appearing every day in the newspapers could not all be untrue. She believed her husband to be troubled and confused, and she could take no more. She packed up her belongings and cleared out of the villa and out of Rome, taking the children with her. Ivor and Gwen Jenkins flew out on the same flight and they all returned to Squires Mount in Hampstead.

Ivor Jenkins could stay no longer as he was absolutely furious with his brother and he left no room for doubt whose side he was taking. Before they left, the two brothers had a monumental row over Burton's behaviour and came to blows. Ivor told his brother he was appalled, and Burton was deeply wounded by what his brother had to say to him that day. They would not speak again for two years.

At the airport, an alert reporter spotted the family, ran up to Sybil and asked for a quote. She looked over her shoulder and told him: "It is best for Rich to be free to work out his own future." With that, she disappeared into customs and was gone from Rome for good.

Meanwhile, back in Rome, the tension on 30th May at the Cinecittà Studios was palpable. No one knew what would happen when Fox vice president Peter Levathes arrived with his colleague Joe Moskowitz. People were worried that he was bringing with him Otto Koegel, the studio's chief legal counsel.

But as luck would have it, Spyros Skouras was in hospital having prostate surgery so the three men had come without clear instructions from Skouras. Wanger quickly sensed this and took advantage. Whatever else he was, Wanger was a wily old fox. He may have been a very poor manager but he was the master of negotiation.

They met at 10:45pm on the evening of 1st June at a meeting room in the Grand Hotel, where they were all staying. Wanger told Mankiewicz it was best if he stayed away from the meeting.

Levathes read out a copy of the minutes of a recent Fox executive committee meeting. Levathes told Wanger that the committee had decided to end his contract effective 30th May and was taking him off the payroll, but he could stay on as producer unpaid if he wanted as long as he paid for his own hotel suite and car. He also told him Elizabeth Taylor's contract would cease to be paid on 9th June. Moreover, he was informèd that, from 30th June, money would no longer be sent to Rome and that production would cease at that time, regardless of progress.

For Fox, it was finally a line in the sand.

Then Wanger took a big risk. Judging that they had no real authority to close down the production, he decided to confront the three men and said to them: "I have no intention of accepting this ultimatum from the company. But I do not intend to argue, the picture is the only important thing and I intend to do everything in my power to finish it properly."

The negotiations suddenly became a very high stakes game of poker with Wanger the only player willing to show his hand. Wanger was bluffing, but the three executives were stunned by his response and had no answer.

They returned to their hotel rooms with their tails firmly between their legs.

For now, Wanger had got away with it. Fox carried on sending US$500,000 a week to Rome and Wanger was sacked although he remained in charge, and the *Cleopatra* fiasco continued.

With that, Wanger left for the Italian port of Ischia, where the battle scenes were due to be shot a few weeks hence. When he returned three days later, he found Levathes, Moskowitz and Koegel had not left Rome and had regrouped. They wanted him and Mankiewicz to sign a memo agreeing to the changes. Mankiewicz refused and walked out, but Wanger, realising he had been sacked and that his signature was worthless, signed.

Happy, they all returned to Hollywood a few days later and closed down a Marilyn Monroe film that Fox was shooting. When he heard that, Wanger realised how lucky he had been.

On 9th June, Elizabeth Taylor had the option to leave the film and Villa Papa. But she did not want to be separated from Burton so she continued unpaid and started paying rent for the villa.

The cast and crew quickly decamped to Ischia for the seaborne battle scenes. Taylor went with them to be with Burton. Naturally, the location shoot was a chaotic and expensive fiasco. There were not enough hotel rooms for the 75 crew and cast. Private pleasure boats crowded the harbour, making shooting difficult. And whether any of it was necessary was debatable as the scenes could have been filmed with models in a big water tank almost as effectively. But it got done the way Mankiewicz wanted it done.

The time in Ischia was not without incident. Burton and Taylor were invited onto the yacht of 73-year-old Italian magazine publisher Angelo Rizzoli, who was a friend of Walter Wanger. Rizzoli was a legend in Italy as he had financed Federico Fellini's *La Dolce Vita* film two years before. Rizzoli said to Wanger: "Why don't you take my yacht for the weekend and get away from life's problems?"

Cruising to Capri for Sunday lunch, there was a large party of Angelo Rizzoli's friends plus Burton, Taylor and Wanger and their friends.

Halfway through lunch, Taylor grew suspicious about what was going on behind a curtain that was drawn behind the entrance to the kitchen. When she questioned it, Rizzoli dismissed her concerns as nothing. But Burton got up and drew the curtain back, which revealed a camera man filming the lunch. It was being done for a newsreel company that Rizzoli owned.

Taylor demanded the boat turned round and returned to Ischia. Wanger was furious with his friend and the party returned to Ischia and the film was handed over.

The incident, although never reported in the press, severely damaged Rizzoli's reputation in Hollywood, which had been at an all-time high after *La Dolce Vita*'s success. No major star or director would ever work with him again and he went to his grave, seven years later, full of regrets over the incident.

The filming of the Battle of Actium at Ischia went on. The highlight was the unveiling of Cleopatra's barge, which had cost US$277,000 to build. An exact working replica, it was the height of folly and added nothing to the film.

It was in Ischia that the paparazzi finally got the photographs they were after. Taylor and Burton were sunbathing on a small boat on the Island of Ischia in Italy on 25th June 1962. The paparazzi were on boats with long lenses and they caught them frolicking on the deck.

Finally, the telescopic lenses of the paparazzi captured the evidence of the affair the world wanted. It was the first incontrovertible evidence of a relationship. Although neither Burton's nor Taylor's face could be seen, there was no mistaking them. The photos were flashed around the world.

The publication of the photos proved the final trigger for the end of Spyros Skouras. It turned out that Skouras had told the 20th Century-Fox board of directors that filming had ceased and the film was completed. The photos were positive proof that this was untrue and that Burton and Taylor were still having a good time at Fox's expense.

It was the final straw and, on 26th June, Skouras was fired, paving the way for Darryl Zanuck to take back control. But Skouras didn't go down without a fight. Even after it was revealed that he had been misleading the board about *Cleopatra*'s costs, he fought a rearguard action and wouldn't leave. It took a four-day board meeting held over a weekend at the Metropolitan Club in New York to dislodge him. In the end, the rest of the board threatened to resign en masse, leaving unless he quit. Skouras didn't want to leave in disgrace and finally, he realised the inevitable and went quietly.

Two days later, Taylor filmed her last scene and Joe Mankiewicz shouted "cut" for the final time. The director and his star, an age old relationship in Hollywood, embraced and the tears ran down her cheeks. It had been an extraordinary two years for her, having begun 22 months earlier when she had taken up residence at The Dorchester in August 1961.

But production still rumbled on without her even after the 30th June deadline. There was a final location shoot planned in Egypt for the land battle scenes between Marc Antony and Octavius' armies.

Although Taylor's role was over, she wanted to travel to Egypt to be with Burton. But Wanger, finally asserting himself, refused to risk any more scandal and would not let her travel. When she said she would pay for herself to travel, Wanger begged her not to for the sake of the film.

Instead, Taylor returned to Rome to pack up Villa Papa and her lawyer, Louis Nizer, announced that she was divorcing Fisher just as soon as the paperwork could be finalised. She also announced cryptically that she had fallen in love and expected to marry the object of her new affections.

No one doubted she would; as what Elizabeth Taylor wanted, she eventually got. That is the way it had always been.

But this was never clear to Burton, who was still deeply uncertain of the future of the affair, however passionate and deep-rooted it was. He wondered whether it was worth the destruction of two marriages? Initially, he concluded it wasn't. But that was for later.

In Egypt, the *Cleopatra* fiasco continued with or without Taylor's presence. Wanger had been promised the use of 5,000 Egyptian soldiers of the Egyptian army by President Nasser at a cost of US$1 a day each. But when they arrived, Nasser reneged and said the new price was US$4 per soldier per day. Wanger turned him down and went to work hiring 5,000 locals instead. In the end, once the locals had been recruited and costumed, they banded together and also demanded US$4 a day, which Wanger then had to agree to. It was the final fiasco.

Filming finally ended on 24th July 1962 and was marked with a party at the San Stefano hotel in Alexandria. After that, they all went their separate ways.

When filming was over, Taylor returned to her house at Gstaad and Burton to his at Celigny, where his family awaited him.

Joe Mankiewicz was relieved to get to the editing suite. Back in Manhattan, when walking home one night after a hard day's work cutting film, he was asked by a journalist about the Burton-Taylor affair and how it had happened with their spouses in such close attendance. He answered: "Why did Burton go after the leading lady is the same as why did the cat go after the mouse? Name the leading lady he did not go after."

# AND GOD CREATED BURTON

# CHAPTER 36

# The Contest

## *The end of Rich and Syb*

### 1963

When the filming of *Cleopatra* wrapped on 24th July 1962, there began an extremely painful eight months during which Richard Burton had to decide between his wife, Sybil, and his mistress, Elizabeth Taylor. Taylor had dealt with her husband and Eddie Fisher had gone back to New York, never to be seen again.

The end of Sybil and Richard took rather longer to come to a conclusion – over half a year longer. Eventually, Sybil made the decision for him and also left for New York, never to see or speak to her husband again. But in between July 1962 and April 1963, there was much drama, much pain and much heartache – not to mention much soul-searching – for everyone involved.

When filming ended in Egypt, Burton flew back to Rome, where he was met at the airport by Elizabeth Taylor, who had been anxiously awaiting his return. She had been banned from the Egypt set by Walter Wanger, and it reflected how fed up 20th Century-Fox had become with the behaviour of its two stars. That immediately manifested itself as Burton looked around for the welcoming team from Fox, which he become accustomed to in the past 12 months, but which was now nowhere to be seen. Jack Brodsky was back in New York and Nathan Weiss, who had replaced him in Rome, was thoroughly fed up with both of his stars' behaviour, as he said: "She was at the airport to meet him, but, you know what, I no longer cared because they are no longer any of our business."

Weiss' attitude was a measure of the trouble that the Burton-Taylor affair had caused Fox and how the studio longed to be rid of both of them. They may both have been following their hearts but, in truth, they had exceeded the limits of all normally accepted behaviour. They had left a trail of destruction in their wake and a lot of people with a sour taste in their mouths, which only the passage of time would wash away. In their own way, both Burton and Taylor were good people but, together, their behaviour in that period had not reflected it at all.

Burton's family was also nowhere to be seen. They had removed themselves from Rome two months earlier and were at Squires Mount in Hampstead, London, reconciling themselves to a life without Burton.

After he had organised the pack-up of his house, Burton left with Taylor for Portofino. But Taylor also left with a bitter taste in her mouth. In her jewel box, she had a set of jewels that Eddie Fisher had bought her from Gianni Bulgari's shop in Rome for her birthday, at a cost of US$90,000 – or so she thought. The jewels – earrings, ring and a brooch in a matching combination of yellow and white diamonds – had been presented to her by Fisher at her 30th birthday party on 27th February 1962. But Taylor had no idea that Fisher hadn't paid for them but merely put them on his account at Bulgari. When Bulgari eventually chased up the debt many months later, Fisher was long gone, past caring, and told Gianni Bulgari to send the bill to his wife, which he did. 40 years later, in 2002, Taylor reluctantly confirmed the story, saying: "I received a bill for the jewellery. Did I end up paying the bill? Mmmm, probably."

With that nasty surprise, Taylor got into Eddie Fisher's old green Rolls-Royce, which he had left behind in Rome, and Burton drove them to Portofino in Italy to spend two weeks with Rex Harrison and his wife, the actress Rachel Roberts. They had become very friendly with the Harrisons during the filming of *Cleopatra* and were grateful for the quiet bolt hole that Rex Harrison offered them so that they could sort out their future.

Their time in Portofino turned into two weeks of soul-searching. At the end of it, they somewhat bizarrely jointly agreed that their affair was just a film-set romance and must be allowed to go no further, and, for the sake of both their families, they agreed to go their separate ways. Taylor's version was that she wrote him a letter to say they must part. But if she did write it, she certainly didn't mean it.

If Taylor had been serious about the split, she would have returned to Los Angeles and that would have been that. However, she chose to go to Chalet Ariel, her house in Switzerland with her children for the rest of the summer.

Back then, Gstaad was a wonderful place, a Swiss playground with people like the Aga Khan giving it patronage by building large homes. It is a particularly magical place during the winter months, when it is blanketed by snow. It has great appeal as a lovely one-street village, full of charming wood chalets made better by the fact that the centre of Gstaad is wholly pedestrianised and cars are banned. The ski slopes and walks are linked by three groups of ski lifts. In those days, it unashamedly catered for the celebrities, then known as the jet-set.

# THE CONTEST

Chalet Ariel was a 16-room house built of oak and perched on a crest overlooking the slopes, with eight acres of land.

It was situated in the Bernese Oberland ski resort of Gstaad and only 70 miles away from Burton's family home at Celigny; an easy one-and-a-half-hour drive. It was no hardship as she loved the house she had bought with Eddie Fisher three years before. They had paid US$280,000 for it as a part-finished shell built by a Texan but never completed. They spent another US$150,000 finishing it off.

Her proximity meant that, although both denied it vigorously, they just carried on seeing each other. The secret meetings went on for four months, from August to December, and became a melodrama in themselves. Although he adamantly denied he was still seeing Taylor, Burton seemingly confided his troubles to everyone and anyone, and even *Time* magazine reported on it. It wrote that Burton was "maddened with guilt" and had taken to repeating to himself over and over again that "my name is writ in water" – Keats' epitaph.

Years later, Burton gave many accounts of what happened in those few months and none of them were true, including a very misleading television interview with David Frost. He told Frost that, in August 1962, there was a three-month cooling off period when he and Taylor didn't see each other, and he even vividly described a romantic lunch on Lake Geneva when they finally reconciled in November 1962. His description of events, probably for Sybil's benefit, was complete nonsense and even he soon thought better of it when, suddenly, in mid-conversation, he told Frost: "I'd rather not talk about that period if you don't mind, it was far too personal and far too tormented."

In reality, he had carried on seeing Taylor regularly – as often as three times a week – following a familiar routine of staying out until 3am and returning to Celigny before dawn. Sybil had no idea what was going on and always assumed he had been out drinking with his friends, as he had always done. She had no idea Taylor was even in Switzerland.

There seems little doubt now that Taylor had deliberately chosen to base herself in Gstaad so she could continue seeing him. Many years later, when it no longer mattered, Burton admitted as much: "Imagine the runs I used to do up here from Celigny and going back in the early hours of the morning." Later, Taylor also said of the time: "It was neither one thing nor the other. He couldn't leave his family. We were all there."

In the beginning, Burton genuinely believed that his liaison with Taylor was akin to his affairs with Susan Strasberg and Claire Bloom, all over again. After all, he had been in love with both those women and had behaved similarly, but not once had he thought of leaving his wife. Then, it gradually dawned on him that those relationships had been pure infatuation but, with Taylor, it was real love. Or, as he kept asking himself: was he actually in fact in love with Taylor's fame and what it could do for his career? In truth, he did not know. All he did know was that his private life and personal well-being were quietly and gradually being torn apart.

And not only for him. During those eight months, Sybil Burton finally realised that the old rule – "I'll never leave Syb" – that had held true for 13 years, no longer applied. The previous Easter, when she had returned to Rome, he had actually asked her for a divorce and then changed his mind. She realised that, for the first time, she was sharing her husband's love and devotion with another woman.

Although there was a degree of acceptance of the situation, Sybil was desperately upset and ready to fight for her husband that summer. And whilst he had made no decision about the future, she would continue to do so. She believed in her heart that he would come back to her and, at that point, she could not contemplate a life without him.

Sybil realised there was massive indecision inside his head. She knew, because he had often told her, that he was uncertain whether his love for Taylor was worth the destruction of two marriages. Certainly, when she had last seen him in Rome, he had believed it wasn't worth it. But by now, she knew he loved Taylor or that he was seriously infatuated with her. There was much discussion that summer between Sybil and her friends about the difference between love and infatuation, both generally and as it applied to her husband. The private debate even found its way into the English newspapers that summer, prompting endless articles on the subject and a national discussion about the differences in the two conditions.

Part of the Burton's extended troubles were caused, ironically, by the lack of any financial pressure. The chasm between them was untroubled by money worries – they had so much of it. After the financial success of 'Camelot' and *Cleopatra*, the Burtons had a sum approaching US$2 million in their bank accounts. Sybil's own personal account had tens of thousands of pounds in it. She had full unrestricted access to it and could go and do whatever she wanted without any reference to her husband. Burton wouldn't have dreamed of using financial pressure to bend Sybil to his will – that was just not his way at all. He told Aaron Frosch if her bank account slipped below £10,000, that he should just put more money in it. The complete lack of any money worries had the reversed effect of most couples going through the trauma of divorce – it gave them both the freedom *not* to have to decide.

At times, Burton appeared desperately to want to make the break from Taylor, but she had him under a spell and was happy to wait it out in Gstaad, confident that she would win in the end. She, too, had no money worries. She had earned well over US$2.5 million on *Cleopatra* and didn't intend to work any time soon unless the right offer came along. She put her pursuit of Burton well above any career concerns.

Elizabeth Taylor also had no problems with her former spouse, apart from the fact that he seemed unwilling to grant her a formal divorce. Taylor and Fisher had separated cleanly and he took up with the actress Ann-Margret. As Taylor admitted in July 1962: "Eddie and I never did live together again."

But Burton was keener to get back to work. He admitted to his friend, American journalist Hollis Alpert, that after a few weeks, he was missing all the fuss and hullabaloo that had surrounded *Cleopatra*, and he missed being the centre of attention. He had become addicted to the attention that Taylor attracted.

But he was also sensitive to criticism that he was only attracted to Taylor because of her fame and what it could do for his career. And, although he denied it, because of her, he was suddenly overwhelmed with movie offers. After *Cleopatra*, Burton was, for the first time, in the superstar bracket and able to command a fee of US$500,000 a film. It was the same sort of money Humphrey Bogart used to make when he was alive.

In October 1962, the right opportunity knocked when he and Taylor were called to Paris by Darryl Zanuck. Zanuck, now firmly back in charge at Fox, had pushed Joe Mankiewicz aside and was personally directing the editing of *Cleopatra*. But Zanuck had no intention of ever re-hiring Burton or Taylor, he simply wanted some re-dubbing work done.

But Burton and Taylor's arrival in Paris together brought every producer with a script to the French capital with an offer. However, one man was in pole position to secure their services, and that was Burton's old friend Anatole De Grunwald. 53-year-old De Grunwald was the former producing partner of Alexander Korda and had produced Burton's first-ever feature film, *The Last Days of Dolwyn*, in 1949.

De Grunwald flew in to Paris from London with an intriguing proposition – a bespoke script, inspired by them, and written specially for them.

# AND GOD CREATED BURTON

De Grunwald, motivated by the events in Rome in 1962, had commissioned playwright Terence Rattigan to write a melodrama. But instead of a film-set, it was based in an airport terminal. The film was called *The VIPs* and, as the name implied, was about very important persons who had all gathered for a flight to New York which couldn't take off because of fog. The story chronicled how a group of passengers, a mixture of celebrities, business people and international aristocrats, were thrown together in the first class lounge at London's Heathrow Airport. The principal character is a rich businessman whose wife is about to leave him for her lover. The supporting characters were all to be played by distinguished actors including, Linda Christian, Louis Jourdan, Elsa Martinelli, Margaret Rutherford, Maggie Smith, Rod Taylor and Orson Welles. In the film, all their characters are unconnected, except by the coincidence of their flight.

To give himself some negotiating room, De Grunwald put it about that William Holden, Laurence Olivier, Ingrid Bergmann and Sophia Loren, as well as Burton and Taylor, were all in the frame for the lead male and female parts. That may have been a possibility but it was unlikely to have been true as the film had been specially written for Burton and Taylor.

Alexander Korda had been dead for six years, so De Grunwald went to MGM for the funding to make his movie. He offered MGM two packages: an expensive one with Burton and Taylor; or a cheap one with Olivier and Loren. As he anticipated, MGM wasn't interested in Olivier and Loren and agreed to provide the funding as long as Burton and Taylor signed up. The possibility of another Burton-Taylor movie following on from *Cleopatra* was an enticing one for any studio.

Hence, De Grunwald's quick trip to Paris.

He arrived in Paris at a very difficult moment, right in the middle of the Cuban missile crisis when no one knew if there would be a tomorrow. It lent a surreal air to the negotiations.

Tactically, De Grunwald was fully prepared for his meeting. He arranged to meet Burton and Taylor together, but only offered Burton the part and told him he would be opposite Sophia Loren. De Grunwald knew this would pique Taylor's interest, and it did. Quickly, she suggested he forget Loren and offered herself for the part.

When she mentioned her fee of US$1 million, De Grunwald insisted he couldn't afford it after having agreed to pay Burton US$500,000 only a few minutes earlier. He told Taylor that Loren would do it for US$150,000. But

Taylor was far too canny to bite on that. She just said to De Grunwald: "Leave it to me."

And that was that. Taylor had been an MGM contract artist for ten years and she knew everyone at the studio. She went straight to the top and even Burton was amazed at the deal she managed to strike. MGM was seemingly prepared to pay any price and, once they had got a sniff of Taylor's interest in the part, they gave in to virtually all her demands. The only downside was Taylor being exposed to a London winter again – but she seemed entirely unconcerned at the all-too-apparent risk she was taking with her health. Her passion for Burton overrode those concerns.

Once the deal was agreed, De Grunwald shuffled in and out of Los Angeles, Geneva, Paris and London to sweat the details and the small print. With an Elizabeth Taylor contract, there was always plenty of small print to be sweated over. In three weeks, he made 34 separate flights and said afterwards: "I am usually exhausted at the end of a production, but this time I was exhausted before we even started."

Burton and Taylor finally signed their contracts on 16th November 1962.

The delays were mostly because of Taylor's complex tax affairs. Burton had introduced Taylor to Aaron Frosch and he was horrified when he saw the sorts of arrangements Taylor had been making to shelter her income from tax.

Taylor's tax affairs were more complicated than usual because of her dual nationality, and she consequently got the full attention of both the American and British tax man. Although she had become a Swiss resident like Burton two years earlier, the US Internal Revenue Service had much stricter rules about what its citizens got up to abroad. Frosch didn't believe her existing tax shelter arrangements would stand up to any sort of scrutiny.

For instance, to receive her income from *Cleopatra*, she had set up a Zurich registered company called MCL Films SA, jointly owned by her three children, Michael and Christopher Wilding and Liza Todd. Frosch thought the Internal Revenue Service would see that as blatant tax evasion. He told her to pay the tax and not take the risk. Frosch was worried as tax evaders went to jail in America. With that in mind, he strongly advised Taylor to give up her American citizenship altogether. She agreed to think about it, but never did. And in the end, that decision probably saved her from prosecution over her tax arrangements on *Cleopatra*, which, as Frosch had spotted, were clearly illegal and ill thought-out. He told her that the way things were currently structured, she would end up paying tax on even her expenses.

For *The VIPs*, Frosch registered her a new Bermuda-based company, called Taylor Productions Inc. He told her that, in order for it to work and to comply with US legislation, it would have to be actively involved in the production of the film, so Frosch arranged for her company to get joint billing with MGM as the producer.

Burton already had his own Bermuda company called Bushell Productions Inc., but he was only subject to scrutiny from the British Inland Revenue and was in full compliance.

The deals saw Burton agree to work on *The VIPs* for ten weeks and get paid US$500,000 with overages of US$20,000 a week. He would also get ten per cent of the gross profits, which would ultimately double his fee. Taylor got US$750,000 and US$50,000 a week overages and the same profit share. After it was signed and sealed, Frosch, a very big admirer and supporter of Sybil, was surprised when Taylor told him she didn't need the money and that she had signed up "just as an excuse to be together" with Burton.

The film was to be made at Elstree Studios in North London and directed by 60-year-old Anthony Asquith. He was an interesting choice for director, being better known as the son of Herbert Asquith, the British prime minister during a period of the First World War.

But just as Burton and Taylor were about to leave for London, a crisis developed. The film's insurance company refused to cover Taylor, or rather it quoted a premium of US$2.5 million to provide cover of US$4 million for the film's budget.

Try as it might, MGM and De Grunwald were unable to find an insurance company that would take the risk at a reasonable premium, which he thought should have been around US$150,000. But word had got around the Lloyds insurance market about what had happened in 1961, and no one wanted to take the risk again. So the MGM studio did something it never did; it went ahead and started the movie without insurance cover on Taylor. Then, the decision was unprecedented but showed just how much power Taylor had over the Hollywood studios.

So, on 6th December 1962, Burton and Taylor took the train from Geneva and came over on the night ferry. They then caught a train to Victoria Station in London. It was Burton's first experience of travelling with Taylor. As well as her three children, she had two secretaries, a nanny and housekeeper, plus a large quantity of baggage. Burton brought just himself.

For the most part, Burton thought the entourage unnecessary, except for one man whom he much admired: Taylor's secretary Dick Hanley, who preferred to be called her 'Chief of Staff'. He was a gentle, unflappable man who had started out as a secretary to Louis Mayer, the founder of the MGM studio. Taylor met him when she worked for MGM in the fifties and poached him straightaway. In those difficult early days with Taylor, Burton relied on Hanley a great deal.

Photographers were waiting for them at Victoria Station and there was almost a pitched battle between them to get a good picture. But the two kept apart and eventually managed to scramble into separate cars, which took them to The Dorchester. It was Burton's first time staying at The Dorchester, although Taylor had been staying there since she was 19 years old. Taylor booked her two usual adjoining suites, called The Terrace and The Harlequin, on the top floor. Her staff usually stayed in the Harlequin, but this time it was reserved in Burton's name, although he would not use it. The suites cost £320 a day for The Terrace, and £215 for The Harlequin, all paid for by Taylor's new production company and billed back to MGM under Aaron Frosch's instructions.

The following days' newspapers had all the details of their arrival and the sleeping arrangements at The Dorchester, but Burton ignored all that and was particularly pleased when they were described in the *Daily Express* as "the hottest screen couple since Spencer Tracy and Katharine Hepburn."

Thankfully, Sybil was in Celigny and missed all the brouhaha. Two weeks later, she arrived in London with Kate and Jessica to stay over the Christmas holidays in their house in Hampstead. Ivor and Gwen Jenkins also returned to London with her.

Taylor and her entourage cleared out of London for Christmas, and she spent much of the holiday with her friend Sheran Cazalet at the Cazalet family's home in Kent. Cazalet was her best friend and had been since they were children. With Taylor away in the country, Burton spent most of the holiday at Squires Mount. Despite the rather difficult circumstances, the whole family spent a happy traditional Christmas together – not knowing, it was to be their last.

Filming of *The VIPs* had begun a few days before Christmas, with MGM anxious to finish as early as the end of February for a June release, to take advantage of the Burton-Taylor publicity around *Cleopatra*. MGM's publicists figured they could just ride on the back of *Cleopatra*.

There was trouble almost immediately when 20th Century-Fox, which had prior call over Burton's services, said it needed him for a week to shoot some extra scenes for *Cleopatra*. But far more seriously, another week was lost when Burton was attacked at Paddington Station in London.

In an incident in the middle of January 1963, never fully explained, Burton was assaulted by a man and left with a badly-bruised eye and damaged vertebrae in his back. There were two different versions of the story; Burton's fictional version and what appeared to be the truth. Burton's story was that he had been at a Wales vs England rugby match at Cardiff Arms Park and was returning by train to London's Paddington Station on the evening of Saturday 19th January 1963 when he was set upon. He said that he was looking for a taxi outside Paddington when he was surrounded by half a dozen yobbos (in those days known as teddy boys) who lunged at him and got him on the ground. He said later: "And then you're helpless. They just kicked me all over. One of them put his boot in my eye."

But his story was certainly untrue because the area outside Paddington station would have been very crowded at that time of night, and Burton was not on his own as he alleged.

Fergus Cashin, a journalist on the *Daily Mirror* and later a biographer of Burton, told a different story. Fergus Cashin was one of the finest tabloid journalists who ever walked, and he could match Burton drink for drink, so they had a natural affinity. Fergus Cashin lived in Shepperton village, and whenever Burton came to film at the studio, they would drink at local village pub called The King's Head. The landlord effectively waived the licensing laws for them. He had been introduced to Burton in 1963 by Peter O'Toole. When they first met in the bar, Burton looked at him and said: "I was wondering when you would turn up. The landlord told us you were living in the village and Peter told me you were an old mate." The friendship, which started that day, would define Cashin's career. Whenever Burton was at Elstree or Shepperton, they could be found every lunchtime and early evening, indulging in their favourite pastime.

Cashin said that there was an argument in the corridor of the train just as it was pulling into Paddington, and an unnamed man bustled an intoxicated Burton into the small toilet cubicle on the train, punched him in the eye and left him sprawled across the toilet floor. Apparently, the unnamed man, before he ran off, said to the other passengers, who came out into the train's corridor after they heard the commotion and saw Burton on the floor: "That's where a shit who's done the dirty on his wife deserves to be." Burton never said who the perpetrator was, but he probably knew him. It was humiliating and he never talked about it except to Cashin.

Cashin's version of the story appeared to be the true one, and the man appeared to have been put up to it by his own volition or by persons unknown.

Burton was unable to work for a week and was very lucky to have escaped virtually uninjured, although he wore an eye patch for a few days. But not that lucky, as he was also left with a hairline fracture of the spine, which went undiscovered for many years. The fracture was to be the start of back problems that plagued him until the end of his life.

The two weeks' lost time started to cause time problems. Both Burton and Taylor could only be in the UK for 13 weeks and came dangerously close to their time limit. They could stay until 20th March safely, but if filming dragged on any longer, they would have to come back after the end of the tax year on 5th April.

To try and get cover for the two weeks he was away, Burton arranged for De Grunwald to hire his brother, Graham Jenkins. Graham looked like Burton and became his film double on *The VIPs*. The ruse actually saved the film and meant Burton and Taylor were able to complete it within their time quota, although it was touch-and-go for a while.

The filming, unlike that of *Cleopatra*, went without incident, despite the fact that Burton was drinking heavily. During that period, his drinking began at breakfast, with one Bloody Mary followed by another, followed by another, followed by another. At lunchtime, he switched to straight vodka on the rocks, and they kept coming all afternoon, served on a silver tray by his valet, Bob Wilson, every quarter of an hour. But somehow, his performance didn't miss a beat.

Taylor also hardly missed a day's filming this time, and Asquith was adept at working around any problems that occurred. Both Taylor and Burton realised that they couldn't mess De Grunwald about as they had Walter Wanger on *Cleopatra*. Terence Rattigan had also written a very tight script.

The atmosphere on the set was also good, unlike that on *Cleopatra*, not least because of the playful insults that Burton and Taylor continually threw across to each other during filming. Typically, Burton would say to her: "I'm pretty fond of that Jewish girl. She walks and looks just like a French tart." She would typically respond: "Does the burnt-out Welshman know his lines?"

Once the Christmas holidays were out of the way, it soon became very clear that Burton intended to spend most of his time at The Dorchester. This was very distressing to Sybil, especially as he virtually moved in with Taylor and started introducing her to family and friends.

It was only for Sybil's sake that they maintained a suite each, as Burton said: "In those days, things were less permissive, so that there was all that fuss about separate rooms in hotels." When Burton made his choice where to live, it became Sybil's worst nightmare – she could no longer ignore the problems in her marriage and pretend they weren't there. All her hopes of his eventually returning home were finally dashed. But she still retained some hope, as he flitted from Squires Mount to The Dorchester and back, just as he had in Switzerland in the summer.

Robert Hardy remembers that period well. One night, Sybil Burton came to his house in Chelsea for dinner with his second wife, Sally Cooper. Sybil was very upset, so, to cheer her up, Hardy mixed some Mint Julep cocktails for the three of them. Mint Juleps can be highly addictive, and so it proved that night as one after the other went down. All three of them gradually got drunk, as Hardy remembered: "Sybil was so plastered that Sally and I tried to get her to stay the night but she said: 'No, I am going to get home.' So I said: 'We'll drive you' – in those days, you would drive no matter how pissed you were. I was pissed, Sally was pissed, Sybil was pissed and we had this great big Dalmatian dog called Troilus." Only the dog was sober that night.

At the time, Hardy drove a green Morris Minor Traveller and the three of them, with Troilus in the back, set off for Hampstead to take Sybil home.

As they drove north up Park Lane, Sybil noticed that there was a light on in the Terrace Suite on the top floor of The Dorchester and started crying. Hardy recalled: "Sybil said: 'There they are.' I said: 'Do you want him?' and she said: 'Only if I can have him back.' And I said: 'I'll get him.'" He swung the little car sharply right and, fuelled by the Mint Juleps and loaded up with gung-ho and full of bravado, he drove to the front entrance of The Dorchester and parked his Morris Traveller right next to all the Rolls-Royces and Bentleys outside.

He remembered: "I charged in, followed by my dog. I was wearing a sweater and jeans and it was 3 o'clock in the morning." Hardy remembers the staff were cleaning and the giant carpet in reception was rolled up whilst the floor was being polished. As he recounted years later, he stood in front of the concierge's desk and said: "Tell Richard Burton that I am here and I mean to see him." The night porter replied: "We are not allowed to put any calls through." That set Hardy off: "I got arrogant and said: 'Do you not know who I am and why I am here?' and so on and so on." The porter looked at him. Hardy was not then the household name and famous face that he is today, but the porter thought he recognised him and on the off chance he might have been as important as he claimed to be, picked up the telephone extension and dialled the night duty manager's number. As Hardy remembered: "They called various people on the telephone and I was beginning to get a bit nervy when a man in full morning dress came stalking from the back, down the stairs and through the hall, and said: 'I wonder if I could be of any assistance.'" By this time, the effect of the Mint Juleps was wearing off at the same rate as the bravado: "I was about to start again, summoning up the courage, when I looked around and Troilus was lifting his leg on the rolled-up carpet and I thought: 'This is not good.' I said: 'Right, I think your service here is disgraceful, he is my closest and oldest friend and it is an utter disgrace that you will not ring him up and say that I am here.'" With that, Hardy and Troilus quickly retreated: "I went back to the car in misery and I had to confess that I had totally failed." A tearful Sybil was returned to Squires Mount and a somewhat crestfallen Hardy drove home silently to Chelsea with his wife, dog and only his most private thoughts for company.

It was then, as the cold night air flowed through the open quarter-light of the Morris, with the London streets empty and silent, that Hardy realised, for the first time, that the marriage was irretrievable.

Stanley and Ellen Baker were also doing everything they could to get their friends back together. On 28th February, they persuaded them both to come to Baker's 35th birthday party – and they did. But a jealous Taylor phoned the Bakers' house three times during the evening, and instead of returning with Sybil to Hampstead, Taylor lured Burton back to The Dorchester that night and Stanley Baker's plan for a romantic reunion failed.

It was then that Baker also realised the marriage was over.

But Burton, it seemed, was the last to know as he continued to agonise and prevaricate. Taylor, however was no fool – she was in love with him but not to the point of the destruction of his life. A moment of truth was coming and, sensing this, Taylor decided to make it easy for him. Rather than risk losing him altogether if he chose Sybil, she said she was prepared to share him and she meant it. And in truth, at that point, so was Sybil. Taylor told him gently: "We don't have to get married. I can be a friend, a sort of mistress, if you like." But somehow, when Taylor said those words, they acted as the trigger Burton had been waiting for – as he admitted years later: "My Welsh Presbyterian puritanical background took over, and a clean break was made."

He picked up the phone immediately and apparently told Sybil he was "choosing Elizabeth" but made no mention of their marriage or divorce. Sybil was shocked but determined that she was not going to be the one to ask for a divorce and believed if the marriage was going to die, he must be the one to finally kill it.

It was Sybil's darkest moment and also a moment of catharsis. She temporarily lost all control of her emotions and found herself alone and emotionally in a very dark place. She took the sharpest knife she could find in her kitchen drawer and went to the bathroom, took ten or so aspirin and, then, in a moment of pure desperation, leaned over the bath and drew the blade of the knife across her wrists, screaming as she did it. It wasn't a suicide attempt; it was a desperate cry for help. Ivor and Gwen, alerted by the nanny, rushed over from their house opposite, put towels round her wrists and rushed her to the casualty department of the Royal Free Hospital in nearby Pond Street, a few minutes away.

Her wounds, albeit not life threatening, were serious enough to leave some large scars. The doctors bandaged her wrists, gave her a tetanus jab as a precaution and no doubt proffered her the usual psychological help such victims receive. Luckily, she was in the excellent hands of Ivor and Gwen, who were anxious to get her back home as quickly as possible and to avoid any publicity. Ivor was at his very best that night and made sure a drama was not turned into a crisis. After he and Gwen had put her to bed and made her swallow a cup of warm Ovaltine, Ivor unrolled an old mattress and that night slept outside her door. Over the years, friends gradually revealed snippets of what had happened that night. As Robert Hardy confirmed: "She did try and cut her wrists – I saw the scars. How genuine an attempt, I have no means of knowing. But she did it."

Around the same time, Hardy met Elizabeth Taylor for the first time when she came to dinner at his house. As he recalled: "Rich rang and he said: 'I'm at The Dorchester and I want to see you, and there is somebody here who wants to speak to you'. He handed the phone to Elizabeth: 'Hi, Tim, can we come round for supper?' I said: 'I have only got sausages and chips, we can go out to the pub.' But we didn't, we had sausages and chips at my house."

It was not an easy evening. Like all his other friends, Hardy was very pro-Sybil but admits now he couldn't help liking Taylor – which he says "didn't come easy" in the circumstances: "Elizabeth was quite beguiling but I was extremely cool because she was a breaker as far as I was concerned. But as I put her into the car at the end of the evening, she said to me: 'Please don't hate me, Tim.'"

Hardy can now recall that moment and those words, in the night chill through the open car window, as vividly as when it happened fifty years ago.

Taylor worked extremely hard to be accepted by Burton's friends. She went to pubs and rugby matches with him and she started to learn Welsh. But she was continually amazed at the loyalty she found to Sybil.

Graham Jenkins was the first of the family members to meet Elizabeth Taylor and remembered: "No one blamed her for what had happened; they all knew him too well. They were simply sad because of what they had both done to Sybil."

Jenkins' own first encounter with Taylor was bizarre. He was invited to dinner with them both at The Dorchester, as he recalled: "Elizabeth, as usual, had taken ages to get ready and when she finally made an appearance, we had to hang around. It wasn't very nice. He turned up as pissed as a newt, called her some awful names and refused to come out with us. I took her to dinner on my own."

For once, Burton's behaviour was excusable. He had just had a terrible alcohol-fuelled exchange of words with his brother Ivor at Squires Mount. The words exchanged had been vicious and Burton returned to the Dorchester shell-shocked. Ivor had told him that Sybil had slashed her wrists. He also said that if he did not come to his senses, he would never speak to him again and that he was 100 per cent with Sybil. In effect, Ivor told him it was now not only either Elizabeth or Sybil, it was also either Ivor or Elizabeth. For Burton, it was a terrible blow to hear those words. Regardless of the fact that he was his brother, Ivor Jenkins was the most moral, upright and honest man Richard Burton knew, and he meant what he said. Ivor, true to his word, would not meet or speak to him for two years, despite remaining on his payroll. For Burton, the split with Ivor was every bit as sad as the split from Sybil.

So Graham Jenkins, a simple Welsh boy by his own admission, found himself out to dinner alone with the most famous woman in the world. He was bowled over, as he later revealed: "I had decided not to like Elizabeth Taylor. But the resolution went by the board almost as soon as I met her. She was, more than I could ever have imagined, a natural woman. That she was naturally beautiful any fool could see…hers was a personality and a strong intelligence which demanded attention and respect. The conversation took the inevitable turn: 'Will you marry Richard?' 'What do you think?' 'I think he's a troubled man.' 'He needs someone to look after him.' 'Isn't Sybil supposed to do that?'" At that, Taylor laughed and told him: "Sybil was yesterday."

Jenkins said: "I realised then I was just a little frightened of Elizabeth. To stand in her way was to risk being hit by an avalanche. At the same time, I could see very clearly how she captivated Rich. When we said goodbye, she gave me a huge kiss and I was captivated."

Two nights later, Taylor invited him to dinner again and once again Burton was too busy drowning his sorrows to join them. Graham became her cheerleader with the family.

In the confusion of his emotions and troubled conscience, Burton was drinking even more heavily than usual, day and night, with no let-up. His general behaviour grew increasingly more worrying. One night, he and Taylor were dining with the director Otto Preminger and some friends at The Dorchester. Burton was paralytically drunk and decided to recite Dylan Thomas at the dinner table. As he stood up and opened his mouth, he was sick all over the table and slumped down. Preminger came to his aid and, as he picked Burton up off the table, he turned to him and snarled: "Fuck off." Preminger recoiled, dropped him where he was and never spoke to him again.

Shortly after the Preminger incident, Graham took his elder brother to one side for a heart-to-heart talk. He basically told him he had to stop drinking and get a grip on his life, telling him: "What did you use to say? You hadn't a care in the world. So what's happened to you?" Burton looked up at him and replied: "I don't know, Gray, I don't know. It's just that, well, all this, it's not what I expected."

It was the moment to choose Sybil, but he was now too far gone to change course as Robert Hardy said: "Even his mistakes were great, which is a nice way of saying he made the most appalling choices. To choose Elizabeth rather than Sybil was lunacy."

After she had recovered from the trauma and her wrists had healed, Sybil decided she had to sort herself out. She left the children with their nanny and Ivor and Gwen and went back to Celigny on her own. She decided to try solitude as an antidote, but that only made her worse as she remembered: "My lowest point came when I'd read myself out. Reading had always relaxed me. There I was in Celigny and I looked down at the page and couldn't read it. Then I knew I was really in trouble. It was awful."

Realising that solitude was not the answer, Sybil quickly returned to London, tried the opposite solution and decided to adopt single status again. Bizarrely, she moved to Chelsea and, as far as it was possible for a 33-year-old, resumed a single girl's life. Around this time, Sybil gave a rare interview to her old friend, the journalist Elaine Dundy, Kenneth Tynan's wife. She admitted she had been going through a desperate time and said: "I knew I was really in trouble. It was awful. I couldn't go anywhere...or do anything because the bloody press was watching, actually watching through the windows." A friend, thought to be Dundy herself, was quoted as saying: "I think that Sybil was so deeply damaged, not only because she loved him and would have died for him, which is not the rarest thing in the world, but because she had tried so hard. What defeated her was to be so dependent on his love, on his being finally there, whatever had gone on in the dark and in the distance, on the fact that he would finally come back to her, and that he didn't."

She made the shock decision to move and based herself temporarily in a rented flat in Brompton Square and embarked on a merry-go-round social life. She found she had a lot of friends who wanted her company and became part of west London's social scene very quickly.

As part of the cure, she threw away the burden of responsible wife and mother, stayed up until all hours dancing at nightclubs and then slept most of the day. She had plenty of money to spend and made a conscious decision to live it up. Spending money recklessly was a small way to punish her husband. During that time, she took several lovers and, for the first time, slept with a man who wasn't called Richard Burton – it was a novel experience for the girl who had been a one-man woman since the age of 17. It wasn't that she had stopped loving Burton, it was simply that she had to experiment with what a new life might be like. According to Dundy and others, she found it was better than she thought. And once she took a lover, some of Burton's spell and hold over her was broken.

She went to every film premiere and theatre first night and became the number one invitee of hostesses across London. Her favourite haunt was the Ad Lib club, which, for a time, was the most fashionable nightclub in town and stayed open until four o'clock in the morning.

She started mixing with a trendy set, which included Princess Margaret and Dirk Bogarde. Old friends such as Stanley and Ellen Baker, Emlyn and Molly Williams and Robert and Sally Hardy rallied round and made it totally clear where their allegiances lay.

On her 34th birthday on 27th March, Bogarde and the actress Alma Cogan organised a surprise birthday party for her at the Ad Lib club. Penny Junor later described it as "the party of all time."

A few days after her birthday, at the end of March, Burton flew back into

# AND GOD CREATED BURTON

London from Gstaad for the day. They met for the final time in their lives in the foyer of the Savoy Hotel on London's embankment. Burton finally told Sybil he had made up his mind and wanted a divorce. They were the words Sybil had been waiting for and signalled that the contest was over. For her, his spell was finally broken. She was no longer in thrall and thanked him for making his intentions clear at last. With that, she got up and walked straight into a taxi that took her home to Squires Mount. She left behind a very heavy-hearted and deeply uncertain but now firmly ex-husband.

Sybil felt like an entirely new woman. The spell really had been broken and, although no one can be really sure, the key, according to friends of the time, appears to have been her taking of new lovers, something she could never have contemplated doing even three months earlier.

From the Savoy, she went straight home and phoned round her girlfriends and said: "I'm going to New York tomorrow. Come and help me pack." Later, she recalled her emotions to Elaine Dundy that fateful night: "I felt I was finally out of the woods when I made my decision to go to America. Such a relief to have made up one's mind. I decided in a moment. That was it."

The following day, she left along with Ivor and Gwen and the two girls. Flying the other way was Aaron Frosch, to make arrangements with Burton for the divorce.

And so it came to pass – 15 months after it all started in Rome, the die had finally been cast and the participants all moved on. The two Burtons, two remarkable people in their own separate ways, who had come so far in the 14 years since 1949, were now two entirely different people.

Sybil made a complete break and cut herself off from the past and her life in Europe for a new start in America. She kept her resolve and, despite many opportunities, never saw her husband again and spoke to him again only once on the telephone. Effectively, the call was to tell him she was settling in New York permanently. Sybil told him she wanted notice if he was ever coming to the city so she could clear out whilst he was there. She said from then on, New York was hers and the rest of the world was his. Burton agreed to her terms.

She moved into an apartment hotel room initially and quickly bought her own apartment at the art deco Eldorado Towers at 300 Central Park West. Eldorado Towers, despite its name, was the perfect choice. It was on the trendy upper west side of New York, situated between west 90th and west 91st street and overlooked the Central Park reservoir.

It proved an inspired place to live and, soon, Aaron Frosch and Roddy

McDowall also bought apartments in the same building, as they liked it so much when they visited her. It was a co-op block but the other residents welcomed Sybil with open arms. The apartment had plenty of room for all six of them.

With Ivor, Gwen and her English nanny in support, Sybil had plenty of time to socialise. Soon, as she had been in London, Sybil became the toast of New York and she found her name was often dropped into the social columns of the New York newspapers. She immediately realised she had made the right decision and found New York refreshing and stimulating and was instantly in demand at dinner parties. She threw herself into New York's social whirl. She had the support of all of her husband's New York friends, not least that of Philip Burton, who, like Ivor Jenkins, also threw his full weight behind Sybil. Philip was absolutely delighted to have his grandchildren in New York all the time. Although Philip was deeply disappointed by the split, he was relieved that it was finally over, saying: "Her strength of mind did much to reconcile me to her decision."

Philip Burton, in his own way, had also become a socialite and an active participant in the New York arts scene. Since he had come to America ten years before, he had fallen in and out of love with an actress called Celeste Holm, who became only the second woman, other than his university childhood sweetheart, to whom he had made love. But with Philip unsure of his sexuality, they had eventually split and Celeste married the actor Wesley Addy. Philip then began a lifelong relationship with the young actor and dancer Richard Alderson, better known by his stage name of Christian Alderson. With Christian's help, Philip introduced Sybil to everyone that mattered in the arts in New York.

By and large, Sybil settled down well in New York. When Ivor and Gwen returned to London, Philip became her rock and support. He took the children out to Central Park almost every day. Sometimes, an enterprising photographer took a photograph, especially when Sybil joined them. Philip found the press intrusion "bothersome" and was often rude to photographers. However, there was a light-hearted moment one morning when a photograph of the family in the park appeared in virtually every newspaper in America. It was of Sybil, Kate and Jessica strolling in the park with Philip the previous day. The caption was identical in every newspaper and described Philip as "an unidentified man." He immensely enjoyed being the "unidentified man", with all the connotations that gave. The "unidentified man" continued to take Kate and Jessica to the park, and they were often joined by Aaron Frosch's three children. And Philip continued to be rude to the journalists and photographers who approached him.

Even people who didn't know Sybil congratulated her on her courage, and it seemed that everyone took her side against her husband. The actress Joan Crawford reputedly came up to her at Saks department store in Fifth Avenue and said three words: "You have integrity."

English actor Edward Woodward, who was appearing on Broadway in the play 'Rattle of a Simple Man', met her at the first-night party of the play and they naturally got together to chat, being two of the few Brits at the party. But, mindful of what had been going on in London and anxious to avoid any mention of her husband, Woodward was so nervous he started discussing the very distinctive suit he wore on stage in the play and the difficulties in obtaining it, choosing it as a safe and uncontroversial subject. Sybil said to him: "Where did you get it in the end?" Without thinking, Woodward blurted out: "Burton." Realising what he had said, Woodward was momentarily speechless, but Sybil, as quick as a flash, reassured him and said: "It's all right, it could have been worse; you could have said: 'Burton the tailor.'" And, after a few seconds to think about it, they both started laughing uproariously.

# THE CONTEST

# AND GOD CREATED BURTON

# CHAPTER 37

# Divorce his, divorce hers

## *The future gets sorted*

### 1963

1963 was a packed year for Richard Burton, dominated by the divorce from Sybil, his wife of 14 years. During that same period, he completed three movies and earned US$1.25 million. But the year as a whole was a minus, as he settled a sum worth US$2.3 million on his wife in the most generous divorce settlement Hollywood had ever seen.

His decision to divorce Sybil had cleared the way for him and Taylor officially to become a couple. With both their former spouses gone to New York, they could finally begin their new life together in relative peace. Elizabeth Taylor was ecstatic that she had finally got her man. Burton was more sanguine and didn't see it in quite the same clear-cut terms she did.

He had lost his whole family when Sybil had departed suddenly for New York, taking their two children along with his beloved brother and sister-in-law with her. They had joined his adoptive father, Philip. They had all, in the process, cut off contact with him and it seemed to him that he had paid a very high price for his new life, whereas Taylor had kept her family intact whilst getting rid of the waste of space that was Eddie Fisher.

When filming of *The VIPs* ended, exactly on time at the end of March 1963, Burton and Taylor swiftly left Britain and returned to Gstaad after using up virtually every day of the 90 days they were allowed to stay for the 1962/63 tax year.

They spent two weeks in Gstaad, reflecting on the recent past and looking forward to the future they now knew they had together. Although Burton was at times overwhelmed with grief from his lost family, it was for the most part a very happy time. Right from the start, their union proved to be a great partnership. Although biographers and journalists have always focused on the bad times, the many good times they enjoyed vastly outnumbered the bad times.

The interplay between Burton and Taylor was, for the most part, extremely warm. Their love was genuine and heartfelt. They always competed with each other, but the competitive interaction was always open and humorous; he was expansive and eloquent and she was subtle and convincing. In fact, Burton used to tell people that his new partner's main talent was her persuasiveness and the fact that she could get what she wanted merely by "look or gesture." But then, no one had ever denied that Taylor had charisma. But she also had a talent for what Burton called "ordinariness" mixed in with it all. He always thought that "ordinariness" was what made her really special.

There were a number of hurdles to overcome before they could be married. The divorces, his and hers, dominated the year.

Burton assuaged his guilt about leaving Sybil by making it clear that her divorce settlement would be whatever she decided it should be. He told her she could have everything if she wanted it and leave him with nothing. But Sybil didn't want everything; she just wanted enough.

And what she really wanted was her life back.

And that was what she found in New York. She waited until she was truly settled in before she turned her mind to the financial settlement.

Straightaway, even though friends told her she must appoint her own lawyer, she insisted there was no question of it. They both appointed Aaron Frosch as their lawyer. It was unusual but it was what Sybil wanted. The marriage may have ended and the emotional trust may have been shattered, but, personally, the bond was as solid as ever. Sybil trusted her husband to do better for her than she would do for herself. It showed what a remarkable pair they were.

So in the last week of August 1963, Philip Burton walked with Sybil to Aaron Frosch's offices in Manhattan for a meeting about the divorce settlement.

Frosch had already worked out a plan according to Burton's instructions; it stated that Sybil was to get a settlement equivalent to the whole of his net worth at the time of the split. That translated to half a million dollars in cash straightaway. She would then get half a million dollars a year for the following two years. Burton would also buy her the El Dorado Towers apartment for cash and put it in her name. The children would both be endowed with separate trust funds and Sybil would have full custody, although she granted Burton free visitation rights.

The whole settlement was worth around US$2.3 million, and it was virtually all Burton had at the time. He got to keep the four houses they owned in Hampstead and Celigny, which Sybil didn't want.

But Burton didn't care that he had been cleaned out by the divorce. He was delighted to give his wife everything, feeling that it was "what she deserved." If she had asked for double, he would have given her double, as he said: "I wanted her to have it all, if she wanted it." Stanley Baker confirmed what happened: "He would have given Sybil every penny he had, if she'd asked. He felt ashamed, you know. He knew he had treated her very badly over the years. And he felt he had betrayed his daughters. I think he was trying to ease his conscience by giving her all she wanted. But I don't believe he ever forgave himself."

After the meeting, Frosch flew straight off to Europe to get Burton's signature on the agreement and that was that. Two weeks after the meeting, Sybil received what was called the "this-is-the-end" letter from Burton, which laid out all the terms in detail. She initialled it and returned it to Frosch.

Sybil then agreed to grant him the divorce he wanted so that he could marry Taylor, and she gave *carte blanche* to Aaron Frosch to arrange it. It was very civilised and, certainly, there had never been as amicable a divorce in Hollywood history, then or since.

Since Burton was temporarily resident in Mexico at the end of 1963, Frosch chose that country as a "tax free location for the divorce." It was filed in Guadalajara on 5th December and finalised on 20th December. Justification was required in Mexican law so the legal documents stated that it was being sought on the grounds of her husband's 'abandonment of the home.' Additional grounds cited were 'cruel and inhuman treatment.' But there was no mention of Taylor in the papers. The documents also stated, almost as an aside, that Burton had frequently been seen "in the company of other women." *Newsweek* magazine called that statement "the throwaway line of the decade."

Sybil Burton was overjoyed when she got the final papers and began to plan the rest of her life. By then, she had no remorse and her marriage was definitely in the past. Years later, Kate Burton remembered: "When my parents broke up, which was when I was four or five, my mother never spoke to my father again. Because that's my mother; her life, that part of her life was over and she felt that there was no point in being friends or trying to maintain a sort of civil friendliness."

Sybil gave a few interviews to mark the end of her marriage and to let the world know she had moved on. She said what had happened in Rome was now a "blank" and that she chose only to remember, "the good times we had there, Rich and I – and with Elizabeth. The rest I forget. I live in the present. I am happy." Lauren Bacall also pitched in on behalf of Sybil, calling her: "A great woman, she had balls, she still has." She added: "She was too good for him."

# AND GOD CREATED BURTON

On 20th December, Aaron Frosch walked round to El Dorado Towers and delivered the notarised divorce papers to Sybil and told her she was no longer married.

With that, the newly reconstituted Burton family in New York, consisting of Sybil, Kate, Jessica and Philip, enjoyed the happiest of Christmases in the new apartment. Christian Alderson joined them for the festivities and there was genuine joy in the air, so different from just a few months earlier. As Philip Burton recalled: "My happiest memories of that Christmas are of being with the children; Grandpa trying to make up for the absence of Daddy."

But Philip was still in no mood to forgive his adoptive son for what he had done to Sybil. When Burton sent a festive message to him, via Aaron Frosch's office, Philip burned it and said: "I wasn't sufficiently adjusted to the new situation even to acknowledge his message."

Philip also made his own life-changing decision that Christmas. On the very last day of the year, he applied for American citizenship, after almost ten years of living in the United States as an alien.

With 'his' divorce finalised, Taylor went about finalising 'hers'. That proved rather more difficult because there was no goodwill apparent at all between the two parties. Eddie Fisher was well aware of the progress of Sybil's divorce proceedings and could sense that Taylor would be desperate to marry Burton once they were concluded. Fisher took his revenge by delaying his divorce for as long as he possibly could – just because he could.

Taylor hired the New York law firm of Phillips, Nizer, Benjamin, Krim & Ballon to represent her. She knew the senior partner, Louis Nizer, because he represented 20th Century-Fox and they got on well. At the time, Nizer was New York's top advocate and recognised in the *Guinness Book of World Records* as the "highest-paid lawyer in the world." But initially, Nizer proved no match for the guile and effrontery of Eddie Fisher. Fisher didn't bother hiring his own lawyer, figuring he could do a better job of negotiation himself.

There were two main tasks for Nizer; organising a financial settlement and the custody of the children, none of whom were Fisher's – although that didn't stop him wanting access.

Financially, Fisher also needed a settlement. Although a successful singer, he had little in the way of assets or wealth, but Taylor was worth around US$10 million, and he wanted it. They also had some companies containing substantial assets in both their names, making a split messy.

Fisher's argument was that he had let go his career when he married Taylor and he wanted compensation for that.

Since the split, he had attempted to salvage his career by making nightclub appearances. He created a new song called 'Arrivederci, Roma' to cash in on his wife's notoriety and created a floor show with the South African dancer Juliet Prowse. She sang a song called: 'I'm Cleo, the Nympho of the Nile,' which effectively made fun of his wife.

Fisher dragged his feet over signing the final divorce papers, which were drafted many times and sent for his signature. Each time, he found a new reason not to sign, frustrating Nizer and continually coming back for more. It was more difficult because he didn't have a lawyer, and Nizer did not do so well when he didn't have an opponent.

Taylor fought him tooth and nail and was determined to keep most of what she had, including all the jewellery, the Gstaad house as well as the green Rolls-Royce, which she had given him as a birthday present.

At the very last minute, Fisher demanded half of MCL Films, which was owned by Taylor's children.

In the end, Fisher accepted a financial settlement of US$500,000 in cash but had to agree to refrain from embarrassing his wife and to give up the rights to the song 'Cleo, the Nympho of the Nile.'

With the financial side finally settled and signed off, Nizer expected a speedy divorce, but he hadn't counted on a rearguard action from Fisher over the children. He wanted some custody rights over Mike Todd's daughter, Liza, and shared custody of newly adopted Maria, whom he hardly knew. Taylor hated him for using her children as pawns in the battle.

Finally, she snapped and told Nizer to "take the gloves off." He designed a plan for a hostile divorce Fisher would find very difficult to contest. So, on 14th January 1964, Taylor filed for divorce in Puerto Vallarta, Mexico, on the straightforward grounds that her husband had abandoned her in March 1962. Abandonment was a charge that was almost impossible to defend or justify in Mexico divorces. It worked and, six weeks later, the divorce was granted. Fisher refused to accept that Puerto Vallarta was legal until it was pointed out to him that, using his logic, Taylor's divorce from Michael Wilding wasn't legal either; nor was her marriage to Mike Todd or himself. He finally relented and gave up his claim on Liza and Maria.

When it was all over, Fisher told journalists somewhat sarcastically: "I wouldn't stand in the way of this earth-shattering, world-shaking romance for anything in the world." In his autobiographies, Fisher later attempted to rewrite history and fantasised about how he would have liked the divorce to have been. But his version certainly wasn't how it had been. After his account was published, one of his own daughters from a later marriage, the actress Carrie Fisher, said she wished she could have her DNA "fumigated."

Whilst all this was going on, Burton was hard at work. He knew once his divorce from Sybil was finalised, he would technically be broke and that he needed money.

As soon as the 1963/64 tax year began on 6th April, Burton and Taylor were back at The Dorchester, this time openly living together. They planned to stay for ten weeks whilst Burton starred in a movie called *Becket*, a commitment he had made a year earlier.

Hal Wallis, the 65-year-old American producer, had approached Burton in Rome in September 1962 with an offer to play the title role of Sir Thomas Becket in the film. It was based on an original 1959 French play called 'Honour of God' by Jean Anouilh. It had been a hit on Broadway, starring Laurence Olivier and Anthony Quinn and directed by Peter Glenville. The play had also been performed in London, starring Eric Porter and Christopher Plummer and directed by Peter Hall.

The story described how Sir Thomas Becket, a man of great skill and wisdom, the chancellor of England and a close friend of King Henry II, was reluctantly appointed Archbishop of Canterbury by the King. As Archbishop and head of the Catholic Church in England, he shifted his allegiance to the Pope and was later murdered by the King's soldiers in Canterbury Cathedral.

The story, set in twelfth-century Britain, was essentially the story of the friendship and then quarrel between two men, and the bigger unseen battle between the King of England and the Pope.

The interiors were shot at Shepperton studios, near London, and the outside scenes at Alnwick Castle and Bamburgh Beach in Northumberland, a north east coastal county of England.

For many, the film was defined by the model of Canterbury Cathedral that was brilliantly recreated at Shepperton, some of it in *papier mâché*.

Wallis told Burton he had secured a US$3 million budget from the Paramount studio and offered him his standard fee of US$250,000. Burton snapped his hand off as it was his sort of film. It was not only the subject matter that attracted him but also Wallis' reputation. He was a producer of legendary status.

The legendary status had been well-earned. For the past 18 years, he had been independent, but before that, was head of production at Warner Bros in the studio's glory years. Wallis had left in 1944, when he got fed up with Jack Warner taking all the credit for his movies. That year, Wallis' *Casablanca* was nominated for eight Academy Awards, and won three. When the award for best picture was announced, Wallis got up to walk to the stage to accept the Oscar. But Jack Warner beat him to it and seized the statuette, almost out of his hands. Wallis remembered bitterly: "I had no alternative but to sit down again, humiliated and furious, and I still haven't recovered from the shock."

When Wallis left, it was a huge blow for Warner Bros, and Jack Warner was forced to watch him make millions for other studios that backed his films as an independent. He very rarely missed. And since then, there had been no Hollywood producer with a better calling card than Wallis.

Playing Becket proved to be one of Burton's better decisions. In an uncharacteristically low-key performance, he became Thomas Becket and defined him as a historical figure for generations to come. Interestingly, the director was Peter Glenville, the very same man who had fired him from 'Adventure Story' 14 years earlier and nearly ruined his career. But Burton bore no grudges and Glenville coaxed a brilliantly subtle performance out of him. *Becket* was a genuine triumph; ask any Burton fan what was Burton's best ever film and half of them will instinctively say *Becket*.

Elizabeth Taylor tried her very best to get a part in *Becket* so she could be on set with Burton, but she could not persuade Hal Wallis. He thought she was trouble, and he thought he was too old for trouble.

The major attraction of the film was the pairing of Burton with Peter O'Toole for the first time. Hal Wallis had been very lucky in that both his leading men had become big stars between him signing them and the start of production. O'Toole had shot to overnight fame as the British soldier T. E. Lawrence in *Lawrence of Arabia*. To make the mix complete, Wallis threw in John Gielgud in a supporting role. It would be one of the few occasions when Gielgud would be completely overshadowed by his co-stars.

The two stars also had something else in common, their capacity for alcohol. O'Toole, eight years younger than Burton was one of the few people in the movie business who could match Burton drink for drink. And it soon emerged that they had a third drinking partner in Elizabeth Taylor, who visited the set most days to keep an eye on her new boyfriend.

Taylor also proved a seasoned drinker, and it became a favourite joke of Burton's that he could drink any man under the table, but not every woman.

Burton repeated the same drinking routine he had begun on *The VIPs*, but with a subtle variation. This time, the Bloody Marys were followed by whisky pick-me-ups for lunch and then wine followed by more whiskies in the afternoon. Graham Jenkins, for one, thought his brother's drinking had reached dangerous levels, as he said: "To be in his company during these marathon sessions was to play life dangerously. When he was feeling good, he could engulf you in a marvellous sensation of well-being. I loved him then and felt as close to him as any brother could be. But the fun times were interrupted by terrifying bouts of depression and ill temper when he became a stranger to us all. No one could tell when the storm would break."

The drinking became a serious problem, and with Hal Wallis often absent from the set, there was no one strong enough to control O'Toole and Burton together, especially not when Taylor was also there. It was a concentration of star power that Peter Glenville certainly wasn't going to challenge. In any case, as Glenville recalled: "Only a couple of mornings' work were lost because of it."

But Burton's drinking did have one very real negative consequence. According to an account by Melvyn Bragg, a crew from *The Ed Sullivan Show* flew over from America to film an interview with Burton to promote *Becket*. But at the prescribed time, Burton was so drunk that he was incoherent and the crew returned to New York with footage Sullivan decided he couldn't broadcast, and a huge publicity opportunity was ruined.

Bragg described Burton's drinking as: "The process of tearing his past out of his mind." Peter Glenville called it "off-set roistering" and believed that Burton drank because "there was something he did not want to face, and which drinking perhaps covered up."

Halfway through filming, the amount of alcohol being consumed was adjudged to have become dangerous and was even recognised as such by Burton and O'Toole themselves – by this time on location in Northumberland. They both made a pact to give it up altogether until the end of filming. The pact didn't hold 100 per cent, especially after dark, but it was a brief respite for both of them.

It was a happy time that was only interrupted by the death of Pope John XXIII on 3rd June 1963. But, after what had happened the year before neither Taylor or Burton mourned his passing.

The spring and summer of 1963, which coincided with the filming of *Becket*, produced some glorious weather. Elizabeth Taylor would usually arrive on set at lunchtime and bring her children to watch filming when they weren't in school. She would then join Burton and O'Toole, and usually around half a dozen of Burton's favourite Fleet Street journalists, for lunch at a pub in the nearby village of Iver.

Afterwards, Taylor would walk round Shepperton village in jeans and t-shirt, sometimes without make-up, with her three children, Michael, Christopher and Liza. Every afternoon, she would go into the village corner shop, run by a character everyone called Ma Rowley and buy ice cream for her children. The other children of Shepperton would flock round and follow her like the Pied Piper. They, too, would be bought ice cream.

After a while, as word got around, Peter Glenville found Taylor's presence wholly distracting and negative to Burton's performance. In the end, Hal Wallis came over from America and politely asked her to keep away from the set for the sake of the film. With that, she cut her visits down to every other day.

But Glenville could do little about the hard drinking journalists who flocked to Iver when they realised they didn't need to make an appointment to just sit and chat with Britain's most famous actor. Most of the questions directed at Burton were about Peter O'Toole, and he told them all, when they asked him about the wisdom of playing opposite the man then regarded as Britain's most promising young star, that: "To work with clever people is not only a pleasure; it's a necessity. You can't win against fools." Burton had nothing to fear from O'Toole. His performance in *Becket* was outstanding, and Hollis Alpert called it: "A model of restrained but emotionally chilling acting."

Alpert was a long-standing American journalist friend of Burton's, but it was during the filming of *Becket* that Burton got to know the *Daily Mirror*'s Fergus Cashin very well and began confiding in him. Over the years, Cashin became the prime source for many of the best stories about Burton, and, ultimately, it was Cashin's writing, more than anything else, that was responsible for the undermining of the veracity of Burton's own diaries.

As for *Becket*, it cost US$3 million to make and only took US$5 million at cinemas worldwide. But with a US$1 million advance from American TV, it broke even. But years later, when home video was introduced, and later, DVDs, it made millions of dollars for the Paramount studio. As for Burton, he got his third Oscar nomination for best actor. And so did Peter O'Toole. But they both lost to Rex Harrison for his performance in the filmed version of *My Fair Lady*. But for many this was his best, certainly for Philip Burton as he said: "His performance caused me to weep with pride."

As *Becket* wrapped, Taylor and Burton had to deal with the cinema release of *Cleopatra*. There was to be no joy in it for them. *Cleopatra's* premiere was at the Rivoli Theatre in New York in June 1963. It was the most publicised film premiere in Hollywood history. But the finished film was a staggering 233 minutes long. The way Joe Mankiewicz had filmed it meant it couldn't be shorter.

Mankiewicz had lost all sympathy with Fox. He had committed the cardinal sin of beginning production without a finished script and writing it as he went along. However fine a director he was, nothing good could ever have come of that.

*Cleopatra* had, as Richard Burton had predicted, made all the old mistakes that had ruined *Alexander the Great*. It was a rambling story instead of being filmed entertainment. It wasn't a bad film, but it just wasn't a good one. Even amateur directors training at UCLA could see what was wrong, and the man who must take the blame is Mankiewicz for shooting it in the way he did. Whilst he was writing it, he thought it his life's work and his crowning glory; but he thought wrong. So much so that when Darryl Zanuck viewed the footage, Mankiewicz was shocked when he took the editing away from him and tried to make sense of it. The final Mankiewicz cut had come in at six hours.

Zanuck took over the post-production of the film himself and applied some unsentimental editing. He couldn't risk the lunatics who had nearly brought down the studio having anything more to do with the process.

The critics thought it dreadful on both sides of the Atlantic. One word was used to describe the film over and over again: "overblown." Rex Harrison undoubtedly upstaged Richard Burton, as his portrayal of Julius Caesar was much more convincing that Burton's Marc Antony. It was also very clear that Burton had been miscast.

The most devastating reviews pertained to Elizabeth Taylor. David Susskind, who hosted an influential chat show on American television, was scathing and stated that she had "set the acting profession back a decade."

Judith Crist in the *New York Herald Tribune* wrote: "Miss Taylor is monotony in a slit skirt. She is an essentially physical creature, with no depth of emotion apparent in her kohl-laden eyes, no modulation in her voice – that too often rises to fishwife levels...in *négligée* or *au naturel,* she gives the impression that she is really carrying on in one of Miami's Beach's more exotic resorts." Taylor didn't mind being called a 'chorus girl' by her critics, but 'fishwife' was too much to bear.

Burton's reviews were only a little better. *Time* magazine wrote: "He staggers around looking ghastly and spouting irrelevance, like a man who suddenly realises he has lost his script and is really reading some old sides from 'The King of Kings.'"

Philip Oakes wrote an extraordinary review in the *London Sunday Telegraph*: "Seeing *Cleopatra* at long last is rather like watching the birth of an elephant. In each case, the interest is clinical rather than aesthetic. In each case, the gestation period runs into years. And in each case, the end product is big, costly, and clumsy. All things considered, I prefer the elephant."

Only *The New York Times* defended the film. Attacking the attitude of the critics, it read: "Sceptics were predisposed to give *Cleopatra* the needle." It called Rex Harrison's performance "faceted" and Burton's "exciting." But no one else thought that.

*The New Yorker* magazine said: "The merciful quick thing to say about *Cleopatra* was that it would have made a marvellous silent picture." It was the ultimate put-down of the actors and, in truth, there was a lot to be said for that view.

Taylor first saw the film when she hosted a special preview, ahead of its release, for the members of the Bolshoi Ballet in early spring of 1963. She was reported as having said afterwards: "The final humiliation was to have to see it."

When he read the first reviews, Burton refused to attend any of the premieres and Taylor went to New York on her own. Neither of them went to the London premiere in protest against the brutality of the critics.

Burton and Taylor both blamed Zanuck, and tried to maintain that their best acting had been cut from the film. Taylor said: "The only things I am proud of, Fox cut out with unerring accuracy."

It was nonsense. But neither was it their fault, as they just couldn't bring themselves to blame their friend, Mankiewicz. Both of them had been much impressed by Mankiewicz and thought that he would get an Oscar for *Cleopatra*. But they were sadly misguided. Burton said: "I think Mr Mankiewicz might have made the first really good epic film." Taylor said: "What has happened to Mr. Mankiewicz is disgraceful, degrading, humiliating and appalling." Mankiewicz also supported his stars and said: "Burton suffered most in the cutting. He gave a brilliant performance, much of which will never be seen." But Mankiewicz didn't seem to understand that Rex Harrison had given the much better performance.

Burton tried to explain what had gone wrong: "In Mankiewicz's version, Marc Antony is a man who talks excessively to excuse his own failure to become a great man. He's extremely eloquent, but at times inarticulately eloquent. The fury is there and the sense of failure is there, but sometimes all that comes out is a series of splendid words without any particular meaning."

Mankiewicz blamed Zanuck for not seeing the need for character motivations. But Zanuck didn't have six hours.

Ironically, there was a chance for success when it was suggested that Fox produce two movies out of it: one, entitled *Caesar and Cleopatra;* and the other, *Antony and Cleopatra* of the type popularised with *Harry Potter* and the *Lord of the Rings.* But such an approach was unheard of then and not seriously considered. But if that idea had been taken up, Hollywood history could have been changed, as it was unquestionably the right thing to do since Mankiewicz had actually unwittingly made two separate and distinctive movies.

Ironically, Darryl Zanuck was ultimately vindicated as *Cleopatra* went on to take US$62 million worldwide at the box office and a further US$7 million from sales to television. Fox got back US$39 million for its US$37 million investment and made itself US$2 million. In truth, Zanuck had rescued the appalling situation into which Spyros Skouras, Wanger and Mankiewicz had landed the studio, and he managed to get back Fox's money.

In the end, Zanuck was very generous, and both Walter Wanger and Joe Mankiewicz got prominent billing as director and producer in the film's opening credits. And for that, they can have had no complaint.

Afterwards, 20th Century-Fox's shareholders wanted to sue former president Spyros Skouras personally for the contract he had signed with Elizabeth Taylor, which was so generous they thought it must be fraudulent. Taylor reportedly took home US$3.5 million, some three times what any star had been paid before. The continuous indulgence of Elizabeth Taylor by Wanger and Mankiewicz had nearly broken Fox.

To the end of his days, Joe Mankiewicz maintained that he had shot a very good film which had all ended up on the cutting room floor, and he urged critics to view his six-hour version, saying: "He [Zanuck] destroyed an extremely good performance by Richard Burton and a well-written one, too, that no one has ever seen. Literally, no one has ever seen."

According to Mankiewicz, before he died, the cans of footage remain to this day in the film vaults of 20th Century-Fox. One day, they might make a very handsome television miniseries, an idea that seems, so far, to have occurred to no one.

It seemed that nothing good happened to Burton around this time. In

# DIVORCE HIS, DIVORCE HERS

September 1963, to coincide with the release of *Cleopatra,* a major interview given to his friend Kenneth Tynan was published in *Playboy* magazine. *Playboy* was then at its zenith and enjoyed a circulation of around seven million in the United States. Its monthly interviews were a very big event.

The interview was conducted in March 1963 in London but didn't appear until six months later. It was done at The Dorchester when Burton was at his lowest point during the filming of *The VIPs.* Burton wasn't doing press interviews at the time because he was in such poor shape from alcohol abuse. But a request from his friend Tynan was different, and difficult to refuse.

Predictably, it was a disaster due to the combination of Burton's expansive, unedited pronouncements and Tynan's indecipherable prose. Years later, Melvyn Bragg described the interview as being "...like the ravings of D. H. Lawrence's less clear-headed heroes." Burton's brother Graham was more direct, calling it "obtuse and contradictory."

In the interview, Burton raved and criticised, amongst others, John Gielgud and Laurence Olivier. He accused them of continually "drying up" during performances. He also attacked the leading playwrights of the day; Samuel Beckett, Arthur Miller, Tennessee Williams and especially Eugene O'Neill, whom he called "hopeless" and added: "He is no good and the phoniest playwright I've ever read." Only John Osborne escaped the lashing.

The interview developed into pure farce when Tynan asked him his views on the sanctity of marriage, to which he replied; "Monogamy is absolutely imperative. The minute you start fiddling around outside the idea of monogamy, nothing satisfies anymore. Suppose you make love to an exciting woman other than your wife. It can't remain enough to go to bed with her; there must be something else, something more than the absolute compulsion of the body. But if there is something more, it will eventually destroy either you or your marriage."

Tynan asked him how he squared his philosophy of marriage in general with his own in particular, and Burton replied: "Speaking for myself, I couldn't be unfaithful to my wife without feeling a profound sense of guilt. I'm not unfaithful to my wife. I never have been, not for a moment. It's wrong to assume I've been unfaithful simply because I happen to live in the same hotel as another woman. What I have done is to move outside the accepted idea of monogamy without investing the other person with anything that makes me feel guilty, so that I remain inviolate, untouched." It was the same stream of consciousness nonsense he filled his own diaries with day after day.

# AND GOD CREATED BURTON

At the end of the interview, a confused Burton could only confess he was "a mass of contradictions." After the interview was published, it was never the same again between him and Tynan, who was heavily criticised by Burton's circle of friends for having conducted the interview, which was tape-recorded, when his friend was so obviously out of sorts under the influence of drink.

When he read the interview, Burton called his friend, the *Daily Mirror* journalist Fergus Cashin, for advice: "Did I say it? You know me by now. Of course, I did. It was an interview at The Dorchester that lasted six hours and six bottles with Tynan's tape recorder going the whole time. I dictated enough to make *Gone With The Wind* look like a slim volume of verse. I'm a confusion of talk. For instance, I heard myself saying on one part of the tape: "Good writing is for the minority, because the minority are the only ones who can judge." And then later I heard myself saying: "Good writing can only be judged by the number of people who read it. The more who read it the better it is."

Outside The Dorchester, Taylor told reporters, who all wanted to question her about the *Playboy* article: "Of course I'm not mad with Richard. I love him and I'm going to marry him. It's just that he suffers from this intoxication of words. It's Welsh verbal diarrhoea. But he is so full of shit."

Around the same time, Graham Jenkins also got in on the act and began giving his own interviews. One in particular got him into a lot of trouble, damaged his reputation and scarred the rest of his life. It came about when he gave a very detailed interview to a *News of the World* journalist, during which intimate aspects of the Burtons' married life were discussed – information that had never before been discussed or revealed.

When the details were picked up and reported verbatim in the New York newspapers, Philip Burton was apoplectic and fired off a letter to Jenkins at his home, as well as consulting a lawyer. Philip was extremely irate and knew it was the last thing Sybil needed as she settled down in New York.

Jenkins later admitted he had been paid for the interview but said he did not realise the writer was a *News of the World* journalist. He said: "An over-trusting nature led me into bad company." Jenkins explained that he had been contacted by a journalist who asked if he could help with an article on his brother for a woman's magazine. He said he met the journalist over lunch and that they got on well together. He agreed to an interview and said: "I was even to be paid for my trouble; not much, it was true, but the thought was welcome." It later emerged he had been paid £200, which in those days was a great deal of money.

The following Sunday, he got a call from Burton who asked him to buy a copy of the *News of the World*. His story was slapped across a *News of the World* spread. It was entitled: 'The Richard Burton story by Graham Jenkins'. And more was promised in the following two weeks.

Burton was furious when he learned Graham had been paid and was also cross about how little it had been, as he said: "Is that all? I can just about understand you wanting to sell out your brother. What I can't forgive is selling me off so cheaply." Burton didn't think it was amusing at all and slammed down the phone. He put his own lawyers to work and the rest of the story got halted at a cost of some £1,000 in legal costs. Burton told his brother: "It cost me more to get them to stop writing than it cost them to start you talking." Graham Jenkins' reputation took a nose dive after that and the family never trusted him again. That episode with the newspaper article still rankles today, even after 48 years.

In September 1963, with the *Playboy* and the *News of the World* articles, as well as the bad reviews, still ringing in their ears, Burton and Taylor flew into Mexico City. It was a convenient time for both of them as it kept them out of Britain and America and away from the attentions of the world's presses, which by then had become a feeding frenzy about every aspect of their relationship and performances in *Cleopatra*.

So Burton had been extremely grateful when he was approached by the producer Ray Stark and director John Huston with an offer to star alongside Ava Gardner in a film adaptation of Tennessee Williams' play, 'Night of the Iguana'. Stark had got a US$3 million budget from MGM and quickly agreed to pay Burton the US$500,000 fee he wanted. Huston recalled: "Ray Stark and I agreed that Richard Burton was ideal for this role."

But there was no part for Taylor, as John Huston didn't rate her acting. When she tried to go over his head to MGM, he stood firm and the studio buckled when Huston told MGM bosses that he thought she was a lousy actress and would be trouble. With that, Taylor gave up and chose not to challenge Huston's view, which would have been difficult with all the negative reviews that were circulating for her performance as Cleopatra.

But she resolved to visit the set every day for the duration to keep an eye on her new boyfriend.

During filming, Taylor perceived a threat from Ava Gardner, then 42 years old but still a "smouldering siren." Nancy Schoenberger said: "With her bold, sensuous beauty, her strong sexuality, and her ability to drink like a man, [she] posed the greatest threat to Elizabeth."

The crew was apparently aware of a "mutual attraction" and it would have been unusual if Burton hadn't made something of it. Taylor made sure she was around as often as possible when Gardner was present.

She had good reason as the film's publicity used the slogan: "One man… three women…one night." It didn't leave much to the imagination.

The film was actually a melancholy comedy about a party of female American tourists on holiday. Burton played a disgraced alcoholic priest who is defrocked for adultery and becomes a tour guide. He is placed in charge of a busload of women tourists, one or more of whom tries to seduce him. His principal seductress was the 17-year-old old starlet Sue Lyon, who had become famous overnight for making a sensuous and controversial film debut as Lolita. It was an all-star cast, including Ava Gardner and Deborah Kerr. Taylor thought she should have been playing Gardner's role.

Huston described Burton's character as "a broken man, drinking heavily." Referring to Burton's drinking habits, Huston quipped to journalists: "A few years later, we might have called it typecasting."

The film was to be shot on location in Mexico near the pretty fishing village of Puerto Vallarta, 320 miles north of Acapulco.

When Burton and Taylor flew into Mexico City's airport on 22nd September 1963, it caused a sensation. A huge crowd awaited them and they could not leave the plane due to a mass of people waiting at the bottom of the plane's steps.

Taylor balked at facing what she described as a "heavy mob." It was a pretty accurate description, but Burton knew they had to try and get through. With them were Dick Hanley and his assistant, Taylor's personal cook, her chauffeur, her nanny, and two of her four children.

There then followed a strange moment when a swarthy Mexican in a large sombrero hat, wearing two guns in a holster, came on board the plane and burst into the first-class cabin. He was Emilio Hernandez, the assistant director of *Night of the Iguana,* and he had come to collect them. But with no introduction, he took Taylor by the arm and just said: "Follow me." Burton instinctively thought Taylor was being kidnapped. He had heard many such stories of what went on in Mexico, so he punched Hernandez to the ground and grabbed one of his guns from the holster. Pointing it at him, he threatened to shoot if he moved. The pilots heard the commotion and rushed in. They disarmed Hernandez on the ground and threw him down the steps of the plane. The stunned and somewhat bewildered assistant director picked himself up and stumbled back to the terminal.

When Burton and Taylor finally disembarked, it was mayhem as they struggled through the crowds with no police or security in sight. In the melee, Taylor lost both her shoes and her handbag.

Finally, the party reached the terminal and the cars which were to take them into Mexico City.

A press conference for Mexican journalists had been planned at the terminal but an angry Burton cancelled it, saying simply: "This is my first visit to Mexico. I trust it shall be my last."

He soon changed his mind a week later when they finally arrived at Casa Kimberley, the house they had rented in Puerto Vallarta. It was the best house in the village and had six bedrooms, with a bathroom for each bedroom. The house was four stories high and on a steep hill that gave a total view of the Bay of Banderas.

Puerto Vallarta was a very quiet fishing port. It was completely unspoiled and had only one phone in the whole village, although Burton soon installed a second at Casa Kimberly. The village's only link with the world was a daily air shuttle that flew in from Mexico City, over 300 miles away.

Like many before them, they were utterly charmed by the beauty of Mexico's Pacific coastline. They fell in love with the empty beaches and the shadow of the grassy mountain that shaded Puerto Vallarta. Melvyn Bragg called it a "Mexican St Tropez." It was hardly that, although it would develop quickly once Burton and Taylor arrived. The heat was intense and the sea was a warm bath – it was a paradise of sorts.

The choice of the mountainous Pacific coast of Mexico for the filming and the all-star cast was a stroke of luck for the villagers of Puerto Vallarta. The arrival of the two most famous people in the world attracted a host of journalists and they all went back and wrote how beautiful it was. From then on, the village never looked back and quickly became a prosperous resort.

Although the unit was based at Puerto Vallarta, the main location of the film was eight miles into the jungle, on a peninsula, in a tiny settlement called Mismaloya, which could be reached only by boat. It was a 20-minute boat ride across the bay and then a 20-minute walk to the set. Ray Stark had built a block of air-conditioned bungalows for the crew to stay in. Giant generators rumbled in the background 24 hours a day.

In the afternoons, those not directly involved in the filming lounged on the beach. And every evening, the whole cast and crew dived into the ocean.

Despite the heat and sometimes difficult jungle type conditions, it was a very easy shoot and a happy set despite the presence for most of the time of Michael Wilding, Taylor's former husband. He was handling the film's publicity and working for Burton's agent, Hugh French. As John Huston confirmed: "Everyone got along really well and there were no tantrums, no fireworks."

But Huston was surprised by Burton's capacity for drink, which he witnessed every day of filming – as Bob Wilson did his traditional act with the vodka. Huston was something of a drinker and a somewhat famous hell raiser himself, but he was staggered at what Burton consumed in a day. Ava Gardner, who also had a reputation for enjoying a drink, said: "I thought I drank a lot, and I thought John drank a lot, but Richard drank more than anyone I ever knew."

Despite the remote location, over 130 journalists visited the set during shooting and at any one time there over 30 staying in the village. With little else to do, every night Burton held court in the local bar and gave the visiting writers his views on everything and anything. There was plenty to talk about and he only became annoyed once, when a writer addressed him as "Mr Cleopatra", a joke which he didn't get.

He enjoyed taunting Taylor during these evenings and loved highlighting her lack of proper acting credentials. One journalist wrote a piece that quoted Burton saying to Taylor: "Give me a line from Shakespeare, any line you can think of. I'll tell you the rest of the speech." She replied: "To be or not to be." He said: "That's too easy. Come on, think of another one."

Knowing what was coming, Taylor tried to change the subject and said: "This is silly, let's talk about something else." He sneered back: "Oh yes, I forgot, you don't know any Shakespeare, do you? Not one bloody word that doesn't come out of the dictionary of clichés."

As she got up to leave, she ended it by saying: "Well, love, we can't all be geniuses." He got the message and shut up, and she came back.

In later interviews, he credited Taylor with calming him down and said: "She makes me less volatile." But she disagreed and said: "He's not less volatile. He just chooses when and where to be volatile with more discrimination."

There was a very sombre moment on Friday 22nd November when news came through to the village that President Kennedy had been assassinated. Burton was devastated. He had met the Kennedys a few times and felt close to them because of 'Camelot' in 1961. He was completely depressed for the whole of the last week of filming and annoyed at the lack of television reception, which meant he couldn't watch President Kennedy's funeral. Every night, he cried on Taylor's shoulder and she comforted him. He was really knocked back and he told her he felt far worse about the President's death than he did about losing Sybil.

The assassination changed his mood and he made the decision to buy a house in Puerto Vallarta, where he felt so at home. After the assassination, he felt as though he never wanted to return to what he called the "real world." He decided the family would stay in Mexico rather than returning to Europe, as they had planned over Christmas. Burton cast his eye over Casa Kimberley and decided to buy it. It cost a mere US$75,000, and almost straightaway they made plans to spend double that amount on upgrading it. Without a new movie to go on to directly after *Night of the Iguana,* they needed somewhere to live, and the thought of leaving Puerto Vallarta in December for Gstaad filled him with horror.

Filming ended at the end of November 1963, and everyone knew that John Huston had put a very good film in the can even without seeing the rushes. Huston instinctively knew how to direct a human drama in a way Joe Mankiewicz never could. The filming came to an end ahead of schedule.

The following year, *Night of the Iguana* raked in US$12 million in cinemas around the world and another US$2 million in TV syndication fees and turned a US$5 million profit for MGM.

That Christmas, the entire extended Taylor family made plans to come to Puerto Vallarta, including Taylor's brother Howard, his wife and their five children.

Ten-year-old Michael and eight-year-old Christopher Wilding, who had been placed in a California boarding school, flew in for the holiday, making a total of nine children in the house for the festive season.

The star of the household that Christmas was little Maria, who was now with them full time after some lengthy operations in Munich to correct birth defects that prevented her from walking properly. The orphan had been discovered by Taylor's friend, the German actress, Maria Schell when she was nine months old. Her official adoption was completed with Taylor and Eddie Fisher as her new parents. Her determination to adopt Maria and give her a new life reflected very well on Taylor as a person. To celebrate, it was decided that, from then on, she would be known as Maria Burton. Like the other Burton family in New York, this disconnected branch also enjoyed a very happy Christmas.

# AND GOD CREATED BURTON

# CHAPTER 38

# Elizabeth conquers the valleys

## *A royal visit to Wales*

### 1963

As soon as *Becket* wrapped at Shepperton, and before he left for Mexico, Richard Burton took his new partner, Elizabeth Taylor, to Wales to meet the Jenkins family for the first time. Meeting the Jenkinses on their home turf could be viewed as a daunting experience. History has recorded that the family followed the example of Burton's friends and rejected Taylor, remaining loyal to Sybil. But this was not true and Burton-Taylor historians seriously erred.

In her biography of Burton, Penny Junor said: "The one thing that brought a smile to Sybil's face about the entire fiasco was the fact that Elizabeth would get the family: there was some justice in the world after all." But there was no evidence to suggest that these were really Sybil's views. Sybil loved Burton's family dearly and, more importantly, they loved her dearly, so Junor's assumptions were at odds with the reality.

Junor went on to call the Jenkinses "warm, kindly people, but the family en masse, with husbands and wives and assorted children, could be very overpowering." That view is also misleading and the Jenkinses were anything but "overpowering." Certainly, in all the interviews with Elaine Dundy, from whom most of Sybil's inner thoughts have been gleaned, she infers the opposite of the view Junor propagated. When she left Burton behind and cut him off entirely, Sybil also felt she had to do the same with his family – but it was done for her own sanity and didn't reflect how she felt towards them at all. In all of Burton's biographies, there is a lot of "assumptive analysis" from writers on this subject, and none of it is accurate.

In fact, one of the beauties of the Jenkins-Williams marriage was the harmony between the families. Just as Sybil returned with him dutifully to Port Talbot, Burton often turned out for Sybil's family and made numerous visits to the town of Northampton, where Sybil's elder sister, Elsie, lived. The truth was that Burton thoroughly enjoyed Sybil's family, and Sybil felt the same way about his.

Sybil's own relationship with the Jenkins family was further enhanced by the lack of a mother-in-law, a normal source of resentment in any family. The natural friction that can develop between a mother-in-law and a daughter-in-law didn't exist, nor did it ever develop. Cecilia James and Philip Burton, the natural in-law replacements, were more like a brother and sister to Sybil, and their relationships were 100 per cent harmonious.

That didn't stop Melvyn Bragg describing Elizabeth Taylor's first visit to Wales as "a brief and difficult encounter." But Bragg also got it wrong, as Taylor had no problems gaining acceptance. The family immediately loved Elizabeth Taylor, and Taylor immediately loved the family, albeit in an entirely different way to the mutual love they also had enjoyed with Sybil. Bragg's view is a notion strongly rejected by the senior members of the family.

From those first meetings, Taylor developed a close and enduring relationship with the family, and one that didn't die when she was divorced from Burton, nor with his death. And as more time passed, the relationship quickly became far warmer and deeper than any they ever enjoyed with Sybil.

The family had been primed by an earlier visit that Burton had made on his own. Eldest brother, Tom Jenkins, described it as: "His coming home. It was like a cry for help." Cecilia James said: "How could we be angry with him? He looked so sad." On his visit, Burton continually told them: "You'll like her." And they did straightaway. So even before they met Taylor, unlike his friends in London, the family in Wales was right behind her.

For the visit, Burton decided not to drive himself, as he had done previously, and they arrived in a chauffeur-driven Daimler limousine. Taylor was dressed to impress, in stark contrast to Sybil's visits. For her, this was politics from the start and she was out to win hearts and minds. She craved acceptance; desperately wanted it; and overwhelmingly won it.

They first drove to Aberavon to visit Elfed and Cecilia James' new house, which Burton had helped them purchase. Burton had only called and told them they were coming the night before, deliberately to avoid any press intrusion. He asked Cecilia to tell the rest of the family but to impress upon them the need for secrecy.

When they arrived in Aberavon there was a very warm welcome awaiting them. Elfed James was standing in the doorway, and there was a great big smile on his face as well as on Burton's as he opened the front gate. Now retired, all of Elfed James' differences with Burton had long been resolved. Now Burton could see things much more clearly than he had as a rebellious 14-year-old and was deeply grateful for everything Elfed had done for him.

# ELIZABETH CONQUERS THE VALLEYS

The two men hugged and kissed, genuinely delighted to see each other again. Cecilia did the same with Elizabeth Taylor; the two women needed no introduction. There was no awkwardness and they both instantly recognised a kindred spirit in the other. In fact, the two women got on like a house on fire immediately. Cecilia took Elizabeth inside the house, and Elfed and Burton chatted outside in the sunshine as neighbours ogled the shiny silver-coloured Daimler parked outside. They recognised it as the same model in which Swansea's mayor drove around and guessed it must be Burton come to visit. But they had no idea that the most famous woman in the world was in their street as well.

There was immediate compatibility between Cecilia and Elizabeth, which there never had been with Sybil. After Cecilia had cooked scrambled eggs and lava bread for lunch, Burton left the two women to bond whilst he explored the local pubs, guided by Elfed, who broke his usual abstinence to enjoy half a pint of pale ale himself.

Taylor's tactile warmth stunned Cecilia. This was Taylor's first taste of what she called "real life" outside of Hampstead, Surrey, Park Lane, Gstaad or Beverly Hills. Talking to Cecilia in her small front room, she realised she had spent all of her life enjoying what she later described as "extreme privilege." Real life was the one thing her fame, beauty and wealth could not provide, and during the trip, it suddenly dawned on her that her life, one surrounded by art and antiques, had been completely taken for granted. She realised she had never experienced a normal life. Coming to Wales turned out to be more than a trip to visit her new partner's family; it turned into a real voyage of personal discovery, something she truly relished.

As they said their 'goodbyes' to Elfed and Cecilia, they went on to Taibach in Port Talbot so Burton could show Taylor where he spent his childhood. She walked up and down Caradoc Street and the adjacent streets, visited the pubs and the fish and chip shops, and shook hands and spoke to everyone who approached her. She also went inside the houses and was shocked by the relative squalor in some of them. She answered any questions that were asked of her and, according to the few people remaining, who still remember her visit, she asked many of her own about her new boyfriend's past.

Port Talbot was then still a charming place before it was irretrievably scarred by the M40 motorway. That evening, the two of them enjoyed an early supper of beef and kidney pie with peas and mashed potatoes in a

Taibach pub with some of his old school friends, now all in their mid-thirties with their own families and with many of their own stories to tell.

Then, around six o'clock, they were driven to Pontrhydyfen, the place of his birth, where they stayed overnight with his sister, Hilda Owen, her husband Dai and the four Owen children, Sian, Megan, Gareth and Gerwyn. Before they went to bed, they visited The Miner's Arms and Burton told Taylor all the old stories; some true, some not. He no longer knew which were true and which weren't, as he had told them so many times. The visit surprised the locals, who had no idea they were in Wales.

Because the visit was a surprise, there was very little press intrusion and when they heard Elizabeth Taylor was in town, newspaper editors simply didn't believe it. Afterwards, Burton told many tall stories to journalists about the visit, including that night when a "grizzled miner reached out and parted her lips to examine her teeth", to which Taylor said: "Just like they were looking at a horse they bought." And he told the story of the miner she slapped after he "pinched her bottom." They both returned to Hilda's house very happy, laughing tears of joy. She favourably compared The Miner's Arms to the bar at the Beverly Hills Hotel in Hollywood, where she had drunk in her teenage years.

They slept in Hilda's tiny guest bedroom upstairs. As the single toilet was downstairs, Taylor asked Hilda if she could have an old fashioned chamber pot under the bed and Hilda fished one out from the shed. Hilda told her that, in the last century, a chamber pot under the bed was regarded as a real luxury when the only other option was a visit outside to the toilet at the bottom of the garden.

The following day, they visited the rest of the brothers and sisters who still lived in the area and got round to most of them, staying an hour and a half at each.

Years later, David Jenkins recalled the visit to his house in Cecil Road in Gowerton, although in his book, he confused it with a much later visit. He described Taylor, the world's most famous woman, sitting in an armchair in his front room with him and his wife Betty, "sipping cups of tea and chatting with careful casualness." He continued: "It was quite an event, of course, having Elizabeth Taylor to tea. You could not help giving quick glances at her eyes, just to check whether they really were all they were claimed to be. She looked stunning, I thought, sitting there in knee-length lavender suede boots which, she exclaimed delightedly, matched our sitting room carpet."

Jenkins, who was a policeman, described the reaction of the residents of Cecil Road: "The neighbours, not least the wife of my superintendent, were installed behind their lace curtains for the duration of the visit and emerged quite by chance as the pair were leaving. To my great amusement, there was a shameless scramble to sit in the chair she sat in."

Burton and Taylor also made a spontaneous visit to Gowerton police station and Jenkins' colleagues didn't attempt to hide their enthusiasm, as he recalled: "The Chief Inspector there rang at once and asked me to bring the celebrated pair to my workplace. Chief Inspector Austin opened a bottle of whisky and the atmosphere was not that of a clinical, busy police station at all. Richard, seeing the booze, said: 'Now, the party's starting' and he, rather than Elizabeth, was the talkative one. But it was she who drew all glances to her. My immediate superior, the late Superintendent Joe Hewlett, said to me: 'My God, Dai, Elizabeth looks simply wonderful. I feel like putting my arms around her.' It was a sentiment shared by many of my seemingly unflappable brawny mates. But perhaps the best comment came from one of our neighbours. 'Oh, such beautiful features. All I can say is she is the reincarnation of the Madonna herself.' Mrs. Austin in particular paid special attention to Elizabeth's appearance and, lo and behold, in the next edition of the *Glamorgan County Police Magazine*, every detail of Elizabeth's outfit was meticulously recorded."

David Jenkins was unequivocal that the visit was a success: "We found her quite charming and not at all ostentatious; a little nervous even, anxious to be accepted by us all. Elizabeth must certainly have been aware of our attachment and supportive feelings towards Sybil. In fact, by then, we had had to do so much adapting that our longing for a vanished past was somewhat diminished. We still felt for Sybil but she had accepted the situation by now, and everybody, with the exception of Ivor, was prepared to move on."

It was a very happy couple who were driven back to London and The Dorchester that night as they snuggled up together in the back of the Daimler and fell asleep. The visit had been problem-free, particularly as there was no intrusion from journalists or photographers. Burton pronounced her visit an unequivocal success, unlike the reception she had received from his friends outside of Wales.

The following day, they were driven down to Oxford to visit Professor Neville Coghill, Burton's old mentor at Oxford University. Coghill was now heavily involved with Frank Hauser's Oxford Playhouse, which Burton had helped get going with his £2,000 investment nine years earlier. For Taylor, it was a totally different experience from Wales and her first visit to the university city. The Oxford Playhouse was continually trying to raise money, and the enthusiasm that was generated for the theatre just by their visit was huge. Taylor encouraged Burton to get more involved and a scheme was hatched for them to play in a future production of Christopher Marlowe's 1592 play 'Doctor Faustus', directed by Coghill himself.

The reception of his friends in Wales and at Oxford helped allay the unhappiness at the rejection from his old friends in London. There, Elizabeth Taylor was only tolerated and there was lip service politeness. It was obvious from the start that Burton's circle of friends outside Wales were 100 per cent behind Sybil. Stanley Baker's wife, Ellen, decided outright to reject a friendship with Taylor.

# ELIZABETH CONQUERS THE VALLEYS

# AND GOD CREATED BURTON

**Above:** Norman Parkinson was commissioned to take Elizabeth Taylor's official 40th birthday photograph. He dressed both her and Burton in black mink coats and positioned them high above the Danube for the photographs taken in the second week of February 1972 in Budapest, where they were shortly to host a grand party. The photos were released on her birthday, Tuesday 27th February. She was wearing the 33.19 carat Krupp diamond.

Douglas Miller/Stringer/Getty Images

**Above:** Richard Burton, Elizabeth Taylor and Michael Redgrave on the receiving line to meet Princess Margaret at the 1967 Royal Film Performance of *The Taming of the Shrew* at the Odeon Theatre, Leicester Square, London, on 28th February 1967.

Getty Images

**Above right:** Richard Burton and Elizabeth Taylor drink a toast after hearing she had won the Oscar for best actress in *Who's afraid of Virginia Woolf?*. They were at the Hotel du Golf di Valescure in St Raphael, France in April 1967 and did not attend the ceremony in Los Angeles.

**Right:** Burton and Taylor with actress Claudia Cardinale at a charity ball in Venice during the 1967 Venice Film Festival, on 11th September 1967.

Willi Schneider/Rex Features

**Left:** The Burtons, photographed on 28th August 1967 on board their yacht, the Kalizma, off the coast of Capa Caccia, Sardinia. They stayed on board during the filming of *Boom!*, in which they both had staring roles.   .

*David Cairns/Stringer/Getty Images*

**Right and below:** The Burtons during the Christmas holidays in December 1967 at Chalet Ariel in Gstaad, Switzerland, in December 1967. Taylor purchased Chalet Ariel in 1959 with her then husband, Eddie Fisher. The Burtons used it as their European base and spent every Christmas there.

*James Andanson/Apis/Sygma/Corbis*

*James Andanson/Apis/Sygma/Corbis*

**Left:** Richard Burton and Elizabeth Taylor at the wedding of Taylor's personal photographer, Gianni Bozzacchi, to her hair stylist, Claudye Ettori, in Paris on 22nd June 1968. Liza Todd and Maria Burton were bridesmaids at the ceremony in the village of Saints.

**Below:** The wedding of Richard Burton's valet, Bob Wilson, to Gladys Mills at Caxton Hall, London, took place on 9th August 1969 and was attended by both Burton and Elizabeth Taylor.

**Left:** The Burtons on the set of *Where Eagles Dare* at Pinewood Studios, Buckinghamshire, England, on 27th February 1968. Taylor celebrated her 36th birthday with a cake presented to her by the film crew.

**Above:** Genevieve Bujold grew very close to Richard Burton during filming of *Anne of the Thousand Days* and spent every moment they could together, despite the close proximity of Elizabeth Taylor.

**Left:** Richard Burton, on the set of *Anne of the Thousand Days* at Shepperton Studios in London, England, takes lunch during a break with his young co-star, the French-Canadian actress Genevieve Bujold, on 28th May 1969.

**Right:** Richard Burton, Elizabeth Taylor and Kate Burton on location in the grounds of Hever Castle, Kent, during the filming of *Anne of the Thousand Days* in June 1969.

**Above:** Members of the Jenkins family, photographed in Wales, where they had gathered to celebrate Independence Day on 4th July 1970 in deference to Elizabeth Taylor. Pictured from left are Graham Jenkins, Hilda Jenkins, Tom Jenkins, Betty Jenkins, Hilary Jenkins, and Hyrel Jenkins.

**Left:** Elizabeth Taylor, Richard Burton and Cecilia James after he was made a Commander of the British Empire (CBE) by Queen Elizabeth II at Buckingham Palace, London, on the same day as his 45th birthday, 10th November 1970.

**Left:** The Burtons exchange a kiss at a hand printing ceremony at Castellaneta, near Taranto, Italy, in 1970.

**Left:** Richard Burton gets in character as he waits to be cuffed by Nigel Davenport on the set of the British movie *Villain*, in November 1970. The low-budget crime drama, in which Burton played a homosexual crime boss called Vic Dakin and co-starred with Ian McShane, has since become a cult classic.

**Right:** Richard Burton interrupts a love scene between Peter O'Toole and Elizabeth Taylor for a photo opportunity during the filming of Dylan Thomas' *Under Milk Wood* in January 1971.

**Above:** Richard Burton relaxes at Chalet Ariel, Gstaad. Taylor had owned the house since 1959, when she had bought it with her then husband Eddie Fisher. They paid US$280,000 for it and it became the place they went to every Christmas.

**Above:** Richard Burton, Elizabeth Taylor and Claudye Bozzacchi, wife of photographer Gianni Bozzacchi, in Acapulco, Mexico in May 1971. The Burtons were in Mexico for the filming of *Hammersmith is Out*.

*Minnepix*

*Reginald Gray/Condé Nast Archive/Corbis*

**Above:** Ringo Starr, Graham Jenkins and Maureen Starkey during the weekend celebrations of Elizabeth Taylor's 40th birthday in Budapest, in February 1972 at the Hotel Intercontinental.

**Left:** Elizabeth Taylor poses with the Taj Mahal diamond necklace, a 40th birthday present from her husband, on the weekend of 24th/25th February 1972 in Budapest. The necklace reportedly cost Burton US$900,000.

*Rhiannon Trowell*

**Left:** Howard Taylor, Cecilia James and Elfed James at Elizabeth Taylor's 40th birthday celebrations in Budapest, on the weekend of 24th/25th February 1972.

**Left:** Princess Grace of Monaco with Richard Burton in Budapest, Hungary, in February 1972. Princess Grace was attending Elizabeth Taylor's 40th birthday celebrations in the city.

**Above:** Richard Burton with Italian director Carlo Ponti at the Moscow International Film festival, where *The Battle of Sutjeska* won best anti-fascist film award, on 26th May 1972.

**Left and below:** In May 1972 Richard Burton was reportedly having an affair with Nathalie Delon on the set of *Bluebeard* to which he later confessed.

**Left:** Burton in character on the set of *The Klansman* in Oroville, California, with a glass of vodka in hand, in March 1974. Burton played an alcoholic on and off the filmset and reviewers called his performance "befuddled." It was the height of his drinking, and at this point in his life he was reportedly consuming two to three bottles of vodka a day.

**Right:** Richard Burton and Robert Hardy starred in the 1974 NBC/BBC co-production of *Walk With Destiny*. Burton played Churchill and Hardy played Ambassador Joachim von Ribbentrop. The programme was called *The Gathering Storm* in America.

**Below:** Richard Burton arrives in his Jaguar E-Type for a day of filming on the set of the television remake of *Brief Encounter* in Winchester, England, in August 1974.

**Above and below:** Richard Burton and Sophia Loren filming the TV miniseries, *Brief Encounter* in England in August 1974. The remake of the 1946 original romantic drama, starring Trevor Howard and Celia Johnson, was produced by Loren's husband, Carlo Ponti. It was a big-budget production made for television and paid for by Hallmark Cards for its new television channel. Burton slashed his normal fee so he could star with Loren. During filming, Burton became mesmerised and infatuated with her and the two enjoyed a sort of romance that was never fully explained.

**Left:** Richard Burton with Princess Elizabeth of Yugoslavia and her daughter, Catherine Oxenberg, after announcing their engagement on 17th October 1974. Burton had got engaged to a woman he didn't really love on the rebound from Elizabeth Taylor. Predictably, it didn't last long.

**Left:** Princess Elizabeth and Richard Burton leave The Dorchester in Park Lane, London, by a side door, on 13th February 1975.

**Right:** Richard Burton and Elizabeth Taylor in Jerusalem, Israel, on 30th August 1975, when they announced their intention to remarry as quickly as possible.

**Above:** Richard Burton remarries Elizabeth Taylor on the banks of the Chobe river beside the remote village of Kasane in Botswana, South Africa, on 10th October 1975. It was the craziest thing he ever did and cost him millions of dollars when he had to divorce her within a few months of the remarriage. She took him for almost everything he had.

**Left:** The twice-married couple arrive at The Dorchester in London on November 1975, for celebrations to mark Richard Burton's 50th birthday.

**Right:** Richard Burton and Elizabeth Taylor at Burton's 50th birthday party, held at the Orchid Rooms of The Dorchester on 10th November 1975. The elaborate party cost Taylor over US$50,000 to put on.

**Above:** James Hunt with Richard Burton and Suzy Miller in London. The racing driver was delighted when his wife found happiness with Burton after they were divorced.

**Above:** Richard Burton in New York City on his return to Broadway in 'Equus'. He is pictured outside the Plymouth Theatre, on 18th February 1976.

**Right:** Suzy Miller was married to the racing driver James Hunt when Burton first saw her in January 1976. Hunt was racing in the South African Grand Prix when Burton phoned to ask permission to date his wife, which was readily granted.

**Above:** Richard Burton with Suzy Miller at a charity ball at the Waldorf Hotel in New York, on 7th May 1976, during the Broadway run of 'Equus'. At the time, the pair were both still married to their respective partners, Elizabeth Taylor and racing driver James Hunt.

**Above:** Richard Burton photographed with his third wife, Suzy Miller, on 22nd February 1977.

CHAPTER 39

# Hamlet on Broadway

*Reputations made, records tumble*

1964

Sir John Gielgud was a last-minute addition to the cast of *Becket*, being filmed during the glorious English summer of 1963. He was appearing in a play in nearby Newcastle while the outdoor filming of *Becket* was being shot in Northumberland. When he learned of it, producer Hal Wallis quickly co-opted Gielgud to play the role of the King of France. Gielgud agreed immediately; he loved working with Richard Burton, even in a supporting role. But Gielgud also had an ulterior motive for accepting the part.

Burton always said the idea of his playing 'Hamlet' on Broadway came about in a casual conversation with Gielgud over dinner in Newcastle. And the unlikely story was true. Gielgud was appearing in a play called 'The Ides of March' in the northern English city. One evening, Burton and Taylor went across to Newcastle to see it and, afterwards, over supper at the Station Hotel, Gielgud casually asked Burton what he was doing to celebrate the 400th anniversary of Shakespeare's birth. When Burton said "nothing," Gielgud told him that he was trying to get a production together of 'Hamlet' in America. Burton remembered: "On impulse, I said would do 'Hamlet' again if Gielgud would direct it. I don't know why I said it. I hadn't the slightest desire to do it again. I'd probably had a few drinks." Gielgud had long harboured the notion of directing a new version of 'Hamlet'; one without costumes.

Burton was sceptical and seriously doubted there was an appetite in New York for profitable Shakespeare, but Gielgud said to him: "Do remember, dear boy, the Americans are the most dreadful snobs. They only appreciate Shakespeare when it is spoken in pure English." Burton bristled at that and retorted: "John, you may have forgotten. I am Welsh." Gielgud responded: "Oh, very well, it is almost the same thing."

Elizabeth Taylor thought it was a brilliant idea and sided with Gielgud. She urged Burton to consider it. Ultimately, Taylor persuaded him to do it, and as she revealed years later: "Richard had felt completely empty, used up as a serious stage actor. Then came the offer of 'Hamlet' and Richard very sweetly gives me all the credit for his accepting that."

# AND GOD CREATED BURTON

Burton had no film commitments for the period and realised that if he was offered 'Hamlet' on Broadway, it would be very difficult for him to turn down. He also guessed that Gielgud was a lot further ahead with the project than he was letting on, and this was his way of sounding him out. He also began to suspect, as the conversation went further along, that Gielgud's presence in Newcastle at the same time as himself was no coincidence either.

First, Burton tried to scare him off by telling Gielgud, rather loftily, that he was now earning a great deal of money in films and would need US$10,000 a week plus a good cut of the ticket sales or his management team would not let him do it. Gielgud was somewhat taken aback but, after a day thinking about it, he said he thought he might be able to swing it.

What Burton suspected, but didn't know for sure, was that Gielgud had already got a deal; it was true that he had approached one of Broadway's most successful producers, 43-year-old Alexander H. Cohen about the idea. So when Gielgud quietly dropped Cohen's name into conversation as the ideal producer, Burton wasn't entirely surprised.

Gielgud was in fact walking a very difficult tightrope. He knew that commercial success would depend on Burton's presence, and although it was to be Gielgud's production, he had to keep Burton believing that he had been, inadvertently, the instigator.

'Hamlet' and Gielgud were intimately connected. The first 'Hamlet' Burton had ever seen was Gielgud's, back in 1943, when he was at Oxford University with the RAF. Burton also felt a natural affinity with Gielgud. Although he had criticised him in the *Playboy* interview, Gielgud had not been offended. He knew what Burton was like when he drank, and so he thought no more of it.

Gielgud's new big idea for 'Hamlet' on Broadway had the potential to be a sensation if he could pull it off. It involved the three and a half hour play being performed in contemporary clothing with no real costumes. It would be performed on stage as if the entire play was a rehearsal run-through, with no scenery, and its success was to depend entirely on the skill of the actors.

It was an audacious concept, and Burton told Gielgud he liked it. The opportunity to do Shakespeare with no wigs and tights was very appealing to him.

But Burton didn't believe that Gielgud would be able to pull it off, so he asked John Heyman, a young British film producer who knew Alexander Cohen, to sound him out. Burton was very surprised when Heyman came back to him almost immediately with a positive response.

Cohen's reputation went before him. He was the only American theatre producer to maintain offices in London as well as New York. It gave him unique links into people like Gielgud, and in a few years, he had become the bridge between the West End and Broadway. He was a natural salesman and specialised in highbrow material and, as such, was the perfect choice to put on 'Hamlet'.

Cohen was also a tough operator who had survived his first ever Broadway production, called 'Ghost For Sale', closing after six nights. Few producers survived such first time shocks – but he had. Cohen was well versed in presenting the classics to American audiences and had promoted a recital tour with Gielgud only the year before, so they knew each other well.

Gielgud handed the negotiations over to Cohen but impressed upon him that it was essential to make it appear that it had all been Burton's idea and that Cohen was responding to him on that basis. Gielgud knew exactly how Burton's mind worked.

But just as Burton didn't believe Gielgud could pull it off, Cohen didn't believe Burton would be interested in returning to the stage; he thought it was too good to be true. But after he heard from Heyman, Cohen suddenly took Gielgud's project more seriously.

So when Cohen booked his call to London, he was expecting to be fobbed off or to be told that "Mr Burton isn't available to come to the phone" – and that would be that. But he was very surprised to be put straight through to Burton on the set at Shepperton. Cohen didn't forget his instructions from Gielgud and played his role to perfection. He let Burton persuade him to be the producer and they arranged to meet the next time Cohen was in London. When Cohen put the phone down, he suddenly realised that Burton was deadly serious.

Cohen flew to London the following week and they had dinner at The Dorchester. Burton told Cohen, in case he had any other ideas, that his agreement was conditional on Gielgud directing. And then he told him that in addition to the US$10,000 a week, he wanted 15 per cent of every ticket sold. Cohen gulped and just nodded.

From then on, Cohen negotiated the commercial terms directly with Aaron Frosch. He managed to get a concession from Frosch that the bonus payment only kicked in after a certain number of tickets had been sold. Frosch agreed but insisted that it was to be retrospective; it was a concession that cost Cohen an extra US$100,000. Whichever way, it was the richest deal in Broadway history.

With that, the deal was done and Burton was destined for America the following January.

Rather than hold rehearsals in New York, which was certain to attract distracting publicity, Cohen decided to rehearse in Toronto, where the play would open at the O'Keefe Center in late February, followed by Boston in March and Broadway in April – exactly the same route that 'Camelot' had taken.

When Cohen put out a press release and announced the production, there was much excitement around the theatrical world, especially amongst Shakespeare aficionados. But Philip Burton, who probably knew more about theatrical Shakespeare than any other man in America, forecast trouble ahead. Burton had not spoken to his adoptive son for two years, but he instinctively knew that his son's interpretation of 'Hamlet' would certainly clash with that of Gielgud.

Rehearsals were scheduled to last for precisely four weeks in the rehearsal room of the O'Keefe, starting on Thursday 30th January 1964.

Burton had agreed to play 'Hamlet' long before he had ever been to Puerto Vallarta, and when push came to shove at the end of January, he did not want to leave his new found Mexican paradise. By then, he had been there for four months and the whole family was thriving, living in paradise. Burton felt that he could have stayed forever in Puerto Vallarta and it was a huge wrench to pack up and move everyone out to Toronto.

In the third week of January, Burton and Taylor flew from Puerto Vallarta, to Mexico City and on to Los Angeles, where they would stay with Taylor's parents before flying out to Toronto. Taylor was firmly by Burton's side and there was no question of his going alone. She was his partner now, and where he went, she went, and vice versa. It had been a year since she had worked, and she told her agents that her priority was now her husband-to-be.

Burton's return to Broadway was big news, and their arrival in Los Angeles had been announced to the press two days before. Valerie Douglas was waiting at Los Angeles airport together with a new bodyguard, called Bobby LaSalle, whom she had hired for Burton. He was an ex-boxer, and he looked the part. But he was brawn with a brain and knew how to handle difficult situations. But he wasn't ready for what he found as they were greeted by a mass of fans all determined to get a look at the most famous couple in the world.

There were well over 50 photographers at the bottom of the plane's steps on the tarmac and at least 500 fans in the terminal and maybe another 500 outside.

They were all trying to touch Taylor and, in the melee, whilst defending her, Burton accidentally whacked a Los Angeles police marshal. But the crowd did not consist solely of fans; there were people protesting against the Burton-Taylor divorces. One held a banner saying "drink not the wine of adultery," and the photograph appeared in many newspapers the next day.

From the airport, they went straight to the Beverly Hills home of Taylor's parents, Francis and Sara. The purpose of the visit was for Burton formally to ask Francis Taylor for his daughter's hand in marriage. But Francis Taylor initially had no idea what he was talking about, as Burton recited his request in Welsh. Eventually, he acceded to the request and told Burton he would change the terms of his will accordingly. At first, Burton thought he was joking but later realised that Francis Taylor changed his will every time his daughter changed her husband.

Then, they moved to Bungalow 5 at the Beverly Hills Hotel for a few days of meetings and interviews. Taylor always stayed at Bungalow 5; if it was occupied when she arrived, the other guests were immediately moved out.

They flew to Toronto on 28th January with their extended full entourage, which now included a secretary for Burton, called Jim Benton, the new bodyguard, Bobby La Salle: Bob Wilson, Valerie Douglas, plus Elizabeth's team of six, as well as Liza and Maria.

They were all checked into the eighth floor of the Sheraton King Edward Hotel in Toronto. This time, there were no scenes at the airport and the arrival was kept secret. Burton and Taylor had a huge five-room suite to share and every detail was recorded in local newspapers, including the room number (850) and the price (CND$65 a day), as well as the fact that it had, on previous occasions, been occupied by both President Kennedy and President Eisenhower.

The 'Hamlet' theatre company arrived from New York two days later and found more than a hundred journalists and photographers waiting for them in the lobby of the King Edward. The press had expected Burton, but he was already at the O'Keefe Center waiting. There was a half hour photo opportunity scheduled for three o'clock, before rehearsals began.

Burton was calm as over 25 reporters surrounded him and, mindful of the *Playboy* fiasco a few months before, he answered their questions sensibly and concisely. He stood in front of them drinking from a polystyrene cup of coffee brought to him by Bob Wilson from the theatre vending machine. It didn't stop one reporter describing Burton the next day as a "burly Welsh actor cradling a drink."

When the photographers were satisfied, the actors went straight into four weeks of intense rehearsals. They were unusual because they were secretly tape recorded by a young actor in the play called Richard Sterne, who later wrote a book detailing the four-week rehearsal period. Sterne was fresh from Philadelphia, and it was his first big part. No one knows to this day whether the recordings were approved by Gielgud or not – or whether Burton knew of them. Sterne infers that they were not approved, but, later, a rather lovely book appeared, written in a style of which no one could possibly disapprove. Sterne had hidden his tape recorder in a large briefcase, which he lugged to every rehearsal, and recorded over 120 hours of Gielgud directing his cast.

And Sterne's was not the only book that eventually appeared on the subject of the rehearsals. Another actor, William Redfield, who played Guildenstern, wrote a book based on his copious notes of the rehearsals. It was called *Letters From An Actor*. It was another good, diary-style account of the process.

Sterne was amazed by Burton's warmth when they first met: "He treated everybody, from the producer down to the doorman, the same." But he was stunned when he met Elizabeth Taylor: "She couldn't have been lovelier," he recalled. Sterne remembered how "awesomely beautiful" she was: "I can still see her coming into the rehearsal hall for the first time. It was maybe a week or so after we'd started rehearsing; she was dressed in a purple pantsuit. You couldn't miss those violet-colored eyes. She sat very quietly; she barely moved, and she watched very attentively."

Taylor sat in for many of the rehearsals and sometimes, if asked, she gave her opinions to Gielgud. At night, in her hotel suite, Taylor read everything she could about Shakespeare and 'Hamlet' and its varying interpretations. Throughout, she seemed captivated by what she called Burton's "poetic brilliance."

William Redfield believed that Taylor was "having the time of her life" amongst real actors and said she was "gobbling up Shakespeare." He added: "This was her first up-close exposure to classical theatre, and she wanted to learn. She steeped herself in the play and its various interpretations."

She also acted throughout as 'mother' to the cast and crew, serving coffee and buns and tending to her future husband's needs. Her presence was a soothing influence on Burton, who was nervous as he had not played Shakespeare for ten years nor stood in front of a live audience for four years.

He also had another concern. It was well known that Gielgud and Burton often had wildly different ideas about how Shakespeare should be interpreted. It was always tricky when Gielgud and Burton worked together; it had been right from the beginning, when Gielgud had directed Burton in 'The Lady's Not For Burning' at the Globe Theatre in London in 1949. They clashed then, even when Burton was just a kid. Now that he was a major star, it was even more difficult.

Graham Jenkins, who had a good feel for the politics of the theatre world, said: "There was a feeling among the critics that director and star were somehow at odds with each other; the Burton energy and passion trying to escape from the restraints of Gielgud's agonising, introspective version of 'Hamlet' – and not quite making it. There is no doubt they had trouble in agreeing an interpretation of 'Hamlet'. Though he took guidance from the director when it suited him, Rich was determined to go his own way. Sadly, it was in a direction in which Gielgud was unable to help him. The result was an undisciplined and unpredictable Hamlet who, at times, had the rest of the cast running round in circles."

Taylor had also noticed that Burton was not completely at ease with Gielgud's direction, nor with the physical and mental demands of the role. But Burton loved Gielgud like a father, and the disagreements, virtually undetectable to others, rarely surfaced. As Richard Sterne confirmed: "Richard adored Sir John and thought he was the greatest Shakespearean actor of all time, the best 'Hamlet' he'd ever seen; he was in awe of him, as we all were in that cast."

But astute observers could sense the undercurrents and Burton's unease in the role.

Burton was also nervous about what was going on outside the theatre in the newspapers. During rehearsals, the papers were full of the Taylor-Fisher divorce saga almost every day. Although they were by now officially divorced, Fisher was contesting its legality, or at least saying to reporters that he was. It was a rather stupid argument to make; if he had been successful and got the divorce annulled, then his marriage to Taylor would also have been annulled because, by Fisher's own argument, her divorce from Michael Wilding was also illegal – making his own marriage to Taylor invalid. It soon became obvious that Fisher was continuing to make media noise only to force a better financial settlement out of Taylor.

Canadian reporters were not a patch on their New York and Rome equivalents but soon got into the swing of the reporting. Basically the story was simple: Taylor said that Fisher was demanding a million dollars of her money; Fisher called Taylor a liar; Burton said it was Fisher who was the liar; and Fisher said that "Burton deserved an Oscar for sheer gall." But that simple 36-word story was spread over four weeks and many tens of thousands of words of newspaper space.

The intense publicity meant that Burton couldn't enjoy the social life that he had always loved when he was appearing in the theatre. He hated his freedom being taken from him and not being able to do something as simple as walk across the street to buy a newspaper.

The presence of Taylor made it impossible for them to go out at night except on the rare occasions when they sneaked out or hired an army of security men to go with them. John Gielgud recalled: "That sort of celebrity is so very hard to cope with. They had to exercise the dogs on the roof. There was a man with a machine gun in the corridor outside their room." Gielgud believed that Burton handled the stresses of it all very well; "Richard handled that marvellously. He was very popular with the company. He took great pains to be nice to everybody. But it must have been a great strain for him." Richard Sterne witnessed it all: "It was dangerous for them to go out. I've never seen anything quite like that. I suppose some of the rock musicians get that treatment, but it's exceptional for theatre people."

One night, Gielgud entertained his stars to dinner at a bistro and recalled there being as many as 200 hundred people waiting outside in subzero temperatures. And now that Burton was famous, he found it difficult to pay for a meal in a restaurant: "It was the cheapest entertaining I ever did. We had a marvellous supper with a lot of champagne. We were about ten or fifteen people, but when I asked for the bill, the management wouldn't give me one. And when we came out, there were two hundred people in the snow, waiting to see them drive away."

"Even when I went out to lunch with him between rehearsals, there'd be four or five of the entourage sitting at adjoining tables, preventing people coming up and talking to him. When I said: 'Please, this is my lunch.' Richard said: 'No, no, they'll pay.' And we sailed out and the entourage was left to pay the bill, which rather embarrassed me."

On Tuesday 11th February, there was a rather distracting, more serious, development. An American Congressman, called Michael Feighan, from Ohio, was calling for the US secretary of state, Dean Rusk, to revoke Burton's visa because of his adultery with Taylor. As it was an official request from a congressman, Rusk's department was forced to take it seriously and to examine it properly.

Although it caused much consternation at the time, there was no chance of it happening. Rusk knew Burton well and, more importantly, knew of his friendship with John Kennedy, who had appointed him as secretary of state. Rusk, who would go on to become the second longest serving secretary of state in history, waved it away and it is doubtful he even spent more than 30 seconds considering Feighan's request. He told his department to wait a week and then put out a statement which duly appeared and said drily: "The Department has found no grounds which would make him ineligible."

But some newspapers backed Feighan and even wanted 'Hamlet' banned from Broadway, calling it "a perfectly shocking play." But the affair had a silver lining for the production, as Feighan proved to be the play's top ticket salesman. After his complaint, ticket sales exploded and Alexander Cohen found he was able to charge as much as US$10 a seat and still sell every ticket.

After four weeks of rehearsals, there was a charity performance on Tuesday 25th February for the benefit of The Canadian National Ballet. Elizabeth Taylor was there for the performance to help soothe Burton's nerves. She caused a sensation and was so distracting that the play took an extra quarter of an hour to run because the audience was cheering and applauding for extended periods, encouraged and excited by her presence.

But despite that, the first performance wasn't a great success and the audience seemed unreceptive to Gielgud's innovative 'Hamlet'. Unused to seeing the play performed in that way, the people of Toronto were not quite sure how to take it. Those who were unfamiliar with 'Hamlet' were thoroughly confused when actors doubled on some parts, wearing the same clothes. And that was one of Gielgud's problems – he always assumed that everybody knew 'Hamlet' line by line and could work it out.

Gielgud panicked and called the cast in early before opening night to try and add a little excitement to the production. In reality, after four weeks of detailed and exhaustive rehearsal, they had got what they had got and would live or die with it.

The opening show in front of Canada's top critics went smoothly, and the audience was mildly enthusiastic at the end despite a delay of a half hour because of Elizabeth Taylor's protracted arrival. As she made her way down to a seat in one of the front rows, the audience stood up, and many stood on the backs of their seats, desperate for a sight of her. Burton complained bitterly to Alexander Cohen: "It was madness such as you've never seen, and people just stare at us as if we're prize animals." After the opening week, it was decided that it was too distracting for Taylor to sit in the auditorium and she attended almost every performance watching from the wings.

The following morning, the reviews in the newspapers were very mixed. Ron Evans in *The Toronto Telegram* called it a "masterpiece." Herbert Whitaker in *The Globe & Mail* said it was "disappointing" and Nat Cohen in the *Toronto Star* called it "an unmitigated disaster." It was very clear immediately that Gielgud's contemporary interpretation of William Shakespeare's 'Hamlet' was not to everyone's taste.

The following day, on Thursday 27th February, it was Elizabeth Taylor's 32nd birthday and she was given a party by the crew on the stage with an enormous birthday cake, decorated with flowers and inscribed: "To our mascot and den mother. Love and happy birthday from the company." Taylor, sensing the moment, ran and got Prince Hamlet's sword. Reciting the appropriate lines from the play, she swung the sword above her head and brought it down on the cake, cutting it cleanly in half.

The jollity soon gave way to serious matters. Some of the detail of the reviews had been devastating, and Gielgud and Alex Cohen sought to reassure the cast and crew at a meeting. Cohen told them that controversy and dissent had been predicted, expected and even welcomed. He assured them there would be no changes to Gielgud's contemporary concept.

But the Toronto audiences never did get it, although that didn't stop them buying the high-priced tickets. The run was even extended to cope with demand. Advance sales were at such a level, and the O'Keefe Center so big, that it easily justified an extra fourth week at the venue.

Gielgud tinkered with the production after it opened but made no major changes and, certainly, there were nothing like the problems 'Camelot' endured. After that, he went on holiday for a fortnight and left them to it.

Burton got very depressed after he left. He knew his performance was not right, yet he didn't know how to sort it out. But he did know someone who could help.

On Saturday 29th February, Philip Burton was enjoying a leap year celebration dinner in New York at the home of his friends, Alfred and Charlotte Baruth. His friend, Christian Alderson, was staying at Philip's house in New York. He had gone to bed early and was surprised to be awoken by a phone call and to hear Elizabeth Taylor's voice on the other end. The Bell phone company had a new facility that allowed calls to be transferred from phone to phone in the New York area and, as soon as he realised he was not dreaming it, Christian transferred the call to where he knew Philip was. Alfred Baruth picked up the phone and was equally surprised as he handed Philip the receiver.

Philip remembered: "I received a phone call transferred from my house. To my great and somewhat unsettling surprise, because I had never met or spoken to her, it was Elizabeth Taylor. As I had anticipated, Richard was having trouble in 'Hamlet'; he said I was the only one who could help him. Would I come up? Not for the first time in the two-year silence of separation, I was torn in my loyalties. Then, Richard came on the line, and that soon settled it. I said I would come the following Saturday."

As soon as he put the phone down, Philip regretted it and realised he could only go with Sybil's blessing, which he was not sure would be forthcoming: "When I later spoke to Sybil about it, she said: 'Of course, you must go. He needs you.'" Philip was mightily impressed with Sybil's attitude and also by Taylor's, as he knew her phone call would have been a very difficult one to make. As he said: "I think that incident bears testimony to the fine qualities of both Elizabeth and Sybil."

A week later, Philip caught a flight to Toronto and Burton sent a car to bring him straight to the theatre where the Saturday afternoon matinee was in progress. Philip remembered: "I both longed for and dreaded our meeting, but it turned out to be quite remarkable; we both behaved as though it had just been too long since we had seen each other: there was no embarrassment. When the matinee was over, we went to the hotel suite. After a nervous delay, Elizabeth came out to meet me. Although it was a tentative meeting on both sides, it was a good one, and it was to lead to a warm and enduring friendship. I was to discover that her character, values, intelligence and talent matched her famous beauty."

That same night, Philip went to see Hamlet: "Richard had been so nervous about my reaction that he had had difficulty in deciding where I should sit and had changed my ticket several times." It turned out that Burton was very nervous about the return of his adoptive father into his life and, for him, it became a very emotional evening. When the performance started, he looked around and could not find Philip in the auditorium – inwardly, he panicked. The interval went well past the usual 15 minutes and the audience started stamping their feet impatiently. Suddenly, Philip was sent for and asked to go to Burton's dressing room. There, he found his son weeping as Philip recalled in his autobiography: "Richard was in such a state that he couldn't go on without a word from me, so I gave him one, and a very strong one. This was so unlike Richard that I have come to believe it couldn't have happened;

I must have dreamed it." But it did happen, and Burton quickly pulled himself together and returned to the stage, albeit 15 minutes late.

Philip was not awfully impressed with John Gielgud's version of 'Hamlet', as he said: "The only advantage I could see in this was that it saved the expense of period costumes." But he was more worried by his son's uncertain performance: "As I expected, Richard's 'Hamlet' lacked confidence because of the conflict between his conception of the part and Gielgud's."

Philip went back to the King Edward Hotel with Burton and Taylor. After a supper in their suite, Taylor went to bed leaving father and son alone. Philip recalled that night many years later: "We talked for hours. I gave him detailed comments and suggestions, but my main purpose was to restore his confidence." The following day, they spoke again until Philip had to leave for the airport to return to New York. On Monday, he was due to be made an American citizen and swear an oath of allegiance before a judge. He also ran an acting school in New York called the American Musical and Dramatic Academy.

So he couldn't stay in Toronto to see the fruits of his work. He said: "It was a great relief to get a phone call from Hume Cronyn after my return to New York: 'What did you do?' he asked. 'He gave a wonderful performance last night. We're all talking about it, and its put new life into the show.'"

The following weekend, Burton and Taylor had an appointment of a different sort – marriage. On Sunday 15th March, they went to Montreal to get married. Burton had hoped that after the marriage, what he called the "state of sin", curiosity about them would diminish and they could get back to leading a normal life. He genuinely believed that it was the "illicit quality of our relationship" that had been attracting the attention. But his hopes were immediately dashed and, instead, he found interest in them as a couple to be intensified.

In truth, some of it was his own fault. On the Tuesday night following the wedding, at the end of that night's performance, Burton brought Taylor onto the stage and introduced her "for the first time on any stage" as "Mrs Burton". He then delivered a line from the play, quoting Hamlet's words to Ophelia: "I say we will have no more marriages." The audience literally thundered its approval and the sound of cheering and clapping could be heard on the streets outside.

On Saturday 21st March, the production closed in Toronto and the company packed up in preparation for the play's transfer for a two-week run at Boston's

# HAMLET ON BROADWAY

Shubert Theater.

On Sunday, the whole company travelled together on a chartered plane that Alex Cohen ha.l rented so he could co-ordinate a big publicity event at Boston's Logan Airport. Taylor also had her publicist, John Springer, and his assistant, Diane Stevens, on hand in Boston.

On the plane journey, everyone was worried whether enough reporters, photographer and fans would turn up, as they believed interest in Burton and Taylor was waning now that they were married. Richard Sterne reported that they all lunched on filet mignon on the plane and had no idea what lay in store for them at Logan airport.

The arrival in Boston proved truly extraordinary. There were five thousand fans inside and outside the airport terminal waiting to greet them. It was too many people, and as the pilot taxied the plane towards the terminal, fans broke through the police barriers on to the runway itself, bringing the aircraft to a complete halt. The pilot refused to move any further with crowds of people in front of the plane. The sheer volume of people meant that Boston's police couldn't begin to cope, and the plane's route to the terminal was blocked. The plane stood still for an hour whilst airport managers decided what to do.

Eventually, they figured the best way to disembark safely was an empty maintenance hangar at the edge of the airport. It forced a change of plan and everyone disembarked into buses and cars, which took them straight into Toronto. Plans for a press conference, autograph signing and photocall at the terminal all had to be abandoned.

John Springer accompanied Burton and Taylor in their limousine to the Copley-Plaza Hotel in downtown Boston, where there were another thousand people waiting outside. It was obvious that fans had been tipped off as to the Burtons' schedule, and Springer strongly denied to Burton that it had been him.

As the limousine pulled up in front of the hotel, the doorman was pushed to one side and the crowd wrenched the door open, making a grab for the couple. The fans grabbed at Burton's clothing and his hair as he attempted to get inside the hotel accompanied by Springer and Taylor. His jacket and then his shirt were ripped off his back. Taylor was pushed and pulled and finally pressed against a wall at the far side of the hotel's lobby. Burton, together with Springer and his bodyguard, had to fight their way through to rescue her. It was not pretty and there was almost pitched battle in the foyer as police arrived and fought to regain control. Eye witnesses say it took five minutes to rescue Taylor and bundle her inside the hotel's lift. Years later, John Springer

537

said it was the scariest moment of his life.

Burton was reportedly furious with Springer as he sought someone to blame. He wanted to know who was responsible. Complaints were made to Boston's police commissioner, Ed McNamara, who hurried round to the hotel to apologise to Burton personally.

Burton was furious and told him: "My wife was almost killed." He threatened to complain directly to Boston's senator, Edward Kennedy, whom he knew personally. He told the hapless McNamara: "I've never seen anything like this before. It's outrageous. We had crowds like this in Toronto, but the police gave us adequate protection."

Burton's haranguing of the commissioner achieved the desired result, and on opening night there was a police curtain around the Shubert Theater. Both Burton and Taylor had police protection, and an armed policeman guarded Burton's dressing room door. It was so efficient that John Gielgud couldn't gain access. When he told him he was the play's director, the policeman guarding the room looked him up and down and said: "Buddy, no one gets in that door."

The opening night performance was delayed to wait for Elizabeth's Taylor's arrival. Alex Cohen had promised to bring her to the theatre. But when he called for her, she was lying on a sofa watching an old film on television called *How Green Was My Valley*. It was a Welsh film made in 1941 and starring Roddy McDowall, who was then a young actor starting out. She had never seen it before and wanted to watch the finish. At a quarter to seven, 15 minutes before the start, she was still in her dressing gown. Cohen said to her: "Elizabeth, please, it's time to go. Do you think you might dress?" Taylor glanced up at him and said: "Not before the movie is over." They eventually arrived an hour late and, as the play had already started, they sneaked in at the back and sat in two seats Cohen had hastily arranged by shifting two delighted theatre goers in the cheap seats to the front stalls.

The next morning, the critics were more generous than in Toronto, although they were still inclined not to like Gielgud's 'Hamlet'. In *The Boston Globe*, Kevin Kelly, Boston's most influential critic, was negative and wrote that the production was "starkly unconventional," questioned its "honesty" and called it "particularly pretentious." But Elinor Hughes told readers of *The Boston Herald* that it was a performance "you should not miss", writing that Burton had "poetry and passion in his bones." Alta Maloney in *The Boston Traveller* said it "was to remain in the memory as a remarkable experience in the theatre."

The final performance in Boston was on Saturday 4th April, and a fortnight later, it opened at the Lunt-Fontanne Theater on Broadway. This time, Alex Cohen kept airport arrival and departure times top secret, and the cast arrived in darkness in New York. Burton and Taylor were driven to the Regency Hotel on Park Avenue under conditions of tight secrecy.

The Regency was brand new and, then, the most luxurious hotel in the world. Burton and Taylor were installed in the Princess Grace suite, an eight-roomed complex on the 20th floor. It became their home for five months. The suite had three bedrooms, three bathrooms and a 12-metre long sitting room plus a well-equipped kitchen and servants' quarters. It was all lavishly decorated in pastel colours in the style of Louis XVI – then becoming very fashionable.

The arrival in New York meant another reunion with Philip Burton. When he arrived, he told Burton that his ex-wife, Sybil, had left the city to stay with friends and would stay away for the whole run of 'Hamlet'. The news bitterly disappointed Burton, who had been looking forward to seeing Sybil and Kate and Jessica. Philip didn't mince his words: he told Burton that Sybil had resolved never to see or speak to him again, and he believed she meant it.

Burton and Taylor enjoyed a convivial time at the Regency, often dining with Philip as they all got to know each other again. It was just as well as they spent far more time in the suite than Burton was anticipating. Whereas Taylor was always happy in her own company, reading or watching television, Burton was not. He was annoyed that he couldn't even cross 46th Street unmolested, or go to Dinty Moore's restaurant for lunch or supper as he always had. Casual drinking in bars was now all but impossible without great subterfuge.

Burton hated being confined to the suite, but he made the best of it. One Sunday, with no performance, Burton was very restless and upset because he couldn't take a stroll in Central Park. Suddenly, Taylor looked up from her book and said: "I'll bet we can do it." They both put on their scruffiest clothes and sunglasses and exited the Regency through its underground car park on 61st Street. The two of them barely made it to Madison Avenue before a crowd of fans came running down the road and they had to leap into a cab to escape.

On New York's opening night, 9th April 1964, thousands of people filled 48th Street and overflowed onto Broadway itself.

Burton had no illusions about the difficulty of the task he faced in New York, as he said: "A Broadway opening is the most terrifying in the world, and I've played in Denmark, in Paris, in London, everywhere you can think of in western Europe. But unquestionably, Broadway is the one that's the most frenetic, the most disturbing, the most exciting and, if you hit the jackpot, the most rewarding."

Rehearsals at the Lunt-Fontanne had gone very well. With its excellent acoustics, Burton's voice sounded wonderful in the auditorium. Richard Sterne was particularly impressed: "He had amazing projection. The timbre of it was quite penetrating and carried all the way to the last row of the theatre. We weren't microphoned then."

But, as in Toronto and Boston, Burton found what he called "a chill and indifferent audience." Although, this time, for a different reason: "There were so many celebrities there they hardly had time to notice us on the stage. They did not pay attention." But the critics were rapt.

Not only were Burton and Taylor on display that night, but the cream of New York society was also there – all attracted to the cultural event of the year. New York's chief of police, tipped off by Ed McNamara, gave Burton and Taylor full protection, including over 100 officers in front of the theatre on opening night, including ten on horseback. They were all needed and it was a mad scramble. After the curtain fell, Burton and Taylor headed back to the Regency to change and they were last to join the first night party at the Rainbow Room on the 66th floor of the main building in Rockefeller Center. There, they found over 600 of some of the most famous and best connected people in the world. At the door, as they were about to enter, Burton famously said to Taylor: "Let's get away from this rubbish."

Even *Newsweek* magazine reported the party, saying: "600 carefully selected celebrities and celebrity watchers gathered to pay homage to Rich and Liz. Everyone wanted to see her." Hollis Alpert wrote: "In all the glory days of Broadway, no one had seen anything quite like it before."

Elizabeth Taylor networked like mad, visiting every table as her husband glad-handed the mayor and the governor and various other dignitaries from City Hall who were in attendance.

But after a half hour, they left, driven out by masses of photographers continually popping off flashguns in their faces. They made their escape through a kitchen, and Alex Cohen was furious with his security staff for allowing the photographers in, saying to them: "This party cost me ten thousand dollars and you let the photographers drive them out?"

Taylor and Burton escaped for a quiet dinner and, for once, an early night. Philip Burton stayed on at the party and had the time of his life, as he said:

"The first night of 'Hamlet' lived up to my high hopes for it, and was followed by a very happy party in the Rainbow Room. Then came the notices. As I confidently expected, they were excellent for Richard, but there were one or two quibbles about the production."

Philip was right; the following morning, the New York reviews were far more positive than those in Toronto or Boston, representing the fact that New York was a more cultured city. *Newsweek* magazine was rapturous, saying of Burton: "The entire performance is overwhelming, a revelation of what Shakespeare can be like; a monument to the actor's art and a new base from which our imaginations can recover from their sleep."

Walter Kerr in the *New York Herald Tribune* had mixed feelings himself: he said he thought Burton "one of the most magnificently equipped actors living," but also that he had acted the part of Prince Hamlet "without feeling." No one knew what to make of that. Richard Watts of the *New York Post* called it a "towering masterpiece" and "stirring and skillful." Howard Taubman in *The New York Times* noted: "Richard Burton dominates the drama as 'Hamlet' should: this is a performance of electrical power and sweeping virility."

But in truth, it didn't matter what the critics said – good or bad. The run was a sell-out and it was immediately extended an extra week into August. Outside, the theatre tickets were changing hands at four or five times their face value.

Throughout, a big police presence was necessary and the chief of police asked Burton to request that Taylor stop attending – she did for a few nights, but it made no difference. Soon, Burton realised that the fans were turning out for him and not for Taylor. As she said to him: "You're the one they're coming to see – you're the Frank Sinatra of Shakespeare." Burton thought the comment was ridiculous and told her so in front of a lot of people.

By then, Burton had established the latest version of 'Burton's Bar' in his dressing room. Although stricter security meant it wasn't as free and easy access as before, a good time was being had by all. Burton held court just as he had four years earlier in 'Camelot' and regaled the cast and crew with his stories. His drinking habits had changed and, instead of vodka, Bob Wilson delivered large martinis before curtain up, and then bourbon on the rocks during intervals, and the Martinis resumed afterwards. Gielgud loved visiting the dressing room after the show for a martini, saying: "Richard is at his most agreeable, full of charm and quick to take criticism and advice, but he does put away the drink, and looks terribly coarse and heavy, gets muddled and fluffy and then loses all his nimbleness and attack."

When it was established that Taylor's presence wasn't making things worse, she went to the Lunt-Fontanne to see the play over 40 times, each time in a different dress. On every other night, she turned up in a limousine to bring her husband back to the hotel. Hundreds of people started gathering to watch her come and go each night.

If it was going to happen, Burton decided to make the most of it and choreographed a leaving-the-theatre production for him and Taylor. That attracted hundreds more fans, who would mass on the corner of Broadway and 46th Street to catch a glimpse. It became almost a ritual and an accepted part of the New York scene.

A routine was established and, at around 9:30pm every evening, policemen turned up with barriers to make a path from the stage door to the limousine, which was parked in the road and contained Taylor. She would arrive to see Burton, who, by then, was well into his last act. An hour and a half later, always around 11:30pm each night, Burton and Taylor would emerge from the theatre under a small marquee. To make sure everybody got a good view, they stood for a few moments in a spotlight that had been specially erected to beam from an opposite building.

The crowd pressed forward against the police barriers as the famous couple hurried to their car. Seconds after the doors closed, the limousine pulled away and the car edged its way through the screaming fans into Eighth Avenue, flanked by mounted police. And the great parade was over for another night.

One night, when Hume Cronyn was in the limousine with Burton, some young fans threw themselves onto the roof of the car and were hanging upside down, peering into the car's windows. The car continued with the youngsters on the roof, and, as Cronyn recalled: "It was the only time in my life that I remember being frightened by a crowd."

Graham Jenkins said: "Rich was not prepared to miss out on the chance to be the centre of attention. No longer Mr Cleopatra, he was Mr Burton in the company of Mrs Burton. For the first time in their marriage, he was seen to be more newsworthy than his wife." *Time* magazine called the nightly exit routine the "fastest, flashiest show around."

Most nights, Burton used to invite guests to join him and share the experience in what he called the "limousine show." Fergus Cashin was in New York at the same time for the *Daily Mirror*'s coverage of the 1964 race riots in Harlem. One night, he was Burton's guest. Burton said to Cashin, who had come straight from Harlem and the front line of the riots: "You smell like an air raid. I heard on the radio they had fire hoses out and the place was burning. It's amazing to think that a real bloody battlefront is just up the road while we are caught up in another madness. It's a weird city."

Elizabeth Taylor, seeking to cement her position with the Jenkins family, also brought Cecilia and Elfed James to New York as a surprise for Burton. She sent them first class air tickets, paid for a room at the hotel and bought a new wardrobe for Cecilia. She also put a limousine at their disposal for their entire week in New York.

On the last night of their stay, they left the theatre with the Burtons. Cecilia recalled it many years later: "I shall never forget. On the last night, as we left the theatre, there were thousands of people, all ages, all backgrounds, all waiting to shake his hand and give him a tremendous send-off. The car was being pushed one way and then another. It was quite incredible. The tears of emotion were running down my face and I turned to Richard and said: 'Oh, Rich, if only mam could see you now.'" He started crying as well, and it was a very precious moment for both of them.

There was also a humorous moment during Cecilia's visit, provided by a reporter from *The New York Times*. He was casually speaking to her and Burton backstage and was told that the traditional Welsh breakfast was lava bread and bacon. The following day, *The New York Times* carried this strange headline: "Actor Burton Brought Up On Seaweed."

Emlyn Williams, who was also appearing on Broadway in a play called 'The Deputy', came to visit. There was some enmity, as Williams had been a big Sybil supporter.

But now that they were married, Williams thought it only sensible to accept the situation.

So when he received a telephone call from Taylor inviting him and his wife, Molly, to the Regency for dinner after their respective performances, he accepted.

When they walked in through the door, Burton leapt to his feet and kissed them both, likewise Taylor. Williams turned to Taylor and said: "The last time we were together, you met Mr. Hyde. This time it's Dr. Jekyll." Taylor quipped: "I think I preferred Mr. Hyde." Williams thought that hilarious, but Burton gave him a queer sideways look. Williams recalled that reunion many years later: "I had been terribly forthright in Rome, but when the years passed by and they really did get married and they were going to be together for life as far as one could see, it was quite rightly all made up. Elizabeth was sweet and very nervous, and it was very touching."

But it was not all sweetness and light. There was one difficult evening in the middle of the run of 'Hamlet', when Burton faced a heckler in the audience who continually booed him. This annoyed him more than it should have and, at the curtain call, he stepped forward and announced: "We have been playing this production for eighty performances. Some have liked it, some have not. But I can assure you, we have never been booed." The audience applauded, but the booer continued.

The booing clicked something in his brain and, for some reason; it put him in a really bad mood. That night, he returned to the hotel alone, as Taylor was in bed with a cold, watching television. He ordered her to turn off the television set, but she ignored him and he said to her: "I was booed tonight. Do you understand that I have been booed? I played Hamlet and was booed."

Taylor, not taking her eyes off the screen, told him to grow up and said that it was all part of the entertainment business. With that, he exploded in a rage and got up from the chair where he had been removing his socks and kicked the television off the table with his bare feet. Then, he kicked it again and jabbed his foot on a sharp bit. The blood now flowed from his big toe, which was badly gashed. It had been extremely stupid to kick a TV set with his bare foot and he needed treatment from the hotel's doctor. Taylor said: "He was like a small atom bomb going off – sparks fly, walls shake, floors vibrate." He was left with 12 stitches, a heavily bandaged foot and he limped for a week. Plus there was a US$500 bill to replace the TV set, for which Alex Cohen refused to pay when he heard what had happened.

Rumours of Burton's volcanic temper and his rows with Taylor spread all over New York.

It prompted one wealthy and rather voyeuristic middle-aged husband and wife to book the almost identical suite on the floor below for the duration of their visit, with the express intention of spying on them. They were interested in listening in on their conversations and, more interestingly, on the high-volume arguments they had heard about. As Hollis Alpert recounted in his biography of Burton: "They would stand on chairs and hold empty glasses to the ceiling to listen in."

The couple, who remained unnamed, were very rich social climbers who did not work. Their motive appeared to be dinner party gossip, which was always a valuable currency in New York.

But they were found out when a friend of Taylor's told her what this husband and wife team had been saying, thinking they were making it up.

Taylor, realising the stories were true, thought that their suite was being bugged. But she quickly realised none of the stories had appeared in the press and that they were just private fodder. So she thought that there must be a simpler explanation. After having the suite swept for bugs, she eventually worked it out and the couple were evicted by the hotel's management. Taylor saw the funny side of it and acknowledged that they must have heard some choice language: "I love four-letter words. They're so terribly descriptive. They just give me a good feeling."

During the play's run, officials from the German Adoption Agency arrived to process the necessary paperwork so that Burton could become Maria's adoptive father, replacing Eddie Fisher on the paperwork. It was a very unusual situation for the officials, and at the end of the lengthy approval meeting, Burton invited them to that night's performance of 'Hamlet'. As tickets were normally impossible to get hold of, it was a huge gesture. To honour the officials that night, Burton performed one of his speeches in German, as he recounted: "I roared into 'To be or not to be' in my best Teutonic. The audience was a bit uneasy, nothing more, and the Germans were pleased but 'sein oder nicht sein: das ist die Frage' was the last thing they expected to hear at the Lunt-Fontanne."

The adoption order for Maria was confirmed soon afterwards and she became Miss Maria Burton, much to Taylor's relief. It was her last link to Eddie Fisher, and she was delighted to be rid of him finally.

Meanwhile, with Sybil absent from New York, Elizabeth Taylor had really bonded with Philip Burton, and the two spent a lot of time together in New York. Philip was now an American citizen and had taken over the non-profit American Musical and Dramatic Academy.

But the Academy was floundering through lack of funds and Philip confided his problems to Taylor. She decided she wanted to help and, together, they hatched a scheme for a poetry recital at the Lunt-Fontanne Theater on Sunday 21st June, a night when there was no performance of 'Hamlet'. Taylor invited New Yorkers to buy tickets at US$100 each to hear her and her husband on stage reciting poetry.

It was a unique event and the very first time Taylor had appeared on stage in a live production.

Philip coached Taylor and found her hugely receptive as she worked all hours for several weeks to perfect her part in the recital.

In the audience was a spectacular cross-section of New York society and celebrities, including Bea Lillie, Lee Remick, Alan Jay Lerner, Carol Channing, Adolph Green, Anita Loos, Betty Comden, Hume Cronyn, Jessica Tandy, Montgomery Clift, Walter Wanger, Kitty Carlisle, Jean Smith and Eunice Kennedy. Taylor's parents also flew in for the occasion.

Burton was in his expensive tuxedo and Taylor took to the stage in a purple off-the-shoulder Grecian style gown wearing her best diamonds. Her hair was piled high and intertwined with purple flowers. At the interval, she changed into the same dress but in white, with fresh white flowers in her hair.

The two recited pieces from Thomas Hardy, D. H. Lawrence, W. B. Yeats, T. S. Elliot and Elizabeth Browning in two acts. Taylor was almost flawless and charmed everyone with a superb performance. When she messed up one line, she didn't miss a beat and said: "Sorry, may I start again? I got all screwed up." The audience loved her.

The evening closed with both of them reading the 23rd Psalm together, and afterwards they received a standing ovation.

Burton was surprised at how good she was, and said at the end of it: "I didn't know she was going to be this good, I've never had an ovation like that before." Emlyn Williams was in the audience and admitted: "She was marvellous. Bea Lillie was sitting in front of me and I heard her say to the person sitting next to her: "If she doesn't get bad pretty soon, people are going to start leaving." But nobody left. Even Philip Burton admitted later that Taylor did the better reading.

The evening raised US$30,000 and Burton had agreed to make a matching donation to Philip's academy, which got a much needed US$60,000.

The recital was a welcome distraction for Burton from the grueling experience of playing 'Hamlet' night after night. At eighteen weeks and 136 performances, it became the longest-running 'Hamlet' ever to play on Broadway. They filled the theatre of nearly fifteen hundred seats every single night. Burton missed only two performances with a throat infection when his understudy, Robert Burr, who looked very much like Burton, took over.

204,000 tickets were sold in New York and it took US$1.45 million during the 18-week run at the Lunt-Fontanne, making it the highest grossing and almost certainly the most profitable presentation of a Shakespeare classic ever in the world. In addition, Toronto grossed over US$400,000 in four weeks in the cavernous O'Keefe Center. Even the much smaller Shubert Theatre in Boston took US$140,000 in two weeks. Burton earned well over half a million dollars for nine months' work; US$240,000 for his 24 weeks' acting and US$300,000 from his profit share. He also picked up a US$250,000 for the movie version, which was released for a short two-day run at 1,000 cinemas in the United States. It had been filmed from the stage production over two nights.

John Gielgud also earned more money than he ever had in his life. But he was most astonished at Burton's stamina and his continually refreshing interpretation of 'Hamlet' throughout the run of the play. Gielgud recalled years later that Burton needed no more rehearsals once the run had started: "I used to write long notes, seven or eight pages and put them on his dressing table, and he would go on the stage and try two or three of them that evening without any rehearsals and discard the rest, quite rightly probably. The amazing confidence with which he just tried two or three new things during the performance amazed me."

In turn, Burton said he believed that Gielgud was the best director he had ever worked with on the stage: "John said that I was very undisciplined, and he is probably right. Then I wouldn't want to be disciplined. I wouldn't want to be that kind of actor who goes on the stage perfectly every night giving the same cadence, the same speech every night for days and days and days on end. I would prefer to be free so that I'm invited to be bad some nights."

Surprisingly, Burton was not even nominated for a Tony award that season, and that surprised everyone who had confidently expected him to win it easily. Even if he could not win, the lack of even a nomination stunned Broadway. It reflected just how mixed opinions were of Gielgud's adaption of 'Hamlet', and how some people still disapproved of the Burton-Taylor union.

But with the financial success ringing in their ears, it was a happy family that flew off to Paris on Sunday 9th August 1964, the day after the play closed.

Aaron Frosch had been growing anxious at how long his clients had stayed in the United States and was glad to see them on their way at last. Frosch made personally sure that they all got on the plane and left the United States.

Fergus Cashin later wrote that 'Hamlet' was "Burton's most spectacular stage success." And in many ways, it was.

# AND GOD CREATED BURTON

# CHAPTER 40

# Wedding number 2:
# Elizabeth Taylor

## *A double helping*

### 1964

O n the morning of Sunday 15th March, Richard Burton and Elizabeth Taylor took off from Toronto Airport in a chartered Lockheed Jetstar private plane bound for Montreal. Also on board was Burton's valet Bob Wilson, the actor Hume Cronyn, Taylor's PR man John Springer, and Taylor's parents Francis and Sara Taylor.

They were en-route to get married later that day.

It had all been very short notice and had begun on Friday morning, when Burton telephoned John Springer and asked him to handle the PR for their wedding on Sunday. He asked Springer to accompany them to Montreal for the ceremony. Burton said simply and directly, as if he was arranging a business meeting: "Will you come with us and deal with whatever has to be dealt with?"

In many ways, Springer wished Burton hadn't told him. For a PR man, to be sitting on such a big secret for two days was a very big ask. Springer was literally bursting to tell people.

It's not clear whether Burton really trusted Springer, and imparting this information to him may have been a test. If it was, then he failed it. No PR man on earth is capable of keeping that kind of secret.

The wedding had been well trailed since Burton had proposed to Taylor in a pub in Berkshire, England, during the filming of *Becket* the previous summer. The proposal had been made in front of *Daily Mirror* journalist, Fergus Cashin and the actor Peter O'Toole. Cashin had scooped the world with the news in the *Daily Mirror* the following morning. He reported that they had all been having a quiet drink at lunchtime when Burton had suddenly, and without warning, looked straight into Taylor's eyes and said: "I want to marry Elizabeth, and I will marry her. There have been all kind of rumours, but that is what is going to happen. No ifs, no buts, she wants to marry me. I want to marry her." Cashin reported that Taylor replied by saying: "You've said it Richard. And you've sent it Western Union. I love you."

# AND GOD CREATED BURTON

The reference to Western Union appeared to be aimed at Cashin and was code for saying he could print the story so that everyone would know.

Burton suggested they seal it by drinking some scotch whisky, but Taylor insisted on champagne. She said: "No. Champagne, nothing but champagne will do."

But the proposal proved to be easier than actually doing the deed. The media noise surrounding Taylor's divorce from Eddie Fisher had made the wedding very difficult to organise. They had originally planned to wait for a New York wedding during the run of 'Hamlet' the following May. But Taylor's ex-husband, Eddie Fisher, had kicked up such a fuss about the validity of their Mexican divorce in the United States, that no minister or official in New York, with the legal power to marry people, would perform the ceremony in case it was later deemed to be illegal.

Every possible venue in the United States was hedged in legal niceties, which Burton's legal advisers thought best not to challenge. It meant marrying within American jurisdiction was out. The whole of the legislation regarding overseas divorces was very vague in the United States. No one directly challenged the validity of an overseas divorce but most States simply refused to recognise it, meaning a validity challenge was pointless as it didn't matter anyway. It was a legal mess that no one ever thought to clarify.

Toronto would have been very convenient, but it would have meant getting authorisation from Ontario's Provincial Secretary, who would have had to check that their divorces were valid in their normal places of residence. The Provincial Secretary decided that both Burton and Taylor's normal place of residence was Switzerland, not Mexico. At first, that was not thought to be a problem until it was found that Mexican divorces were not legal in Switzerland. It was all very arbitrary.

The next best place was Quebec province and, amazingly, it had no such problems so they chose Quebec's capital, Montreal, for their ceremony. But just to be safe, they decided to hold two ceremonies. Since they both had Mexican divorces, they took advantage of the more liberal Mexican marriage laws, and 'Hamlet' producer Alexander Cohen managed to arrange a ceremony at the Mexican Consulate in Montreal. It would be followed by what Burton called a "make-sure" ceremony on Canadian soil at the Ritz-Carlton hotel, where they would also spend their first night as man and wife.

On board the short flight from Toronto to Montreal, Burton was drinking heavily and appeared to be very agitated. Taylor said to Hume Cronyn: "Why's he so nervous? We've been sleeping together for two years."

When the plane came in to land, Burton looked out of the square little window by his seat and saw a crowd awaiting them. He looked at Springer. The promised secrecy had developed a leak, and he wondered if he was looking at it.

But Montreal's citizens were very civilised and the crowd wasn't big enough to cause them any problems, so they were soon on their way in the two cars that were waiting. First, they headed to the Ritz-Carlton where, in order to maintain secrecy, they were booked in as Mr and Mrs Smith. When Taylor asked why 'Smith', Burton explained to his soon-to-be bride that it was a very English joke, but admitted that as he was Welsh it really should have been 'Mr and Mrs Jones.' She didn't get the joke at all and he quickly gave up trying to explain.

They were booked into Suite 810, the Ritz-Carlton's famous bridal suite. A separate room had been booked for the bride to get ready for her Sunday afternoon weddings. As soon as Mr and Mrs Smith had checked in, they went to their respective rooms; Burton to the suite and Taylor to her room with her mother.

Burton went into the bedroom of the suite to be dressed by Bob Wilson, who was to double as best man. Both donned pleasant-smelling, colourful floral buttonholes for the ceremonies.

At the appointed hour, the men sat around waiting for the bride to appear. An hour went by as they downed a few ice cold martinis, which were Bob Wilson's specialty. As the hour dragged on, Burton got more and more fractious. Finally, he shouted out: "Isn't that fat little tart here yet? She'll be late for the last bloody judgment."

A little too late, Burton remembered that Francis Taylor was in the room. Taylor looked at him like thunder and must have wondered whether it wasn't too late to remove his daughter from the arms of this uncouth Welshman. But he let it pass and realised that it was the drink talking.

When Elizabeth Taylor finally appeared, it was clear she had been worth waiting for. She was wearing a yellow chiffon gown and a headdress of Italian hairpieces entwined with hyacinths and a yellow ribbon. It had been designed by the *Cleopatra* designer, Irene Sharaff, and was supposed to be a replica of the yellow gown she had worn in the first scene she and Burton shot together in *Cleopatra*. For jewellery, she had chosen the emerald and diamond brooch Burton had bought her from Gianni Bulgari in Rome and matching a diamond and emerald necklace and earrings, his wedding present to her that day, also from Bulgari. She looked sensational and every inch the international film star that she was.

By now, they were very late for their date with the Mexican Consul General and they all jumped into the two cars and sped off. The Consul General had put a canopy up in his little garden for them to stand under. It was a lovely scene in the scented garden as he duly pronounced them, under Mexican law, man and wife. After much hugging and kissing, the Consul General's immaculate, white-coated butler brought out champagne in silver goblets. Explaining they were short of time, Burton thanked the Consul General, grabbed the Mexican marriage certificate and sped off back to the Ritz-Carlton.

They went straight back up to the suite, where they were immediately married by an unnamed Englishman who was apparently a Unitarian Minister. He said to them: "You have both gone through great travail in your love for each other." To which they both nodded, signed his register and grabbed their second marriage certificate of the day, as Bob Wilson put a glass of champagne in the minister's hand.

It was all very bizarre but Burton thought, between the two ceremonies, there must be some sort of legality as he reflected just how confused the business of international marriage and divorce really was.

Burton was 38 and Taylor was 32, and they were now man and wife. When it was all finally over, Elizabeth Taylor was absolutely delighted that she had got her man. Richard Burton was her dream come true and had been since 22nd January 1962, when they had first kissed in Rome. She was also pleased that she was no longer Mrs Fisher.

As the news broke across the world, the Jenkins family sent a joint family congratulatory telegram to the Ritz-Carlton. Burton sent a reply back with a one-line message: "And they said it wouldn't last."

It was Burton's second marriage, but Taylor's fifth. Strangely, after the ceremony, she chose to utter precisely the same words that she had said after the first four marriages: "I truly believe in my heart that this marriage will last forever." After a moment's thought, she added: "I know I have said that before, but this time I really do think it is true."

Then they all sat down to a wedding breakfast. At the meal, Burton waxed lyrically about his new wife: "She is like a mirage of beauty of the ages; irresistible, like the pull of gravity. She has everything I want in a woman. She is quite unlike any woman I have ever known. She makes me not want to know any other woman, believe me, sincerely. I think of her morning, noon and night. I dream of her. She will be my greatest happiness – forever, of course."

In reply, Taylor was far less eloquent and told their guests: "The two of us act like we're 17-year-olds. My favourite time is when we're alone at night and for hours we giggle, and talk – about maybe books, world events, poetry, the children, when we first met, problems, daydreams and dreams. We love to watch old movies on TV to regenerate our souls. Sometimes, I wake up in the morning with my eyes absolutely swollen shut from crying at some wonderfully old movie the night before."

They spent that night in Montreal and flew back to Toronto the following morning for the performance of 'Hamlet' on Monday night. When they got back, they found Burton's dressing room filled with presents from the company; particularly, an array of kitchen equipment – pots, pans, choppers and a rolling pin.

On Monday morning, newspapers all over the world reported the marriage on their front pages. It was one of the few days in history when every newspaper in the world had precisely the same story on its front page. Taylor was quoted in many of them saying: "We knew then that there was only one way, indirectly, that we could make it up to all the ones who had suffered: by being good to each other and loving each other. But it has to be not just for now. In 25 years, 50 – then our marriage will have meaning; then all of the unhappiness will at least have been for something."

But the last word was left to America's best known gossip columnist Walter Winchell, who had his own syndicated radio show. He quipped: "Imagine, marrying every husband you meet."

# AND GOD CREATED BURTON

# CHAPTER 41

# Trouble at the top

## *The year to forget*

### 1964- 1965

The Burtons flew straight to Paris from New York, arriving on Sunday 9th August 1964 to begin filming a movie called *The Sandpiper*. It was Elizabeth Taylor's first starring role for nearly two years and she was eager to get back to work. Taylor had finally had enough of being a full-time wife and the film was chosen purely because the studio was prepared to employ both her and Burton, pay them their going rates and make the film outside the United States.

Everything else was secondary to those three considerations, and the resulting second-rate movie reflected that.

The request to shoot the film outside the United States was difficult for the studio, MGM, to comprehend as the story was actually set on a California beach. But such were the ways of Hollywood that the studio signed off on the request to film it in France. The Burtons did make one concession; they would return to America to film the beach exteriors on the Big Sur in California. The cost of recreating the Big Sur in a French studio was just too high and too stupid for even Hollywood to contemplate.

Taylor received her normal US$1 million fee and there was US$500,000 for Burton. They had also received a joint offer of US$2 million to make a film in Israel, but because of the uncertain political situation in the Middle East, they declined.

When Taylor stepped off the plane from New York, she said to a reporter who asked why she was in Paris: "It's always a giggle to pick up a million dollars."

*The Sandpiper* was a project of producer Martin Ransohoff and was to be directed by Vincente Minnelli. The script was written by the legendary Dalton Trumbo.

But right from the start, it was clear the script was poor and had been written on one of Trumbo's off days. *The Sandpiper* was a drama about a young artist, a bohemian woman, living on the beach with her four-year-old illegitimate child. An Episcopal married priest takes the child into his school and becomes involved with the woman. The priest finds himself in love with his wife as well as the artist. Burton played the priest, Taylor the bohemian artist and Eve Marie Saint played Burton's wife. Charles Bronson also had a supporting role.

Burton didn't like the precept of the film or the script, but Taylor talked him into doing it with her. Declaring that he knew what was coming, he said: "We knew this one would be bad before we started, as the dialogue was so awful."

Burton clashed with Minnelli throughout the film and didn't hesitate to tell Trumbo what he thought of his script either. Both men were Hollywood legends in their own way and were not used to being spoken to in that manner. But neither was strong enough to stand up to him although, in the end, Burton gave up and said to Minnelli: "For the money, we will dance."

The problem was that both men were well past their best and should have retired years earlier. They were both hanging on to past glories.

The film ended up being overblown and facile. After it was finished, Burton claimed he had received a telegram from a leading critic, whom he didn't name, which read: "Have just seen a run through of *The Sandpiper* – run and hide." The reviews were predictably scathing. *The New Yorker* called it "a very silly movie." *Newsweek* said it was the "biggest egg in years."

Its only redeeming feature was the theme tune. Initially called 'Love Theme From *The Sandpiper*', it became a huge hit record for Tony Bennett as 'The Shadow of Your Smile' and one of the most iconic tunes of all time.

The theme music saved the film, and it went on to make a large profit for MGM. The final cost was US$5.3 million and it grossed US$14 million at cinemas worldwide. Eventually, there was a US$4 million profit after television fees and sales of the soundtrack.

Before they left Paris, Taylor took Burton to one of Paris' top bespoke tailors and bought him a new wardrobe. It cost her US$5,000 and became his Christmas present.

After filming was finished in Paris, they took the Queen Mary to New York on their own and caught a train to Los Angeles, ready to shoot the exterior shots on the Big Sur beach. They had two reasons to celebrate on that train ride. Firstly, they read the script that would change their lives and define their careers, and secondly Burton had finally achieved one of his ambitions to be a published author. He had written a book called *A Christmas Story*, a semi-fictional autobiography of his childhood, that had just been published. It was more of a leaflet than a book and wasn't particularly inspiring, but it gave him the satisfaction he had long craved.

# TROUBLE AT THE TOP

At the end of filming the exteriors in California, the Burtons fled to Puerto Vallarta for six weeks of sun before returning for Christmas in Gstaad. Burton was due back in Europe in January to film *The Spy Who Came In From The Cold*.

But Christmas of 1964 was not a happy holiday. It was dominated by discussions about Burton's youngest daughter, Jessica; a situation which had finally come to a head after she had been put into an institution and the family had agreed not to visit her.

The story of his daughter, Jessica, had been a blight on Burton's life for over five years; ever since Burton's sister, Catherine Jenkins, a state registered nurse, recognised some problems soon after she was born on 29th November 1959. The problems, obvious to Catherine Jenkins, took two years to be acknowledged by doctors.

By the time she was two years of age, Burton's wife, Sybil, found Jessica was continually misbehaving, sometimes uncontrollably. As she passed three, then four and finally five Sybil had to face up the fact that Jessica was retarded. In those days such children were labelled spastics. But Jessica was not deformed in any way and she was an exceptionally beautiful child. The problem was that her mental capacity had not developed and Burton told friends, trying to describe what was wrong, that she had the mental capabilities of a very smart dog. He said: "The shock to me of being told my child had the intelligence of a reasonably clever dog was considerable."

Burton was always away filming and most of the burden fell on Sybil as she gradually learned the inescapable truth about Jessica's condition. After years of tests, specialists finally diagnosed autism as the problem. Then autism was a little understood condition. Autistic children are perfectly normal, physically and intellectually, but because of inner trauma, they shut themselves off from the world and their only form of expression is anger. Autism also varies in intensity.

Sybil was absolutely devastated the day she was told by an autism specialist that Jessica's autism was 100 per cent. The specialist told Sybil there was no cure and that Jessica would always be very difficult to handle.

By the time Burton was aware something serious was wrong, he and Sybil had split up and by the time he realised the true nature of the condition, he was married to Taylor. Kate, a bright, happy child, grew up with little knowledge of her sister's problems. It soon became very evident that Jessica would need special care forever and would not have a normal life.

# AND GOD CREATED BURTON

The Jenkins family were never told anything about her condition and Jessica was mostly kept away from them. They eventually started to wonder where she was and when David Jenkins asked Burton about her, he just looked back at him "darkly" and said nothing. Burton found it upsetting just to talk about it, so he didn't. Graham Jenkins remembered: "Outwardly, she appeared a normal, healthy child, if somewhat withdrawn. She never smiled or showed pleasure in the silly games children enjoy. In New York, she spent all her waking hours staring, uncomprehending, at the flicker of the television screen."

There was also talk that the autism had been set off by the trauma surrounding the marriage break up. Sybil sometimes alluded to the problems caused by photographer's flashbulbs going off in Jessica's face – triggering abnormal behaviour. David Jenkins said: "We do know that Jessica had just begun to talk when Richard left; then, abruptly, all communication ceased. She became locked in her own mysterious world, where she has remained ever since." That possibility haunted Burton for the whole of his life.

At first, Sybil tried to treat Jessica as normally as possible, taking her out to the movies or to eat and to be with other children, but she became more disruptive as she got older. If they went outside of her apartment in New York, Jessica often caused a disturbance and could even be violent. She was often hard to restrain. Eventually, Sybil began to find it very upsetting to be with her daughter and to never see her smile or talk. She also found her increasingly difficult to control.

Sybil was advised by specialists in America that, sooner or later, Jessica would have to go to a special institution. They recommended the Devereux Center in Long Island, a specialist institution run by the Devereux Foundation. At Long Island, all the nurses had special training to cope with autism and to give their patients as normal a life as possible.

Ivor and Gwen Jenkins, who were childless, took over most of the burden of looking after Jessica and regarded her as their own. When the decision was made for Jessica to be put into an institution, Gwen was devastated and was insistent that Jessica was responding and making headway. Gwen believed Ivor Jenkins was able to communicate with her in a limited way. But they lost the three-way argument with the doctors and her parents, and Jessica was moved to Long Island.

At first, Sybil visited Jessica often, as did Burton when he was in New York.

But when they visited, they found she didn't recognise them and doctors said she was locked in a world no one would be able to penetrate. As Sybil described it: "Nobody knows what autism really is. That's the hell of it. It's a sort of mental illness. Jessica lives in a world of her own. She doesn't recognise me or Rich or anybody. There's no way of telling just how much she understands."

During the Christmas holidays in 1964, Elizabeth Taylor began discussing with Burton a plan to take Jessica out of the Devereux Center and to bring her to live with them permanently. She figured they could afford to employ specialist nurses to care for her 24 hours a day.

Taylor was encouraged by the success she had enjoyed with Maria, who was born a cripple and was now leading a normal life because of her intervention. Taylor genuinely believed that she could intervene again and make a difference to Jessica's life and maybe even cure her.

Gianni Bozzacchi, who was Taylor's personal photographer, confirmed that Taylor wanted to bring Jessica into their household, where she could be looked after by a hired nursing team. But Burton told her she did not know what she was talking about. Taylor, however, didn't give up on the idea and pursued it for a long time. In the end, she backed off when Burton told her Sybil would never give her permission.

Today, there is a very well-endowed trust fund that is believed to have grown to well over US$10 million to provide for 51-year-old Jessica's care.

The bad news about Jessica was that it was just a portent of what was to come in 1965. The year started promisingly enough with the beginning of filming for *The Spy Who Came In From The Cold*, based on a novel by John Le Carre. But for varying reasons, it was fraught with difficulties every step of the way.

Originally, Burton and Taylor had meant *The Spy Who Came In From The Cold* to be the first film they produced together. But when Le Carre's agent put the film rights up for auction, they bid, but not high enough.

The rights were eventually bought by the partnership of director Martin Ritt and the actor Paul Newman. The book seemed a sure-fire winner as a movie and the competition to get it had been fierce. Le Carre preferred to sell it to some creative individuals rather than to a studio. Ritt and Newman were both high minded, principled individuals who fitted his requirements.

Ritt got the budget of US$5 million from the Paramount studio and told Paramount he wanted Richard Burton for the lead part of Alec Leamas. But first, he had to win an argument with John Le Carre, who wanted Trevor Howard or James Mason for the part – the director won.

# AND GOD CREATED BURTON

Burton, as usual, played hard to get and Hugh French sensed desperation when Ritt, who had never met Burton, approached him. Instead of Burton's usual half a million dollars, he asked for three quarters of a million. Ritt wasn't a great negotiator and when Paramount resisted, he took the actor's side. As he admitted: "I fought for Burton and, finally, Paramount agreed to pay it."

As soon as they got back to Gstaad from Puerto Vallarta, Burton flew to London to meet Martin Ritt, the director for the first time. They had lunch at The Dorchester with Claire Bloom, who was to play the role of Leamas' communist girlfriend in the movie. Burton hadn't seen Bloom for nearly six years and not since she had married Rod Steiger in 1959. It could have been a tense reunion but they were both cordial to each other.

Burton did not find much personal chemistry with Ritt, a man he had expected to like a lot more than he did. Ritt, who was a non-drinker and non-smoker, bridled at Burton's indulgence. He found non-stop drinking and smoking distasteful. Ritt couldn't hide his distaste and Burton felt that he was being patronised and hated it.

Burton flew back to Gstaad and would return three weeks later to begin work. Three months' filming was scheduled to start at Shepperton Studios in London and then to continue at the Ardmore Studios in Dublin, Ireland, and finally to finish in Holland at Schiphol.

*The Spy Who Came In From The Cold* was the story of Alec Leamas, a weary, disillusioned and expendable British spy whose body is still alive but whose spirit is slowly dying of self-disgust. No longer a young man, he is exhausted by life's experience. The plot of the story sees Leamas engage blindly in one last game of double-dealing behind the Iron Curtain. The role of Alec Leamas was not natural territory for Burton. He specialised in playing heroes, and Leamas was no hero – or at least not an obvious one.

Claire Bloom played the female lead of a communist librarian, called Nan, who is in love with Leamas. Before filming began, there was one change to the script, insisted upon by Elizabeth Taylor. Bloom's character in Le Carre's book was called Liz, and Taylor would have none of it. So it was changed to Nan.

At the end of January 1965, both Burton and Taylor took up residence at The Dorchester. Taylor introduced Burton to Marjorie Lee, the hotel's entertainment manager. Lee eventually became a friend and unofficial aide to the Burtons and organised many social occasions on their behalf.

The stay at The Dorchester was only for two weeks, just long enough for some interiors at Shepperton and exteriors in London's Trafalgar Square to be shot.

On the way to Ireland Burton decided to take Taylor back to Wales for the first time since they were married. But what he really wanted to do was go to Cardiff Arms Park for the England-Wales rugby match on Saturday 16th January. He called it "reconnecting with his roots."

They were driven down to Wales in Elizabeth Taylor's white Rolls Royce Silver Cloud by her chauffeur, Gaston Sanz. They checked into the Queens Hotel in Cardiff and met up with Burton's brother, Graham Jenkins, who had tickets to the match. Taylor dressed for the occasion in an all-red outfit, complete with a red bowler hat. They cheered as the Welsh rugby team trounced England, and both of them joined in the singing.

During the match, they were left alone by fans who really didn't know they were there. It was a brilliant afternoon if you were a Welshman, and they returned to the hotel to find a mass of fans celebrating the victory. They were jostled by the good natured crowd, who refused to let them leave until they had had a drink with them. Graham Jenkins remembers what happened: "It was without doubt, one of the worst experiences of lack of crowd control that I have ever known. The crowd just wouldn't let us get out." In the end, some members of the Welsh team also staying at the hotel formed a cordon and got the Burtons out through the kitchen entrance.

Realising that it was not a good idea hanging around, they went to Port Talbot to visit the family.

But this time, the word was out and the press was on the case. The visit turned into a media circus and a convoy of journalists and photographers followed the Burtons' car around Wales.

When they got to Pontrhydyfen, the place was heaving with people anxious to catch a glimpse of Taylor. Hilda Owen, Burton's sister, recalled that there were "busloads coming in to see them." Once again, they stayed the night with Hilda and her family in Pontrhydyfen and ate the traditional Welsh meal of lava bread. The trip was most memorable for the amazing gooseberry tart that Hilda produced from her larder for pudding.

The following morning, they got into the Rolls-Royce and caught the ferry to Dublin, where they checked into the penthouse suite of the Gresham Hotel. From the penthouse windows, they could see a cinema across O'Connell Street. It was playing *Cleopatra*, and the couple were surprised by the large queues waiting to get in to see it.

The rest of the entourage, including little Maria, flew in the next day and filled up two floors of the Gresham Hotel. The entourage was growing the entire time and now consisted of Taylor's secretary, Dick Hanley, and his assistant, John Lee; Burton's valet, Bob Wilson; Taylor's personal make-up artist, Ron Berkeley; Burton's bodyguard, Bobby LaSalle; Taylor's chauffeur, Gaston Sanz; and Burton's secretary, Jim Benton; plus a tutor, governess and nanny for Maria.

Very early on in the shoot, it was obvious that the film was blighted by the decision to film it in black and white in an era in which colour had begun to dominate the cinema. It was an international spy drama, so the decision was inexplicable and seemingly made in the name of art. It was a shame, as it precluded the film becoming a commercial as well as a critical success.

In spite of that and the obvious tension and lack of empathy between Burton and his abstaining director, there was little doubt that *The Spy Who Came in from the Cold* was going to be a good film.

Which was just as well, as it was a far from happy set during filming.

Burton blotted his copybook early on by bad-mouthing Ritt to the young actress Joanne Woodward, who was also Paul Newman's wife. In conversation with her, Burton called Ritt "that prick of a director." Woodward immediately turned her back on him and made her displeasure known.

Ritt dismissed the remark and got on with filming. But he and Burton argued openly on set and Burton attempted to stamp his authority on the directorial process. Ritt refused to let him.

Years later, Ritt talked about his differences with Burton: "I wasn't sympathetic to his lifestyle, nor Elizabeth's. She was there much of the time as an onlooker, constantly drinking from a champagne bottle. She'd open a bottle as early as eleven in the morning. Richard was fine until lunchtime, and then he'd join her, and by the time he was back, he had a buzz on from too much wine. I had made a commitment to the picture, to achieve the most that could be gotten for it, and I wanted the same from everybody." Ritt admitted: "It was not a happy picture. I'm sure he felt that I didn't appreciate him enough."

For all of the two months that the Burtons occupied the penthouse suite at the Gresham, it was far from an easy time. First, Maria caught the measles, which was more scary than usual because of her prior medical problems. Then, a tragedy befell Taylor's chauffeur of 12 years, Gaston Sanz, when his 16-year-old son was killed in a shooting accident in Paris. Sanz was a tough individual, who had fought with the French resistance during the Second World War and been personally decorated by General De Gaulle. He fell apart when he heard of his son's death.

Taylor flew to Paris to console him and to accompany him to the funeral and, later, the inquest. It was an extraordinary gesture and Sanz later said of her: "Only her compassion and support saved me from myself. I wouldn't be here now if it wasn't for her." Whilst she was in Paris, Taylor had some expensive jewels stolen from her hotel suite.

The troubles got worse. When Sanz returned to Dublin, with Taylor in the back seat of the Rolls-Royce, he accidentally hit and killed a pedestrian. It wasn't in any way his fault, but it still cast a shadow.

Then, a final blow came in the middle of March, when Taylor's father, Francis, suffered a serious stroke. She flew off to Los Angeles to be with him as he was expected to die. She spent a whole week at his bedside at the hospital and nursed him back to health.

To cap everything off, near the end of filming, Taylor herself was in the hospital with the recurrence of a spinal injury and some new gynaecological problems.

Burton chose to drown all these troubles with scotch whisky brought to him continually by Bob Wilson. He drank heavily throughout the shoot, which created even more differences with the director.

But the relationship between Ritt and Burton wasn't the only factor causing problems. Filming was dominated by the coolness between Burton and Bloom. The atmosphere was effectively poisoned by Taylor, who did not trust her husband around his former mistress. Taylor reasoned that as Bloom had been, in the past, the only serious threat to Sybil before her, then she was probably still a threat, despite the fact that she was now married to Rod Steiger. It became clear that, of all the people from Burton's earlier life, Taylor hated Claire Bloom the most. Melvyn Bragg explained it best: "Elizabeth Taylor was like a one-woman emotional KGB: he was under twenty-four-hour surveillance. She monitored every wink."

Burton responded to his wife's unease by trying to prove the opposite by snubbing Bloom continually. He was cool to the point of rudeness.

Taylor's jealousy and possessiveness and Burton's crass behaviour towards her upset Bloom substantially. Martin Ritt took Claire Bloom's side and blamed Burton for the atmosphere on set. As he said: "He wasn't very nice to her; understandable, I suppose, with Elizabeth there."

Taylor was overprotective and mothered Burton throughout the shoot. When she wanted him, she just screamed out his name and he came running. She worked Burton up into a permanent state of anxiety on the set. It was clear to everyone that she was besotted with him to the point of unhealthiness.

Finally, Bloom snapped and made her feelings known in an interview with the columnist Sheilah Graham, who was visiting the set. Graham wrote a daily column, called 'Hollywood Today', published in 178 newspapers across America. She often flew long distances to visit the sets of Richard Burton's films, where she knew there would always be juicy stories. Eventually, the 61-year-old became a one-woman chronicle of Burton's life and times, and her columns are now far more useful than Burton's own diaries when trying to understand his life.

Bloom was entirely candid when she spoke to Graham on set. She said of her former lover: "He hadn't changed at all except physically. He was still drinking, still boasting, he was still late, still reciting the same poems and telling the same stories as when he was 23. They were both rather aloof to me. During the month's shooting in Ireland, I was never asked to dinner by the Burtons. He was interesting, years ago, but now I found him rather boring, as people are when they have got what they always wanted...a beautiful wife, money, and a great career. In the early days, he would have included a wish to be the greatest actor in the world. It was obvious that he was going to be a huge star, which is not the same as being a great actor. He has confused them. He thinks they are the same."

When he read what Bloom had said and was asked for a comment by the journalist Hollis Alpert, Burton responded: "I can tell you in just four words: 'Hell hath no fury.'"

The two women met properly only once, when John Le Carre cheekily brought Bloom as his date to dinner in Burton's suite at The Gresham. As Burton biographer Sam Kashner put it, the dinner became a "gunfight between two great raconteurs", with Le Carre and Burton both taking turns telling stories to impress Taylor and Bloom.

But Taylor got fed up staring at Bloom across the table and retired to bed halfway through. Through the intercom, which linked all the rooms in the suite, she called Burton to join her. He ignored her requests and finally she appeared at the door and they began having a huge row in front of Le Carre and Bloom. The two of them made their excuses and left.

John Le Carre told another story that has appeared in many Burton biographies and is presumed to be true. He recalled the first time he met Taylor after he had been urgently summoned to the Burtons' penthouse suite at an early hour of the morning to meet her. Le Carre arrived to find Burton sitting on his own in the suite's lounge area. As he described it: "I heard the intercom crackling with Elizabeth's voice. 'Richard?' 'Yes, darling?' 'Who's there?' 'The writer.'"

Burton disappeared into the bedroom to fetch Taylor and they proceeded, as Le Carre described it, "...to have a mother and a father of a row all heard though the intercom loudspeaker. There were sounds of slapping. Eventually, she arrived in this sort of fluffy wraparound dressing gown you send away for, barefooted, rather broad-arsed, but extremely cuddly, extraordinarily attractive – those beautiful eyes, far more beautiful off-screen than on. And she gave me one of those little-girl handshakes."

After all the slapping noises, Le Carre had expected Taylor to emerge from the bedroom with a red face. Instead, it was Burton who emerged all bruised and battered, having clearly received the slapping from Taylor.

Le Carre was surprised how much Burton aged during the filming. It was his 40th year and he deteriorated in front of his eyes, from the start of filming at Shepperton to the final beach scenes at Scheveningen in Holland. Le Carre had hit the mark with his observation, and years later, it became clear that the shooting of *The Spy Who Came In From The Cold* marked the start of a physical decline that was to continue unabated for the next 18 years.

One actor who had an entirely different experience with Taylor was Robert Hardy, who also appeared in *The Spy Who Came In From The Cold*. He will always remember the moment when Elizabeth Taylor won him over for all time. When he arrived at his hotel in Holland, as he recalled: "There was a note on my pillow – 'We are in the American bar - Rich and Liz.' So I went downstairs and there was this enormous room; of the sort you would expect to see Mussolini at the end sitting down on a raised platform. It was a creepy hotel because it had been Gestapo headquarters during the occupation. Elizabeth turned around and held her arms out and kissed me on the mouth, and of course that was the end of standing-off. It was such magic. She was, when she wanted to be, the most sexual being that you would ever come up against."

The critics gave Burton a unanimous thumbs up for playing Alec Leamas; he played the role so well, he was in danger of becoming typecast. Leonard Mosley, who went on to write a very fine biography of Walt Disney, and who had been a huge Burton critic in the past, was then working for the *Daily Express* and wrote: "It compensated for every bad part he has ever played and every indiscretion he has ever committed off the screen or on. If he doesn't win an Oscar for it this year, there is not only no justice left in Hollywood but no judgment either." Burton gained a fourth Oscar nomination, but did not win.

When filming ended, the whole family went on holiday to the Côte d'Azur for two months to get over the stressful time in Ireland and to put its recent problems behind them.

It proved a blissful holiday and Burton thoroughly loved the time with the children, who were growing up fast and were still at the age where they could be enjoyed. Taylor watched proudly as her children bonded with her husband. It was the family unit she had always hoped for and now had.

They were all so happy: Michael Wilding, the eldest was demonstrating musical talent. Christopher Wilding was turning into a very good looking boy, with his mother's violet eyes and dark eyelashes. Taylor was pleased that the early hostility the two boys had showed to their new stepfather, some of it encouraged by Eddie Fisher, had vanished. Now fully recovered, Maria was becoming very close to the only man she ever knew as a father. But diminutive Liza was the star of the family. She was a mini-Elizabeth and shared her mother's love of animals and horses. She also loved to take charge, just like her mother.

The major subject of discussion on holiday was the formation of a new production company so that Burton and Taylor could produce their own films. Their appetites had been whetted by Ritt and Newman's success with *The Spy Who Came In From The Cold*.

That summer, the Burtons put together their new production company to make the first film, to be called *The Greatest Train Robbery in the World*, based on the British train robbery that had taken place in Buckinghamshire two years before.

They hired Sam Wanamaker to direct it, and Burton would play the gang's leader. Strangely, it would be the first time he played a criminal. He said: "I come from the humblest of Welsh families…yet I've almost always played princes and kings… I'm looking forward to getting back to a working-class part." Then, he said something really strange: "I remember at the time of the robbery feeling rather good that we, the British, had brought off the biggest raid ever made, and I've never met anybody who wasn't delighted that the robbers managed it."

Filming was scheduled to begin in November 1965, four months hence, by which time they would be back from Los Angeles, where they were shortly to go and film *Who's Afraid of Virginia Woolf?* Both he and Taylor were very excited about it.

But before they left for Los Angeles, Burton received some news he personally found very disturbing. Aaron Frosch phoned him out of the blue to tell him that Sybil had remarried and that his financial obligations to her were consequently over. Frosch expected Burton to be delighted with the news but quickly became aware he wasn't – far from it. When Burton demanded to know details, Frosch told him that his 36-year-old ex-wife had married a pop singer called Jordan Christopher who was 11 years her junior. Frosch explained that her new husband had been born in Macedonia but brought up in Ohio. He took all this in and was silent for around 30 seconds. Then, through gritted teeth, Burton told Frosch he was pleased to see Sybil move on with her life and to pass on his best wishes. But inside, he was devastated and felt like he had been hit by a truck. It had been less than two years since they had split, and now his wife was married to another man, 16 years younger than him. It was beyond his comprehension. He slammed the phone down hard.

Burton's first reaction was to telephone Stanley Baker to see if it was true. Baker told him it was and that he was glad for Sybil. Hearing that, Burton went hysterical at the other end of the phone. According to Baker, he told him: "You've got to stop it. Go out there, Stan, and stop her marrying that boy. Please don't let her get married." Baker held the phone away from his ear, scarcely believing what he was hearing.

When he put down the phone to Baker, Burton launched into a routine that was to make John Cleese so famous ten years later. He put his head between his legs, clasped his hands underneath his knees and hopped around the room backwards, making a funny screaming noise as he went. It was the only way he knew to express the anger and frustration he felt at the news.

When Taylor heard the commotion, she came in to find out what was going on. When Burton told her, she just said: "Oh that." Taylor had already heard the news from one of her girlfriends in New York.

The news was a massive blow to Burton's ego, and to say he was unsettled by it would be an understatement. Later, he said he had no idea why he took the news so badly but admitted it had come as a complete surprise and that he had never contemplated Sybil getting remarried, let alone being happy with another man who wasn't him.

He suddenly felt very insecure and kept wondering if he had done the right thing in marrying Taylor. In the back of his mind he had always known Sybil would take him back. Now he knew that option was closed off and it completely destabilised him. He couldn't think about anything else for almost four days.

There were no such thoughts at El Dorado Towers in New York, where the new Christopher family had settled. Sybil had rediscovered all her old energy for living and even spoke publicly to her friend Elaine Dundy about her new husband: "I was attracted to Jordan right off, very strongly; but I couldn't believe it, wouldn't let myself even think about it. It was the age difference that shocked me about my feelings. What I kept saying to myself all the time was: 'Sybil, what are you doing, you, a simple Welsh Methodist lass with a rock and roll star?'"

The Jenkins family were delighted and they sent Sybil the same congratulatory telegram they had sent their brother when he married Taylor. And when Graham Jenkins started speculating about how long Sybil's marriage to Jordan Christopher would last, he was immediately cut off by his older brother, Tom, who said: "You don't have to worry about Sybil. She's not a girl to make the same mistake twice." Tom had summed it up perfectly and, indeed, as he predicted, the marriage endured and has been happy for 46 years.

Kate Burton later admitted that her mother and her new stepfather had agonised about the age gap and quickly decided it didn't matter. As she said: "They both worried at first about how long the marriage might last. But it did. And he became a remarkably good second father."

When the marriage was announced, it delighted the old Sybil fan club in London and they came out with their support in the press. Despite Burton's reaction, Stanley Baker was Sybil's most vociferous supporter and said: "In this superficial world we live in, there is so much nonsense talked, so much pretence, and yet here was one girl who had none of that. She was a genuine person with great humour, wit, intelligence and warmth. And an attractive woman, a very sexy woman."

Two years after the divorce, Baker was still telling journalists how stupid Burton had been to ditch Sybil: "Richard knew a lot about life in this business and must have realised how superficial it is, how long certain things can last and what your values are. Yes, it is extraordinary that the marriage has broken up, and it shows how wrong you can be about people. I just thought – and it appeared not only to me but to everybody – that Richard and Sybil were two peas in a pod, dead right for each other." It was the most direct snub he could make to Taylor without actually mentioning her name, and it delighted his wife Ellen when she read it.

After Baker, there was no one more delighted than Emlyn Williams: "I admired her tremendously. My fear had been that if she were going to make the break she would disappear into the Welsh valleys and become just a sad little lady. But not at all. She had always behaved so beautifully, and it was marvellous that she was to become a great personality on her own. It was a happy ending to a very bumpy journey."

Burton's discomfiture was made worse by Sybil's growing success as a business woman. She had started a very successful business with the money he had given her in the divorce.

In May 1965, Sybil opened a discotheque called Arthur on 54th Street and became queen of America's disco scene. One columnist described her as "the white tornado of the jet-set" and said she had "extraordinary flair." It was Arthur that had indirectly caused her to meet her new husband. The Arthur house band was called The Wild Ones, fronted by Jordan Christopher and, gradually, he and Sybil had fallen in love.

The inspiration for Arthur had come when Sybil had developed a taste for nightclubs during her last few months in London in 1963. In fact, the concept of Arthur was based on the Ad Lib club in London where Sybil had enjoyed so many good times before moving to New York.

In New York, one of her regular haunts was Strollers. It was Jeremy Geidt at The Strollers Club that became her inspiration. After her divorce came through, he sat her down and said: "Well what are you going to do next?" Together, they conceived the idea of setting up as a production team and taking over the upper floors of The Strollers Club in order to open a theatre.

Geidt told Sybil she had taste, and she also found she had a flair for casting. He was right and, as the co-director of The Establishment Theatre Company, she was responsible for the off-Broadway productions of 'The Ginger Man', 'The Knack' and 'Square in the Eye'.

The theatre was a big success and easily paid its way under her direction. That led to Sybil eventually taking over the lease of the whole Strollers building and turned it into a discotheque.

Although she had enough money to do it herself, she asked people to invest and they did so willingly. Arthur's shareholder roster included Sammy Davis Jr and, through him, Frank Sinatra, both of whom invested US$1,000 each, as did Roddy McDowall, Julie Andrews, Leonard Bernstein and Stephen Sondheim.

Almost immediately, Arthur became the in-place to go to and Sybil became the most celebrated hostess in town. The Wild Ones, fronted by her husband, also became New York's most popular band for a period. It all came together for her.

# AND GOD CREATED BURTON

Her secret was a democratic door policy and it encouraged young, hip, working class people to come. They loved to mix with Sybil's sophisticated friends, some of whom came every night. They included Tennessee Williams, Truman Capote, Andy Warhol, Rudolph Nureyev, Stanley Baker, Robert Hardy, Emlyn Williams, Rex Harrison and Dirk Bogarde. Quite quickly, Arthur became the hardest club in New York to get into. Crowds gathered outside the unpretentious building each night hoping to gain admittance, and, if not, to at least watch those who did.

It was hard to define exactly what was the secret of Sybil's success at Arthur. But the subtly-coloured lights flashing from the ceiling and the amplified music shaking the floor were all part of the mix. Sammy Davis Jr observed: "It's like the Black Hole of Calcutta – only with no air."

Arthur was different from other discotheques. It had class, a touch of elegance that came from Sybil's presence and the many friends she entertained there. Sybil had always had a gift for friendship, and that turned out to be the most needed talent for running a successful night club. She said in an interview when Arthur opened: "I knew if I came here, I'd be all right. If New York had failed, I'd have been in real trouble."

But it was Andy Warhol who made Arthur famous when he called the club "all dark brightness." Warhol, who ran a magazine called *Interview*, had become one of Sybil's closest friends. He described Sybil as "an upbeat, outgoing woman; the energetic English type that wants everybody to have fun."

With that kind of endorsement, Arthur became a magnet for celebrities including regulars such as Sophia Loren, Bette Davis and, as Warhol famously said, "everybody but Liz Taylor-Burton."

Warhol's endorsement of Sybil was a surprise, as he had been up to then a worshipper of Taylor in his art and his writing. His silk screens of her were already sought after and had helped define his work.

None of this went unnoticed by Burton and Taylor, and when they were in New York they desperately wanted to visit Arthur and to bury the hatchet with Sybil, as well as to meet her new husband. Philip Burton warned them this would never be possible. Ignoring him, Burton put in a request to visit through Aaron Frosh and, just as Philip had said, Sybil told them to stay away.

Success was Sybil's ultimate revenge on her husband. Her elevation was as welcome as it was unexpected. It gave her a glamorous image and she became a social power player in New York. Eventually, she became associated with sister clubs in Los Angeles, Dallas, Detroit and San Francisco, which she advised on. Sybil sold the club four years after she started it, when criminal gangs started to dominate the local unions and infiltrated the club scene. By then, she and her new husband were very wealthy as a result.

Sybil had a very successful life and eventually a daughter called Amy was born of their union. For Sybil, the ghost of Jessica had been exorcised when Amy arrived. She could now be truly happy again.

Burton would eventually recover from the shock of Sybil's remarriage, and as soon as their holiday was over, they were both back at work in Los Angeles working on Ernest Lehman's version of Edward Albee's disturbing play 'Who's Afraid of Virginia Woolf?'

It was the study of the marriage of a bitter, aging, childless couple, fuelled by alcohol, who use a young couple to wage a war of anguish and emotional pain against each other. The couple, called George and Martha, are bent on destroying each other's lives as part of a game in which they seek to expose their partner's weaknesses and to exploit them. Burton played George, a middle-aged, ordinary, college history professor. Taylor played Martha, a plump domineering woman who is married to George but protected by virtue of the fact that she is the daughter of the college's head.

The negotiations between Ernest Lehman and Burton and Taylor had started in late July 1964. The Burtons were on their way to California to film the exterior shots at Big Sur for *The Sandpiper*. They had decided to travel by train overnight on the Super Chief, and Taylor read the script whilst Burton buried his nose in his books.

After she had finished it, she handed the script to her husband without saying anything. Burton remembered: "I thought I'd have a glance at it. It was late, ten o'clock at night and I thought that perhaps I'd read an act and finish it in the morning. But I was compelled to finish it."

And then, he read it again and, afterwards, woke his sleeping wife. He told her: "I think you're too young for the part. I don't think you're enough of a harridan. Maybe you don't have the power to play Martha but you've got to play it to stop anybody else from playing it. I don't want any other actress to do it. It's too good a part."

Taylor said she thought she would be offered the part but was doubtful whether it was for her. But Burton had no doubts and told her: "This could be your 'Hamlet.'" They discussed it until dawn broke and the train pulled into Los Angeles.

Meanwhile, in LA, Ernest Lehman, the producer, who was also one of

Hollywood's most successful screenwriters, had been mulling over how to write a screenplay of the production, which had been a huge hit on Broadway.

Once Taylor had read the script, Hugh French, Burton's agent, got on the case. He offered his client to Lehman for US$1.1 million plus US$100,000 a week overages and a ten per cent share of profits. The more Lehman thought about Taylor as Martha, the more he liked it. But he could not fathom Burton as George, the professor.

With that, Lehman went to see Jack Warner and told him he wanted to offer the role of Martha to Elizabeth Taylor. Warner shouted back at him: "She's too young for it and she'll cost too much."

Then, without a word, he went through the door behind his desk that led to his private bathroom, and left Lehman alone and wondering where he had gone. But it was a standard Warner technique when he wanted to ponder a perhaps too-hasty decision without appearing indecisive in front of a visitor. He returned two minutes later and stunned Lehman by telling him to hire Taylor for the part, offering no explanation for his change of mind.

Hugh French negotiated for her and a deal was quickly done. The start date was mid-1965, when Burton was scheduled to shoot *The Spy Who Came in from the Cold*. But Taylor did not want to be separated from Burton or her children for that long. So before leaving Los Angeles to go to Puerto Vallarta for a few weeks, they stopped off at the Beverly Hills Hotel and met with Ernest Lehman to discuss a delayed start. Surprisingly, Lehman didn't see that as a problem at all. In truth, he had already anticipated it. And before they arrived, Ernest Lehman had received a call from Hugh French who told him: "Richard has given the matter of playing George some thought. Now he is convinced he can do it."

Lehman had earlier decided that Jack Lemmon was his choice for the role. He had sent the script to him and Lemmon had indicated his interest. But a few weeks later, Lemmon's agent had called back and said: "I don't know how to tell you this, and I don't know who Jack's been talking to, but he'd rather back away from it." That left the door wide open for Burton.

When they arrived, Taylor thanked Lehman for her US$1.1 million fee and then told him: "Ernie, I'd have done this role for nothing, you know. But Hugh French told me to say a million wasn't enough. We took you, we really took you." Then, she proceeded to persuade Lehman to hire her husband and pay him US$750,000 plus US$50,000 a week overages and ten per cent.

Surprisingly, he agreed just like that; having anticipated it and agreed it with

Jack Warner in advance.

The Burtons arranged to come back out to California at the end of June 1965. They rented a Hollywood mansion that stood at the back of the Beverly Hills Hotel on Carolwood Drive, in Bel Air's Holmby Hills. It was big enough to hold the entourage and also get all the facilities of the hotel.

With his stars in place, Lehman could finally get a proper budget from Jack Warner and hire a director. Warner gave him a very generous budget of US$7.5 million, which would make it the most expensive black and white film ever made. And by luck or judgment, Mike Nichols was signed on as a first time director. Nichols, at that time, was known only in the theatre, where he had been directing successful comedies on Broadway.

Burton couldn't have been more pleased. He loved Nichols and had known the young director on Broadway. They had become friends when Burton was playing in 'Camelot'. Taylor and Burton had lobbied behind the scenes for him to get the job, and he was to prove an excellent choice.

Lehman did a superb job of turning Edward Albee's play into a film script. It was ready to go by the start of July 1965. Graham Jenkins described the script of the film as "a professional commitment to a three-month slanging match in front of the cameras."

The production began on 6th July 1965 on the Warner Bros lot at Burbank. Nichols insisted on doing things his way and there were three weeks of rehearsals before the cameras were even turned on. It was an unusual start to a film, but insisted upon by Nichols, who wanted everything perfect.

Principal photography began on 26th July and lasted a month, until the unit flew to Massachusetts to do exteriors and interiors at Smith College. By the time they returned to Los Angeles, they were well behind schedule.

Both Burton and Taylor's performances were superb, amongst the very best of their careers. They really got into their characters and became their characters. It was almost like projecting their own personas 20 years forward, and they thoroughly enjoyed doing it.

In particular, Burton's performance as George was described in *Variety*, the Hollywood trade paper, as "superlative." "I *am* George," he said to Mike Nichols, and thoroughly enjoyed working with a fine script and a producer and director he respected. Every opportunity he got, he told Nichols and Lehman how great they were.

Elizabeth Taylor had to put on a great deal of weight to play Martha. She also had to be aged by 20 years with make-up and wigs. It was also undoubtedly the performance of her life.

On 25th November 1965, Richard Burton celebrated a very special birthday – his 40th. Warners threw a big party for him on a Burbank sound stage. Taylor gave him America's hottest new car, the Oldsmobile Toronado, for his birthday and wrapped it in a huge red ribbon. It was very special, as it had been obtained before the new model had been officially released by General Motors. Taylor had persuaded GM's president, Jim Roche, that it would be worth it for the publicity and Roche agreed. He also omitted, as she had very cleverly calculated, to send her a bill for the car.

Ernest Lehman's birthday present was a first edition of the essays of Francis Bacon. Nothing could have made Burton happier and he cherished it. Mike Nichols gave him a puppy, which pleased him much less. Not that he didn't like the puppy. He just felt that he and Taylor had enough of them already. In retaliation, he went out the next day and bought Nichols four mice in a cage.

Filming finally finished on 13th December 1965, overrunning the schedule by 35 days.

The Burtons were owed US$750,000 dollars in overages between them. But when they found out that Nichols' contract with Jack Warner called for any overages to come out of his fee, they both waived them.

A wrap party was held on the soundstage, but even then, most of the cast and crew had to wait until Mike Nichols got one last take with Burton and Taylor, who were already having withdrawal symptoms from their characters, George and Martha.

The Burtons gave their own farewell party on the eve of their departure at their mansion on Carolwood Drive. They hired a full orchestra to play for their guests and it was an immensely happy occasion for the cast and crew.

Interestingly, at the party, both Burton and Taylor separately requested a private word with Lehman. And both of them, without the knowledge of the other, told him the same thing. They told him they were going to miss playing their roles of George and Martha, which they had been doing non-stop for five months. They both said that they had strangely enjoyed being their respective characters and that they would find it had to revert back to their real personas. Burton told him: "I feel rather lost."

With that, they headed home for the holidays.

Professionally, the film was a triumph. Burton turned out a superb performance and everyone agreed it was Taylor's best ever. They were both nominated for Oscars, but she won and he didn't. The best actor Oscar that year went to Paul Scofield for *A Man For All Seasons*. It was a travesty. Scofield was very good in his film, but Burton was better in his. It was his fifth nomination and his fifth straight failure to win.

The machinations and overruns on *Who's Afraid of Virginia Woolf?* meant that *The Greatest Train Robbery in the World* fell by the wayside – never to resurface. And, for the moment, so too did Burton and Taylor's dream of producing their own films. They weren't too bothered. In the interim, many competing film projects about the great train robbery had emerged to queer their pitch, and they all decided it was for the best.

The year, which had been terrible in so many ways, therefore ended well.

And there was more good news to come early in the New Year. Burton broke back into the list of top ten actors at the box office during 1965. And suddenly, he was attracting huge interest from publishers who wanted him to write his autobiography now that he had turned 40. They told him it would undoubtedly be a big seller. Hugh French was offered a US$100,000 advance for the book. But Burton had no intention of writing it. Instead, a young entertainment journalist called Ruth Waterbury wrote a quick paperback of the Burton story to date. Waterbury, who was the former editor of *Photoplay* magazine and founder of *Silver Screen* magazine, actually wrote two paperbacks, the first called *Elizabeth Taylor: Her Life, Her Loves, Her Future*, followed quickly by *Richard Burton: His Intimate Story*.

Burton agreed to sit for some interviews. In the process, he rewrote the history of his childhood, which Waterbury obliged him by printing verbatim. It was a version of his truth that no one in his family would recognise. 1965 had been a year packed with incident, and for the most part a year to forget. But 1966 looked so much better. And so it was to prove.

# AND GOD CREATED BURTON

# CHAPTER 42

# Return to Oxford

## *Fiasco amongst the spires*

### February 1966

Since he had gone into tax exile in 1957, Richard Burton had often dreamed noble dreams and thought noble thoughts but very rarely acted upon them. The noble dreams and the noble thoughts were always put to one side when people offered him hundreds of thousands of dollars to make movies – which they frequently did, and it was always the source of dilemma. The scorecard in his profession was, at the end of the day, always money.

Every so often, he would go back to the stage but only for a substantial amount of money. But despite this unpromising track record, there is little doubt that his natural inclination was to not take the money, although he always did.

Pre-tax exile, when there was no incentive in Britain in the 1950s to earn money, he did return to his art in 1953 and 1954. But after he moved to Switzerland, when Hollywood or Broadway were prepared to pay him as much as US$25,000 a week to perform – he returned no more.

But that didn't stop him continuing to talk about one day giving up Hollywood and retiring to become an academic in Oxford; lost in his books and writings and imparting his great knowledge to others. It was how he always envisaged himself – in thought, if not in reality – just like the oft-thought idea of making noble films of Shakespearean subjects such as 'Macbeth', 'Coriolanus' and 'King Lear'.

'King Lear' was his greatest obsession. He continually fantasised about playing Lear on the stage and on film. But the more he thought about it, the further away it seemed, as he said often: "I have to play Lear as a kind of obligation, I am, after all, the kind of authentic dark voice of my tortured part of the world, Wales. And Lear is the only Welshman of any interest that Shakespeare wrote about. Lear, when he lets off steam, when he really lets go, is utterly Welsh. Hamlet is not. Hamlet is English, but Lear is a Welshman." Despite that ambition, he never did play Lear.

So it was against this background, that, for three wonderful weeks in

# AND GOD CREATED BURTON

February 1966, he returned to his alma mater to provide the sleepy English city of Oxford with a theatrical spectacle the like of which it had never before seen – nor ever has since.

For years, Richard Burton had been making promises – willingly-given heartfelt promises – that he would return to Oxford University to help the cause of the arts; notably to support the Oxford Playhouse, which he had helped re-establish many years earlier when it had been down on its luck. He received many requests to support all sorts of arts projects, either with his cash or his time, but he turned them all down in favour of Oxford as he considered the city his spiritual home from the days he attended the university in 1944.

The Oxford Playhouse was run by Professor Neville Coghill and it broke even year to year on an operating basis, but it never had anything left over for capital expenditure or development. So it was gradually crumbling. It needed cash urgently; some £100,000 for a development programme. And Burton promised to help.

Finally, in February 1966, he was able to do it. There was a natural gap in his schedule but it was a very tight one, with no margin for error. Burton had three weeks before he and Elizabeth Taylor were due in Rome to appear in Franco Zeffirelli's film version of *The Taming of the Shrew.*

The plan to raise the money was a fascinating concept. The basic idea was that he would come to Oxford for three weeks and spend two weeks rehearsing and one week performing with members of the Oxford University Dramatic Society (OUDS).

Then he would take the entire cast, props and costumes over to Rome and shoot a movie based on the play, which he would finance. He had got the idea from the film version of *Hamlet* at the Lunt-Fontanne theatre in 1964. That production had been made directly and rather crudely from the play, and Burton thought he could do it better and make some money for the Playhouse.

The timing was good, as Professor Coghill was now 66 years old and about to retire. He was in his final year at Merton College. As his legacy, Coghill wanted to leave the Playhouse in good financial shape. Burton was very happy to be able to help.

Burton figured that between the live play and the movie, he could raise the £100,000 Coghill required. That was the theory anyway.

So on 1st February 1966, Burton and Taylor drove down to Oxford in his new convertible Rolls-Royce for his wife to be formally introduced to the professor. Elizabeth Taylor and Professor Coghill bonded immediately – he adored Taylor and she reciprocated.

The play they chose to put on was 'Doctor Faustus' by Christopher Marlowe, written 400 years earlier. Burton would play the title role and Elizabeth Taylor would play Helen of Troy, which was essentially a non-speaking cameo role. Taylor had never acted on the stage before and didn't feel able to commit to a bigger role.

They took the best rooms in the Randolph Hotel, which was just down the road from the Playhouse in Beaumont Street. Burton brought his valet, Bob Wilson, along as well.

Coghill had prepared the ground well. By the time Burton and Taylor arrived, the rest of the cast had been rehearsing for months with Burton and Taylor's parts being played by understudies. The students wanted to do their very best as the production had naturally attracted a lot of attention and there was in the city a state of excitement at the prospect of Burton and Taylor appearing at the Oxford Playhouse. All the actors were members of the Oxford University Dramatic Society, and they had got the play word perfect with Burton's understudy, Bob Scott, before he arrived.

As soon as they arrived, Burton and Taylor called a cast meeting in their rooms at the Randolph. The entire student cast turned up and Taylor took their drinks orders and served them herself. Penny Junor described the scene: "Elizabeth seemed somewhat over-awed by the place, and being surrounded by so many people with brains. Richard simply had a new audience for his stories; he was sharp and witty and kept everyone entertained."

After the daily rehearsal, the two of them mixed with the students where possible and joined in university activities. Burton and Taylor set out to enjoy their three weeks in the city and treated it almost as an 'intellectual' activity holiday.

Neville Coghill organised a press conference to promote the play and help sell tickets, and it was an opportunity for Burton to perform in front of the press, which he thoroughly enjoyed. He told the assembled reporters about his history with Professor Coghill and how much he owed him – which was why he was there. He said: "I was going to come back after the war, but instead I became what for lack of a better word is known as a star." Of Professor Coghill's upcoming retirement, Burton joked: "Since he started me off, I think I should finish him off." Taylor added: "I have never acted on stage before, so I'm starting the easy way. It's a marvellous opportunity."

He told them he thought the last speech in 'Faustus' was "the greatest speech in the history of literature."

Burton really felt he had a special relationship with 'Faustus', as he explained: "'Faustus' is the one play I don't have to do. Dr Faustus is a man who sells his soul to the devil in exchange for knowledge and power but who forgets his worthy aspirations, is taken in by toys and has a childish delight in showing off."

Richard Burton had no hesitation in recognising himself in that description. Just as he had told Ernest Lehman: "I am George", he told Neville Coghill: "I am Faustus". And it was true.

Melvyn Bragg, admittedly with the benefit of hindsight, later drew a convincing parallel between Burton's character and Faustus: "It coincided with a truer analysis – that of a man being drawn slowly but, it appeared, helplessly into a deeply seductive and romantic circle of self-destruction." It certainly was uncanny how Burton was continually drawn to parts with such parallels to his own life.

But Burton put no real work into the part or the production, and barely bothered to learn his lines. He just went through the motions, and the rehearsals were one big show-off. No one realised what was happening because they were all enjoying themselves so much. The university actors were not experienced enough to be spontaneous on stage and were too easily thrown. Suddenly, a very tight play with the understudy was reduced to something less than perfect.

So rehearsals were a shambles, although terrific fun for the actors, and it was not until the first night that Burton did any preparation. Neville Coghill was dragged along in the excitement and kind of lost the plot as well. He was dizzy with excitement at hosting the two most famous people in the world in Oxford. It had turned him into a local celebrity and the talk of the city. The normal creativity and iron discipline he installed into a production was simply not there on 'Doctor Faustus'.

Burton thought he already knew the play off by heart and so did Coghill, who was directing. But when it came down to actually doing it, he didn't. Burton ad-libbed throughout rehearsals and, on every run-through, it was a different play. Burton admitted: "I've been wanting to play Faustus for more than twenty years. I know the part but not as well as I thought." As Paul Ferris said: "A lot of Marlowe's lines started coming out as Burton lines." Melvyn Bragg said: "He treated the event as a spree."

The play opened with a charity presentation for the critics and was a true shambles. Graham Jenkins described the first night as "a classic of theatrical confusion." He said: "What should have been treated as a dress rehearsal or, at best, a cheap price preview, was mounted as a full scale charity premiere.

There were technical difficulties backstage and a delayed start."

But it was humorous incompetence and it threatened to turn 'Faustus' into a rank comedy, especially when Elizabeth Taylor entered the stage surrounded by mist and fog provided by a dry ice machine. The operator of the dry ice machine was inexperienced and instead of a path of mist for Taylor to walk in on, the machine billowed out thick smoke and she was completely obscured by the dry ice. The audience could see nothing but Taylor's feet, which exposed her modern Gucci shoes under the period costume. The laughter was palpable.

Coghill had assumed that the critics would understand and be tolerant of the style of production it was. But they weren't. They had expected and anticipated greatness but had seen ineptness and mediocrity.

Not only was the production chaotic, but front of house organisation also fell down spectacularly. Because the theatre capacity was only 600 and tickets were highly priced, at £1.18s each (£1.80p), Neville Coghill made a tactical mistake by restricting the critics to one ticket apiece, meaning they had to come down to Oxford on their own, without wives or partners. They couldn't even buy extra tickets because they were all sold out. He lost their goodwill.

It was a huge mistake, and by the time the critics arrived, they were already seething at the situation and ready to take revenge for what they considered a personal snub by Richard Burton. Not only that, but when they found their allocated seats, someone else was sitting in them and they had to scrounge around for somewhere else to sit. There was no one to help them and they wandered around aimlessly. Some critics took the view that Burton was humiliating them on purpose to get back at them for past bad reviews.

The front of house fiasco was not only restricted to the critics' tickets. Some tickets had been overprinted with an incorrect later starting time, which meant a portion of the audience arrived 15 minutes late. Many of the critics blamed Burton personally for the fiasco.

The critics, predictably, took great pleasure from slamming the production. Of the ten national newspapers covering the play, eight criticised it heavily. Only Harold Hobson in *The Sunday Times* and John Crosby in *The Observer* were kind. Hobson understood what it was all about and critiqued it to those standards.

# AND GOD CREATED BURTON

Alan Brien, in the *Sunday Telegraph* took it all very personally and gave Burton the worst review of his life: "Long ago, I compared Mr Burton's Old Vic delivery to that of the man in the I-Speak-Your-Weight machine, too perfectly modulated to be real. Now that effortless flow has been interrupted by his new habit of pausing in the middle of almost every phrase as though dictating to a secretary whose shorthand is rusty." Irving Wardle in *The Times* said it was "a sad example of university drama at its worst."

The other critics laid into Coghill for a "tedious production" and Burton for "walking through the part." Another called Elizabeth Taylor "impossibly pretty in a flimsy nightie on a carpet of smoke" and said her performance was like a "cunning soft-sell for lingerie."

Burton said of the reviewers: "What do you expect from a pig but a grunt?"

And Burton was right. The critics had missed the point. The production was never about the performance; it was about putting on entertainment that would sell high-priced tickets to raise cash for the Oxford Playhouse, which it did.

But Burton also knew the critics were right and it was a signal for him to buckle down and do some work.

Neville Coghill was extremely cross with how the critics reacted, particularly as the performance improved beyond recognition as the week progressed. After two nights, it had settled down, by which time the critics were long gone. And by the end of the week, it was very good, leading Francis Warner of St Peter's College to write in the *Western Evening Mail* that 'Faustus' was "the greatest performance of Burton's career." It was never going to be that, but by the end it was very acceptable.

Wolf Mankowitz, the distinguished playwright and screenwriter, was apoplectic at how the critics had treated Burton and his friend Neville Coghill. He wrote a furious letter to *The Times* and *The Guardian* newspapers, which read: "It is, surely, that by contributing his superb talent and incredibly valuable and highly sought after time to a student production, Mr Burton has made it possible for several generations of young theatrical talent to work with greater freedom and in better circumstances."

The Jenkins family, who all came to see the production, were also put out. David Jenkins said: "A spirit of optimism, excitement and generosity was clear for all to see, and the carping of critics over this endeavour has always annoyed me."

But perhaps the only critic that mattered to Burton was Neville Coghill, and he said he thought it was brilliant – which in context it probably was.

And all the effort they made did not yield the expected financial rewards either. With only 600 seats available every night, after six performances, the financial surplus was only £3,000 and Burton, as he had promised, matched it. But he could have earned the Playhouse ten times that amount in a week by going to Hollywood and appearing in a TV miniseries. So, as a money-raising exercise, it was a disappointment.

But Professor Coghill was delighted and announced all sorts of grand plans for the money, very few of which made any practical sense. But he appeared almost giddy after nearly a month in the Burtons' company. How different it was from that moment in April 1944, when the 18-year-old, Richard Burton had sheepishly knocked on the door of his study and the professor had been more inclined to throw him out than to listen to what he had to say.

Much greater things were expected from the film version that was planned to be made in Rome in August, after the Burtons had finished shooting *The Taming of the Shrew*.

Coghill organised his actors to go to Rome to film the play in the summer holidays. It was amateur-dramatics-meets-Hollywood, and Burton and Coghill had high hopes of making it work and raising £100,000 for the Oxford Playhouse from the box office receipts.

Burton co-directed with Neville Coghill. They used exactly the same student cast, and the film was effectively the play performed on a Rome sound stage.

But almost immediately, the costs started racking up. Union rules dictated that the student actors had to be paid £45 a week. They all needed to be accommodated in Rome for six weeks and given expenses. To guarantee quality, Burton spent a small fortune hiring Gabor Pogany as director of photography and John de Cuir as production designer.

The least Burton hoped to get for his money was a quality picture. But he and Coghill were hopelessly inexperienced movie directors and, in truth, had little real idea about how to do it. His brother, Graham Jenkins, summed up Burton's talents as a director honestly: "He created a mess, with more special effects, as a technician pointed out, than 50 average films. And this time, the responsibility was his alone."

Suddenly, Burton realised how difficult it was directing a movie and, also, how he had been less than kind dealing with directors in the past. In truth, he had no idea of the difficulties they faced.

And the mess he created was also an expensive mess. The production

AND GOD CREATED BURTON

ended up costing £300,000 which, translated into dollars, was getting on for US$800,000. It was a serious amount of money even for him, and it all came out of his own pocket.

The filming soon got out of control and it became a mini-*Cleopatra*, with Aaron Frosch spending more and more cash as the weeks rolled by. When time ran out in the Rome studios, it had to shift expensively to Shepperton in order to get finished.

Burton was producer, star and co-director, and he found it all too much. The production turned into a nightmare from which he could not escape, and everyone was having a great time on his money – all except him as he kept looking around and wondering what the final sum would be. There were also huge problems with the script Coghill had written and, as Hollis Alpert recounted: "Burton had to surmount the mediocre stretches of the play with borrowings from other works of Marlowe and effects concocted out of swirls of mist, guttering candles and billowing draperies."

When the film was finished, it was viewed by all the major Hollywood studios as Burton tried desperately to find a distributor. But no one liked it and no one would take it.

Meanwhile, it was premiered in Oxford on 15th October 1967, and to promote the film, Burton and Taylor, together with Neville Coghill, were interviewed by the BBC's David Lewin on live television.

Straightaway, Lewin, who had a reputation for being a sharp interviewer, asked Burton whether he had turned his back on the English stage and sold out to Hollywood. The question, and the way it was put, upset Taylor and her response and reaction to it became a classic moment, often repeated in documentaries and clips even today, 45 years later.

It all started when Lewin asked Burton a very long-winded question: "You must at some time have faced the question of whether you should have continued as an imposing and even, in the view of some, great stage actor, or moved into the realm of films, which is perhaps more commercially rewarding, but not as rewarding artistically. Any regrets?" Taylor: "Oh, excuse me, Richard that makes me so angry. Because he has not left the stage. That's absolute, bloody rubbish. Last year, he just got finished doing a play for Oxford on the stage. The year before that, what was he doing on Broadway? That was the stage. How can you say he left the stage?" Burton, somewhat shocked, looked round at Taylor and muttered words to the effect that she should pull herself together and leave the interview to him. But she was in no mood for it.

Lewin countered: "That is not a continuous career like Paul Scofield's or Laurence Olivier's." Taylor responded that Olivier's career was "not continuous either, on the stage. He does film appearances for money. And so does Paul Scofield."

When Lewin asked if Burton identified with Faustus, Elizabeth was further incensed: "You bastard, David, I knew you'd ask that. Would I be selling out if I deserted film for the stage?" Neville Coghill, sitting at the end, just smiled – he was out of his depth.

Eventually, Burton answered the question and said: "Everyone is offered a choice. Most men, regardless of their backgrounds, are faced at one time or another with an obvious, easy one, or a more difficult, rewarding one." He added: "It is by no means selling out when one was able to command a larger audience." He told Lewin that his roots were still in the theatre, which he said he was proving by "being at Oxford playing Dr Faustus."

The interview attracted huge ratings and made Lewin's career. It also helped the film, which fared better in Britain than it did anywhere else in the world – despite the fact that the British critics all hated the Dr Faustus film as much as they had the Dr Faustus play the previous year.

*The Times* described Burton and Taylor as "travelling together down to hell on a moving staircase, a journey enlivened by writhing, intertwined torsos at whom Mr Burton furtively glances as if they were corset advertisements on the London Underground." The newspaper summed the film up by saying: "It is a combination of self-indulgence and visual vulgarity."

Somehow, after a year trying to find an American production company willing to release it, Burton managed to get Columbia Pictures to distribute the film and pay for the marketing and the prints. But Columbia's marketing executives were horrified. They would only put it on in art house cinemas and not mainstream houses as Burton had hoped.

Even the American premiere was held at the Rendezvous, an art house cinema in New York. A bunch of hippie like characters turned up to watch the opening with the critics and, outside, the Burtons' appearance attracted two thousand fans who staged a mini riot.

The American critics absolutely hated the film and could find nothing redeeming in it at all. Renata Adler of *The New York Times* wrote: "*Doctor Faustus* is of an awfulness that bends the mind." She added: "The Burtons are clearly having a lovely time; at moments, one has the feeling that Faustus was shot mainly as a home movie." *Time* magazine described it being like "lots of undergraduates bringing their wives back to the old school and hamming it up for home movies." Pauline Kael in *The New Yorker* wrote: "*Doctor Faustus* becomes the dullest episode yet in the great-lovers-of-history series that started with *Cleopatra.*"

Burton dismissed them all, saying: "I could have written the notices before they appeared. The English critics are the most snide in the world. They are sneaky, mean and spiteful but, this time, the Americans went one better."

*Time* magazine was particularly hateful and reserved most of its wrath for Taylor's performance. It said she had done nothing but "wander around looking beautiful" but then added: "When she welcomes Burton to an eternity of damnation, her eyeballs and teeth are dripping pink in what seems a hellish combination of conjunctivitis and trench mouth." Taylor said she thought the *Time* review ridiculous and detected jealousy: "People don't like sustained success. After all, we make an awful lot of money and some people just resent us."

Columbia Pictures cut its losses and quickly removed the film even from its art house slots after audiences dwindled to an average of less than half a dozen people at each of its showings. In the end, the film took US$110,000 in America and US$500,000 in the rest of the world – and even that was a miracle in itself.

In the end, when the final accounting was done, Burton lost US$1 million on *Doctor Faustus*, including the £100,000 the Oxford Playhouse got. Coghill had spent the money before it had been received, and when it didn't materialise, Burton had no choice but to make it good. His investment was a total write-off with no income to offset against the production costs. It couldn't even be given away to show on television.

The shock of a nearly complete write-off should have brought home the perils of independent production to Burton. He had never before experienced such a complete failure, but he could easily afford to lose US$1 million as he had so much. So he didn't really learn the lesson. He got very upset when his brother Graham pointed out that the loss on *Faustus* was "tax deductible." Burton shouted at him something very impolite, which Jenkins sanitised years later in his book: "I've spent all these years trying not to pay tax. Now you tell me I should have stayed at home and made nothing."

But in the end, the money was not the main loss. The loss to his reputation was far higher. The fact that the two biggest names in Hollywood could have been involved in such a catastrophic production was damaging to their reputations. *Variety* called the film "one of the most desperately non-commercial enterprises in the history of motion pictures."

Surprisingly, Burton was not put off by the Faustus fiascoes and discussed working with Neville Coghill again on a film of 'The Tempest' and also roped in John Gielgud. But they fell out when Gielgud wanted to film it in the remotest part of Scotland and Coghill insisted it had to be filmed in the Caribbean island of Tobago. At that stage, Burton backed out of the project realising its folly. To end what he saw becoming another fiasco, he sent Coghill a telegram that read: "*Tempest* could not possibly begin for at least a year and a half or two years because of other commitments." And that was that. He was saved from himself – but only just – as there is no doubt that, had the Coghill-Gielgud production of *The Tempest* gone ahead, it would have been a true disaster.

The financial disaster of *Doctor Faustus* took years to clear up as Elizabeth Sweeting, then the Oxford Playhouse's manager, recalled: "I have never encountered anything so complex in my whole life." But in the end, the theatre got its money and is now a vital part of Oxford's cultural scene. Today, the only relic of Burton and Taylor's involvement is a small 50-seat rehearsal building called the Burton-Taylor Studio, a permanent memorial of that remarkable period in 1966.

# AND GOD CREATED BURTON

## CHAPTER 43

# The Dream Years

## *No 1 at the box office*

### 1966-1967

The best years of Richard Burton's life were unquestionably 1966 and 1967. Creatively, financially and personally, he was untouchable. He was number one at the box office, the number one earning actor and was very happily married to the most famous woman in the world. It really didn't get any better than that.

Their combined earnings that year were nearly US$20 million, easily making Burton and Taylor the highest earning individuals in the world, being paid the equivalent of anything the world's most successful businessmen of the time, Paul Getty and Aristotle Onassis, were earning. No one could match them.

They were also effortlessly picking up nominations for Baftas, Oscars and Golden Globes. They were the toast of Hollywood, and any past sins were forgotten.

They even returned to Rome.

After *Cleopatra* had finished, Richard Burton and Elizabeth Taylor had sworn they would never go back to Rome. That resolve lasted precisely three years and, in March 1966, they were installed in another magnificent house on the Appian Way. Burton said by way of explanation: "We got middle-aged, I suppose, and forgot."

They were there for the making of *The Taming Of The Shrew*. It was a film they had agreed to make more than a year earlier, when the great opera director Franco Zeffirelli brought them the project while they were in Dublin filming *The Spy Who Came In From the Cold*.

The cosmopolitan Italian was famous for staging extraordinary operatic events. In Britain, he had directed 'Romeo and Juliet' and 'Othello' at the Old Vic.

Being Italian, Zeffirelli instinctively thought that fellow Italians Marcello Mastroianni and Sophia Loren should play the lead roles in *The Taming Of The Shrew*. But his agent, Robbie Lantz, who had originally conceptualised the film, had other ideas. When Lantz suggested the Burtons, Zeffirelli didn't think they could possibly be interested. But Lantz was a very clever man and knew Burton would be tempted by a Shakespeare project, and indeed he was. Years later, Zeffirelli said: "I knew Richard would definitely be interested, but I wasn't sure about Elizabeth."

So Zeffirelli and Lantz both travelled to Dublin and met the Burtons in their suite at the Gresham Hotel. Zeffirelli was totally honest and told them he had wanted Mastroianni and Loren but that Lantz wanted them. He also told them he had never before directed a movie and that this would be his first attempt. Burton was enormously impressed by his honesty and warmed to him immediately. He was also very impressed by Lantz and wished his own agent, Hugh French, was as good at pressing his client's position.

Burton was unfazed by Zeffirelli's lack of movie experience. He told him he had seen one of his operas and that he recognised talent when he saw it.

Zeffirelli later said that when he observed the living chaos of Burton and Taylor's suite at the Gresham, he knew immediately that they would be a perfect Katharina and Petruchio, the film's principal characters.

They had come calling at exactly the right moment, as all Burton and Taylor had been talking about since they had arrived in Ireland was producing their own film. Burton asked Zeffirelli about financing and offered to put in half the cash. Zeffirelli told him he had Paramount lined up and that he would discuss it with them.

Lantz took over the negotiations with Paramount and, in the end, negotiated a US$4 million budget, with half of that assigned as Taylor and Burton's fee, which they would waive as their contribution to the budget. The producing deal, worked out by Lantz, was that they would get 25 per cent of the gross cinema and TV receipts instead. The Burtons and Zeffirelli became co-producers, under the aegis of a new company called Royal Films International, fulfilling their long-held dream

But Zeffirelli was very surprised when Burton suggested that he discuss the script with Philip Burton. At the time, Zeffirelli was directing an operatic version of *Cleopatra* in New York called 'Antony and Cleopatra' and was already consulting with Philip on it; they knew each other well. Zeffirelli said: "I met Philip and I left realising how lucky Richard had been to have such a father-figure to rely on when he was young. It was obvious that Richard idolised the man."

And so it came to pass, a year later, as soon as they had finished filming *Who's Afraid of Virginia Woolf?* and had fulfilled their obligations in Oxford, the Burtons flew to Italy with their support staff, consisting of Dick Hanley,

# THE DREAM YEARS

John Lee, Bob and Sally Wilson, Ron Berkeley, Gaston Sanz and Bobby LaSalle.

They arranged to rent a lavish house in Rome set in huge grounds, notable for its dazzling swimming pool. It was comfortably far enough away from the heat and bustle of Rome, and not far from the studio, owned by Italian producer Dino de Laurentiis, where filming was to take place.

The house was a typical Italian old style flat-roofed Roman villa that had been restored to very high standards. It was surrounded by thickets of dark cypress trees which thinned out closer to the house to reveal beautifully landscaped gardens with renaissance terraces and spectacular verandas. The house was staffed with a multitude of highly trained servants. As David Jenkins recalled: "It was a display of ostentation and luxury."

The entire family moved in for the spring and summer shoot – including their four children: Michael and Christopher Wilding, aged thirteen and eleven; Liza Todd, aged nine; and Maria, aged five.

This time, the Burtons weren't taking any chances and the house had been specially chosen for maximum security. It was a time when there was a real terrorist threat in Italy from an organisation that called itself 'The Red Brigade' and specialised in murder and kidnapping. The house, set well back from the road, had been designed to be secure from a terrorist attack and was completely fenced off and obscured by high hedges. At the entrance, there was a lodge with heavily fortified, electrically-operated, security gates.

With kidnapping in Italy at a peak, no less than eight armed security guards were on duty around the house at all times. But the only real threat seemed to be from the paparazzi, armies of which were continually camped outside the house. Whenever the Burtons moved, so too did the paparazzi, chasing them all over the city and often at high speed.

Aside from the constant concerns about security and the need for the children to be monitored continually in Italy, it was to prove an idyllic spring and summer in Rome as the Burtons filmed their first jointly-produced movie together. The house staff were exceptionally friendly, and Enzo, the cook, doubled up as a children's entertainer while Karen, one of the servants, took charge of the children and spent the entire summer with them.

The atmosphere at the house was largely responsible for Burton and Taylor's contentment. It was relaxed and magical, and all the worries of a household and everyday hassles were dealt with for them. For five months, it seemed as though the world had stopped and they had got off. It had a very positive effect on their relationship and they were a united, contented married couple.

# AND GOD CREATED BURTON

That idyllic summer proved to be the height of their personal relationship as they enjoyed a summer of love together with hardly a cross word. It moved Taylor to say: "They say it won't last; that it's a self-limiting affair. We're just going to have to prove them wrong – in 20 years' time, when we're still together, they'll be forced to admit they were wrong." She genuinely felt it. Taylor recalled the six-month shoot in Rome as "one long honeymoon."

Taylor later described the lifestyle they enjoyed that summer: "We just lead a very simple life. When we come back from the studio, we just like to relax."

As joint producers of *The Taming Of The Shrew*, they had a real purpose in their lives for the first time. Burton was in his element at the house, and the total fulfillment he was experiencing at his work during the day transferred itself to his private life in a very noticeable way. Burton rehearsed with Taylor every evening, helping her master Shakespearean verse.

The relaxed atmosphere was very apparent to Mike Nichols, who came to stay at the house with his latest girlfriend, Mia Farrow. Nichols immediately noticed the happy mood.

He also observed how Burton fostered a loving environment, insisting that all family members greeted each other with a kiss at the beginning and end of each day. A courtesy that extended to any visitors passing through. If the children forgot, Burton did not, and his paternal reminders became a ritual as he would say: "Where are the kisses flying around here this morning?" and the children would shuffle around kissing each other. It was marvellous to see.

The happiest day in Rome that summer was Liza's tenth birthday, when her parents presented her with a donkey. Both parents stood and watched and enjoyed their daughter's pleasure and, eventually, Burton couldn't contain himself as he took charge of organising donkey rides round the garden for the whole family and snapped pictures of them with his brand new Polaroid instant camera, which were then all the rage.

The donkey later became famous and was pressed into service during the film, and Taylor fell off it, hurting her foot in the process. She fractured a small bone in her left foot, which was placed in plaster for two weeks.

There was only one sadness during this period. After two years of marriage, there was no sign of Taylor becoming pregnant. By now, Burton had realised he was not particularly fertile, and although he loved his daughters dearly, he badly wanted a son. He wanted a genuine Burton-Taylor variant in the family. The closest he came to it was Liza Todd. He recognised a kindred spirit in Mike Todd, her father, and was every bit as close to Liza as he was with his real daughter, Kate. And that bond stretched to Kate. When Kate visited the villa that summer, she and Liza were as one.

Interestingly, the subject of having a child together was something he and Taylor never discussed with each other; it was more comfortable to discuss it with other people. As Taylor told Burton's brother David: "We so much want a child together, but it just can't happen." Jenkins said Taylor left it at that and didn't elaborate. It is likely then that Burton had realised he was infertile and that it was probably caused by his prodigious alcohol intake, and it was just too painful for the two of them to discuss.

As producers and actors, Burton and Taylor found themselves looking forward to each working day. Richard Burton would be driven each morning by Gaston Sanz in the Rolls-Royce, followed by a security detail and the paparazzi, arriving promptly every morning at 7:30am, ready for his first take at 9:30am. Sanz would then return in the car and wait for Taylor until 10:45am, delivering her to the studio at 11am. The regular routine was risky because of kidnap threats, but Burton refused to change his schedule.

The studio had four enormous soundstages, which Franco Zeffirelli had transformed into 16th century Padua. Burton found Zeffirelli a delight to work with most of the time, although in truth it was a love-hate relationship throughout the film. He quickly got used to his ways and found him to be a typical wound-up Italian, with hang-ups galore. He only got fed up once with Zeffirelli's continual carping about his screen credit. Now that he was a producer, all those sorts of petty squabbles were brought to Burton's door. Burton told the Italian to sort it out with Columbia. It was a typical producer's put-off and demonstrated that Burton was learning fast about dealing with the talent.

Interestingly, Zeffirelli was continually writing Burton letters throughout the production, even though he saw him every day. It was his way of communicating. But Burton forgave him everything when he saw the daily rushes.

*The Taming Of The Shrew* was a Shakespearian drama of marital strife. Taylor played the role of Katharina, the shrew, with Burton playing Petruchio, who tames the shrew. It was a remake of a Douglas Fairbanks and Mary Pickford version made in 1928. That version had not been a success.

Burton aimed to rectify that and, as producer, he assembled a wonderful cast, including Michael York, Michael Hordern, Cyril Cusack and Victor Spinetti.

Michael York, who has Burton to thank for giving him his first serious role, was in awe of the whole set-up: "On my first day, I remember thinking: 'My God, these are the kings and queens of Hollywood, and at the top of their profession.' There was an overwhelming sense of glamour about them, intensified by the way they lived, you know, with their dressing rooms with dazzling white carpets and all of their butlers and maids, and so on . . . the Rolls-Royces, the jewels. They behaved like movie stars; old-fashioned movie stars. But I also found them to be enormously kind. There was also a sense of family. For instance, whenever her children were around, they were popped into costume, and then onto the set as extras."

Zeffirelli filmed *The Taming Of The Shrew* in a comic Italian style, disregarding tradition and indulging himself with vast, ornate sets and lavish costumes. The old archaic speech and almost half of the Shakespearean original lines were radically changed and plenty of horseplay substituted.

When Burton saw the rushes of one scene, in which he uttered the famous line: "For I am he am born to tame you, Kate, and bring you from a wild cat to a Kate conformable as other household Kates", he knew the film was going to be a big hit.

Taylor herself was a sight to behold, in a teased-out wig and clinched bodice with a plunging décolletage. Zeffirelli made her spit out her lines against Burton's Petruchio, and it came out so naturally. As Melvyn Bragg described it: "Shakespeare's original play was cut in half, romped up and acted *con brio*. It is an irresistible knockabout version with Burton like a jolly but stern father watching 'his girl' take the jumps."

Zeffirelli perfectly caught a real sense of fun in Shakespeare's play, and the marvellous rapport between Burton and Taylor was clear on the screen. In fact, Burton and Taylor together put on a virtuoso performance of the classic drama.

One observer thought that they weren't really acting but "playing real life a few centuries ago in costume."

Burton had a certain reputation for playing Shakespeare, but Taylor easily matched him. David Jenkins called it "a visual feast, far removed from the austere majesty and grimy battle-scenes of most films of Shakespeare. This was a Bard to revel in as well as admire."

Burton seemed to thrive as a producer, taking his responsibilities very seriously and having meetings seemingly here, there and everywhere, with everybody. Many of the people involved in the film were old favourites of the Burtons such as Irene Sharaff, the costume designer; Alexandre de Paris, the hairdresser; and Dick McWhorter, the production manager.

Burton had never dealt directly with McWhorter, De Paris or Sharaff before. He found it quite difficult, calling Sharaff "a funny contradiction and enormously concerned with her own dignity."

Much of the making of *The Taming Of The Shrew* was recorded in his personal diaries, which were used by many biographers to chronicle his life. But great doubt must be placed on the accuracy of Burton's diaries and whether they were written contemporaneously or much later. The doubt comes as he was in Oxford when he was writing up entries for Rome and, chronologically, they make no sense. In truth it is likely that these diaries were written up much later, as it is hard to see how he had time in Rome. If the diaries weren't contemporaneous and the dates weren't correct, then they become little more than observations rather than a record. And Burton appears to betray himself when he writes in the past tense rather than the present. There seems little doubt that the diaries were being kept up for an eventual autobiography, whenever that might be. But whether or not it would ever be publishable remained in doubt, not least in his own mind. The one talent he never possessed was that of a writer, but it didn't stop him continually trying.

During that summer, Senator Robert Kennedy, to whom Burton had grown very close after the death of his brother, visited the Burtons in Rome. Kennedy confided in Burton that he would in all likelihood run for president in 1968. Burton promised that he and Taylor would do all they could to see that he was elected. It was a mark of the rehabilitation they had undergone in America in the past two years that Kennedy came calling for their support.

But it had become clear that after the humiliation of *Cleopatra* and the public divorces, the success of 'Hamlet' on Broadway in 1964, a transformation of their images in the minds of the American people had taken place, especially amongst New Yorkers. Straight after 'Hamlet', Taylor had noticed that everything seemed different in the public's perception of them. She sensed a real change in how she and Burton were seen. She said: "There is no deodorant like success. Richard and I are going through a period now, I feel, in which a lot of people are beginning to realise that we're not monsters. Some may even like us for being honest."

Kennedy, the Burtons and Zeffirelli hit Rome one night, and Burton and Kennedy found they shared a mutual love of poetry. According to Melvyn Bragg, they both began to compete over recitals of the sonnets: "Burton eventually won by employing his old party trick – reciting the fifteenth sonnet word for word, backwards."

When the time came for Kennedy to leave, there was a very warm farewell. Robert Kennedy was Richard Burton's kind of politician.

With the filming of *The Taming Of The Shrew* on a tight schedule, neither Burton nor Taylor could attend the premiere of *Who's Afraid of Virginia Woolf?* on 22nd June in New York's Criterion theater. The film had overcome various problems with the censors, who objected to the sexual realism and some of the language.

Long ago, Burton had arranged the premiere to be a benefit night for Philip Burton's American Musical and Dramatic Academy (AMDA) and was mortified when he couldn't attend. Jack Warner was pleased to deputise for them and happy to take some of the credit for what was clearly going to be a very big box office hit – although, at that time, he had no idea how big.

There was also more disappointment for Philip as he had to share the cash with the National Haemophilia Foundation. Richard Burton had been diagnosed as suffering from mild haemophilia, and the charity had begged him to help publicise the disease, about which remarkably little was known. So when Burton asked his adoptive father to share the big night with the charity, he could hardly refuse, although his AMDA organisation desperately needed all the money he could get. Sensing this, Burton's lawyer, Aaron Frosch, stepped in and arranged for the US$10,000 shortfall to be made up.

*Who's Afraid of Virginia Woolf?* opened to absolutely glorious reviews; *Newsweek* hailed Burton's performance as "a marvel of disciplined compassion. With the self-contained authority of a great actor, he plays the part as if no one in the world had ever heard of Richard Burton."

*Time* magazine said: "Burton is superb, shrewdly measuring out his powerhouse talent in a part written for a less heroic actor. Elizabeth Taylor is loud, sexy, vulgar, achieves moments of astonishing tenderness."

*Village Voice* described Burton's acting as "possessing heroic calm, which other actors could use for a textbook", and raved about the "inscrutable ironies flickering across his beautifully ravaged face." It said: "Without Burton, the film would have been an intolerably cold experience." Of Taylor, it said: "Elizabeth's performance scorches the paint off the walls and puts to rest any doubt about her as not just a movie star but a serious, first-class film actress."

The film eventually won six Oscars, including best actress for Elizabeth and best supporting actress for Sandy Dennis. Burton was nominated for best actor but failed to win again.

The film may have been the most expensive black and white movie ever made but it also turned into the most profitable. It took a staggering US$40 million at the box office worldwide, and television companies paid another US$5 million for later TV showings. Warner Bros took home US$24 million and made US$16.5 million profit, more than it had made on any movie before. Burton and Taylor picked up an extra US$3.3 million on top of their normal fees.

Amidst the seemingly inexhaustible supply of good news that summer, there was some bad.

At the end of July, Taylor had a shock when her close friend, the actor Montgomery Clift, died of a heart attack in bed on 22nd July. He was only 45. He had been found by his houseman, who immediately phoned Roddy McDowall, who called John Springer to break the news to Taylor. Along with McDowell, Clift was Taylor's best friend in the world. When Springer told her, she fainted, was sedated and put to bed. The next day, she put out a statement: "I am so shocked I can barely accept it. I loved him. He was my dearest friend. He was my brother."

When the five months of filming of *The Taming Of The Shrew* came to an end, Richard Burton couldn't have been happier with what he achieved in Rome. He hired Maurice Binder to design the title credits. Binder was the best in the business and created the James Bond title credits, which had revolutionised the art.

Zeffirelli returned to New York to carry out his editing magic for a 1967 release date and to dub a version for the Italian and French markets.

As Burton suspected, *The Taming Of The Shrew* proved to be a mighty success; the third in a run of three straight hits, and following on from *The Spy Who Came In From the Cold* and *Who's Afraid of Virginia Woolf?*, all three were nominated for every award going in 1965 and 1966; it was the peak of his career.

But the highlight for the Burtons came when it was announced that *The Taming Of The Shrew* had been selected for the Royal Command Performance screening at the Odeon Cinema in Leicester Square on Monday 28th February 1967. The next day, it was also announced that the French premiere would be held at the Paris Opera House, followed by a government sponsored gala reception.

For Burton, getting the Royal Command Performance was the greatest honour he could imagine and it was a cue for a big weekend celebration that would start at eight o'clock on the evening of Friday 25th February and end at ten o'clock on the morning of Tuesday 1st March with virtually non-stop partying in between. It was certainly the biggest and best party staged in London that year. Burton also combined it with Taylor's 35th birthday celebrations on 27th February and decided to make it a Jenkins family occasion. He managed to conjure up a list of 40 family members from Wales to come to London for a weekend at The Dorchester. All brothers, sisters, cousins, aunts, uncles, nephews and nieces were invited, and he booked 14 suites and large rooms to accommodate them all.

Burton vowed to make it a weekend to remember. The Jenkins family was certainly not used to what they called "the Dorchester lifestyle". David Jenkins described it as "revolving doors, sumptuous bars and attentive waiters, hovering reverently with cocktails at one's elbow."

The weekend started when a fleet of Rolls-Royce Silver Clouds collected the Jenkins family from Paddington Station, where they had all arrived together from Wales. They were whisked to The Dorchester to freshen up for a gala welcoming dinner that evening. That Friday evening, the chefs laid on a feast for them and the sound of merry singing Welshmen reverberated round The Dorchester until the early hours of the morning. When they finally crawled into the lift to go to bed, neither Burton nor Taylor could remember when they had last had such a good time.

The next day, the Jenkins men all went to Twickenham to see England play Scotland in a rugby union Calcutta Cup match. The Rolls-Royces then came back to take the Jenkins women to Harrods, where Burton had opened up a seemingly unlimited credit account for them all. Surprisingly, their purchases proved very modest.

On Saturday, there was another dinner, and on Sunday, Taylor's birthday party started in the early evening and carried on into the following morning. Burton gave his wife a spectacular diamond and emerald bracelet he had bought at Gianni Bulgari's shop in Rome for US$320,000. Burton wasn't surprised when Bulgari insisted he paid for the jewels rather than put them on his account. When the party wound down at around four o'clock, everyone went to bed and stayed there until early Monday afternoon.

The Royal Command Performance was on Monday evening. Burton had bought 40 tickets for his family and another 100 or so for the friends he had invited. Everyone came to The Dorchester for cocktails first, and then the Rolls-Royces, supplemented by additional Daimlers, pulled up alongside the red carpet. There were so many cars that by the time the first one hit the red carpet, the last one had only just left the hotel. The line of Rolls-Royces and Daimlers blocked traffic in the West End for over half an hour.

Everyone in the family was asked to sign autographs as they went up the red carpet. Somehow, the fans recognised his family, especially his brothers. They signed everything put under their noses without complaint. Most of the fans thought Graham Jenkins was Burton, and he made sure his signature was indecipherable to avoid disappointment.

Princess Margaret was in attendance, and the Odeon Leicester Square looked superb in all its magnificent art deco splendour. Burton and Taylor and the cast and crew turned out in their best white tie evening wear to greet Princess Margaret.

When everyone was seated, and before the film was run, Burton stood in front of the audience, introduced Taylor and made a short speech he had written himself. The 40 or so family members in the audience gazed up at him and his beautiful famous wife, proud of their extraordinary relations and not quite believing where they were and what they were seeing. For them, it was all a dream; they knew him simply as a little boy from Pontrhydyfen.

The press had been writing nonstop about the Jenkins family from Wales, which they said had "taken over the entire Dorchester". Burton warmed to that theme, telling the audience: "My real name, of course, is Jenkins and my wife is known as Lizzie Jenkins. Sitting up there in the circle is Maggie Jones. When we took over the Dorchester, it was only a desperate attempt to try to keep up with the Joneses." He was referring to Princess Margaret, whose married name was Jones. Laughter, applause and loud cheers were evident throughout the showing and afterwards.

The evening was a huge success and raised £36,000 for the Cinema and Television Benevolent Fund.

Afterwards, the cars returned and ferried all 150 of the Burton party back to The Dorchester, where he had taken over the ballroom for a giant party. The 150 were joined by as many again who couldn't make the film showing, including Sophia Loren, Christopher Plummer, Gina Lollobrigida, Stanley Baker and Laurence Harvey. Princess Margaret and her husband, Lord Snowdon, also stayed to the early hours.

The room had been booked through to ten o'clock the following morning. The time was significant for that was when Burton and Taylor had to leave to catch a private jet to take them to Paris for the French premiere of *The Taming*

*Of The Shrew.* They had no intention of going to bed that night.

They checked into the Lancaster Hotel on the Champs-Elysées and the first thing Burton did was summon the boss of the jet charter company to his suite. He informed him that he and his wife had so enjoyed his flight that they wanted to buy the plane. Told that the De Havilland 125 would cost US$960,000, Burton wrote the startled man a cheque there and then for the full amount.

That evening, the Burtons went to the home of the Duke and Duchess of Windsor and enjoyed an early supper with Baron and Baroness Guy de Rothschild.

Meanwhile, whilst the Burtons, the Windsors and the Rothschilds were enjoying their consommé, gendarmes set up barricades to keep several thousand fans from storming the Opera House. Many had arrived the night before just to make sure of a good position to catch sight of Elizabeth Taylor when she emerged from her car.

The premiere was another enormous success and the European media turned out for a brief press conference between the showing of the film and the party. One journalist annoyed Burton when he insisted on calling him "the fifth Mr Taylor."

At the gala, Taylor wore a borrowed diamond necklace from De Beers which had been designed by Van Cleef and Arpels; it was reportedly worth US$1.2 million.

The party was attended by Prince Rainier and Princess Grace of Monaco, Princess Elizabeth of Yugoslavia, the Duke and Duchess of Windsor, Rudolf Nureyev and Guy de Rothschild plus a host of socialites who lived in Paris. President de Gaulle himself could not attend due to ill health but he wrote them a personal letter, which was presented to Burton by one of his ministers.

That night, Burton was very proud of his wife and said: "They hardly photographed anybody else" and he admitted: "The flattery we were subjected to was very rich and heady. It, however, I hope, has not gone to our heads."

The reviews received by the film that week were lacklustre but, this time, the critics proved themselves out of synch with public taste. *Time* magazine wrote: "Zeffirelli has succeeded in mounting the liveliest screen incarnation of Shakespeare since Olivier's *Henry V*", but added: "Burton pursues his Kate with a weary, beery smile that promises temptation and trouble."

Hollis Alpert, writing in *Saturday Review*, wrote: "Miss Taylor had to contend with her husband at his absolute best in a role for which he is so extremely suited. Well, not only has she managed it; she has come through the ordeal with honour." But there was stronger dissent from Judith Crist of the *New York World Journal Tribune* who didn't care for the film or the Burtons: "It's a shaky and unpoetic contraption, little more than a vehicle for a couple of players to exhibit their talent for merriment and romping in excelsis – and, too often, in excess."

*Variety*, the film industry trade paper called the film "an uninhibited wife-beating lark."

The Academy didn't like it much either; it was only nominated for three Oscars and failed to win any.

But the film made money. Melvyn Bragg says they got a US$12 million return on their US$2 million investment. It was an oft-quoted figure but it's hard to see where that came from. With TV syndication fees, the film grossed US$15 million. The studio got back US$9 million and, on 25 per cent of first dollar gross, Burton and Taylor received US$4.8 million, leaving the Columbia studio with a profit of US$2.2 million.

After the success that year, Burton and Taylor were swamped by meetings with agents with film propositions for both of them together. This annoyed Burton, as he said: "I do wish you chaps could get it into your heads that although we've done five films together, that doesn't make us Laurel and Hardy."

But the reality was that Burton and Taylor were the number one actors at the box office in 1967 and, after successive hits, were in huge demand as a double act.

# CHAPTER 44

# The big money years

## Financial hits, creative misses

### 1967-1970

After a run of three excellent films, Richard Burton's luck couldn't hold – and it didn't. His agent, Hugh French, was mainly to blame. French had taken his eye off the ball and become drunk with the success and the money he had earned with the Burtons. His ten per cent commission on their earnings had earned him more than US$5 million over the past eight years. The money and the success had gone to his head and he came to believe he was god's gift to agenting. The judgment and the talent that had made him a top agent deserted him, and it affected his clients' careers adversely.

The problem was exacerbated by both Burton and Taylor's increasing remoteness. As they became bigger and bigger stars, they became less accessible to people. The entourage of secretaries and servants that followed them around increasingly kept them away from contact with the outside word. Telephone calls were no longer connected; letters no longer read, let alone replied to; and the normal flow of producers, directors and agents discussing deals virtually ceased. It left Hugh French as their sole contact with the creative community, and he became their gatekeeper at the precise moment his own talents were fading. Inevitably, it meant he selected their projects and, as a result, deterioration set in.

Some magnificent film projects were not properly evaluated, including a film version of *Camelot* which Richard Harris got; *The Fixer* from director John Frankenheimer, which went to Alan Bates; and perhaps the biggest loss of all was MGM's musical remake of *Goodbye Mr. Chips*, which went to Peter O'Toole. Instead, Burton chose to do a film called *The Comedians*, which was unquestionably, by any measure, the worst of the bunch.

There was also an element of hubris. Burton and Taylor radiated power; they were on top of the world. They had created a monster and let it take charge of their lives. So the creative mess that followed can only be laid at their own door.

Many people, including Rex Harrison and Robert Hardy, blamed the entourage for what happened, and there is much truth in that. Enjoying the vicarious success of Burton and Taylor, the entourage caught the always fatal disease of self-importance. Most of them became prima donnas, fawning to Burton and Taylor but behaving appallingly to the outside world.

This disease spread throughout the entourage, from Valerie Douglas to Aaron Frosch and the thirty or so people Burton and Taylor employed to look after their affairs. Simultaneously, Burton and Taylor retreated into a cocoon where they saw the world through only these people and had no idea it was happening. It suited the entourage as they became the ones to wield the power.

As well as Hardy and Harrison, close friends like Alec Guinness, John Gielgud and Emlyn Williams found themselves increasingly cut off from contact and subsequently stopped bothering with the couple. So many of their close friends, people who had known them from the 1940s and 1950s, lost contact in this period. Alec Guinness said it was "very rum." Guinness, 11 years older than Burton, had been a friend since the fifties, when they were both employed by Binkie Beaumont at HM Tennent. Guinness felt it was as though Burton had constructed a wall around himself: "He didn't seem to know half of what went on, which must have been terrible for Richard, who was a most gregarious person."

Rex Harrison was more blunt and personally offended. He famously said: "Why do the Burtons have to be so filthily ostentatious?" Melvyn Bragg observed in his own biography of Burton: "There are too many stories of the entourage appearing to behave in a high-handed manner. It is doubtful whether that sort of thing got back to Their Majesties. It seemed to be becoming a court based on the over-protective and self-inflated model of the 18th-century German princelings."

Robert Hardy was the most distressed. Used to popping in and out of Burton's home at Hampstead and then The Dorchester for 20 years, he suddenly couldn't even get through on the telephone. He said: "Messages weren't returned. In the end, I sent a telegram and that wasn't answered."

Whatever the cause, the effect was clear and it greatly blighted the life of Richard Burton for the next ten years until Suzy Miller, his third wife, sacked most of the people working for him and restored some sanity to his affairs. Removing the entourage became Suzy's greatest gift, but by then, unfortunately much of the damage had been done and couldn't be reversed.

The first manifestation of that was a film called *The Comedians*, which was to be directed by Peter Glenville. It was further complicated by the fact that sandwiching those negotiations were two personal tragedies.

On Friday 21st October 1966, Burton was having lunch when Bob Wilson brought him news of a terrible mining disaster in the Welsh village of Aberfan, not far from where he had been raised.

There had been a catastrophic collapse of a colliery slag heap that had slid down and crushed a school, killing 116 children and 28 adults. It was to prove Britain's worst ever peace time disaster. The slag heaps were comprised of waste extracted from mines and piled up on adjoining land. They became part of the Welsh landscape and were not thought to be dangerous. But the one that towered over Aberfan had an underground stream running through it which, after two days of heavy rain, undermined its integrity and caused it to collapse.

The National Coal Board, run by an ineffective chairman called Lord Robens, was almost entirely to blame for the disaster. Robens had failed to act on any of the warnings about the possibility of a collapse until it happened.

Burton was deeply affected by the tragedy and wanted to fly to Wales immediately to assist in the rescue. But he was prevented by his advisers, who told him there was nothing he could do at the scene and they were worried about his ongoing tax status. Instead, he immediately began to mobilise a fund to raise cash for the families of the bereaved.

When Burton finally learned what had befallen the young pupils of the Pantglas Junior School that morning, he broke down and cried. It turned out that they had arrived at school as usual at nine o'clock on Friday morning; it was the last day before half-term holiday. They had attended assembly and sung the hymn 'All Things Bright and Beautiful' before going to their classrooms. Simultaneously, the slag heap, 40 feet deep, rolled down the hill. The only warning they had was a great noise outside, but they didn't know what it was. With no windows on that side of the school, they couldn't see it approaching. The classrooms were on the side of the building nearest the landslide. The huge moving mound of slag slammed into the side of the flimsy classrooms and the children were crushed at their desks. Just five minutes earlier, those buildings had been empty.

When the landslide ended, there was utter silence in the village. As parents realised the school had been hit, they rushed to the scene and began digging through the rubble with their bare hands, trying to find their children. But it was truly hopeless and only a few children were pulled out alive in the first hour, but no survivors were found after 11 o'clock that day.

Burton felt helpless but did the only thing he could by helping to organise a disaster fund. He contacted all the famous people and entertainers he knew to take part in a special television show to raise money to help the village recover from its huge loss.

So, on 19th November 1966, Burton and Taylor flew into London's Heathrow in their jet with Peter Sellers and his wife, Britt Ekland, on board. They were all to appear in the special show.

In the end, the Aberfan disaster fund raised £1.6 million, well over US$3.75 million, and much of it was thanks to Burton's efforts.

But there was also a sting in the tail. Lord Robens removed £150,000 from the fund to make the rest of the slag heaps, overlooking Aberfan, safe. Burton was apoplectic when he learned of it, but there was little he could do as the funds were overseen by the coal board. Burton had failed to make the safeguards when he helped set it up. But Robens saw no shame in what he had done.

The Aberfan disaster came straight after another shock when Burton's youngest sister died unexpectedly. Edith Cook was 43 years old when she went in for a heart valve replacement corrective operation. It was not a life threatening situation but she died from a blood clot that formed a week after the operation had taken place. Her death was very sudden, and Edith left behind her a devastated family – her husband, Ron Cook, and three children: Caroline, Barbara and Anthony.

Burton flew into London with his brother Ivor for the cremation at Golders Green Crematorium. It was a rare gathering of all the Jenkins brothers together – Richard, Ivor, David, William, Tom, Graham and Verdun. Although they didn't know it then, it would be the last time all seven of them gathered together in one place. David Jenkins recalled: "Edie was the first of the 11 of us to die, and the fact that she was one of the youngest made the event especially poignant."

Soon afterwards, Burton flew to Paris to talk seriously with Peter Glenville about his new film called *The Comedians*, developed from Graham Greene's novel about political dictatorship in Haiti. Glenville was to be producer and director and Greene would write the screenplay. Glenville, who was trying to get into the more lucrative world of films after his success with *Becket*, got backing from MGM to film the novel in the obscure west African country known as Dahomey. Burton agreed to star in *The Comedians* because he admired Graham Greene's writing. He was also able to get Taylor a co-starring role because, together, they were such a hot ticket. It seemed completely irrelevant whether she was suited to the role or not. The script and story was adapted to suit her.

As it happened, the role was unsuitable for Taylor because it was a small part for a star of her stature. Of the 20 weeks' filming, she was only needed for five of them. Consequently, it was the first time Burton was paid more than Taylor. He got US$750,000 and she took US$500,000.

Interestingly, Taylor's career had started to decline just as Burton's came into ascendance. Now in her mid-30s, as a female actress, she was getting old and was regarded by Hollywood as being in decline; whereas Burton, approaching his mid-40s, was at his peak.

Glenville wanted the younger Sophia Loren or Anouk Aimee for the part and seemed determined to get her – so Taylor halved her fee and the studio intervened to overrule Glenville.

Glenville remembered: "She wasn't keen about him going away to Africa without her. The role of the woman was not large and wasn't really suitable for her...my choice was Anouk Aimee. Obviously, it was not a million-dollar role. But then Elizabeth's agents came along with the suggestion she play the part on more favourable terms."

The reduced fee, however, caused problems everywhere. Within the Hollywood community, the fee reduction was treated like an international incident and egos had to be smoothed.

Taylor's version of events leading up to it was different from Glenville's. She said: "Peter conned me into it and got me at half pay. He said: 'You realise of course that Sophia Loren is dying to do it. You wouldn't want anyone else to do those kissing scenes with Richard.'"

Glenville said he agreed to use Taylor but warned: "A glamorous superstar might topple the balance of the story."

Dahomey, a tiny republic, once French, was chosen to re-create Haiti, where the novel is set. The Burtons arrived in Cotonou, the capital of Dahomey, in mid-January and stayed there through February. They resided in an air-conditioned bungalow facing the ocean and flew in and out of the country on their new jet as their schedule allowed.

During the shoot, they spent a lot of time with the country's ruler, a man called President Soglo. He put the presidential compound at their disposal. Elizabeth Taylor affectionately called him *"mon general"*.

# AND GOD CREATED BURTON

Set in the Haiti of "Papa Doc" Duvalier, the film was a steamy cocktail of politics and sex, laced with some voodoo. Burton played the part of Mr Brown, a seedy English hotel-owner running an empty hotel. As Haiti slips into barbarism, he has an affair with Taylor, the wife of an ambassador, played by Peter Ustinov. Alec Guinness also had a supporting role.

The film, released at the end of the year, was poor. Greene was a much better author than screenwriter and, as Hollis Alpert put it, he "lost touch with his material." But the real problem was that both Burton and Taylor were miscast.

The film took around US$8.5 million at the box office on a budget of US$4 million. The pulling power of Burton and Taylor at their peak and a brilliant marketing campaign meant it made money for the studio.

During the filming of *The Comedians*, Gianni Bozzacchi, a photographer, joined the entourage as Taylor's personal photographer. He became a good friend of both Burtons. Bozzacchi learned his skills from his father, Bruno Bozzacchi, a famous restorer of photographs in Italy. He shot some beautiful images of Taylor over the years, unfortunately mostly in black and white.

After the exteriors were shot in Dahomey, the film's interiors were shot in a studio in Nice in March 1967, and it was a cue for some high living on the French Riviera. During that time, they struck up an enduring friendship with Prince Rainier and Princess Grace of Monaco. They also spent a lot of time with the Duke and Duchess of Windsor.

The time was another very happy period, and they were ensconced in a magnificent house called La Fiorentina on the Côte d'Azure near Monte Carlo, which Taylor had rented before when she was married to Mike Todd. The house, owned by Gianni Agnelli, was one of the most beautiful houses in the world and easily the best on that stretch of the French Mediterranean coast.

Once again, the Burtons were having such a good time ensconced in the south of France that it led to another incident that blighted both their careers. Taylor was due to travel to Los Angeles for the Oscars on 10th April 1967 as part of the *Who's Afraid of Virginia Woolf?* party. The film had garnered 13 nominations, and she was expected to win an Oscar for best actress. She was the clear-cut favourite in her category and her attendance was taken for granted.

Thirteen nominations was extraordinary, and it remains the only film in the history of the Oscars to be nominated in every possible category. It was eligible in thirteen categories and got thirteen nominations: best picture, best actor, best actress, best supporting actor, best supporting actress, best director, best adapted screenplay, best art direction/set decoration, cinematography, sound, costume design, music score and film editing. It is a record unlikely ever to be beaten and is a mark of how significant the film was.

Taylor was just about to fly to Los Angeles when Burton told her that he had dreamed about her being killed in a plane crash and asked her not to go. She said: "He dreamed the plane I was flying back to California in crashed – and he saw me dead. We've almost never been separated and now he doesn't want me to go. He's my husband and I'm not going...He gets into a terrible state when I'm away, especially when he gets tanked up. He just needs me..."

She cabled Jack Warner and told him of her change in plans and, within hours, received a wire begging her to reconsider. It said simply: "Do not burn the bridges you have built." Burton's response was appalling and he reportedly said: "Piss on him."

But she did not go and it was a terrible snub for Hollywood. So much so that many people never forgave her.

People speculated about the real reason she had cancelled her trip. One commentator said he believed it was because Burton was jealous of his wife and would be "most uncomfortable sitting in an audience watching his wife receive an award that he wouldn't get."

When Taylor won as expected, Anne Bancroft accepted the Oscar for her. Bob Hope then humiliated her by cracking a joke seen and heard by millions of TV viewers: "Leaving Richard Burton alone on the French Riviera is like leaving Jackie Gleason locked in a delicatessen."

Afterwards, she realised the huge error she had made but by then it was too late. To everyone, it seemed like Burton and Taylor were now bigger than Hollywood itself and that the tail had begun to wag the dog. All the image rebuilding of the past three years was undone.

As soon as *The Comedians* was finished, the roles were reversed and Taylor got involved in a starring role of her own in the film version of Tennessee Williams' play 'The Milk Train Doesn't Stop Here Anymore'. For reasons best known to Hollywood, the film version was to be called *Boom*. It was brought to her by her friend, the producer John Heyman, and it was his first major project with funding from Universal Pictures. It would also be Burton's first film for the legendary Lew Wasserman and his Universal studio.

Taylor loved the project because it was written by her favorite playwright, Tennessee Williams, with whom she had worked twice in the past on *Cat On*

# AND GOD CREATED BURTON

*A Hot Tin Roof* and *Suddenly Last Summer*. The basic plot was that of an older wealthy woman becoming obsessed with the arrival of a younger man.

The director Joseph Losey, Heyman's co-producer Norman Priggen, and Tennessee Williams all flew to Portofino where the Burtons were on holiday, cruising in a chartered yacht. The yacht was late and they spent a week kicking their heels waiting for it to arrive.

Despite Burton's earlier comments about them not being Laurel and Hardy, Hugh French seemed to coerce producers and directors into casting both of them in projects, regardless of suitability. Taylor told Priggen that she wanted Burton in the film. Although the part was perfect for Taylor, it was not for Burton and he was terribly miscast in the younger man's role. At 42, Burton was considerably older than the character should have been, but Taylor was adamant and Losey agreed. The decision was a disaster and made the casting of Taylor as the older woman ridiculous – Burton was seven years her senior. From that point on, no matter how good the script and the directing, the film wasn't credible and so it proved.

It was difficult for John Heyman, as he was a friend of both Burtons. Joseph Losey, the director, had always wanted the much younger actor James Fox for the role.

*Boom* was reputed to be the first film where Burton was paid US$1 million. Taylor got the same amount and somehow the budget ballooned to US$10 million.

*Boom* was filmed in Sardinia right in the middle of the Red Brigade scares in the summer of 1967. One night, Burton disappeared and the worst was feared when he could not be found. The police were called in and an island-wide search was mounted. At 10 o'clock, he was found with Bob Wilson, his valet, outside a bar, standing on a table reciting Shakespeare. He was apparently holding a competition for an audience of bemused Italians, with the prize of a drink to the person who could tell him which of Shakespeare's plays his recitals came from.

The whole family stayed on their new yacht, Kalizma, during filming. The older children, by now at boarding school in England, flew out for the summer holidays.

The filming was blighted by the constant fear of kidnapping, and the children were thought to be the main target. The premium for the insurance policy obtained from Lloyds to insure the Burton family in Sardinia was huge. It cost over US$2.5 million for US$15 million of cover and Universal had no choice but to pay. The insurance also had to cover the costs of abandoning the film if there was an incident.

The huge policy also got publicity in the newspapers and it was as if a bounty had been put on the Burton childrens' heads. A small army of armed guards was hired by the studio to look after them. More guards were needed for the US$2 million worth of jewellery Taylor had to wear in the film, which she personally borrowed from Gianni Bulgari's shop in Rome. Normally, the jewels would have been paste but Taylor wanted real ones. And what Taylor wanted, Taylor almost always got – whatever the cost or the inconvenience.

The yacht environment did not ensure harmony, and unlike Rome the year before, the couple spent the holiday drinking and arguing. The environment was too free and easy and they could drink without consequence. Alcohol was the sole cause of the arguing. Taylor was drinking as heavily as Burton. She began with Bloody Marys almost as soon as she was up in the mornings. At noon, she moved on to Jack Daniels. In the evenings, it was champagne.

Burton, who, despite his prodigious consumption, rarely missed a day's filming, was so far gone that he completely missed the very first day on set – literally unconscious after a session.

*Boom* told the story of a very wealthy widow who is dying and living in a large mansion on a secluded island with only her servants for company. Into her life comes a mysterious handsome young stranger with a weakness for dying widows. The stranger was played by Burton and the film explores the confrontation between a woman who has everything and a penniless poet who has nothing. Noel Coward also had a starring role. Taylor also secured her brother, Howard, a marine biologist, a part in the film for a thousand dollar fee. Howard was on holiday with his family and was delighted at his temporary stardom and the money.

Most of the action took place in and around the wealthy widow's house, which was built on a Sardinian hill overlooking the coastline. MGM lavished US$500,000 on the house with its spectacular whitewashed walls, a vast terrace, and open archways, where muslin curtains swung back and forth in the wind. The house cost so much because it was built of special travertine marble, which came from the same quarry that had been used for Rome's Coliseum.

Tennessee Williams also wrote the screenplay and, sadly, he was not up to the task. Williams couldn't shape his characters properly on film as he had on stage. Characters with no redeeming qualities do not come across well on celluloid. As Burton's brother Graham, who was always a good judge of creative issues, said succinctly: "They seemed just rich, self-indulgent bores." But Williams himself blamed miscasting for the film's failure: "Dick was too old and Liz was too young. Despite its miscasting, I feel that *Boom* was an artistic success and that eventually it will be received with acclaim."

Burton and Taylor's reputation saw the film open big, but no one liked it and word of mouth was bad. Hit films in America rely on word of mouth and on cinemagoers returning to see a film twice or even three times if they like it, an American peculiarity.

Hostile word of mouth and very poor reviews killed it quickly. The trade magazine *The Hollywood Reporter* called the film "an ordeal in tedium." Judith Crist wrote that Burton looked "more like a bank clerk on campy holiday, kimono and all, than a poet." Fergus Cashin called it: "an extravagant failure...a project weighed down with opulence."

*Time* magazine said: "They display the self-indulgent fecklessness of a couple of rich amateurs hamming it up at a country club frolic, and with approximately the same results."

Within ten days of it opening, it was finished and cinemas were empty. Because of the high insurance costs, the budget had ballooned to US$10 million by the end of filming. In the end it took just US$2 million at the box office and less than a million in the rest of the world. The TV syndication rights were almost worthless and Universal lost around US$7 million on the venture.

The failure of *Boom* was a serious wake up call for the Burtons and Hollywood. It was their first commercial failure together. Every other one of their joint films had made money.

After *Boom* was finished, Burton returned to Rome to play a cameo role in a film called *Candy* starring Marlon Brando. Burton was repaying a favour Brando had done for him years earlier. Burton had always had a special rapport with Brando, and their friendship was one of the strongest and deepest in Hollywood.

*Candy* was a comedy described by one critic as "trendy nonsense". It was based on a satirical novel about a young girl's sexual escapades. Brando had gathered together a disparate bunch of people to play small roles in the film, including Ringo Starr, John Huston, Charles Aznavour, Walter Matthau, Sugar Ray Robinson, James Coburn and Elsa Martinelli. Burton played a lecherous Welsh poet presumed to be modelled on Dylan Thomas. The film was panned by the critics, but it was a smash hit at the box office. With a small budget of US$4 million, it took a staggering US$16.4 million in American cinemas and

US$4.5 million overseas.

The Kalizma yacht would have come in very handy for Burton's next film, called *Where Eagles Dare*, as the Burtons wanted to take it up the River Thames and stay on it during filming. But he had ordered a very expensive refit and it was stuck in dry-dock. So he chartered a similar yacht called the Beatriz for the duration of filming. It was moored at Tower Bridge in London and cost US$2,500 a week.

The film was to be shot mainly in London, and Taylor managed to get another film called *Secret Ceremony* to be filmed at the same time in London.

The two films were both being shot at Elstree and Borehamwood; *Where Eagles Dare* at what was then the MGM studios, and *Secret Ceremony* at the then ABC owned studios. *Secret Ceremony* was due to begin two weeks after *Where Eagles Dare*.

*Where Eagles Dare* was developed by an up-and-coming producer called Elliott Kastner and financed by MGM. Kastner's formula was to assemble a writer, actors and director and then sell the whole package to a studio. Inspired by the very successful *The Guns of Navarone*, Kastner commissioned a script by the British fiction writer Alastair Maclean, and first sold the idea to Burton. He told him it was a *Boys' Own* type adventure with a convincing storyline: "I told him he should do a movie that had some meat and potatoes, that it was not a weighty tome. It was a good solid action-sweat movie. I talked him into it, based on doing something different."

Burton negotiated himself the most extraordinary profit-sharing deal that reportedly saw him earn US$8 million, his highest ever fee for a film. His brother Graham said: "The deal was to relegate all his earlier films into the league of minor earners." He added: "I was with him when he received a financial update on *Where Eagles Dare*. He glanced at the paper then pushed it over to me with his finger pointing to the bottom line. His earnings were in excess of eight million."

Burton's co-star was Clint Eastwood and they were supported by some top drawer British actors, including Peter Barkworth, Donald Houston and William Squire. Burton thoroughly enjoyed working with Eastwood and said: "I did all the talking and he did all the killing. Eastwood responded: "I just stood around...firing my machine gun, while Burton handled the dialogue."

Burton flirted with Polish actress Ingrid Pitt throughout filming at Elstree and when Taylor wasn't around used to give her a lift home to London in his Rolls-Royce, stopping at every pub along the way. He developed a little routine for Pitt's benefit, as she remembered to Burton biographer Michael Munn: "Always there would be someone who would come up to Richard and say: 'Aren't you . . ?' and he would say in a gruff voice: 'No, mate." And they would say, 'I didn't think you were.'"

Another old girlfriend, Mary Ure, was also on the film. She had become a well-known actress and divorced John Osborne to marry Robert Shaw. When Taylor was absent, she and Burton resumed their very casual fling.

The outdoor sequences were filmed in Switzerland and Austria, and Taylor made sure she could accompany her husband. She organised what she called food runs, which were in fact champagne picnics. Wrapped up head-to-toe in sable fur, she would lead a line of waiters, carrying silver trays of food, up a snowy hillside to where the crew were filming.

*Where Eagles Dare* was an old fashioned adventure; escapist entertainment of the best kind. The critics couldn't criticise it, as it was what it was and the best of its genre. But afterwards Burton seemed somewhat ashamed of the film, saying he had done it only to "amuse his children."

When *Where Eagles Dare* wrapped, Burton was due to move straight on to another film in London called *Laughter in the Dark*, directed by Tony Richardson, who had previously directed him in *Look Back in Anger*. The film was based on Vladimir Nabokov's 1932 novel, and Burton played an art dealer.

But, a fortnight after filming had started, something very strange happened and Burton was fired. The official story is that Richardson threw Burton off the film. Apparently, Burton had turned up half an hour late to shoot a scene on a Sunday morning, and Richardson lost his temper and they swore at each other. Burton was incensed because it was all done in front of his daughter Liza Todd. Burton walked off the set never to return after Richardson told him to "fuck off", which Burton assumed was his dismissal from the film. The young actor, Nicol Williamson, replaced him and the incident was airbrushed from its history.

The official version of events was almost certainly not true. When filming started, the film did not have studio backing and certainly didn't have enough money to afford Burton at the time. It appears that financial backing hoped for was not forthcoming and Burton agreed to an exit that would not embarrass Richardson. A press release was issued that read: "Woodfall Film Productions announces: 'Richard Burton is leaving the set of *Laughter in the Dark*, to be replaced by Nicol Williamson.'"

But the story had a pleasant ending for Burton. Whilst filming on location at Sothebys, he bought a Degas drawing for £58,000 and a Monet for a similar amount. The two items rocketed in value very quickly.

In between, Burton and Taylor spent one of the most enjoyable days of their year on 15th June 1968 at the wedding of Sheran Cazalet and Simon Hornby which was held at the magnificent Cazalet family home called Fairlawne in the English county of Kent. Taylor and Cazalet were childhood friends from the days when her father was an art dealer in London.

She was the daughter of Peter Cazalet, the Queen Mother's racehorse trainer. It was a steeped aristocratic family. Her husband was the son of Michael and Nicolette Hornby, scions of the one half of the founders of the WH Smith retail empire.

It was the society wedding of the year and the Burtons spent their time in the company of Noel Coward. Their presence was like a magnet for the British press, who headed down to Kent for the day.

They had plenty of opportunity for photographs. Knowing her friend was habitually late, Sheran Cazalet told Taylor the 11:30am wedding was due to start at 10:30am. But, for once, Taylor turned up punctually and when Burton realised the ruse, he directed his wife to the local village pub, where the landlord was startled to find Elizabeth Taylor, Richard Burton and Noel Coward across his bar ordering a vodka and tonic each.

Burton was not out of work for long and he was soon attached to a film called *Staircase*, an entertaining comedy produced and directed by Stanley Donen. It was adapted from a play by Charles Dyer and started shooting in Paris in September 1968. The play told the story of two aging, homosexual hairdressers trying to come to terms with middle age and a deteriorating relationship. Burton played Harry and Rex Harrison was Charlie, living together in the east end of London when Charlie is prosecuted by the police for indecent behaviour.

It was not an easy role, and Burton and Harrison sat down together and apparently they each said to the other: "I will if you will."

The film reunited Burton with Darryl Zanuck's 20th Century-Fox studio for the first time since *Cleopatra*. Any old differences had been forgotten, especially as Zanuck was also financing Taylor's new film as well. Amazingly, Taylor also managed to arrange for her new film, *The Only Game in Town*, directed by George Stevens and co-starring Warren Beatty, to be shot in Paris, although it was set in Las Vegas. Graham Jenkins said: "If they couldn't make films together, they made sure they were in the same town at the same time to make their movies."

Burton persuaded Donen and Zanuck to pay his usual US$1.25 million fee. The film was set in a hairdressers shop in London but filmed in Paris because Burton's time allowed in England had run out after *Where Eagles Dare*. Burton and Taylor moved into the whole of the top floor of the Plaza-Athenee hotel on the Avenue Montaigne near the Eiffel Tower as Fox set about building a fake Las Vegas and a fake London at two studios in Paris.

Zanuck was euphoric about the daily rushes and believed he had a big hit on his hands with *Staircase*. But he was wrong, and it was not destined to be a hit. America's cinema going public was not ready to see a funny film about two homosexuals camping it up. The combination, on film, of Burton and Harrison, both obviously heterosexual, misfired. Audiences laughed in the wrong places as Burton and Harrison came out with every gay cliché known to man.

Rex Harrison couldn't believe it afterwards, as he said: "The gimmick was that he and I – two of the better known heterosexuals in the business – would do our damnedest to play homosexuals without in any way being camp. I can't imagine now why I agreed to do it – what on earth we thought we were doing, the pair of us, playing two long-married homosexuals as straight as we could, and trying so hard not to camp the piece up or appear like a couple of outrageous queens, is beyond me."

Nor did Taylor's *The Only Game In Town* fare much better. Both scripts were nowhere near good enough.

When filming ended, in late November 1968, Burton's film career was suddenly pulled up short. After a string of flops, the studios had suddenly stopped rushing forward with million dollar cheques. In a four year period, his only hit film was *Where Eagles Dare* and studio chiefs in America put that down to Clint Eastwood.

If truth be told, many people in Hollywood thought Burton was a bloated has-been. And as Taylor approached 40, she was far less attractive to studios than she once had been. Taylor's offers of work had completely dried up.

The demands for films to be shot in adjacent locations were also increasingly difficult to fulfil. By the time the Burtons realised that the mood had changed, the pipeline had dried up. It was then that Burton finally realised how useless Hugh French had become. But it was too late.

Burton's schedule was empty and he tried to talk away the problem to Barry

Norman, then a young show business reporter on the *Daily Express*: "Last year, I had a few months off in Mexico, the first holiday I'd had in fifteen years, and I suddenly realised that doing nothing was marvellous."

When the Paris filming was completed, early in 1969, they flew to Los Angeles, where Taylor checked in at the Cedars of Lebanon Hospital to have tests for her back condition. Then they went to Puerto Vallarta for an indefinite stay. There was only one film in the book for the whole of 1969 and 1970, called *Anne Of The Thousand Days*.

In the end, Burton and Taylor spent five months in Puerto Vallarta. They enjoyed it so much that they did not want to leave to go to London, but in May 1969, they finally departed Mexico for London via Los Angeles.

Hal Wallis had come to Burton's rescue with a project that had been five years in the making. Wallis had put together a package for a new Henry VIII film called *Anne Of The Thousand Days*. It was the story of Anne Boleyn, one of the Tudor king's eight wives, and of her failure to produce a son and heir. Anne Boleyn was beheaded after exactly a thousand days of marriage. Burton played Henry VIII for the first and only time in his career. He was co-starring with Anthony Quayle, Michael Hordern and William Squire. Boleyn was played by Genevieve Bujold, a startlingly ethereal 26-year-old French-Canadian unknown. Kate Burton, now 12 years old, and Liza Todd had small non-speaking parts as maids.

*Anne Of The Thousand Days* was adapted from Maxwell Anderson's play with a screenplay by three unknown writers. The screenplay wasn't up to much and Burton's portrayal of Henry VIII was, in truth, good but not great. He felt it was a boring script and agreed with the description by one critic that it was "a plod through Tudor history". The director, Charles Jarrott, was inexperienced and it showed.

Despite that, Burton received his sixth Oscar nomination, which surprised him greatly and he told people: "The words don't sparkle; it's not *Becket*." He added: "It should have been retitled 'Anne Of A Thousand Hours'."

It was on the set of *Anne Of The Thousand Days* that he had his first major romantic involvement since his marriage to Taylor. The object of his affections was Genevieve Bujold.

Taylor operated a zero-tolerance policy when it came to infidelity and Bujold was Taylor's first big test – although she would face many more in the years to come. She managed to keep her husband, who was never going to run off with Bujold, but she could not prevent what was going on despite being on set every day and spending every minute she could with her husband.

She reportedly said to Burton on the very first day of filming, as she observed her husband and Bujold eyeing each other up: "Watch it, buster, or you'll be singing soprano soon.'

Their big chance came in June, when Taylor was hospitalised and then confined to bed with piles. She was unable to come to the set.

Bujold was a Claire Bloom/Susan Strasberg lookalike and Burton was naturally attracted to her and she to him, even though she was supposedly happily married to a film director called Paul Almond. Burton told people that Bujold reminded him of Vivien Leigh. She and Burton embarked a low-key affair but it became more than just a casual fling and it carried on for many years after the film had finished shooting.

Taylor did her very best to prevent it. She had desperately wanted to play the part of Anne Boleyn, and with a weaker producer she may well have been able to bully Universal Pictures into it. But Universal had lost a fortune on *Boom* precisely because of miscasting, and this time it would not budge. Hal Wallis told Taylor flat that she was not getting it and she had to accept it.

Burton always denied he was ever unfaithful to Taylor and many biographers, including Melvyn Bragg, were generous enough to give him the benefit of the doubt. He denied he was unfaithful to Taylor to the end of his life despite all the evidence to the contrary. He said at the time of his affair with Bujold: "It was all very tiresome, I had never betrayed Elizabeth." But then he thought about it and added: "Not at that point."

However, his comments on fidelity were very surprising to the crew of *Anne Of The Thousand Days* who daily witnessed his shenanigans, especially the continual rocking motion of Burton's caravan during breaks on location at Hever Castle when Taylor was away ill.

Burton vehemently denied all the gossip for Taylor's benefit, saying: "That was all rubbish. It was a bigger problem for Gin (his nickname for Bujold) because she had Elizabeth training her sights on her."

Bujold eventually won a Golden Globe for her performance in the film. Many people thought her acceptance speech rather mischievous when she said: "I owe my performance all to Richard Burton. He was generous, kind, helpful and witty. And generosity was the one great quality."

Charles Jarrott chose diplomatically to describe what went on between the two co-stars as: "They had a little flirtation." And he admitted: "Elizabeth was extremely uptight about this."

After the film was finished, Burton pined for Bujold. And Taylor could sense what had happened. It was not a happy time as the Burtons went straight back to Puerto Vallarta, where they would spend most of 1970.

Bujold, to her great credit, never denied the relationship, but would never confirm it either and Burton could rely on her complete discretion despite the fact that it eventually wrecked her marriage.

When filming finished in October, Universal went into fast track and released the film for Christmas 1969. But Taylor, furious about Bujold, refused point blank to allow her husband to attend the premieres and he was forced to remain in Puerto Vallarta. As a concession for the London premiere, she sent her 12-year-old Liza Todd in his place. She was at boarding school at Heathfield in England and got special permission to attend for the evening. Permission was forthcoming when she asked the headmistress to be her guest.

In the end, the film received only one Academy Award, for costumes, even though it was nominated for best picture, screenplay, photography, music, best actress, best supporting actor and, of course, best actor. BAFTA completely ignored the film.

Despite all the reservations, Philip Burton really liked it when he saw it and said: "I was so thrilled by Richard's performance that I felt sure he would get an Oscar for it. Apart from Richard's Henry VIII, there was a special joy for me in the film: eleven-year-old Kate appeared with other children in a scene where they watched the King passing by."

And so ended the era of the Burton-Taylor domination of Hollywood. There were no more great film offers and Hollywood was effectively finished with them. But the franchise they had created would enable them to enjoy a long and lucrative decline in cobbled-together projects that would keep them in the style they had become accustomed to.

But for the next 12 months, neither of them worked and, instead, embarked upon a period of pure hedonism, drinking themselves stupid, enjoying their money and gradually falling out of love.

# AND GOD CREATED BURTON

# CHAPTER 45

# Fabulous wealth

## *The art of being very rich*

### 1966 - 1974

There are various estimates of what Burton and Taylor earned together in the eight years between 1966 and 1974, but the most accurate appears to be around the US$78 million mark.

It was more money than they could comprehend and the Burtons were living a life of unimaginable self-indulgence. The stories of their casual and often frivolous spending abounded. Soon, they had so much cash they could buy whatever they wanted at whatever price.

For three years of those eight years, between 1966 and 1969, he was probably the highest earning individual in the world, or certainly in the top three, and there was absolutely no doubt they were the highest earning married couple in the world. So much so that they could easily outbid the world's biggest spender, Aristotle Onassis, for diamonds and anything else they wanted to buy.

Just because he could, Burton bought both he and his wife his and hers matching Kojah fur coats. It took 42 Kojah mink pelts to make the coats. They were so valuable they had to be specially stored, smothered in mothballs. They cost US$125,000 for the pair.

Their level of personal spending prompted a *New York Times* editorial which read: "In this age of vulgarity marked by such minor matters as war and poverty, it gets harder every day to scale the heights of true vulgarity. But given some loose millions, it can be done – and, worse, admired." Responding to the *New York Times*, Taylor told a journalist: "I know I'm vulgar, but would you have me any other way?"

In the summer of 1966, the Burtons chartered a 150-foot yacht called the Odysseia, for a brief week's cruise with their children in the Mediterranean. They had just finished shooting *Doctor Faustus* in Rome and it was their first ever cruising holiday. They weren't sure if they would like it. But they all enjoyed their time on the yacht so much that they wanted to extend it for another week – they didn't want to get off. But that posed a problem as it was chartered to another customer whom they were due to meet and hand the yacht over to in the port of Santa Marguarita in Spain.

So Burton cabled Valerie Douglas and told her to arrange for the next charter customers to spend a week in Spain at his expense. He agreed to compensate them handsomely so the Burtons could carry on cruising. That extra week cost him a staggering US$27,000 to arrange in charges and compensation. He also had to put off three film executives who had arrived in Santa Marguarita to discuss a movie. They also kicked their heels for a week in a Spanish hotel.

When the Odysseia finally arrived in Santa Marguarita, a week later, Burton was full of apologies for the trouble he had put everyone to. Then he told them that his wife had fallen in love with the Odysseia, and he was going to buy it for her. He apologised to everyone for any inconvenience he had caused and reportedly told them: "But you know how it is when Elizabeth wants something."

Burton had already cabled Aaron Frosch and told him to get the owner to meet them at the port, and he negotiated the transaction there and then. All existing charters were cancelled, including the hapless man who had been waiting in Santa Marguarita. But he went home happy, with a big cheque in his pocket, almost enough to buy a yacht of his own.

The 60-year-old, 150-feet, 280-tonne Odysseia had a colourful history. But whether the history recounted by Burton many times to his guests was true or not, no one knows. The way Burton told it was that the yacht had been built for an eccentric Englishman, principally so he could install his organ. The Englishman, according to Burton, liked to take the yacht out to sea in stormy weather to get exactly the right atmosphere so he could play Bach to himself on the organ.

What was true is that it had been pressed into service in both the First and Second World Wars as a patrol boat in the Mediterranean and after the war was refitted as a pleasure yacht for holidays.

The yacht had seven bedrooms and three bathrooms and a capacity, when full, to sleep 14 guests. It was staffed by a captain and a crew of seven. Burton paid US$192,000 for it and also took over employment of the crew. Before the deal was signed, the owner warned Burton it would cost US$30,000 a year to operate. In the event, it cost treble that and more.

Finally, when the transaction with the owner was completed, Burton found time for his meeting with the men from Hollywood, Joseph Losey and Norman Priggen. They were shown aboard to find Burton on the aft-deck, leaning against the bar that formed part of the bulkhead. There was no sign of an organ.

# FABULOUS WEALTH

The purpose of the meeting was to negotiate a fee for him and Taylor to appear in Losey's next film, *Boom*. The conduct of the negotiations was a good example of just how much money they couple had. The eventual fee would be US$2 million for both of them for three months' work. As part of his negotiation and a demonstration of how much they were earning, Burton fished around in a pile of papers on the bar. Eventually, after much rustling, he pulled out a cheque made out to Taylor from Warner Bros, which he had been using as a bookmark. It was a part-payment for her profit participation royalties for *Who's Afraid of Virginia Woolf?* The cheque was for US$2.05 million. He simply told them: "This will give you an idea."

After the yacht came the jet.

In 1967, private jets were a relatively new thing and up to then had only been used by big corporations such as Ford Motor Company to ferry around executives. The notion of a private individual owning their own plane was almost unheard of. The era of jet aeroplane travel was itself in its infancy, so much so that the vast majority of Europeans had never even flown in an aeroplane.

Then one morning, Richard Burton and Elizabeth Taylor took their first European trip on their own in a private jet from London to Paris. They were immediately hooked, and as soon as they arrived in Paris, they bought the jet in which they had flown over – for US$960,000. Taylor christened the plane 'The Elizabeth.' She said: "I bought it so we could fly to Nice for lunch."

They could easily afford it; by then, their bank accounts had US$10 million in them.

The purchase of the jet was the first visible sign of the extravagance for which they became famous. And from then on, it was downhill. The transaction had been so easy that Richard Burton understood that anything he wanted he could have. Nothing was out of his reach and nothing was unattainable.

After a few months of ownership, the Burtons were dissatisfied with the fit-out of the Odysseia after inspecting some other yachts. So the following year, Burton booked the yacht into a Genoa shipyard to be completely refitted at a cost of some US$240,000, more than it had cost them to buy it.

Taylor hired a designer called Arthur Barbosa to design a new interior in Regency style. Taylor had been introduced to Barbosa by Rachel Roberts, Rex Harrison's wife, and he had designed their Portofino home.

The master bedroom suite got the most attention, and a new giant bed and wall-to-wall bookshelves were installed. Burton loved the fact that his books now travelled with him

The yacht was fitted with modern radar equipment for the first time and a sound system that cost US$10,000. The whole yacht was fitted with deep pile Wilton Super Peerless carpeting, then the best in the world, at a cost of US$2,500. There was also space on deck for a Mini Moke that could be craned ashore and used to get around.

There was also a secure gun room where a small arsenal was stored, including four sub machine guns. Whenever the yacht was in Italy, it was guarded by four swarthy men who brandished the guns.

When it was finished, the whole yacht resembled an Edwardian palace, which is precisely what Taylor wanted. Burton would often stay up until the early morning hours just walking the decks and wandering below, admiring his yacht. He couldn't stop looking at it in wonder.

After the re-fit, they rechristened the yacht the Kalizma after their three daughters: an amalgam of Kate's, Liza's and Maria's names. Only Jessica seemed to have been forgotten.

Burton told journalists he had had the organ removed and replaced with a bar. He also told them that he had calculated that if they could stay on the yacht instead of hotels they could actually save money. Acquiring the yacht meant that the personal staff employed by the couple went over 50 for the first time.

So much money was sloshing around that Aaron Frosch formed two new Bermuda registered companies to keep it all in. Frosch was well aware that much of the money they were spending was money the taxman would normally have taken. His advice to them had been so good that they paid no tax at all. But that didn't stop him being continually worried about tax demands he might receive, and he took every precaution he could. He kept the diary of their movements across the world meticulously, on some occasions down to the last minutes. More than once, he had to phone them to move out of a country on a few hours' notice, sometimes just to fly out and back in overnight. It was the price they paid for not paying tax. Taylor called her new company Interplanetary Productions Ltd and Burton's was named Atlantic Programmes Ltd. He said at the time: "I want to be rich, rich, rich, or at least as rich as my wife."

Sometimes it looked as if they were just trying to find ways to spend money; it was coming in so quickly. The one area they didn't overindulge in was houses, although between them they owned seven; three in London, two in

Switzerland and two in Mexico.

Puerto Vallarta had really taken off since the Burtons had bought a house there in 1963. From a remote fishing village with one telephone line, it was now a thriving vacation resort.

The Burtons now owned two houses in Puerto Vallarta after they built a second house on the opposite side of the small road. They became his and hers houses, connected by a bridge over the road. The bridge spanned the swimming pool area at the original house to the first floor of the new house. It was an exact replica of the Bridge of Sighs in Venice. A top London interior designer called Jill Melford was brought in to make it "sumptuous", as Taylor put it.

Some of the torrent of cash was invested in various businesses. They bought shares in the company that managed their jet in Switzerland. They invested in a retail business run by a relative of Sybil's. Ron Berkeley's wife Vicky Teil had an idea to start a boutique in Paris and they backed that to the tune of US$50,000. They were also in on the early days of commercial television in Wales, where they invested £125,000 in Harlech Television, a consortium that included Lord Harlech and Stanley Baker. It won the ITV franchise for Wales and the West of England; Burton became a non-executive director. They bought a 685-acre plantation on Tenerife in the Canary Islands and a ten-acre horse-breeding farm in County Wicklow, Ireland.

But the most money was invested in the intangible worlds of art and jewellery. It was popular with both of them as the investments also made good presents and solved birthday and Christmas gift-giving problems.

Burton had no idea about art and relied totally on Taylor to buy what she liked. Taylor had always bought paintings when she saw an opportunity. Her father advised her on what to buy and Burton also encouraged her as she built the collection, including one year paying record prices for a Monet, a Degas and a Modigliani. Eventually the paintings were sent on loan to a gallery in Geneva because of the problems of storage and insurance.

But Burton didn't understand art at all. He had no appreciation of it and couldn't tell one painting from another, as he readily admitted: "My trouble is I can't understand art. I've tried and tried, but I still can't tell the difference between a Rembrandt and a Picasso. Some time back, Elizabeth bought a Van Gogh for around £100,000. I said to her: "A hundred thousand pounds? 26 inches by 12? Good God."

While in London in 1963, Taylor decided to surprise Burton with a Van Gogh painting that she bought in Sotheby's on Bond Street for £92,000. Incredibly, she simply took it back to The Dorchester in a taxi wrapped in brown paper. On the way, she stopped to buy picture hooks and a hammer. She then carried the painting up to the suite herself, where she hammered in a hook above the fireplace and hung the painting herself, ready to be viewed upon her husband's return.

Eventually, many of the paintings were hung on board the Kalizma because security around the yacht was so good. A Monet dominated the main salon, a Picasso and a Van Gogh hung side-by-side in the dining area, and a Vlaminck was in the stairway leading to the children's cabins. A Utrillo and a Rembrandt were hung in the master bedroom suite.

Works by Renoir, Rouault, Rembrandt, Degas and Pissarro were scattered around the guest cabins. When her father died, Taylor inherited an Augustus John, which she placed in the upper saloon. But Burton most loved the Jacob Epstein bust of Sir Winston Churchill that was on the main deck.

Burton's luxury was books, and these were worth very little. His fascination had no value at all. Years after he died, his entire collection was sold off and raised only £14,000. He admitted: "The only thing you can give me and be certain that I will enjoy it is a book."

But it was jewellery where Burton splashed the most of his cash, and in his lifetime it is estimated he bought Taylor jewels that cost him US$4 million. Taylor had a fascination with jewellery and a way of demanding that men bought it for her as gifts. In her lifetime, she received significant diamonds from Mike Todd, Burton and Michael Jackson. Others such as Malcolm Forbes, George Hamilton and Eddie Fisher also gave her expensive jewels.

Although he knew nothing about fine art, Burton did have a nose for jewellery; a talent he used to great effect, as Taylor revealed: "Richard knew everything there was to know about jewellery. The more he learned about the background and history of a piece, the more fascinated he became with it. He actually appreciated fine jewellery every bit as much as I did. It gave him such joy to see the expression on my face when he would present me with something he had spent hours selecting just for me." Taylor believed that appreciation stemmed from his being a miner's son, and she said that because he knew the value of coal, he also knew the value of diamonds.

Burton made a few smaller purchases costing between US$100,000 and US$250,000 in the years between 1962 and 1967 and he had already given her several exquisite pieces, including an emerald and diamond brooch from

Bulgari that she had worn at their wedding in Montreal. It had matched the emerald and diamond ring he had given her the year before, in Puerto Vallarta, when he was filming *The Night of the Iguana*. He would later add two emerald and diamond bracelets to the set, sometimes called "The Grand Duchess Vladimir Suite", also from Gianni Bulgari's shop in Rome. But it was all small-time compared with what came in the few years between 1968 and 1972.

The first significant purchase was the most special of all; the 33.19-carat Krupp diamond. The Krupp was named after its owner Vera Krupp. She was the second wife of Alfried Krupp, who had unexpectedly died in 1967 at the age of 58. The diamond was put up for sale as part of the settlement of Alfried Krupp's estate.

The diamond also had a touch of notoriety as the Krupp family had been involved with the deportation and forced labour of Jewish people during the second world war. Vera Krupp's husband had served three years in prison for his war crimes. Taylor, who had converted to Judaism in 1959, before her marriage to Eddie Fisher, said: "I thought how perfect it would be if a nice Jewish girl like me were to own it."

The Krupp was considered to be the world's most perfect specimen of a diamond. The mark of its beauty was in the exquisite way it had been cut in the 1920s. It was an emerald cut, with perfect proportions of length and width; so much so that people confused it with a style known as an Asscher cut.

Burton flew to New York specially to bid for the diamond at the Parke-Bernet Galleries in New York on 16th May 1968. When he got there, he found himself bidding against the fabled New York jeweller Harry Winston. But Burton figured that if Winston wanted it then it must be worth it, and he didn't put an upper limit on the purchase. He just kept on bidding until it was his. It finally was for US$307,000

The 33.19-carat, oblong diamond literally took Taylor's breath away when Burton presented it to her. He gave it to her on the Kalizma, moored on the River Thames, and later Burton erected a small plaque on the yacht's deck to mark the occasion.

Taylor was overjoyed and she described the Krupp's shape as "so complete and so ravishing as steps leading into eternity and beyond. It sort of hums with its own beatific life." J. Randy Taborrelli, one of Taylor's biographers said of the Krupp: "It shimmers as if it's actually alive, with every color of the rainbow." The Krupp remained the favourite and probably the most valuable piece in Taylor's collection until her death.

It's true to say that the Krupp became the most famous diamond in the world over the next five years. It was by no means the biggest but it was regarded as the most beautiful. The artisan who cut it, probably in Amsterdam, was never named but his skill was the secret of the jewel's appeal.

It certainly caught the eye of Princess Margaret, Queen Elizabeth II's sister one night. She asked Taylor: "Is that the famous diamond?", knowing full well it was. Taylor lifted up her hand so the diamond caught the light. The princess said: "It's so large, how very vulgar." Taylor responded: "Yes but ain't it great?" in the best vulgar voice she could summon up. Then Princess Margaret asked to try it on and wasn't overly keen to give it back as it dazzled on her finger.

But the really big purchase came in the autumn of 1969, of a 69.42-carat pear shaped diamond known then informally as The Annenberg Diamond. Regarded as the most valuable diamond in the world, it was owned by the late Harriet Ames, the wife of stock broker Paul Ames. She was the daughter of Moses Annenberg and sister of Walter Annenberg, the publisher and then the US ambassador to Britain. Harriet had died suddenly of a heart attack, which led to the diamond being put up for auction at the Parke-Bernet Galleries on Madison Avenue in New York.

Everyone was interested in it and the favourite to buy was Greek shipowner Aristotle Onassis, who had recently married Jackie Kennedy. Everyone thought Onassis would win it easily and simply bid until he got it.

It was only when the Burtons read about Onassis' interest in the diamond that they became interested. When she heard about it, Taylor called Ward Landrigan, the head of Parke-Bernet's jewellery department, and told him: "I want it. I really want it. I'd even be willing to pay a million for it." With that, Burton saw it as a challenge to get it. But so did everyone else as Taylor effectively had announced what her final bid would be. Ward Landrigan flew the diamond across the Atlantic for Taylor to view in Gstaad.

The original rough diamond had been mined in 1966 in the Premier Mine in South Africa. It was 241 carats and was originally cut by Harry Winston to 69.42 carats in the shape of a pear.

Harriet Annenberg had worn it as a ring.

Burton asked Aaron Frosch to attend the auction for him and bid. He set a top figure of US$1 million. Onassis dropped out at US$780,000. Harry Winston was out of his depth, and at the end there was only Robert Kenmore, the owner of Cartier, and Frosch bidding in US$50,000 increments. Frosch stopped at US$1 million as instructed, and it went to Kenmore with his last bid of US$50,000.

Burton was sitting drinking in a pub in England when he heard that Frosch had lost the diamond. Burton was furious that even a million dollars wasn't enough to buy it. So he instructed Frosch to go back and buy it from Kenmore at any price. Sensing the publicity value, Kenmore agreed that Cartier would sell it to the Burtons for a sum publicly revealed to be US$1.1 million. But the reality was much more and it is said by insiders that Burton had to pay US$1.2 million to finally get it. The sale was announced on 25th October 1969. Burton agreed to let Kenmore display the diamond in Cartier's Fifth Avenue shop window for a week before it was delivered to him in Switzerland. Cartier immediately took out a full page advert in the *New York Times* telling people to come and look. The *New York Times* quoted Burton as saying: "It's just a present for Liz."

Disliking the setting in a ring, she immediately commissioned Cartier to make a v-shaped necklace of graduated pear-shaped diamonds, mounted in platinum to house the diamond.

She wore it for the first time at Princess Grace's 40th birthday party on 12th November 1969. But she never really liked it, and the Krupp remained her favourite. It caused her to sell it in 1978 to the New York dealer Henry Lambert for US$5 million. Today, it would be worth upwards of US$30 million, and Taylor admitted she regretted the sale.

Burton also bid on another fabled jewel at Parke-Bernet known as La Peregrina, a pear-shaped pearl. It was a very special piece, said to be over 400 years old, and with what looked like a perfect provenance. But was the ancient pearl the same as the one up for sale? – many people thought not, including 77-year-old General Francisco Franco, the Spanish dictator, who believed La Peregrina was safely, amongst the Spanish crown jewels, locked up in his vaults.

The provenance was, on the surface, as flawless as the pearl itself. It had been discovered by a slave in the Gulf of Panama and at the time of its discovery, it was the largest perfectly symmetrical pear-shaped pearl in the world.

The pearl was handed to Don Pedro de Temez, the administrator of the Spanish colony in Panama and carried to Spain and presented to King Philip II of Spain. The slave was given his freedom as a reward.

The King presented his bride, Mary I of England, with the pearl. After her death in 1558, the pearl was returned to Spain's royal family, where it remained as part of the Spanish crown jewels for the next 250 years. It was reputedly featured in two paintings by Velazquez, worn as a brooch by Queen Margarita, the wife of Philip III, and suspended from a long necklace belonging to her daughter-in-law, Queen Isabel.

In 1808, the elder brother of Napoleon Bonaparte, Joseph, was installed as the King of Spain by his brother. Five years later, he was overthrown and he stole La Peregrina and took it with him back to France. The Bonaparte family later sold it to the Duke of Abercorn. The Abercorns owned it until 1969, when they put it up for auction at Parke-Bernet in London.

Burton won with a bid of only US$37,000. And there the story goes murky. There was immediate speculation about the provenance because of the very low price of US$37,000 fetched by the jewel at the auction. It was clear that others did not believe it was the real La Peregrina, although no one was particularly going to take the word of General Franco.

But Parke-Bernet stood by the provenance and the pearl was delivered to Las Vegas, where the Burtons were staying on the top floor at Caesars Palace hotel. Taylor couldn't have been more delighted when it arrived, and she believed that La Peregrina was the perfect example of the expression of a "mystical connection" she had to jewels.

La Peregrina had originally been set on a pearl-and-platinum chain necklace, but, three years later, Taylor commissioned Cartier to create a new setting of a double-stranded pearl-and-ruby choker, made with 56 matched oriental pearls. Burton was so inspired by its history that he decided, at some time in the future, he would write a historical novel based on the pearl's story.

In her book published in 2002, called *My Love Affair with Jewellery*, Taylor tells the story of what happened when La Peregrina was delivered to Caesars Palace. She wrote, in her own words: "It was on a delicate little chain and I was touching it like a talisman and sort of walking back and forth through our room at Caesars Palace. So I was dreaming and glowing and wanting to scream with joy, but Richard was in one of his Welsh moods and his joy...well, he was a Welshman so sometimes his joy was perverse and he would become dark. But when I'm happy, I show it and scream it and yell it, and I wanted to throw myself at him and kiss him all over. But because I knew Richard very well, I had to play it by ear, and I knew this was not the moment to become too demonstrative. Just the same, there was no one to talk to and no one to show the jewel to and I was going out of my mind.

"At one point, I reached down to touch the jewel – and it wasn't there. I glanced over at Richard and, thank God he wasn't looking at me, I went into the bedroom and threw myself onto the bed, buried my head into the pillow and screamed.

"Very slowly and very carefully, I retraced all my steps in the bedroom. I took my slippers off, took my socks off, and got down on my hands and knees, looking everywhere for the pearl. Nothing. I thought: 'It's got to be in the living room in front of Richard. What am I going to do. He'll kill me.' Because he loved that piece. Anything historic was important to him. This pearl is unique in the world of gems. It's one of the most extraordinary pieces there is. And I know that he was proud inside, which was why he was being like this cartoon with a black cloud over his head and raindrops falling.

"So I went out and sort of started humming 'la la la', and I was walking back and forth in my bare feet, seeing if I could feel anything in the carpet, I was trying to be composed and look as though I had a purpose because, inside, I was practically heaving because I was so sick. So I looked over at the dogs… and I saw one chewing on a bone. And I did the longest slowest double take in my head. I thought: 'Wait a minute, we don't give our dogs, especially the puppies, bones. What is he chewing on?' And I just wanted to put my hand over my mouth and scream again. But no, I just casually opened the puppy's mouth and inside its mouth was the most perfect pearl in the world. It was – thank God – not scratched."

That was an elaborate story – oft told. But was it true?

Robert Hardy told an entirely different story of almost exactly the same incident, which he personally witnessed; not in Las Vegas but on the decks of the Burton's yacht, The Kalizma, which was then moored on the River Thames at a place known as Traitor's Gate.

As he recalled, in his own words: "I went and stayed on the yacht. I was filming quite near London and they came to pick me up in the tender on the dockside by the Tower of London. Everything went well, we all drank a lot and Richard went to bed early because he was filming."

But before that, Hardy and Burton had enjoyed a fierce argument over his portrayal of Henry VIII in *Anne of The Thousand Days*, which he was currently filming. Henry VIII actually had red hair and a red beard. Burton told Hardy he had refused to dye his hair the red colour required for historical accuracy.

Hardy recalled: "When I suggested that this was irresponsible – playing a man who is portrayed in paintings, by Holbein and others, quite clearly as a red-headed man with a red beard – as all the Tudors were, he said: 'Christ no, fuck that.' I told him it was dreadful and not the way that I thought about characters that I was going to play, and we disagreed and he went to bed."

Hardy later described Burton's attitude as a "disinclination to agree."

Hardy and Taylor sat up enjoying a last drink and then she retired and Hardy had a nightcap talking to the crew, as he takes up the story: "Suddenly, Elizabeth darted out of the cabin and said: 'Oh my god, it is ghastly – I have lost La Peregrina' and she held up the necklace and said: 'It's fallen out. I have searched and searched and now I must take the crew and they must search and search until they find it. I don't know what to do, Rich must never know.'"

Hardy was no help as he was filming the next morning and retired to his cabin. As he remembered: "And so I went to bed and was having my breakfast in the morning thinking: 'My God, I wonder what has happened because there will be a monster explosion about all this' and she came out and said: 'It's okay, I have found it' and she held it up."

She explained that one of her dogs had been caught chewing it: "She gave it to me and I held it in that bright light in the early morning. I could see that toward the thinner end, there was a complete flake that had been taken out by the dog's teeth."

And there the story ended. Or so Hardy thought.

That is, until many years later, when Hardy was lunching at Claridge's in London with an old friend called Paul-Louis Valere, whom his elder daughter Emma worked for in Paris. The discussion turned to Richard Burton and Hardy told him the story of La Peregrina.

Suddenly, Valere shouted: "It is not right." He snapped his fingers and the waiters at Claridge's brought a telephone out on a trolley. He dialled a number and had a discussion with Dowager Queen Ena of Spain, to whom Valere was related by marriage. She told him: "I am sitting at my dressing table and if I reach out to my left, I can pick up La Peregrina; the real Peregrina."

In 2002, when Taylor's book was published, Hardy learned of the story Taylor told as having taken place in Las Vegas, the same event which he had witnessed, but in London. Later, a journalist was shown Taylor's La Peregrina and said it was intact and there was no sign of any missing pieces.

Robert Hardy was an eye witness to what really happened. Why Taylor made up the Las Vegas story is a mystery to this day - as is the provenance of the La Peregrina in her jewellery collection.

The final big purchase was a birthday present for Taylor's 40th on the 27th February 1972. For that special occasion in Budapest, Burton acquired the Shah Jahan yellow diamond, a seventeenth-century gem from India once owned by the emperor responsible for the building of the Taj Mahal.

He bought it from Cartier, who brought it to show him during a stopover at Kennedy Airport in New York. Better known now as the Taj Mahal diamond, it cost him a reputed US$900,000. The Persian necklace had been made in 1627 for Nur Jahan, wife of the Emperor Jahangir, the father of Shah Jahan. Shah Jahan was given the diamond by his father and he then gave it to the woman who was the favourite of his wives, Queen Mumtaz, for whom the Taj Mahal was built. It is inscribed in Parsee with the words: "Love Is Everlasting."

The Taj Mahal diamond was Taylor's crowning glory and never again was she given anything so magnificent. In many ways, she felt she had enough as she said: "You can't possess radiance, you can only admire it."

The purchase of the Taj Mahal diamond proved to be the high watermark of their conspicuous consumption. By then, both were in decline as actors. High inflation had set in across the world, devaluing their wealth and their earnings. They still both earned a million dollars a movie. But the buying power of a million dollars by the late seventies was a fraction of what it had been ten years earlier.

Years later, long after Burton was dead, Taylor looked back at those heady days and said: "When I think about the sixties, I'm glad that I knew the wildness, glamour and excitement when I was in my prime: the parties, the yachts, and the private jets and the jewellery. It was a great time to be young, alive and attractive, and to have all those goodies. I enjoyed it."

# AND GOD CREATED BURTON

# CHAPTER 46

# Terrible tragedy

## *A year of sorrow*

### 1968

U p until 1968, Richard Burton had led a charmed life. But on 5th June, it suddenly ended and 1968 was to prove a year of terrible tragedy from which he would never truly recover, as five tragic events completely changed his life in ways he would never have thought were possible.

It all began on Wednesday 5th June, when the first hammer blow came without any warning whatsoever.

It was 11 o'clock in the morning, during a break in filming, when Bob Wilson tapped him on the shoulder. As Burton looked up at his faithful valet, he knew that face. It was the same face that had delivered the news about the Aberfan disaster two years before. Wilson said simply: "I'm sorry sir, Bobby has been shot." Burton didn't need to be told any more to understand, and couldn't help but notice the tears in Bob Wilson's eyes as he said the words.

Robert Kennedy was a champion of black Americans and a hero to Wilson.

Burton was shocked to his core by the news. He had become inordinately close to Kennedy over the past three and a half years – ever since he had become the senator for New York. He had supported his senatorial campaign strongly.

Burton immediately went to find a television and a radio set to get the latest news on his condition and to find out what had happened. He discovered that Kennedy had been shot by a lone gunman, a 24-year-old year old Palestinian immigrant called Sirhan Bishara Sirhan, in the basement of the Ambassador Hotel in Los Angeles. The shooting had taken place shortly after midnight, straight after Kennedy had declared victory in the democratic primary.

Kennedy was being treated in the Good Samaritan Hospital in Los Angeles, but Burton immediately knew from the prognosis and the half hour medical bulletins, that Kennedy was unlikely to survive and that if by some miracle he did, he would be a complete vegetable. As he listened to the radio, it reported Kennedy had gone into theatre an hour before. He couldn't work anymore that day and went home at around two o'clock after he heard Kennedy had survived the surgery and was in intensive care. He sat glued to the television set waiting for news with the radio set on as well. Taylor left him alone; she knew when to back off. Later, he turned down the sound and just stared at the pictures of his friend dominating that evening's newscasts. As he sat in silence, he reached for a closely bound typed manuscript that Bob Wilson had placed at his feet. It was a document entitled '13 Days', Robert Kennedy's personal account of the Cuban missile crisis in October 1962, which had brought the world to the brink of nuclear war. Kennedy had sent it to Burton a few months earlier in order to get his opinion, as he intended to publish it as a book. Now as he read it again, his tears falling on the pages as he did, he slugged back scotch after scotch brought to him by Wilson, each time with a silent toast to his fallen friend. Eventually, he slumped down and Bob Wilson carried him to his bed.

At around 11 o'clock the following morning, the news he had been waiting for came over the radio. It announced Robert Kennedy had died in Los Angeles at 1:44am local time.

It was a shocking moment. In that instance, all hope in the world seemed to have disappeared and he felt the death of a man he was so compatible with very keenly. Both men were the same age, at 43, and had been born within ten days of each other. Their political ideals were so close as to be indivisible. He was also a man who's intelligence matched his own.

Burton's mind wandered back to when he had first met Kennedy, when he was playing in 'Camelot' in 1961. Then in 'Hamlet' three years later and in Rome only two years before. He thought about that magical night out in Rome when they had both got drunk and recited Shakespearean sonnets. Although as a foreigner he had been barred from contributing directly to Kennedy's election campaign, he had steered his donations through his wife's parents and had indirectly been a big contributor to the Kennedy campaign. Burton had shared Kennedy's dream just as it might have been his own.

Finally that night, near midnight, his thoughts wandered back to 1961 when Robert Kennedy had come backstage to his dressing room at the Majestic Theatre and recited back to him a verse from the lyrics, written by Alan Jay Lerner, that he so loved: "Each evening, from December to December, before you drift to sleep in your cot, think back on all the tales that you remember of Camelot. Ask every person if he's heard the story and say it loud and clear if he has not, that once there was a fleeting wisp of glory called Camelot." Kennedy had nicknamed the White House 'Camelot' in 1961, and his 1968 campaign had really been about recreating that brief shining moment that was

Camelot. It was a dream that Burton shared, and now he realised that with Robert Kennedy's death, the dream of Camelot really was over. It was very, very hard for him to take in.

Although Elizabeth Taylor was not nearly as close to Kennedy as her husband; she was also very upset and swore that something needed to be done about America's gun laws. Her response was to buy a full page advertisement in the *New York Times* advocating stricter gun control laws.

It took Burton a full two weeks to begin to recover from the death of his friend.

In 1968, there was another development in his life that Burton was none too keen on. He heard murmurings that people close to him were considering writing books that were supposedly memoirs of their own lives but were effectively back door biographies of Burton himself. Not wanting that, he told them all to desist and they mainly did. That is all except one man whom he felt he could not tell what to do; his adoptive father, Philip Burton.

Philip had been approached by a wily publisher, Bill Decker of *The Dial Press* in New York. Decker had wined and dined him and persuaded him to write a memoir, which to all ends and purposes was a book about Richard Burton as much as Philip tried to resist it.

Philip sent him the draft manuscript for comment and Burton wrote a devastating critique, which he never actually gave to him. He claims he forgot but it is more likely he thought twice about hurting Philip's feelings as the criticism in the note was relatively harsh and did not pull any punches. It was, however, a brilliant critique and Burton at his very best. He headed the typewritten note: "Written in an honest attempt without malice and without special favour."

He called parts of Philip's manuscript "prissy, pious and pretentious." He called the style "convoluted, pedantic and frequently opaque." He said parts of the book had "meagre substance", and added that at times the "style is frighteningly self-conscious and ponderous." Another chapter was described as "perishingly dull." He called the chapters as a whole "ill-arranged" and, to summarise, said Philip's observations of life were "not very interesting."

The book was published in 1968 and was poorly received. Burton had been right.

On Sunday 21st July of that same year, another major blow struck when Elizabeth Taylor went into hospital for a hysterectomy operation. He wrote in his diary two days later: "Elizabeth had her uterus removed on Sunday morning. The operation began at 9:30 and ended at 1:00." The matter-of-fact entry marked one of the most awful days of his life. It meant that there would never be, could never be, a bloodline called Burton-Taylor; a human being with the genes of one of the greatest actors and greatest actresses of the 20th century. It was their greatest dream when they married and something more precious than anything their millions could buy. It was the one thing they wanted to buy but couldn't. And he could hear his wife's pain in the next room, where he sat and waited overnight.

When the time came for her to leave the hospital, he mused in his diaries that "at least [he] hadn't lost her", though it hit them both hard that they would never have "their own child." Taylor said: "A child with Richard – I would have wanted that above everything in the world." And she meant it – above anything. She referred to the surgery as "the destruction of my womanhood."

Three days later, on Wednesday 24th July, there was more bad news which would prove to be the trigger to the worst tragedy ever to befall him. It started when Burton received a telephone call from Janine Filistorf, who, together with her husband, ran the Café de la Gare restaurant in Celigny. The Filistorfs were great friends of Burton, but this was not a social call. She told him that his gardener, Andre Besancon, who was about to retire and enter a nursing home, had hanged himself in Burton's garage at Le Pays De Galles in Celigny.

Besancon had worked for Burton from the time he had bought the house in Celigny in 1957, some 11 years. Although Burton had declined to go to his own father's funeral a few years before, he now made immediate plans to fly to his gardener's funeral in company with family members Ivor, Gwen, Kate, Liza and Brook Williams.

It was a strange decision, and there was absolutely no need for him or any of them to go. It seems certain it was an excuse for Burton to escape the London hospital where Taylor was recovering and to go off in the jet for an adventure to Switzerland. Taylor didn't want him to go at all and made him promise that he would stay at her Gstaad house rather than Celigny, which held, for her, so many bad memories of Sybil.

But Burton ignored his wife's pleadings to stay, claiming he had been very close to Andre Besancon. The seven of them flew on Burton's jet from London to Geneva on the day of the funeral. After it was over, they checked Gwen Jenkins and Liza and Kate into a hotel on the shores of Lake Geneva and planned to drive to Gstaad for the night. The following morning, they would drive back, collect the girls and fly home.

But before that, they decided to go to the Café de la Gare for supper and some drinks. It was to prove a fatal mistake. Supper at the Café de la Gare was much looked forward to. It had a very special dish on its menu called 'Fillet of Lake Geneva Perch', prepared with a special secret recipe given to the Filistorf family years earlier.

All three men ordered the dish and inevitably had rather too much white wine to accompany the fish. Burton's reputation for drinking was well known, and Brook Williams also enjoyed it. But few knew of Ivor Jenkins' liking of drink. It was his big weakness in an otherwise blameless life.

Although airbrushed away and never ever mentioned by the family, Ivor drank like a fish and took any opportunity he could to get intoxicated. In truth, Ivor's drinking problem was no different from that of his brother.

Details of what happened have always been sketchy but, apparently, the Burton party drank 18.5 litres of wine. It seems likely that they were joined by other friends, as it would be impossible for three men to consume that much. But, even so, it is clear that they drank at least three bottles of wine each and were completely incapable as a result.

Their condition made it impossible to drive to Gstaad. By the time they decided they were too drunk to drive, they had two options: check in at the same hotel as the girls, or open up Celigny for the night. By then, it was three o'clock in the morning and they decided they were too drunk to drive even the few miles to the hotel and so they decided to stay the night at Celigny.

But Celigny had been closed up and Burton hadn't set foot in the house for two years. It was full of memories of Sybil and would be an emotional return for the two brothers, who had only recently been reconciled after the traumas of the divorce.

Ivor had always taken Sybil's side over the divorce and had refused to talk to his brother for nearly three years after he left Sybil and took up with Elizabeth Taylor. The row had culminated in Burton visiting Ivor at his house in Hampstead and being refused entry after an hour of pounding on the door and begging to be let in. Although it had all since been smoothed over and Ivor and his wife Gwen had become friends with Taylor, it was still raw under the surface.

The Café de la Gare is situated by a railway bridge just across the railway tracks from Le Pays de Galles. Apparently, it was raining heavily when Ivor volunteered to walk up the hill to the house to open it up and turn the outside lights on for the other two. He told Burton and Williams he would return for them.

It was pitch black and there were no lights on as Ivor got to the house, and by all accounts this is what happened: when he got to the house, Ivor was looking for the outside light switch when he put his foot on a new grille outside the back door designed to remove snow from boots in the winter. The grille was slippery and it slid along the ground when he put his foot on it, causing him to fall over. As he fell, his chin caught a windowsill and instantly snapped his neck. Any other time, he might have just bruised himself or sprained an ankle at most. But because he was incapably drunk, he just fell straight down and fate took a hand.

For the first time, the excessive drinking practiced by Burton and his brother had come unstuck and caused a real tragedy. Ivor lay on the ground outside the house unable to move, and no one was near enough to hear his cries for help.

It seems that Burton and Williams carried on drinking at the Café de la Gare for at least another hour until it closed, and they stumbled up to the house and found Ivor lying on the floor. Somehow, they managed to call an ambulance.

By then, the 61-year-old Ivor was in poor condition but still alive, and he was taken to the intensive care unit in the Cantonal Hospital in Geneva. They could not operate immediately because of the amount of alcohol in Ivor's system. By the time he was wheeled into the theatre, it was too late to save his spine.

There was very little that could be done. It was only because he was so fit that he managed to survive the accident at all. Surprisingly, no one in the family was told about the accident, and by the time they did learn of Ivor's true condition, an air ambulance had flown him back to Britain to Stoke Mandeville, the spinal injury hospital in Buckinghamshire.

He was paralysed from the neck down, and although every effort was made, hardly any progress was possible. His sister Catherine, a nurse, devoted herself to a recovery that never came. Burton paid for the best treatment at Stoke Mandeville, but he remained paralysed.

After a few years, when it was plain that Ivor was not responding to treatment, he and Gwen moved to Switzerland to live in Gstaad where two nurses rotated to be with Ivor all the time. The quality of the air in Switzerland improved his breathing and made the end of his life more pleasant. Catherine gave up her job and nursed Ivor when it was clear he was near the end. Catherine later recalled Burton visiting their brother: "It was agony for him to watch Ivor. He was such a proud man and there was no dignity in it. He had always been such a dignified man. Richard used to visit when there was usually sport on the television. But if there was no sport on, he was like a cat on hot bricks. Then he would have to talk to Ivor, and he just didn't know what to say. The whole thing was so painful for all of us – four years of absolute hell."

Ivor Jenkins finally passed away on 19th March 1972, and Richard Burton heard the news whilst he was in Budapest making a film called *Bluebeard*. After the funeral, his widow, Gwen, went back to live in the house at Squires Mount in Hampstead, London, and life gradually returned to normal. Brook Williams replaced Ivor in Burton's life and took over all his duties effectively as his road manager and went on the payroll.

But the funeral failed to bring closure to the mystery of the circumstances of Ivor's death. When it came to recording what had happened that fateful night in Celigny, Burton's biographers were told all sorts of lies by various family members. The necessity for the lies naturally cast doubt on what really was thought to have happened.

An unsuspecting Penny Junor was deliberately misled. Paul Ferris didn't believe what he was told and subsequently hardly wrote anything at all. Hollis Alpert, Fergus Cashin and other journalists were told that Ivor had been injured in a car accident. Some were told a heavy snowfall had caused the accident, although it was the middle of July.

Graham Jenkins wrote a very elaborate and almost wholly untrue, albeit probably innocent, description of what happened in his biography of his brother. Whether Graham was misled or went along with a cover-up is uncertain. He does give the impression that he was misled, and that he didn't believe the version of events he was told. He appeared torn by loyalty to his family and the truth.

Graham Jenkins described in the book how he saw Ivor for the last time in February 1972 in Switzerland, less than a month before he died. They spent 72 hours together, as Graham revealed: "I sat by his bed and we talked. We must have said more to each other in those three days than in the previous 30 years. On the last night, he refused to let me go to bed. We talked on right the way through to breakfast."

When he got home, Graham realised that Ivor had never talked about the accident itself, how it happened or anything that went on that night. As he said: "How curious it was. He had revealed so much of himself, but not once in our long exorcising sessions had he said a single word about the accident that was to be the death of him."

David Jenkins was also kept in the dark and later admitted when he wrote about the accident: "There are conflicting versions." David was a policeman and must have suspected that there was something amiss in what he was told. Considering it was an accident that ultimately involved the death of his brother, it was a shocking state of affairs. But it was not the first or the last time David was involved in covering up less-than-savoury family matters. David said by way of explanation: "As far as I can establish, Ivor went ahead to open up the house, which involved switching on the mains electricity from somewhere in the grounds. There was some sort of metal grille you had to step on in order to do this. Ivor, uncharacteristically, tripped. He fell awkwardly and broke his neck. He was never to walk again."

It's very clear David Jenkins doesn't believe he was told the truth. But as a former policeman and of very strong character, he was not the sort of person to accept that situation. So the account in his book appears highly disingenuous. Whilst the truth may well have been kept from Graham, who was not trusted by the family after the *News of the World* incident five years earlier, David would have been told.

Having got that clear, it is pretty apparent that Graham Jenkins does not believe the explanation that Ivor slipped on a loose grille. From close examination of all available evidence, it does appear that the events are loosely true up to the moment Ivor fell. But who was there when it happened and why it happened is now anyone's guess.

The most viable explanation that has emerged over the years is that Burton and Ivor got into a fight over Sybil when they got back to Celigny. It was the first time they had been back to the Celigny house together since Sybil had left it nearly six years before. It was effectively haunted by memories. It appears that something one of them said may have sparked a fist fight between the two intoxicated brothers and Ivor went down on the floor, breaking his neck.

What is known is that Burton disappeared for ten days after the accident and could not be found. If the story of the fight was true, there was a real danger Burton could have been charged with manslaughter if Ivor had died. Certainly, if he had died, the Swiss police would have investigated and the story they gave would not have stood up to any sort of scrutiny. It appears that Burton did not return until he knew Ivor would survive. It is likely that Graham, who is no fool, realised this. David Jenkins would certainly have done so.

But whatever the real circumstances of Ivor's death, there is no question that it was an accident – albeit the circumstances are a mystery. David Jenkins said: "Richard was never able to talk to any of us about it. He was utterly devastated by the accident and by Ivor's helpless misery during the remaining four years of his life." Curiously, Burton's diaries are missing for the eight years after Ivor died and maybe, if they haven't been destroyed, the truth is written in them. But now, close to 44 years later, it doesn't really matter.

Even after the four tragedies in 1968, there was still one more to come.

On the evening of 20th November 1968, Richard Burton answered the telephone in his suite at the Lancaster Hotel in Paris. He found his mother-in-law, Sara Taylor, on the other end.

It was not an easy call for her to make, and she was very grateful to find Burton had answered the telephone rather than her daughter. Sara told her son-in-law that her 72-year-old husband, Francis, had died in his sleep. Although he had not been in good health for some time and had suffered strokes in 1965 and 1967, there had been no warning.

Burton told Sara Taylor to put down the phone and that he would tell his wife the bad news. He went into the bedroom where she was reading and sat down beside her, took her hand and told her as gently as he could. She just screamed and said: "No, not Daddy." Although Francis Taylor had never been a loving or demonstrative father, he had been very supportive and always at his daughter's side when she needed his help.

Taylor said much later that receiving that news was the single worst moment of her life. Burton recalled in his dairies: "Elizabeth was inconsolable in her grief – like a wild animal."

A few hours later, she phoned her mother and they were able to have a reasonable conversation. Taylor told her mother how she had been planning a surprise Caribbean cruise on the Kalizma over Christmas for them both.

After that, Burton put her to bed and a doctor sedated her whilst he arranged flights for the following morning. The next day, the Burtons flew to Los Angeles to attend the funeral. The funeral was conducted by a Christian Science minister at Westwood Memorial Park, where Francis Taylor was interred. Six days later, they flew back to Europe and Taylor returned to work.

And Burton prayed that it was the last of 1968's terrible tragedies, which had combined to turn it into such a wretched year.

# AND GOD CREATED BURTON

# CHAPTER 47

# The Turkey Shoot

### *Five terrible movies*

#### 1970 - 1972

At the end of 1969, when shooting of *Anne Of The Thousand Days* was over, the Burtons retreated to their house at Puerto Vallarta. *Anne Of The Thousand Days* effectively marked the end of Richard Burton's mainstream film career. His wife's had already ended two years earlier with the filming of *The Only Game In Town*, with Warren Beatty.

Burton was 44 and Taylor was 37, and as far as Hollywood was concerned, they were all washed up. Never again would either of them be offered work on a big Hollywood movie. From then on, they could only get work from independent producers with financing from outside of Hollywood. Burton hoped it would be temporary and mused hopefully in his diaries: "I am afraid we are temporarily (and I hope it is only temporary) out in the cold and fallen stars. What is remarkable is that we have stayed up there so long."

Suddenly, they were both pariahs and their agent, Hugh French, had no answer to it. Burton finally realised how useless French had become and made moves to find a new agent. He sincerely regretted burning his bridges with Robbie Lantz and didn't feel he could go back to him again, and so he was stuck with French.

During this period, Burton peppered Aaron Frosh with questions about his net worth and the sort of income he could look forward to if he had to stop working. Frosch told him he had around US$6 million in cash and as much again in assets. He said Taylor had a similar amount. He told them, invested wisely, it might bring them a joint annual income of US$1 million but he warned that their living expenses were currently running at between US$600 and US$800,000 a year.

Burton wasn't completely finished – he still had the potential to earn millions but as inflation took hold in western countries and the US dollar and Swiss franc appreciated against sterling and other weaker currencies, a million dollars was worth a fraction of what it had been worth in the fifties and sixties. And it was by no means certain that movie actors would continue to earn such big salaries. Hollywood was having severe problems as television continued to bite into its revenues. One writer described Hollywood at the time as being in "hysterical disarray", and production starts and investment by the big studios were at an all-time low.

In reality, the studio system era was over and its replacement was not yet clear. Television was dominant and many people questioned the purpose of cinemas altogether as audiences fell and kept on falling with no end to the decline in sight. It was by no means certain that cinema-going as a concept would survive

Burton sensed it all keenly and three months into 1970 noted his changed circumstances in his diaries. It hit home when he suddenly found something he could not afford to buy – a Gulfstream jet. He took a trip on the Gulfstream owned by Frank Sinatra and, when he wanted to buy one, was told the price was US$3.5 million and he knew he couldn't afford it. It was the first tangible sign of a changing tide.

At the beginning of April, he and Taylor went to the Oscars ceremony in Los Angeles for their last hurrah in Hollywood. Much to his surprise, he had been nominated for best actor for *Anne Of The Thousand Days*. Astonishingly, he was favourite to win. Frank Sinatra sent his Gulfstream over to Puerto Vallarta to collect them and bring them to Los Angeles. But for the sixth time, there was no Oscar glory. John Wayne won – not on merit, but sentimentality.

They flew straight back to Puerto Vallarta afterwards.

In May, with nothing else to do, and for a big fee, both he and Taylor returned to Los Angeles again to appear on the Lucille Ball show, a long-running comedy show called *Here's Lucy*. They were guests and were expected to participate in various comedy routines. But Burton found proper American comedy to be gruelling work and rather unbecoming. As soon as it was over, they couldn't wait to get back to Puerto Vallarta.

The lack of offers of work was a cue for Burton to make his first sustained attempt to give up drinking. And from this point, his life would be dominated by periods of failed abstinence. But it was a landmark decision of sorts. For the rest of his life, he no longer drank continuously.

His first dry period was to last for over five months before he reverted back to his old ways.

He also managed to get his first movie deal for nearly a year, albeit very much a b-movie project that Universal threw his way when no other big star would touch it.

# THE TURKEY SHOOT

Thrift and economy were the new watchwords in Hollywood and Harry Tatelman, a television producer at Universal, saw his chance. Tatelman was famous for the *77 Sunset Strip* television drama series. He hatched a plan for a new film using some old footage from a Universal movie called *Tobruk* – a Rock Hudson war picture – that had been made four years earlier.

Tatelman went down to the Universal film vaults and found thousands of feet of unused film of dive bombers and desert battlefield scenes that had never been used and that no one knew what to do with.

Tatelman had the idea that he could quickly make a new film, which he called *Raid on Rommel*, using the footage. He made a plan to shoot for just three weeks in the Mexican desert. Everything was on the cheap, including Richard Burton, who admitted it was a "way of getting back into the swing of things." Desperate to work, he agreed to work for a percentage of the gross receipts instead of taking a fee. It was the only way he could get back in the game. Burton was well aware of what he was getting into, as he admitted: "The writing is sufficiently credible to get us from one explosion to another. There is to be no overt attempt to give it any artistic merit whatsoever."

The film was to be shot in intense heat in San Felipe and would be a very unpleasant 23 days in the sun. As he was on a cut of the first dollar gross at the cinemas, he figured he would make at least US$500,000 even if the film flopped. For that, he was willing to be discomforted in the desert heat.

Because of illness, Taylor could not accompany him for the start of filming. She had recently been hospitalised after a routine operation. As soon as she realised that it was an all-male cast and that there were no young, unattached women on the set, she relaxed and visited the set for a few days before returning home. It was the first time they had been separated for more than a few days since December 1963.

Filming started on 20th June 1970. But Tatelman had made a crucial mistake. He had hired 72-year-old Henry Hathaway to direct the film. Hathaway was a director well past his prime, who, like Burton, needed work. Instead of opting for unproven youth, Tatelman had gone for experience. It was a huge mistake as Hathaway, by then, had completely lost whatever talents he once had.

When the film was finished, the rough cut was viewed by Universal's chairman, Lew Wasserman. Wasserman straightaway realised it was terrible and not even worth the million dollars it had cost Universal to film. It was a second-rate war movie and Hathaway had made it worse by shooting it like an old-fashioned B-picture. In desperation, he ordered Universal's marketing department to "go all out" promoting it using Burton's name. The publicity department asked Burton to narrate radio and some TV commercials for the film. Burton was incredulous and told the hapless publicist: "Good god, man, do you think I'm a double fool? It's bad enough that I made the picture. Why would I want people to see it?"

The film was released in 1971 and flopped immediately. Predictably, the critics gave Burton a real hammering and wondered what he was thinking of putting his talent on display in such rubbish. They were pretty unanimous that it was the worst film he had ever been involved in. *Time* magazine wrote: "Burton's voice remains one of the most distinctive and controlled in the world. But he is no longer in charge of his face." Whatever that meant, it was true. Burton did not have many real regrets in his life, but making *Raid on Rommel* undoubtedly became one of them.

After *Raid on Rommel*, Burton stayed dry but was truly frightened by what had happened to his career. He was not helped by the economic situation with Hollywood in a financial mess and almost all the British studios closed up. His biggest fear was to end up as a television actor, so he grabbed any cinema movie he could to avoid television.

So he panicked once again and agreed to do another film for very little money up front. In England, two young up-and-coming American producers, Alan Ladd Jr and Jay Kanter, gave him the lead in a low-budget crime thriller called *Villain*.

Their first choice had been Robert Stack, the TV star of *The Untouchables*. But Stack wanted a US$175,000 fee and Ladd and Kanter decided they couldn't afford him. When Burton agreed to do it for nothing up-front – they snapped him up.

This time, Taylor came with him and, realising they were no longer earning vast sums of money, they rented a house in North London instead of staying at The Dorchester. At the time, both were frightened by what had suddenly happened to them. They began living their lives differently, believing they might have to make their money last.

But when Burton saw that having given up drinking was not making producers warm to him, he started up again. He also believed he was a much better actor with a few drinks in him, and he had his performance in *Raid on Rommel* to prove it.

*Villain* was made on a tiny budget of US$2 million and financed jointly by MGM and EMI.

Taylor also landed her first film part for two years in a movie called *Zee & Co*, adapted from an Edna O'Brien novel, financed by Columbia Pictures and co-starring Michael Caine. Taylor's fee was slashed and she was getting a quarter of what she had previously been earning. She only accepted it because it was filming in London at the same time as *Villain*.

In *Villain*, Burton played a London gang-leader, modelled after the notorious east London gangsters Reggie and Ronald Kray. His character was called Vic Dakin, who was a sadistic man who murdered for fun. He was also a homosexual, and Ian McShane played his reluctant lover. Dakin's gang got up to all sorts of old-fashioned crime capers attempting to outwit a very convincing police detective, played by Nigel Davenport, who was the real star of the film. In truth, *Villain* was no better than an average episode of *The Sweeney* in England or *Kojak* in America, but for what it was, Burton was very good in it. And it certainly was not the rubbish that *Raid on Rommel* had been.

Paul Ferris said: "*Villain* was good in places in a modest, B-picture manner, but Burton added nothing to it except his name in first place, the same size as the title. It might have been any competent actor with raddled features who could snarl in guttural cockney." Ferris got it precisely right, and eight years later, Bob Hoskins showed what could be done with a British crime drama in *The Long Good Friday*. *Villain* did well enough in Europe but flopped in America, where the cockney accents had to be re-dubbed in order to be understood.

For reasons best known to itself, The *New York Times* homed in on the film. It flew one of its top writers, Bernard Weintraub, from New York to the set in London. During the making of the film, Burton gave Weintraub an interview which included the immortal declaration: "Fame is pernicious and so is money." At the end of the piece, Weintraub gave this opinion of Burton: "Despite the bravura voice and style, he appears, at this point, oddly vulnerable, even frail. Somehow, the shadows of the past have deepened. The drinker, the lover, the celebrity have flattened into a surprisingly weary figure." Weintraub had delved deep into Burton's psyche and was merely reflecting what Burton himself was thinking.

Weintraub appeared to somehow sense he was writing Burton's career obituary, and in many ways he was.

The *New York Times* again showed undue interest in Burton when it came to review the film. It was headlined: "Whatever Became of Richard Burton?" Vincent Canby wrote: "*Villain* is Richard Burton's latest and least interesting bad movie." Canby then went on to deliver a postmortem on Burton's 20-year-career since he had first come to America. It was so very clear that the most influential newspaper thought it was all over for him.

Interestingly, *Villain* made a small amount of money when it was released in 1971. It is now a cult classic and caught the video era perfectly. Ten years later, it could be bought and rented on VHS video cassette, and it brought in five times what it had cost to make from rentals and sales.

Halfway through *Villain*, Burton and Taylor had grown tired of economising and quickly moved back into The Dorchester, vacating their rented house. They figured if they were going to go down, they may as well go down in style. The entourage was recalled and they resumed where they had left off two years earlier.

Robert Hardy recalled it well when Burton invited him to dinner. He told his friend he would only come if it was just the four of them and not a huge crowd. He said: "I'd love to come and see you if ever there's a time when there will just be a few of us, as I'm afraid your giant organisation defeats me." Burton responded: "Come on Friday when there'll just be us and the children."

But Hardy was astonished when he arrived for the intimate dinner with his old friends and found around 100 people in the suite and spilling out onto the roof terrace. He remembered there being a giant mound of caviar on a table and, at four o'clock in the morning, Burton standing up and announcing: "The rest of you can go now; I'm going to fuck my wife." It was a magnificent moment and "if only the cameras had been turning", thought Hardy.

When *Villain* finished, Burton was sad in a manner in which he had not been over any other film. He had thoroughly enjoyed playing Vic Dakin with the film's collection of up-and-coming British actors. It was a friendly cast and crew, with Burton at the centre of it, especially when he had abandoned abstinence and started drinking again in the middle of the film. Years later, Ian McShane, who played his homosexual lover, recalled a jokey moment on set when Burton said to him: "I'm very glad that you're doing this film." McShane replied: "So am I, Richard." He said, "You know why, don't you?" McShane said: "Why?" Burton said: "You remind me of Elizabeth."

Gradually, Burton and Taylor adjusted to their new status in the world, and relaxed. They had plenty to do and it proved to be a busy time in London. The filming of *Villain* coincided with the marriage of Taylor's oldest son, Michael Wilding Jr to Beth Clutter. They wed at Caxton Hall in October, the same venue where Taylor had married Wilding's father 18 years earlier. Michael

Wilding had not been an easy teenager, developing into a typical rebel of the time. At 17, he had effectively rejected his parents and gone his own way, including announcing his intention to marry a hippy girl called Beth Clutter two years his senior. His mother could hardly object, considering her own marriage record. Clutter was rumoured to be pregnant. Over 500 people were outside Caxton hall, not to see the bride and groom but the new mother-in-law. Predictably, the marriage lasted less than two years.

A much happier occasion was Burton's 45th birthday, on 10th November 1970, when he went to Buckingham Palace with Taylor and his sister Cecilia James to be made a Commander of the British Empire (CBE) by Queen Elizabeth II. Afterwards, dressed up in a morning suit and top hat, Burton, Taylor and Cecilia posed proudly with the medal. But secretly, Burton had hoped for a knighthood; but, in those days, that was an impossibility for a tax exile.

With no film offers coming his way, Burton was once again forced to agree to perform in a film for nothing, this time in exchange for a very dubious profit-sharing arrangement.

Andrew Sinclair, a contemporary historian whom Melvyn Bragg described as a "polymath", had bought the film rights to Dylan Thomas' radio play 'Under Milk Wood'. Sinclair intended to direct the movie himself and write the screenplay. His previous experience was limited to one film, called *When Winter Comes*.

Sinclair naturally approached Burton as he had performed in the original broadcast of the radio play and was Dylan Thomas' greatest supporter. It was a film offer Burton couldn't say 'no' to easily. He discovered he had three weeks left in the 90 days he was allowed to stay in Britain by the Inland Revenue, and he told Sinclair he would do it.

But there was a snag when Aaron Frosch ordered him point blank not to do the film and to get out of Britain. Frosch was worried that, if the film overran, Burton might be tempted to stay and finish it and to try and leave the country surreptitiously on his jet. Frosch realised how disastrous it could be if the credibility and integrity of his diary was threatened. Burton ignored the warning but promised Frosch he would leave on the due date, come what may.

Frosch was right to be concerned. If the Inland Revenue had caught Burton fiddling just once, it could have claimed he had been dishonest in every one of his 13 years of tax exile and declared his exile status invalid. Then, in the worst case, it could have made him pay £8 million in back taxes, plus punitive penalties – enough to break him. The thought worried Frosch sick, but of course it didn't worry Burton at all. Frosch was also mildly superstitious of it being Burton's 13th year in tax exile. He didn't like to tempt fate.

So Burton decamped to Wales for the film version of Dylan Thomas' *Under Milk Wood*. He played the part known as the First Voice, and Peter O'Toole played the role of Captain Cat. Elizabeth Taylor played Rosie Probert. The famous opening line defined the production: "To begin at the beginning."

Not many films had ever been adapted from radio plays, and Sinclair raised a £300,000 budget to make the picture. What wasn't generally known was that Burton had secretly underwritten the £300,000 budget before the film started. But his guarantee wasn't needed, as the government-sponsored British National Film Finance Corporation put in £190,000 and merchant bank Hill Samuel put up the balance of £110,000.

Sinclair paid his three main stars £10,000 each and paid the rest of the cast, including Victor Spinetti, Glynis Johns, Vivien Merchant, Sian Phillips and Ryan Davies, the union scale rate. But he gave them all first dollar gross deals on cinema ticket sales, which soon became irrelevant when it became apparent that he had given away well over 100 per cent of the revenues before the film even started production.

The whole film, shot in the Gwaun Valley in Wales, was made in just 40 days with many of the locals appearing as extras. Burton was there for three weeks and he thoroughly enjoyed his time in Wales with his friends. But as the phone calls from Frosch grew in frequency from one a day to two a day and then every hour and, finally, every half hour, he and Taylor got on their jet and left Cardiff with only hours to spare before their 90 days was up for the 1970-1971 tax year.

But Frosch was still worried and cursed his client for cutting it so fine. No one had ever properly defined the system for measuring the 90 days allowed in Britain for tax exiles. Frosch just crossed his fingers hoping that no one ever did define it.

During filming, Burton grew increasingly close to Andrew Sinclair and he respected his innate intelligence. The repartee between them during filming was non-stop. One day, Burton said to him: "You're lucky I'm sober, Andrew." Sinclair, quick as a flash, shot back: "Define sober." Burton smiled and said: "Never more than one bottle of vodka a day." After a quizzical look from Sinclair, Burton clarified it: "I am not drinking on your film. That means only

**Above:** Suzy Miller and Richard Burton's official photograph taken for inclusion in the programme for the tour of the Camelot revival in June 1980.

**Above:** Richard and Suzy Burton with Suzy's twin sister, Vivienne, on the set of *The Wild Geese* in Africa, on 19th October 1977.

**Above:** Suzy and Richard Burton, Luisa and Roger Moore, and Hardy and Anita Kruger celebrate Moore's 50th birthday on 14th December 1977 during filming of *The Wild Geese* in Africa.

**Right:** Richard and Suzy Burton attend a premiere in New York City on 19th May 1980.

**Left:** Victor Luna, Elizabeth Taylor, Richard Burton and Sally Burton in the dressing room of the Lunt-Fontanne Theatre after a performance of 'Private Lives' on 7th July 1983. For a brief period that year, Taylor was engaged to Luna who would have been her sixth husband if the marriage had gone ahead.

**Left:** John Hurt, Suzanna Hamilton and Richard Burton in costume on location for the film *1984* by George Orwell in Chippenham, England. They were posing for a press photo shoot to publicise the film.

**Above and right:** Richard Burton with daughter Kate Burton on the set of the American miniseries *Ellis Island*, which was filmed at Shepperton Studios, London, England in the summer of 1984. These photographs were taken in July 1984, a month before he died. Burton had a cameo role and his daughter was the lead actress. He played a United States senator and Kate his on-screen daughter.

**Above:** The main house at Le Pays de Galles with Sybil's red MG parked in front.

**Above:** The guest lodge at Celigny that was occupied by Ivor and Gwen Jenkins.

**Above and left:** Café de la Gare is situated at the bottom of the hill from Richard Burton's house at Celigny. Burton drank or dined there most days that he was resident at Celigny and got to know the proprietor Paul Filistorf extremely well. On Friday the 4th August 1984, Burton dined there for the last time with his wife Sally and John Hurt.

**Above:** The original sign on Le Pays de Galles (Wales) that Ivor Jenkins put up in 1957.

**Above:** Richard Burton's study on the top floor of his house in Celigny. The study contained most of his books, which were on special slide-out shelving units that his third wife, Suzy, had installed in 1977, during a makeover of the house. The rest of his vast collection of books, including the Everyman series given to him by Elizabeth Taylor, were stored in an outbuilding in the grounds.

**Funeral in Celigny: Thursday 9th August 1984**

**Left:** Kate Burton, Brook Williams, Verdun Jenkins, Catherine Jenkins, Liza Todd, Sally Burton and Maria Burton stand before the coffin just before it is lowered into the ground in Celigny, Switzerland, on 9th August 1984.

*Jacques Langevin / Sygma / Corbis*

**Right:** Ushers carry Richard Burton's coffin from the church in Celigny to its resting place in Celigny's cemetery, on 9th August 1984. The coffin was bedecked in red and white flowers depicting a Welsh dragon.

*Geoffrey White / Daily Mail / Rex Features*

*Geoffrey White / Daily Mail / Rex Features*

**Left:** Crowds gather along the route as Richard Burton's coffin is conveyed to the small protestant church in Celigny, Switzerland, on the morning of Thursday 9th August 1984, three days after he died.

*Francois Schenk*

**Above:** Richard Burton's grave in the protestant church in Celigny. He bought the plot five years earlier, when it was decided he must be buried in Switzerland for tax reasons. He also bought the two adjoining plots to prevent attempts by Elizabeth Taylor to buy a plot so she could be buried next to him. As much as he may have loved her in the past, he wished for peace in his passing.

*Aiden Sullivan /Mail on Sunday/Rex Features*

**Left:** The scene at the Welsh memorial service for Richard Burton held at the Bethel chapel in Pontrhydyfen on 11th August 1984. Over 400 friends gathered in the chapel with over twice that number gathering on the hillside to listen to the service over a tannoy.

**Above:** Sally Burton arriving at Richard Burton's London memorial service at St-Martin-in-the-Fields Church in Trafalgar Square in London on 30th August 1984. Two more memorial services were held in Los Angeles and Pontrhydyfen in Wales

**Below:** Suzy Burton arrived late at the memorial service at St-Martin-in-the-Fields Church in London on 30th August 1984. There were no seats left until Robert Hardy found her one. She was deeply distressed even though she and Burton had been divorced for three years.

**Above:** Elizabeth Taylor and Cecilia Jenkins arrive together at the London memorial service at St-Martin-in-the-Fields Church in London on 30th August 1984. The service was organised by Burton's oldest friend, the actor, Robert Hardy.

**Above:** Elizabeth Taylor surrounded by the Jenkins family in Pontrhydyfen, Wales, on 19th August 1984. She flew into Wales after visiting Burton's grave in Celigny, ten days after the funeral, which she did not attend. (left to right) Burton's brothers and sisters, Cecilia James, Hilda Owen, David Jenkins, Verdun Jenkins and Graham Jenkins.

**Above:** Graham Jenkins and his wife, Hilary, unveil a new art installation honouring his brother at a site commemorating Welsh legends in Cwmafan, Port Talbot, Wales, on 1st May 2010.

**Above** Lord Rowe-Beddoe, one of Richard Burton's best friends and president of the Royal-Welsh College, with Dame Elizabeth Taylor and Prince Charles at a gala evening at Buckingham Palace to mark the 60th anniversary of the Royal Welsh College of Music and Drama. At the event, held on 29th April 2010, Dame Elizabeth was moved to tears as she presented a bronze bust of her late husband to Prince Charles. The bust is now at the new Richard Burton Theatre in Cardiff.

**Below:** Kate Burton, photographed at the New York premiere of her latest film *Remember Me*, on 1st March 2010. She lives in the United States with her husband, Michael Ritchie, and her two children, Morgan Ivor, born in 1988, and Charlotte Frances, born in 1998.

**Above:** Penny Junor wrote the first biography published after his death in 1985. It was a matter-of-fact workmanlike look at his life entitled *Burton - The Man Behind the Myth*.

**Left:** Robert Hardy, lifelong friend of Richard Burton, photographed at his home in Oxfordshire on Wednesday 9th March 2011.

**Above:** Rhianon Trowell, Richard Burton's niece, photographed at her home in Oxford on Saturday 12th March 2011.

**Below:** Kate Burton and her mother, Sybil Christopher, photographed in 2008. Kate is a successful actress and Sybil, who is now 82, co-founded the not-for-profit regional theatre situated at Long Wharf in Sag Harbor, New York, in 1991.

**Above:** Melvyn Bragg wrote the only officially authorised biography of Richard Burton published in 1988 called *Rich* as a joint collaboration with Burton's widow Sally.

one bottle of vodka a day. I am sober on two. But when I'm drinking, it's three or more."

Another time, he said to Sinclair: "You and I may be intellectuals, Andrew, yet Elizabeth is more intelligent than both of us."

Although he loved praising Taylor, and did it habitually whether she deserved it or not, he often eulogised over her purely for effect. But this time, he did have a point. Taylor had no intellectual pretensions but she did have a remarkably instinctive intelligence that defied analysis and which often gave her an unfair advantage over genuine intellectuals such as her husband and Sinclair.

Sinclair did a good job of handling the finances and had £15,000 left in the bank when all the bills were paid. But the film bombed. Just like *Doctor Faustus*, it had very narrow appeal and it ran in art-house cinemas for a just a week before the audiences dwindled. It proved impossible to sell it to television and it took less than US$1 million at cinemas worldwide

The film lost its backers all their money and there was little left for the actors – but it was very popular in Wales. And, even though the film never made much money, it was generally agreed to be an admirable production. Arguably, its greatest achievement was Burton winning a favourable review from Judith Crist, now working for *New York Magazine*. She wrote that the film was "a triumph of visualisation of the verbal visions and vignettes the poet created." She added: "No question but that Burton was born to recite Thomas' luxuriant and flowing poetic realities and lusciously lilting prose; his voice washes over the screen, penetrates to the very heart of the matter."

Many of the other critics also wrote favourably, including Pauline Kael in *The New Yorker*. "I enjoyed sitting back and listening. Sinclair brings the material emotionally close. You feel the affection of the cast and you share in it."

*Newsweek* magazine wasn't so charitable and missed the point of the film entirely. It thought the casting of Taylor as a Welsh prostitute was ridiculous and dismissed her performance: "Fortunately, Elizabeth Taylor, as Welsh as Cleopatra, plays only a small part; her harsh, yowling cadence a bit of intrusive tourism."

But the intellectuals of Wales loved it, and David Jenkins said: "I, for one, delighted in seeing Richard in something worthwhile."

There was more sadness in both of their lives when Taylor's long-standing secretary, Dick Hanley, who had been with Taylor since the start of her career, died at the age of 65. Hanley was homosexual and is thought to have succumbed to an early version of AIDS, a disease no one then had any notion of. Richard Burton had an extremely high regard for Hanley and his talent for diplomacy was greatly missed. He was replaced by a man called Raymond Vignale, whom Burton found he detested almost as much as he had liked Hanley.

After he left Britain, Burton found another turkey awaiting him. All great actors believe they can be great film directors, but they very rarely are. Burton realised his limitations on *Doctor Faustus* in Rome and never tried it again. But come 1971, there came another fine British actor, Peter Ustinov, seemingly keen to find out the hard way about the limits of his directing skills.

Ustinov had put together a project called *Hammersmith Is Out* with producer Alex Lucas and screenwriter Stan Whitmore. The film was to be made very cheaply and financed by a man called J. Cornelius Crean, who was apparently a manufacturer of mobile homes and fancied himself as a Hollywood mogul.

Ustinov sensed that Burton and Taylor, both down on their luck, might play the leads for very little money up front. He was right – especially when he agreed to film it in Mexico.

They were paid around US$300,000 each with a hefty share of the first dollar gross. The film was shot in Cuernavaca, not far from Puerto Vallarta, and filming began in May 1971.

It was a black comedy about a certified madman called Hammersmith, who escapes from an asylum and sets off on a destructive adventure across America making him and two of his associates rich and powerful. Burton played Hammersmith, roaming America doing evil and prospering, and Taylor played a blonde waitress who conspires with her boyfriend, played by Beau Bridges, to help front the evil empire he creates. The film begins and ends with Hammersmith in the asylum. Burton originally had high hopes for what was a reasonably interesting storyline which, handled properly, could have made a very good film.

But Ustinov was no director. He didn't know what he was doing and seemed unaware of his own limitations, thereby botching the film. With no effective guidance, Burton and Taylor were left to their own devices and were consequently terrible. Burton never did well playing an unsympathetic character and Taylor was too old for the part of the waitress.

It wasn't the worst film they ever played in together, but it was their worst performance.

As ever, Melvyn Bragg described it best: "They look like two heavyweight champions who had fought each other to exhaustion but cannot quit. She is out of it and Burton is further away from a character than ever in his life."

The film proved significant because it was, discounting cameos, the ninth and last cinema movie they starred in together. Their joint franchise, that had seen some big successes, was finally finished off by the box office returns of *Hammersmith Is Out*.

Release of the film was held up for a year because of a dispute between Cornelius Crean and producer Alex Lucas. Crean, who was no fool, couldn't believe the film was so bad and didn't want to pay the producer his fees.

Interestingly, Ustinov later tried to rewrite history and blamed Burton and Taylor for the film's failure. But the responsibility was all his, although, ironically, it did moderately well at the box office, especially outside America.

But the main loser was Elizabeth Taylor and, as her 40th birthday approached, her serious film career was over and she started drinking more heavily than normal to compensate. Without exception, Hollywood's biggest female stars are all highly attractive women whose careers fade with their birthdays. Most Hollywood actresses have mental crises around their 40th birthdays. Inevitably, when they are no longer the dream ticket and Hollywood rejects them, they fall into depression, start drinking and face mental health problems as a result; the most recent example being the travails that have befallen Catherine Zeta-Jones. Like Zeta-Jones in modern times, Taylor had a very long way to come down. And she suffered greatly for it.

Burton was so desperate not to be cast in anything on television that he took any movie offer that seemed remotely credible, including his next project, a biopic of a young Marshal Tito financed by the Yugoslav government entitled *The Battle of Sutjeska*. It was essentially a war film and he got the part because Tito was said to be struck by a "remarkable resemblance between him and the Welsh actor." Graham Jenkins called it "inspired casting" and insisted his brother did resemble the young Tito during the war.

The Yugoslavs offered Burton US$1 million and he couldn't turn it down as it was the first decent cash offer for almost three years. It was impossible for him to assess the script before signing because the 250-page script was written entirely in Serbo-Croat.

The script was finally translated and sent to the British producer John Heyman, who, at the time, was acting as Burton's informal manager. Heyman found the script "truly atrocious" and called up Burton and said: "Really, Richard, you can't do this." But Burton had no other offers and no choice if he wanted to work.

His contract was with the Yugoslav Ministry of Culture and the film was made by the Yugoslav government's own film company, staffed entirely by Yugoslav nationals. The producer, Nikola Popovic, also offered Taylor a cameo role but she wisely declined to have anything to do with the film after reading the script.

*The Battle of Sutjeska* told the story of how Marshal Tito and his army were under siege in a mountain stronghold surrounded by overwhelming German forces during the Second World War.

The original screenplay was so poor that before filming began, Burton called in Wolf Mankowitz to rewrite it. Mankowitz advised Nikola Popovic to buy the film rights to a book called *The Embattled Mountain* by William Deakin, on which he could base a new screenplay. The changes caused the budget to rise alarmingly.

In September 1971, the Kalizma cruised into Cavtat, a harbour town south of Dubrovnik, with Richard Burton on board ready to start work. The Burton-Taylor entourage, some 30 people, were put up free of charge at Belgrade's finest hotel. Burton commuted to the location on President Tito's own helicopter.

Filming did not start well because of poor organisation and Burton was forced to draft in professionals from London to help. With no proper control over the budget, the cost had soared and, eventually, the money allocated to it completely ran out with barely three quarters of the film made. Production was suddenly suspended and it would be another three years before the film was released.

Burton was relieved as he had grown very frightened of the daily helicopter rides into the mountain location. Each day, he would be flown by military helicopter to the movie's location at the site of the original World War II battle in which Tito and 20,000 partisans broke through the German siege.

On one occasion, Taylor was waving "goodbye" to her husband when she had a premonition and ordered them out of the helicopter just as he was about to take off with Ron Berkeley also aboard. She later wrote about the incident in a book: "Suddenly, something came over me: 'Guys, get out of there – Richard, get out of there, just get out.'" Burton apparently did as he was told and got into another helicopter. And according to Taylor, the helicopter crashed in the mountains later that day, killing everyone on board.

There was a more tangible incident which Brook Williams recalled to the writer Michael Munn: "We had finished filming for the day at a place called Kupari, and we all piled into the helicopter – Richard, Ron Berkeley, Gianni Bozzacchi and our interpreter, a nice lady called Vesna. The cloud was so low that the pilot could barely see. Rich, Vesna and I sat behind the pilot, and Ron and Gianni sat at the rear. We were barely passing mountain peaks on both sides. Then, suddenly, there was a complete white-out – nothing could be seen but the cloud. It was terrifying. And then it began to rain – a torrent. Then the pilot realised we were heading straight for a mountain peak. He was a good pilot and flung the helicopter to the right to miss the peak and found we were heading into another mountain. Then we pulled to the left and just missed the rock face. The co-pilot was keeping lookout; we were flying blind. I shut my eyes tight. I couldn't bear to look. Ron had already got himself into a crash position, curled up on the floor in a tight ball. I could hear Richard whispering: 'Holy shit, holy shit.'

"Suddenly, we seemed to drop – I thought we were going down, but the pilot had decided to get as low as he could as quickly as he could so he could see the mountain road, which we followed. It was harrowing. And I'd never been so pleased to see a road in my life."

Eventually, the film did get finished in 1973 but wasn't released outside of Yugoslavia and, aside from a few showings at the New York Cultural Centre in 1976, hardly anyone saw it.

Although there were no offers of work for Taylor, offers now began to flow in for Burton as the global economy picked up and as producers sensed that his financial demands had become more reasonable.

Burton still had big drawing power for movie financiers, and the directing and producing partnership of Joseph Losey and Norman Priggen came calling for him to play the lead role in their new film, called *The Assassination of Trotsky*. The film was financed by a consortium of investors and they wanted Burton and were prepared to pay him a million dollars. Burton had actually been Losey's third choice after Dirk Bogarde and Marlon Brando, had both turned him down.

The storyline was simple enough; it was about the murder of Leon Trotsky, the former Russian leader in exile at his hideaway in Mexico in 1940, by agents of the current leader Joseph Stalin – a true story. Trotsky was murdered with an ice pick by a man whom he had befriended. The screenplay was by the novelist Nicholas Mosley.

Despite the bad experience on another Losey/Priggen film, *Boom*, which had started his Hollywood decline, Burton trusted Losey and Priggen and thought the material had promise so he signed up without seeing a script. If truth be told, he was just grateful someone wanted to pay him at all. His co-stars were Alain Delon and Romy Schneider.

The exteriors of the film were all shot in Mexico but the Mexican government intervened, worried about its relations with Russia. The Mexican president himself had to approve scenes shot in the country. Consequently, a lot of the film was shot in Italy, where a complete replica of Trotsky's villa in Mexico was built on a Rome sound stage.

Burton did most of his filming in Rome and occupied a suite at the Grand Hotel for the six weeks for which he was required. Although Burton grew a pointed beard, he didn't look much like Trotsky and, again, was miscast.

Burton was trying to give up drink once and for all during the early part of filming. Penny Junor, in her biography of Burton, maintains that he was a poorer actor when sober: "Burton was not so good when he was sober. He was too tense, awkward in his movements and hesitant on dialogue. The character did have long speeches but, under normal circumstances, Richard could have coped with them. Sober, he had to break them up and take them bit by bit."

At least that was until Peter O'Toole arrived in Rome and Burton missed a day of filming. When he didn't turn up on set, Priggen remembered finding Burton and O'Toole in the bar of the Grand Hotel "drunk as skunks, lying on the floor, fondly embracing one another and singing happy birthday to each other."

A furious Priggen ordered O'Toole out, and with the aid of the bell boy, carried Burton to the bed in his suite upstairs. Priggen was amazed when he made it to the set the following day.

But Burton was not the only one in trouble with drink. Joe Losey was having problems with his second marriage and brought his problems to work. He had also taken to the bottle. The film suffered when his mind wandered, as Burton recalled: "Joe is definitely not himself. He doesn't seem to know the script as well as he usually does. Time and time again, I or the continuity girl have to remind him of things that are very obvious."

As a result, it was a very poor film and more like a documentary than a drama. It was labelled "worthy but uninspiring" by Burton. Predictably, the film was panned by the critics, and one suggested it should be marketed as a "cure for insomnia." David Jenkins went to see it in Wales and came away very confused: "The subject matter was of academic rather than popular interest...instead of making a puzzling and complex character fascinating for the audience, the film only confuses and, unforgivably, bores."

The movie's reception was so bad it was actually booed at the New York Film Festival.

*The Assassination of Trotsky* was Burton's fifth box office dog in a row. No career could possibly survive that, but somehow Burton's did. Although Hollywood no longer wanted to know him, he somehow kept moving from film to film, being paid to make movies that no one wanted to see.

And there was one very happy moment during filming when Michael Wilding Jr presented his mother with Leyla, Elizabeth Taylor's first grandchild. As his wife cradled the baby, Burton was delighted for her but couldn't help wondering what might have been.

# AND GOD CREATED BURTON

# CHAPTER 48

# The seven year itch

## *Elizabeth turns 40*

### 1972

Elizabeth Taylor's 40th birthday on 27th February 1972 presented Richard Burton with a real problem – how to celebrate? The filming of *Bluebeard* was in full swing; he was stuck in Hungary and his options were very limited. So he made the best of it and decided to throw the party of all parties over the weekend of 24th to 28th February in Budapest.

In truth, Budapest in February was not a great venue for a party – but they were stuck; he couldn't leave because of filming and had to make the best of it – and they did.

The party had two purposes: to celebrate the birthday and to make a big splash in the press in order to confirm that the Burtons were still a force in show business. They had never had any need to do that before and had always had the opposite problem of attracting too much attention. Now they needed the publicity and it was a mark of just how drastically things had changed for them that they felt the need to pursue it.

Burton also wanted to make his wife feel special for the weekend. By the seventh year of their marriage, he had been getting an itch and had started seeing other women again. Not nearly as many as in the old days, but still enough to feel some guilt. As their eighth wedding anniversary approached, he was still keen to keep the marriage working.

Burton decided to make the venue the Inter-Continental Hotel, where they were staying. The old Duna hotel had been rebranded as an Inter-Continental but it still was well below normal international standards. Taylor did her own quick fix and hired the designer Larry Barcher, from Paris, to redecorate the Inter-Continental Hotel function rooms.

The invitation sent out by telegram read: "We would love you to come to Budapest, as our guest, for the weekend of 26th and 27th February to help me celebrate my 40th birthday. The hotel is very Hilton but there are some fun places to go. Dress slacks for Saturday night in some dark cellar and something gay and pretty for Sunday night. Dark glasses for languorous in between. Lots of love, Elizabeth and Richard. P. S.: Could you RSVP as soon as possible to Inter-Continental Hotel, Budapest, so I know how many rooms to book."

The trick of the party was to get as many A-list celebrities as possible to come. But only a small handful responded, and of the 50 or so invited, only David Niven, Michael Caine, Ringo Starr, Susannah York and Frankie Howerd responded positively. The rest were elsewhere and committed to something – or, more likely, didn't fancy spending a weekend in Budapest at the height of winter. The words "very Hilton" seemed to put off a lot of people.

People were also put off by the Burtons themselves. A lot of their long-standing friends had been cut off from them by the entourage and when they suddenly, out of the blue, got an invitation to attend Taylor's 40th, they were disinclined to go. They had always blamed Taylor for cutting Burton off from his old friends, and the absence of people like John Gielgud and Laurence Olivier spoke volumes. The truth was that they were snubbed by a lot of people who declined to come as a sort of revenge over the way they had been treated in the past.

The response was very disappointing and the party was only saved by Princess Grace of Monaco's acceptance. She was committed to come, as Burton and Taylor had gone out of their way to attend her 40th celebrations in November 1969 three years earlier.

The party list was bolstered by lesser names such as Emlyn Williams, Stephen Spender and Victor Spinetti, as well as old friends such as Neville Coghill and Gianni Bulgari, and seven foreign ambassadors – but the celebrity count was very thin, indeed. All the children came except for Michael Wilding, who wasn't really getting along with his mother at that point.

The cast of *Bluebeard*, mostly women, were also invited until Taylor disinvited them all at the last minute. She believed many of them were having, or wanted to have affairs with her husband and didn't want them at her party. In the end, of the seven girls whom Taylor called the "*Bluebeard* broads", only Raquel Welch gatecrashed the party.

Taylor took care and got a lot of pleasure planning her gala weekend. The celebrations started when Norman Parkinson arrived ten days earlier to take her official 40th birthday photograph. Parkinson was the top fashion photographer of the day. He positioned Taylor and her husband on a balcony high above the Danube and decked them out in matching black fur coats with the Krupp diamond ring prominent.

The photo was spectacular for the time and was sent out with an embargo of

27th February. It was duly printed in every newspaper on her birthday.

Although no journalists were invited to the party, they were encouraged to come to Budapest by Burton and Taylor's publicists. Press conferences and photo calls were arranged, and Burton and Taylor showed off the US$900,000 Taj Mahal diamond Burton had purchased for her birthday. Both Burton and Taylor went out of their way to make themselves available to the press as they talked up themselves and the party.

A BEA Trident jet had been chartered to bring over English guests, and a small squadron of private jets brought in guests from European airports. All the guests had to do was turn up at their chosen airports and get on board a chartered private plane.

Marjorie Lee at The Dorchester organised the British end, where the vast majority of guests met up at London on Friday morning to get on board the Trident.

The previous afternoon, 14 members of the Jenkins family had taken the train to London and were collected from Paddington Station by four Rolls-Royces. They had their own party that night, and the following morning were driven to London airport and boarded what they thought was a normal flight to Budapest.

The Jenkins family were unaware it was a specially chartered flight, and only when they were airborne, half an hour into the flight, did they realise everyone on board were Burton's friends. As David Jenkins remembered: "Gradually, the connection dawned on us: the entire aircraft was occupied by Richard's and Elizabeth's guests. Not surprisingly, there was a festive atmosphere right from the moment of take-off."

At Budapest, Burton himself was standing on the runway to meet the plane. Despite the low A-list acceptance, he was really looking forward to having many of his friends and family in the same place for four days. As they all embraced on the tarmac, David Jenkins told his brother that he was looking forward to meeting Princess Grace and recalled what happened next: "No sooner had we arrived at the hotel than I was whisked down to her suite to be introduced. I was not disappointed. She was charming and excellent company, as well as being almost startlingly beautiful."

Princess Grace had become great friends with the Burtons over the years. She was genuinely fascinated by the Jenkins brothers and they all got to know her well. Princess Grace was also hugely attracted to Richard Burton, and always had been. However, she would be the last person to take that attraction any further. But she couldn't help feeling it like so many of the women at the party that weekend. At 46, Burton was in decline physically but still immensely attractive to women, which is why Taylor was so determined to keep his co-stars in *Bluebeard* away from the party.

Ed Dmytryk, the director of *Bluebeard*, observed it: "There is no doubt he had this quite phenomenal effect. Whatever the case, they fell for him."

The guests that did come were soon delighted they had. The Hungarians made them feel very welcome. They were all given cards identifying them as belonging to the Burton party and giving them unlimited free access to all the hotel services. Burton kept telling his guests he hoped they hadn't brought any money, because they wouldn't be needing it.

Taylor even arranged for the hairdressers in the main lobby to stay open 24 hours a day.

To brighten up the drab guest rooms, Taylor personally decorated each one with flowers and Burton organised the drinks according to his guests' preferences. There was what was described as a loaded tray in each bedroom, bearing champagne, whisky, wine and vodka. Burton had resolved not to drink at all that weekend but he didn't intend any of his guests to remain sober.

The first night was low-key to give everyone time to settle in, and everyone was invited up for drinks in the Burtons' top floor suite so they could all get to know each other. In an adjacent room, Burton set a cinema up to play films of old Welsh rugby internationals, borrowed from the BBC.

That night, Burton took personal delight in introducing Maria, now 11-years-old, to her Welsh relatives, many of whom were meeting her for the first time. Maria was surprised they all spoke to each other in Welsh. They all thought it uncanny how much Maria resembled Kate and wondered if there was something they didn't know – in Welsh, of course.

On Saturday night, the real celebrations began. The party was held in the hotel's old wine cellars. The supper buffet was authentic Hungarian goulash, sauerkraut and sausages.

Basements always make good party venues, and this one was perfect. Taylor had gone to a great deal of trouble to dress up the basement to a theme she called "candlelight and cobwebs." The fake cobwebs were spectacular and had been created by *Bluebeard*'s set designers. Burton told his guests that the "cobwebs cost a dollar a time to put up."

Music was provided by a top Hungarian pop group whose favourite number was 'I Left My Heart In San Francisco', which they sang at least a dozen times. But when the Welsh contingent started singing hymns, the band quickly picked up the tunes and were soon playing along as if they had spent weeks rehearsing.

On the stroke of midnight, to officially mark Taylor turning 40, 'Happy Birthday' was sung, first in English, then in Welsh. The Welsh version reverberated around the cellar and Princess Grace dropped her regal bearing and joined in. She told Burton she loved being surrounded by what she called "real people."

Taylor made an impromptu speech, saying; "I think it is fantastic to be 40. 40 always sounds important. The big four-o. It's halfway or more through life, but I find it appealing. I've always wanted to be older." David Jenkins recalled her speech: "She sounded as if she meant it, I thought. Not that she looked anything like middle-aged; she positively sparkled all weekend, and not just because of the diamond. She and Richard seemed fine together. He was drinking, but not to excess, and threw himself wholeheartedly into hosting the event."

The evening was a little marred by Emlyn Williams' 37-year-old son Alan, who had come with his recently widowed father and his brother, Brook. During the course of the evening, he made it clear in a very loud voice that he strongly disapproved of the junketing. He was left-leaning and after a few drinks began voicing his opposition to the party, to anyone who would listen. He demanded to know why so much money was being wasted in idle frivolity while many Hungarians were wondering where to find their next meal. At first, Burton ignored him and told other guests they must "tolerate" his views. Burton dismissed him as a "left-wing pinko bogeyman", whatever that was and explained he was a novelist who had written about the Hungarian revolution and that his "heart was in the right place."

But he was only tolerated up to a certain point. Eventually, he buttonholed Elizabeth Taylor and asked her how much she knew about the Hungarian Revolution of 1956. When it appeared she knew very little, he started lecturing her in a loud voice and Burton was forced to intervene. He sought to quieten him with the minimum unpleasantness but when Taylor started getting upset, he signalled to Bob Wilson and Gaston Sanz. They grabbed both his arms, lifted his feet half an inch from the floor and removed a protesting Williams from the party and dumped him outside in the icy cold night. Burton considered throwing him out of his room at the hotel, but in deference to his father, didn't.

Taylor also had a left-leaning rebel son who had stayed away from the party in protest, so she knew first-hand how difficult it could be.

Sensing discord, a journalist called Nicholas Tomalin grabbed him that night whilst he was still in party mood and Alan Williams let fly. More or less every word he said was reported in newspapers the next morning, making a bad situation worse – especially when Williams called Elizabeth Taylor "a beautiful doughnut covered in diamonds and paint." The newspapers focused on him instead of the party.

To defuse the situation, Burton announced he was making a US$45,000 donation to the United Nations children's charity Unicef, the exact same cost as the party. It worked and Williams' protests were quickly forgotten.

But it was very embarrassing for Emlyn Williams, and the following morning, walking by the Danube, he attempted to talk some sense into his son, telling him this was neither the time nor the place. Williams made his son write an apology to Elizabeth Taylor, and the affair blew over as Alan Williams stopped drinking for the weekend and sat quietly keeping himself to himself.

The official day of celebration was Sunday, and the main party was held that night in the rooftop restaurant on the 12th floor of the hotel. The room was decorated like a nightclub with thousands of red and gold balloons and masses of white lilies, hyacinths, cyclamen, daffodils and red tulips, described as "an explosion of flowers" in newspapers. A 30-piece orchestra had been specially flown in from Paris to entertain guests and the atmosphere was very special.

The Burtons couldn't disguise their joy at having Princess Grace sharing the occasion with them.

At around ten o'clock, Burton grabbed a microphone and announced "a surprise for Princess Grace." He read out what he called a "proclamation" inviting her to become Princess of Wales as well as of Monaco. The document was passed around, duly read and solemnly signed by each member of the Jenkins family. Princess Grace received it shortly after midnight and was moved to tears by Burton's reading of the proclamation, which was followed by the emotional rendering by the Jenkins brothers of "We'll keep a welcome in the hillside." After that, she led a conga line around the ballroom.

Edward Dmytryk didn't really know the Burtons that well, but said afterwards: "It was the most wonderful party I have ever been to."

It garnered the column inches around the world which made it worthwhile, and for a period the Burtons were making headlines again. When the guests departed on Monday afternoon, many were in a sorry state after four days of bingeing. The Jenkins brothers returned to their regular jobs in South Wales and faced a few days of coming down from their high. It was a weekend they remembered for the rest of their lives.

# AND GOD CREATED BURTON

# CHAPTER 49

# Total career collapse

## *Four more turkeys*

### 1972 -1973

Richard Burton and Elizabeth Taylor arrived in Budapest in the first week of February 1972 and checked into the presidential suite of the Hotel Inter-Continental. As soon as they arrived, Taylor launched into organising her 40th birthday party, and their few weeks in the city was dominated by the preparations.

Burton had been really looking forward to being in Budapest for the ten weeks of the shoot, as he mused in his diary: "I am looking forward to it with excitement. The very name Budapest smacks of romance and tragedy and wild Magyar music. It cannot, simply cannot, be dull. Regardless of friends' warnings that it is the most depressing capital in Europe, I shall start out, at least, refusing to be talked into disliking it before I find out for myself. And again, the communist experiment is eternally fascinating. There must be some alternative to the idiocy and rat-race murderousness of 'democracy' and I'm pretty sure that communism is not it, but it is different so one more look at one more communist country."

Burton was there to film *Bluebeard*, a comedic drama that Graham Jenkins called his brother's "fourth shot at giving new meaning to the phrase 'disaster movie.'"

The deal had been put together by the producing father and son team of Alexander and Ilya Salkind and would be directed by Edward Dmytryk. It was a good team and should have guaranteed a good movie. But they were at the mercy of their financiers, who pulled the purse strings.

It was financed by Hungarian and Italian investors who believed a film with Richard Burton frolicking with a bevy of naked and half-naked women for two hours couldn't fail to do well.

The Salkinds' method of financing was to get investors to cover the budget and then seek a quick return by collecting money from distributors around the world up front. Burton's name helped to pull off some of those deals.

The film was based on the novel *Bluebeard* by Charles Perrault, a remake of a 1944 film. It told the story of a wealthy aristocrat, a count, who murders his many wives to cover up the fact that he is sexually impotent and how, when his latest wife discovers her predecessors in a freezer, she tries to avoid the same fate.

*Bluebeard* was Burton's 40th film in 28 years and was the sort of movie he swore he would never do. He decided upon it simply because he had no other offers and had never before made a horror film. But the film turned out to have very little horror in it. Graham Jenkins called it a "blatant attempt to cash in on the soft porn market." When Dmytryk was asked about the insertion of nudity, he explained it away by saying: "If I didn't do it, someone else would, so I did a few scenes but kept it tasteful."

The financial deal was not a great one. Burton was paid US$80,000 up front but had a percentage right off the top from the very first ticket sold, as Ed Dmytryk said: "There was no way he could lose. Whether the film lost money or not, he was bound to make a large bundle."

Once again, Burton didn't read the script before he signed up. According to Dmytryk, he didn't seem to care what it was, provided that he was working: "He had made several poor films in a row, but he made no complaints about their quality. Whether it was good or bad, he worked in the same professional way. If he sold himself, he gave full money's worth."

But filming was dominated by Burton's persistent drinking, which was steadily getting worse as his marriage to Elizabeth Taylor began to deteriorate. During the shooting of *Bluebeard*, he relied heavily on his chauffeur Gaston Sanz, who came to his rescue time and time again. When Burton became very drunk, he often turned nasty and had no discrimination. He needed protection from the people he insulted, as Ed Dmytryk recalled: "I had worked with other stars who drank, but none who started as early as Burton did. Spencer Tracy's were periodic. Gable didn't start his drinking until 5:30 in the afternoon, so you could get a day's work in. Monty Clift didn't get mean, he would just fall apart and you'd say 'cut' and wrap for the day."

But Dmytryk found Burton to be something else entirely.

Dmytryk says many days and half days were lost because of Burton's drinking. He remembered when Kate Burton and Liza Todd visited the set together and saw what was happening to their father: "One morning, they both came to his dressing room and pleaded with him to stop drinking. He promised he would, but he wasn't able to keep the promise for long. It must have preyed on him, not being able to keep his promise to two such wonderful kids. He hadn't yet reached the point of where he was aware of it, but it was his body's need now. And from his youthful appearance when I first met him, I could see him getting older week by week. We covered it up with the usual lighting tricks."

There was an incident during filming when Burton attended a dinner at the British Embassy. Among the other guests were the Swiss and Dutch ambassadors with their wives plus the American attaché. It started well, with Burton reciting Dylan Thomas to the teenage sons of the British ambassador.

At dinner, he didn't touch his food, but kept drinking and, then, without any warning, he turned to the wife of the Swiss ambassador, who was sitting next to him, and said to her: "You remind me quite distinctly of a hungry vulture." The ambassador quickly changed the subject of conversation in order to get Burton's attention. But Burton fixed his eyes on the Swiss ambassador and said: "You Swiss are a very bad lot." It was an extraordinary thing to say considering he was living in Switzerland at the time. His remarks were the makings of a diplomatic incident until Taylor said sharply to her husband: "Richard, Richard." He suddenly pulled himself together and said: "I think I'd better go home." Gaston Sanz was standing by for just this eventuality and quickly lifted his boss from his chair and escorted him to the car. Sanz took him back to the Inter-Continental and put him to bed. Then he went back for Taylor, who, as cool as a cucumber, carried on enjoying the dinner party. Dmytryk, who was also at the dinner party, said: "Elizabeth seemed to drink probably as much as he did, but she wasn't nearly as much affected by it, so far as one could see. She was stronger than Richard in every way."

And alcohol caught both of them out in a big way when David Frost arrived to film an interview for American television. They should never have gone ahead with the interview in the condition they were in, but they trusted Frost and thought he was "one of them." They believed he would edit out the nonsense. But he didn't, and the public spectacle that appeared on television – watched by some 25 million people – was highly embarrassing. It defined Richard Burton's image and reputation for a whole decade. It was the *Playboy* scenario all over again, but much, much worse. Dmytryk recalled: "Richard was at ease and loquacious in the interview; Liz was very shy. She had been drinking, and it didn't show at first, but then her speech got slower and there were long pauses between her words. That was the only sign she'd had too much. Frost could have edited the tape so it wouldn't show, and it was mean of him that he didn't."

Taylor was drinking Jack Daniels from a beaker during the actual interview. But she came out of it better than Burton.

# AND GOD CREATED BURTON

Aside from the interview with David Frost, the filming of *Bluebeard* became Elizabeth Taylor's worst nightmare. For the entire film, her husband was surrounded by beautiful young women at exactly the same moment she was losing her allure in her 40th year. It was made worse by the fact that he appeared to have lost none of his sex appeal. It created a huge pressure cooker in Budapest, as Taylor fought on multiple fronts to keep her man.

The women, whom Taylor called the *"Bluebeard* broads", were led by the international sex symbol Raquel Welch and sexy French actress Nathalie Delon. In fact, all eight wives of *Bluebeard* were stunning women; among them were Virna Lisi, Joey Heatherton and Sybil Danning. The rumour was that Burton chased them all.

Burton happily played the field during the film and thoroughly enjoyed the attentions of the so-called *Bluebeard* broads. Raquel Welch was his first target. No one knows for sure what happened between them but the crew were fairly certain something did. In the old days, Burton would have made no secret of his conquests but now he had to be discreet. Dmytryk said: "I know he was very much taken with Raquel Welch. Whatever happened between them, I can't say. I wasn't there with them." Burton eventually admitted he was unfaithful to his wife during filming and that he was attracted to the younger women in the film.

Ed Dmytryk confirmed that Burton retained his remarkable skills with the opposite sex. At Taylor's birthday celebrations, he remembered when a girlfriend of one of the guests danced with him and they talked for 10 minutes. She came over to Dmytryk afterwards, starry-eyed, and just blurted out: "He loves me." Dmytryk said this was not an isolated example: "He had this amazing effect on women. He would talk to them for a few minutes and they'd be convinced that either he'd fallen in love with them or would very soon. I never could quite figure it out, but it was all in the way he looked at and talked with them."

But it was on the film set every day that Taylor faced the most competition. The first problem came during a scene with a local actress called Dora Zakablukowa, who was naked in bed with Burton. Taylor, who was watching, believed that Zakablukowa was putting far too much effort into the scene. She suddenly snapped, and in full view of the crew and her astonished husband, walked up and slapped Zakablukowa round the face mid-scene with the cameras still rolling. It was truly extraordinary and the footage of it still exists somewhere. Taylor said afterwards by way of explanation: "There was someone who put too much passion in certain scenes and, moreover, she was naked. I smacked her face for her pains. And Richard, I don't know how many plates I broke over his head." Ed Dmytryk recalled it well: "Richard and the actress were enjoying it, and Elizabeth saw what was happening and, well, she landed one on the girl." He added: "Richard was behaving very oddly. It was like he was trying to goad Elizabeth. Or maybe he had just lost interest in her."

Graham Jenkins, who witnessed many of the shenanigans in Budapest, said: "His acting in bed was convincing enough to cause Elizabeth some irritation, but to those who lacked a personal interest, the sequence of attempted couplings was hilarious."

But it was not Dora Zakablukowa or Raquel Welch whom Taylor had to worry about. During filming, it was Burton's burgeoning relationship with Nathalie Delon that became the real threat to their marriage. One night, he whisked her off to dinner after a night shoot and left Taylor as well as the director and crew waiting on the set for him to return. The two of them just walked off the set and into Burton's Rolls-Royce, leaving everyone else wondering what had happened. It was extraordinary behaviour.

Taylor was so furious that she called Aristotle Onassis, who, it just so happened, had called her earlier with an invitation to dinner in Rome. Onassis was in Rome without his wife, Jackie Kennedy, and he immediately sent his jet to Budapest to collect Taylor.

When she checked into the Grand Hotel in Rome later that night, she phoned Burton in their suite and screamed at him: "Get that woman out of my bed." Burton looked round at Delon and wondered how she could possibly have known. He denied it and put the phone down.

He realised then that Taylor had spies everywhere amongst their entourage reporting back to her.

As Michael Munn, one of Burton's biographers, said: "There wasn't a move he made that she didn't know about." Burton suspected he knew who had betrayed him to his wife and fired both of them the next morning. But when Taylor returned, she hired both of them back.

However, there was trouble on the set the next day. Dmytryk was stunned by Burton's walk off the set and cancelled the next day's shooting whilst he awaited Burton's explanations. The following afternoon, after he had sobered up and Delon had returned to her own room, Burton was horrified at his conduct and sent Dmytryk a note, which read: "Dear Eddie, please believe that the Richard you saw last night is not the real Richard Burton."

Dmytryk was still furious and refused to take Burton's phone calls: "He kept calling and calling, and I wouldn't answer my phone. But finally I did, and he apologised profusely, and we went back to work the next day."

Despite all that, *Bluebeard* was a happy set and filming ended on time and on schedule. But it was a lousy film, as Dmytryk readily admitted: "I know *Bluebeard* didn't turn out well for any of us, but we were happy making it."

But by the end of the shoot, Burton's drinking was getting out of control. He appeared to be undergoing a classic mid-life crisis. Once he had begun drinking again, he became frustrated, and halfway through the shoot, his brother Ivor finally died. He also seemed to be tiring of his wife and wished he was a single man again. He said: "Once I started being attracted to other women, I knew the game was up." Indeed, it was from that moment that the marriage began to crumble.

After *Bluebeard* wrapped at the end of April, there was once again no more work on the horizon apart from finishing off the *Battle of Sutkjeska*, which didn't take long.

Burton was now so desperate that he did something he had long resisted; he accepted a role in his first 'made for television' film. He dressed it up as fulfilling a commitment to Harlech TV, where he and Taylor were both substantial shareholders.

The project was a two-part miniseries called *Divorce His, Divorce Hers*. It was two 90-minute films about the break-up of a marriage seen from the perspectives of both the husband and the wife. The films were produced by John Heyman and the main funding came from ABC network in the United States, and Harlech had very little to do with it. Heyman raised half a million dollars, which was thought to be Burton's money, and a million came from ABC. Harlech only put in US$75,000 and was very much the junior partner. One of ABC's conditions was that Taylor played opposite Burton in the lead female role.

ABC at the time was run by Barry Diller and Michael Eisner, who had invented the made-for-TV movie concept. They thought that the combination of Burton and Taylor in a made-for-TV movie would be a real ratings winner in America. And when they suggested Taylor as a condition for the financing, neither man could hardly believe it when the answer came back as a "yes." They simply couldn't understand why stars of Burton's and Taylor's calibre would want to make such a low-rent movie for ABC.

The plan was to make the films in Britain, but production was switched to Rome and Munich to suit Burton and Taylor's personal tax considerations. Taylor had begun making a film in London called *Night Watch* immediately after *Bluebeard* and had used up most of her time quota.

John Osborne was hired to write an original script, and because it could be set anywhere, Burton wanted the story to be international. But Osborne wrote the script his way, as he recalled: "The most important aspect of it seemed to be that most of the locations should be in Mexico, Acapulco or the south of France, where the Burtons' yacht was conveniently moored. I ignored this instruction. When I presented the script, a kind of resentful hysteria seemed to break out."

That was a good analysis of what happened and, when he ignored the brief, Osborne was fired. John Hopkins, a specialist television writer, was hired to rewrite Osborne's script.

To direct, Burton and Heyman selected Waris Hussein, a 34-year-old Indian-born director. He was one of the talented new breed of television directors then emerging. On paper, he was a very good choice, but in reality, he was too young to take on a big international assignment. He was simply not up to directing two big stars like Burton and Taylor, both of whom were at their arrogant worst during the making of the movie.

Throughout filming, they were arguing and drinking as their marriage disintegrated before Hussein's eyes. It became apparent that Burton and Taylor were playing dangerously close to home in a film about a marriage break-up as seen by both partners. Burton and Taylor's rows, during their drunken lunches, continually held up filming. They appeared to have no shame and the rows they were having on set were almost overlapping the rows they had in the film – as Burton's brother Graham said: "There were times when they hardly knew whose lives they were talking about."

Burton behaved very badly during filming, refusing to acknowledge the schedule and turning up on set when he felt like it. When he decided he'd done enough filming for the day, he simply walked off the set where Gaston Sanz was waiting to drive him home. There were no goodbyes; he simply left.

Hussein admitted: "It was a bad time for all concerned. I think that a lot of what happened was due to their own personal unhappiness." Many years later, Hussein gave a long interview to Paul Ferris and refused to blame anyone but himself for what happened. "From early on, it was clear it was going to be a disaster. I suppose I should have left then. I couldn't have closed down the production, but I could have walked away from it."

It became clear that Burton was very close to the edge of his sanity throughout filming. Heyman and Hussein were worried that imposing any discipline might push him over the edge and they would lose the film. Around this time, Burton admitted for the first time that he was an alcoholic and that he was seeking help, as he said: "I need all the help I can get. I'm talking to doctors who know about this sort of thing. They say I can pull round."

Despite their difficulties, Burton and Taylor both put on a united front for Burton's 47th birthday. It coincided with the day filming ended and there was a joint wrap/birthday party in Munich. Taylor arranged for a huge picture of both of them to be hoisted above the set with a bubble on it from her mouth that read: "Happy birthday, Richard. I love you." For his birthday present, she bought him an original copy of a book by Goethe, although Taylor had no idea who he was. As she admitted: "I don't know who Goethe is, but I hope he likes it."

When the two films had wrapped, their co-star, Carrie Nye, gave a devastating behind-the-scenes interview to *Time* magazine, in which she told the truth about what had gone on. The article was terrible for the Burtons but didn't hurt the ratings when both films aired on successive nights on ABC on the 6th and 7th February 1973. As Diller and Eisner predicted, they scored very high ratings although both were very poor films. *Time* magazine's critic called it: "A matched pair of thrilling disasters." *Variety* wrote: "*Divorce His, Divorce Hers* holds all the joy of standing by at an autopsy."

As soon as filming finished on *Divorce His, Divorce Hers*, the Christmas holidays couldn't come soon enough and the Burtons went to Puerto Vallarta to recover.

But as 1972 closed, so too, effectively, did their marriage and it was never to be the same again.

Astonishingly, it took Burton three full years to make the break from Elizabeth Taylor, and at the end of it, he would be exhausted and a broken man and right back where he had begun.

But before then, for the next three years, Richard Burton would endure a miserable existence as his personal life and his career went down the toilet. It would be 1976 before he would emerge from a three-year nightmare which would have finished a lesser man off for good. But Burton was not a lesser man, as he had proved time and time again. But he would need every ounce of resilience and more for what was to unfold over the next three years.

# TOTAL CAREER COLLAPSE

# AND GOD CREATED BURTON

# CHAPTER 50

# The end of Elizabeth Taylor

## *... for the time being*

### 1973 - 1974

And so the three-year saga began: two break-ups, two reconciliations, two divorces and a remarriage would take place before it was all over. It was played out in two parts over three years; three years of some extreme highs but mainly excruciating lows.

What was the point of having so much talent, so much money and enjoying so much good luck if it all ended like this? It was a question Richard Burton asked himself many times in those three years.

During this period, he was trying desperately to shake off what he saw as his three destructive addictions: alcohol, cigarettes and Elizabeth Taylor. And at the time, he wasn't at all sure which was the most dangerous. What he did know was that all three were slowly killing him.

Somehow, Burton pulled himself together over the holidays and in early 1973, he was well enough to travel to Rome where he was due to make a film for Carlo Ponti called *Massacre in Rome*. He was to star with Italian heart throb, Marcello Mastroianni. Taylor had also managed to get a film being shot in Rome at the same time. It was called *Ash Wednesday* and was being produced by Dominick Dunne.

In his 48th year, it was clear Burton could no longer drink like he used to. There was a physical problem and also a mental one – he discovered a 47-year-old drunk was not tolerated the way a 30-year-old or even a 40-year-old drunk might be. If he had led a normal life, the problem would have been solved for him. But because he was Richard Burton, he could do what he liked and there was no brake on his activities. He was able to get away with it because of people like Gaston Sanz, Brook Williams and Bob Wilson, who continually covered for him and plucked him from the situations he got himself into. Time and time again, they stepped in to rescue him from himself before he did real damage and before he suffered the consequences.

But conversely, they were also responsible for his drinking. Wilson was there with a constant supply of vodka; Williams also. When he wanted a drink, they just brought him one and didn't question it.

And he found there was relentless pressure to carry on working even though he no longer needed the money. They had over 50 people on their payroll and that drove the relentless filmmaking and the need for more and more activity. Certainly, financially, there was no longer any need. Even the movies where he received no upfront fee were proving highly lucrative. Of all the films he had done since 1969, only *Under Milk Wood* and *Villain* had been losers for him financially.

Now, Carlo Ponti, one of Italy's top film producers but probably better known for being the husband of Sophia Loren, had come to Burton's rescue with the offer of *Massacre in Rome*.

Ponti was the only producer who would employ Burton after details of what had happened on *Bluebeard* and *Divorce His Divorce Hers* got around. David Frost's television interview in America and Carrie Nye's devastating article in *Time* magazine had rendered him virtually untouchable. Burton was very grateful to Ponti and they became lifelong friends as a result.

*Massacre in Rome* was potentially a great film. It was thought to be a run-of-the-mill war film, but was in fact a tense, thought-provoking drama that deserved much more attention than it received.

The film was based on the recently published book *Death in Rome* by Robert Katz, which Ponti had snapped up before it was even printed, recognising a great story.

The film was set in 1944 during the Second World War and was based on the true story of the killing of 320 Italian hostages. It was a wartime reprisal following an incident when Italian partisans killed 32 SS troops in Rome. The reprisal killings were on Hitler's direct orders using a ratio of ten Italians for every one German. Precisely 320 Italians were shot at the Ardeatine caves in Rome on 24th March 1944. Burton played the German Gestapo colonel ordered to carry out the executions on randomly selected victims.

The book, when it was published, was controversial because it recorded how the Vatican had stood by and issued no condemnation. The Pope's family sued Robert Katz for criminal libel and he was accused of defaming the memory of the Pope Pius XII. The case lasted seven years before being dismissed.

Although filmed on a tight budget, the director George Pan Cosmatos was able to get a great performance out of Burton, undoubtedly his best for perhaps five years. After he saw the rough cut, Ponti was so pleased that he dipped into his own pocket to hire Ennio Morricone to write the musical score.

Unfortunately, for varying reasons, the film had a limited release outside of

Italy, and its distribution was badly mishandled. It also suffered from a change of name from *Death in Rome* to *Massacre in Rome*, which was thought to give it more commercial appeal. Years later, it eventually became a big success being rented out when VHS video cassettes became popular.

When it wrapped, Burton stayed on in Rome with Taylor whilst she finished *Ash Wednesday*. Without any work to distract him, he was drinking very heavily in the suite at The Grand Hotel. Brook Williams remembered it well: "It really irritated him. He wasn't used to waiting around for her to finish work. He got very bored and got drunk a lot."

Taylor was, at this time, going in the opposite direction. The David Frost interview had shaken her and she was gradually weaning herself off alcohol.

With one drinking more and more, and the other abstaining more and more, the marriage started to disintegrate.

Burton's family in Wales were very worried about what was happening. Normally, they would be hearing happy stories about the family looking forward to the summer holidays, instead they were reading press reports about excessive drinking and public rows. With Ivor dead, his elder brother, Tom, tried to step in and help. But Burton sent him a telegram that read: "Worry not. All is well between us." But the opposite could not have been more true.

The first manifestation of a split came when *Ash Wednesday* wrapped and Taylor left Rome for California on her own, leaving Burton with Maria in Rome where she was in school.

The Kalizma was waiting around in the South of France, but they made no plans to join her.

The marriage was hanging by a thread and Taylor's solo departure was a pivotal moment. From then on, what followed was inevitable. She had made the first move, as Burton later admitted: "I had told her to go 'get out' and to my astonishment, she went."

When she got to Los Angeles, she threw off the yoke and went out every night with old friends such as the actors Peter Lawford, Laurence Harvey and Roddy McDowall. Her relationship with Burton had become very staid and she relished a change of scene. One night, she went to the Candy night club in Beverly Hills and was introduced to a man she liked by Peter Lawford.

Taylor was desperate to get away from Burton, as she said later: "We were killing each other. And for why? I couldn't just sit there and let it happen." Burton told reporters who wanted to know why his wife had left Rome: "When a woman like Elizabeth loves you, she is not happy until she owns your soul.

And me, I demand absolute loyalty. I demand obedience. I must have my own way. Our natures do not inspire domestic tranquility."

But after she went, Burton didn't know what to do. As Graham Jenkins vividly described in his biography of his brother: "Rich was befuddled, not knowing what to do next. After a week, he was mooching about his hotel suite when he found his daughter Maria, now aged 12, packing a suitcase. 'What are you up to, love?' 'I'm going to New York to be with Mommy.' 'Are you packing for me too?' 'No.'"

Maria left with her nanny.

Now on his own, he cleared out the suite at The Grand and flew to New York. When he got there, on a whim he drove down to Aaron Frosch's house in Quogue, Long Island. Frosch had a guest house at the bottom of his garden. Burton loved going to stay with friends who had separate guest houses in their gardens. He somehow felt empowered living a responsibility-free life in other peoples' gardens.

After a few days of talks with Frosch, he tracked down Taylor who was with her mother and asked her to come to Long Island. Taylor made it a condition that he wouldn't drink whilst she was there. He agreed.

He told her he would pick up her up from Kennedy airport. When she arrived, he was there waiting in the back of a chauffeur-driven car but Taylor immediately knew he had been drinking. She froze but had no choice but to get in the car and go to Long Island with him. When they arrived, there followed two hours of furious rows, with Frosch trying vainly to referee.

Taylor, realising the situation was hopeless, ordered a car to take her into New York. She asked Frosch to phone ahead and tell The Regency she was coming. As she was leaving, she told him to work out the financials for their divorce. Frosch, who was suffering from the early stages of multiple sclerosis, was appalled by what he had just witnessed.

It was a very distraught Elizabeth Taylor who arrived back in New York that evening. Someone at the hotel tipped off the newspapers that she was back in town and they gathered in the lobby. As soon as she arrived, she telephoned John Springer and asked him to come to the hotel. She told him she wanted to announce tonight that she and her husband had separated. Springer asked why it was so urgent but she wouldn't say.

The man she had met in Los Angeles was called Henry Wynberg. Wynberg was Dutch and was divorced with a young son. He was five years younger than her and she knew she could not take that relationship further whilst she was attached to Burton. She needed another man in her life and he was the one. She desperately wanted a new start, or so she thought, and she wanted to make the split official as quickly as possible.

So on 3rd July, Taylor wrote a press release in her own hand on the notepaper of The Regency Hotel. Springer helped her compose it. When they were happy with the wording, he made some copies and handed them out to the now huge crowd of journalists waiting in the lobby of the Regency. It read: "I am convinced it would be a good and constructive idea if Richard and I separated for a while. Maybe we loved each other too much. I never believed such a thing was possible. But we have been in each other's pockets constantly, never being apart except for matters of life and death, and I believe it has caused a temporary breakdown of communication. I believe with all my heart that the separation will ultimately bring us back to where we should be – and that is together. Wish us well, please, during this most difficult time."

Melvyn Bragg called it: "A confidential letter addressed to millions."

The following day was Independence Day, a national holiday, and Burton had no idea what she had done until a horde of journalists and photographers suddenly arrived and set up camp outside Aaron Frosch's house, waiting for a reaction from him. But a reaction to what? He had to read the newspapers himself to find out what was going on and the separation was news to him as well.

Taylor's statement made headline news around the world at a time when America was in crisis over President Nixon and Watergate. Anyone reading the newspapers that day might have wondered which was the bigger crisis.

So it was a very surprised and shocked Burton who ventured outside to face the world's press. He had been drinking but managed to hold himself together as he said: "There is no question of our love and devotion for each other. I don't even consider Elizabeth and I are separated. It is just that our private and professional interests are keeping us apart. I even have Elizabeth's passport in my possession. Does that look as if she has left me?"

With that, he went back inside as journalists waited outside for further developments. Meanwhile, Nigel Dempster, the 32-year-old diarist on the *London Daily Mail* had hot-footed it to New York once he had heard the news. He was about to get the story that would make his name and soon get him his own column.

Whilst the world's press were at the front of Frosch's house, Dempster managed to get himself to the rear of the house after he realised that Burton was living in the guest house at the bottom of the garden. It was ten o'clock in the morning when he knocked on the window of the bathroom. The glass was frosted but he could hear Burton inside shaving with his electric razor. Burton opened the window to see who it was. He knew Dempster slightly and was glad to see a friendly face from London so invited him in. Burton was drinking vodka and orange and offered Dempster one, which the diarist thought politic not to refuse. He told Dempster he had not spoken to his wife since her "extraordinary statement" and that he actually had no idea what she was talking about. He said: "She's planning to go back to California to see her mother again and then to stay with her brother in Hawaii. Am I going to Hawaii? Not on your nelly. It's a terrible place."

Burton said he was "amused" at the latest revelation from "this mystifying woman he had married." But he told him: "It was bound to happen. You can't keep clapping a couple of sticks together without expecting them to blow up." The next morning, Dempster had a world exclusive for the *Mail*'s daily diary column. David English, the *Daily Mail*'s legendary editor, wasn't interested in more Nixon/Watergate stories being sent to him by his other reporters; all he wanted was Burton-Taylor stories, and Dempster delivered. That one story made Dempster's career. Burton added for good measure: "Elizabeth is like a spoiled child; she enjoys undermining me. One gets tired of it. A man must have some peace. The problem is that Elizabeth and I have grown apart intellectually. I have only 24 hours a day. I read, write and film. Elizabeth is constantly seeking problems of one kind or another. She worries about her figure, about her family, about the colour of her teeth. She expects that I drop everything to devote myself to these problems. I cannot."

Meanwhile, Taylor checked out of The Regency and flew to California to be with her mother, who was not in the best of health. She was also due to have a showdown meeting with her eldest son, Michael Wilding, whose life was in a mess. Three years earlier, at the age of 17, Wilding had unwisely married a woman two years his senior, who was pregnant. He had taken her to live in a commune at a Welsh farmhouse. Not surprisingly, the woman soon tired of the situation and took their daughter, Leyla, off to Hawaii. With his wife gone, he began a relationship with a girl called Johanna Lykke-Dahn, who quickly became pregnant. For good measure, he had also acquired a police record for growing marijuana.

Whilst Taylor did her best to grapple with that situation, she started dating Wynberg and they were soon sharing a bed. That was a new situation for

Taylor. Her secretary, Raymond Vignale, who had replaced Dick Hanley, was delighted she had ditched Burton for Wynberg. He had been encouraging her to leave Burton and was quoted as saying: "Henry was more fun – he could dance all night while Richard preferred to sit at home." Years later, Vignale changed his story and said he tried to dissuade her from returning to Wynberg and told Taylor's biographer C. David Heymann: "I didn't like him. I thought he was using her. I told her if Dick Hanley were still around, he would have told her the same thing. But Elizabeth was headstrong. She did what she felt like doing."

Meanwhile, Burton spent the next few weeks commuting between Long Island and Manhattan and was not short of female company himself. Burton just loved living in Frosch's guest house, where he found a sort of security with Frosch's wife, Bobby, and their daughters, Juliana, Phoebe and Suzanna. Quogue was conveniently situated about 70 miles from New York City.

Whilst there, he discussed his future with Frosch and he decided he needed specialist help to try and cure his alcohol addiction. Frosch quickly contacted a medical staffing agency who found him a doctor and a nurse who specialised in these situations and were willing to travel to Europe and to be with him 24 hours a day. And most importantly, they were able to start immediately.

Burton was due to leave for Rome in August to start work on his next film, *The Voyage*, produced by Carlo Ponti. Ponti was currently the only producer who would employ him.

Burton had arranged to stay at his guest house in Rome during filming, but not until August. So Burton telephoned Ponti and asked him if he could come a month early. He explained that he wanted to begin his detoxification process in seclusion. Ponti consulted his wife and she agreed. In fact, she was delighted. Sophia Loren wasn't averse to having Richard Burton come and stay for the summer. Like most women, she had always found him immensely attractive.

He arrived with Bob Wilson, Gaston Sanz, plus the doctor and his nurse. They were all accommodated in the guest house on the estate. Burton had already started the detoxification regime in New York and he spent the whole of the summer in seclusion, emerging only for filming.

Burton put himself completely in his doctor's hands and went on a rigorous diet. The programme permitted him to enjoy occasional glasses of white wine in an attempt to inject some self-control into his drinking. The experience was shocking for him, but being allowed a small amount of alcohol enabled him to cope and to slowly wean his system off it.

Gradually, he settled down to his new regime. He rose early every morning and swam in the Ponti's pool. Loren invited him for lunch in the main house every day. They sat on the terrace and ate. Afterwards, they played scrabble, sometimes until the sun went down. She found him very stimulating and he found her very beautiful. Burton had never before been jealous of another man, but he was jealous of Ponti that summer.

Graham Jenkins personally witnessed the kindness the Pontis showed his brother that summer: "These two were incredibly kind to Rich. Carlo Ponti believed in his talent and Sophia Loren in his humanity, and though both had their faith strained to breaking point, they remained loyal. To stay on the wagon, he needed someone near him who was witty, diverting and extremely patient. It had to be a woman, and a beautiful woman at that. Sophia Loren, unpaid and unthanked, accepted the role."

Burton gradually became infatuated with Loren. It was a situation Loren was used to and, as with all her other admirers over the years, his ardour was not returned. In any case, he had not shaken off the ghost of Taylor.

On the one hand, Burton was glad to be rid of his wife and, on the other, he missed the life she had provided for him. He gradually began to realise that she was the star of the relationship and that he missed being married to her much more than he missed her love. It was a strange fixation, made worse when he read in the newspapers about the good time she was having in California being squired by Henry Wynberg. When some journalists cornered Burton in a rare outing to Rome, he called Wynberg a "used car salesman," a moniker that stuck to Wynberg for the rest of his life.

A fortnight later, Taylor was due back in Rome to start work on her new film called *Identikit*. Aaron Frosch had been working non-stop to try and effect a reconciliation. He had kept Taylor up to date on the medical team Burton had hired and on the detoxification process. Hearing the progress, she reluctantly, at Frosch's urging, agreed to go and stay with Burton in Rome. But she still kept her booking at The Grand Hotel just in case.

A delighted Frosch convinced John Springer to issue a press release with the good news. It said Burton had given up alcohol and that he and his wife were to be reunited at the first possible opportunity.

She flew in on a private jet to Rome's Ciampino airport. The former military airport was now used just for private aviation and was very small. Reporters and photographers, who had somehow got wind of her flight, were swarming everywhere. As the plane came to a halt, they got between the plane with Taylor in it and the green Rolls-Royce containing Burton, 50 metres away.

He sat in the car and she in the plane for 20 minutes. Eventually, a security team arrived and cleared a path. When she emerged from the plane, she looked absolutely spectacular. She had slimmed down dramatically and was wearing a tight orange t-shirt and even tighter blue jeans. On her finger was the Krupp diamond, flashing in the sunshine. The two had an emotional reunion in the back of the car, and Taylor was relieved when she realised he was sober.

They went back to the Ponti's guest house and were given a huge welcome by Carlo and Sophia, who did their very best to smooth her path. But after exactly nine nights, it had all collapsed and there were some fierce rows. The Pontis kept trying to paper over the obvious cracks in the relationship but it was hopeless. She packed up and moved to the suite that was waiting for her at The Grand.

Taylor was devastated that the reunion didn't work even though her husband had been sober the entire time. Up until then, she had thought it was alcohol that had caused the split, but for the first time she realised there were also some more fundamental problems.

Taylor had genuinely wanted things to be right between them again. But it appeared that as soon as Burton had her again, he didn't want her.

Burton told a reporter without directly mentioning Taylor: "If two people are absolutely sick of each other, or the sight of one another bores them, then they should get divorced or separated as soon as possible. Otherwise, life becomes intolerable, waking up every morning and having breakfast with the same miserable face."

It did seem to reflect what he really felt.

John Springer had flown into Rome to brief journalists on the reconciliation and had flown back after a week. He was bemused to find that by the time his plane touched down in New York, his clients had split up again.

As a consequence of the upheavals, Taylor was late on set for her first day of filming on *Identikit* the following day. She finally arrived at five o'clock in the evening. Expecting to find some fed-up people, she was surprised when the cast and crew cheered her onto the set. Clearly upset, she was very moved and made a short speech asking for their "forgiveness." Afterwards, she told reporters that she had thought she would never have another day like the day Mike Todd died: "I was wrong. Today is the second saddest day of my life. I am desolate."

Taylor was in pieces and told a group of journalists about her problems coping with other women who lusted after her husband: "There were several women and they weren't the ugliest. At first it amused me. But there comes a point when you shouldn't overdo anything. I am a jealous woman and, finally, the smallest glance or the smallest smile would cause me to come apart inside. I could no longer bear being deceived. We quarrelled, regardless whether someone was present or not. Our quarrelling finally destroyed our love. I am very quarrelsome. I always wanted to be in the centre and loved being desired by men. That gave me the feeling of being even more beautiful. Richard couldn't stand it. He had a murderous jealousy and, because of this, we several times hit each other. Maybe I've been wrong not to take greater care of my figure. He always told me it wasn't important if I was a little stout and I always believed him. I am not so sure now."

Two days later, Henry Wynberg joined her in Rome.

Burton was certainly was not short of female company as old and new girlfriends flocked around him now that he was single again. His favourite companion during this period was Jeanne Bell, the black model who had caused a sensation when she appeared unclothed in *Playboy* magazine. But abstinence from alcohol significantly reduced his sex drive and what he really wanted was companionship from friends and family. He was desperately lonely and encouraged his family to come and visit, including his brother Graham who observed the detoxification process firsthand. They shared a bedroom and Graham recalled that his brother's last words before falling asleep each night were: "Another day, another day. Drink, you devil, I've beaten you." They both hoped it was true.

In August, filming was due to start on *The Voyage* opposite Sophia Loren and Marcello Mastroianni. But Mastroianni walked off the set after a few days when he realised that Burton and Loren were being given the top billing and that he was relegated to a supporting role.

Ponti suspended production for two weeks whilst he replaced him, and Burton took the opportunity to fly to New York. He was now feeling much better and getting restless. In New York, he dallied with a young fashion designer called Barbara Dulien. He then flew to Long Island to visit Aaron Frosch and then Philip Burton, who lived in Ashbury Park, a suburb of New York.

Whilst with Frosch, he discussed the possibility of him marrying Sophia

Loren and asked what the financial implications would be. Frosch realised that he had become totally infatuated with the Italian actress. But Frosch was astute enough to work out that the relationship was mostly in Burton's head and did not take him seriously.

Soon, Ponti recalled him to Rome and he resumed his routine at the lodge, once again emerging only for filming.

In his absence, Ponti had recast Mastroianni's character with the Scottish character actor Ian Bannen. It was crazy casting and Ponti seemed temporarily to have lost his judgment over such things.

*The Voyage* was a romantic melodrama set in turn of the century Sicily. Directed by the legendary Vittorio De Sica, it told the story of an old wealthy Sicilian family. Burton played Cesare Bragi, whose father's will had profound consequences for his destiny. In keeping with his father's wishes, Cesare allowed his brother to marry his own sweetheart, played by Loren. But after his brother died unexpectedly, Cesare realised he had another chance if destiny would allow it.

It was a very Italian film, but with the two main male characters played by a Welshman and a Scot, everyone was miscast. In late September, the cast and crew of *The Voyage* moved down to Sicily to film the exteriors. The Kalizma sailed to Sicily to meet Burton.

After two weeks of filming in Sicily and with her husband absent, Burton made his play for Loren – much as he had with Julie Andrews in 1961, 12 years earlier. It was only when he was rebuffed, that he suddenly and belatedly realised that Loren wasn't interested in anything beyond friendship. Her marriage to Ponti was rock solid and she wasn't about to break it for him.

Deciding he was cured of his alcohol addiction, he ended the contract of his doctor and nurse and sent them back to New York. Fitter and stronger after three months of abstinence, he found he could keep to the white wine regime prescribed by his doctor and keep his drinking under control.

Then, in the third week of November 1973, came a new drama. Elizabeth Taylor returned to Los Angeles after filming had wrapped on *Identikit*. She had just attended the funeral of Laurence Harvey, who had died of stomach cancer. Suddenly, news came through to The Kalizma that Taylor had been taken to hospital in Los Angeles with a cancer scare. She telephoned Burton in Sicily and asked him to come and be with her. He immediately went to a rather bemused Carlo Ponti and asked permission to be released for a few · days so he could fly to his wife's bedside.

When she had called, Burton, who had spent the past four months trying to forget Taylor, found he was actually very pleased to hear her voice. He tried to explain: "There is this strange woman, very strong, very odd, very perverse, very curious, who says: 'Can I come back home?' or something like that and I said: 'Oh sure.'"

It turned out that she had been admitted to University of California hospital suffering from stomach cramps. She was x-rayed and it showed a cyst on one of her ovaries. The next day she underwent surgery but the cyst was non-malignant. Afterwards, she was transferred to the Scripps Institute Clinic in La Jolla to convalesce.

Burton arranged to charter a Mystere private jet that would fly him to Los Angeles with the minimum hassle, wait for him and get him back to Italy quickly.

Burton's brother Graham was on board the Kalizma whilst this drama was going on, and before leaving, Burton ordered the yacht's captain to sail the yacht to Naples where he said he would meet them in three days' time. Jenkins remained on board as he remembered: "I sailed in a lonely state wondering how much more drama could be packed into two lives."

Two days later, they weighed anchor in Naples and, soon afterwards, Burton reappeared with Taylor just as if nothing had happened. As Graham recalled: "It appeared she was not desperately ill after all. Maybe just desperately in love. When they came aboard the Kalizma, I had never seen them look happier. We had a wonderful meal together, joking and laughing about old times, hardly able to believe what I was witnessing. I wished them all the joy in the world."

When Jenkins asked Taylor about her seemingly remarkable recovery, she told him it happened after Burton had turned up at the clinic: "You've never seen anybody heal so fast. It was as if the grand maestro had placed a hand over my incision and healed me up."

It transpired that Burton had arrived at the hospital and found Henry Wynberg in attendance. Burton ordered him out and slept overnight in a cot by Taylor's bed. The next day, he told a delighted Taylor he was taking her back to the Kalizma. And that is what he did.

Whether Taylor had dreamed up the whole illness to woo him back to her after tiring of Wynberg was never clear to Graham Jenkins. As he was leaving to return to Wales, Burton shouted after him: "Tell them at home the bad times are over."

When the weather turned cold in early December, they left the Kalizma and went to Taylor's house in Gstaad for Christmas and all appeared to be well again. They flew to Switzerland for Christmas in a blaze of love and togetherness. Taylor was overjoyed and quoted in the newspapers as saying: "Richard and I are back together again and it will be the happiest Christmas of my life. I believe in Santa Claus again."

There was a small cloud when *The Voyage* was released for the holidays and died an early death at the cinemas. The *New York Times* said of it: "Even if Mr Burton and Mr Bannen had been Italian, they would have been wrong for this movie. They are too old and their temperaments do not suit the cinematic landscape. Miss Loren's age is not right but, worse, she has no role."

At the beginning of 1974, the Burtons went from Gstaad to Hawaii and then to Puerto Vallarta until the beginning of March, when Burton was due to start a new film. There, they celebrated Taylor's 42nd birthday on 27th February. The good times lasted until Burton began drinking again, which he soon did.

Burton arrived in Oroville in northern California in early March 1974 to make a film with Lee Marvin called *The Klansman*. The film was based on a novel by William Bradford Huie about racial violence in Alabama. Effectively, it was the story of the Ku Klux Klan before the civil rights movement. Burton played a Southern liberal landowner who opposes the Ku Klux Klan. Marvin played the sheriff trying to maintain law and order between the Klan, the local Negroes and Burton. Terence Young, who had made his name directing two James Bond movies, was the director.

Significantly, Burton had left Taylor behind, and she said she would join him later.

The film was important because it was financed by Paramount and was the nearest Burton ever got to a Hollywood movie again. But he couldn't have made a worse impression. By March, he had built his alcohol consumption back up to one, then two and finally three bottles of vodka a day. As a result, he arrived on the set in terrible condition.

And he couldn't have walked into a worse situation for an alcoholic. His co-star Lee Marvin was renowned as the biggest drinker in Hollywood. Naturally, the two men got on famously and at lunchtime on the first day on set, they apparently drank 17 martinis each.

Almost immediately, Burton started running round with an 18-year-old waitress called Kim Dinucci. She was famous locally for being Miss Pepsi of Butte County. The story of Burton and the waitress was picked up and published in the *San Francisco Examiner*. The story said he had met the waitress on the street in front of the local jail and invited her onto the set. But he quickly dumped her and began romancing Anne De Angelo, a 33-year-old hotel receptionist who was married. Her husband, a bartender called Tony De Angelo was very unimpressed and came after Burton with a shotgun and had to be restrained by the film's security team. Years later, De Angelo was interviewed: "Burton promised Anne he'd take her to Switzerland once he finished filming. It was just a line, but Anne fell for it – she was walking on air for weeks thinking Burton really loved her. Then he left without her, and I watched her fall utterly apart. She couldn't take the humiliation so she divorced me, left Oroville and moved to Monterey." Burton admitted later: "I didn't know what the hell I was doing."

Soon women were passing in and out of Burton's trailer like on a conveyor belt, just like the early days at 20th Century-Fox, 20 years earlier. Except, this time, they were local women and not famous movie stars.

With all this going on, Elizabeth Taylor arrived on the set. She was horrified at the drinking and the women. Burton didn't seem to care what she thought and she quickly realised that their relationship was over. She stayed just long enough for the 16th March 1974, when they celebrated their tenth wedding anniversary. Before she left, she pulled Valerie Douglas to one side and effectively handed over the problem of her husband. She strongly advised Douglas to book Burton into St John's Hospital in Santa Monica. She reportedly said: "Either that or he's a dead man."

With that, she left and flew to Los Angeles and checked into Bungalow 5 at the Beverley Hills Hotel. The first phone call she made was to Henry Wynberg.

Taylor then had John Springer deliver another of what Burton now called "The Elizabethan Proclamations." She announced "that with deep regret the reconciliation had failed and the marriage had died of irreconcilable differences." Burton wondered why she felt the need to keep announcing they had split: "Surely, propinquity must breed some kind of durable affection, even only for the weaknesses."

Taylor's departure and her statement was the cue for hundreds of journalists to descend on the set of *The Klansman*, and the film's publicists were delighted with the attention. They didn't seem to understand that Burton needed protecting from journalists – not to have them thrust upon him – he was in no condition for that. But the publicists didn't care; they simply wanted publicity as long as the film was mentioned. It was a recipe for disaster, and that is precisely how it turned out.

Consequently, Burton's drunkenness was witnessed firsthand and reported by all. His reputation, or what was left of it, was trashed across America.

Robert Kerwin of the *Chicago Tribune Magazine* wrote of Burton on the set: "His thin wrists branch out of a baggy shirt. His loose brown trousers are an old man's trousers. The once robust and forceful face has a powdery pallour. The irises are bright blue but the whites are deeply red, with only flecks of white. On his face is a dazed grin as if he's been shocked awake under those heavy lights in the midst of surgery."

The film's publicists just threw him to the wolves and allowed him to be interviewed whilst drunk and swigging vodka neat brought to him on a tray by Bob Wilson – a fresh glass every quarter of an hour. They effectively allowed him to commit professional suicide right in front of their eyes.

Burton was drinking in some ways to dull the pain he was in from acute sciatica and problems with the nerves in his left arm. At the end of the filming, he was walking with a pronounced limp and had to be held up by Bob Wilson. It became obvious he was a seriously sick man. Terence Young said: "It was painful to see this great actor disintegrating before all our eyes." Lee Marvin observed: "The man was suffering. Who knows what it is? He has to fend off so many people that his mind is hardly his own anymore."

Young added: "Richard was at his all-time low and on the verge of drinking himself to death, and Lee was doing his best to catch up." Young found he had to get most of his scenes filmed in the mornings before his stars were "totally bombed." It was a wholly ludicrous situation and more than once, he thought of abandoning the film.

Finally, when Burton could no longer stand on his own without help, Young insisted that a doctor be called to the set. The doctor could only tell Valerie Douglas that Burton would be dead within the month without urgent treatment. That was all Douglas needed to hear and she told her boss that his next destination was the St John's Hospital in Santa Monica. This time, there was no choice and he knew it.

As soon as the last scene was finished, Burton was driven to the airport and put on a private plane to Los Angeles. He was taken straight from Los Angeles airport to the clinic. Terence Young said at the time: "'I think I saved his life. If we hadn't moved that fast, Richard would be dead today." Valerie Douglas kept up the pretence and told journalists Burton had been admitted to the clinic for a condition she called "influenza tracheobronchitis." But no one believed it and everyone knew what he was there for. Graham Jenkins recalled he was in a really bad way when he was admitted: "He could hardly walk without someone holding him up; he could hardly talk without someone finishing his sentences, and he could not sleep without someone handing him the glass and the tablets."

Doctors were horrified by his condition. As soon as he arrived, they ordered a blood transfusion. Initially, the doctors at the clinic did not think they would be able to save him and believed he was too far gone. They didn't mince words when they delivered their grave prognosis, but Burton didn't take them seriously and replied: "I am not afraid of death, I am just amused that you think I can be killed off this easily." He added: "Don't forget I come from Welsh mining stock and I am only 48 years old. My father was the greatest boozer in our valley and he lived until he was 83, and then he died not from drink but from a stroke." Burton really believed that he could drink himself silly every day and live a long and happy life.

For the first few days of treatment, he was allowed three, then two, glasses of wine a day until he was taken off it completely. Almost immediately, he began to shake – so much so that he had to be fed intravenously. He was given multiple blood transfusions to try and quickly cleanse his system of alcohol. It was a painful and undignified process. He remembered later: "After I was taken off drink altogether, that was bad; very bad. I had to be fed through a tube, I would shake so much. People are supposed to see pink snakes and spiders on the ceilings or crawling up the walls when they are being dried out. I didn't. I just could not sleep. I could get off for 45 minutes and then I'd have a nightmare – always the same nightmare and I'd be awake again."

During his stay, there was a desperately sad encounter. Walking in the hospital grounds, by pure chance he came upon someone he had last seen in 1958 – 16 years earlier. It happened as he emerged from the building for a walk, helped by two orderlies. The woman, who was just going in, paused and said: "Richard". "Yes," he said, wondering who it was. She said: "It's Susan, Susan Strasberg." By now she had been married and divorced, and was visiting her daughter at the hospital. They stood looking at each other silently until Strasberg just said: "It was lovely seeing you," and walked away.

Burton had been booked into the clinic for ten days but in the end, the process took six weeks. By the end, he had dropped three stone in weight. Bob Wilson and his wife, Gladys, took him to Puerto Vallarta to lie low and recuperate. Whilst all this was going on, Taylor was negotiating with Aaron Frosch over the divorce she was now determined to have. Frosch resolved to split their assets in half. But Burton gave Frosch *carte blanche* and told him to let Taylor have what she wanted. She took full advantage.

In late April, John Springer issued a statement on Taylor's instructions. It read: "Elizabeth and Richard Burton have requested Aaron R. Frosch, their long-time attorney, to proceed to legally terminate their ten-year marriage due to irreconcilable differences. Frosch will seek the divorce in the canton of Berne, Switzerland, where the Burtons have been legal residents for many years."

By this time, Burton had neither seen nor heard from Taylor for three months. They were on opposite sides of the world, and divorce was now inevitable. She had taken up with Wynberg full time and was cruising on the Kalizma with him, visiting all their old haunts along the Mediterranean coast. Burton only became annoyed when he read that Taylor and Wynberg had been seen in Monte Carlo with Prince Rainier and Princess Grace.

Burton stayed put in Puerto Vallarta, making only the occasional trips to New York and Los Angeles for meetings or when he needed more books.

The grounds for the divorce were 'irreconcilable differences'. At the end of June, Burton flew to New York and prepared to return to Europe as soon as he knew the divorce had been granted.

On 26th June 1974, Burton and Taylor were divorced by a village judge in Saarinen, Switzerland. Under Swiss law, the participants in a divorce were required to attend in person. Burton was excused by a medical certificate from his doctors stating that illness prevented him from appearing in person. Taylor turned up wearing a brown silk suit and hiding her eyes behind a pair of huge sunglasses. The 30-minute hearing was mainly procedural with the judge asking her only one question: "Is it true that to live with your husband was intolerable?" She answered: "Yes, life with Richard became intolerable."

The financial settlement had already been agreed. Taylor got ownership of the yacht and Casa Kimberley. She kept all her jewellery, which was valued at US$7 million and she also got all the paintings. They each kept whatever cash they had. Taylor was also awarded sole custody of Maria Burton.

With that, she stepped from the courtroom and briefly went to Gstaad before flying to join the Kalizma, where Henry Wynberg was on board waiting. They resumed their summer-long cruise up and down the Mediterranean.

In London, Burton's old friend Emlyn Williams was in his apartment in Chelsea reading about the divorce in the newspapers. He mused to himself: "I wonder who will get custody of Brook?"

The next day, Burton left New York and boarded the SS France for a six-day trip across the Atlantic. He was coming to London to begin filming a television movie for Carlo Ponti, a remake of *Brief Encounter*. Journalists found out about his departure and were waiting at the gangplank. He told them he had conquered his demons and that he felt ten years younger. Of Taylor, he said: "Frankly, she'll be better off without me. I intend to roam the globe searching for ravishing creatures." And with that, he got on board to begin that search.

Meanwhile, the Hollywood trade magazine *Variety* reviewed *The Klansman* in its latest issue, calling the film "a perfect example of screen trash that almost invites derision."

# THE END OF ELIZABETH TAYLOR

# AND GOD CREATED BURTON

# CHAPTER 51

# A single man again

## *Adapting to changed circumstances*

### 1974 - 1975

Richard Burton was a man of very changed circumstances when he returned to Europe in July 1974. He disembarked at the port of Cherbourg on his way back to Celigny to make his home there for the first time in ten years. He no longer owned a yacht or an art collection, nor any diamonds, and his bank account no longer had as many noughts on the end of it as it had previously. He was also minus a wife.

To reflect his changed circumstances, he radically reduced his entourage down to just five people; Bob Wilson, Brook Williams, Valerie Douglas and two secretaries.

He had returned to Europe to appear in a television drama called *Walk With Destiny*, a joint BBC and NBC co-production financed by the Hallmark Greeting Cards company. He had arrived back in plenty of time to give him three months in Switzerland, open up the house and get his new life in order.

Whilst he was settling back in at Celigny, a film director called Alan Bridges suddenly appeared at his front gates. The day before, Burton had taken a phone call from Sophia Loren asking if he would see Bridges and hear what he had to say. Bridges flew into Geneva with a script in his briefcase and Burton read it sitting in the garden while Bridges chatted with Brook Williams inside the house. Burton had two months of inactivity before he began *Walk With Destiny*, and Bridges wanted to make full use of that time. He made Burton a quite remarkable offer. He said there was US$500,000 on the table if he could drop whatever he had planned and get to England for the next six weeks.

Bridges had a big problem. He had already started filming a remake of *Brief Encounter* in Winchester when his male lead, Robert Shaw, was suddenly forced to withdraw from the production. *Jaws*, the debut picture from Steven Spielberg, was shooting in Martha's Vineyard and had overrun its schedule due to the inexperience of its first time director, and Shaw, the film's star, was needed for another month. *Jaws* was a big budget movie costing US$7 million and Universal Pictures agreed to pay compensation of US$300,000 to

# AND GOD CREATED BURTON

Bridges, which was US$100,000 more than he was paying the actor to star in *Brief Encounter* in the first place. It effectively gave him US$500,000 to find a replacement – adding the compensation sum to Shaw's fee.

Sophia Loren, who was the female lead in *Brief Encounter*, suggested Burton as an ideal replacement. Before leaving for Celigny, Bridges had made his enquires of Burton's agent, Hugh French, who told him he could just about fit it in before he started work on *Walk With Destiny*.

It was an offer Burton could not turn down, as he said: "Sophia came on and, in that gently imperious voice, persuaded me."

As he read the script that sunny afternoon, however, he must have known it would be a pretty hopeless film.

It shouldn't have been. The original *Brief Encounter* was a 30-year-old classic film from the pen of Noel Coward. The original starred Trevor Howard and Celia Johnson, both of whom had defined the parts.

It was being revived as a made-for-TV movie by the 57-year-old American producer Cecil Clarke. Clarke had a stellar reputation and there was then an unlimited appetite for television movies in America. The made-for-TV movie concept, invented by Barry Diller, had started a huge production boom and in the process revived the film industry around the world. *Brief Encounter* had a US$1.5 million budget.

Burton played the part of a married doctor who has a brief encounter with a married housewife at a suburban railway station. It was an ordinary man meets ordinary woman story. And there it came undone, and the miscasting became very apparent. There was just nothing ordinary about Richard Burton or Sophia Loren. It was ridiculous miscasting.

The film was shot in August 1974 on location at Winchester, Hampshire, a pleasant county of England. The interiors were shot at Twickenham Studios near London.

When Burton arrived in Winchester, he just wanted to get on with filming and to get it done with the minimum fuss. He was more concerned with keeping to his new health regime. He was not drinking and was trying very hard to exercise and keep in shape. If he didn't, he realised there would have been little point to the six weeks he had spent in St John's.

But it also meant there was little joy in his life, apart from when his 16-year-old daughter, Kate, came to visit the set on summer vacation.

It was also clear he was morose without a partner and was on the lookout for a new wife.

# A SINGLE MAN AGAIN

On the set, he did a remarkable interview with *Ladies Home Journal* magazine and a journalist called Roger Falk. The resulting article, published three months later in a double feature alongside a profile of Elizabeth Taylor by the famous writer Truman Capote, was entitled: "Richard Burton: Life without Elizabeth"

During the interview he wrote out a spoof advertisement and handed it to Falk and said it described his situation. It read: "Intelligent well-to-do actor, aged 49, twice divorced, seeks nice lady aged between 28 and 38 to have baby by him. Will pay £20,000 if it is a boy child or £10,000 for girl child. Mother will then legally surrender all rights over child. Apply: Richard Burton CBE." A somewhat bemused Falk took the piece of paper and asked him if he could print it, Burton mischievously said: "Sure." Elsewhere in the article, he was quoted as saying: "You think women have been my passion. The real passion in my life has been books."

The article also noted how Burton was being stalked on set by photographers and journalists eager for his attention and he said: "I'm fair game; anybody who can make a spare penny out of me is entitled to do so when I make so much money out of other people."

Now that he had lost all pretentions of being a big Hollywood actor and shed all his superstar trappings, he was amazed by how much people would pay him for just a few weeks' work. He had worked out that, despite his fall from the big time, if he worked full time it would be perfectly possible to earn between US$4 and US$5 million a year.

Burton spent an enjoyable six weeks during some uncommon balmy summer weather filming *Brief Encounter*. He tried desperately to interest Sophia Loren in his advertisement, to no effect. That summer, Burton drove himself around in his Jaguar E-Type. Now that he wasn't drinking, he could safely drive again.

*Brief Encounter* was a disaster as a film. But when it was shown on the NBC network, it achieved very high ratings purely because of the presence of its two stars. That didn't stop Graham Jenkins, who over the years was his brother's most astute critic, dismissing it as "an absurdity." When it was shown in England, Clive James, then emerging as a top critic at *The Observer* newspaper asked: "Would an Italian beauty queen with a wardrobe of exotic if badly chosen clothes pretend to be the humdrum wife of a British solicitor and make goo-goo eyes at a raddled Welsh thespian trying to pass himself off as a promising physician by dyeing his hair with black boot-polish?"

Burton didn't care what they thought and just banked the cheque. When

*Brief Encounter* wrapped, he had a week spare and spent it at The Dorchester. He had received a big money offer from some European financiers to make an unnamed film, and he waited for a contract to sign and a cheque for US$1 million. But it never materialised and, as Burton said, the project foundered because the consortium had "more accountants than actors."

Then he went straight into the filming of *Walk With Destiny*, which was effectively a 90-minute dramatised documentary film about a period of Sir Winston Churchill's life before the outbreak of the Second World War. The BBC would make the film and co-finance it with the NBC network. It was also sponsored by Hallmark Greeting Cards, which ensured a big budget.

Even so, it was no easy thing in that period to persuade backers to agree to having Richard Burton in a production, but Hallmark liked him. The problem was insurance and the premiums to cover him were huge.

For the Churchill role, Burton was championed by 56-year-old Jack Le Vien, an Oscar-winning documentary producer of some repute. Le Vien had sealed the deal with him during a trip to Puerto Vallarta the year before. He visited Burton at Casa Kimberley, where he was convalescing after his stay at St John's. Burton invited Le Vien to dinner one night along with the American consul and his wife. During dinner, Burton entertained them by imitating Sir Winston Churchill and acting out portions of the *Walk With Destiny* script. Le Vien recalled that, suddenly, Burton slumped and fell asleep mid-sentence as if he had been knocked out. Without any explanation, Gladys Wilson grabbed him before he fell and took him off to bed as the guests made their excuses and left.

Le Vien was not encouraged by what he had witnessed that night and considered withdrawing his offer, but Hallmark insisted it wanted him and would take the risk.

*Walk With Destiny* was a dramatic reconstruction of Churchill's life from 1936 to 1940, based on his own memoirs. It was arguably the most exciting time of Churchill's career and was destined to be remade many times, most memorably in Robert Hardy's *The Wilderness Years*. Hardy was the definitive Churchill as one observer said: "More like Churchill than Churchill himself."

Burton made a passable Churchill and, interestingly, Hardy also starred with him in *Walk With Destiny* as the German ambassador, Joachim von Ribbentrop.

Apparently, Churchill, before he died, knew about the project and had asked for Burton to play him, remembering their dressing room encounter at the Old Vic during 'Hamlet' in 1954.

Burton was ideally placed to play Churchill and had total familiarity with the subject, having read every volume of his multi-part biography, which was being written by Churchill's son Randolph and later, Sir Martin Gilbert.

Everyone believed that Burton idolised Churchill and one of his most treasured possessions was his Jacob Epstein bust, the only artwork that had escaped Elizabeth Taylor's clutches in the divorce.

*Walk With Destiny* was one film for which Burton thoroughly enjoyed doing the publicity, as he recalled all his encounters with Churchill and expounded his undoubted knowledge of the subject. Burton may have enjoyed it, but the director, Herbert Wise, did not find filming easy. First, Burton refused to shave his head or wear a hairpiece and played Churchill with a full head of hair, which was not historically accurate. He also missed the first day of filming when he had a reunion with the vodka bottle – which, fortunately, was an isolated event.

It was also Burton's first production shot on videotape as opposed to film, and he did not adapt particularly well to the new process. Herbert Wise felt he was not trying hard enough and grew frustrated. It was not a particularly happy set, as Wise said: "I don't think he liked me and I didn't like him." The script was written by Colin Morris, who later recalled Burton's "sourness, gloom and lack of humour."

After filming was over, and before the programme was broadcast, there came what probably can safely be described as the most unsavoury and unpleasant incident in Burton's whole life.

A few days before *Walk With Destiny* had its first showing on NBC at the end of November 1974, an article written by Burton appeared in the Arts section of the *New York Times*. The article was headlined: 'To Play Churchill Is To Hate Him.' In it, Burton wrote that Churchill was a "monster"' and called him "a vindictive toy-soldier." He wrote that "in the course of preparing myself to act the part of Winston Churchill, I realised afresh that I hated Churchill and all his kind. I hate them violently."

Calling him a "coward", Burton compared Churchill unfavourably with Hitler, Stalin and even Attila the Hun and Genghis Khan.

The wartime bombing of the German city of Dresden was cited as evidence that Churchill had committed genocide on civilians, as Burton argued: "How could he have ordered the enchanting and innocent city of Dresden razed to ruins?" Burton also theorised that Churchill compensated for his timidity by being bold.

# AND GOD CREATED BURTON

A second article appeared in *TV Guide* on the same lines, calling Churchill "short, obese, vigorous, pugnacious, something of a vulgarian, power-mad and afraid of nothing, either physically or morally – the former by nature, the second by a lack of sensitivity to other people's feelings." Burton wrote: "Churchill was intellectually barren, superficially educated, maniacally industrious and of a physical constitution to marvel at. He drank steadily all day long with time off for sleep – champagne, whisky, brandy – and lived for more than 90 years. His last device to the free world he served so well might well have been to leave us his liver to wonder at."

And he finished by describing him as "just an actor like myself, but with a wider audience."

Strangely, he also said that Churchill was "one of the few people, the two others were Picasso and Camus, who have frightened me almost to silence when we came face-to-face." But he didn't explain that the first meeting he ever had with Churchill was his request to use Burton's lavatory at the Old Vic. People who knew the story wondered just how frightening that could have been.

The *TV Guide* article was arguably more offensive than the one in the *New York Times*.

The Churchill family was very upset, and Jack Le Vien revealed that when Burton had tea with Lady Churchill, he had "expressed only the greatest admiration for Sir Winston."

But Burton, at certain points in his life, had a proclivity for criticising and being nasty about people he really loved – if the mood took him. He had done the same in 1954 when he violently verbally attacked his adoptive father, Philip Burton, when speaking to Rosemary Kingsland, his underage mistress. Thankfully, Philip was dead by the time the words were published.

The desire to attack those he loved occurred only infrequently through his life and, of course, most famously with Laurence Olivier, Michael Redgrave, and John Gielgud during the filming of *Wagner*, years later.

But attacking Sir Winston Churchill was of a totally different dimension and turned many people off Burton for life.

At the root of the attack appeared to be an incident in Wales 45 years earlier. It was no secret that Churchill was not liked in the Welsh valleys. He was Home Secretary in 1930, when striking miners attacked a pithead at Tonypandy and threatened violence. To keep the peace, Churchill sent units of soldiers to the Rhondda and ordered them to stand-by in case the situation got out of control.

The situation did get violent but the troops were not needed. Nevertheless, the perception was that Churchill had ordered troops to attack the miners, when he had done no such thing.

Robert Hardy and Sheran Cazalet fired off angry telegrams to Burton, but he ignored them both. Hardy believes that Burton had a chip on his shoulder resulting from that incident in Tonypandy, as he said: "There was a sharpness and a bitterness that sometimes surfaced in Rich. I do not know what the cause of it was, but I think it was the unfairness of life; I think this was his socialist chip. Rich could display rage, a controlled fury at the unfairness of life. He'd say: 'Churchill was the most wonderful man but, by God, he sent in the army' and something sparked him off."

By the time the articles appeared, Burton was in Rome when the fury of the world came down on his head. Shaun Sutton, the BBC's head of drama said the BBC would never again use his services. Sutton even considered cancelling the showing of *Walk With Destiny*.

Norman Tebbit, then a rising young Conservative member of parliament, said Burton was: "An actor past his best, indulging in a fit of pique, jealousy and ignorant comment." Another MP said: "If there were more Churchills and fewer Burtons, we would be a very much better country."

In London, *The Times* newspaper wrote: "Burton has damaged himself in the eyes of the British people and does not deserve to recover."

Hallmark Greeting Cards was mightily embarrassed when it was revealed that its own public relations manager, Jack Meelan, had pushed the *New York Times* and *TV Guide* to commission Burton to write the article to get publicity for the upcoming broadcast.

Astonishingly, Burton had sent the articles to Meelan first, to send to the *New York Times*, and the hapless PR man hadn't seen the dangers. When he received the piece, Meelan told the commissioning editor of the *New York Times* that he didn't think the paper would want the article, as he called it "irrational." They asked to see it anyway and were delighted to publish it, realising the attention it would get.

The president of Hallmark Greeting Cards was eventually forced to write to the *New York Times* to dissociate himself from Burton's views. What happened to Meelan isn't recorded.

Burton told reporters who cornered him in Rome, that he withdrew nothing of what he had written. And the true cause of his resentment finally came out when he called Churchill "a bogey-man who hated us, the mining class, motivelessly. He ordered a few of us to be shot, you know, and the orders were carried out." When a reporter asked about the comparison with Genghis Khan and Attila the Hun, Burton thought about it for ten seconds and said simply: "Well, they were all killers. Perhaps we all are."

But perhaps the worst consequence came from the board of directors of Harlech Television; they all took grave offence at his remarks and demanded Burton's resignation. They didn't care who he was and declared they would not be sitting round a table again with such a man, regardless of how many shares he owned. Interestingly, they had never sat round a table with him anyway; in the ten years since he had joined, he had never once attended a board meeting. Lord Harlech wrote to Burton at Celigny and asked for his resignation. He received it by return.

Meanwhile, amidst all the drama, Burton had found himself a new girlfriend, called Princess Elizabeth of Yugoslavia, the 37-year-old daughter of exiled Prince Paul and Princess Olga. She was also a cousin of the Duke of Kent, Prince Michael of Kent and their sister, Princess Alexandra.

Princess Elizabeth was an intelligent, very attractive woman, with three children of her own – one by her husband, Neil Balfour, and two by her former marriage to an American called Howard Oxenberg.

Burton first met her through Elizabeth Taylor, and they had always flirted with each other. Taylor didn't think anything of it because of their long friendship. When Burton was back in London in August 1974 for *Brief Encounter* and *Walk With Destiny*, he called her up. Their first date was the visit for tea with Clementine Churchill at Hyde Park, and it went from there.

Princess Elizabeth was playing with fire and soon, she was in Burton's bed. Any association with Burton was very reckless as she was happily married to merchant banker Neil Balfour and they had a four-year-old son together. But like many women before her, she was smitten.

Three weeks later, Princess Elizabeth walked out on her husband and said she was going to spend the rest of her life with Burton. He agreed, saying: "I'm going to marry her; I want her to be my wife. I want to be with her for ever and ever and ever. I love her, I truly do. I love her so much, so deeply, it hurts."

But like Loren just a year before, he had quickly become infatuated, and that infatuation only lasted a few months. He took her on a romantic trip to Morocco to celebrate their engagement. They were supposed to be getting married as soon as possible, as soon as she could exit her marriage to Balfour.

The so-called engagement stretched out to three months and there is little doubt that Princess Elizabeth fell hopelessly in love with Burton while he treated her with continual and growing disrespect. In fact, he spent much of his time trying to avoid being in her company and was helped when his 90 days allowance ran out and he was forced to return to Switzerland. But somehow, Aaron Frosch managed to have some of the previous year's allowance transferred, which Burton hadn't used because of his illness. So he came back.

Amazingly, around this time, Burton was signed up for another film by the same producer and director team that had made *The Klansman*. The experience for Terence Young and Bill Alexander could not have been worse the first time around, but they came back for more. For reasons best known to both of them, they once again took a chance on Burton. Young said: "I'd heard Richard was sober and, besides, it was his name that got us the money to make the film."

The film was called *Jackpot* and was backed by a company called the Irwin Trust Company Ltd. It was based on a novel of the same name. Young and Alexander assembled an all-star cast of Burton, Robert Mitchum, James Coburn and Charlotte Rampling, and started filming in the south of France in February 1975. But right from the start, there were cashflow problems, and production stopped and started. The budgets had not been fixed before the filming started – never a good thing.

But Burton didn't care, he was enjoying himself in a suite at the Negresco Hotel in Nice, alternating between two women, Jeanne Bell and Princess Elizabeth, both of whom were down in the south of France for varying periods. Both seemed to be oblivious to the other's presence.

In the film, Burton played a character who tries to defraud an insurance company out of millions of dollars by faking an accident that cripples him for life. He then effects a recovery by way of a miracle cure, mostly by praying. The filming carried on haphazardly until June as money arrived in dribs and drabs. But by July, it was all over and Burton hadn't got his money. He sued the producers for US$125,000 in back pay.

It was during the filming of *Jackpot* that Burton gave another interview to the journalist David Lewin and famously told him: "Most actors are latent homosexuals and we cover it with drink. I was a homosexual once but not for long. But I tried it. It didn't work so I gave it up." Lewin always insisted that Burton was being serious – although, of course, he was not.

# AND GOD CREATED BURTON

Burton quickly fell out of love with Princess Elizabeth although she wouldn't let him go and proved quite tenacious at holding on. After he returned from Nice, he found himself playing a cat and mouse game with her across London to the extent that he was forced to leave his suite at The Dorchester and move back to his house at Squires Mount, which she didn't know about.

Princess Elizabeth was a neighbour of Robert Hardy's in Chelsea, and he recalled his part in the drama after they met at a party at Argyle House and began talking about Burton: "She told me that she was pretty much in love with Richard and that Richard was in love with her. If only she could find Richard." Hardy thought this strange, as he had left him not two hours before: "I said I know where he is, and she said: 'Oh, you couldn't go and get him, could you?' and I, like a lap dog, said: 'Of course I can.'"

Hardy had had too much to drink but jumped into his car and drove straight up to Hampstead. When he got to Squires Mount, Burton was in his dressing gown: "He did not welcome me because he obviously had a bit of skirt somewhere which he was hiding away, and we sat down and he said: 'Have a drink. What do you want?' And I said that I had come as an emissary from Princess Elizabeth and that she wants you to come down. 'I can't, I can't', he replied. So I said: 'What shall I tell her?' 'Tell her I will come later'. And I thought: 'Thanks very much, indeed.' So I had a drink, crept back to my car and drove back to Argyle House to deliver the message."

The end came when Princes Elizabeth finally got the message. He was drinking again, increasingly frequently, although nowhere near as much as before. The game was up when she opened a copy of *The Daily Express* and there was a huge photo of Burton arm-in-arm with Jeanne Bell.

Princess Elizabeth phoned and told him it was over. Surprisingly, Burton became interested again and he hurried off to The Dorchester to make his excuses about the photograph. She kept him waiting downstairs in the lobby for two hours until she finally allowed him to come up. He had been drinking in the bar solidly for two hours, and she realised it was hopeless and sent him on his way and out of her life. Her final words were: "I didn't realise that it takes more than a woman to make a man sober." Whatever that meant, it was certainly true.

With that, Burton returned to Switzerland and began an eight-month affair with Jeanne Bell, who came to live at Celigny with her 13 year old son, Troy. Burton enrolled him in a local school. Bell was now his official girlfriend and couldn't have been more different from Princess Elizabeth. She was originally from Houston and had become a minor celebrity in America when she became the first black woman to pose naked for *Playboy* magazine. She described her new role in Burton's life as "a helpful companion."

With her support, Burton went on his third serious program to stop drinking. He hired a new Swiss doctor, who put him on a regime of sedatives and tranquilisers along with proper diet and exercise. During that period, he drank nothing but milk or soda water.

But there was more drama to come. Amazingly, as soon as she realised that Princess Elizabeth had departed her ex-husband's life, Elizabeth Taylor began to take an interest in him again. Taylor began phoning the house at Celigny from Leningrad, where she was making a film called *The Blue Bird*. Ostensibly, her affair with Wynberg was as strong as ever, at least as far as he was concerned – they were engaged to be married. For him, it was a question of 'when', not 'if.'

When she started phoning and Burton realised what she was up to, he just laughed. As he sat in his garden and gazed at his beautiful black girlfriend lazing around in the sunshine in her pink bikini, he couldn't comprehend any scenario in which he would get back together with Taylor. It just wasn't possible.

But Taylor had other ideas. In August, she arrived back in Switzerland and went to her house at Gstaad, anticipating a re-run of 1962. Even though both were effectively living with different partners, the game was afoot again.

# AND GOD CREATED BURTON

# CHAPTER 52

# Re-marriage

## *The second time around*

### 1975

For the remainder of 1975, Richard Burton did no more film work. Although his career had been reestablished as a made-for-TV movie star at US$500,000 a picture, there had been no more offers after *Jackpot's* production had abruptly ended.

But he was in a far better position than his ex-wife who, since the divorce, couldn't get any paid work at all. She could only work if she settled for a percentage of the gross. She even had to pay her own expenses. In the middle of 1975, she was shooting a film called *The Blue Bird* in Russia. Filming had been completed on 11th August and had been a fiasco, as she said: "It was a disaster; in five months, I did about a week's work." But it was all she could get. The alternative was announcing her retirement, and she was not about to do that.

Amidst the gloom that same evening, she received a telex from Burton, who was in Celigny. It asked about the possibility of her coming to Switzerland for what he called "an important meeting." Henry Wynberg handed the telex to Taylor after he had read it. He wasn't at all concerned by Burton's request. After a year together, Wynberg considered that his and Taylor's relationship was very "tight" as he put it. It never crossed his mind, or anyone else's, that she would consider a reunion with Burton.

But in the middle of August 1975, Richard Burton and Elizabeth Taylor found themselves in the same place as they had been 12 years earlier. He was in Celigny and she was in Gstaad, only 70 miles apart. What had changed, except everything?

For their reunion, Burton and Taylor chose neutral ground – the Hotel Beau Rivage in Lausanne, right by the lake – and they met there on 15th August 1974.

Henry Wynberg genuinely thought she was going to a business meeting to tie up loose ends with their lawyers after the divorce. He had no idea they were going to discuss getting back together again. It was so incredible that he would not have believed it if she had told him.

# AND GOD CREATED BURTON

But both Burton and Taylor had no doubts why they were at the Beau Rivage. Kitty Kelley, Taylor's biographer, described it: "He arrived without his *Playboy* playmate and she came without her used-car salesman."

Burton had been in Celigny all summer, but Taylor had returned to Switzerland only a few days before.

At the Beau Rivage, no business was discussed and they just fell into each other's arms. Burton wanted to take a room there and then and re-consummate the relationship, but Taylor was far too canny for that. She wanted a commitment first.

Burton was totally beguiled by Taylor that day. She was looking very svelte as a result of being ill in Russia with dysentery. She had lost nearly two stone and had never been thinner. Burton desired her more than ever before. And she ruthlessly used that desire to ensnare him.

So, incredible as it sounds, they got straight down to discussing how they could get rid of their current partners and get together again – this time forever. They decided that both Wynberg and Bell would have to be bought off. Burton said he could handle his end, but Taylor said she would need help to disentangle herself from Wynberg. They had set up some business ventures together that would need to be curtailed.

So three days later, on 18th August, Burton went to Gstaad and met Henry Wynberg for the first time. Again, Wynberg thought he was coming to a business meeting to tie up more loose ends on matters that, this time, also concerned him. As far as Wynberg was concerned, he and Taylor were shortly to be married and he had no notion what was about to come out of Burton's lips when he sat down for the meeting. As Peter Lawford, Wynberg's best friend, later recalled: "I believe Henry had no idea what was going to take place. It was a bombshell for him – and for me."

The breakup with Wynberg was more complicated than might have been anticipated. Taylor and Wynberg had set up a joint venture to enter the perfume business using Taylor's name as the brand.

Burton had to negotiate a price to buy him out of that business, and he did. Considering how shocking it was, the negotiations went swimmingly and, within a few days, both of their partners were gone; Bell went back to New York with her son and Wynberg went back to Los Angeles. Bell is believed to have left Celigny with US$100,000, and Wynberg left Gstaad US$500,000 richer, both sums paid by Burton. To get their money, the condition was that they had to leave the next day. Both of them, separately unaware of what was happening to the other and facing the stark inevitability of it all, packed their bags and got out.

When Wynberg arrived back in Los Angeles, he was sanguine about what had happened: "I was her lover and people always assume that when a love affair is over, the lovers become enemies, not friends. I will always be her friend." That is what he thought then. Later, Wynberg would be unhappy about how he had been treated and would launch a legal suit against Taylor over ownership of the perfume business. As for Jeanne Bell, she accepted her lot and has never said a word about it, then or since.

With those loose ends tied up and the business concluded, on 21st August, John Springer announced to an astonished world that his clients were back together, in love again, and that remarriage could not be ruled out.

Burton did not want to remarry, but Taylor was determined to have it her way. Kitty Kelley said: "It took Elizabeth approximately six weeks to convince Richard Burton to remarry her. Rationally, he knew it was the worst thing he could possibly do to either of them, but emotionally he could not resist." Taylor wrote Burton a letter which was eventually published – it read: "I know we will be together in every biblical sense forever, so why are we afraid of that legal bit of paper?...Someday, somewhere, you son of a bitch, something will make you realise that you can't live without me."

After the announcement, Taylor left no one in any doubt about what she intended; she spoke of Burton as "my former husband – oh, I mean, my future husband – oh, I don't know what to call him. I can't say 'my fiancé' or 'my roommate'. Isn't life full of ironies?"

The newly reunited couple, with no work on the horizon, decided to travel for pleasure and to go places they had always wanted to go to. They flew first to Israel to undertake a tour of the country and support various charitable initiatives. When they got to Jerusalem, they checked into the King David Hotel and, for once, had to settle for the second best suite as Henry Kissinger, the US Secretary of State, was already in residence with his wife, Nancy.

The arrival of Burton and Taylor caused a sensation in Jerusalem and it was just like the old days again. Israeli fans hadn't heard about the decline in their careers. Wherever they went, they were mobbed. They also became firm friends with Kissinger and his wife. He offered them the use of his own security team, which consisted of 70 US Marines. Kissinger was apparently star struck by the couple and hosted an official US government reception for them in the hotel.

# AND GOD CREATED BURTON

Before they left, they performed at a benefit concert in Israel, where Taylor read out 'The Story of Ruth' and Burton read the 23rd Psalm. After a week in Israel, they returned to Gstaad. Soon afterwards, they decided to attend a celebrity tennis tournament in Johannesburg, South Africa, to raise funds for a local hospital. Peter Lawford and Ringo Starr also flew out to attend the tournament. The publicity generated by such visits was enormously valuable to the charities concerned.

In Johannesburg, there was more drama with a very familiar ring to it. Taylor went into hospital after a fall with sore ribs. Her chest was x-rayed and, although the ribs were intact, she was told there was a shadow on her lung which needed to be investigated. South African doctors told Burton they feared that she could have lung cancer. They scheduled more detailed scans the following day.

Taylor was distraught and she faced a terrible 24 hours as she awaited the results of the definitive tests. She said: "I thought all through the night, it's funny when you think you don't have long to live how many things you want to do and see, and smell, and touch. How really simple they are. I had about 12 hours to contemplate death, and a nasty one at that – cancer of the lungs."

Her account of that period was later published in *Ladies Home Journal*, where she described how she and Burton "held each other with a kind of awe" that night as they contemplated the worst.

But it turned out to be nothing at all – not even remotely a serious problem. The specialist's report stated that the shadow on her lung was caused from old scar tissue, a legacy from having tuberculosis as a child. Taylor was ecstatic when she heard the news, and the performance she put on was equal to any of her best work in the movies. Memorably, she said to Burton: "I have my life back. I mean you, Richard."

She had worked her magic and, straightaway, Burton got down on one knee and proposed remarriage. She accepted like a flash and later recalled the moment: "He got down on his knees. He said: 'Will you marry me?' I fell about with laughter and said: 'Sure, honey bunny.'"

She had somehow convinced him that they were either "destined" or "doomed" to stay together forever.

Afterwards, anyone reviewing the events of those 48 hours might have had some concerns. Burton, who had resisted remarriage, immediately changed his mind when Taylor was given the all-clear from cancer. Taylor had been into hospital many times since then and had been x-rayed countless times.

# RE-MARRIAGE

The issue of the shadow must have come up before. When doctors told her about the problem they had found, she could simply have told them about it – but for some reason she kept silent. Johannesburg was the one place in the world where her medical records could not be accessed easily because of the apartheid sanctions.

Paul Ferris was certainly suspicious that all was not what it seemed and he wondered what sort of game Taylor was playing and to what lengths she would go to ensnare her man. Ferris said: "The next day, she was told it was not cancer after all. How the disease could have been suspected and then excluded on the basis of x-rays studied overnight is not clear. But perhaps it was meant to be symbolic as Burton proposed marriage."

Some people to this day believe she planned the whole thing to trick Burton into remarrying her. That the remarriage was against his will is not in doubt, and how he allowed it to happen no one really knows. But from the evidence, it appears he was tricked into it by a very wily woman pulling every emotional string she could. Suffice to say, she ensured that they immediately left for Botswana after she was discharged from the hospital. They went on a safari holiday with remarriage in mind.

With the proposal in the bag, in the next few days, Taylor persuaded Burton to remarry her immediately in the remote village of Kasane, on the banks of the Chobe River in the Chobe Game Reserve in Botswana.

Later, Burton said he was overcome by the romance of the setting. It was idyllic, but he admitted: "I kept asking myself: 'What am I doing here?'"

For the ceremony on 10th October 1975, the bride wore green, a dress that had been given to her by the late Ivor Jenkins before his accident. It was a kind of Druid garment, trimmed with beads and bird feathers. In her hair, she had green leaves and beads. The groom wore a red shirt, red socks and white trousers.

They were married by Ambrose Masalia, the African District Commissioner from the Tswana tribe, who doubled as the local district commissioner. At the ceremony, Masalia asked them if "they understood the consequence of marriage." They replied "yes" almost in unison. When it was done, they drank a loving cup watched by two hippopotamuses and a rhinoceros. Burton later remembered: "It was like a huge dream...Odd place to be married, in the bush by an African gentleman. It was very curious. An extraordinary adventure, doomed from the start of course."

It was Taylor's sixth marriage ceremony to her fifth husband, and his third ceremony to his second wife. She said afterwards: "He's changed. He's so different, so loving. He's not drinking as much. I think, this time, it can work." As was usual on these occasions, she announced they would be together "always" and he responded: "Without you, I was a ghost."

It seemed as if nothing had changed, and in reality, nothing really had. She was still manipulating him and he was happy to be manipulated.

Taylor wrote to him on their wedding night: "How about that? You really are my husband again and I have news for thee, there will be bloody no more marriages – or divorces. We are stuck like chicken feathers to tar – for lovely always. Do you realise that we shall grow old together and I know the best is yet to be."

It was hopelessly optimistic yet, at that moment, they were both lost in some sort of dream world.

To celebrate the marriage, Burton gave Taylor a diamond ring that cost a reputed US$500,000. She then talked about selling the ring again to give to the poor of Africa to celebrate their marriage. It was reported widely that she would do that – whether she ever did is unknown.

What is known is that with the cost of the ring and the pay-offs to Wynberg and Bell, Burton had spent US$1.1 million on getting his wife back. It had cost her nothing.

Philip Burton was shocked and surprised when he found out what had happened in Botswana, and said: "It seemed as if all was as it had been, but when I recalled Richard's letters and what he had told me, I had grave doubts about their future together."

Philip was not the only one; his was a universal reaction. The wedding was christened by journalists "The Burton-Taylor Nuptials – Act Two", for want of anything better. Only the Jenkins family in Wales welcomed the news. They were happy to have their "beloved Elizabeth" firmly back in the family bosom.

Newspaper columnists around the world were aghast at the turn of events. Ellen Goodman famously wrote in *The Boston Globe*: "Sturm has remarried Drang and all is right with the world…In an era of friendly divorces and meaningful relationships, they stand for a marriage that is an all-consuming affair, not a partnership. None of this respecting each other's freedom, but instead saying: 'I can't live without you.' Wow."

They planned to go on a traditional safari for the honeymoon but Burton's constitution was too weak to cope with the jungle environment and he quickly contracted malaria. The trip was abruptly cancelled. To treat him properly, drugs were needed that were not available in Botswana. Taylor was recommended to a qualified American pharmacist called Chenina Samin, later shortened to Chen Sam. She was helicoptered in and expertly nursed Burton back to health. Taylor was deeply impressed and offered her a job on the spot. Chen Sam became Taylor's PA and friend, and served her well for many years.

As soon as he was well enough, a month after the remarriage, Burton and Taylor flew back into London on the morning of the 10th November 1975, where Taylor had planned a spectacular 50th birthday party for her new husband. Taylor had phoned Marjorie Lee from Botswana to ask her to organise the party and spent hours on the telephone giving her the names of all the people to be invited. As usual, there was never reference to any sort of budget. Throughout their years at the Dorchester, both together and separately, neither had ever inquired about the price of anything. But then, neither of them ever directly paid a bill there either. The bills were all sent to Aaron Frosch, who simply paid them.

The party was held in the famous Orchid Room at The Dorchester. Burton and Taylor were delayed and didn't arrive back in England until hours before the party. But their daughters, Liza and Maria, were already there and they sorted out all the arrangements.

For Burton's 50th, no expense was spared. The entire entrance area to the Orchid Rooms was decorated to resemble an East End of London street market. Inside, there were old fashioned wooden barrows full of all Burton's favourite food, like fish and chips and sausages and mash. Graham Jenkins described it: "They chose what I can only describe as an upmarket cockney theme. To carry the buffet of sausage and mash, tripe and onions, ham, turkey, pork and, of course, chips, the Orchid Room was occupied by a fleet of multi-coloured coster barrows. These were given a suitably luxurious setting by the addition of gold hangings and tablecloths."

The Jenkins family was again out in force, welcoming Taylor back into the family. They simply adored Taylor and she them. She positively revelled in the family's affection.

250 guests attended the party and drank as many bottles of champagne. Burton, making his fourth serious attempt to give up drinking, sipped mineral water and seemed surprised to see so many of his friends and family gathered in one place. In true tradition, the party went into the early hours and he led the singing, which Graham Jenkins described as: "As fine a rendering of the Welsh language as to be heard outside the valleys."

The following day, Burton checked into the Wellington Clinic near the famous Lord's Cricket Ground, in North London, for further treatment for his malaria. The doctors found Chen Sam had done a remarkably good job and got the malaria out of his system. Taylor said of her reclaimed husband: "I love him, deeply and truly and forever. He has the most remarkable recuperative powers I've ever seen, which is probably why he is still alive – thank God."

After Burton came out, Taylor went back into the London Clinic for renewed back and neck pain from which she was suffering. Burton took her into the hospital in a wheelchair and was about to leave, when she shouted: "Where are you going buster?" When Burton told her he was going back to The Dorchester, she told him to think again. She insisted that he stay with her at the clinic. But this time, he didn't want to. He felt pressured and she felt upset, and they had their first big row since the remarriage, and he left.

It was already the beginning of the end. They very quickly discovered that they were the same people they had been when they divorced; with the same insecurities, egos and needs. They had foolishly thought they could have a new start, but nothing had really changed. It was obvious at that moment that the remarriage had been a disastrous mistake.

When Taylor came out of the London Clinic, they made a quick trip to Wales to deliver Christmas presents and then flew to Gstaad for Christmas.

Once there, they spent less and less time together. Back at Chalet Ariel, they slept in separate bedrooms in separate wings of the house. The rows grew to be longer and more painful than before. Whereas previous rows had ended quickly, now they extended from one day to the next, picking up the next morning exactly where they had left off the night before. In the end, they gave up speaking to one another – only two and half months after they had remarried.

By then, Burton hadn't worked for nearly a year and he was bored. He had agreed to return to Broadway the following February and was looking forward to going there on his own. A catalyst was needed to bring the disastrous remarriage to an end, and it wasn't long in coming.

# RE-MARRIAGE

# AND GOD CREATED BURTON

# CHAPTER 53

# Suzy Miller

## *The racing driver's wife*

### 1974 to 1975

Suzy Miller was a very striking woman who always made a brilliant first impression, particularly for those men who appreciated willowy, small-breasted blondes. She was not classically beautiful but had the effervescent appeal of an English country girl. Her looks, presence and effect on people were very much the same as the late Princess Diana's. Princess Diana, also never classically beautiful, managed to captivate everyone she met – and Miller had exactly the same effect.

She had spent much of her childhood in Southern Rhodesia with her expatriate parents and her twin sister, Vivienne, as well as a brother called John. As a child, she took piano lessons and became a concert standard pianist. She also was an excellent cook.

Her father, Frederick Miller, had been a high-ranking officer in the British army and then a lawyer and barrister employed in the British colonies. Her childhood had been spent in a number of different countries. But it was under the African sun, with her father working as a judge in Kenya, that Suzy developed into a truly attractive young woman; a real 'head turner', as James Hunt would later describe her to his friends back in London.

By the time the family returned to England, she was a young woman. Frederick Miller bought a farmhouse in Basingstoke, Hampshire, but Suzy, Vivienne and John all moved to London. Without any obvious career prospects, she soon signed up for some modelling work and found she was constantly in demand. She was the perfect dimensions to be a model at 5'10" tall. As well as being good looking, she had an easy personality and was at home in any social circle. She was musically minded and had an instinctive warmth and gentility, although she was not an intellectual of any sort.

In 1974, having just turned 24, Miller suddenly moved to Spain for a lifestyle change. She had been modelling non-stop in London for two years and had made some money. She had also attracted the attention of some unsuitable boyfriends and had moved to Marbella for a change of pace. But in Marbella, she suddenly found herself alone and without friends.

AND GOD CREATED BURTON

She resolved to make some new friends and began playing tennis at the Lew Hoad club in Fuengirola, where, at the bar one day, she set her eyes on an extraordinarily beautiful young man wearing nothing but a pair of very brief shorts and holding a tennis racket.

Although she didn't know it then, her eyes had alighted on one of the world's most eligible bachelors, the 25-year-old racing driver James Hunt. A product of the English public school system, Hunt was an inordinately good-looking man whom women constantly referred to as "beautiful." As a highly talented racing driver, he drove for the eccentric Lord Hesketh's private Formula One racing team.

Hunt was also newly arrived in Marbella in 1974. He had come for tax reasons. With an annual income of US$250,000 a year, he could no longer afford to pay the punitive British taxes. It was the same problem which had also driven Richard Burton out of England 17 years earlier.

Hunt had also found himself lonely and without friends. Although young women were attracted to him like a magnet, he didn't consider them friends and as soon as he had had sex with them, they were soon ejected from his house.

But a few weeks after arriving in Marbella in the spring of 1974, Hunt began rethinking his shallow personal life. Even though he was only 25, for some reason he suddenly decided he should be married. For a consummate playboy who slept with two or three women a day just for sport, it was not the soundest thought he had ever had.

Hunt regularly gave people his views on marriage and expounded his belief that conventional thinking on the subject was wrong, especially with regard to racing drivers. He thought it was a "stupid myth" that drivers had to have a stable home life in order to cope with the stresses and strains of racing.

But his recent move to Spain seemed to have changed his mind. Initially, he was lonely, and, within a week of arriving, he appears to have bought into the "stupid myth" and gone actively looking for a wife. He suddenly announced that he wanted a wife to "help my career and ease my life in exile." In fact, the last thing Hunt needed was a wife. His lifestyle meant he met a lot of women, and it wasn't unusual for him to have sex with more than two of them in a day – often complete strangers. His sexual appetite was voracious, and he had never found a woman who could keep up with him.

His search for a wife was a short one and ended when he set eyes on Suzy Miller that day at the tennis club. Almost immediately, Hunt and Miller began seeing a lot of each other. Hunt was still living out of a suitcase in a hotel, and she had an apartment on the coast overlooking the sea. Their mutual isolation was what initially drew them together.

Miller was very different from Hunt's previous girlfriends. Undemanding, she was quiet and had a thoughtful manner. At first, Hunt attempted to treat her like all his previous flings – in a casual manner – but she bridled against it. And the more she bridled, the more Hunt wanted her. She was not prepared to be his casual girlfriend.

Like many women approaching their mid-20s, Suzy wanted a husband. The fact that Hunt was a famous racing driver held no appeal at all, but she saw him as perfect husband material.

Miller had no affinity for motor racing whatsoever. She had left modelling because she recognised what a shallow world it was and, from what she could observe, motor racing wasn't all that dissimilar. She was desperately keen to have children, and all she really wanted was a serious relationship with a suitable man. Content to devote her life to one man, Miller imagined a partner who would provide her with security and whom, in return, she could look after.

Hunt, however, just didn't get it and Miller quickly threw him out. For the first time, Hunt found himself feeling hurt and lovesick. Realising that he actually might be in love with her, he said: "I talked myself back into her affections."

But Hunt had learned little and soon ended up back at the hotel on his own once again. The relationship continued with its ups and downs, and the more she rejected him, the more he desired her. It was an old trap, and Hunt fell right into it.

After a three-week separation, which included the weekend of the British Grand Prix at Brands Hatch in England, he found himself intensely missing her. All he could think about that weekend was being naked in bed with her – and this time, his thoughts were not of lust but of love. Over the three days, he became more and more obsessive in his thoughts.

On the evening of Sunday 20th July 1974, he arrived back in Marbella from London. He drove straight from the airport to her apartment and proposed marriage. As he remembered: "Knowing that the prospect of marriage would swing Suzy around, I went back to her and proposed." It was a desperate measure and reflected the extent of his infatuation. He had truly lost his senses. Miller accepted without hesitation and immediately telephoned her parents and sister with the news. She watched as a sheepish Hunt also telephoned his own astonished parents. The engagement was properly announced a week later and a wedding date set for the end of the Formula One season, in October. The roller coaster had started, and there would be no getting off.

Miller wanted to get married right away, but that was impractical and Hunt wanted to catch his breath and put some time between the engagement and the wedding day.

Immediately after the proposal, he expressed some regret to his friends, saying he was not quite sure what he was doing. Although he wanted Miller to be his girlfriend, he found he was still sexually attracted to other women. Miller, however, was perfect at family occasions and for parading as his partner. She added a great deal of value to him, and he knew it. So he resolved to try his best to reform himself in order to make the relationship work.

But there were inherent problems. He loved having sex with her but found that it was over too quickly. Hunt was a sex addict before the term came into common usage, and he was unfaithful to her almost from the start.

But Hunt found that, once he had proposed, there was no escaping and, at that time, he did not even particularly want to escape. He enjoyed home life with her very much. He was in love with her, or so he thought, and was undeniably proud of having landed her.

Friends at the time conceded that Hunt was unsure of himself where women were concerned, and his interest in them typically extended no further than the bedroom. He had a giant appetite for sex and looked to feed wherever he could. On a physical level, he was unequalled. Emotionally, however, he was an amateur. According to friends, he would often suggest in conversation that he was not sure what love was. Later in his life, he denied ever having been in love with Suzy. As his close friend the journalist Gerald Donaldson observed: "The emotional component of a relationship for James was still virgin territory."

At the engagement party held at his brother Peter Hunt's apartment in London, he kept telling people: "I don't know why I'm doing this." But as he looked around at the happy family scene, he realised that it had gone too far and he couldn't get out of it. To people who knew him well, he appeared very weak and confused – at odds with the confident Hunt whom everyone knew.

Hunt wanted desperately to cut and run and to remove himself from the whole dreadful situation, but seeing no way out, he turned to drinking. For the full four days leading up to the wedding, he was never once sober. The night before the ceremony, he had hardly any sleep as he stayed up most of the night drinking himself silly in preparation for the big event. And, on the day of the wedding itself, the situation was an utter farce. At 6 o'clock that morning, Hunt woke up and poured himself the first of many beers. Before leaving to go to the church, he knocked back a couple of Bloody Marys in quick succession in order to keep him going until lunch. By the time he walked up the aisle he was hopelessly intoxicated. Some say he had done it deliberately because he would otherwise not have been able to go through with the ceremony.

Hunt couldn't cope, as he admitted: "I just couldn't handle the whole scene, so I went out and got blind, roaring drunk. For four days, I went on the most stupendous bender of my life."

Lord Hesketh continued to assure him that "it would all work out in the end." Afterwards,

Hesketh vehemently denied having encouraged the marriage: "I think the truth of the matter is that James had rather changed his mind by the time he got to the church, and he wouldn't have been the first or last person to have done that and survived." But Hesketh admitted: "He said it to me on the way to the church, and I said: 'It's a bit late now.' It was a very big wedding. I said: 'You know, everyone feels like this.'"

Lord Hesketh paid for the wedding, which was held at the Church of the Immaculate Heart of Mary, better known as the Brompton Oratory, in Kensington. Suzy Miller was Catholic, which dictated a Catholic church, and Hunt converted to Catholicism for the ceremony. The grand setting was entirely appropriate for the society wedding of the year. Hesketh, who was best man, arranged a full orchestra to play the music, and the invitations had stressed that nothing short of full morning suits were required. More or less every racing driver of distinction was invited, including Graham Hill, Stirling Moss, Jackie Stewart, John Watson and Ronnie Peterson.

As for Hunt, he would say afterwards that he remembered little of the event. At the wedding reception, Hesketh and Horsley supported him when he had to stand up to deliver the speech. According to other guests, he was virtually incoherent as he addressed the invitees and it was all rather embarrassing. Suzy just smiled her way through it all, convinced it would be different now that he was a married man. Given how much he had had to drink that day, the portents were not auspicious.

The following day, they left for their honeymoon in Antigua and, once

AND GOD CREATED BURTON

more, the occasion proved to be anything but straightforward. The essential incompatibility of the newly married couple was immediately apparent by the presence in Antigua of his racing team manager, Anthony Horsley, and his wife. Horsley had also married just a few weeks earlier and the two men planned a joint honeymoon in Antigua, in the Caribbean Sea.

It was no accident of dates. Hunt simply didn't want to be alone with Suzy for a fortnight. He knew she would want conversation and he knew it would have little to do with motor racing, which was all Hunt talked about.

While both their brides had dreamed of a romantic honeymoon on the golden sands of Antigua alone with their new husbands, the two men seemed to prefer each other's company. It was an entirely selfish gesture.

When they returned to Spain as man and wife, things did not improve. Hunt was absent most of the time. Suzy just wanted them to settle down and enjoy each other's company. She longed for a relationship, followed by three children and a settled family life. Miller desired nothing more than to be a wife and to build a home. The result, however, was catastrophic: the harder she tried to please him, the more he tried to shake her off.

The new Mrs Hunt did her best to be a racing driver's wife. But, mostly, she led her own life and her husband led his. He became consistently unfaithful and was not particularly good at hiding his infidelities. And she learned not to ask. Hunt recalled later: "It was a matter of clashing lifestyles and personalities. I am very much into racing and doing my own thing, and I move very fast. She wanted a slow pace, a good solid base and a solid relationship. Ironically, these were the very things I married her for in the first place."

Within a few months, Suzy realised that the marriage was not going to work. Still, she was prepared to give it time in the unlikely event that she might be wrong. At races in early 1975, Suzy admitted she was "bored stiff", saying to friends: "I literally felt like a spare part. I was just there for the show."

The couple began to spend more and more time apart. Sensing that the union was coming apart, Hunt's parents, Wallis and Susan, travelled to Marbella for a long stay to try to make running repairs to the marriage. Upon their arrival, their son was absent and he appeared only sporadically thereafter. Susan Hunt was entirely on Suzy's side. She knew precisely where the fault lay, conceding: "Suzy is absolutely gorgeous, most of his girls are. But I can see that, for James, to be married is impossible. His lifestyle doesn't suit it. I'm bound to say I love him dearly, but I'd hate to have him for a husband." Susan Hunt had just about summed it up.

Hunt tried to explain what had gone wrong: "I thought that marriage was what I wanted and needed to give me a nice, stable and quiet home life, but in fact it wasn't. And the mistake was mine. I really wanted to go racing on my own, and it wasn't much fun for Suzy to sit at home and wait for me all that time. It was also a terrible hassle for her to come racing because race meetings were probably the most relaxing time in my schedule. The rest of the time, you tend to be leaping on aeroplanes once a day and that made it even worse. It's bad enough organising one person to get on an aeroplane; organising two gets to be twice as much hassle. It got to the point where it was a problem for Suzy to come travelling and a hell of a deal for her to stay at home. It was making life miserable in the extreme for her and, since I felt responsible for her, it was making me miserable too.

"If she stayed at home while I rushed around the world, it was boring for her. If she came with me, it was no fun for her. I was always looking over my shoulder to see if she was there, and she was always struggling to keep up with me. It was a heavy deal for both of us."

Hunt knew he had to get out of the marriage and he prayed for a miracle. The miracle he hoped for, quite simply, was that she would meet someone else. Hunt did not want to desert her and was also wary of the money situation. In the case of a divorce, Suzy would have been entitled to a large share of his wealth, which he had moved to Spain to protect. A divorce would have relieved him of half of fortune, as much as US$250,000. He literally couldn't afford a divorce, but as he said: "I was very, very anxious not to hurt her. There are nice ways and nasty ways to do things, and I hope I can never be a hurtful person."

Meanwhile, Suzy began to feel the same. Facing the possibility that James was not for her and that she had likely married for the wrong reasons, she wanted out as well. The marriage may as well have ended there and then, but it dragged on for another eight months as Suzy looked for a new partner. Finally, despairing of the likelihood of a miracle, Hunt offered to buy Suzy a smart apartment in London and to give her an allowance, with a divorce to follow when it suited them. He was prepared to pay heavily to get out of the marriage, but she didn't need the money and was reluctant to make it official. Suzy was certainly not going to get divorced and be single again – that was not on the menu at all. So they continued to live together in Marbella although, by July 1975, they had for all intents and purposes gone their separate ways.

And as they went their separate ways, Hunt got the bills for his wife's travelling, which he didn't like. On one of the few occasions they were both at home, they had a heated argument about the cost of transatlantic telephone calls on her hotel bill. The hotel bills added up to nearly US$8,000, with two thirds from telephone costs.

Meanwhile, Hunt was seen with a new girl called Jane Birbeck in London, although in reality she was just one of many. He was careful to be discreet as he didn't want anything in the newspapers that might upset Suzy or the Miller family – or his own family for that matter.

Lord Hesketh finally conceded that he had been wrong about the marriage: "I'm not sure James was perfectly suited for married life, really."

In mid-December, the two of them packed a suitcase, locked up the house and left for the airport bound for Gstaad. They had randomly accepted an invitation to spend Christmas in the ski resort with friends. At the same time, Richard Burton and Elizabeth Taylor were also preparing to leave The Dorchester for the airport, also bound for Gstaad.

There was nothing random about Richard Burton's decision to be in Gstaad at Christmas; it was something he always did. But for Suzy Miller, it was a meeting with her destiny. A divorce and a wedding would shortly follow.

# SUZY MILLER

# AND GOD CREATED BURTON

# CHAPTER 54

# Blinding flash of reality

## Suzy arrives in the snow

### 1976

In December 1975, Gstaad was the place to be. At that time of year, it was an absolutely magical place if you were in love. But Richard Burton and Elizabeth Taylor no longer were. And neither were James Hunt and Suzy Miller. Burton and Taylor walked around their house at Chalet Ariel avoiding each other. Hunt and Miller were never even in the same place. Burton went out for long walks with his friend and assistant, Brook Williams, and Suzy Miller wandered around Gstaad on her own, deep in thought about her future. If Burton walked and Miller wandered, eventually they were bound to bump into each other and so it came to pass. But it would take two weeks.

Meanwhile, Burton and Taylor had moved into separate bedrooms for the first time since they had met, 14 years before. Symbolically, it marked the end of the love affair. They knew this was to be their last Christmas together and they jointly decided that when Burton flew off to New York in late January to begin rehearsals on his new Broadway play, Taylor would not be going with him.

Likewise, the Hunts had ended up in Gstaad because they also realised it was their last Christmas together as man and wife. With the state of their relationship, they didn't want to stay at home in Marbella on their own; they didn't want to go to their families either, with all the explaining that might mean. But for their last Christmas together, they didn't want to be apart either.

Like Burton, Hunt would be flying off alone once the holidays were over. At the end of 1975, Lord Hesketh's Formula One racing team had closed down and he had secured a new drive with the McLaren-Ford team as its number one driver. Come January, he would be going to South America to challenge for the world championship for the first time.

In Gstaad, Miller and Hunt, like Burton and Taylor, effectively went their separate ways. Hunt was in serious training for the 1976 Formula One season and spent all day at the gym or running in the snow. At night, he didn't drink and, consequently, didn't socialise. Without alcohol, Hunt was a different man. Suzy also knew he was surreptitiously seeing local girls he met at the gym. Miller ended up very depressed for the first time in her life, and spent most of

731

the days on her own wandering around Gstaad looking miserable.

A few days after the New Year, Hunt flew to São Paulo to compete in the Brazilian Grand Prix, the opening race of the 1976 Formula One season. The first few races of the year were outside of Europe, and he would be gone for a month.

He left his wife continuing her lonely wanderings looking for a new boyfriend, and there was no better place than Gstaad in January to find one.

She first set eyes on Richard Burton as they were going in opposite directions on a ski cable lift. She knew exactly who he was, but he had no idea who she was. There was no chance to speak, but they both exchanged wry smiles.

Burton felt like a clap of thunder had gone off in his ear. He was awestruck by Suzy Miller and turned to Brook Williams, who was with him, and said: "Who is that vision that has just passed by?" Of all the magnificent women in Gstaad that holiday, and there were many, Burton was struck by the sheer presence of Suzy Miller. He admitted he was "transfixed", as he would say later: "I turned around and there was this gorgeous creature, about nine feet tall. She could stop a stampede."

Luckily for Burton, Williams knew exactly who she was and was acquainted with her socially. But then, Williams knew everybody. He was immediately able to tell Burton that she was 27 years old and the wife of James Hunt, the famous racing driver. Burton had never heard of Hunt. But Suzy Miller was well aware that the man smiling back at her formed one half of the most famous married couple in the world.

Burton recalled: "I was wondering when she would turn up again, but Brook knew her a little and my luck was in." As luck would have it, Burton and Williams ran into her again a few days later on the main street in Gstaad. This time, they stopped to chat. Williams seized the opportunity to invite her to a house party they were attending that night. She grabbed the invitation with both hands and was desperate to penetrate the Gstaad party scene in order to get to know the man who couldn't stop smiling at her. Burton may by then have been 50 years old, but his smile was as devastating to women as it had ever been. And Brook Williams couldn't help but notice the way Suzy Miller's face lit up when she received the invitation.

Miller quickly realised that his second marriage to Taylor was over already. Although she was at the party, she and Burton hardly spoke and it was clear that there was little warmth between them.

At the party, Burton sat at one end of an overcrowded table and Suzy was at the other end of another table. As the party became more crowded and more people squeezed on the benches, Burton and Suzy found themselves next to each other and were properly introduced.

During the conversation, Burton confided to her that the second wedding had been a terrible mistake and that it had become apparent almost immediately. Miller recognised the dilemma immediately and told Burton it was precisely what had happened to her marriage; within days, she had also realised that it was a mistake. Although nothing physical happened between Miller and Burton, the relationship between them started that night.

Burton was captivated by her, particularly as she, having lost a contact lens, ended up crawling around on the floor to look for it amongst the guests' feet. He thought this hilarious.

Williams invited her to come to the house the following day for lunch and, after that, Suzy started visiting Chalet Ariel regularly to meet Burton. The affair between them began almost immediately. He was 50 and she was 27, and it was Suzy's first dalliance since her marriage to Hunt. The age gap appeared large but, as Burton said: "She was mature far beyond her years."

From the day they were introduced, Burton and Suzy became virtually inseparable. Burton remembered: "She started coming to the house two, three and then four times a week."

Although both their brief marriages were effectively over, the union was immediately problematic. As far as the outside world was concerned, both the Hunt and Burton marriages were happy. But Burton needed Suzy Miller desperately: his life was a mess, he was drinking heavily again and he needed to be taken care of.

Elizabeth Taylor immediately noticed the fresh-faced and uncomplicated Englishwoman coming to the house and quickly guessed what was going on. But Taylor had also realised that her marriage to Burton a second time round was a farce, and that it was stupid to fight it.

Miller and Taylor were two very different women, with very different talents and interests, but, despite the predictable rivalry, Taylor instinctively recognised that Suzy was something special and witnessed the way she fussed over her husband. One evening at the château, in a particularly memorable exchange, Taylor said to Suzy: "You'll only last six months with Richard." To which Suzy replied: "Perhaps, but those six months will be very worthwhile."

Taylor, to her surprise, found that she was rather relieved at Burton's affair and at the acknowledgement that her marriage to him was finally over.

She went straight out and hit the local discotheque. There, she found an attractive 37-year-old Maltese advertising executive called Peter Darmanin holidaying without his wife. She brought the flaxen-haired young man back to Chalet Ariel to stay with her and wouldn't let him go.

For a week, it was an extraordinary time with both Burton and Taylor sleeping in the same house, but with different partners.

In the third week of January, Burton had to leave for New York to attend rehearsals for a new play in which he was due to star at the Plymouth Theatre, on Broadway. Suzy presented him with a dilemma. He couldn't really take her to New York, and she couldn't go home to Marbella either. So he arranged for Brook Williams to take her to Lausanne; to the home of Gunter Sachs, one of the richest men in Europe. Sachs was one of Europe's great playboys and the heir to a vast fortune. He and Burton were great friends.

He arranged with Sachs for Suzy to be a houseguest for a few weeks to give him time to tell Taylor that their marriage was over. Then he would send for her.

Burton didn't want his relationship with Suzy turning into a media feeding frenzy, which he knew was easily possible. Burton knew she would be safe and have a good time at Sachs' extraordinarily lavish home by the lake in Lausanne.

Meanwhile, as Burton left Chalet Ariel for the last time and flew to New York, Taylor stayed on in Gstaad, continuing her affair with Darmanin. Knowing he would eventually have to return to his wife in Malta, she wanted to make the most if it.

Throughout it all, Suzy had been keeping her husband, who was in South America, fully informed over the telephone of her developing affair, and to say that he was delighted would have been an understatement. In fact, when she first told him that Burton had invited her to go to New York, James Hunt had simply replied: "Fine, off you go." When Hunt put down the telephone receiver, he just hoped and prayed it would last. Richard Burton was the answer to his prayers.

As soon as his plane took off from Geneva to New York, Richard Burton also breathed a sigh of relief. He had left Elizabeth Taylor behind for the last time and could look forward to a new life with Suzy Miller. He could not have been happier.

Burton's foray to New York would be the first time he had stood on a stage since 'Hamlet' in 1964, 12 years earlier. There was more at stake than just the play. In the intervening years, Broadway had missed him. It was down on its luck and was looking forward to Burton's arrival as a potential saviour.

When he got there, he found the glory years of Burton and Taylor had worn out. Now, in middle age, the fans waiting on street corners were counted in the hundreds rather than the thousands. The glamour of Broadway had faded.

Burton was to play in Peter Shaffer's gruelling drama called 'Equus'. 'Equus' was about a boy who blinds six horses because they witness him indulging in sexual intercourse with a very young woman. Burton played Martin Dysart, a provincial psychiatrist who treats the boy. The play, directed by John Dexter, was first shown at the Old Vic in London and was brought to Broadway by producer Alexander H. Cohen.

Burton's opportunity came when Anthony Perkins, who was playing Dysart, told Cohen he would have to leave the production in February 1976. Burton wasn't a shoo-in for the role as John Dexter didn't want him. But somehow, the director's view was pushed to one side.

The deal came about principally because of Burton's new agent, Robbie Lantz. The Hugh French era had finally come to an end, and both he and Elizabeth Taylor had signed with Lantz.

They had first met Lantz in 1965, when he had approached them along with Franco Zeffirelli with a deal to become involved in *The Taming Of The Shrew*. Lantz had been very impressive and both Burton and Taylor had wanted him to become their agent and replace Hugh French, whom they believed had got above himself and become far less effective as a result. But Burton got clever and told Lantz that he and Taylor only paid five per cent commission to agents, although they in fact paid French ten per cent and always had. Lantz looked at them and said: "Let's talk again when you can afford me." And that was that. Eventually, as French deteriorated, Lantz came back into their lives and they paid him the standard ten per cent.

The 59-year-old Berlin-born agent was a short, gnomish figure with large glasses who spoke with a thick German accent. He was an independent agent with a roster of clients that included Leonard Bernstein, Bette Davis and Yul Brynner. Lantz was a genius and had worked hard to revive Burton's career.

Lantz was Peter Shaffer's agent, and that gave Burton the introduction to 'Equus'. The agent convinced Shaffer to overrule Dexter and recommend Burton to 'Equus' producer, Alex Cohen.

A meeting was arranged in London, at the Squires Mount home of Gwen Jenkins, Burton's sister-in-law. Lantz invited the producer, Cohen, to renew his acquaintance with Burton over lunch. But it was not to be without drama.

When they both got there, Burton was upstairs so they sat down and Gwen served them a drink whilst she prepared lunch.

But when Burton came down, he was rolling drunk and in no state for a meeting. During the lunch, he fell off his chair and on to the floor. Luckily for Burton, Cohen was well used to this sort of behaviour and, together, he and Lantz put Burton to bed to sleep it off.

Lantz and Cohen carried on negotiating without him and a deal was settled for Burton to take over the lead in 'Equus' at US$60,000 a week for 12 weeks with the option for another two. Burton also agreed to do the film version Shaffer had planned for US$500,000 at some date in the future.

But Cohen had taken a huge gamble hiring Burton. The role of the Dysart, the psychiatrist in 'Equus' was the most difficult of parts. Graham Jenkins summed it up when he said: "The man of reason, Dysart, pitted against the primitive spirit of the boy who, against all reason, blinds six horses can, in the wrong hands, come across as the most dreadful rubbish."

Peter Shaffer agreed: "'Equus' is the most private, the most deeply erotic of all my plays." But Alec McCowen in London and Anthony Perkins and Anthony Hopkins in New York had played the part with great acclaim, so it was Richard Burton's to mess up.

Publicly, Burton was full of bravado and said to Alex Cohen: "I bet you a thousand kisses to one that I will earn a standing ovation at every performance." But privately, he was very, very scared about playing Dysart and returning to the stage after a decade away, at the age of 50. As he readily admitted: "I thought if I don't take the plunge now, I probably would never go back. I'd never been so bloody scared in my life."

Cohen was delighted to have Burton back and he could see the dollar signs flashing round again. No one had any idea how profitable Burton's 'Hamlet' had been 12 years before. He had seen nothing like it since, as he admitted when they met in Gstaad later to sign the contract.

Burton asked Cohen to help him keep off the drink, and he agreed.

Later, when Cohen had left, Burton walked through the snow around the grounds of the Chalet Ariel reading Shaffer's script, mesmerised by its speeches. He had always responded to the power of words and recalled later: "I walked through the snow in the woods thinking about Dysart, muttering Dysart, spouting Dysart."

Just before he left, Taylor told him he was mad to return to Broadway, saying: "You have the guts of a blind burglar – you know they'll be gunning for you." Burton thought it ironic. 12 years earlier, Taylor had encouraged him to take the lead role in 'Hamlet' against his will – now, she was seeking to discourage him. But he was going to do it no matter what she said. In more ways than one, it was his destiny.

# CHAPTER 55

# Springtime in New York

## *Equus is a triumph*

### 1976

A week later, Richard Burton checked into his regular suite on the 20th floor of the Lombardy Hotel on 56th Street off Park Avenue. As soon as he was settled, he called Suzy Miller in Lausanne and told her he believed it was safe for her to come to New York. But he warned her that he had not yet been able to tell Elizabeth Taylor about the situation, and if the press got hold of the story, there could be trouble. But he decided to take the risk. The moment he had arrived in New York, he found he missed Suzy desperately, and she crossed the Atlantic the next day to be with him. She moved straight into his suite.

Somehow, Burton harboured the notion that Taylor was going to be terribly upset about his affair with Suzy Miller and that he must keep it secret until he told her. In reality, Taylor already knew and couldn't have cared less. She had her spies everywhere, and the minute Miller arrived in New York, Taylor knew about it.

Back in Gstaad, Taylor was having the time of her life with Peter Darmanin. The Maltese turned out to be a genius between the sheets, and since Burton's departure, she and her lover had hardly left the bedroom.

Burton and Suzy spent two discrete weeks together in New York. When people asked her who she was and what was her connection to Burton, she told them she was a friend of Brook Williams. When they went out to dinner, Williams came too.

Only one or two well-connected journalists noticed anything out of the ordinary was going on. In South America, David Benson, motoring editor of the *Daily Express* asked James Hunt why his wife was in New York hanging around with Richard Burton. Hunt admitted there were strains in the marriage, but that she was an old friend of Burton's and it was no more than that. At this stage, no one guessed that Suzy Miller was Burton's new girlfriend.

It was a heady time for Burton in New York. His arrival had excited the whole city and everyone was waiting for his stage debut as the psychiatrist Martin Dysart in 'Equus'.

# AND GOD CREATED BURTON

Suzy and Burton spent a great deal of time in his suite at the Lombardy getting to know each other. Like Taylor and Darmanin, they also spent a lot of time in bed. Burton told her all about his extraordinary life. What surprised her most was the amount of money he earned. She thought racing drivers were the highest paid performers in the world, but she soon realised that Burton was paid in four weeks what it took her husband an entire year to earn. Burton promised her there would be no more quibbling over her phone bills, and she believed him. They seemed automatically to assume this was going to be a permanent union. It was unsaid.

After two glorious weeks with Burton in New York, Suzy left for England to visit her parents and to tell them her news in person. Before she left, Burton had proposed and she had accepted.

After Suzy left, Burton called Taylor, who was still in Gstaad, and asked her to come to New York. He told her he had something very important to say to her. He had also organised a 44th birthday party for her on 27th February – but he didn't tell her that. Burton was incredibly nervous and didn't feel able to tell Taylor about Suzy over the telephone, mistakenly believing she would be very upset.

Meanwhile, Burton was having trouble in rehearsals for 'Equus'. It was proving a struggle for him to grasp the ordinariness of the part of Martin Dysart. Dysart was just an ordinary man, and Burton didn't play ordinary men very well.

Burton was very nervous about the part. He was worried about whether his vocal chords were up to it; worried whether he could remember his lines in the demanding role with a lot of long speeches. When Kenneth Tynan visited him and asked him why he was putting himself through it, he said that, although he was frightened of the stage, he must return to it.

And according to his pact with Alex Cohen, Burton was not supposed to be drinking – but, secretly, he was. Although he strongly denied it in later years, Brook Williams was secretly bringing alcohol into him during rehearsals.

On the 25th February, Taylor flew into New York from Europe. Burton, Robbie Lantz and Aaron Frosch all went to meet her at the airport. Burton asked his two friends to come along for moral support, and they obliged

They had two limousines: one for the people and the other for luggage. But when Taylor appeared with her assistant, Chen Sam, through the gate, they were followed by a line of porters carrying no less than three dozen pieces of luggage. Aaron Frosch realised it would not fit in the car and ordered a van.

On the drive into the city, Burton and Taylor did not speak and Lantz brought Taylor up to date about his work for her. Frosch stayed to wait with the luggage. When they got to the Lombardy, Taylor went straight to the separate suite that had been booked for her. She was jet lagged and went straight to bed.

The following evening, Burton invited Taylor to his suite and sat quietly tapping his fingers on the table as they looked at each other sheepishly. Eventually, Taylor asked: "What is wrong, love?" Then he said it: "I want a divorce."

Taylor looked at him blankly, wondering if this was indeed the same man she had married just 12 years earlier. At that moment, it seemed like a lifetime ago. And they seemed like complete strangers meeting to cancel a business deal. Then, Burton told her about his relationship with Suzy. Taylor just shrugged. He omitted to mention the birthday party he had planned for her two days later.

After a few minutes' contemplation, Taylor blew her top. She screamed at him and said she was not at all upset about Suzy and was already aware of it and had been for days. But what she was really furious about was that Burton had made her travel all the way across the Atlantic to tell her about it. Taylor screamed at him: "You mean you brought me all this way to tell me that?" The two had a furious row which failed to subside even when Burton told her about the birthday party he had planned. Taylor believed he had made that up when he had seen how angry she was.

Storming out, Taylor returned to her room. She called her assistant and told her to book a flight for the following day to the west coast. On impulse, she then called the room of Alexander Cohen to see if the birthday party story was true. He confirmed that it was, and she told him to cancel it. She didn't believe there was any party planned and remained convinced that Burton had called Cohen to tell him what to say after she had left his room.

Cohen was the first to hear the news that she was leaving on the midday plane, and she asked him to issue a statement confirming that they were to divorce.

Her fury with Burton was not abated, and her next call was to Aaron Frosch telling him to draw up two sets of divorce papers – one for her and one for Burton. Even though he was the lawyer for both of them, she told him to set tough terms, believing Burton would do anything to dissolve the marriage quickly. On that score, she was entirely right. In the end, Burton surrendered almost all of his assets to her and was to pay dearly for that trip he had made her take across the Atlantic Ocean.

Burton breathed a sigh of relief when Taylor left his suite. She had seemed almost happy with what he had to say. He put a call into Suzy's parent's house in England and spoke to her father for the first time. He told Suzy he was missing her and needed her to get back to New York as fast as she could.

Meanwhile, Burton turned his attention back to the rehearsals for 'Equus' which were going from bad to worse. And Burton was drinking much more than he should have. At 50 years of age, he no longer had the capacity he had even five years before. He was now an old man and had not adjusted his intake to cope. He found he could no longer drink and act; it simply didn't work anymore.

John Dexter was growing increasingly frustrated with Burton and decided to go for broke and to remove the kid gloves he had been using on the actor. He felt he had nothing to lose. It was just days away from when he would take over from Anthony Perkins, and he was nowhere near ready.

Dexter decided on shock treatment and told Burton he would be playing Dysart in the forthcoming Saturday matinee, a whole week before he was due to replace Perkins. Dexter told him: "I'm going to put you on Saturday afternoon when the audience won't be expecting you." Burton replied: "I won't be ready on Saturday afternoon." Dexter said: "You'll be ready on Saturday afternoon, and you'll go out on stage and you'll do it. On Monday night, the press will be in and there'll be no excuses. On Saturday, you'll be able to get away with murder."

It had been years since a director had spoken to Burton like that, so he just ignored him and carried on as before.

Dexter finally lost his temper, and within full earshot of the rest of the cast and crew, delivered a long monologue about all that was wrong with Burton and his acting. He started with the words: "Richard, you're disgracing yourself..." and ended with: "...you're a lazy, drunken fool." Burton just stood there open mouthed and listened. Dexter knew it was a pivotal moment and that if Burton walked out, he had no replacement. But he felt it was the only chance he had, so he took it. He knew he had to say it in front of the entire cast and company to make Burton realise the seriousness of the situation.

Burton, for all his irresponsible ways, knew Dexter was right and that he had to do something about his desperate existence and dependence on alcohol. He urgently needed Suzy to return from England to give him support, and he counted the hours until she arrived. She had arrived in his life just in time, and he knew it. Burton's extraordinary luck had struck again.

When the Saturday matinee came, it was announced that Anthony Perkins would not be appearing and the audience groaned quietly. But then when the announcer said Richard Burton would be taking his place, they roared in approval.

But Burton was terrible and his performance a fiasco. The audience still loved it because they loved Burton and he was Broadway's biggest star. When John Dexter went back to Burton's dressing room and Burton asked him how he had been, Dexter said; "Absolutely bloody dreadful." Dexter came out of the dressing room and found Robbie Lantz and Peter Shaffer outside. He told them firmly: "Now don't go in there undoing all my good work. He's got to know how bad he was."

And Burton did know. By now, Suzy was back and Burton knew what he had to do. Burton had always had the incredible ability to pull himself together at the very last minute when things seemed at their very worst and about to collapse irretrievably. That time had come again.

In days gone by, he would have called up his adoptive father, Philip Burton, and asked him to get on the next flight for a coaching session. But those days were over. Philip was getting old and had a heart condition. He could no longer travel far from his home in Key West, Florida.

But when he returned to his suite at the Lombardy that evening, he knew exactly what he had to do. He grabbed Suzy and called Brook Williams into his room. They re-arranged the furniture in the suite to match the layout of the stage, and while Brook read and played all the other parts, Richard sweated and drove himself through his lines. Suzy watched and applauded and gave him new confidence. And instead of ice cold martinis, she brought him another ice cold refreshment – milk.

Meanwhile, Elizabeth Taylor, about to depart and realising it was finally over with Burton, suddenly felt very sad. Before she left, she sneaked into his dressing room and wrote on the mirror in an eyebrow pencil: "You are fantastic, love." Burton left it there for the whole run of 'Equus'.

The same day, she flew to Los Angeles and straight into the arms of a former boyfriend, called Henry Wynberg. She found she hardly missed Burton at all. When Taylor was asked by journalists about the swap of partners and her new relationship, she said: "What was I expected to do? Sleep alone?"

By the time Monday night came, Burton was a new man. He was on a high.

He had stopped drinking, knew the script backwards and gave a first night performance that won him a standing ovation, just as he had promised Cohen. As soon as he got back to his dressing room, he called Los Angeles and wished Taylor a happy birthday. With that, he went to dinner with Suzy Miller.

The critics, who were all in to see his first performance that night, were ecstatic. Walter Kerr in the *New York Times* described it as: "The best work of his life." But John Dexter still refused to praise Burton, telling him it was much better but still not good enough. He said: "There was too much emotion; too much of the pulpit and the pub."

The 12-week run was completely sold out and Cohen triggered his two-week extension, which quickly sold out as well. And as Burton promised, there were standing ovations every night. The crowds returned outside the theatre and Burton revived his limousine exit performance with Suzy, although on a much smaller scale.

Robbie Lantz said: "He revitalised not just the play but the whole of Broadway. In what had been a lacklustre season, business picked up all round." The mark of success came when Cohen was able to raise seat prices by US$5 as soon as Burton took over the part.

Burton was also serious about giving up alcohol and started to avoid invitations where he might be tempted, preferring quiet dinners with Suzy. He credited Suzy for his new sober state: "She didn't stop me drinking. She didn't hide bottles. But she encouraged me not to drink because she knew I didn't want to drink. She steadied me. She may have even saved my life. Booze would have killed me, I am sure, if it had not been for Suzy."

One evening, when there was a big party he wanted to avoid, he asked Alex Cohen: "Do you mind if I say that Suzy and I have a date with you?" "Fine" replied Cohen, "but who's Suzy?" Burton said: "You are naïve, aren't you?" It then finally dawned on Cohen that the tall blonde who happened to be staying at the same hotel was his new girlfriend.

Meanwhile, journalists were also starting to get wind of the relationship between Richard Burton and James Hunt's wife. But, perhaps predictably, the first reports to surface in print were of an affair between Suzy and Brook Williams.

One writer who was fooled was the man reputed to be the world's most astute gossip columnist, Nigel Dempster. In his fabled column in the London *Daily Mail*, Nigel Dempster revealed the breakup of the Hunt marriage and wrote that his wife Suzy had flown to New York where she was "being escorted by Emlyn Williams' son, Brook, who is one of the Burton entourage."

Despite it being wrong, it was news because it signalled the Hunt marriage was over, and the *Daily Express*' David Benson found himself in trouble for being scooped by Dempster. Benson immediately rang Hunt's brother, Peter Hunt, in London, as Hunt himself was in transit to Johannesburg for the South African Grand Prix. Benson recalled: "He professed to be astounded by the report, denied it absolutely and said he knew nothing of this man called Williams. He told me that there was nothing unusual in the fact that Suzy was in New York while James was in South Africa; that they were both friends of the Burtons and that Richard and Elizabeth had invited them both to visit them when they were in New York."

But Peter Hunt was lying to Benson; he knew exactly what was going on. Benson accepted his denial and phoned the *Daily Express* news desk and told them there was no truth in Dempster's story. The denial only stood for a day.

As soon as Taylor had left for Los Angeles, Burton dispensed with any discretion and Suzy was openly on his arm. Manhattan can be a very small place, and Burton and Suzy made no attempt to hide their closeness. Initially, however, American reporters were completely baffled as to who Suzy was.

Burton did not care to enlighten them and enjoyed the press' discomfort at them not being able to caption the many photos of the two appearing in the four New York daily newspapers.

Eventually, the journalists worked out that the striking blonde was the wife of racing driver James Hunt and that she had clearly broken up Burton's marriage to Elizabeth Taylor. There was no bigger media story than that in the last week of February 1976.

In New York, after his performances, Suzy and Richard would dine with friends or on their own. Burton took her to the same bistros and restaurants to which he had taken Elizabeth Taylor ten years earlier. Burton was immensely proud of his new girlfriend's magical effect on people. When he walked into a restaurant with her on his arm, people applauded. When she excused herself, the women of New York followed her into the restroom to get a closer look at the green-eyed English beauty who had enraptured New York society overnight.

With the news suddenly out, and Suzy and Burton no longer a secret, James Hunt was in for a shock when he landed at Johannesburg airport for the South African Grand Prix.

When Hunt got off the plane, he drove to the Sleepy Hollow Hotel where he was staying for the build-up and preparation before he moved to the Kyalami Ranch Hotel for the actual race. The hotel was staked out by a throng of jostling journalists and photographers – none of them interested in the race. Everywhere he went, he was followed by journalists who had flown in specially to work on the story.

Formula One racing as a sport was popular all over the world, but not *that* popular. Suddenly, there was huge media interest, including from the *Punjabi Times*, who had never before sent a reporter to cover Formula One.

Meanwhile, David Benson was furious with Peter Hunt, who had lied to him. He decided to phone James Hunt directly, but Hunt also proceeded to tell him a pack of lies. He told him that he had been speaking to Suzy the night before and that there was nothing between her and Burton. Benson recalled: "Hunt had never before lied to me to my knowledge and I'd known him from his very early days and done a great deal to promote his career. So I had every reason to believe James. I suppose, deep down, I liked Suzy so much and I thought that they made such a good couple that I wanted to believe James. He was rather jovial about the whole thing. Nevertheless, I instinctively suspected that Hunt was not really telling the truth and I fed my feelings back to the *Daily Express* news desk."

The *Express* news desk contacted its own bureau chief in New York, a man called Ivor Key. Key investigated and confirmed Benson's suspicions, writing a story headlined: 'Off We Go Again – Booze, A Beautiful Girl And Another Burton Bust-up'. The article read: "Off we go once more on the Burton marriage merry-go-round. First, Richard Burton is back on the booze, with racing driver James Hunt's 26-year-old wife, Suzy, at his side. Second, Liz Taylor is packing her bags to go home to mother in Los Angeles. Third, Suzy Hunt has said she is considering divorce, although her husband, now in South Africa, says that's news to him."

When that story was published, Benson got back on the phone to Peter Hunt. Benson recalls: "'Look, Peter', I said, 'I have had a great friendship with you and James and this story about Suzy is bouncing around the world and must come out in the open sooner or later. Why not tell me straight exactly what is going on? It's perfectly obvious that this is no friendly little deal of Suzy staying with Burton in New York.' Peter replied: 'All right, David, I'll square with you. Suzy wants to marry Burton. I think she's a very silly girl, but there it is. She's told James and he has said he won't stand in her way.' I grumbled about not being told that at the start and immediately phoned James in South Africa, where he confirmed the story and gave me a quote about his co-operation if Suzy asked for a divorce."

Benson then wrote a story that appeared on the front page of the *Daily Express* on 26th February 1976, headlined: 'Suzy To Marry Burton.' Benson and the *Daily Express* were now back on top and leading the world with the story. The story read: "Suzy Hunt, wife of British racing driver James Hunt, is seeking a quickie divorce in America so that she can marry Richard Burton. This follows the actor's latest breakup with his second-time wife Liz Taylor. He and 27-year-old Suzy are staying at the same New York hotel. Burton, too, was said to be in a hurry to get a divorce." The article then contained everything the Hunt brothers had told him.

The article legitimised the story and it seemed that, suddenly, everyone wanted to know how Hunt felt about his wife keeping company with Richard Burton. Hunt pretended to be desolate. At the gates of the hotel, he read out the following statement: "Naturally, I am perturbed by all the publicity about my wife in Europe and America, but I must concentrate 100 per cent on the Grand Prix. If there is a problem, it is just going to have to wait until after the race. Meanwhile, I'm far too busy sorting out the car and keeping myself fit." With that, he handed out the press releases and immediately sprinted off on a six-mile training run, followed by puffing hacks who soon gave up the chase.

It was one of the most satisfying workouts of his life. He was finally free, exactly 16 months after his wedding day in London. In fact, the Miller-Burton relationship that had developed so quickly into a proposal of marriage and a request for a quickie divorce came as a huge relief for Hunt.

Meanwhile, Suzy and Burton found they couldn't leave their Lombardy Hotel suite because over 50 reporters and photographers were in the corridor.

As the news broke, Burton decided to break the ice with Hunt and called him in South Africa, effectively to apologise. Hunt remembered Burton being rather embarrassed and tongue-tied on the telephone, which he found strange. In truth, Burton couldn't quite believe that Hunt was being so casual about letting go of his beautiful wife. He expected him to be bitter towards him and devastated. But he simply said to Burton: "Relax, Richard. You've done me a wonderful turn by taking on the most alarming expense account in the country." A bemused and somewhat relieved Burton replaced the receiver in his hotel room and turned to Suzy and smiled. She said to him: "I told you James is fine about all this." Burton still could not understand.

They had effectively split some six months earlier, in July 1975, so it was by no means traumatic as Hunt said at the time: "Her running off with Burton is a great relief to me. It actually reduces the number of problems I have to face outside my racing. I am mainly concerned that everyone comes out of it happy and settled." In fact, there was no disguising Hunt's utter relief at what had transpired, as he confessed: "I prefer to be on my own at races because, really, there's enough to do looking after me. It's more than I can handle to keep myself under control at a race meeting without trying to look after someone else as well and have more responsibilities and worries. I find that if I want an early night before a race, or if I want a couple of hours to cool off and relax before dinner, I can do no better than to read a book or listen to music and therefore it's better to be on my own." Resolving not to get tempted into marriage again, he told journalists: "Meanwhile, it is probably a good thing that I am still technically married. I have that as a safety valve. It will stop me from doing anything silly again."

The intense media interest carried on all weekend and Hunt was equally prominent on the front pages of the newspapers as he was on the back. His team manager confessed: "James loved every minute of it."

After the race, Hunt flew home to London, then Spain and planned to call into New York on his way to the US Grand Prix to sort things out with Suzy and to meet Burton. Hunt said as he left: "I have spoken to her on the phone and I am hoping we can have lunch together tomorrow and talk over the whole problem and the question of Richard Burton. It's all very personal and there's nothing else I can say right now." When they put down the phone, Hunt took a taxi to Battersea and flew by helicopter to Heathrow to catch a Pan Am flight to New York.

In reality, it was a brief stopover on his way to Los Angeles airport. As news got round New York that "the husband" was flying in, reporters filled up the Lombardy lobby and pounced on Hunt as soon as they recognised him. He was shocked to find himself surrounded by photographers and journalists asking him questions while his wife was upstairs in Burton's suite. Suzy eventually appeared and they went off in a taxi together to meet Burton. It was basically a meet-and-greet with nothing of substance discussed. But, perhaps a bit ironically, Hunt had wanted to meet Burton to "approve him" as suitable for his wife. At that first meeting, Hunt was impressed by Burton's sensitivity. Burton even thanked Hunt for having given him Suzy. Thoroughly approving of Burton, Hunt said he hoped to meet him again soon.

When they returned to the Lombardy, the number of reporters and photographers had doubled, and Hunt hightailed it back to JFK airport to catch his flight to Los Angeles.

# CHAPTER 56

# Divorce number 3, wedding number 4

## *Liz makes way for Suzy*

### 1976

'Equus' finally closed at the end of June and, once again, Aaron Frosch shuffled Richard Burton out of New York before the US Internal Revenue Service became too interested in the US$800,000 he had earned for his five months' work on the stage. Suzy accompanied him back to Switzerland.

Suzy had spent most of spring and early summer in New York with Burton, save for a two-week trip back to Europe. At the end of March, she had returned to Marbella to sort out the logistics of the split from James Hunt.

The visit was an eye-opener. Free of the responsibilities of their relationship, they enjoyed a lovely few days together in the sunshine they had once taken so much for granted. They talked properly for the first time.

Hunt confessed to her the anguish he had gone through over their marriage. He told her he had recognised that he liked "consuming life in a rush", whereas it was now clear to him that she had wanted the exact opposite.

Hunt was also secretly worried about the cost of the divorce, but Suzy assured him that she did not want a divorce settlement and that Burton would take care of the financial arrangements for her. All their joint possessions stayed with Hunt, including the piano; and when the time came to leave, she carried all her personal possessions off in a few suitcases. They met only once more as man and wife for coffee at a restaurant in Malaga to sign the divorce papers.

From Marbella, she flew to Geneva and drove to Celigny to see her new home for the first time. Suzy had been looking forward to going to Celigny. The house had been unused since 1962 and she wanted to get a handle on the scale of the refurbishment she knew would be necessary. She was met at the gates by the caretaker, Harley Decorvet, who lived nearby. His master's homecoming was the moment Decorvet had been awaiting for 12 years, and he was delighted to meet Suzy.

Just as Suzy had expected, the house was a 1960s time capsule which had been frozen in time from the moment Sybil had left it and gone to New York. Immediately, she began planning the changes and meeting with builders.

On her way back to New York from Celigny, she stopped off in England to see her parents and to say a 'goodbye' to James Hunt's family. They all wished her well. Hunt's mother, Sue, was particularly sad to see her go.

She also had a date with the motoring editor of the *Daily Express*. Up until then, she had not spoken to any reporter about the events of the past few months. But James' brother, Peter Hunt, owed David Benson a favour after the terrible lies he had told him. Suzy knew Benson from her days on the motor racing circuits with her husband. She realised that he had been at the forefront of the story, and he had always treated her well in his reporting.

So when Peter Hunt prevailed on Suzy to come to his office to speak to Benson, she agreed. It was convenient because she also had some paperwork to sign at Hunt's office regarding the divorce and financial separation.

So Benson was rewarded with an interview with Suzy, and he remains the only journalist ever to have sat down to talk with her in the 36 years that have followed.

Benson himself recalled what happened: "As an old friend, she greeted me with a warm embrace. I took notes on the interview, writing down the precise words she wanted to appear: 'You are the first newspaperman I have talked to about the break-up. You understand the difficulties I have in discussing my private life in public so I want to talk to you about them and, then, if you print them, that will be it once and for all.' Suzy was particularly distressed about a report in a rival newspaper that suggested she had given Richard Burton a ring – 'I want to correct that. I didn't give Richard a ring and I wouldn't do anything like that; it's too vulgar. Also, Richard did not break up my marriage to James, it was already over when I met Burton, and James had already asked me for a divorce. All I want now is to complete the separation with as much dignity and friendship as possible. James and I are still good friends, and I hope we will remain so. I did not go to Spain to try and effect a reconciliation. The home that you knew us in, David, we were only renting, and the lease ran out. James has now rented a new house and he was moving all of our things out of our old home. It was the right time for me to collect my things and sort them out.'"

When Benson asked her what had gone wrong in the marriage, she told him that James was just not ready for it: "'His racing career put enormous demands on him and, at this stage, his career must come first. He tried awfully hard not to hurt me. Fortunately, everything has turned out for the best for all of us.

James is happy and I am happy. It sounds corny, but put this down David: he [Richard] is a very special person and we are very, very happy together.'"

Suzy confirmed to Benson that she and Burton intended to get married, but, because of the legal problems with various divorces, she didn't want to have it printed at that time. Benson agreed to the informal embargo.

The resulting story was another world exclusive for the *Daily Express* and it was covered over a double-page spread on Saturday 24th April. After that, Benson never saw Suzy again.

Afterwards, Suzy flew back to New York to be with Burton until 'Equus' completed its run. She found she loved New York life; the arts and going to dinner at the apartments of people like Leonard Bernstein. Suzy was very musical and got on well with Bernstein and, in particular, the composer Jay Alan Lerner. She moved easily in their company.

Despite the age difference, Burton and Miller were a perfect foil for each other, providing exactly what the other needed. Suzy was quite unambitious and didn't crave fame or fortune in the slightest. She wanted Burton for exactly who he was. Equally, Burton loved the quiet and unassuming, quintessentially English woman. He was delighted at the seemingly endless happiness she exhibited in sitting and listening to his stories and poetry, all of which were rather good. She was an all-attentive, all-adoring audience, and Burton loved it. He also loved listening to her play the piano, marvelling in her ability to play faultlessly any piece of music he chose.

She also kept him sober. Stressing that she planned to have children with him, she did her best to ensure that their father would be around to see them.

As he grew older, Burton wasn't a pleasant drunk, and his personality would change for the worse after even one drink. She had been used to a drinker like Hunt, who simply became increasingly sillier as he drank. But Burton was an altogether different proposition, and she realised she had to keep him off it entirely. Burton did later readily admit that she had saved him from the brink of self-destruction.

Over that period, Burton telephoned James Hunt several times to sort out the details of the divorce. Burton was surprised by how well they got along. Both men were charmed by each other. Hunt, in particular, found Burton not at all like the man portrayed in the newspapers. He said at the time: "He was a very nice guy, not at all the monster the press made him out to be. He called himself my father-in-law, and he's been a very nice father-in-law ever since."

With the divorce pending, Burton and Suzy made a trip to England so that each could meet their respective families. The meetings were a huge success. Burton became great friends with Suzy's father, Frederick Miller, and found that they shared similar interests. Miller, like Burton, was very well read and owned a considerable library of books, which Burton loved perusing. Sharing similar literary tastes, Burton and Frederick would go for long walks in the Hampshire countryside discussing books they had read and owned. Only Suzy's brother, John, who lived in Los Angeles, was absent, but Burton did meet Suzy's twin sister, Vivienne Van Dyke, and Vivienne's young daughter, Vanessa. The Burtons and the Millers could not have been more compatible.

At the same time, Burton took Suzy down to Wales to meet his family. Equally, Suzy got on very well with Burton's Welsh family and his sisters. They particularly admired the subtlety with which Suzy kept their brother from drinking. In Wales, Suzy found that she also had to get used to the many people who accidentally kept calling her Elizabeth. And eventually, she realised that quite a few of them really believed she was Elizabeth. But when she had worked it out, they were usually far too deep into a conversation for her to be able to enlighten them without severe embarrassment.

Whilst the Jenkins family met with her approval, many of his friends did not.

In Marbella, Suzy had become accustomed to the people who surrounded James Hunt. She put up with them because they were mostly old school friends who had known him long before he was famous. But she was not prepared for the mass of hangers-on and sycophants that surrounded Burton. Where Hunt's friends had been quality people, she recognised Burton's followers as mostly low-quality individuals. She felt they just told him what he wanted to hear and encouraged him to drink. As soon as she was Mrs Burton, she resolved to do something about it.

On 29th July 1976, the divorces of both Taylor and Burton and Hunt and Miller were completed in Port-au-Prince, the capital of Haiti, in the Caribbean. There, foreigners could be divorced in a day, although the status was not always universally recognised. The two marriages were ended with payment of a US$7 fee and a tap of the gavel by the Haitian judge when it was all over. Immediately afterwards, Taylor issued a statement that read: "I love Richard Burton with every fibre of my soul. But we can't be together. We're too mutually self-destructive." But as with all Taylor's public pronouncements on marriage and divorce, her words could only really be taken with a pinch of salt.

Burton paid all the legal costs and, as predicted, Taylor took him for almost everything he had. She even delayed signing the divorce papers until she got precisely what she wanted. She demanded and got all the jewels, all the paintings and almost all the property – everything she hadn't got in the first divorce two years earlier. She also got full ownership of the Kalizma and Casa Kimberley. Taylor also got the financial benefit of the companies they owned, including Taybur Productions, Oxford Productions, their shares of Harlech Television and the Vicky Tiel Boutique in Paris.

Taylor effectively left Burton with the US$800,000 he had earned in 1976 since the split, and the house in Switzerland which Taylor decided she didn't want.

At the same time, financial arrangements in the shape of trust funds were made for all their children, including 15-year-old Maria who was at the International School in Geneva; 18-year-old Kate, who was at Brown University in the United States; 19-year-old Liza, who was studying sculpture in London; 21-year-old Christopher, who was attending the University of Hawaii; and the 23-year-old Michael, who was now married and a saxophone and flute player with a rock band based in Wales. 15-year-old Jessica was in Pennsylvania being treated for autism, and at that point it was still hoped that one day she might emerge.

Suzy Miller had no such complications to deal with.

After settling Taylor's demands, Burton insisted that he sign a prenuptial agreement with Suzy that guaranteed her a million dollars in cash plus a suitable house if their marriage failed. After his divorce from Taylor, however, he realised that he didn't actually have a million dollars in cash, so he bought her a half million dollar insurance policy on his life. She was well-provided for and the divorce didn't cost James Hunt a penny.

None of this was at Suzy's urging but Burton insisted on it after learning of the death of his closest friend, the actor Stanley Baker, on 28th June 1976. He was called by Baker's widow, Ellen and told that his fellow Welshman and lifelong friend had lost a long fight against cancer. Baker was 48, three years younger than Burton.

Baker had been diagnosed with lung cancer six months earlier, in January 1976, and had undergone surgery in February to attempt to cut it out. Baker was a heavy smoker and it was too far gone. He moved to Malaga in Spain to recuperate with his wife, Ellen. But at the end of June, he caught pneumonia and was too weak to fight it.

It took Burton two days to stop crying over his old friend. He then recounted to Suzy how they had started out together as actors in Liverpool during the war years.

In response to his death, he typed out an obituary for *The Observer* newspaper and proceeded to upset his widow, Ellen, with its tone – especially when he described Baker as "tallish, thickish, with a face like a determined fist prepared to take the first blow but not the second," whatever that meant.

The piece was long and rambling, and in parts incoherent. But it was a poetic account of their friendship and was described as "a hymn to the working class culture of South Wales", which they had in common.

With Baker's death, Burton finally came face to face with his own mortality. He was particularly upset that Baker had been knighted that very year but did not live long enough to be dubbed by the Queen at Buckingham Palace. It made Burton determined to leave Suzy secure in case anything similar were to befall him.

In August, Burton and Suzy were filming *The Exorcist II*, directed by John Boorman, when they suddenly decided that the time had come for them to get married. Just as it had been with Burton's first two weddings, it was a sudden decision. On Saturday 21st August 1976, they flew to Arlington, Virginia. Virginia was one of only three states that recognised a Haitian divorce.

There were no diamonds, no lavish gifts, and they exchanged simple gold bands. The wedding service, conducted by Judge Frances Thomas Jr., lasted precisely four minutes.

They then flew back to New York and had dinner with ten close friends at Laurent, the restaurant attached to the Lombardy Hotel. They spent their wedding night in the same suite they had occupied during 'Equus' earlier in the year. Almost immediately, they stopped using contraception and began trying for a child.

At the precise moment of their wedding, James Hunt was playing golf at Gleneagles in Scotland. No one who was witness to his demeanour that day would have believed he had just lost one of the world's most beautiful women to one of its most seductive men.

For the record, he told a local journalist: "Richard Burton came along and solved all the problems. I learned an awful lot about myself and life, and I think Suzy did too. We all ended up happy anyway, which is more than can be said for a lot of marriages." For Hunt, it was the final release, as he said afterwards: "For the first time, I am mentally content with my private life. Suzy is largely responsible for that."

Meanwhile, across the Atlantic, Burton gushed about his new wife to anyone who would listen. It was hard to believe that the new husband and the ex-husband were indeed talking about the same woman. It must have been the most pleasurable divorce and remarriage in history.

After the wedding, Burton bought Suzy a new holiday home in Puerto Vallarta. They called it Villa Bursus after both their names, hence Bur-Sus. He called it her Valentine's Day present.

Then they settled into Celigny, where Suzy got to work on the house. It was to be her first real home. She loved the fact that she had an unlimited budget to spend and went into full focus re-modelling and redecorating the house, making it comfortable and removing any lingering memories of his earlier marriages and of Ivor Jenkins' accident.

The most significant change to the house was the conversion of the attic, which the builders transformed into a spacious study for Burton, with a fireplace and special bookshelves to hold his growing library. When it was finished, a delighted Burton said to Suzy: "Was it not Francis Bacon who said books make the best furniture?"

But perhaps the biggest change overseen by Suzy was the downsizing of Burton's life. As she became established in his life, she tackled the hangers-on and told them they were no longer welcome. Inadvertently, she included Brook Williams in this purge. Or, at least he thought she had.

Suzy had decided that Burton's friends were the reason he drank so much and that they made it too easy for him. Contrary to what people thought, Suzy did not drive Williams away, but she told him firmly that the secret bar he ran for her husband had to be closed down. Williams had long been in denial about this, and Suzy upset him with the direct manner in which she brought up the subject. But it needed to be done, as his daughter Kate Burton readily acknowledged: "I think Suzy provided a very important gift to him. She made him able to leave Elizabeth."

Suzy made Celigny a very happy place to be. Music filled the house whenever they were there. Burton bought a new grand piano and Suzy played for at least two hours a day. He spent most of the day reading, and she was happy as his companion. He loved to hear the sounds of the piano wafting up the stairs as he read.

So much so that when they had to travel to a studio or a location for filming, the only luxury Burton demanded in his trailer or dressing room was a baby grand piano for Suzy to play.

Burton simply couldn't have been happier after his marriage to Suzy. As he told journalists: "Although I like to be thought of as a tough, rugby-playing,

Welsh miner's son, able to take on the world, the reality is that this image is just superficial. I am the reverse of what people think. Suzy is a crutch to me. Without Suzy, I might very easily have been dead. When I met her, I was on the edge of self-destruction and Suzy saved my life. I met her just when I was putting my hand up for help for the last time."

Suzy stayed on good terms with James Hunt, and Burton found he liked him a lot when he got to know him.

When Burton and Suzy travelled to Marbella, they stayed with Lew Hoad, the former Wimbledon tennis champion, at his club – which also happened to be the place where Hunt and Suzy had first met – and they socialised with Hunt whenever possible. One night in Marbella, he invited them for dinner and Hunt introduced Burton to his neighbour, Sean Connery. But it was a clash of two giant male egos and they did not get on.

Burton also mixed easily with all of Suzy's friends, including, oddly, Bette Hill, the widow of Formula One great Graham Hill and the mother of Damon Hill, who was also a world champion driver. She accompanied the couple to many social occasions whenever they were in London. At the Evening Standard Drama Awards in 1977, Burton passed Bette Hill a note that read: "Thank you for saving Suzy for me." It reflected everything he felt.

# AND GOD CREATED BURTON

# CHAPTER 57

# Life with Suzy

## *A different kind of life*

### 1976 - 1981

As Robbie Lantz took charge of Richard Burton's career, he faced a major rebuilding job. Under Hugh French's stewardship, Burton's career had been run into the ground. Lantz's first priority was to get Burton into a mainstream Hollywood movie again. He wanted him in a film financed by a major studio at a good rate of pay. The strategy was to get his new client into a studio film, any studio film, where he could prove he was still capable of holding an audience. Everyone except Lantz thought this was impossible and, against the odds, he pulled it off.

Warner Bros was making *Exorcist II: The Heretic*, the sequel to the fabulously successful original *Exorcist* film. Lantz got Burton the lead role opposite Linda Blair. The deal was a coup and it was Burton's first studio financed and produced film for seven years. No one but no one had believed he would ever work for a major Hollywood studio again.

Lantz secured him a big payday of US$750,000 plus US$250,000 for overages, which meant he walked away with US$1 million. With the inflationary spiral of the early seventies, a million was not what it used to be but it was a big morale boost at the time. For Burton, it was a return to the big time.

But it soon became clear that the film was going to be a disaster. Burton made his excuses in advance and told Roderick Mann of the *Los Angeles Times* that he was doing this "horror film" because his daughters had loved the original *Exorcist* and had urged him to do the sequel.

Burton played a priest trying to guard Linda Blair from some unfathomable forces of evil, but what the evil was, no one knew. Burton said after his first week on set: "I'm not sure what this is about." Filming went on for a staggering 23 weeks at Warner's Burbank studios in California as the British director, John Boorman, appeared to get completely lost in the material.

Boorman was expected to treat the supernatural in intelligent new ways but the final result was baffling. He also spent money like water and it ended up costing twice as much to make as the big blockbuster *Jaws*. Burton was moved to call it "the worst large-budget film ever made." It was a bewildering film and few people seemed to understand it, including the director.

Burton was very bemused when Boorman couldn't decide how the film should end and deferred his decision by shooting multiple different endings. As Burton explained: "They must have shot ten different endings." Burton told Janet Maslin of the *New York Times*: "I'd become so beaten down by the California sunshine and smog that I said: 'I'll do any ending.'"

The ending that Boorman eventually used saw Burton in a house, lying on a bed with Linda Blair when suddenly the roof of the house caved in. With that, the bed collapsed and slid into an abyss that had conveniently appeared. Boorman had meant to give the film "a visionary quality", but he had misjudged either his material or his audiences. Boorman admitted: "I made the wrong film." But he omitted to define what the right film might have been. Melvyn Bragg didn't mince his words when he called it: "Not quite the worst, but certainly the stupidest film ever made." Paul Ferris called it "one of the silliest plots ever seen in the cinema."

The main problem appeared to be Boorman himself. He seemed out of his depth in a major studio movie and nervous to the point of chronic indecisiveness. He also regarded himself as a creative *artiste*, and the aura he attached to himself became a chronic burden when he had to carry it around. The shoot was allowed to go over six months when half that time would have sufficed.

Burton said of it: "After a few weeks of filming, Susan could see I was very unhappy about it. I would come home and read the stupid lines aloud and Susan would say: 'Never again will you do rubbish like this. It is not worth it, not even for a million dollars.'" Suzy was furious that he had, in her opinion, "humiliated himself."

*Variety*, the Hollywood trade magazine wrote: "*Exorcist II* is not as good as *The Exorcist*. It isn't even close. It is guaranteed to keep audiences on the edge of their seats, wanting to go home." *Newsweek* said it was a "dispiriting spectacle." *New York magazine* said: "Whereas it is impossible to designate even approximately the worst film one has ever seen, there is a very strong probability that *Exorcist II* is the stupidest major movie ever made." After the film was jeered at previews in New York, Boorman was forced to re-edit it.

But despite the carping from just about everyone, the film was still a commercial success, costing US$14 million to make and delivering a worldwide gross of over US$50 million, and a resounding profit for Warner Bros. There were enough fans of the occult for it to be a success.

# LIFE WITH SUZY

It was late October before John Boorman had finished messing around with *Exorcist II* and Burton and Suzy flew off to Canada to finally make the film version of *Equus*. It was an Elliot Kastner production and Peter Shaffer's play matured under Sidney Lumet's outstanding direction. Lumet was the exact opposite of John Boorman. He knew his own mind and he was an economic filmmaker, never taking ten minutes when five minutes would do.

Lumet caught on film the moving confrontation between the boy, played wonderfully by Peter Firth, and the psychiatrist who is trying to unravel the boy's mind, played by Burton.

Burton's character, Martin Dysart, had eight long monologues in which he speaks to the camera. As one critic said, they "punctuated" the film.

Because Burton and Lumet had bonded creatively, Lumet was able to film those eight monologues, the heart of the film, in a single day. And some of them were truly extraordinary renditions. No one could forget "Why me, why me? First account for me" as rendered by Burton in one take. One could be forgiven at that stage for forgetting the plot of the film – there was no acting involved. It appeared to everyone that Burton was asking the question of his own life. The power of his acting was overwhelming.

Melvyn Bragg called it "a more than creditable performance" but it was indeed much more than that. And Hollywood thought so as well when he was nominated for a seventh Academy Award. In *Equus*, Burton was back in the reckoning as one of the world's major actors. He was moving gradually to recover the ground he had lost in the second half of the Taylor years.

It was also a very happy set and Burton was good humoured and sober throughout the shoot. His relationship with Suzy, now almost a year old, had matured successfully and he was living a totally different kind of life to the one he had enjoyed with Taylor.

The film was a moderate box office success but underperformed compared with its quality. Graham Jenkins nailed the problem: "*Equus* failed to translate well to the screen because too much realism shifted attention from the emotional conflict at the heart of the story." But *Variety* summed it up: "*Equus* is an excellent example of film-as-theatre."

By the end of 1976, they both returned to Celigny. Burton had had a very good year, earning US$2.2 million. He returned to Switzerland feeling happier than he had for 15 years.

The union with Suzy Miller had enabled him finally to break free of Elizabeth Taylor's shackles and the psychological manacles she had placed on him in

1962 were finally unlocked forever. He gradually began to realise what a negative affect she had had on him.

He was enjoying life again and went briefly to London to narrate a 26-episode series called 'Vivat Rex: Chronicles of an English Crown' for BBC Radio. The story of English royalty told through the eyes of Shakespeare, Marlowe and other great playwrights were just up his street.

Apart from that, they enjoyed an idyllic six months together doing nothing at all in Celigny – apart from playing a normal married couple in real life, something Burton had never done much of before.

Suzy had taken charge of his life and Valerie Douglas joined them for a long period to help get his business and financial affairs in order.

In some ways, the pause in his career was an enforced one because there were no offers on the table. Suzy refused to let him appear in any more "rubbish." She just wouldn't let him sign up for any more poorly-scripted films. She, together with Douglas, read every script he was offered, and he did not even take the meeting if they considered the script to be poor.

One script that got past during this period was *The Medusa Touch*, a screenplay by director Jack Gold and John Briley based on Peter Van Greenaway's 1973 novel of the same name. The theme was telekinesis, a mysterious power to make objects move without touching them. Burton played a lawyer who discovers that by sheer force of concentration he can influence people and events. His mental powers are so great that he can make buildings fall down and aeroplanes fall from the skies.

Even so, Burton took some persuading to do it. He was not against sci-fi movies but he was very wary. He realised that the film could have been preposterous in the wrong hands, so Burton had to make sure Jack Gold was not another John Boorman.

To persuade him, Gold flew into Geneva to see Burton who, with Suzy, took the local train into the airport for the meeting. Burton told Gold he had checked him out with other directors. He said he was cautious because he didn't want to be caught doing another *Exorcist*. But when he heard that Elliot Kastner was involved, he became far more amenable. Burton admired Kastner and respected his judgement.

After lunch, Suzy left to go home and Burton went with Gold to his hotel room to go through the script. They all met for dinner that night and shook hands on three weeks' work for US$500,000.

So in mid-1977, Burton and Suzy travelled to London to shoot *The Medusa*

*Touch*, which Warner Bros was again financing. Warner had no qualms about Burton. Burton was gradually getting his reputation back in order and word had got around.

Instead of staying at The Dorchester, Suzy did the sensible thing for a change and rented a house in Windsor very close to the set.

On set, Burton was a totally different man. There was no drinking and no lusting after women. The presence of an old girlfriend, Lee Remick, on the set presented him with no problem.

He'd go back to his trailer between takes and Suzy would make him tea and feed him cake she had made the previous day.

But life was far from perfect. She felt that the secret of his future was his having kicked his alcohol dependency. He was allowed moderate intakes, a maximum of two glasses of wine a day, but the problem was that once he had consumed the first one, he wanted another and then another. His age and condition meant he had lost all tolerance, and a few glasses could tip him over. Suzy felt she had to watch him all the time to make sure he didn't lapse. She quipped: "If I wasn't his wife, he'd need me as his nurse."

Brook Williams also spent time with them. Although Suzy had fired the rest of his retinue, she had formed an understanding with Williams.

She warned him about giving any alcohol to her husband and Williams agreed to desist, but he didn't like it. If Williams griped about her, Burton continually told his occasionally grumpy assistant, who hankered after the old days, that Suzy had saved him from near-death. He said: "Suzy didn't stop me drinking. She didn't hide bottles. But she encouraged me not to drink because she knew I didn't want to drink. She steadied me. She may have even saved my life. Booze would have killed me, I am sure, if it had not been for Suzy."

There is no doubt that Williams had been part of the problem before and, gradually, he came round to understanding that.

*The Medusa Touch* was a very well-crafted movie and did well at the box office. Buried in the cast were some fine character actors such as Alan Badel, Jeremy Brett, Michael Hordern, Gordon Jackson, Robert Flemyng and Derek Jacobi. The casting director, Irene Lamb, did an exceptional job getting such talent together and it showed in the film. In 1976, *Exorcist II* and *The Medusa Touch* represented the two far ends of Hollywood competence, and Burton had experienced them both in the same 12 months.

Burton's next film in 1977 was the one for which most people will always remember him, *The Wild Geese*. Getting the part was Robbie Lantz at his best.

Lantz was proactively hunting for good parts that would reestablish Burton back in the Hollywood mainstream, something Lantz felt was essential

Lantz cold-called the producer, Euan Lloyd, and pitched Burton for the part. Lloyd was intrigued and Lantz flew over to London specially to meet Lloyd. He took the script straight to Venice, where Burton and Suzy were. Burton spent a few days examining it from every angle and authorised Lantz to secure him the part. However, Lloyd, an extremely affable man, didn't bite. He had asked people about Burton and was frightened by what he heard. The stories from the set of *The Klansman* had got around.

*The Wild Geese* was due to be filmed in the African bush under less than ideal conditions and in intense heat, and Lloyd knew what that could do to a man. He didn't want to risk Burton becoming undone and having to cancel the movie.

He had already signed up another notorious drinker called Richard Harris. But Lloyd felt he was protected. Almost all of Harris' fee for the movie was being held in escrow against strict guarantees of abstinence on the film set. Lloyd finally agreed to hire Burton if he would accept the same terms.

But once that was agreed, it was Burton's turn to become reluctant. He told Lloyd that he wouldn't work on a set where black people were segregated from the whites. Lloyd assured him that the set would be mixed and he would not tolerate apartheid in any form. He was as good as his word, and the 200 crew and the 50 in the cast, a mixture of Africans and Brits, all worked and lived together, a rare novelty in South Africa at the time.

Lantz negotiated him US$750,000 for a maximum of 14 weeks' filming. Lloyd signed him on subject to insurance approval. Lloyd expected problems over Burton's drinking, but after seeing medical reports, the film's insurers excluded cover for any delays/cancellation caused by Burton's back problems. Lloyd said: "If his back went, we would be finished...But we all wanted him and so we took the risk." With that, Burton got the part; arguably with the benefit of hindsight, the most important of his film career.

On the way to South Africa, Burton and Suzy went to New York to meet with Alexander Cohen who wanted to put on a Broadway production of 'King Lear'. King Lear, the greatest Shakespearean role, was Burton's ultimate acting ambition. He agreed to do an eight-week run after *The Wild Geese* had wrapped. But it foundered when Burton refused to do any matinees saying his health was only good enough for six nights a week. Cohen balked at this. The production would cost US$700,000 to mount, and it would have been almost impossible to recoup with only six performances a week. Cohen didn't think it could be profitable at that so the production was cancelled and Burton never did achieve his long-time ambition to play King Lear.

*The Wild Geese* was based in the Northern Transvaal at a spa resort called Tshipise. To get there meant flying into Johannesburg and then taking a small plane another 700 miles into the northernmost part of South Africa.

The resort provided reasonably comfortable living conditions. The four stars had their own comfortable air conditioned bungalows with lush gardens for the ten weeks or so that they were on location. Lloyd shipped a grand piano onto the set so that Suzy could play, and most evenings they socialised with Roger Moore and his wife, Luisa; Richard Harris and his wife, Ann; and Hardy Kruger and his wife, Anita.

But Burton went to bed every night early and sober. There was never a moment's problem on set because of alcohol. Lloyd recalled: "He said he wouldn't drink, and he didn't". When Harris and Burton greeted each other on set for the first time, Harris said: "We'll let Roger Moore do the drinking for the three of us."

*The Wild Geese* was a fictional film about a band of mercenaries based on the real-life story of Colonel Mike Hoare. Hoare was technical adviser on the film and Burton was playing him. Burton's character was called Colonel Faulkner and he commanded a mission to rescue a deposed president from the hands of a corrupt dictator. The director was Andrew McLaglen and Reginald Rose turned in a screenplay with some superbly written dialogue.

Lloyd had assembled a very good cast of Roger Moore, then in his heyday as James Bond, and South African actor Hardy Kruger. All had equal billing. It was a friendly and good-humoured set and the NCOs and the ranks of the mercenaries were all skilled British character actors, many of whom knew each other from earlier films together.

Also starring in the film was Stewart Granger, Burton's old foe from Hollywood. It was a risk reuniting Burton and Granger after what had happened with Jean Simmons. Burton had also made a few disparaging jokes about Granger's acting career over the years. But it proved to be water under the bridge for both of them.

There was a memorable scene between them early in the film where Burton, as Colonel Faulkner, accepts a drink from Granger, playing a powerful merchant banker called Sir Edward Matherson, who challenges him about it. Burton replies that he never drinks when working and adds: "There's a special clause in my contract which says that my liver has to be buried separately, with full honours." Granger stares back at him hard and says: "I'm not a humorous man, Colonel Faulkner." At that moment, they both could not have failed to be thinking about the real life confrontation in Granger's study 25 years earlier.

There was a punishing shooting schedule in intense heat and, on cue, Burton started to experience trouble with his back. They lost an entire day of filming as a result. Euan Lloyd knew just the solution and flew in Africa's equivalent of Dr Max Jacobson to come to Burton's rescue.

Jacobson, known in America as Dr Feelgood, used powerful and addictive drugs to eliminate pain. His methods were disapproved of by the medical establishment and the drugs not approved. This didn't bother Lloyd, who flew a doctor called Professor Kloppers into the airport at Tshipise. Kloppers arrived at noon and went straight in to see Burton. Within an hour, after a couple of injections, Burton was a new man and suffered no more back trouble for the rest of the shoot.

During filming, Burton was prone to bizarre behaviour in the heat. Penny Junor described one such incident in her biography of Burton. Christopher Wilding and Glyn Baker, both 19-years-old, had small roles in the film. Christopher was Burton's stepson and Glyn was Stanley Baker's son. Burton told people Glyn Baker was his godson but that was one of his tall stories. His godfather was actually the comedian and sometime classical singer Harry Secombe.

One day, Suzy, encouraging family closeness, invited both Christopher and Glyn to lunch on a non-filming day. When they arrived, Burton was asleep in the garden, so they played Scrabble with Suzy. As Junor described it: "Suddenly, Richard burst in: 'How dare you disturb me when I'm reading Lear?' 'What do you mean, reading Lear?' said Christopher, scathingly. 'You were asleep. You were snoring.' 'I can't bear to be with you non-intellectuals,' roared Richard. 'Then I think I'd better leave,' said Glyn. 'No, you're semi-intellectual. You can sit down.'" Junor put it down to the fact that Burton felt "threatened by youth." She thought he was jealous of them being round Suzy. And perhaps it reminded him of when he and Glyn's father had been 19-year-olds appearing in their first production in Liverpool in 1944.

During the whole of filming, there was only one occasion when the Harris/Burton non-drinking pact with Euan Lloyd was broken. It came at Roger Moore's 50th birthday party on 14th October 1977. The party was held in the bush and featured six giant barbecue fires. First Richard Harris and then Burton started drinking with the excuse of it being Moore's 50th. Lloyd decided to step back and let it go.

Burton had invited his friend David Rowe-Beddoe down for a few days on set, who witnessed it all: "I was in South Africa for business and I flew to where they were filming. It was a fascinating night. Richard was not drinking and Richard Harris, you can imagine, was not the best of influences. I thought Richard was drinking a glass of water but it was a glass of vodka, and within a very short period of time you could see he was legless and making no sense to anybody. It must have been 11 o'clock in the evening."

The two Richards were reciting poetry to each other and having a great time.

No one expected much the following morning. But Burton was up by 5am and on set, ready for make up at 5:30am. Rowe-Beddoe recalled: "Richard was already in the shower singing and humming. He had this power of recovery which was enormous. Here was our man going to work, no problem at all. And that is one of the dangers, I understand – that if you can recover so quickly, it doesn't encourage you to be more disciplined in what you imbibe. "

Both men apologised profusely to Euan Lloyd for the lapse and promised it wouldn't happen again, and it didn't.

Burton greatly enjoyed shooting *The Wild Geese* and he turned in a superb performance. Suzy also got a tiny non-speaking part during one scene in a casino. When the film was finally released, it easily took in much more than its budget of US$10 million and made a healthy profit for its backers. Over the years, it returned five times what it cost to make.

It was a relief to return to London after three months in Africa, and Burton was straight into his next film, called *Absolution*, which was shot at Pinewood Studios and on location in Shropshire. It was an Elliot Kastner production and Burton felt he couldn't refuse the part. He had an incredible bond with Kastner and did everything he asked of him. It was written by Anthony Shaffer, brother of Peter, who had written *Equus*.

But there were delays caused by financing, and during the delay in February 1978, Burton took Suzy to Puerto Vallarta for the first time. During their stay, they bought a house further up the mountain from Casa Kimberley. From there, they went to Los Angeles for the Oscars. Burton thought he had his best chance ever with *Equus*. He was now officially the most nominated actor in film history, and he lost out once more to Richard Dreyfuss.

Meanwhile, the financing problems on *Absolution* were sorted out, but by then Burton was reluctant to return to England from Puerto Vallarta. Elliot Kastner eventually persuaded Burton when he told him it was costing him

US$20,000 a day, out of his own pocket, for every day he didn't turn up.

Burton played the part of a priest at a Roman Catholic school, who hears the confession of a boy who has committed a murder. It was not a great film and had trouble getting distribution. When it eventually opened in 1981, it was dismissed by one critic as a "pretentious melodrama."

With the collapse of plans for him to play King Lear on Broadway, Andrew McLaglen co-opted him into a film he was directing called *Breakthrough*, a sequel to Sam Peckinpah's *Cross of Iron*. It was a violent World War II story told from a German perspective.

It was filmed in Germany and Burton played the title role of Sergeant Steiner, with Robert Mitchum and Rod Steiger co-starring. It was an excellent film but was rather overshadowed by *The Wild Geese*, which came out about the same time. It also suffered when compared against the original and because of its rambling storyline. But Burton picked up a cheque for US$750,000 for his role, which rather reflected the raging inflation of the time more than his pulling power.

With Suzy and Valerie Douglas taking full control of Burton's career, Robbie Lantz gradually faded away. The two women vetted every script and rejected most of them as not good enough. In that period, they turned down *The Sea Wolves*, and the part went to Gregory Peck.

In truth, they were no better at picking scripts than anyone else. Together they made some terrible choices such as turning down *The Sea Wolves*, which he should have accepted, and accepting *Circle of Two*, which certainly should have been turned down. Suzy gradually dispensed with the rest of the entourage that had made it through the first purge. John Springer and Ron Berkeley were frozen out of the inner circle, and Bob Wilson also went.

Brook Williams recalled: "The trouble was that she'd made a lot of us who had been with Rich for such a long time unwelcome. His publicist, John Springer, gave up because he couldn't get close to him. And Ron Berkeley, who'd been doing Rich's make-up and hair forever, had gone because Susan did all that herself."

Springer agreed: "To what degree Susan was influencing him is hard to know, but it did look as though she was weaning him away from the people with whom he had been associated. The one she became closest to was Valerie Douglas, who up to then had been a kind of gofer for Richard, and who she now trusted more and more with the details of his career. Richard blandly chose not to know what was happening."

The firing of almost everyone except Brook Williams meant his filmmaking capacity was much reduced. Without the infrastructure backing him up, the slowing down of his filmmaking schedule was inevitable. In many ways, it was a good thing as his health was slowly deteriorating and his back pain was apparently incurable. He was continually battling with a crippling illness.

During this period, Burton and Suzy spent much more time at either Celigny or the new house in Puerto Vallarta. Suzy's twin sister, Vivienne Van Dyke, had split from her husband and she and her daughter, Vanessa, also lived with them during this period of inactivity. Consequently, between 1979 and 1981, Burton only made two films, and both were dreadful.

In the summer of 1979, Burton shot *Tristan and Isolde* in Ireland. It was a costume drama where he played a character called the King of Cornwall. Suzy's vetting process came really unstuck and Graham Jenkins called the film: "One of the dreariest pieces of nonsense in the Burton canon. Rich lost both ways, professionally and financially."

After that, Burton and Suzy went to Ontario to film *Circle of Two*, with sixteen-year-old Tatum O'Neal. She was the youngest leading lady to have played opposite Burton. He played a 60-year-old artist in love with a 16-year-old schoolgirl. It involved him playing love scenes with a girl 38 years his junior and younger than his daughter Kate. He said of the experience: "At my age, they should have paid me danger money." In Burton's own words, *Circle of Two* was supposed to be a delicately balanced story but it just didn't come off under the direction of Jules Dassin. In the end, it was just embarrassing.

Around this time, Aaron Frosch also came under the Suzy glare. She realised her husband had no idea about his finances and, with Douglas's help, she set out to find out more. During this period, Frosch was put through the hoop and asked to explain everything he had done with Burton's money over the years.

The first financial statements he produced were wholly inadequate and many of Burton's assets were missing from it. Frosch was far too casual for the new regime in Celigny. Eventually, thanks to Suzy's tenacity, she got his financial affairs in order. Frosch had got used to doing what he liked and never having to justify his actions, and there was no system of financial reporting. Valerie Douglas helped her, and transferred her loyalties from Frosch to Suzy.

As 1979 closed, the four years he had spent with Suzy had proved to be good ones for Burton. Suzy Miller had saved his life in every way. She had rescued him from the clutches of Elizabeth Taylor, rebuilt his reputation and made his life whole again. His only failure were the films she had chosen for him. Arguably, she was worse at that than he was.

# CHAPTER 58

# Medical catastrophe

*Divorce from Suzy as alcohol exacts its price*

1981

In early 1979, Burton was asked by theatre impresario producer Mike Merrick to appear in a touring revival of 'Camelot', nearly 20 years after the original first played. Merrick had first become aware of Burton when he had handled the American marketing of John Le Carre's *The Spy Who Came In From The Cold* in 1965.

Alan Jay Lerner had suggested Burton for the part, although in reality he did not think he would do it. Lerner warned him: "I've asked him before and he'll never do it. It's a waste of time." Merrick wasn't going to take no for an answer, as he recalled: "We contacted his manager, Valerie Douglas, and she said he would be willing to meet with me in Switzerland.

"I called Lerner and told him of the development and he was delighted, to say the least. I insisted that he meet me in Geneva, as I had never met Burton and wanted Lerner's presence to give validity to the plan. We met at a hotel in Geneva with Susan and Richard, and by the end of lunch, as I said to Richard: 'Well, we hope that we have Richard Burton so we will be able to announce it and plan to start a tour next year.' He looked at me with those blazing blue eyes and said with the Burtonian baritone: 'I assure you, you have Richard Burton.'"

Burton should have said 'no'. He was too old, at 52, to consider such a physically demanding part in a touring production with all the extra problems that involved. King Arthur was a particularly strenuous role at the best of times. But Merrick offered Burton US$60,000 a week for a 12-month American tour. It added up to US$3 million, and few actors could turn that down – especially as it was a chance to return to the stage and visit parts of America he had never seen. It was simply too hard to resist and so he signed on. He also liked Mike Merrick and enjoyed working with him.

Merrick disagreed with the notion that Burton was too old: "He was on top of his game during rehearsals and magnificent in Toronto and all the successive cities we played on tour. His health problems, with his spine and back, exacerbated to a dangerous point near the end."

Merrick hired a 27-year-old unknown actress called Christine Ebersole to play Guinevere when Julie Andrews ruled herself out as far too old. As it was, the storyline had to be slightly rejigged to reflect Burton's greater age.

'Camelot' opened in Toronto on 6th June 1980 at the O'Keefe Center and the audiences flocked. Many were the same Canadians who had first seen it in 1960. This time, they were 20 years older.

As always with Burton, there was drama – and this time it was with the 'Camelot' programme. Merrick had inadvertently published a photograph of Burton and Elizabeth Taylor inside the programme. Suzy flipped when she saw it and insisted it be cut out. So the theatre ushers faced a long night before the opening, individually removing the photograph from each programme with scissors.

Apart from that, the opening couldn't have gone better and Henry and Nancy Kissinger, now firm friends, threw them a party afterwards. The production moved to Broadway.

Although Burton's physical problems were becoming more and more apparent, they didn't detract from the performance. Every performance was sold out and the critics were unanimous about Burton. The *New York Times* summed it up: "This actor doesn't merely command the stage, he seems to own it by divine right."

The New York run was briefly interrupted when Tom Jenkins, the first born of the Jenkins siblings, died at the age of 78. Burton and Suzy flew to Wales for the funeral at Margam Crematorium in Port Talbot. The Cwmafan male voice choir sang him out with two of his favourite hymns. David Jenkins called the singing: "The most powerful and impassioned I have ever heard." Suzy couldn't believe the passion with which the Welsh saw off their dead and was in tears for the entire service, as Burton remembered later: "Susan was overwhelmed by the singing; the whole valley was out in force." It also seemed to have a magical effect on Tom's only daughter, Mair, who had been married for 20 years. She suddenly found herself pregnant for the first time at the age of 41. The only dark moment came when Graham Jenkins then led Burton off to the Pontrhydyfen Rugby Club for the wake. Suzy was filled with horror and knew what was to follow, and it did.

Suzy was desperately frightened of her husband drinking anything but white wine. Apart from the occasional lapses, Burton's drinking was well under control. As soon as they returned to New York to resume 'Camelot', he was fine again.

Inevitably, the 'Camelot' tour was dominated by Burton's health. At the start, he looked in the rudest health and posed for publicity photos with Suzy and Mike Merrick, looking as good as he ever did.

Burton put everything he had into the touring production of 'Camelot'. After one performance, when there were production problems in Chicago, he stormed out and refused to have dinner with the director Frank Dunlop. Later, when Dunlop got back to his hotel, there was a message waiting for him, which read: "The King called, apologises for acting like a peasant."

But he was doing eight performances a week and as the tour went on, his neck ached and gradually his right arm became more and more useless. He was also suffering at various times from arthritis, sciatica and gout.

He also ached for a drink to help dull the pain, as he mused in his diaries at the time: he was constantly dreaming of "a double ice-cold vodka martini, the glass fogged with condensation, straight up and then straight down, and the warm food of painkillers hitting the stomach and then the brain and an hour of sweetly melancholy euphoria." At the end of the entry, he added: "I shall have a Tab instead – disgusting."

But the reality was that he now relied upon a cocktail of painkillers just to keep him going. And they didn't mix well with alcohol.

Alcohol only caused a problem one night early into the Broadway run. One evening, he seemed to be staggering around the stage and there was a shout from the audience: "Give him another drink." The stage manager quickly realised that there was something wrong and the curtain came down. Burton's understudy quickly took over. He was not drunk but apparently had enjoyed two glasses of white wine, his daily maximum, with Richard Harris before the show opened. It had not mixed well with his painkillers on an empty stomach.

Mike Merrick remembered: "Richard insisted on going to the theatre that night, even Susan could not stop him."

The following night, he was back and as good as ever. And, from the standing ovation he received before the performance started, it was clear that New Yorkers now loved him, whatever his faults.

The following week, he appeared on the US chat programme *The Dick Cavett Show* to reassure his fans he was in good shape.

Suzy accompanied him for the whole of the 'Camelot' tour as it lurched from city to city and success to success. Mike Merrick found he could virtually charge what he liked for tickets and still fill every seat. Merrick explained: "Because it was a limited run and the attraction of Burton in person was so great, scalpers bought large batches of tickets and sold them for hugely inflated prices."

Burton's physical bravery during the 'Camelot' tour was extraordinary but, inevitably, the constant battles with his health and the constant possibility that he might drink again took its toll on the marriage. The bloom had gone off it although he dearly loved his wife and she dearly loved him back. But there was only so much a young 32-year-old, however capable, could take.

The love story started to unravel along with his health.

After nine months, Mike Merrick could also see the writing on the wall. He approached Richard Harris and asked about his availability to take over the role of King Arthur if anything happened to Burton. Merrick's actions were prescient, as a few days later something did happen.

On 26th March 1981, the show was playing in Los Angeles when Burton suddenly collapsed. He had chronic pains in his arms and was rushed to St John's Hospital in Santa Monica, where he was found to be suffering from a viral infection. It was apparent that Burton's run in 'Camelot' was over for good and Harris was ready to take over. Merrick recalled: "Richard Harris did not take over the role of Arthur until it was certain that Burton could not continue; a sad, sad day."

An expert neurosurgeon was flown across America, from Florida, to examine Burton. The subsequent diagnosis was serious; the specialist found he was suffering from severe degenerative disorders of his cervical spine. He was told he required immediate major surgery or it could be fatal. However, the operation had to be delayed until Burton recovered from the viral infection. The doctors in Santa Monica just about managed to keep him alive and, five days later, when he had stabilised, he was discharged temporarily to recuperate and get his strength up for the operation.

At the time, there were rumours all over Los Angeles that he had cancer and had been sent home to die. So it was decided that a formal press release would be issued, making it clear what was wrong. On 2nd April, it was announced that he had formally withdrawn from 'Camelot' and the release gave details of his medical status. Valerie Douglas explained: "Doctors felt he would be more comfortable and rest better at home to recover from the vestiges of a severe viral infection. They don't want any of that floating around when they operate."

Three weeks later, on 22nd April, a team of four surgeons operated on him. They performed a procedure called a cervical laminectomy. Before he was wheeled into the operating theatre, the doctors warned that the operation could fail and leave him in even more pain than he already was. There was also a running risk of paralysis. Suzy persuaded him it was worth the risk.

What they discovered when they opened him up was grave. The whole of his spinal column was coated with crystallised alcohol. The surgeons had never seen anything like it. They had to scrape it off before they could rebuild the vertebrae in his neck. It was a dangerous and delicate operation, carrying with it the constant risk of paralysis from the slightest mistake during the surgery. But the surgeons were the best in the world and they didn't make mistakes.

Suzy was camped out at St John's day and night, and the Jenkins family, including his sister Catherine, a state registered nurse, flew over from Wales during the recovery period. In truth, he was not expected to survive the operation but, somehow, he did. Suzy stayed by his side, and two weeks after the operation, he was fit enough to leave hospital. When he emerged from hospital, he was a physical wreck. Unable to take painkillers for his back due to their harmful side effects, Burton suffered huge discomfort in the aftermath of his operation. They were forced to remain in Beverly Hills until he was given the all-clear by his doctors to fly back to Celigny. When they got home, a physiotherapist was permanently on hand. Burton was ordered to have six months of total rest.

During that period, for the first time, he started to rebel against the abstinence from alcohol. But Suzy fought back. She knew that just one mouthful of spirits meant instant insensibility. And occasionally, when her back was turned, he did stray with disastrous effects.

Burton was desperately bored and he accepted an offer from the BBC to be part of the commentary team for Prince Charles' marriage to Lady Diana Spencer on 29th July 1981. It was against doctor's orders.

During that trip, Graham Jenkins recalled an incident at The Dorchester when Suzy called him to help with her husband, who was paralytic after only a few mouthfuls of vodka. They were due to fly back to Celigny, and Suzy was frantic. Eventually, they got him on the plane.

The frequency of such incidents increased and they started to argue – sometimes the arguments became unpleasant. Feeling the force of Burton's thunderous temper, Suzy became worn down by his constant abuse. Suzy asked Valerie Douglas to come to Celigny to help her look after him. Brook Williams observed the problem: "He'd been suffocated by Elizabeth's constant need for attention, and with Suzy he was suffocated by being the one getting all the attention."

Burton hated being an invalid. Brook Williams thought the operation had made him worse: "They should never have put him under the knife. It did him no good. He was in terrible pain and the neck muscles were permanently damaged for the rest of his life. He couldn't raise his arms up in the air or reach across the table for the marmalade. But you never, ever, heard him complain." Williams also thought the constant physiotherapy was counterproductive and putting more strain on his body.

But that summer, he did find a diversion. He got involved in a project with his friend David Rowe-Beddoe to rescue the Old Vic Theatre. The Old Vic had run into tremendous financial problems after the seventies recession and had eventually been forced to close down. That summer, Burton felt he would never return to mainstream acting again and looked around for something else to do and found the Old Vic needed his help.

Rowe-Beddoe explained what was planned: "The theatre was closed. It was dark and we were negotiating the lease on The Old Vic – myself, Richard and John Heyman. The whole concept was 'Richard Burton Classic Theatre' and it had a wonderful ring to it. It was highly bankable."

The plan was to attract big-name actors to come and perform at the Old Vic in their favourite productions and then film it, as Rowe-Beddoe explained: "The concept was to stage three or four plays a year and to create a video of each play to start a library."

Burton and Rowe-Beddoe roped Philip Burton in as a consultant, as Philip recalled: "He wanted my co-operation in an ambitious new scheme. It immediately involved me in morning-to-night work for three weeks; if it had matured, it would have kept me busy for the rest of my life. I was to supply Richard with lists of plays, chiefly revivals, suitable for production first in London and then in New York, to be followed by films derived from the productions." But Philip was not too confident the project would succeed and was quite relieved when it ended. As he said: "After all my work, the whole thing came to nothing – in fact and in payment. I was relieved for Richard but a bit sorry for myself."

A year later, Burton pulled the plug on the project completely. He travelled down to Rowe-Beddoe's house in the south of France and told him in person that his health just wasn't up to it. Rowe-Beddoe was shattered by the news: "He pulled himself out of it. It was a great blow. John had spent a lot of time;

we had all spent time. And it was a very exciting theatre project. He just got frightened. He was terrified. And there was no way we could persuade him."

In mid-September, Burton and Suzy returned to St John's in Los Angeles for a post-operation check-up and to review his progress. The doctors did not detect a huge improvement and they had to accept that the operation had not been as successful as they had hoped in relieving his condition.

But overall, he was doing well until 2nd October 1981, when he collapsed with a perforated ulcer and was rushed back to St John's for an emergency operation.

Suzy was with him constantly, although she started to sense for the first time that the end might be near. The ramifications from the illness gradually started to destroy the marriage. After the treatment, he was again unable to immediately resume taking the painkillers.

In hospital, Burton became irascible and unpleasant, and Suzy struggled to cope. Catherine Jenkins and Suzy's parents also flew in to provide support. Suzy confided in Catherine about her intention to leave at some time in the future. Upon leaving, she wanted Catherine to step in as her husband's nurse. Shortly afterwards, Catherine returned home, ready to return if Suzy called. But the anticipated call did not come.

For the first time, Burton found his wife less than perfect, and her attentive ways were becoming a burden. She tried her best and seldom let him out of her sight, constantly running her fingers through his hair for assurance as she always had. She brought him chicken soup and tea continually, as it was all he could eat and drink. He was soon discharged from hospital but remained in Los Angeles for observation.

But Burton had attacked Suzy verbally one time too many. He was wracked with pain and continually failed to appreciate her efforts to support him. By the time he was able to resume taking the painkillers, it was too late. David Rowe-Beddoe recalled: "It was a difficult time and she was a very brave person and I think she acted in the most immaculate manner."

Finding him increasingly difficult to live with, Suzy simply began to fall out of love with him. The perpetual fight to keep him sober was a losing battle and, faced with the recognition that she had no future but as a widow if he continued to drink, she decided to bow out before that happened.

It was around this time that the film director Tony Palmer came to visit, along with his producer Alan Wright. They came with an intriguing proposition and offered Burton the title part in a new miniseries set to start filming four months hence, called *Wagner* – a biopic of the great German composer Richard Wagner. It would be filmed at multiple locations across Europe from February to September, with a cast including Laurence Olivier, John Gielgud, Ralph Richardson and Vanessa Redgrave.

Palmer had originally contracted Albert Finney for the part but Finney wouldn't give Palmer a start date. To Burton, it all seemed too good to be true and he said to Palmer quizzically: "Am I going to get paid for this?" Palmer replied: "Yes, but not what you normally get." With that, he offered Burton US$1 million for the seven months' work, which he accepted. Crucially, it gave Burton something to look forward to.

But by the time that came around, Burton and Suzy would no longer be together. It all came to a head when there was an incident that effectively ended the marriage. Suzy has never spoken of it, even to very close friends. She has only said it was caused by "a huge betrayal" and has never gone any further.

Suzy was said to be absolutely devastated by the "betrayal" but kept her counsel and her cool. It was the tipping point and she decided she had had enough. She planned her exit carefully and was not about to leave her husband alone with his problems. She was, however, straightforward and told him what she intended.

When Burton and Suzy returned to Europe they went on their normal pre-Christmas trip to see the Jenkins family. But this time they visited Cecilia, who had been widowed after her husband, Elfed's, death. She had moved to Hadley Wood, near London, to live with her daughter Marian.

Suzy had planned her exit meticulously. She delivered her husband to Hadley Wood and then made her exit to her parents at Aldermaston, in Berkshire.

Suzy asked Catherine to meet her at Hadley Wood, and the two took Cecilia into their confidence. After supper, Burton retired to his bedroom early. He knew what was coming and left the women to make the arrangements.

The three women talked long into the night. Suzy told them she had finally decided to leave her husband and could not cope any longer with the complex demands of the relationship. She told them her own health was suffering badly as a result of it. She was, as she admitted, "at the end of her tether." She had finally reached her limit.

But it was clear that Suzy felt deeply for Burton and that she was obsessed with his care. She needed to make sure that Catherine could take over administering his drugs on a daily basis. He was taking ten different drugs at the time. Catherine assured her she would take very good care of her brother.

After a few days, Suzy left quietly to go to her parents' house, and the marriage was effectively over. Burton was in many ways relieved when she had gone. They had grown apart and he would now be able to plan his new life. But the night before she left, he was very depressed that yet another marriage had failed. He felt utterly helpless.

That afternoon, Cecilia sat down for a chat with her brother: She said to him; "I'm very sorry, Rich." He flashed her that irresistible smile and replied; "Oh, it's all right, Cis. It's only six years they stay with me after all." But it was all bravado. Inside, he was devastated that she had gone.

Astonishingly, when Suzy went away, Burton started drinking again. He was back on the spirits and it temporarily seemed to restore him to health. Philip Burton confirmed: "Richard had taken to the bottle with his old zest." Philip was astonished when he saw him during a television interview early in January 1982: "He was doing an interview on television and, to my great relief, he looked better than I feared he would."

Burton stayed in Hadley Wood for a week and returned to Los Angeles with Brook Williams. A few weeks later Suzy also returned to Los Angeles.

Meanwhile, Burton travelled to Vienna with Brook Williams and Ron Berkeley to start filming *Wagner*. Mike Merrick was with him the night he and Suzy parted for the last time: "My wife, Annie, and I were with Susan and Richard at their rented house in Beverly Hills the night before he left for Europe to start filming *Wagner*. They did not say they were parting but that he was going alone to start shooting the film and that she would 'hopefully' join him in a few weeks."

After he went, Suzy departed from Los Angeles for Puerto Vallarta. At this stage, Burton wanted Suzy to return and she told him she was still making up her mind.

Four weeks into filming, on 20th February 1982, Suzy sent him a short telex saying she was not coming back and wanted a divorce. He was with the actor Franco Nero when he received the telex and immediately went on a drinking session like none before. As he drank himself into oblivion, the torn-off telex from Suzy lay nearby.

Burton was devastated by Suzy's message. And so were Mike and Anne Merrick who adored Suzy. As Merrick said: "Susan was the personification of caring and devotion. A truly sensitive and loving wife with a large responsibility as the wife of a great star who was ailing. Annie and I are, to this day, close friends with Susan, a lovely woman, living in Europe."

When the news got out, there was immediate speculation that Burton and Taylor would get back together. In the intervening years, Taylor had married and divorced John Warner, an American politician, whom she had married after Burton. Now she was on stage in London starring in a play called 'The Little Foxes.' She made no secret of her ongoing affection for her ex-husband.

Burton fuelled those rumours when he left the *Wagner* set for a few days and flew into London to be with Taylor at her 50th birthday party on 27th February. Burton was reported to have spent the night with her at her rented house after he failed to return to his hotel until the following morning.

If there was any hope of getting back together with Suzy, by that action he quickly removed it. Before that, Suzy might have returned to Burton had he asked her; but that sealed it.

Afterwards, Burton held a drunken press conference at the Dorchester Hotel in London, telling reporters: "Susan, my wife? Taller than a ghost – and just as remote, I may say. She is so English; hopelessly, hideously remote."

At the beginning of 1983, Burton returned to Port-au-Prince in Haiti for a divorce from Suzy; much as he had seven years earlier when seeking a divorce from Taylor. Suzy was given US$1 million in cash and their holiday house in Puerto Vallarta as a settlement. He kept his home in Celigny and the rest of his money.

The reason for the quickie divorce soon became apparent; Burton, it seemed, now wanted to marry another – an attractive Englishwoman called Sally Hay, a 34-year-old film production assistant he had met on the set of *Wagner.*

# CHAPTER 59

# The beginning of an end

## *Sally sparks personal revival*

### 1982

hen Richard Burton arrived on the set of *Wagner* in Vienna at the end of January 1982, almost immediately he noticed the pretty continuity girl, who director Tony Palmer seemed unable to do without. Sally Hay was here, there and everywhere. But she was for later, if at all. Burton was still hoping to be re-united with his wife, who was in Puerto Vallarta. He was in regular telephone contact with Suzy although everyone knew she had left him. There was disappointment on the set that she had not come with him, as Sally herself recalled: "I was disappointed about that as I had been looking forward to meeting her."

Then there was Elizabeth Taylor; she was also in regular contact, astonishingly hoping for a third wedding and pestering Tony Palmer for a part in *Wagner* so she would have an excuse to fly to Vienna. Burton, meanwhile, was running round in time-honoured fashion with an Italian journalist. His daughter Maria was also getting married in New York to a model agent called Steve Carson, and he didn't really approve. So he also had that to worry about.

Sally remembered the moment she saw Burton for the first time: "Now there was no doubt about it, Richard Burton was gorgeous. He was also pleasant on set, making the crew feel at ease. There was no starry grandeur about the man at all."

After about three weeks into the shoot, she thought that Burton was staring at her although they had had no contact, as she said: "It rather spooked me as I considered him to be way out of my league." She didn't think she had a chance.

Burton had his hands full in that first two months of filming. *Wagner* was a great epic, the story of the German composer's life, filming in 27 locations in six countries across Europe. Director Tony Palmer had made his name with highly-acclaimed documentaries. But *Wagner* was the first drama he had directed, and he was nervous. Burton sought to help and had studied the great composer before he arrived. Palmer praised the thoroughness of Burton's research: "He had a library of Wagner books with him and he was a stickler for accuracy." Palmer was delighted how Burton looked when he was made up and costumed: "We did a photo of Burton as Wagner – modelled on a famous photo – and they were uncannily alike. They both had very large heads."

The first few weeks were taken up with the big scenes, which featured the three knights of the British theatre: Sir Laurence Olivier; Sir Ralph Richardson; and Sir John Gielgud. It was a momentous occasion and the very first time they had acted together. Although they had all been in Olivier's film *Richard III*, they had never appeared in the same scenes together.

Burton had been looking forward to their arrival with child-like excitement, although by the time they came to leave they were no longer speaking.

As usual with Burton, there was more drama off set than on, and to mark the occasion of all four of them being together, they decided they would each host a dinner party on successive nights to celebrate.

There was some one-upmanship and also some trepidation over Burton's drinking. Richardson entertained first, but surly waiters spoilt his party. Next, Gielgud's was let down by indifferent food. Olivier had no problems with the food or the waiters but everyone was late because of his poor directions to the restaurant he had chosen.

But they were all relieved when Burton didn't touch a drop of alcohol at any of the dinners.

Finally, Burton thought he would show them how it was done and held his dinner party at the famous Palais Schwarzenberg. He asked Tony Palmer, Vittorio Storaro, the designer Shirley Russell and Lady Richardson to join them, making a party of eight.

Although he wasn't drinking, Burton had a full glass of white wine by his side at the table; it remained untouched. He drank water throughout.

For two hours, Burton held the party captivated with his stories. It was dinner party conversation at its very best and a historic last time when the four greatest actors Britain had ever produced would be together on a social occasion. By then, Richardson was 78, Gielgud 77 and Olivier 75 – it was never to be repeated.

Melvyn Bragg described it as a "crescendo of splendid mimicry and anecdote and competitive out-quoting and fun." Tony Palmer, recognising the occasion, had all four of them sign the menu that night.

Burton thought he ought to make it unforgettable and proceeded to do so. He suddenly yawned and his hand shot out, almost by reflex, and he grabbed the glass of wine and downed it in one. The whole table went silent as if they knew what was coming. Another glass and then another followed, and five minutes later, he was transformed from affable host into attack dog. As Melvyn Bragg put it: "He became as vicious as he had been generous, as savage as he has been affectionate."

He called Olivier a "grotesque exaggeration" and made snide remarks about Gielgud's homosexuality. He then told Richardson he could only act with cue cards – amongst many other insults. The three old actors stared at him in utter silence.

Burton had gravely insulted all three of the giants of British acting and although, afterwards, everyone tried to make light of a very embarrassing situation, they were all mightily offended.

Finally, Palmer managed to take Burton away: "Eventually, I took Richard by his hand and took him out to get a taxi. He said, 'I blew it didn't I? Oh my God, I blew it.' I said: 'Yes, Richard, you did.' But it was entirely accidental."

But Olivier didn't think so and on the way out, he said cuttingly to Palmer: "I know now why you chose Richard to play Wagner." When he left Vienna, Olivier gave a farewell party to which everyone was invited – everyone except Burton.

Finally, after it was officially announced that he was separating from Suzy in late February, Burton made his move on Sally during filming in Lucerne. It started when he asked Palmer if she could type up some letters for him. Then his new assistant, Judith, invited Sally to a dinner party at his hotel that evening. But it was not until the middle of March that Burton asked her to come to dinner on her own. She soon ended up in his bed, as she admitted: "I was not going to say 'no' but I had no idea if the relationship would continue after filming ended."

But she was encouraged when he invited her to move into his hotel suite for the duration of filming.

Shortly afterwards, Palmer asked her to switch from being continuity manager to Burton's liaison assistant on the film. She agreed. Her ordinariness was very refreshing for Burton after the glamour of his two previous wives and people meeting her for the first time saw Sally as a return to the old days – reminiscent of the stability of Sybil. Emotionally, he was almost back to where he had started, and somewhere he probably should never have left. Palmer said: "He liked her because she was absolutely straightforward and simple."

Filming finally finished on *Wagner* after seven months and Tony Palmer was delighted with what he had got in the can, as he said: "I can't think of anybody who could have brought it off better than he did. Apart from anything else, they [Wagner and Burton] were so alike – the women, the drink, the grandiloquence, the sense of destiny."

And Palmer, aside from the dinner party, was delighted with Burton's personal conduct; of the 158 shooting days, Burton had only missed two of them.

When filming ended, Sally fully expected to return home to Barnes in London and she began packing up her Volkswagen in preparation to leave.

She had little idea how much Burton had become attached to her. As Burton told Brook Williams: "She can do everything; she can cook, speak French – there's nothing she can't do. She looks after me so well. Thank God I've found her, Brookie."

And he was not about to lose her. When the last scene was shot, he asked her to come and live with him permanently. It was what she had hoped for in her wildest dreams, and they were suddenly an official couple. It was an amazing turnaround in her life and, soon, the British press became very interested in the ordinary English girl who had competed with Elizabeth Taylor and won Richard Burton.

They discovered that 34-year-old Sally Hay had grown up in Birmingham in the West Midlands of England. Her father had been the motoring correspondent for *The Birmingham Post*. She was raised a Catholic and was educated privately, preferring sport to academic studies.

Cars dominated her early life and her father took her to race meetings all over England, including famous tracks such as Silverstone and Brands Hatch. As she remembered, she never knew what car her father would be driving each day and she recalled him coming home in successive days in a Jensen Interceptor, then a Hillman Imp, according to what he had to road test for the newspaper that week.

She spurned the opportunity to attend university to take a secretarial course, and her street smarts landed her a job in the newsroom of the BBC in Birmingham.

She was a natural production assistant, being a good organiser and quick thinker. As she said: "I loved the immediacy of the work, the live gallery work and the pressure of getting the programme on air on time and, more importantly, closing on time."

But there were clouds, and before she was 21, she was surprised to realise that her father was an alcoholic. She remembered: "From having a father I greatly admired, I began to have a father who was an embarrassment."

From then on, she wanted to get away and, at 23, like all the talent in the media world, she eventually did. She moved to London in 1971 to work as a production assistant on the current affairs programme *24 Hours*. She moved around the BBC's current affairs department to work on *Panorama* and *Newsnight*. She was paid enough to put down a deposit to buy a small flat in Barnes in west London.

Then she was laid low when a love affair went wrong and she suffered from a bout of depression. He had been the man she wanted to marry and, afterwards, she was diagnosed with clinical depression, from which she was to suffer regularly thereafter.

At the end of the seventies, she left the BBC to pursue a freelance career just as commercial television was taking off. She worked on assignments all over England, and production companies were very eager to hire her. Then she met Tony Palmer, who was then editor of Southern Television's arts programme called *First Edition*. He hired her on a six-week assignment and liked her straightaway: "I thought that she was very, very nice and sexy too, I have to say."

It was good timing as Palmer's own career was taking off and he offered her a job on his new film version of the opera 'Death in Venice.'

Then, when Palmer started planning *Wagner*, he offered her the job as continuity manager, based in Vienna for seven months. She couldn't believe her luck and said: "It was a gift of a job and would mean that with pre-production work in Vienna, I would be out of the UK for nine months. So in October 1981, I loaded up my Volkswagen and drove to Vienna."

She was on her way to her destiny.

Her trip to Vienna took three days and she played The Beach Boys and The Beatles on her cassette player the entire way. She hoped the job on *Wagner* would take her out of television and into the movies, and she arrived in Vienna full of optimism. But she had absolutely no notion what was about to happen to her. At 34 years of age, she had given up on marriage and was entirely focused on her career.

So when Richard Burton asked her to accompany him to Los Angeles, where he was due to get a scheduled health checkup, she readily agreed to abandon her old life and to come and join his.

She arranged to get her Volkswagen back to the UK and got on the plane.

# AND GOD CREATED BURTON

# CHAPTER 60

# The Final Curtain

## And wedding No 5 to Sally

### 1982 - 1984

After *Wagner*, Richard Burton had no work scheduled at all. His diary was completely empty, so he took off with Sally. And once they were free of the film set, their relationship became more intense and developed into a full-blooded romance as they settled easily into one another's company. But first, they had a date at a hospital. As Sally explained: "Richard and I went to Los Angeles, where he went to hospital for treatment of his back and neck condition."

They went to stay in a house that Burton had rented on a long-term basis, as it was convenient for St John's Hospital and it gave him a base in Hollywood.

They then left for London, where Burton had promised to meet up with Elizabeth Taylor to see her production of 'The Little Foxes', which was running in London.

Taylor was desperate to see him, in more ways than one. Unable to get any work in films or even television at that point in her career, she had formed a theatre company called The Elizabeth Taylor Theatre Company in partnership with producer Zev Bufman.

She had a business proposition for Burton in which they would appear together in a new stage adaption of Noel Coward's 'Private Lives' on Broadway. Burton was intrigued and told her he would think about it. She also had a more personal proposition for him, but she put that on ice for later when she saw Sally at his side.

Sally was constantly wary of Taylor. Since the announcement of Burton's separation from Suzy, Taylor had been waging a campaign to get him back.

But this time, Burton resisted and kept his distance from her. This was partly in deference to Sally but also his own growing realisation that he was being manipulated.

To prove that, he startled Sally with a proposal. It was very sudden as Sally recalled: "He asked me to marry him."

The proposal was a bit moot as he was already married to Suzy and the complications of that marriage would need a little unravelling before he was ready to tie the knot again. Sally also wasn't the marrying kind and had proved that before she met Burton, and afterwards. She had been thrust into an unfamiliar world with a man who drank heavily. She had been through that experience with her father and found it had ruined their relationship.

She advised caution and said: "He seemed to like being married, having tried it a few times, but I said we should wait a year for me to make sure I found his kind of life one I could live with." She added quickly: "But it did not take me long to adjust to his kind of life."

And what a life that was. Aside from the restrictions of his doctors, Burton was a truly free man. He could go anywhere and do anything he wanted without having to worry about money. Since his second divorce from Taylor, he had already replenished his back accounts and earned US$12 million in those six years since she had cleaned him out.

Sally found that her new boyfriend had one of the most recognised faces in the world. He was known more or less everywhere, given the best tables in restaurants and sent to the front of every queue. Restaurant bills also frequently disappeared and, at airports, he was given treatment beyond that of VIPs. When they travelled, Sally felt as though she was with the most important man in the world; a man everyone seemingly wanted to meet.

The only downside to this life was his drinking. On the few occasions he drank, he would insult his well-wishers, and the goodwill would instantly disappear. He would insult her as well but as long as she could handle the insults, she could handle him.

From July to December of 1982, they had a glorious six months travelling the world, interspersed with spells at Celigny. They went anywhere and everywhere they wanted.

But everywhere they went, Elizabeth Taylor was never far away from their lives, and they were linked forever by her children, who were very close to Burton. Sally encouraged Burton to continue to see Taylor's children: "I felt it would be much better if Elizabeth's children could see Richard and he could enjoy seeing them. I also wanted to get to know them as I felt they should be part of our lives."

After a few months, they ended up in Los Angeles again.

As soon as Taylor realised Burton was back in LA, it didn't take her long to get in touch. She phoned Burton's manager, Valerie Douglas, saying she would like to meet up to discuss business.

With no new offers of work, Burton was getting restless. He had no need to be worried about money, but his Welsh working class roots had always dictated he worked. To that end he was willing to listen to anything Taylor had to say.

Sally remembers going to Taylor's house for an afternoon with Burton, Brook Williams and Robbie Lantz. She swam in Taylor's pool and, as she said: "Brook told me that he watched Elizabeth, who was watching Richard watching me swimming in the pool."

Taylor did have a proposition that interested Burton; a proposition that Sally later described as "throwing a spanner into their works."

Taylor and her partner, Zev Bufman, made a serious proposal to Burton for a new Broadway revival of 'Private Lives', a drama set in the 1930s and written by their friend Sir Noel Coward, who had died in 1973.

Burton was all ears. He had discussed 'Private Lives' many times with Noel Coward, who had always expressed a wish that Burton and Taylor would one day play it.

'Private Lives' was a brilliant story about a divorced couple who are now married to different younger people and discover that they are separately honeymooning with their new spouses in the same hotel in Deauville.

It featured two sets of characters: Elyot and Sybil; and Amanda and Victor. Both couples are starting their new life together in an adjoining hotel room with a shared terrace. Elyot and Amanda have been divorced for five years but now have new younger partners. Burton played Elyot, Taylor played Amanda, and their two co-stars were John Cullum and Kathryn Walker playing the younger partners.

In reality, both Burton and Taylor were far too old for the roles, but in many other ways, it suited their real life personas.

Burton was very excited about it, especially when his ex-wife's business partner offered to pay him US$70,000 a week to play Elyot. The first proposal was a short Broadway run in order to make a film of the production, but it quickly developed into a longer Broadway run and then a tour of the United States, and the film was forgotten. Burton was attracted by the money and the fact that the play was a genuine drama with few stresses for the actors. He was also attracted by the prospect of returning to the Broadway stage with Taylor. Burton couldn't say 'no' to the money or the glory.

The only other serious offer he had was from Anthony Quayle to return to the newly re-opened Old Vic for £500 a week. It was certainly an easy choice between the two.

# AND GOD CREATED BURTON

Interestingly, despite the money on offer, Robbie Lantz, who was both Taylor's and Burton's agent, was dead set against the deal. Years later, Lantz recalled the meeting in which it was all decided: "I walked into the room and Elizabeth very excitedly said: 'Robbie, we have decided to move forward with the best idea ever. Just wait until you hear it.' Then, after a big, dramatic pause: 'Elizabeth Taylor and Richard Burton in "Private Lives."'"

"I made a face: 'No, I don't think it's a good idea at all. In fact, I think it's a terrible idea.'" To this, Burton said: "But Noel Coward always wanted us to play it", and Lantz sneered back: "Oh yeah? When?"

Taylor was horrified by Lantz's reaction and asked him to talk with her privately in the adjacent room, leaving Burton with Zufman. Lantz told her: "Elizabeth, this is a terrible mistake. Neither one of you is in any shape to do this kind of delicate drawing room comedy right now." Taylor ignored his objections and replied: "Of course, it's right for us. And we'll just make oodles of money. I promise you, Robbie, this shall work."

It was clear to Lantz that there was no talking them out of it. He did not think either of his clients were comedy actors and believed it was inappropriate. He also thought it could lead to more personal problems between them. He was so against it that he told them in all conscience he could not take a commission on a deal to which he was so vehemently opposed. He declared: "This can lead to nothing but misery for you and Richard, and, as your agent and more importantly your friend, I absolutely refuse to profit from it." That shocked both of them as the deal was worth US$500,000 to Lantz in commission alone. But Taylor wasn't to be put off. She thought about it and said to Lantz: "I've been taking chances all of my life, Robbie, as you well know. And here's another one. I know our public, they will love it."

It gradually dawned on Sally that 'Private Lives' could just be a scheme for Taylor to break their relationship and get back together with Burton. In truth, it probably was, and the first part of the plan was very successful when Burton signed a contract for a nine-month run that would earn him nearly US$3 million. It was a lot of money but Sally realised that, for the best part of 1983, Burton would effectively be Taylor's employee. She wondered if their relationship would survive it.

Sally recalled: "Somehow, a three-week stint of taping 'Private Lives' became a nine-month tortuous tour." She didn't hide her feelings at the time: "It took me a while to realise that Elizabeth thought she and Richard would reunite at some point during the tour; that somehow fiction would turn into fact. That, I

792

suppose, was her master plan. She must have been furious that I was sticking by his side."

Before it started, Burton and Sally flew back to Europe and spent their first Christmas together at Celigny. Tony Palmer, the man who had introduced them, came to stay. It seemed appropriate.

The pressure to marry became even more intense when they both went to Port-au-Prince to secure his divorce from Suzy in January 1983. Whilst they were there, Burton decided he liked the climate and the laid-back pace of life. So he bought a new holiday home in the posh part of Port-au-Prince to replace the house in Puerto Vallarta that Suzy had taken possession of as part of the divorce settlement.

After Haiti, they went back to Los Angeles where Burton still retained his rented house. There, they got ready for 'Private Lives' and nine months on the road with Elizabeth Taylor – certain to be an interesting experience.

Before that, Burton made time for *Alice in Wonderland*, a television adaptation of the old stage production, in which he played the White King. He was supporting his daughter Kate who had the title role for her television debut on the American channel PBS at the age of 26.

Meanwhile, Zev Bufman's marketing machine had been going full speed, hyping up the return of Taylor and Burton to Broadway. It seemed that nothing was off limits.

Taylor took full part in the publicity drive. She told them that 'Private Lives' was strictly a business venture. She would laugh and say that she had no designs on her ex-husband when every journalist asked her the same question. But Burton wondered who had put the idea in the journalists' minds in the first place.

Bufman was in overdrive, as recalled by J. Randy Taborrelli years later in his biography of Taylor: "The advance publicity was so overhyped that theatre critics seemed to be rubbing their hands together, just waiting to pounce on it with all fours."

The marketing worked, and a staggering US$2 million was taken in advance ticket sales long before the play opened in May 1983 at the Lunt-Fontanne Theatre.

By the second week of March, Burton and Taylor were in New York rehearsing for the play, directed by Milton Katselas. And the trouble began straightaway. Burton had learned his lines for the play to perfection, but at first rehearsal, it didn't appear that Taylor had even read the script, let alone learned her lines. Katselas didn't prove a very inspiring director and Burton thought his treatment of the play was wrong.

Burton wrote about the experience extensively in his diaries and admitted that the attraction between him and Taylor had all but disappeared. For public consumption, he praised her to the hilt and often stated she was the love of his life and that she would be until death. He always said that the reason they were apart was that they could no longer live together. The truth was startlingly different. He wrote in his private diaries that she was starting to "bore" him, adding: "How terrible a thing time is." Sally recalled: "The experience on 'Private Lives' utterly destroyed Richard's relationship with Elizabeth, even on a friendly basis, and made me feel all the more secure."

Taylor herself was drinking heavily in this period and was addicted to certain prescription drugs of which Burton was unaware.

The play opened at the Shubert Theatre in Boston on 7th April for a month's run. Every seat was sold and, despite the problems, Burton was looking forward to opening on Broadway.

The first night at the Lunt-Fontanne was on 8th May 1983. The opening was, by all accounts, badly handled and the production crew were simply not ready. The start was 30 minutes late and the intermission overran. But at the curtain, Burton and Taylor nevertheless received a standing ovation. Whatever the chaos behind the scenes, New Yorkers loved them.

Frank Rich in the *New York Times* led the appalling reviews. He said 'Private Lives' as reprised by Burton and Taylor had "all the vitality of a Madame Tussaud exhibit." Rich continued: "Life doesn't imitate art in 'Private Lives' – it obliterates it. Early on, we see that, unlike Elyot and Amanda, Mr Burton and Miss Taylor have little lingering affection for each other – or none that they can either convey or fake on stage." And just when it seemed it couldn't get any worse from Rich, it did: "When Mr Burton finally crosses from his side of the terrace to embrace Miss Taylor in Act 1, he approaches the task with the stealthy gait of Count Dracula stalking a victim."

Peter Egan, the well-known British stage and television actor, thinks it was more fundamental than that: "They were too old for the parts, and apart from the age factor, they could not handle the diamond cut delivery that Coward's writing demands."

But what Frank Rich had to say made no difference, and box office ticket sales surged the next day. It was immediately obvious that the public reception wasn't about the play; it was about Burton and Taylor. It was a public spectacle, albeit hugely damaging for their careers as serious actors.

Lantz had been right. But by then, they were stuck with it. Burton in particular immediately regretted his involvement despite all the money he was making. Sally said: "Richard hated the Taylor/Burton version of the play but, not surprisingly, the audiences lapped it up. It was a purely commercial venture with no artistic merit but the audiences came in droves to see the Liz and Dick show. The producers must have been very pleased."

But the reality was that it was nowhere near as profitable as Taylor and Bufman had hoped. Broadway ticket prices had not kept up with inflation during the previous decade, but costs had. Taylor was also paying herself the same US$70,000 a week Burton was getting. The play was making money on Broadway, but it was clear the touring version in smaller theatres would probably lose money.

When Taylor realised that Burton was no longer interested in her, she got morose. She met a man called Victor Luna, a Mexican lawyer, and went through the motions of a relationship. She was also suffering from her addictions and getting ill. When that happened, because she was such an integral part of the play, that night's production had to be cancelled and refunds made. The show began to clock up large losses that were coming out of Taylor's own pocket.

In late June, they were playing in Philadelphia and Taylor was ill, and then she announced she was going away for four days with Victor Luna to recuperate. A whole week's shows had to be cancelled. Burton was stunned by the unprofessionalism and almost walked out. Instead, he told Sally that the year was up and that they could now get married.

Sally recalled: "Elizabeth was off sick. Richard had five free days. He said: 'Let's get married' and I didn't think he meant it." This time, Sally put up no objections: "I couldn't believe life could be so good to me."

With that, he took her off to Las Vegas where Haitian divorces were recognised and a marriage could be arranged in hours.

They were quietly married on Sunday 3rd July 1983 in the Presidential Suite of the Frontier Hotel by a Presbyterian minister called Reverend Phillips. Sally became the fifth Mrs Burton. Brook Williams was best man and it was witnessed by Valerie Douglas. They spent their wedding night in the spectacular US$1,000-a-night bridal suite of the Frontier Hotel.

On Monday morning, Burton telephoned his adoptive father, Philip and told him the happy news. Philip took the opportunity to tell his son he had just seen *Circle of Two* and it was much better than the critics had portrayed.

Philip's verdict cheered Burton enormously, not that he needed it that morning – one of the happiest he could ever remember. He put Sally on the phone to speak to her new father-in-law

Not so Elizabeth Taylor's morning; she was stunned when she read in the newspapers what had happened. She sent flowers to the newly married couple and then, almost in retaliation, announced her own engagement to Victor Luna. She couldn't hide her disappointment. As Sally recalled: "Elizabeth must have been devastated when Richard and I travelled to Las Vegas."

Only one thing slightly spoiled the day for Sally; in hindsight, she realised the dress she had chosen for the wedding ceremony had been wrong. As she admitted herself: "I'm wearing the most boring dress. But I thought I might as well get something that's useful – no one-off designer number."

Back in Philadelphia, Taylor, as the producer, was obliged to host a celebratory party for the newly married couple. It also doubled as a celebration of her engagement to Victor Luna. Robbie Lantz was at the party and recalled: "Actually, the show they were doing offstage was much more entertaining, I thought, than the one they were doing onstage."

Soon after the wedding, with the production headed for a long run in Los Angeles, Burton tried to get out of his contract. He had been offered a part in John Huston's latest film, called *Under the Volcano*, beginning in August. Burton was under contract to Taylor and Bufman's Elizabeth Taylor Theatre Company, and asked to be let out. He thought Taylor could be persuaded to release him from his contract, but he thought wrong. She simply said to him: "Richard, I think it would be very wrong to disappoint our fans, so I have to say 'no.'"

Burton was bitterly disappointed but didn't let it show and carried on with the play, which continued to be punctuated by Taylor's illnesses.

The last performance was in November 1983 in Los Angeles, nine months after it began. The final show was almost unscripted; Burton and Taylor made it up as they went along and the audience loved it. The final curtain calls were very emotional and although they didn't know it, fate dictated that it was to be the final time they would perform together. Afterwards, Taylor waited in the dressing room for Burton to come and say goodbye, but he never came and she said her goodbyes to the whisky bottle instead.

Despite the US$3 million he banked, when it was all over Burton swore he would never ignore Robbie Lantz's advice again.

Shortly afterwards, Taylor ditched Luna and booked herself into the Betty

# THE FINAL CURTAIN

Ford Clinic to try and kick her addictions. It was there that she met Larry Fortensky, and the rest was history.

The newly married Burtons went straight to Los Angeles to pack up the house as the lease was running out at the end of 1983. They invited Burton's brother David Jenkins, who had retired from the police force, to join them for an extended holiday. Afterwards, they travelled to Haiti for Christmas to set up their new home and enjoy a much delayed extended honeymoon. Whilst they were there, the pressures of life disappeared and they looked forward to many more holidays in their new Haitian home.

They had all the time in the world to enjoy it, and Burton had no work booked. And after the stresses of 'Private Lives', he wasn't particularly looking for any. They finally returned to Switzerland in the early spring of 1984.

And then Paul Scofield broke his leg.

Burton received an offer to replace him in a film called *1984*. It would be his first supporting role in 30 years. *1984* was a British-produced film and Burton was asked to play the part of O'Brien. The film was already six weeks into production, with John Hurt in the lead role of Winston Smith, a rebel against the system who is physically and psychologically tortured by O'Brien. Cyril Cusack and the up-and-coming actress Suzanna Hamilton also starred.

Burton saw it as a means of re-establishing himself as a serious actor after the farce of 'Private Lives', and it called for just three weeks' filming in May at an abandoned RAF airfield in Wiltshire. The film was directed by Michael Radford, whom Burton recognised as a kindred spirit. But Radford did not want a typical Burton performance, nor did he want – perhaps for the first time – the famous Burton voice. Radford asked Burton to perform the character as written and, after a struggle, he got it. Eventually, Burton called Radford to his trailer and said: "Listen, I've been waiting 20 years to do a film without the Richard Burton voice, and I can see this is going to be the one." Sally remembered: "It was an experience Richard thoroughly enjoyed. He explained to me that, too often, directors thought they had got the great actor Richard Burton on their set and left him to find his own way."

To make the point, Radford had a set-chair made up with the name 'Richard Jenkins' on the back. Burton thought it hilarious, and asked if he could keep it.

And so, after a very happy three weeks, Burton and Sally headed for London and what would be his swansong, which happily involved his 26-year-old daughter, Kate. Against Burton's advice, Kate had decided to embark upon a career as an actress. She had spent three years at Yale drama school to learn her craft. Her first big break was a revival of 'Present Laughter', in which she made her Broadway debut.

After that, she had won a major role in a three-part seven-hour long miniseries called *Ellis Island* for the American TV network CBS.

*Ellis Island* was about immigrants in New York at the beginning of the 20th century. Kate was cast as the daughter of a rich senator, and Burton agreed to take the modest role of the unscrupulous senator. It was filmed mostly on a soundstage at Shepperton Studios and on location at the old Billingsgate fish market in London. Sally remembered it as a "lovely family time."

During filming, Burton and Sally stayed at The Dorchester for three weeks and got re-acquainted with old friends. The future looked bright and he had already agreed his next film; his first big role for over two years and his biggest payday in a decade. Euan Lloyd had reprised plans for a sequel to *The Wild Geese*, called *Wild Geese II*. Burton would play his old role as Colonel Faulkner, hired to reform his mercenary army to rescue Rudolf Hess from Spandau prison. Hess would be played by Laurence Olivier. Filming was due to start in September 1984 in Berlin.

During that time Elizabeth Taylor who was in London rang up fresh from the Betty Ford Clinic with Victor Luna back in tow. She invited Burton and Sally to lunch. After the lunch, which wasn't particularly satisfactory, they got back to The Dorchester and Burton turned to Sally: "I didn't think I would ever feel this or say this, but I don't want to see her ever again." By then Burton was tired of Taylor's games. A few weeks later Liza Todd was getting married in New York and Burton decided not to travel to the wedding. When Sally asked him why he just said it was because of Taylor. At the end the schism between them was total.

In the middle of July, they bade farewell to Kate and to The Dorchester and headed back to Celigny for a month's holiday before they set out for Berlin and the set of *Wild Geese II*.

And the days counted down to Sunday 5th August.

# THE FINAL CURTAIN

# AND GOD CREATED BURTON

# CHAPTER 61

# Funeral in Celigny

## *The final act*

### 7th August to 30th August 1984

As soon as Valerie Douglas arrived at Le Pays De Galles in Celigny, she took sole charge of events. She set up her office in Richard Burton's library in an old stable block in the grounds, found the key to the door and locked it.

The conversion of the old stables had been a happy bolt hole for both Burton and Sally. Many a winter's day had been spent there with an open fire roaring away and both of them silently lost in their books. Now, it became the nerve centre for planning the aftermath of Burton's death.

It was Valerie Douglas' command centre and she firmly told Sally that, as executor of Burton's estate, she was legally in charge of what happened next. Sally had no idea what she was talking about but was in no fit shape to argue with her.

But they both agreed that they wanted a quiet funeral, with just Burton's children in attendance. But what seemed reasonable to them would seem entirely unreasonable to others.

Sally was in a terrible state; she had been absolutely devastated by the sudden loss of her husband. She had spent virtually every minute of the past 26 months in his company – hardly ever leaving his side. It made his sudden and total loss difficult to bear.

Although she had known him the least amount of time compared to his family and ex-wives, she had spent the most time in his company in the recent past and so, for her, the shock was the greatest. As she said: "I was completely lost, stunned, disbelieving, quite unable to function in any rational manner. But everyone else was similarly affected, which made the preparations for the funeral difficult if not chaotic. It was a horrendous thing to negotiate with so many difficult and different personalities trying to make their point."

In short, she couldn't cope – although she realised she had to.

Douglas effectively told the Jenkins family not to come and to stay away. She told Graham Jenkins on the telephone: "It would be best for all of us if the whole affair was kept low key. Surely you can see that?"

But, like Sally, Valerie Douglas was not thinking straight. She was as much a part of Burton's family as anyone, and there had always seemed little doubt that Douglas had been in love with Burton for the 32 years she worked for him.

There was an unseen fight for his memory between the blood relations and the people who had been closest to him.

But it simply wasn't in Douglas' power to invite or disinvite anyone to the funeral. When they spoke on the telephone again, she and Graham Jenkins had a confrontation. He said to her: "What are you frightened of? Surely you can't object to close family. If we're not eligible to attend, who is?" Douglas thought about it and said: "Well, if you must, you must." Jenkins said "Thank you" and put the phone down.

Both Sally and Valerie Douglas wanted to put Burton's body into the ground with as little fuss as possible. They needed to grieve and they didn't want a circus; they wanted a private funeral. Unfortunately, they didn't realise that it just wasn't going to be possible. Richard Burton was Richard Burton, one of the most famous men in the world; and his funeral was always going to be a circus and there was nothing anyone could do about that.

Next, Brook Williams had a go at Graham Jenkins – asking the family to stay away. Williams was also in shock; he had lost the man who had been his surrogate father for over 20 years – the man who had been his whole life. He was also taking his orders from Douglas and had no choice but to go along with whatever she wanted. He called up Jenkins and said: "Graham, love, you know what it's like at this time of year. I've been trying to book rooms for you and your family, but all the hotels are packed out. It's the tourists; they're everywhere." Jenkins was disgusted and replied: "Forget it, Brook. I'm sure you have other things to worry about…I can fix everything from this end."

Williams, seeing Graham's determination and realising the folly of his request, said: "There's no need for that. We'll arrange something. It's just that, well, it's all very difficult."

From then on, the three of them accepted that the family was coming and resolved to make them as welcome as possible under the circumstances. Williams and Douglas took care of all their arrangements, just as their brother would have wanted.

But they all drew the line at Burton's ex-wives, especially Elizabeth Taylor. She would not be attending the funeral. Although Burton made a great public show of affection for Taylor throughout his life, they all knew it wasn't the reality.

The family was also having trouble coming to terms with the fact that their brother would not be buried at the place of his birth in Pontrhydyfen – especially as Burton had already arranged a plot in the Welsh cemetery.

The decision to be buried in Celigny was simple; it was for tax reasons and all his heirs would benefit from it. If Burton had been buried in Wales, the British Inland Revenue might have had a claim on his estate for inheritance tax. It was as simple as that.

Eventually, all the problems were resolved and, the following day, on Tuesday 7th August, the majority of the Jenkins family arrived in Celigny. The rest followed the day after. Each time, the arrangements were the same as Brook Williams met them at the airport with security passes identifying them as family, and cars awaited to take them all to Celigny. On both days, each time the family's cars moved off, as many as ten cars containing photographers and journalists took off after them.

The gates of Burton's home, Le Pays De Galles, were shut tight and protected by armed security guards in dark blue outfits, all wearing sunglasses. Everyone's security passes were examined before the cars could move up the hill into the house.

Those arriving first on the Tuesday faced a very difficult time when they walked through the front doors of Le Pays De Galles. They were met by Valerie Douglas and immediately introduced to Sally's mother Mary Hay. Douglas informed them that Sally was in her bedroom and would come down imminently.

When she did appear, wearing her dressing gown, they could see immediately what a desperate state she was in. Sally was a woman in a state of total shock, as Graham Jenkins described: "Her face was stone white. Her eyes stared as if she was in a trance. She did not say a word."

It had only been 72 hours since she had lost her husband, and although she had coped well in the immediate aftermath, she was now in a bad state.

Although everyone else had long anticipated the day when Richard Burton would drop down dead, and even wondered why it had not come earlier, the thought had never occurred to Sally. She had only known him for two years and believed they had a long and happy life in front of them.

When she saw how she looked, Cecilia rushed over to Sally and put her arms around her, but she just looked straight ahead and did not respond. There was some small talk going on around her, which Sally appeared not to hear.

Valerie Douglas ended it by steering the family out of the house and back into the cars and on to their hotel. They were all booked in at Hotel Port d'Alleves, overlooking the lake.

Graham Jenkins had been badly affected by what had happened at the house. After he unpacked, he went down to the bar to drown his sorrows. He was distraught and hated being treated liked a stranger, as he put it, at "my own brother's funeral." As he recalled: "The conflict of emotions left me with a sense of painful bewilderment."

Sally later regretted much of what happened with the family, but said: "We were all grief stricken and, like me, no one was making much sense. It caused a great deal of friction, which magnified our grief to breaking point."

Graham Jenkins believed that Sally thought that the family from Wales were "all locked in a conspiracy against her; that by claiming some part of the memory of Rich we were trying to steal what was rightfully hers."

But the truth was much simpler than that; Sally was simply consumed by grief from having her husband, whom she loved dearly and in whose pocket she lived, suddenly snatched away. The Jenkins family was consumed by a totally different kind of grief. Nobody could understand what had happened to them. Alongside this, Valerie Douglas and Brook Williams also had their totally different kind of grief to deal with.

Douglas had arranged a family meal for that night at the house, which would be prepared by the kitchens at the nearby Café de la Gare and brought up to the house. Everyone promised to attend.

At dinner that night, Verdun Jenkins held court and told stories about his brother, which cheered up Sally enormously.

As they were leaving the house that night, Valerie Douglas said to the brothers: "Don't forget, I want to talk to you guys tomorrow. I have some news for you." They presumed she was talking about the will, but never did find out what she wanted.

The next day, three of Burton's children arrived: Kate and her boyfriend, Michael Ritchie; Liza Todd with her new husband, Hap; and Maria Burton with her husband, Steve Carson. Neither Michael nor Christopher Wilding turned up, which surprised everybody. The children all stayed in the main house with Sally and her mother, and Brook Williams and Valerie Douglas shared the guest chalet in the garden.

The following day, the Jenkins brothers went to the small protestant church to practice their singing for the service. David Rowe-Beddoe had flown in from Portugal to play the organ. Rowe-Beddoe, who was a classical music scholar at

Cambridge, had to write out all the hymns and orchestrate and score them from scratch, which he did on some manuscript paper he purchased in Geneva.

On Wednesday, there was speculation that Elizabeth Taylor might actually come to the funeral. It was doubly difficult because she was in constant contact with her daughter Liza. When Graham Jenkins returned to Le Pays de Galles that night, Liza was speaking to her mother and handed the phone to Jenkins. Taylor told him: "I won't be at the funeral tomorrow, Graham. I'm sure that's best for everyone."

Sally did not want Taylor anywhere near Celigny, and she knew her husband wouldn't have wanted it either. And therein lay the conflict. Burton had almost entirely cut himself off from Taylor before he died. He had gone to the extent of buying both burial plots on each side of his own in order to stop her ever being buried next to him. Sally knew this, but the Jenkins family did not. The relationship between the Jenkins family and Taylor had always been strong, and she had nurtured it over the years. They all hated Sally's opposition to her and couldn't understand why it persisted.

On the day of the funeral, the family gathered at Le Pays de Galles to be given places in the convoy of funeral cars. The church was accessed by a long track and was situated amongst trees. In amongst the trees was the small cemetery. As the cars came closer to the church, the crowds thickened and they were forced to stop some 50 metres short of the church entrance and walk.

The whole surrounding field was swarming with journalists and photographers, and there must have been around 300 in attendance to cover the funeral. Tony Palmer had arrived to film the funeral officially and his was the only TV camera allowed into the churchyard.

When they finally reached the church, Cecilia whispered to her brothers: "Who would have thought that Rich would become so popular."

Meanwhile, Sally, who was in the car immediately behind the hearse, had problems getting her husband's coffin into the church; such was the crush of people. In the end, the ushers had to carry Burton's coffin through a private garden, over a wall and into the church by a side entrance.

Inside, it was a humble church, very like a Welsh chapel with a curved wooden ceiling with coconut matting and a coke-burning stove in the aisle.

Sally wanted everyone to stand for five minutes of silence before the ceremony properly began. It was her private time to remember her husband. Throughout, she just stared at his coffin, lost in her own thoughts.

# AND GOD CREATED BURTON

In his own biography of his brother, published some years later, Graham Jenkins made some very crass comments about that five minutes' silence. The comments reflected the difference between Sally's grief, which was total, and the family's, which was certainly not the wall of grief that had hit Sally.

The funeral service was conducted by Pastor Arnold Mobbs, a Presbyterian minister who had christened Kate and her sister Jessica in the same church a quarter of a century before. He had known Burton since he had moved to Switzerland in 1957. Although Burton himself was agnostic, he had cultivated a relationship with the pastor.

The service itself was very simple. Kate Burton read Dylan Thomas' 'Do Not Go Gentle Into That Good Night', and Graham Jenkins read chapter 13 of the First Epistle to the Corinthians, in English and Welsh. The Jenkins family led the singing, and the hymns were all sung in Welsh. Accompanied by Rowe-Beddoe on the organ, they put on the same performance which every Jenkins sibling had been played out on. There was no sound like it in the world.

Afterwards, ushers carried Burton's coffin to his grave.

When the family got there, they found it surrounded by photographers who had formed a sort of amphitheatre of flashguns. It was the circus that Sally had fought so hard against but, in the end, couldn't prevent. Richard Burton was finally laid to rest dressed in red; his coffin carried a large wreath on top in the shape of the Welsh dragon.

After the ceremony, there was a reception at the Café de la Gare, which Sally couldn't face and she went straight back up the hill to the house.

There was another family dinner at the house that night, the third in a row before they all went home the following day.

There then followed an extraordinary sequence of four memorial services; two in America and two in Britain. Between them, they were attended by most of the major figures in show business.

The first came two days after the funeral in Pontrhydyfen on Saturday 11th August. Held at the Bethel Chapel and presided over by the Rev Eric Williams, it was Wales' goodbye to its most famous citizen. Over 400 friends of Richard Burton squeezed inside and three times that number listened to the service over a loudspeaker outside. Thousands more watched from the grassy hillsides that surrounded Pontrhydyfen.

Elizabeth Taylor didn't turn up until a week later. She went first to visit Burton's grave at Celigny and then to his family at Pontrhydyfen. She spent the night at Hilda Owen's house in Pontrhydyfen, just as she had when she was married to Burton. The following morning, she stood on the doorstep and declared: "I feel as if I am home."

On 24th August, there was a memorial service in Los Angeles at the Wilshire Theatre, organised by Mike Merrick. It was attended by Suzy. Eulogies were given by Kate Burton, George Segal and Richard Harris. Susan Strasberg and Clint Eastwood were in the congregation. Outside, one of Burton's dearest friends from the old days in Hollywood, Pamela Mason, said: "We should feel bad that he has gone, good that he was here."

Straight afterwards, Mike Merrick also organised an East Coast memorial service at the Lunt-Fontanne theatre in New York, which Sally also attended. The street had to be blocked off by the police as the crowd was so big.

On 30th August, Robert Hardy organised London's memorial service in the church at St Martin-in-the-Fields. The church was jammed to capacity. Outside, the whole of Trafalgar Square came to standstill as fans gathered to see three of Richard Burton's four wives came together to mourn him. Suzy arrived late, as did John Gielgud. But Laurence Oliver declined his invitation altogether, still smarting from that dinner in Vienna two and a half years earlier.

78-year-old Emlyn Williams delivered the eulogy.

Only Sybil, who had long ago blanked her first husband out of her life many years before, failed to attend any of the memorial services.

The succession of memorial services proved to be a welcome diversion for Sally, and it was to be a month before she returned to Celigny to face all its memories. She slowly began to recover, as she said: "As the weeks went by, I began to realise I had left my old world behind. I had not been long in Richard's life and that was now lost to me. It was impossible to see a way forward or to find a place where I would feel at ease and fit in.

I adored being with Richard and I adored being married to him. It was a wonderful time and I enjoyed every minute of his stimulating company. Yes, he did fall off the wagon at times and, when he did, it was difficult. However, he would pull himself back after three days and return to a life of endless cups of tea and books."

After he was dead, the television channels in England endlessly broadcasted an interview Burton had recorded not long before he died. In it, he seemed to sense that the end might be near, and when he was asked what, if anything, he would change if he had his life to live all over again. He replied: "I wouldn't change anything. I have had the most incredible life."

# AND GOD CREATED BURTON

# INDEX